D0917884

A Reader for College Writers

Eighth Edition

Santi Buscemi

BVT Publishing

www.BVTPublishing.com

Publisher and Managing Director: Richard Schofield

Production and Fulfillment Manager: Janai Escobedo

Designer and Typesetter: Stephanie Elliott

Managing Editor: Anne Schofield

Copy Editor: Tara Joffe

Proofreader: Teresa Daly

Permissions Coordinator: Jade Elk

All rights reserved. Printed in the United States of America. No part of this book may be used or reproduced in any manner whatsoever without written permission, except in the case of brief quotations embodied in critical articles and reviews. For information address BVT Publishing, P.O. Box 492831, Redding, CA 96049-2831.

Copyright © 2020 by BVT Publishing

LAB BOOK^Plus ISBN: 978-1-5178-0808-2

Textbook^Plus (Loose-Leaf Bundle) ISBN: 978-1-5178-0807-5

eBook^Plus ISBN: 978-1-5178-0806-8

Loose-Leaf ISBN: 978-1-5178-0804-4

Soft Cover ISBN: 978-1-5178-0805-1

Brief Contents

Table of Contents

Section One
Organization and Development

Chapter 1

The Central Idea   **3**

Chapter 2

Paragraphs: Mastering Unity, Coherence, and Development   25

Chapter 3

Special Paragraphs: Writing Introductions and Conclusions   61

Section Two
Word Choice and Sentence Patterns

Chapter 4

Word Choice—Using Literal and Figurative Language Effectively   **91**

Chapter 5

Sentence Structure: Creating Emphasis and Variety   119

Section Three
Description and Narration

=== **Chapter 6** ===

Description   149

=== **Chapter 7** ===

Narration   179

Section Four
Exposition

Chapter 8

Illustration   205

Chapter 9

Comparison and Contrast   229

Chapter 10

Process   257

Chapter 11

Definition   283

Section Five
Argument and Persuasion

Chapter 12

Argumentation   **323**

Chapter 13

Persuasion   **353**

Appendix 1

Grammar Review   381

Appendix 2

The Research Process   419

PREFACE

A Reader for College Writers is a brief yet comprehensive guide for students in first-year collegiate composition courses. The text, now in its eighth edition, retains its original purpose: to help students read carefully, respond thoughtfully, and use those responses as creative springboards for writing. As in the past, research continues to affirm the close relationship between analytical reading and effective writing. This textbook makes emphatic use of that connection.

NEW TO THE EIGHTH EDITION

Though the purpose of the text remains the introduction of rhetorical and linguistic principles to help students organize and develop college-level discourse, there is also additional material in appendix 1 to help students learn grammar, sentence structure, and other skills important to the editing process.

A second appendix includes a discussion of important skills and principles related to the writing of collegiate research papers using MLA (Modern Language Association) style. Coverage of the research paper ends with a full-length annotated student paper that illustrates all the basic principles and formats in the latest MLA style.

As such, *A Reader for College Writers* has now become an introduction to collegiate writing that includes a rhetoric, a reader, a grammar and editing manual, and a research guide.

MORE THAN EIGHTEEN NEW READING SELECTIONS

The essays and poems in the collection represent a range of cultural and academic interests and are enhanced in this edition by eighteen new major reading selections, as well as other shorter pieces. New to this edition are authors such as Sam Pickering, Gail Sheehy, Senator Bernie Sanders, Aldous Huxley, former attorney general Jeff Sessions, Walter Williams, Robert Reich, James Jeans, and Lawrence Reed. The two chapters on argumentation and persuasion contain contemporary essays offering opposing views on important controversial issues: sanctuary cities and raising the minimum wage to $15 per hour.

PROVEN FEATURES OF *A READER FOR COLLEGE WRITERS*

FOCUS ON CRITICAL READING AND WRITING

The introductory section, Getting Started, introduces the fundamentals of analytical reading and collegiate writing by stressing that reading and writing are processes and that there is a natural connection between the two. Moreover, the pedagogy in each chapter introduction and accompanying each reading selection shows students how to exploit this connection. Several sample student essays, which illustrate techniques for analysis, annotation, summary, and synthesis, appear in Getting Started. Another student piece in Getting Started illustrates the writing process step-by-step through note taking, outlining, drafting, revision, and editing. Finally, a sample student paper, annotated with notes that help students introduce, cite, and document their research, caps off the research-paper discussion in appendix 2.

ROBUST SUPPORT FOR READING SELECTIONS

Each reading selection is prefaced by an author biography, by questions and comments under "Preparing to Read," and by a vocabulary section. Each of these features provides a context for reading and reinforces the notion that critical reading—like writing—is a process. Each reading selection is followed by suggested websites for further reading, questions for discussion, items for thinking critically, and suggestions for journal entries, all of which help students understand the reading and draw inspiration from it for their own writing. In addition, the responses students make to the suggestions for journal entries can double as prewriting for the formal, sustained essays they create in response to the suggestions for sustained writing, which appear at the end of each chapter.

Extensive Coverage of Argument and Persuasion

In addition to complete coverage of traditional methods of argumentation and persuasion, the two chapters in section 5 discuss both Toulmin and Rogerian argument. Paired readings on contemporary controversial issues appear in chapters 12 and 13 in that section.

Inclusion of Student Writing

Every chapter contains at least one student essay, with excerpts of the student's rough and final drafts compared in the chapter's introduction. Many students using this book have welcomed this side-by-side analysis because it convinces them that the only way to produce successful academic prose is through a meticulous process that includes careful revision and editing. These selections also serve as inspiration by encouraging current users of the text to produce the best writing they can. Indeed, some even express the hope that their writing might appear in a future edition of the text.

Additional Materials Regarding the Editing and Research Processes

As noted earlier, the text now offers coverage of major grammatical, sentence structure, and other editing concerns, as well as a full introduction to research paper writing using MLA style. This appendix includes an annotated student research paper that students can use as a model of excellence. Although this added material is new to the text, it has been classroom tested by the author and several of his colleagues in college classrooms. As a result of the addition of these two features to the eighth edition, students need purchase no other text to become proficient in freshman writing.

Acknowledgments

I sincerely appreciate the comments and suggestions from my colleagues across the country who have reviewed this text ever since its inception. Among my colleagues and friends at Middlesex County College, I would like to thank Barry Glazer, James Keller, Yvonne Sisko, Renee Price, Helena Swanicke, and Shirley Wachtel for their support and loyalty. I would also like to thank the many students who contributed their work for presentation in this text; I have learned so much from them. I would also like to thank the editors and staff at BVT Publishing—Janai Escobedo, Jade Elk, Stephanie Elliott, Teresa Daly, and Tara Joffe—for their patience, their outstanding support and guidance, and their confidence in me and my work. Finally, I want to thank my family—Elaine, Pamela, Matthew, and Molly—for supporting and encouraging their "Paka" in whatever work he engages.

Supplements and Resources

INSTRUCTOR SUPPLEMENTS

A complete teaching package is available for instructors who adopt this book. This package includes an **online lab**, **instructor's manual**, **PowerPoint™ slides**, and **chapter exercises**.

Online Lab	BVT's online lab is available for this textbook on two different platforms—BVT*Lab* (at www.BVTLab.com), and LAB BOOK™ (at www.BVTLabBook.com). These are described in more detail in the corresponding sections below. Both platforms allow instructors to set up graded homework, quizzes, and exams.
Instructor's Manual	The Instructor's Manual helps first-time instructors develop the course, while also offering seasoned instructors a new perspective on the materials. Each section of the Instructor's Manual coincides with a chapter in the textbook. The conversational format begins with a brief description of the chapter and a broad lecture overview. Key terms and definitions are then defined. Finally, the manual presents answers and suggested responses for the questions for each reading in the chapter.
PowerPoint Slides	A set of PowerPoint slides includes about thirty slides per chapter, including a chapter overview, learning objectives, slides covering all key topics, key figures and charts, and summary and conclusion slides.
Chapter Exercises	Downloadable exercises are available for each chapter. These exercises provide valuable application of the important grammatical and structural concepts presented throughout the book.

STUDENT RESOURCES

Student resources are available for this textbook on both the BVT*Lab* platform and the LAB BOOK platform, as described below. These resources are geared toward students needing additional assistance, as well as those seeking complete mastery of the content. The following resources are available:

Flashcards	BVT*Lab* includes sets of flashcards that reinforce the key terms and concepts from each chapter.
PowerPoint Slides	For a study recap, students can view all of the instructor PowerPoint slides online.
Additional LAB BOOK Resources	The LAB BOOK platform offers detailed section summaries developed by the author. Study tools such as text highlighting and margin notes are also available. These resources are not available in BVT*Lab*.

BVT*Lab*

BVT*Lab* is an affordable online lab for instructors and their students. It includes an online classroom with grade book and class forum, a homework grading system, and a host of student study resources.

Course Setup	BVT*Lab* has an easy-to-use, intuitive interface that allows instructors to quickly set up their courses and replicate them from section to section and semester to semester.
Class Forum	Instructors can post discussion threads to a class forum and then monitor and moderate student replies.
Student Resources	All student resources for this textbook are available in digital form within BVTLab. Even if a class is not taught in the lab, students who have purchased lab access can still use the student resources in the lab.
eBook	BVT*Lab* includes both a webBook™ and a downloadable eBook (on the Vital-Source® platform). For some product bundles, BVT's LAB BOOK can also be accessed from within BVTLab, offering enhanced eBook features and study tools for students, as described below.

LAB BOOK

LAB BOOK is a web-based eBook platform with an integrated lab providing comprehension tools and interactive student resources. Instructors can build homework and quizzes right into the eBook. LAB BOOK is either included with eBook^Plus or offered as a stand-alone product.

Course Setup	LAB BOOK uses the BVT*Lab* interface to allow instructors to set up their courses and to replicate them from section to section and semester to semester.
Advanced eBook	LAB BOOK is a mobile-friendly, web-based eBook platform designed for PCs, Macs, tablets, and smartphones. LAB BOOK allows highlighting, margin notes, and a host of other study tools.
Student Resources	All student resources for this textbook are available in the LAB BOOK, as described in the "Student Resources" section above.

CUSTOMIZATION

BVT's Custom Publishing Division can help you modify this book's content to satisfy your specific instructional needs. The following are examples of customization:

- Rearrangement of chapters to follow the order of your syllabus

- Deletion of chapters not covered in your course

- Addition of paragraphs, sections, or chapters you or your colleagues have written for this course

- Editing of the existing content, down to the word level

- Customization of the accompanying student resources and online lab

- Addition of handouts, lecture notes, syllabus, and so forth

- Incorporation of student worksheets into the textbook

All of these customizations will be professionally typeset to produce a seamless textbook of the highest quality, with an updated table of contents and index to reflect the customized content.

Shutterstock

Getting Started

Outline

GS.1   How to Use This Book

GS.2   Becoming an Active College Reader

GS.3   Using the Writing Process: A Tool for Discovery

GS.4   The Making of a Student Essay:
       From Prewriting to Proofreading

A Reader for College Writers contains short readings by professional and student authors. Each paragraph, essay, and poem is accompanied by discussion questions, suggestions for writing, and other instructional aids.

The reading selections act as springboards to your own writing. Some supply facts and ideas you can include in your own work. Others inspire you to write about similar subjects by drawing details from your experiences, observations, and readings. In short, this book helps you make connections between reading and writing, and it shows you ways to improve both. The rest of this Getting Started (GS) introduction is divided into the following sections:

GS.1 How to Use This Book

GS.2 Becoming an Active College Reader

GS.3 Using the Writing Process: A Tool for Discovery

GS.4 The Making of a Student Essay: From Prewriting to Proofreading.

GS.1 How to Use This Book

The paragraphs, essays, and poems you will read are accompanied by instructional aids: (1) a note on the author and on the text's origins, (2) material that prepares you to read, (3) a vocabulary list, (4) discussion questions, (5) critical-thinking questions, and (6) journal entry suggestions (short writings). Also, at the end of each chapter, you will find Suggestions for Sustained Writing (essay writing). These materials help you make the most of your reading and get started on your own writing. Here's one way to use *A Reader for College Writers*; your instructor might ask you to use another:

1. The book is divided into five sections; each has at least two chapters. Begin each section by reading its introduction, for it contains important information.

2. Read each chapter, which explains principles and strategies of writing illustrated by the reading selections in that chapter.

3. When you get to the individual reading selections, notice that each is preceded by an author biography, a section called Preparing to Read, and a vocabulary list. These help you review each selection.

4. Read the selection itself. As you read, make notes in the margins, underline important ideas, and mark unfamiliar words or ideas, which you can look up before you reread the selection.

5. After you have reread the selection, answer the Questions for Discussion and the Thinking Critically items. You may record your answers on paper, in a computer file, or in the margins of the text.

6. Respond to at least one of the Suggestions for Journal Entries. Put your responses in a journal (notebook)—paper or electronic. Making regular journal entries is important. First, writing is mastered only through regular practice, which making journal entries provides. Second, your journal contains responses to the readings, so it helps you make what you have read your own. Most important, keeping a journal helps you gather information for longer projects. Almost all the Suggestions for Sustained Writing (at the end of each chapter) refer to journal entries; so, keeping a journal means you will already have taken the first step in completing a major writing assignment.

7. Choose one of the Suggestions for Sustained Writing as a prompt for a formal essay. Read each suggestion carefully; then choose the one that interests you most.

8. If your teacher asks you to use library or Internet research in a paper, you might want to review Modern Language Association style, which is explained at style.mla.org and in the Research Process appendix at the end of this book. If you are unsure about certain writing terms in this book, look them up in the glossary at the end of the book.

GS.2 Becoming an Active College Reader

GS.2a Preparing to Read: Survey

GS.2b Reading and Taking Notes: Engage the Text

GS.2c Writing an Informal Outline: Strengthen Your Grasp of the Text

GS.2d Conversing with the Text: Read It Again

GS.2e Summarizing: Make What You Have Read Your Own

GS.2f Responding and Critiquing: Evaluate What You Have Read

GS.2g Synthesizing: Bring Ideas Together in a New Statement

The more you read, the better you will write. Like writing, reading is an active process. Effective readers don't just sit back and absorb words. They *digest, interpret,* and *evaluate* what they read. They interact with the text by considering both *stated* and *unstated (implied)* messages. They question *facts* and *assumptions,* evaluate *evidence,* ask *questions,* and apply their own *insights* and *experiences* to what they read.

In college, you will read textbooks; essays in newspapers, journals, and anthologies; scientific materials; poetry, fiction, and other literature; and academic, professional, and government websites. Many people read such materials without fully understanding them the first time. If this happens to you, don't worry. Read them a second and third time, discuss them with classmates, or put them aside for a while to allow ideas to develop. (Doing so is like writing multiple drafts of an essay, getting feedback from others, and putting the paper aside before rewriting it.) Most important, don't be afraid to ask your instructor for help both in class and in tutorials.

HELPFUL TIPS

Special Tips on Reading Selections in This Book

- Prepare for a reading selection by first reading the author's biography, the vocabulary words, and the Preparing to Read section, all of which come before the selection itself.

- Take notes while you read. You can do this by listing or outlining ideas on your computer or a notepad. Two good ways are by making notes in the margins of the text or by keeping a double-entry notebook. Both methods are explained below.

- Answer the Questions for Discussion and the items under Thinking Critically, which appear after each reading selection. Then complete at least one of the Suggestions for Journal Entries.

GS.2a Preparing to Read: Survey

Surveying, also called *previewing*, is an essential first step; it reveals much that will help you read more effectively and easily.

- Begin by looking for clues in the title, especially in essays or scholarly articles. Titles often contain hints about content, purpose, and thesis.

- If a biographical or introductory note precedes the essay or article—as with selections in this book—read this first. It will help you understand the cultural, historical, or other context in which the text was written, and it might provide clues to the author's thesis (main idea). If it tells you when and in what publication the item first appeared, you might be able to conclude something about the author's purpose and audience.

- Sometimes, essays state their theses (main ideas) in the *introductory* or *concluding paragraphs*. So, you might want to read these paragraphs at least twice. The introduction can also provide clues about the organization, purpose, and supporting ideas in the essay.

- If the item contains *subheadings* or *subtitles*, read them. They will provide insight into the essay's organization. Then, *skim* every paragraph for ideas that support the thesis. Often, supporting ideas are expressed as conclusions drawn from evidence. So, look for words and phrases such as *therefore*, *thus*, and *as a result*, which often introduce such ideas.

EXERCISE 1: *Practice what you have learned.*

Survey a chapter in a textbook, an article in a newspaper or magazine such as *US News & World Report* or *National Geographic,* or an article assigned by your instructor. You can also read articles from such popular magazines online.

GS.2b Reading and Taking Notes: Engage the Text

Some texts can be understood on the literal level; they mean exactly what they say. Others require you to draw inferences (conclusions) for yourself. In such cases, different readers may come up with different, but equally valid, interpretations. Generally, the richer and more complex the text, the more subject it is to interpretation. As you read something for the first time, keep the following in mind:

- This time around, focus on the literal meaning alone.

- Use a pencil to underline words and phrases and to make notes in the margins. When you read the text a second time, you might want to change, delete, or clarify notes by erasing old material and adding new.

- If you come upon unfamiliar words or references, don't worry. Reading, like writing, involves discovery. But don't break your focus and look up these items immediately. Underline or circle them, but look them up in a dictionary or online later.

- Mark the thesis and important ideas that support the thesis.

- In the margins, write comments about points you don't fully understand, find interesting, or want to question.

Study the notes and comments a student made when she first read the following essay, entitled "The Case Against Free College," by Elizabeth Marcello, who was a senior at the College of William and Mary when she wrote this piece. Originally posted on CollegeConservative.com, it discusses the question of shifting the burden of college tuition from the student to the government. The issue in this essay was an important part of the political platform put forth by Senator Bernard Sanders of Vermont when he campaigned for the Democratic Party's nomination for president in 2016. (A statement of Senator Sanders's philosophy follows in section GS.2g.)

The Case Against Free College
Elizabeth Marcello

Meaning? Over the past several years, young Americans have faced a <u>daunting</u> economy upon completing their undergraduate degrees and after being thrust into a seemingly jobless country. Underemployment has <u>stifled</u> **Meaning?** development and innovation. Tuition, room and board, and general living expenses are a nightmare to the current college student, never mind the high interest rates we will face upon repaying our loans. Quite frankly, American college students are panicking. **Thesis?**

1

Is this true? Check on Internet Across the sea, Germany has abolished its tuition fees, making college education completely free. How <u>surreal</u>. It was only natural that young **Meaning?** people here in America stopped and said, "Wait, why not us? Why do I have to pay?" Of course, the absence of tuition is incredibly appealing to any student trying to get a great education, **Good Point!** especially in an economy that isn't at its best.

2

But that's just it. With the absence of tuition fees, no one will be getting a free college education that is actually great, or even decent. Logically, here is what free college will look like in America: <u>If public colleges were to abolish</u> **Why? Is this** <u>tuition fees, we would be kissing the quality of</u> **her thesis?** <u>our education goodbye.</u>

3

I attend the College of William & Mary, a public institution in Williamsburg, Virginia. William & Mary is considered to be a "Public Ivy League" school, meaning our academics are **She seems to** just as strong as Harvard's, Princeton's, Yale's, etc. **know her stuff!** Currently, the tuition fees for William & Mary account for 43.1% of the operating revenue. Funds from the state of Virginia only account for 13.4% of such revenue. The school's revenue is applied largely to the payment of the professors here, along with the services offered to the students and other general maintenance tasks.

4

5

I'm lucky that I'm receiving such an amazing education and at a state-level cost. But if we stop paying tuition, who picks up the burden? It is not possible to rely on donations, so will the state of Virginia then foot the bill? Or will the federal government pay?

Good questions!

6

Neither the federal nor state government is in any financial shape to add the debt of abolishing just one school's tuition, never mind that of all of the public institutions. To do so would only hurt us, the young students, in the long run, because we would be seeing the effects of this debt later in life when our taxes are raised <u>exponentially</u> as we try and pay off loans, start families, and buy cars and houses.

Meaning?

Good point! This idea supports thesis.

7

It is obvious that, if we were to rely on the government to fund education, funds would become stretched. We would see <u>tangible</u> consequences in the number of services offered to students that are already free. Further, if the goal is to take the burden off of the students, then the salaries of our professors might also be targeted, making it less attractive for quality instructors with unique experiences to join our academic community.

Meaning?

8

I've gone through the logical, fiscal argument against "free college," but there is a broader argument to be made as well. The fact that there are now students demanding the total abolition of tuition indicates the growing level of American <u>entitlement</u> (as if there wasn't enough entitlement to begin with). Society jumps at the word "free" without thinking of the consequences, and increasingly pines for more tangible rewards with less actual work. The fact that implementing drug-testing into the process of receiving welfare is a controversial topic indicates how far we have wandered from the American dream, which brought so many people from around the world to our nation.

Meaning?

Another supporting idea. Makes sense!

Another take on the issue, but it too supports thesis.

9

Where did the determination to be one's own success go? It went when we started interpreting welfare as the haphazard <u>doling out</u> of resources rather than as a safety net for those going through rough times. It went when we stopped expecting able-bodied persons on welfare to try and seek out employment. Now, we hand out money for the sake of existing, and we take that money away from those who are working hard to put their resources and talent into the system for the benefit of society at large. I have seen so many hardworking, generous people suffer since the

Meaning?

implementation of the <u>Affordable Care Act</u>—families who used to be able to get the care they needed but now cannot afford it since premiums have skyrocketed. These hardworking people who expected nothing from the government are the ones suffering now; they are the ones responsible for funding universal healthcare, yet they cannot get the quality care they deserve.

Check out ACA on Internet.

    Everything in American politics circles back around. The entitlement mentality that demanded universal healthcare is the same that demands free college education. We have seen a decrease in the quality of healthcare since the implementation of the Affordable Care Act; is it not logical to predict the same decrease in the quality of educational institutions if we abolish tuition?

Seems logical, but I need to read more about success of ACA.

10

EXERCISE 2: *Practice what you have learned.*

Use a pencil to take notes on an editorial on a controversial issue in a newspaper or other periodical. You can find many of these online. Underline the thesis and supporting ideas, and ask questions or make comments by writing brief notes in the margins.

GS.2c Writing an Informal Outline: Strengthen Your Grasp of the Text

After your first reading, look over the words, phrases, and sentences you have underlined or marked, and read your notes in the margins. This review alone can provide enough information to create an informal outline and strengthen your understanding of what you read. (Such an outline is like the informal outline you make before writing an essay, as explained in section GS.3c.)

1. State the essay's thesis in your own words.

2. List each major idea the author uses to support the thesis.

3. Under each supporting idea, include one or two important details the author uses to develop that idea.

An Alternative: Keep a Double-Entry (Summary/Response) Notebook

The double-entry notebook is another way to summarize and respond to a text. It can help you become a more efficient reader, and it will help you when responding to the Suggestions for Journal Entries, which appear after each reading selection in this book.

1. Before you begin reading, draw a line from top to bottom on a notebook page, dividing the page in half.

2. Label the left column *Summary*; the right, *Response*.

3. As you read the text of an essay or poem, summarize the major ideas in the left column. (A summary condenses—puts in briefer form—what you have read and expresses it in your own words.)

4. In the right column, write a response to each summary statement you made on the left. These responses can take various forms, but they will probably be similar to the notes you made in the margins of the text. You might (1) ask a question, (2) disagree with an opinion, (3) identify the central idea (thesis), (4) mark a phrase you like (5), note a word or reference you will have to look up later, or (6) explain how something in the text relates to you.

Here, "The Eagle," a poem by Alfred Lord Tennyson, is followed by a notebook entry summarizing and responding to it.

The Eagle

He clasps the crag with crooked hands;
Close to the sun in lonely lands,
Ring'd with the azure world he stands.

The wrinkled sea beneath him crawls;
He watches from his mountain walls,
And like a thunderbolt, he falls.

Summary	Response
Stanza 1: Grasping a large rock, an eagle stands on a high and lonely cliff.	The eagle is "close to the sun." He's higher than we are, but very alone. Why are his feet called "hands"?
Stanza 2: The eagle looks down at the sea from on top of a mountain. He drops down quickly, furiously.	Why is the sea "wrinkled"? Because he's so high up? When he falls, what is he going after? Food? An enemy? "Thunderbolt" is a great word. He's an incredibly majestic, powerful animal—and dangerous, maybe?

GS.2d Conversing with the Text: Read It Again

As you read the text again, pretend you are having a conversation with the author. The text is the author's part of the conversation; yours is making marginal notes that do the following:

*   Add information that helps you understand a point, state agreement or disagreement, or express your own point of view.

*   Draw conclusions from the material and add insights or facts from your own observations or reading.

*   Challenge opinions, statistics, "expert" testimony, or other evidence the author uses.

*   Challenge illogical conclusions. For example, if the author claims that a college president with a doctorate in history would not support technical education, you could certainly challenge that as illogical.

*   Question the author's use of undocumented sources. If you read that a study shows that listening to rap music makes children aggressive, you might ask, "What study?" "Who conducted it?" "Where was it published?"

- Comment on the author's tone and language:

    1. Is his or her language objective, or is it "loaded"? In other words, does it call up emotions that might interfere with the readers' reasoned response to the material?

    2. Does the author express a legitimate concern, complaint, or purpose, or is his or her position compromised by self-interest, personal feelings, or ignorance?

    3. If the purpose of the essay is to persuade, is the author's approach biased? Does it tell the reader everything needed to make an informed judgment, or does it withhold important information or present it in a misleading way?

- Revise the notes you made during your first reading.

Note: Be skeptical; don't believe everything you read. Even villains and liars have published books and articles. Questioning, challenging, and demanding proof are signs of an enlightened reader.

Here are the notes and comments a student made on her second reading of "The Case Against Free College." You will notice that she has defined terms, found out more about some of the references the author makes, and added opinions about the issue.

The Case Against Free College
Elizabeth Marcello

Over the past several years, young Americans have faced a <u>daunting</u> economy upon completing their undergraduate degrees and after being thrust into a seemingly jobless country. Underemployment has <u>stifled</u> development and innovation. Tuition, room and board, and general living expenses are a nightmare to the current college student, never mind the high interest rates we will face upon repaying our loans. Quite frankly, American college students are panicking.

Meaning? = challenging

Meaning? = held back

Introduction has vivid vocab; makes you want to read more.

Thesis?

Across the sea, <u>Germany has abolished its tuition fees</u>, making college education completely free. How <u>surreal</u>. It was only natural that young people here in America stopped and said, "Wait, why not us? Why do I have to pay?" Of course, the absence of tuition is incredibly appealing to any student trying to get a great education, especially in an economy that isn't at its best.

Is this true? Check on Internet- Yes, Internet says no tuition fees in Germany

Meaning? = strange

Good point!

But that's just it. With the absence of tuition fees, no one will be getting a free college education that is actually *great*, or even decent. Logically, here is what free college will look like in America: <u>If public colleges were to abolish tuition fees, we would be kissing the quality of our education goodbye.</u>

This is in fact her thesis

1

2

3

I attend the College of William & Mary, a public institution in Williamsburg, Virginia. William & Mary is considered to be a "Public Ivy League" school, meaning our academics are just as strong as Harvard's, Princeton's, Yale's, etc. Currently, the tuition fees for William & Mary account for 43.1% of the operating revenue. Funds from the state of Virginia only account for 13.4% of such revenue. The school's revenue is applied largely to the payment of the professors here, along with the services offered to the students and other general maintenance tasks.

Why?—Read on; she explains!

She seems to know her stuff!

Good use of statistics here.

4

Good questions!

I'm lucky that I'm receiving such an amazing education and at a state-level cost. But if we stop paying tuition, who picks up the burden? It is not possible to rely on donations, so will the state of Virginia then foot the bill? Or will the federal government pay?

Good point! This idea supports thesis.

5

Neither the federal nor state government is in any financial shape to add the debt of abolishing just one school's tuition, never mind that of all public institutions. To do so would only hurt us, the young students, in the long run because we would be seeing the effects of this debt later in life when our taxes are raised <u>exponentially</u> as we try and pay off loans, start families, and buy cars and houses.

Another supporting idea. Makes sense!

Meaning? = increasing quickly

6

It is obvious that, if we were to rely on the government to fund education, funds would become stretched. We would see <u>tangible</u> consequences in the number of services offered to students that are already free. Further, if the goal is to take the burden off of the students, then the salaries of our professors might also be targeted, making it less attractive for quality instructors with unique experiences to join our academic community.

Meaning? = solid, real

7

Meaning? = cries out for

I've gone through the logical, fiscal argument against "free college," but there is a broader argument to be made as well. The fact that there are now students <u>demanding</u> the total abolition of tuition indicates the growing level of American entitlement (as if there wasn't enough <u>entitlement</u> to begin with). Society jumps at the word "free" without thinking of the consequences, and increasingly pines for more tangible rewards with less actual work. The fact that implementing drug-testing into the process of receiving welfare is a controversial topic indicates how far we have wandered from the American dream, which brought so many people from around the world to our nation.

Another take on issue, but it too supports thesis.

"Entitlement"! I've noticed that lots of people, not just my peers, think the world owes them.

8

Meaning? = distributing

9

Where did the determination to be one's own success go? It went when we started interpreting welfare as the haphazard <u>doling out</u> of resources rather than as a safety net for those going through rough times. It went when we stopped expecting able-bodied persons on welfare to try and seek out employment. Now, we hand out money for the sake of existing, and we take that money away from those who are working hard to put their resources and talent into the system for the benefit of society at large. I have seen so many hardworking, generous people suffer since the implementation of the <u>Affordable Care Act</u>—families who used to be able to get the care they needed, but now cannot afford it since premiums have skyrocketed. These hardworking people who expected nothing from the government are the ones suffering now: they are the ones responsible for funding universal healthcare, yet they cannot get the quality care they deserve.

Check out ACA on Internet; also known as "Obamacare."

Seems logical, but I need to read more about success of ACA.

Everything in American politics circles back around. The entitlement mentality that demanded universal healthcare is the same that demands free college education. We have seen a decrease in the quality of healthcare since the implementation of the Affordable Care Act; is it not logical to predict the same decrease in the quality of educational institutions if we abolish tuition?

10

From what I've been reading, lots of questions about ACA.

EXERCISE 3: *Practice what you have learned.*

Reread the editorial you read for exercise 2. Converse with the author of this editorial by underlining words and sentences and making additional marginal notes. You might also delete notes you made in the previous reading. Then, review and, if necessary, revise the informal outline you made in your first reading.

GS.2e Summarizing: Make What You Have Read Your Own

Summarizing restates the text's main and supporting ideas in your own words. It requires you to wrestle with the author's language and transform it into your own. Thus, it forces you to put into concrete form ideas and insights that otherwise would have remained vague. Summarizing improves comprehension; if you can summarize accurately, you can be sure that you've understood a selection.

Unlike a paraphrase, which only restates the original in new words, a summary also *condenses* the original. Depending on length, a chapter in a textbook or an article in a journal might be summarized in a few paragraphs. A summary of an essay of 1,500–2,000 words might span about 150 words. Read the following tips on writing summaries. Then, read "Writing an Outline for an Extended Summary," which is followed by a student summary of the "The Case Against Free College."

- After rereading the text, review the marginal notes and ideas you have marked.

- As a general rule, begin your summary by stating the essay's thesis (explicit or implied), its purpose, and its intended audience.

- State each of the supporting ideas used to develop the thesis.

- Depending on the thoroughness required, include one or two examples of the details used to develop each supporting idea.

- If you need to use some of the author's own words, introduce them appropriately and place quotation marks around them (see The Research Process in the Appendix.)

- Don't summarize each paragraph one by one. Authors often develop supporting ideas with details spread over a few paragraphs, so summarizing every paragraph is often unnecessary. (A summary is a condensation, not the restating of every detail.) Including too much detail can be misleading because it places emphasis on minor aspects of the essay, and it shows that the reader's grasp of the text is weak.

A short or concise summary can be used to take notes for inclusion in a research paper. Such summaries usually contain one to three sentences that express the paragraph's or page's main and supporting ideas. On the other hand, if you are summarizing an entire article, website, or chapter of a book, you might first want to create an outline of the text, listing the text's thesis (main or central idea) and then all the ideas that support that idea. You can also list opinions and other ideas that develop these supporting ideas. You might even want to include explanatory details in your outline. Of course, all of this will be in your own words. Here's an outline of "The Case Against Free College," followed by the student summary of the essay based upon that outline. (You will find more about outlining in GS.3 Using the Writing Process: A Tool for Discovery.)

Outline for a Student Summary of "The Case Against Free College"

Thesis is stated in first paragraph.

I. This is a response piece to students who, upon learning that Germany has made public college tuition-free, ask why can't the U.S. do the same?

Thesis: According to Elizabeth Marcello, who wrote this essay for CollegeConservative.com, tuition at public colleges should not be free.

First supporting idea

II. Free tuition for public higher education will decrease academic quality.

Ideas and details that develop first supporting idea

A. Government, neither federal nor state, can afford to make up the deficit that eliminating tuition would create.

B. This deficit would negatively affect faculty salaries, in turn attracting less-qualified professors.

Second supporting idea

III. The demand for free tuition is just another aspect of the "entitlement" mentality, which is hurting the nation.

*Ideas and
details that
develop second
supporting idea*

A. This is a mentality adopted by people who believe they have the right to sponge off the government without paying their fair share.

B. It hurts those who work hard, pay taxes, and contribute to our society.

C. Such is the mentality behind "Obamacare," which has resulted in higher health costs for hardworking Americans, who are now required to subsidize healthcare for others.

Conclusion IV. Author concludes by emphasizing her most potent argument: Free tuition will decrease the quality of higher education.

Louis Virga
Professor Reilly
ENG 101-34
10 November 2018

Student Summary of "The Case Against Free College"

Elizabeth Marcello's article argues that college tuition should not be free. This opinion piece was published on the CollegeConservative.com website in response to students who, when hearing tuition in public colleges in Germany was now free, asked why the same shouldn't be done in the United States. 1

Marcello argues that eliminating tuition payments at public colleges will decrease the quality of education at those institutions. At William & Mary, the college she attends, more than 43 percent of the institution's operating costs are covered by tuition, and she argues that neither the federal nor the state governments are in a financial position to assume this cost. 2

If, in fact, students no longer paid tuition, the resources of state and federal governments would be stretched so thinly that faculty salaries at public colleges would suffer, thereby attracting fewer qualified professors and negatively affecting the quality of education at those schools. 3

But this is only one of the reasons Marcello opposes free tuition. The movement behind it is part of a larger problem. Too many Americans, she asserts, have an "entitlement" mentality, and they find it perfectly acceptable for some people to take from the public treasury without deserving to do so, while others work hard and contribute their fair share to society. As an example, she cites the Affordable Care Act (ACA), otherwise known as "Obamacare." Too many hardworking Americans are being taxed to support universal healthcare. However, these same people, who "expected nothing from the government," are unable to afford the kind of medical care they are entitled to because the ACA has caused their health insurance premiums to rise exorbitantly. 4

Marcello concludes by comparing the effect of the ACA with what public higher education will experience if tuition is free: a marked decrease in quality. 5

Be Original: Avoid Plagiarism

You can find out more about summarizing, paraphrasing, and quoting in The Research Process in Appendix 2 of this book. For now, make sure your summary is your original restatement of the text and that it contains no traces of *plagiarism*—that is, passing off words or ideas of another person as your own.

The two items that follow summarize the first paragraph of Elizabeth Marcello's "The Case Against Free College." The first contains unintentional plagiarism; the second does not.

Unintentional plagiarism: In America, many college graduates face a challenging <u>economy</u> because of the high <u>jobless</u> rate, which also hinders <u>development</u> and <u>innovation</u>. Moreover, ordinary college costs have become a <u>nightmare</u>, not to mention the fact that <u>college loans with high interest rates</u> will have to be paid off once one graduates. <u>Students in America's colleges are in a panic because of all of this.</u>

More original summary: College students in this country have much to be concerned with. First, the costs of attending an institution of higher learning are oppressive, and students must deal with paying back their college loans, which come with hefty interest costs, after they graduate. Once out, these students also face the problem that there might not be a job waiting for them, for the economy is not producing enough new jobs.

The underlined words in the first example come from Marcello's essay. In addition, this first version follows the original's organization too closely. The second example is fresher, both in language and organization. It shows that the student has understood the content of the editorial.

Using the Split-Screen Function to Paraphrase and Check for Plagiarism

Most computers offer a split-screen function, which can aid in checking for plagiarism in paraphrasing and summarizing material. This tool allows you to review the original version of a text on the top half of the screen. (This works best for original material in electronic form. Otherwise, you will have to type it in yourself, which you might want to do anyway, especially when taking notes for research.) You can then paraphrase or summarize that text on the bottom half of the screen. Each half can be scrolled through separately, allowing you to compare specific sentences carefully to make your version more accurate and to eliminate unintentional plagiarism.

EXERCISE 4: *Practice what you have learned.*

Write a summary of a newspaper or periodical editorial or opinion piece. Try using your computer's split-screen function.

GS.2f Responding and Critiquing: Evaluate What You Have Read

You can respond to the ideas in a text, you can critique (evaluate) its message and presentation, or you can do both. In a *response*, you comment on the author's ideas by agreeing, disagreeing, drawing comparisons, adding new evidence, presenting another point of view, raising questions, applying these ideas to other things you have read or observed, or doing all of the above. You engage the text just as you do when making notes in the margins, but now your part of the conversation is more formal. You are creating your own text, which might complement, add to, or reject the original text. In fact, it might do a combination of all these things.

In a *critique*, you evaluate the text's message and its presentation. Although the words *critique* and *criticism* are related, a critique is not just negative; it can mention both strengths and weaknesses. Begin by reviewing your marginal notes and your summary. If necessary, go back to the text itself and reread it. Revise the notes you have already made in light of criteria (measuring sticks) you are using to evaluate what you have read.

Criteria used to evaluate a text can differ from reader to reader. Following are only a few questions you might ask as you critique a text. Perhaps these questions will help you create some of your own criteria. After you have read all the questions, read the student critique of Marcello's "The Case Against Free College," by Louis Virga, which follows the suggested criteria.

Suggested Criteria for Evaluating Text

- What are the author's credentials? Is the publication in which the essay was first published reputable?

- Are the essay's thesis and purpose clear and reasonable?

- Are supporting ideas logical and well developed?

- Does the author make unsubstantiated claims?

- Does the author use evidence from studies or experts to support the thesis without naming these authorities?

- Is the author impartial, or does he or she use language that appeals to the reader's emotions and self-interest? If the latter, is this language simply strong and moving, or is it unfair or biased?

- Does the author use information that is incomplete or incorrect?

- Does the essay lack important information that you know might contradict one of its supporting ideas or even its thesis?

- Does the author raise important questions and answer them adequately? Does he or she address opposing arguments fairly?

- Is the language of the essay appropriate to the intended audience? Does it contain jargon or other language that is unnecessarily complicated?

Louis Virga
Professor Reilly
ENG 101-34
19 November 2018

Making College Free: Critique of "The Case Against Free College"

Elizabeth Marcello's arguments against making tuition free at public colleges in the United States are both clear and persuasive. The author wrote the article when she was a student at the College of William & Mary in Virginia, a state-supported institution, at which more than 40% of the college's operating costs are covered by student tuition.

1

Marcello poses two arguments against free tuition, both of them convincing. The first is that if the state or federal governments assumed the costs students would have paid, colleges would find themselves quite underfunded, for, as Marcello says, the budgets of both the states and the nation can ill afford such an expense. With government paying the bill, college budgets would have to be slashed. This would lead to a less-qualified faculty because the more talented people would choose other, higher-paying professions. In the end, the quality of higher education would suffer. Her second argument has to do with the "entitlement" attitude that many Americans have. To show us the effects of this mentality, she mentions the Affordable Care Act, which takes money from "those who are working hard to put their resources and talent into the system," so that others might enjoy this "entitlement." Finally,

2

she compares the effects of the ACA with what will happen as a result of making public colleges tuition-free.

Marcello's arguments and the ideas and statistics she uses to back them up are quite solid. However, she might have spent more time explaining why federal and state governments are so hard-pressed to dole out more money. Her argument would have been a little more pointed had she reminded the reader of the country's multi-trillion-dollar debt or had she cited statistics about income and real-estate tax rates in her own state of Virginia. More could also have been said about the Affordable Care Act and its consequences. Here, Marcello could have used information from any number of recent articles criticizing "Obamacare." Finally, she might have brought up one or two opposing arguments and addressed or attacked them. Doing so would have been especially effective in terms of responding to the pleas of so many students whose college costs are exorbitant and who rightfully desire some relief.

Nonetheless, this is a convincing, well-written essay, which approaches its readers with language that is clear, to the point, and easy to access. What is especially impressive is her insight into the effects of free tuition and her analogy of them with those of the Affordable Care Act. Of course, the essay was posted on CollegeConservative.org, so it is quite obvious where Marcello's political sympathies lie, and one has to wait to hear arguments from the liberal side to make a fair judgment on this issue. Nonetheless, Marcello's essay is objective, well-thought-out, and interesting.

EXERCISE 5: *Practice what you have learned.*

Write a critique of an essay, article, or textbook chapter you have been reading. Begin by reviewing the Suggested Criteria for Evaluating Text, listed earlier in this section.

GS.2g Synthesizing: Bring Ideas Together in a New Statement

Learning to synthesize or to bring ideas together from different sources is a logical step in developing critical reading skills. Synthesizing requires the coherent *restating, combining,* and *reconciling* of information from different sources.

In various college courses, you may be asked to evaluate one writer's position against another's, compare or contrast ideas on the same issue, and even create an entirely new perspective after reading several different discussions on an issue. However, this new product should be more than a collection of borrowed elements; it should also reflect your own thinking, perspectives, and experiences. Just as important, it should be developed and organized in a way that suits your purpose.

Read "It's Time to Make College Tuition Free and Debt Free," posted on BernieSanders.com. Senator Sanders made this idea part of his platform during his campaign for the Democratic presidential nomination in 2016. Then, read Matthew Roberts's "Paying Our Way," a student essay that synthesizes materials from the Sanders post and Marcello's "The Case Against Free College."

It's Time to Make College Tuition Free and Debt Free

In a highly competitive global economy, we need the best-educated workforce in the world. It is insane and counter-productive to the best interests of our country and our future, that hundreds of thousands of bright young people cannot afford to go to college, and that millions of others leave school with a mountain of debt that burdens them for decades. That shortsighted path to the future must end.

Bernie Sanders will fight to make sure that every American who studies hard in school can go to college regardless of how much money [his or her] parents make and without going deeply into debt.

Here are the six steps that Bernie will take to make college debt free:

Make tuition free at public colleges and universities. This is not a radical idea. Germany eliminated tuition because [its government] believed that charging students $1,300 per year was discouraging Germans from going to college. Chile will do the same. Finland, Norway, Sweden and many other countries around the world also offer free college to all of their citizens. If other countries can take this action, so can the United States of America.

In fact, it's what many of our colleges and universities used to do. The University of California system offered free tuition at its schools until the 1980s. In 1965, average tuition at a four-year public university was just $243 and many of the best colleges—including the City University of New York—did not charge any tuition at all. The Sanders plan would make tuition free at public colleges and universities throughout the country.

Stop the federal government from making a profit on student loans. Over the next decade, it has been estimated that the federal government will make a profit of over $110 billion on student loan programs. This is morally wrong and it is bad economics. Sen. Sanders will fight to prevent the federal government from profiteering on the backs of college students and use this money instead to significantly lower student loan interest rates.

Substantially cut student loan interest rates. Under the Sanders plan, the formula for setting student loan interest rates would go back to where it was in 2006. If this plan were in effect today, interest rates on undergraduate loans would drop from 4.29% to just 2.37%.

Allow Americans to refinance student loans at today's low interest rates. It makes no sense that you can get an auto loan today with an interest rate of 2.5%, but millions of college graduates are forced to pay interest rates of 5–7% or more for decades. Under the Sanders plan, Americans would be able to refinance their student loans at today's low interest rates.

Allow students to use need-based financial aid and work study programs to make college debt free. The Sanders plan would require public colleges and universities to meet 100% of the financial needs of the lowest-income students. Low-income students would be able to use federal, state and college financial aid to cover room and board, books and living expenses. And Sanders would more than triple the federal work study program to build valuable career experience that will help them after they graduate.

Fully paid for by imposing a tax on Wall Street speculators. The cost of this $75 billion a year plan is fully paid for by imposing a tax of a fraction of a percent on Wall Street speculators who nearly destroyed the economy seven years ago. More than 1,000 economists have endorsed a tax on Wall Street speculation, and today some 40 countries throughout the world have imposed a similar tax, including Britain, Germany, France, Switzerland, and China. If the taxpayers of this country could bail out Wall Street in 2008, we can make public colleges and universities free.

A Synthesis of "The Case Against Free College" and "It's Time to Make College Tuition Free and Debt Free"

Louis Virga
Prof. Reilly
ENG 101-34
10 December 2017

Paying Our Way

One of the most important issues facing American college students today is the high cost
of college. Along with this, many students face the difficult problem of paying back college
loans after graduation. Some politicians are now advocating the extension of free tuition to
students who attend American public colleges and universities. Among the most prominent
of these is Sen. Bernie Sanders, Democrat of Vermont, whose position is outlined on his website BernieSanders.com. However, solid arguments opposing this opinion have been made
by many other people, including Elizabeth Marcello, who, while attending the College of
William & Mary, posted "The Case Against Free College" on a conservative website. Both
Sanders and Marcello offer insight into dealing with the burden of college expenses and
student debt.

Sanders points out that, in Germany and other countries, college tuition is now free.
Marcello agrees, but she calls this state of affairs "surreal," pointing out that eliminating
student tuition would place the burden on state and federal governments, which are already
strapped for cash. At William & Mary, the college that Marcello attended, the state of Virginia covered only about 14% of the school's operating budget, while student tuitions covered more than 43%. If, in fact, the state had to subsidize public colleges more than it does
now, it could not provide the difference unless it raised taxes on its wage earners, a move
that would penalize graduates once they entered the work force. Even so, new tax revenues
would not be enough to cover the total contribution that student tuition provides, and the
colleges would have to slash their budgets. This, according to Marcello, would result in the
hiring of less-qualified faculty (more talented people would elect to enter professions other
than college teaching), thereby lowering the quality of higher education.

Sanders also argues that interest rates on student loans should be lowered, so as to make
the burden of paying back these loans less difficult. In addition, however, he would "require
public colleges and universities to meet 100% of the financial needs of the lowest-income students." This means that college expenses other than tuition would also be free for a portion
of the population. While Marcello does not address this proposal directly, she does argue
against the "entitlement mentality," which bristles at the notion that welfare recipients should
have to undergo drug testing to qualify for their benefits. It's this mentality, she argues, that is
behind the Affordable Care Act (ACA), passed by the Obama administration, which extends
health benefits to the uninsured while making it nearly impossible for "hard-working, generous people … to get the care" they need because the ACA has caused insurance premiums to skyrocket. Comparing the effects of eliminating the need for students to contribute to
their education to those of the ACA, Marcello predicts disaster for public higher education
in America.

Marcello's arguments are hard to deny. Indeed, given the fact that the majority of Americans believe the ACA needs revising or repealing, the analogy that Marcello makes is convincing. On the other hand, some of Senator Sanders's positions should be given a fair hearing. For example, why can't the interest rates on college loans go back to where they were
in 2006? And if the government bailed out Wall Street in 2008, as he says, why can't it help
students in our public colleges? One thing is for sure: the problem of rising costs for higher

education is one of the greatest challenges our nation faces. We need to approach it from a variety of perspectives and consider varying—even opposing—opinions if we are to solve it.

Works Cited

"It's Time to Make College Tuition Free and Debt Free." BernieSanders.com, n.d., berniesanders.com/issues/its-time-to-make-college-tuition-free-and-debt-free/. Accessed 5 Dec 2017.

Marcello, Elizabeth. "The Case Against Free College." CollegeConservative.com, 9 Oct. 2014, thecollegeconservative.com/2014/10/09/the-case-against-free-college/. Accessed 5 Dec 2017.

Crediting Your Sources

When you use other authors' materials in a synthesis, you must provide parenthetical citations, thereby informing your reader that the material is not your own. *You must do this whether you paraphrase, summarize, or quote directly.* Follow standard guidelines such as those published by the Modern Language Association (style.mla.org) or by the American Psychological Association (www.apastyle.org) or by another professional group, as required by your instructor.

EXERCISE 6: *Practice what you have learned.*

Find another essay or editorial that relates directly to the topic or issue addressed in an essay or editorial you have read recently. Synthesize ideas from what you have read with your own ideas.

GS.3 Using the Writing Process: A Tool for Discovery

This section explains steps in the writing of an essay:

GS.3a The Writing Process: An Overview

GS.3b Prewriting

GS.3c Outlining

GS.3e Drafting and Revising

GS.3f Editing and Proofreading

GS.3a The Writing Process: An Overview

Both writing and reading are processes. (Refer back to GS.2 Becoming an Active College Reader.) The writing process can be explained in four steps: *prewriting, outlining, drafting/revising,* and *editing/proofreading.*

Prewriting, also called *invention,* consists of two activities:

- Deciding upon your intended audience (your readers), purpose, and style

- Gathering information

Professors Gilbert Muller and Harvey Wiener explain the importance of this first step:

> Few writers begin without some warm-up activity. Generally called prewriting, the steps they take before producing a draft almost always start with thinking about their topic. They talk to friends and colleagues; they browse in libraries … ; they read newspapers

and magazine articles. Sometimes they jot down notes and lists in order to put on paper some of their thoughts in very rough form. Some writers use free-association; they record as thoroughly as possible their random, unedited ideas .... Using the raw, often disorganized materials produced in this preliminary stage, many writers try to group related thoughts with a scratch outline. ("On Writing.")

In addition to helping you answer important questions about your writing project, prewriting provides insights about how your ideas might be organized and leads to the second step in the process: outlining.

Outlining provides a blueprint or framework through which to present information in an easy-to-follow manner. As you will see in section GS.3c, you can choose from two types of outlines: formal and informal.

Drafting and revising are the heart of the process. In general, you should begin drafting after deciding on purpose and audience, gathering information, and making an outline. Remember that first drafts are also called *rough drafts*. So, spend time revising—completely rewriting and restructuring—your first, second, and third drafts until you are sure that your paper says what you want it to say clearly and completely.

Editing and proofreading may come last, but they are extremely important. Neglect them and you risk embarrassing yourself or confusing and frustrating the reader.

These steps are neatly defined, but they are not always separate. For example, while editing, you might realize that you need to add more information or correct a serious organizational problem. If this happens, don't worry. Go back and make the changes. That's how the process should work.

GS.3b Prewriting

This section explains (1) how to determine purpose, audience, and style and (2) how to gather information.

Determining Purpose, Audience, and Style

Determine Your Purpose

Writing is practical; it always serves a purpose, whether it be to produce a technical report, to explain a scientific process, to argue about a social issue, or simply to make an entry in a diary. Purpose determines the major approach or method a writer uses and the form the document will take. To explain the workings of a cell phone, you might use a technique called *process analysis* to list the steps in the transmission of sound over a wireless system. If you are trying to convince the state legislature to increase funding of school athletic programs, you would probably use *persuasion*. If you are simply making a diary entry, you might use *narration* to record events in the order they occurred.

However, pieces of writing rarely use only one method or approach. For example, a *process analysis* paper that explains how cell phones work might also use *definition* to explain what a transmission tower is. It might *contrast* land-line and wireless phones. In short, even though a piece of writing relies on one major approach, it can also use others, depending on the writer's purpose.

In first-year college writing courses, instructors sometimes specify the purpose of an assignment and even require students to take a specific approach. At times, however, professors ask students to choose their own purposes and then decide for themselves on how best to achieve them. All of this is part of maturing as a writer. Although we often think of writing as a matter of sticking to the rules of grammar and mastering the techniques of rhetoric, good writing also requires the ability to make judgments. For example, you must decide on a topic's particular focus, identify relevant information, and determine ways to fulfill your purpose.

A writer develops judgment only through experience—trial and error. So, don't get discouraged if you suddenly discover that you have chosen the wrong approach or have to redefine your purpose. Go back and rethink things. Then, start again. Of course, this might require doing more information gathering by using one of the prewriting techniques explained in the next few pages. It might also require you to get rid of some information gathered earlier because it is irrelevant to your new purpose. However, this is normal—writing is a process of discovery and revision.

The best time to think about your purpose for an academic essay is before you begin gathering information. After carefully considering the assignment, write a statement of purpose (a sentence or two) on an index card or scrap of paper. Keep in mind that you might revise this statement later—after you have gathered information, made an outline, or even written a first draft.

Consider the Audience

The audience for any piece of writing is its readers. Consider your audience even before you begin gathering information. Let's say your purpose is to convince your classmates to use the library's online periodical database to find information on their majors. You might first have to define *periodical* and *database*. You might have to explain that periodicals come in various types: magazines, professional journals, and newspapers. You might also have to convince your readers of the ease with which databases can be used.

On the other hand, what if you are trying to convince college librarians to subscribe to a particular online database? You certainly would not explain terms like *periodical* and *database*. Doing so would bore and insult them.

The primary audience for any college paper is the instructor. However, you might be asked to discuss your work in a small writing group or with the entire class. If so, you must consider your whole audience—both instructor and students—and you might need to include explanatory information and definitions of special terms that you would not have included had you been writing for your instructor alone.

Even if you are writing only for your instructor, evaluating the needs of a reader can get tricky. Most college composition instructors have advanced degrees in English or related disciplines. Thus, you can assume that they are well trained in their field. But can they be expected to be knowledgeable in other specialized areas? Would they know the process by which atoms are split or be familiar with the latest theories relating to prison reform? If you choose to write about popular music, can you assume that your instructor knows the difference between hip-hop and gangsta rap? Again, try to determine your audience's needs before you begin gathering information, but remember that you can revise your evaluation of your readers any time in the writing process. You will learn more about evaluating an audience in section 5 of this book.

Use Formal Style in Academic Writing

Style refers to the level of language you use. Essentially there are three levels. But *formal style* is preferable in academic writing

Informal style is used when writing to a limited audience—a close friend, a classmate—in emails, short notes, or personal letters. Such writing may contain colloquialisms, or conversational expressions used only in certain locales. Informal style also allows for slang and private language, which have special meanings within a limited group and which change rapidly. It can also contain clichés, common phrases heard over and over again. Consider this passage from a student's email to a friend:

> Most guys in my frat are pretty brainy, and they hit the books hard. But they aren't that stuck up, not like the Geek Patrol we knew at Jefferson High. In fact, they're cool! They even tutor kids whose grades are tanking.

Terms like *guys, brainy, stuck up, Geek Patrol, kids,* and *tanking* are examples of informal language.

Familiar style is used in short business memos, in letters to the editors of newspapers, and in emails or letters to older relatives or acquaintances. Here is a version of the above paragraph as it appeared in the student's letter to his former boss:

> You would like the students in my fraternity. They are fairly smart, and they really put their noses to the grindstone when they want to ace a big exam. However, they're not snobs. In fact, they often tutor other kids who are having trouble with their studies.

This version is somewhat more formal. It does not include slang or private language, but it does use colloquialisms such as "ace a big exam," and a cliché—"noses to the grindstone." In the familiar style, it also addresses the reader directly by using the word *you.*

Formal style belongs in academic papers, in answers to essay questions, and in business letters and reports. Notice that the writer now replaces all colloquialisms, slang, and clichés and that he no longer addresses the reader directly by using *you.* The vocabulary is more sophisticated than the relaxed choice of words in the two previous versions.

> Students in my fraternity are quite likable. They are intelligent, and they are also diligent, studying hard, especially when it comes to major examinations. However, they are not snobs. In fact, they often tutor other students who are having difficulty with their studies.

Try to use formal style from the moment you begin drafting your paper. However, you can always eliminate slang, colloquialisms, and nonformal elements when you edit.

Gathering Information for Writing

You can use seven techniques to gather facts, ideas, and opinions for any assignment, especially for journal entries, like those responding to the Suggestions for Journal Entries after each reading selection in this book. A good way to start a journal entry is to read the notes you took in the margins of a reading selection. (You can learn more about note-taking in GS4, The Making of a Student Essay: From Prewriting to Proofreading.) Then, just follow the Suggestions for Journal Entries, which often recommend using one of the information-gathering techniques explained here.

Listing involves putting down details that you believe are most important, startling, or obvious about your chosen topic. At times, you can compile a list simply by putting down whatever comes to mind. Here's one that student Aggie Canino made when asked to describe the effects of a storm:

- Clogged rain sewers
- Giant trees down, across lawns, roads
- Wires down, no telephone, no lights, flooding
- 50-mile per hour winds, thunder, lightening
- Ligtening destroys old oak on neighbors lawn
- Bridge washed away, road closed traffic detured.
- Terrifying sounds
- Dog hides under bed
- Flooded basements
- Lasts one hour
- Howling wind, frightening
- Thunder, lightening
- Complete darkness at 2 pm
- Crack utility poles
- Flooded streets

Your list may be repetitious and have spelling errors, but don't worry about such problems now; you can correct them later. Just concentrate on your topic and record details.

After you run out of things to say, stop writing and read your list. Cross out information that is repetitious and correct spelling. As you do this, new details will pop into your head; use these to add specifics. For example, Aggie expanded "crack utility poles" to include "white sparks flying from downed power lines," and she expressed the terror she felt as she heard the "splintering of a sixty-foot oak struck by lightning" and the "breaking of windows into which tree limbs flew."

Focused freewriting is a common technique to help overcome writer's block, a problem that results in staring at a blank paper while trying to come up with something to say. Freewriting involves writing nonstop for up to ten minutes and recording ideas that come to mind at random. Focused freewriting is similar, but it involves concentrating on one topic. Let's say you want to freewrite by focusing on a storm. Your results might look like this sample, which captures a student's memories of Hurricane Sandy, which hit the eastern United States in 2012.

> The clogged rain sewers were overflowing, and there was a lot of flooding with strong winds knocking down power lines. Thunder cracked and lightening flashed. Giant tree limb fell across the road and a birch was bent double and there were lots of flooded basements. The storm lasted so many hours. Several downed power lines threw threatening sparks and flashes across the road. My street was blocked; a large oak had fallen across it. We lost our electricity for a week. The crash of thunder shook my bones. My dog hid under the bed. We were terrified.

Again, don't worry about grammar and other errors at this time; just focus on your topic and record ideas quickly. As always, read your journal notes immediately after you've recorded your ideas. Doing so helps cut out repetition, rework parts that require clarification, and add details that come to mind in the process.

Clustering can turn a broad subject into a limited and manageable topic. Also called *mapping* or *webbing*, it is another effective way to gather information. Like focused freewriting, clustering uses free association. Here's what to do:

1. In the center of a blank piece of paper, write the word or phrase that stands for the broad topic you want to write about. Let's say it's dance. Then, think of subtopics such as ballet, ballroom dancing, folk dancing, or modern dance. Arranging these subtopics around a general subject might result in a diagram that looks like this:

Ballroom dancing   Ballet   Dancing as exercise

Modern Dance   DANCE   Dancing in the movies

Folk/ethnic dancing

2. Write down details related to these subtopics; continue until you run out of things to say. Draw lines between each of your subtopics and the ideas and details that relate to them. Here's what your paper might look like when you are finished.

Dame Margot
Fontaine
Joffrey
Great
Music
Aerobic
exercise
Stamina
Weight
loss
Ballroom
dancing
Ballet
Dancing as
exercise
George
Balanchine
DANCE
Dirty
Dancing
John
Travolta
Martha
Graham
Modern
Dance
Dancing
in movies
Jose
Limon
Folk/Ethnic
dancing
Ginger Rogers &
Fred Astaire
Hula
Morris
dance
Bolero
Highland fling
Tarantella
Irish jig
Polka
African ritual dances
Square dance
Hopi snake dance

Notice that some subtopics have been given more attention than others. That just means that you might know more about folk/ethnic dancing than ballroom dancing. In fact, clustering helps focus on the topic that the writer knows most about or is most interested in.

Of course, you might stop at this stage, review your notes, and even write a working thesis statement for a paper on ethnic dancing. Or, you might focus your topic even further by getting more specific. Let's say you are particularly interested in African ritual dancing and want to learn more about it through Internet or library research. You can extend your cluster by focusing on that subtopic. Here's what that cluster might look like:

Headdresses

Evolution of African dancing

Mask

Costumes

Body movements

Masks

Body painting

Fertility dances

African ritual dancing

Harvest celebrations

Leaps, jumps, thrusts

Drum music

Singing

Mime

Team dancing

Religious aspects

Seasonal dances

Drawing a subject tree is another way to settle on a manageable topic and gather information. As with clustering, start with a broad topic. Then, divide it into two or three subtopics or branches. Next, subdivide each branch until you have limited your topic sufficiently and have gathered enough information to write a working thesis statement and an outline.

As you draw a subject tree, you will naturally put down more details under subtopics with which you are most familiar or in which you have the greatest interest. For example, the writer who created the subject tree for "uses of computers" would probably choose to write an essay on the ways computers help students and teachers.

Industry

Manufacturing

Record Keeping

Payroll

Personnel files

Robotics

Quality control

Inventory control

Business/Professions

Business letters

Writing

Accounting

Memoranda

Reports

Sales tax files

Accounts payable/ receivable

Manuals

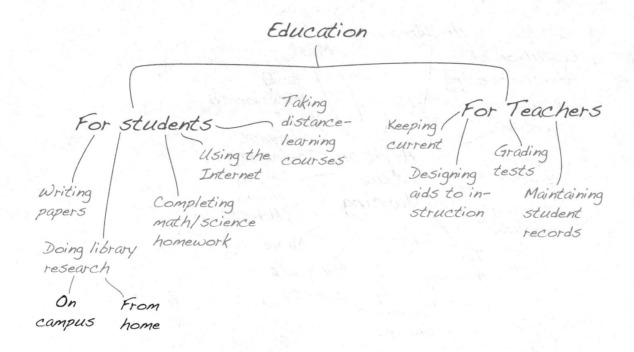

Brainstorming is a tool used to gather information in a small group, and it results in a random collection of words and phrases written across a page. Often, people working together can gather far more information than someone working independently. One of the most effective ways to begin brainstorming is to ask the journalists' questions; reporters ask these when they plan their stories: *What happened? When did it happen? Who did it? Where did it happen? Why did it happen?* and *How did it happen?* An easy way to remember questions that journalists use is to think of them as the five Ws and the H.

Journalists' questions work best if you want to tell a story or explain how or why something happens or should happen. However, you might have to think of different questions if you have other purposes in mind. Say you want to describe Uncle Charlie; you might ask: *What does he look like? Who are his friends? What kind of job does he have?* In any case, remember that prewriting is also called invention, so invent as many kinds of questions as you like.

Not all questions yield useful information. However, the answers to only one or two might suggest ideas and details to other members of your brainstorming group. In a little while, a mental chain reaction will occur, and you will find yourself discussing ideas, facts, and opinions that seem to pop up naturally.

EXERCISE 7: *Practice what you have learned.*

Pick a topic related to your academic major or to a long-time interest. If you are majoring in nursing, you might focus on pediatric nursing or emergency-room nursing. If you are a psychology major, consider the causes of anorexia nervosa. Or focus on a hobby or sport such as model railroading, camping, or basketball. Begin gathering what you already know about this topic through listing. Then, using the same topic, try clustering or drawing a subject tree.

Interviewing requires you to ask appropriate questions of people who know about your topic. Like brainstorming, interviewing gives you other perspectives from which to view your topic, and it often yields new and valuable information.

The kinds of interview questions you ask should be determined by your purpose. If you want to learn why something happened, what someone did, or how something works, you might begin your interview with questions like those journalists ask: *Who, When, What, Where, Why*, and *How*. Just make sure that the person you interview is knowledgeable and is willing to spend enough time with you to make your interview worthwhile. When you schedule your meeting with this person, discuss your purpose and the kinds of questions you might ask. This will enable him or her to prepare thoughtful responses.

Finally, come to the interview prepared. Write down a few important questions ahead of time. You can use these in the interview to get your subject talking. If your questions are clear and interesting, you should gather more information than you bargained for. On the other hand, don't be upset if the interview doesn't go as planned. Your subject might not answer any of your questions but simply discuss ideas as they come to mind. Such interviews can be very successful—just take good notes!

Summarizing is an information-gathering technique that condenses another writer's ideas and puts them into your own words. It can be used to combine information you have read with details gathered from your own experiences. Just be sure to use your own words throughout the summary. Also, if you use this information in an essay, give the source of the material credit by mentioning the author's name or the title of the work. For example, if you decide to summarize a paragraph from Richard Marius's "Advice to new Writers" (an essay in chapter 1), you might begin: "As Marius argues. … "

EXERCISE 8: *Practice what you have learned.*

Read Richard Marius's "Advice to new writers" in chapter 1. Then summarize this essay, paragraph by paragraph. Try to capture the content of each paragraph in one sentence.

GS.3c Outlining

After gathering information and deciding on a working thesis, many writers construct an outline, which makes the writing of a rough draft easier. Think of an outline as a blueprint, which guides you through the drafting process.

For most short essays, an informal or scratch outline is sufficient. However, if you are writing a lengthy essay, such as a library research paper, you might want to use a formal outline, which can also serve as a table of contents. Ask your instructor if you should have an outline and, if so, what type. In any event, spend a few minutes on a working thesis statement, your essay's central idea. Then, jot down at least a scratch outline of the essay's main points. (You will learn more about writing thesis statements and developing paragraphs in chapters 1 and 2.)

Writing an Informal Scratch Outline

Let's say you reviewed the notes you took when you completed a clustering exercise about African ritual dancing. Realizing that the most important aspect of what you know about such dancing is that it is energetic and fascinating, you decide to write an essay whose working thesis might be, "African ritual dances, which I observed in Zimbabwe, are dramatic." As you review your notes a second time, you realize that several of the ideas you jotted down in your clusters do not relate to your working thesis. For example, the fact that certain dances are seasonal does not support or develop your thesis, so you decide not to mention it. Instead, you focus on aspects of the dances that are dramatic. At the same time, you realize that the working thesis needs to be expanded to include other aspects of the dances that will make your paper more accurate and specific. So, you revise the thesis. Here's a sample scratch outline for such a paper:

> Revised Thesis: African ritual dances, which I observed in Zimbabwe, are the most dramatic, colorful, and exciting folk dances I have ever seen.
>   1. Colorful masks
>   2. Frightening costumes
>   3. Bodies painted in bright colors, eye-catching patterns
>   4. Joyous music
>   5. Vivid body movements

This outline is no more than a brief list of details pulled from the clustering exercise completed earlier. However, it provides a pattern the writer can follow to construct a first, or working, draft.

Writing a Formal Outline

A formal outline differs from a scratch outline in that it is more complete and more consistent in structure. A formal outline on African ritual dancing might look like this:

I. Introduction
   A. Folk dances differ in form and purpose from culture to culture.
   B. Many European and American folk dances reveal much about the cultures in which they originated.
   C. Thesis: African ritual dances, which I observed in Zimbabwe, are the most dramatic, colorful, and exciting folk dances I have ever seen.

II. Dancers wear bizarre masks intended to startle and even frighten the audience.
   A. Patterns painted on these masks are vivid and varied.
   B. They take odd shapes and are often very large.
   C. Many are rectangular or pointed; others resemble shields used in warfare.
   D. Some triple the size of the wearer's face to make him appear monstrous.
   E. Some look like faces of animals; others suggest that the dancer may have come from another planet.

III. The costumes are rich, complex, and colorful.
   A. Some are made of animal skins; others are woven from native vegetable fibers.
   B. All are extremely colorful.
   C. The costumes make use of fascinating geometric patterns.
   D. Huge headdresses are worn, sometimes resembling animal heads.

IV. Drum music gets the heart pounding; the air is sometimes filled with song.
   A. The musicians keep the pace energetic, often adding to the dramatic effect.
   B. A chorus of women singing sweetly often accompanies the dancers.

V. The real spectacle comes in the dancers' acrobatics.
   A. Each dancer conveys a message or story through vivid movement.

    B. Performers run, stomp, and leap high into the air.

    C. Some prance around on stilts, standing 15 feet tall.

    D. They even approach members of the audience, pretending to threaten them with lunges and howls.

This formal outline is very different from the scratch outline:

- It contains more detail. Each of its major sections is subdivided into more specific subheadings.
- Each heading is a complete sentence. In fact, the writer might use each of these as the topic sentence of a paragraph. A topic sentence expresses a paragraph's main or central idea. (You will learn more about topic sentences in chapters 1 and 2.)
- Sections of the formal outline are identified by number or letter. The major headings have Roman numerals (I, II, III). These are subdivided into items with capital letters (A, B, C,), and these are followed by Arabic numerals (1, 2, 3). It isn't necessary to divide each major heading into an equal number of subheadings. For example, IV is divided into two subheadings, but V is subdivided into four. Actually, the pattern to follow is straightforward:

    I. (Roman numeral)

        A. (Capital letter)

            1. (Arabic numeral)

                a. (Lowercase letter)

- Each unit is divided into at least two subunits. Never place only one subheading below a more important heading. If you can't divide a heading into two or more subdivisions, leave it alone

Not	But	Or
I.	I.	I.
A.	A.	A.
1.	1.	B.
B.	2.	
	B.	

    Whether you make a scratch or formal outline, remember that an outline is only a guide to drafting an essay. As you begin your first draft, stick to your outline closely, but don't be afraid to add new information, make changes in organization, replace or delete parts, or revise your working thesis. Of course, if you are writing a long paper and want your outline to serve as a table of contents, you will have to revise it to reflect changes you have made. But this can be done later. Just remember that writing is a process of discovery; the deeper you get into it, the better you will understand what you have to say.

Writing Other Types of Outlines for Special Purposes

Here are some other kinds of outlines you might use depending upon the purpose of your paper.

An Essay That Makes More Than One Point in Its Thesis

If your thesis makes more than one point, you might expand upon each of those points in a separate body paragraph or groups of paragraphs. Here's a blueprint based upon Siu Chan's essay "Suffering," which appears in chapter 1.

Paragraph 1: Introduces the essay and states its thesis.

[Living] in Cambodia from 1975 to 1979 was the worst time in my life:

    Point A   **Point B**

I was allowed little personal freedom, I witnessed the death of

Point C

my family, and I nearly died of starvation.

Paragraph 2: Develops point A.

When the communists took over, the government destroyed nearly all my <u>personal freedom</u>.

Paragraph 3: Develops point B.

During those years, <u>I lost six members of my family.</u>

Paragraph 4: Develops point C.

I can still remember a three-month period in which <u>I nearly starved to death.</u>

Paragraph 5: States essay's conclusion.

Having gone through [that suffering], I can appreciate the life I have now.

An Outline for an Essay That Supports an Opinion

As you will see in chapter 12, one of the best ways to argue an opinion is through the conclusion-and-support method. Start by stating your opinion in a thesis (also known as a conclusion in argumentation). Then, in the essay's body paragraphs, discuss ideas that support the thesis in detail. In other words, explain why you hold this opinion. Of course, some supporting ideas may need more than one paragraph to be adequately developed.

Sometimes, writers of argument papers find it effective to anticipate and respond to the opposing point of view in addition to supporting their own arguments. In the outline that follows, the writer does this in paragraph 5.

Paragraph 1: Introduces essay and states thesis.

Term limits should be established for all elected government officials: local, state, and national.

Paragraph 2: Develops first supporting idea.

Limiting the time politicians can serve prevents them from becoming too powerful.

Paragraph 3: Develops second supporting idea.

Term limits create an opportunity for a greater number of people to serve, thereby making government more representative.

Paragraph 4: Develops third supporting idea.

Term limits would remove the incumbents' name-recognition advantage over lesser-known candidates at election time. This would make it easier to infuse government with new ideas new people would bring.

Paragraph 5: Anticipates and answers opposing argument.

Opponents of term limits argue that politicians with seniority can do more for people back home than newcomers can. However, this just supports the notion that long-time office holders have too much power.

Paragraph 6: Concludes the essay by summing up and restating the thesis.

EXERCISE 9: *Practice what you have learned.*

Review the notes you made for exercise 7. Then write a formal or informal outline for an essay that might use this information.

GS.3d Drafting and Revising

Start the first draft several days before the paper is due. This will give you time to revise, edit, and proofread it without rushing.

Drafting

- Begin drafting by reviewing decisions you made about purpose, audience, and style. With these in the back of your mind, reread the notes you took when gathering information through listing, researching, or another method discussed earlier. Check your working thesis and your outline and make last-minute changes if necessary. For example, when rereading your notes, you might discover that you left out an important point when you wrote the outline.

- Keep your working thesis and your outline in front of you as you begin to draft. Following your outline, put down important ideas and concrete details paragraph by paragraph. Include as much information as you can. If you repeat yourself or write more than you need to, no matter. You can remove words, sentences, and even whole paragraphs when you revise. And don't worry about grammar or spelling errors; you can correct them when you edit.

- If you get tired before completing this draft, take a break. However, finish it before beginning another project. Once you have done so, put the rough draft aside for twenty-four hours if possible. When you get back to it, you will approach it with a clearer head.

Revising

- Read your rough draft two or three times. Revise your working thesis if you believe that what you wrote in your paper no longer matches what is in the thesis. As you will see, the final draft will often reveal exactly what you meant to say in the first place. This is only one reason writing is called a "process of discovery."

- At this point, you might decide to add details that will make your paper more convincing. If so, return to prewriting and gather this information. Then, in your second draft, add this information to an existing paragraph or give it a paragraph of its own.

- Read your second draft. Do you need still more information? If so, find and add it. Next, rewrite paragraphs that are too long or that contain information irrelevant to the thesis. Combine short paragraphs that relate to the same point. Change the positions of paragraphs if doing so will make your paper easier to follow or more logical. Do the same with sentences; add to, combine, separate, and reposition them as needed. (Chapters 2 and 5 discuss paragraph and sentence structure.)

- Don't be afraid to cut information you don't need. Perhaps you have repeated ideas. There is no sin in that; eliminate one version. Perhaps you have offered three examples when two will do; remove the third. Just remember that all writing is rewriting.

GS.3e Editing and Proofreading

Editing means reading the best of your drafts to correct errors in grammar, punctuation, sentence structure, and mechanics. It also means cutting out wordiness and eliminating diction problems. **Proofreading** is a final check for spelling and typographical errors.

There are many ways to edit and proofread. Some writers read their papers backward, sentence by sentence. Others read aloud to friends to make sure that they haven't left out words and that their sentences make sense. Some read their final drafts several times, concentrating on one major editing problem each time. For example, they read once to correct sentence-structure errors such as fragments and comma splices. They read a second time for grammar, a third for punctuation, and so on. However you proceed, take your time. A paper might be organized and well developed, but if it is not edited and proofread carefully, it can suffer from errors that distract and confuse readers. For more on editing and proofreading try this website: Purdue University Online Writing Lab (owl.english.purdue.edu).

EXERCISE 10: *Practice what you have learned.*

In exercise 7, you were asked to gather information on a particular topic. In exercise 9, you were asked to write an outline using this material. Follow your outline to draft a short essay that uses information you have collected. Revise this essay at least once. Then edit and proofread it.

GS.4 The Making of a Student Essay: From Prewriting to Proofreading

This part of Getting Started traces the writing of a full-length essay by first-year nursing student Deborah Diglio. As her essay proves, she sees writing as a process of steps that need to be followed carefully.

> **GS.4a** Prewriting to Gather Information
>
> **GS.4b** Making a Scratch Outline
>
> **GS.4c** Writing a Working (First) Draft
>
> **GS.4d** Revising the Working Draft
>
> **GS.4e** Editing and Proofreading

GS.4a Prewriting to Gather Information

The process began when Diglio was inspired by Carl Sandburg's "Child of the Romans," a poem about the difficult job of an Italian immigrant who maintains the stone bed on which railroad tracks lay.

Child of the Romans
Carl Sandburg

The dago shovelman sits by the railroad track
Eating a noon meal of bread and bologna.
A train whirls by, and men and women at tables
Alive with red roses and yellow jonquils,
Eat steaks running with brown gravy,
Strawberries and cream, éclairs and coffee.
The dago shovelman finishes the dry bread and bologna,
Washes it down with a dipper from the water-boy,
And goes back to the second half of a ten-hour day's work
Keeping the road-bed so the roses and jonquils
Shake hardly at all in the cut glass vases
Standing slender on the tables in the dining cars.

Responding to a journal assignment from her instructor, Diglio used focused freewriting to gather information about a job she once held. Here's what she wrote in her journal about waitressing.

> People ordering food. The night was going by fast. Nervous. First nights can be scary. Keep a pleasant attitude. I could do the job easily. Training period over; I was on my own. I needed this job. We needed the money. I felt confident, too confident. I can now laugh at it. Not then. Society may not place waitressing high on the social ladder, but you have to be surefooted, organized, you have to have a sense of humor and a pleasant personality. You have to be able to learn from your mistakes. Eventually I did learn, but then I thought I would die. The old woman left her walker in the corner. How did I know it wasn't a tray stand? Still, I should have. Why didn't I just look more closely? Why didn't my brain take over? And the old folks didn't mind. We should look back at ourselves and laugh sometimes.

As you can see, there is no particular order to Diglio's notes, and like most freewriting, it uses quick phrases as much as full sentences. Nonetheless, an event that might make interesting reading is coming through. So is the idea that Diglio learned something from the experience and can now look back at it with a smile.

GS.4b Making a Scratch Outline

After discussing her journal entry with her instructor, Diglio decided to tell her story in a full-length essay. She reviewed her journal entry and thought about a working thesis. After adding notes to her original entry, she made this scratch outline:

> Working thesis: Sometimes we need to look back at ourselves and laugh.
>
> 1. Describe the restaurant, set the scene.
> 2. State the thesis.
> 3. Describe the job.
> 4. Tell what happened that first night.
>   How well it went at first—thought I was a "natural."
>   The old couple and their walker.
>   I wanted to crawl into a hole.
> 5. What I learned from my mistake.

GS.4c Writing a Working (First) Draft

Diglio's outline served as a blueprint for her first draft. Each paragraph in that draft corresponds roughly to the five major headings in her outline. However, the act of writing inspired her, and as she wrote, more details and ideas came to mind.

This proves an important point: an outline—especially a scratch outline—can be used only to get started. Don't be a slave to your outline; if the act of writing adds new details or takes you in a new direction, so be it. Again, writing is a process of discovery, and good writers change their minds at many points.

When Diglio finished her first draft, she read it over, a process that helped her recall even more details, which she squeezed in between paragraphs and sentences and in the margins of her paper. The result was messy, so she retyped the working draft, as shown below. This early draft of her paper contains more detail and is better written than her journal entry or outline, but it is only a start. Note that this draft contains many errors. No one would suggest that these are acceptable, merely that early drafts often contain such errors.

Waitressing

It was a typical Saturday night. I was standing there paying no attention to the usual racket of the dinner crowd. The restaurant was crowded. I was waiting for my next table. I try to listen to the sounds around me. I hear the stereo.   1

In come my eight o'clock reservation, fifteen minutes late. There is an elderly woman with them. She reminded me of something that happened when I started working there many years before. Recalling that story taught me to look back and laugh at myself.   2

When my second child was born. It became clear that I needed to find a part-time job to make ends meet. A friend said I should waitress at the restaurant where she worked. I thought about it for a few days. I decided to give it a try.   3

I bluffed my way thru the interview. A new chapter in my life began. Since then I have learned from many mistakes, like the one I am about to describe. My friends told me that I would look back and laugh at that night. I guess, after fifteen years, the day has come!   4

I followed another waitress for a few days, and then I was on my own. All went well the first week. When Saturday night came, I had butterflies in my stomache. I was given four tables not far from the kitchen. It was an easy station. Oh, God, was I happy, however I still felt awkward carrying those heavy trays. Before I knew it, the restaurant was packed, resembling mid-day on wall street. I moved slowly, organizing every move. I remember the tray stand at my station. It looked a little different than the one I was trained on. It had nice grips for handles of which made it easier to move around. I was amazed at how well things were going. I was too confident. I remember thinking I was a born natural. Then, this jovial looking old man came over, and taped my on the shoulder, and said, "Excuse me, dear, my wife and I loved watching you work. It seems that your tray stand has been very handy for you, but we are about to leave now, and my wife needs her walker back." I wanted to crawl into a hole and hide. What a fool I had made of myself. I was so glad when that night ended.   5

Since then, I have learned from many mistakes such as the one I just described.   6

GS.4d Revising the Working Draft

The essay above makes for entertaining reading, but Diglio knew it could be improved. She revised is several times to get to the last draft (but not the final version) of her paper, which appears below. This draft is not perfect, but it is more complete and polished than the one you just read. Again, it contains unacceptable errors, which were corrected in editing.

Lessons Learned

It was a typical Saturday night at Carpaccio's Restaurant. I was standing there, paying no attention to the merrymaking of the dinner crowd. Just two of the restaurant's twenty-five tables were vacant. As I waited for my next table, I absorbed a few of the sounds around me: clanging trays, the ringing of the cash register. I could even hear Dean Martin belting out a familiar Italian song in the background.

Finally, in come my eight o'clock party. As they were seated, my attention was drawn to an elderly woman with a walker slowly shuffling behind the others. She brought back a memory I had locked away for fifteen years.

After the birth of my second child, I needed to find a part-time job to make ends meet. A friend suggested I apply for a waitressing job at a new restaurant where she worked. I decided to give it a shot. I bluffed my way through the interview and was hired. A new chapter in my life began the next evening.

After trailing an experience waitress for a few days, I was allowed to wait tables on my own. All went well that first week. When Saturday night came, the butterflies in my stomach were set free. I was given the apprentice station that night, four tables not far from the kitchen. Oh, God, was I relieved, however I still felt awkward carrying the heavy trays.

Before I new it, the restaurant was packed; it resembled mid-day on wall street. I moved slowly, organising every step. I remember how impressed I was with the tray stand at my station, it looked different than the one I was trained on. It had nice grip-like handles, of which made it easier to manuver. I was amazed at how well things were going. I began to believe I was a natural at this job.

Then, a jovial, old man approached, tapped me on the shoulder, and said, "Excuse me, dear, my wife and I loved watching you work. It seems your tray stand has been very handy for you, but we are about to leave now, and my wife needs her walker back."

At first his message did not register: "What was he talking about!" Then, it sank in. I had set my trays on his wife's orthopedic walker. I stood there frozen as ice, but my face was on fire. I wanted to crawl into a hole; I wanted to hibernate.

Since then; I have learned from many mistakes such as the one I just described. I have learned to be more observant and more careful. I have learned to guard against overconfidence, for no matter how well things are going, something will come along eventually to gum up the works. Most of all, I have learned that the best way to get over honest, embarrassment is to look back and laugh at yourself.

As this draft shows, Diglio made important revisions. She

- Changed the title to clarify purpose; "Waitressing" didn't reveal her main point.

- Moved the central idea—the point she wanted to make—to the end. This allowed her to tell the story first and then explain its importance clearly.

- Added details to make her writing exact and vivid. In the later version, she names the restaurant and explains that just two of its "twenty-five tables were vacant," not simply that it was "crowded." She even mentions that "Dean Martin [was] belting out a familiar Italian song."

- Divided paragraph 4 into several new paragraphs, each of which focuses on a different idea, makes a new point, or tells another part of the story.

- Removed unnecessary words to eliminate repetition.

- Replaced some words with more exact and interesting substitutes. For example, in paragraph 1, the dinner crowd's "racket" is changed to "merrymaking."

- Combined short sentences to create longer, smoother ones and to increase variety.

- Corrected some—not all—problems with spelling, verb tense, sentence structure, punctuation, and mechanics.

GS.4e Editing and Proofreading

Although Diglio's last draft is better than her first, she wanted to remove annoying errors that could interfere with the readers' appreciation of her work. Using a pencil, a dictionary, and a handbook of college writing, she corrected problems in grammar, spelling, style, and other areas. Here's what two paragraphs from that draft looked like after she edited them. The cross-outs indicate material removed; items in bold indicate material added.

> After trailing an experienc**ed** waitress for a few days, I was allowed to wait tables on my own. All went well that first week. When Saturday night came, the butterflies in my stomach were set free. I was given the apprentice station that night, four tables not far from the kitchen. Oh, God, was I relieved; however, I still felt awkward carrying the heavy trays.

> Before I knew it, the restaurant was packed; it resembled mid-day on W**w**all S**s**treet. I moved slowly, organi~~s~~**z**ing every step. I remember how impressed I was with the tray stand in my station~~;~~**.** it looked different ~~than~~ **from** the one I was trained on. It had nice grip-like handles, ~~of~~ which it made it easier to maneuver. I was amazed at how well things were going. I began to believe I was a natural at this job.

Of course, a paper full of such corrections is too sloppy to submit in a college class. So, after correcting her final draft in pencil, Diglio typed one last, clean copy for her instructor.

The methods you use to write a paper may be different from those Diglio used. They also may be different from ways your classmates write. And no one says that any of the steps explained above has to be done separately from the others. In fact, some folks edit while they revise; some continue to gather information as they write their third and fourth drafts. Nevertheless, writing is a serious business, and completing only one or two drafts will never enable you to produce quality work.

Acknowledgments

"It's Time to Make College Tuition Free and Debt Free." Bernie Sanders, n.d., berniesanders.com/issues/its-time-to-make-college-tuition-free-and-debt-free/.

Marcello, Elizabeth. "The Case Against Free College." *The College Conservative*, 9 Oct. 2014, thecollegeconservative.com/2014/10/09/the-case-against-free-college/. Reprinted with permission of *TheCollegeConservative*.

Muller, Gilbert H., and Harvey S. Wiener. "On Writing." *The Short Prose Reader*, 13th ed., McGraw-Hill, 2013, p. 1.

Sandburg, Carl. "Child of the Romans." *The Complete Poems of Carl Sandburg*, Revised and expanded edition. Copyright © 1969, 1970 by Lilian Steichen Sandburg, Trustee. Reprinted by permission of Houghton Mifflin Harcourt Publishing Company. All rights reserved.

Tennyson, Alfred Lord. "The Eagle." 1851.

Section 1

Organization and Development

Getting Started taught you that collecting enough information—making sure you know as much about your subject as needed—is an important first step in the writing process. Next, you must determine what you wish to communicate about your subject and how to use your information to make your point clearly and effectively. Making such decisions is what the three chapters in section 1 discuss.

Chapter 1 explains two crucial steps early in the writing process: focusing and limiting the information you've collected so that you can decide on a central idea. Sometimes referred to as the *main* or *controlling idea*, the central idea of a paragraph or essay expresses the main point its writer will develop. Begin deciding on a central idea by reviewing information you collected in your journal through focused freewriting, clustering, or another prewriting technique. Then evaluate these details to determine what they tell you about your subject and what specifically you want to say about it. The more information you collect about your subject, the easier it will be to find an interesting central idea. Once you have a central idea, you will find it easier to decide which of the details you first gathered should be included in your writing and which should be left out.

Chapter 2 explains how to make the paragraphs in the body of your essay unified, coherent, and well developed. If an essay is unified, all of its paragraphs relate directly to its thesis, a statement of its central idea. If a paragraph is unified, each piece of information relates directly to its topic sentence, the paragraph's central idea. If an essay or paragraph is coherent, it is easy to follow, for the writer has included logical connections between paragraphs and sentences within a paragraph. If a piece of writing is well developed, it contains enough detail to support or prove its central idea.

Chapter 3, Introductions and Conclusions, offers suggestions for creating other types of paragraphs—namely, those that make effective openings and closings for essays.

The reading selections in section 1 contain examples of the important principles of organization and development explained in each chapter. They are also a rich source of subjects for your own writing. However, like other sections in this book, each reading selection has a value of its own. Whether written by professionals or by college students like you, they are interesting, informative, and even touching. Here's hoping they will inspire you to read and write about a variety of subjects, especially those you care about most.

Shutterstock

1

The Central Idea

Chapter Outline

As a writer, you need to know how to organize information in a form that is easy to follow. The best way to do this is to arrange, or focus, the details you have collected around a central idea.

1.1 Identifying the Central Idea

The **central idea** is often called the *main idea* because it conveys the writer's **main point**. It is also called the *controlling idea*, for it controls the kinds and amounts of detail a paragraph or essay contains.

Think of the central idea as the focal point to which all the information in an essay or paragraph points. Just as you focus a camera by aiming at a fixed point, you focus your writing by making all the details in it relate directly to the central idea. Everything you include should help prove, illustrate, or support that idea. You can also think of a central idea as an umbrella. It is the broadest or most general statement; all other information is more specific and fits under it, as shown in the illustration.

FIGURE 1–1   **Central Idea = Focal Point**

My Life is
full of risks.

risk at work
risk driving old car

risk playing lottery
risk attending Devry

Read the following two paragraphs; all the information in them focuses on or points to their central ideas (shown in italics). The first is taken from a student's essay; the second, from President John F. Kennedy's inaugural speech in 1961. Notice that the central ideas are broader than the details that support them.

> *My life is full of risks.* As a stair builder who works with heavy equipment, I risk cutting off a finger or a limb every day. Each Monday and Thursday, I risk four or five dollars on the state lottery. Every time I take my beat-up Chevy for a drive, I risk breaking down. However, the biggest risk I've ever taken was my decision to attend DeVry University this year. (Kenneth Dwyer, "Risks")

> *In your hands, my fellow citizens, more than mine, will rest the final success or failure of our course.* Since this country was founded, each generation of Americans has been summoned to give testimony to its national loyalty. The graves of young Americans who answered the call to service surround the globe. Now the trumpet summons us again—not as a call to bear arms, though arms we need—not as a call to battle, though embattled we are—but a call to bear the burden of a long twilight struggle, year in and year out, "rejoicing in hope; patient in tribulation," a struggle against the common

central idea
The idea that conveys a writer's main point about a subject; it may be stated explicitly or implied. Also known as the *main idea* or *controlling idea*.

main point
The point that a writer focuses on in a thesis or topic sentence.

enemies of man: tyranny, poverty, disease, and war itself. (President John F. Kennedy)

In most cases, the central idea of a paragraph is expressed in a **topic sentence**; the central idea of an essay is expressed in a **thesis statement**. Sometimes, however, the central idea is so obvious that the author need not express it formally. In such cases, the central idea is *implied*. This is often true of narration and description. However, it can apply to any type of writing. Note that in "A Typical Morning" (one of the reading selections in section 1.6a), the central idea is implied.

Nonetheless, as a college writer, you should always try to state your central idea outright, either in a topic sentence (for a paragraph) or thesis statement (for an essay). Doing so will help you organize your work effectively. Often, the central idea can be expressed at the beginning of an essay or paragraph, though this is not always the best place for it. For example, if you need to give readers some explanatory detail first, you might state your central idea in the middle or even at the end of your writing. Delaying the central idea can create suspense; it can also avoid turning away readers who, at first, might be opposed to an opinion you are presenting.

1.2 Writing a Preliminary Topic Sentence or Thesis Statement

Creating an effective central idea for your writing is a process. Begin by jotting down a preliminary (working) version of your central idea on scratch paper or in your journal. This is a *working* version because you can and often should make significant changes to it after you have begun writing your paragraph or essay.

Of course, before you draft the working version of a topic sentence or thesis statement, you need to choose a subject to write about. By its very nature, a subject is general, abstract, and incomplete. A central idea, on the other hand, is specific, concrete, and complete. Notice how much more meaningful the subject "skydiving" becomes when turned into a central idea: "*Skydiving* can be dangerous."

To turn any subject into a working topic sentence (paragraph) or thesis statement (essay), you must first *focus* your discussion of that subject by saying something concrete and specific about it. You can then *limit* your topic sentence or thesis in such as way as to keep the length of the paragraph or essay manageable.

1.2a Focus Your Discussion

A good time to draft a working topic sentence or thesis is after reviewing the notes you made in your journal through listing, focused freewriting, or other information-gathering (prewriting) techniques you learned about in Getting Started. While this information is fresh in your mind, ask yourself:

- What is my *purpose*? What do I want my writing to accomplish?
- What is the *main point* I wish to make about my subject?
- What *details* can I use to develop this main point?

Your purpose may be to entertain your readers with a colorful story or description, to explain a process, to contrast two types of popular music, or to convince the reader to adopt an opinion on a controversial issue. Once you have determined your purpose, you can decide which of the details and ideas that you have gathered through prewriting will help you achieve that purpose.

Let's say your purpose is to describe the state forest you hiked through on a fall weekend. After reviewing your notes, you decide to talk about the brilliant oranges, yellows, and reds of the falling leaves. You also think about describing the family of deer

topic sentence
A clear and explicit statement of a paragraph's central idea.

thesis statement
A clear and explicit statement of an essay's central idea that often appears in an introductory paragraph but is sometimes found later in the essay.

that scampered by you. You even plan to include the tire that was dumped on the side of the trail. Finally, you want to explain that you felt more calm and relaxed at the end of the hike than at the beginning. However, you decide not to write about your three-hour trip to the park in a pickup truck or about the friend you met as you were leaving. They have nothing to do with the forest.

Now, ask yourself what the most important or interesting aspect of your subject is. Perhaps your hike helped you relax after a long week of studying. This will be your main point, the point you will make about your subject: "Hiking through Sandburg State Park helped me relax after a tough week at school."

Focusing turns an abstract, general idea into a central idea for a paragraph or essay. Notice how much clearer ideas on the right are as compared to subjects on the left.

Subject	**Central Idea**
Rock music	Rock music can damage one's hearing.
Alternative fuels	Alternative fuels can reduce our need for foreign oil.
Cell phones	Cell phones can be expensive, annoying, and even dangerous.
Majoring in biology	Majoring in biology can prepare a student for a career in medicine, dentistry, or laboratory research.
Types of Chinese food	Szechuan, Hunan, and Cantonese food differ in several ways.

Focusing also provides a starting point for the first draft of an essay because it helps you decide which details in your prewriting to include and which to discard. Let's say your working thesis is "Hiking through Sandburg State Park helped me relax after a tough week at school." You might discuss the vibrant colors of the leaves and describe the deer you encountered. But would you also include a description of the old tire you saw? No, you would certainly discard this information.

1.2b Limit Your Discussion to a Manageable Length

Typically, students are asked to write short essays, usually ranging between 350 and 750 words. That's why it's important to limit your central idea. Otherwise, you won't be able to discuss it in enough detail to make your point effectively.

Let's say you choose to contrast two popular makes of automobiles. In a short essay, it would be foolish to discuss cost, performance, handling, comfort, reliability, safety features, *and* sound systems. A far more reasonable approach is to cover only two or three of these items. In fact, you might even limit yourself to cost; then you can divide your topic into more specific subsections like purchase price, yearly maintenance costs, and gas mileage. Here's what the thesis for your paper might look like: "The 2018 Mountain Marauder is far more economical than the 2018 Cross-Country Bandit."

1.2c Some Tips on Writing Topic Sentences and Thesis Statements

- Make sure your topic sentence or thesis is a complete sentence. A complete sentence contains a subject and a verb, and it expresses a complete thought.

  Not: Computers and being a successful college student.

  Or: Using computers to succeed in college.

  Or: How computers can help students succeed in college.

  But: Computers can help students succeed in college.

- State your main point directly; don't announce it.

  Not: I am going to write about how computers can help students succeed in college.

  Or: This paper will discuss the fact that computers can help students succeed in college.

  But: Computers can help students succeed in college.

- In most cases, readers will naturally assume that what you are writing about is your own opinion or is what you believe. There is no need to explain that.

  Not: I believe that computers can help students succeed in college.

  Or: It is my opinion that computers can help students succeed in college.

  But: Computers can help students succeed in college.

- Make sure your topic sentence or thesis clearly states the point you want to make about your subject.

  Not: Computers affect student performance in college.

  But: Computers can help students succeed in college.

1.3 Controlling Unity and Development

The central idea is sometimes called the controlling idea, for it helps determine the kind and amount of information a paragraph or essay contains. This is explained further in chapter 2. For now, remember that a piece of writing is unified if all the information relates to its central (controlling) idea. It is well developed if it contains all the information it needs to prove, illustrate, or support that idea.

1.4 Revising the Central Idea

Always revise the working or preliminary version of your thesis statement or topic sentence as you go through the writing process. Like taking notes or writing a rough draft, writing a working thesis statement or topic sentence is intended only to give you a starting point and a direction. There is no rule that prevents you from stopping at any point in the process, looking back at what you have done, and changing it as often as you like. So, don't be afraid to revise or change it at any time. Writing always involves discovery. The more you write and revise, the more likely you are to understand your subject and to revise what you *thought* you had wanted to say about it.

Study the three drafts of the introductory paragraphs from "Echoes," an essay by student Maria Cirilli. Each time Cirilli revised her work, she came to a clearer understanding of her subject and of what she wanted to say about it. This can be seen best in the last sentence, Cirilli's thesis. Her complete essay appears later in this chapter.

Cirilli—Draft 1

I hardly remember my grandmother except for the fact that she used to bounce me on her knees by the old-fashioned brick fireplace and sing old songs. I was only four years old when she died. Her face is a faded image in the back of my mind.

In contrast, I remember my grandfather very well. He was 6'4" tall. He possessed a deep voice, which distinguished him from others whether he was in the streets of our small picture-perfect town in southern Italy or in the graciously sculptured seventeenth-century church. He appeared to be strong and powerful. In fact he used to scare all my girlfriends away when they came to play or do homework. Yet, I knew that there was nothing to be afraid of.

Is this thesis clear? Does it tell what the essay will say about Cirilli's grandfather?

Cirilli—Draft 2

I hardly remember my grandmother except for the fact that she used to bounce me on her knees by the old-fashioned brick fireplace and sing old songs. I was only four years old when she died.

In contrast, I remember my grandfather very well. He was 6'4" tall, a towering man with broad shoulders and a pair of mustaches that I watched turn from black to grey over the years. He possessed a deep voice, which distinguished him from others whether he was in the streets of our small picture-perfect town in southern Italy or in the graciously sculptured seventeenth-century church. He appeared to be strong and powerful. In fact, he used to scare my girlfriends away when they came to play or do homework, yet he was the most gentle man I have ever known.

The last sentence of draft 1 has been removed.

Detail has been added to describe him better.

Thesis is clearer, but will the essay discuss fear?

Cirilli—Draft 3

I hardly remember my grandmother except for the fact that she used to bounce me on her knees by the old-fashioned brick fireplace and sing old songs. I was only four years old when she died. Her face is a faded image in the back of my mind.

In contrast, I remember my grandfather very well. He was 6'4" tall, a towering man with broad shoulders and a mustache that I watched turn from black to grey. His voice was deep, distinguishing him from others in our small picture-perfect town in southern Italy. To some, my grandfather appeared very powerful, and he used to scare my girlfriends away when they came to play or do homework. In fact, he was strong, but he was the gentlest and most understanding man I have ever known.

Detail about church removed; not needed.

Thesis stands alone in its own sentence; much clearer.

Cirilli reuses this sentence from draft 1.

Thesis expanded; now includes "most understanding."

1.5 Practicing Writing Central Ideas

To turn a subject into a central idea, you must make a main point about the subject. In the left column are subjects that might be discussed in a paragraph or essay. Turn them into central ideas. Start by asking yourself what is most interesting or important about your subject. Express your central idea in a complete sentence, which has a subject and a verb and which expresses a complete idea. The first item is done for you.

Central Idea

Subject	**Main Point**
1. A successful diet	takes will power
2. College textbooks	
3. Working while attending college	
4. Listening to music	
5. Buying a used car	
6. Budgeting one's time	
7. Adopting a pet	
8. Alcoholism	
9. My family	
10. Cell Phones	

The principles just discussed are illustrated in the following reading selections. Read each selection carefully, take notes, and respond to the Questions for Discussion and Suggestions for Journal Entries that accompany them.

1.6 Reading Selections

1.6a Four Paragraphs for Analysis

The four paragraphs that follow show the importance of focusing on a central idea. Written by different authors, they discuss different ideas, but each focuses on the main point and develops it through details.

Author Biographies

Carl Sagan (1934–1996) made major contributions to the U.S. space program and was twice cited for them by NASA. He was a prolific writer and winner of a Pulitzer Prize in literature for his book *The Dragons of Eden*. Other important works by Sagan include *Broca's Brain* and *Cosmos*, which is taken from the television series of the same name.

Stephen Fox is the author of "The Education of Branch Rickey," an essay published to celebrate the fiftieth anniversary of Jackie Robinson's breaking of major league baseball's color barrier in 1947. Rickey was the owner of the Brooklyn Dodgers at the time. The paragraph that follows is from that essay.

Ernest Albrecht is a college professor, theater critic, and author of several books on the circus.

Denise Kormondy was a college freshman when she wrote "A Typical Morning," which discusses her early morning tugs-of-war with her father.

Preparing to Read

1. As the following four paragraphs show, a writer who wants to express a central idea in a topic sentence need not start with that sentence. Depending upon the paragraph's purpose, he or she might provide a few sentences of background information first. To create emphasis, a writer might even wait until the end of the paragraph to state the central idea. Sometimes he or she might even choose not to express central ideas at all and, instead, allow readers to draw their own conclusions. In such cases, the central idea is said to be *implied*. That's just what Kormondy did in her paragraph from "A Typical Morning."

2. As you read the first sentence in Sagan's paragraph, try to identify his main point. Keep this in mind as you read the details that follow in the rest of the paragraph. They relate to this point.

3. The paragraphs by Fox and Albrecht mention several names, such as Branch Rickey, Jackie Robinson, Brooklyn Dodgers, and Madison Square Garden. If you are unsure of how these terms contribute to the paragraph's meaning, look them up on the Internet.

Vocabulary

conjured (verb)   Imagined.

controversial (adjective)   Causing disagreement, disputable.

debris (noun)   Waste, litter.

enigmatic (adjective)   Mysterious, puzzling.

harbinger (noun)   Sign of things to come, forerunner.

hippodrome (noun)   Arena for horses.

lathe (noun)   Machine for shaping wood.

megaton (noun)   One million tons.

roustabouts (noun)   Workers, laborers.

unprecedented (adjective)   Exceptional, extraordinary, never happening before.

wary (adjective)   Careful, cautious.

The Nuclear Winter

Carl Sagan

Except for fools and madmen, everyone knows that nuclear war would be an unprecedented human catastrophe. A more or less typical strategic warhead has a yield of two megatons, the explosive equivalent of 2 million tons of TNT. But 2 million tons of TNT is the same as all the bombs exploded during World War II—a single bomb with the explosive power of the entire Second World War but compressed into a few seconds of time and an area of 30 or 40 miles across.

The Example of Jackie Robinson*

Stephen Fox

Fifty years ago this fall, Branch Rickey announced that Jackie Robinson had signed a contract to play with the Brooklyn Dodgers organization, thus breaking the "color line" that had kept African-Americans out of white organized baseball in the 20th century. With that single stroke, the crafty 63-year-old white man and the wary, explosive 26-year-old black man helped spark a social revolution. Intensely controversial at the time, the signing of Robinson now seems a harbinger of the postwar civil-rights movement three years before the integration of the armed forces, nine years before the Supreme Court's *Brown* decision, ten years before the Montgomery, Alabama, bus boycott.
*Editor's title.

Sawdust

Ernest Albrecht

As a ten year old, I watched as miniature mountains of the magical debris took shape around my father's lathe or his table saw, and with hardly any effort at all I imagined three rings and a hippodrome track sprinkled with the stuff in various colors. Having once conjured that, it didn't take much more effort to envision the ropes and cables that the circus roustabouts spun into a fantastic web transforming the old Madison Square Garden on Eighth Avenue and 49th Street [New York] into an exotic world of wonder and fantasy. That is why, of all the changes that progress has wrought upon the circus, I lament the loss of the sawdust the most. Rubber mats may be practical, but they have no magic.

A Typical Morning

Denise Kormondy

When I heard the alarm, I turned it off, put the light on, and turned over. I convinced myself that I was going to get out of bed, but I knew I wouldn't—I never do. Before I could fall back to sleep, I heard my father asking if I were awake. I assured him that I was, and I pulled the covers over my head. As I lay there, I noticed that the light at the top of the stairs was going on and off. That's one of my father's favorite tricks. I yelled down to him and insisted that I was up. I even turned on the television, but that didn't seem to fool him either. As I was falling back to sleep, he announced that it was snowing and, being half asleep, I believed him. Never mind that this was happening in the middle of September. I looked out the window, but it was too dark to see anything, so I ran downstairs. Needless to say, there was no snow, but at least I was out of bed.

Read More on the Web

To learn more about what you have just read, visit these websites.

- University of North Carolina Writing Center: writingcenter.unc.edu/faculty-resources/classroom-handouts/thesis-analysis
- St. Cloud State University Literacy Education Online: leo.stcloudstate.edu/acadwrite/thesistatement.html
- Carl Sagan: carlsagan.com
- Jackie Robinson Foundation: jackierobinson.org
- Circus World Museum: circusworldbaraboo.org

Questions for Discussion

1. What are the topic sentences in the first three paragraphs?

2. In your own words, what is the central idea of Kormondy's paragraph?

3. Would the selection from "Nuclear Winter" have been as effective had the topic sentence appeared in the middle of the paragraph? At the end of the paragraph? Explain your answer.

4. What important information does Fox provide before the topic sentence in "The Example of Jackie Robinson"?

5. What is the main point of "Sawdust"? Why does Albrecht wait until the end of the paragraph to reveal it?

Thinking Critically

A central idea can act as an umbrella under which the details in a paragraph or essay fit. The central idea in the following paragraph about the planets is not stated in a topic sentence; it is only implied. After reading this paragraph, write out an appropriate topic sentence of your own.

The planet Mars takes its name from the Roman god of war.

Mercury is the Roman god of commerce; Venus is the goddess of love.

Pluto is named for the god of the underworld.

Neptune rules the sea, and Jupiter reigns as king of the gods.

Even the planets Saturn and Uranus borrow their names from ancient deities.

Suggestions for Journal Entries

1. This journal entry is in three parts:

   First, pick a limited subject you know a lot about. Here are some examples: waiting on tables, last year's Fourth of July picnic, your bedroom at home, feeding a baby, your car, studying math, your Uncle Mort, going to a concert, watching baseball on television.

   Second, decide what are the most interesting or important points you can make about that subject. Choose one of these as the main point of a central idea.

   Third, write that central idea in the form of a topic sentence for a paragraph you might want to write later.

   Do the same with three or four other limited subjects you know about. Here's what your journal entries might look like when you have finished:

   - **Limited subject:** Feeding a baby

     Main points: Sometimes messy, always fun

     Topic sentence: Feeding a baby can be messy.

   - **Limited subject:** Uncle Mort

     Main points: Old, handsome, outgoing, considerate

     Topic sentence: Uncle Mort was one of the most considerate people in my family.

   - **Limited subject:** Last year's Fourth of July picnic

     Main points: Much food, many people, lots of rain

     Topic sentence: Last year's Fourth of July picnic was a washout.

Suggestions for Journal Entries (Continued)

2. Using the Internet, find a short but interesting essay on a professional athlete, on the circus or another form of entertainment, on nuclear energy, or on any subject that interests you. In your own words, write the central idea of each essay's paragraphs in a numbered list. Then summarize one of the essay's paragraphs (you can find out about how to summarize in Getting Started, section GS.2e). Pick a paragraph that is at least three sentences long.

1.6b Echoes

Author Biography

Born in a small town in southern Italy, **Maria Cirilli** immigrated to the United States in 1971. She earned her associate's degree in nursing from a community college. Cirilli completed her bachelor's in nursing at the University of Medicine and Dentistry of New Jersey. After writing "Echoes" for a college composition class, she revised it several times to add detail and make it more powerful.

Preparing to Read

1. Cirilli chose not to reveal the central idea of this essay—her thesis statement—in paragraph 1. However, the first paragraph is important because it contains information that we can contrast with what we read in paragraph 2.

2. The two main points in the thesis (paragraph 2) are important because they give us clues about the topic sentences in the body paragraphs that follow.

Vocabulary

distinguishing (adjective)   Making different from.

exuberance (noun)   Joy, enthusiasm.

manicured (adjective)   Neat, well cared for.

mediator (noun)   Referee, someone who helps settle disputes.

negotiating (adjective)   Bargaining, dealing.

placate (verb)   Pacify, make calm.

siblings (noun)   Sisters and brothers.

solemnly (adverb)   Seriously.

tribulation (noun)   Trouble, distress.

vulnerable (adjective)   Open, defenseless.

with a vengeance (adverb)   Earnestly, forcefully.

Echoes

Maria Cirilli

I hardly remember my grandmother except for the fact that she used to bounce me on her knees by the old-fashioned brick fireplace and sing old songs. I was only four when she died. Her face is a faded image in the back of my mind. — 1

In contrast, I remember my grandfather very well. He was 6'4" tall, a towering man with broad shoulders and a mustache that I watched turn from black to grey. His voice was deep, distinguishing him from others in our small picture-perfect town in southern Italy. To some, my grandfather appeared very powerful, and he used to scare my girlfriends away when they came to play or do homework. In fact, he was strong, but he was the gentlest and most understanding man I have ever known. — 2

I still see him weeping softly as he reads a romantic novel in which his favorite character died after many trials and much tribulation. And I will never forget how carefully he set the tiny leg of our pet bird, Iario, who had become entangled in a fight with frisky Maurizio, our cat. Once, my brother and I accompanied him to our grandmother's grave at a nearby cemetery that was small but manicured. As we approached the cemetery, my tall grandfather bent down from time to time to pick wild flowers along the road. By the end of the journey, he had a dandy little bouquet, which he placed solemnly at my grandmother's grave while bountiful tears streamed down his husky, vulnerable face. — 3

My grandfather was always available to people. Mostly, he helped senior citizens apply for disability or pension benefits or file medical-insurance claims. Several times, however, he was asked to placate siblings who had quarreled over a family inheritance. Many angry faces stormed into our home dissatisfied with what they had received, but they usually left smiling, convinced by my grandfather that their parents had, after all, distributed their possessions fairly. — 4

At times, he could even play Cupid by resolving disputes between couples engaged to be married. Whether the problem concerned which family would pay for the wedding or who would buy the furniture, he would find a solution. As a result, our family attended many weddings in which my proud grandfather sat at the table of honor. — 5

On Sundays, there was always a tray of fresh, homemade cookies and a pot of coffee on our oversized kitchen table for visitors who stopped by after Mass. Seeking advice about purchasing land or a house, they asked my grandfather if he thought the price was fair, the property valuable, the land productive. After a time, he took on the role of mediator, negotiating with a vengeance to obtain the fairest deal for both buyer and seller. — 6

I remember most vividly the hours we children spent listening to our grandfather's stories. He sat by the fireplace in his wooden rocking chair and told us about the time he had spent in America. Each one of us kids would aim for the chair closest to him. We didn't want to miss anything he said. He told us about a huge tunnel, the Lincoln Tunnel, that was built under water. He also described the legendary Statue of Liberty. We were fascinated by his stories of that big industrialized land called America. — 7

As I grew up and became a teenager, I dreamt of immigrating to America and seeing all the places that my grandfather had talked about. His exuberance about this land had a strong influence on my decision to come here.

A few months before I arrived in America my grandfather died. I still miss him very much, but each time I visit a place that he knew I feel his presence close to me. The sound of his voice echoes in my mind. — 8

Read More on the Web

To learn more about what you have just read, visit these websites.

- "Being a Grandfather—The Joys and the Lessons Learned," *The Good Men Project*: http://bvtlab.com/5bSMa

- How to Be a Good Grandparent," *Our Everyday Life*: http://bvtlab.com/ES79g

- Susan Heitler, "Becoming a Grandparent": http://bvtlab.com/F9898

Questions for Discussion

1. What important information does Cirilli give us in paragraph 1?

2. What is her thesis? Why does she wait until paragraph 2 to reveal it?

3. Pick out the topic sentences in paragraphs 3 through 7, and explain what each tells us about Cirilli's grandfather.

4. What evidence does the author give to show that her grandfather was "gentle"? How does she prove he was "understanding"?

5. What about the fact that Cirilli's grandfather scared her girlfriends? Why does the author give us this information?

6. Why is "Echoes" a good title for this essay?

Thinking Critically

1. Reread the three drafts of Cirilli's introduction, which appear earlier in this chapter (section 1.4). In your journal, write a paragraph that explains the major differences you see among the versions. Use the notes in the margins as guides, but write the paragraph in your own words. If you read carefully, you will find even more differences than those described in the margins.

2. Cirilli tells us that her grandmother's "face is a faded image in the back of [her] mind." Why did she put this line back into the third version after taking it out of the second (refer to the drafts in section 1.4)? Explain in two or three sentences why keeping this line is important to Cirilli's essay.

Suggestions for Journal Entries

1. Use focused freewriting to gather information that shows that someone you know practices a particular virtue. Like Cirilli's grandfather, your subject might be gentle or understanding. Then again, he or she might be charitable, hardworking, generous, or considerate of others. Reread paragraph 3 or 4 in "Echoes" to get an idea of the kinds of details you might put in your journal. After completing your entry, read it carefully and add details. Finally, write a sentence that expresses the main point you made and that might serve as a topic sentence for a paragraph using this information.

Suggestions for Journal Entries (Continued)

2. Think of someone special in your life and write down a wealth of details about this person. Use brainstorming, interviewing, or any other information-gathering techniques discussed in Getting Started. Then, discuss this special person in three or four well-written sentences. Like the topic sentences in "Echoes," yours should focus on only one main point you want to make about your subject or about your relationship with this person.

1.6c Suffering

Author Biography

Siu Chan was born in Cambodia of Chinese parents. Her father owned a small business in Phnom Penh, the capital, where Siu lived with her parents and her five brothers and sisters. In 1975, her life changed drastically. That was the year that the Khmer Rouge, the movement headed by communist leader Pol Pot, took control of the country. The atrocities committed by this group resulted in the extermination of millions of native Cambodians and other people, with millions more displaced from their homes and sent to live in work camps. In fact, the communists nearly evacuated the city of Phnom Penh and redistributed the people in rural areas.

  This essay, which Siu Chan wrote while in college, tells of her experience during the four years she lived under the tyranny of the Khmer Rouge. In 1979, she and three younger brothers and sisters escaped from Cambodia into Vietnam, traveling by bus, boat, bicycle, and on foot. They spent five years in Vietnam before immigrating to the United States, where an uncle who sponsored them was waiting. During this time, Siu worked two jobs to help support her family and attended college part-time, majoring in accounting. As she explained to her writing instructor, she worked seven days a week and has not had a day off in over three years.

Preparing to Read

1. Chan states a thesis in her first paragraph. It contains three main points. Make sure you understand each before going on to the rest of the essay.

2. This is a five-paragraph essay. Paragraph 1 is the introduction, with the essay's thesis statement. Each of the three main points in Chan's thesis is the basis for the topic sentence you will find in each body paragraph—2, 3, and 4. Paragraph 5 is the essay's conclusion.

3. Think about the significance of Chan's title. Doing so makes reading her essay easier.

4. The horrors the Khmer Rouge created in Cambodia are documented in *The Killing Fields*, a film that you can learn more about on the Internet.

Vocabulary

authorities (noun)   People in charge.

craved (verb)   Desired.

malnutrition (noun)   Inadequate diet, lack of food.

nourishment (noun)   Proper food, sustenance.

tyranny (noun)   Oppression, dictatorship

Suffering

Siu Chan

Whenever I think about the word "suffering," the first thought that comes to my mind is the time I   1
lived under the dictatorship of the Khmer Rouge from 1975 through 1979 in my homeland of Cambodia. It was the worst time in my life. I was allowed very little personal freedom, I witnessed the death
of my family, and I nearly died of starvation.

Starting in 1975, when the Communists under Pol Pot took over, the government destroyed   2
nearly all personal freedom. Families were split apart, with each member being forced to live separately. Even my two-year-old brother was taken away to live with a group of children the same age. We
were never able to visit each other, and when my parents passed away I wasn't even able to see them
for a final goodbye. In addition, the communists forced me into slave labor. I got up at 3:00 a.m. every
day, sometimes to work on a roadbuilding project for which I carried water and earth and sometimes
to dig a hole for an artificial pond. Our work day sometimes ended at 11:00 p.m. Moreover, I was
allowed to speak only one language: Cambodian. At home, we had spoken Chinese. The authorities
would not allow any criticism of the government, and I had to be very careful about what I said and
did. Otherwise, they would kill me.

During those four years, I lost six members of my family. First my grandparents passed away   3
about two months apart. They were old and ill. Because my country had experienced war and tyranny
for many years, they could not get the medicines they needed. Approximately four months later, my
uncle died; he was overworked and did not have enough food to eat, so he became ill. There was no
medicine to help him either. One year later, my little brother died after suffering from a fever for one
full week. Again, no medication was available. After another six months, my parents also died one
month apart. They starved to death.

I had to eat food that the communist government gave me whether it was good or not. Usually it   4
was just plain white rice, sometimes with a few wild vegetables mixed in, but it was never enough to
fill me up. I can still remember a three-month period during which I nearly starved to death. The rice
crop had failed because of flooding, so I had to go into the woods to search for tree roots and other
wild foods. But they satisfied me only temporarily, and they did not have enough nourishment to keep
me healthy. I began to suffer from malnutrition, and my body became swollen. In fact, I was so hungry
for real food that I sometimes burst into tears. I craved food all the time. I even dreamt about it. I
would have been very satisfied with only a bowl of plain rice or a slice of bread.

Throughout those four years, I suffered a great deal. I cannot find the appropriate words to   5
describe that horror. However, having gone through it, I can appreciate the life I have now. My spirit
and my mind get stronger each day. I learned not to waste anything—especially food—when I was
in Cambodia, and I am doing well in the United States. I work hard and I have even started going
to college. What's more I feel confident about the future. My suffering has prepared me to face any
obstacle.

Read More on the Web

To learn more about what Siu Chan faced, visit these websites:

- Cambodian Genocide Project:
  cambodiangenocideproject.weebly.com/organization.html

- Cambodian Genocide: World without Genocide: worldwithoutgenocide.org/genocides-and-conflicts/cambodia

Questions for Discussion

1. What is Chan's thesis? What are the three main points found in that thesis?

2. Identify each of the topic sentences Chan uses in paragraphs 2, 3, and 4.

3. Explain how the details in paragraphs 2, 3, and 4 relate to their topic sentences.

Thinking Critically

1. Why do you think the authorities allowed people to speak only Cambodian?

2. What questions might you ask Chan if you had the opportunity? Write your questions in the margins beside the essay.

Suggestions for Journal Entries

1. Recall a personal experience in which your freedom was limited or your well-being was threatened because of the power someone had over you. Use clustering, drawing a subject tree, or listing to record the details of this experience.

2. Recall a battle with a serious illness from which you or someone close to you suffered. What caused it? What were its symptoms? What kind of suffering did it cause? Was the illness ever overcome? If so, how? Try using focused freewriting to record these details.

1.6d Advice to New Writers: Revise, Revise, Revise

Author Biography

Richard Marius (1933–1999) directed the expository writing program at Harvard University. He began his career as a historian and professor of history at the University of Tennessee and authored several historical studies and biographies, including those of Sir Thomas More and Martin Luther. He also wrote several novels, including *The Coming of Rain*, as well as guides to grammar and writing for college students and professionals. "Advice to New Writers: Revise, Revise, Revise" is from *A Writer's Companion*, a splendid guide for both beginning and experienced writers.

Preparing to Read

1. Although Marius hints at his thesis in the first sentence, he states it outright at the end of the essay. Look for it there.

2. Marius draws two analogies (comparisons) between writing and sports in this essay. Find the places where he does so, and try to explain how these analogies help him get his point across.

Vocabulary

disciplines (noun)   Areas of study, academic subjects.

evokes (verb)   Brings up, calls to mind.

prose (noun)   Writing that is not poetry; the kind you now are reading.

unblemished (adjective)   Perfect, without error, untarnished.

woo (verb)   Persuade, entice, court.

Advice to New Writers: Revise, Revise, Revise*

Richard Marius

No writer gets it right the first time. No writer I know writes easily. We don't begin at the beginning, write steadily, and get up at the end—whenever that may be—with an unblemished manuscript ready to go off to the publishers. Most of us struggle to get ideas, labor with blood, toil, tears, and sweat to get them into some kind of order, wrestle them down onto the page, and then decide that we've made some wretched mistakes, that we have repeated ourselves, that we have written some sentences so incomprehensible that they make us ashamed, and that perhaps we should have been forest rangers or bankers or welders—anything other than what we are, writers with this addiction to our craft. I've never been surprised that a great many great writers are also alcoholics. No, I do not advise drinking as a means to creativity. Drinking has destroyed many a good pen. But I can understand the frustration that writing evokes. Writers are like baseball players; they fail so often that to get it right one-third of the time seems like the peak of success.   1

Writing is an effort to woo readers. Readers nowadays are in an almighty hurry. They will seldom struggle to understand difficult writing unless they are forced to do so. Samuel Johnson, the great eighteenth-century writer, said, "What is written without effort is in general read without pleasure." Today what is written without effort is seldom read at all.   2

Here is a fact: Writing takes time—lots of time. Good writers don't dash off a piece in an hour or two. They observe. They take notes on what they observe. They think about what they want to say. They plan. They write first drafts. They revise, both structurally and on the level of the sentences. That is, they move sections of their work around, seeking a better natural flow of their prose. Or they go over and over their sentences, searching for the right word, eliminating words and phrases they don't need. Sometimes they delete whole sentences and even whole pages. Even small writing tasks may require an enormous investment in time. Even in this age of technology, computers can't do your work for you. You may use the computer to do the work that finally only you can do.   3

So it is with all disciplines. A great athlete may run a marathon in a little over two hours. But to train for those two hours requires months of preparation. If you want to be a writer, you must be serious about the task, willing to dedicate all the time it takes to your work, revising it again and again.   4

*Editor's Title

Read More on the Web

Consult these websites for more about the nature and rewards of writing:

- Purdue University Online Writing Center: owl.purdue.edu

- University of North Carolina Writing Center: writingcenter.unc.edu

- St. Cloud University's Literacy Education Online: leo.stcloudstate.edu

Questions for Discussion

1. What is Marius's thesis?
2. What are the topic sentences in paragraphs 1, 2, and 3?
3. Explain how each of these sentences supports the thesis.
4. Explain the analogies (comparisons) that the author draws between writing and athletics. How do these analogies help him make his point about writing?

Thinking Critically

1. Think about the way you approach a writing task, even the writing of a short email. Do you think about your reader? Do you plan? Do you gather notes? Do you struggle to get just the right word? Or do you dash it off as quickly as possible, not caring about how effective your writing will be?

2. How would you evaluate your writing skills? How can following Marius's advice improve them?

Suggestions for Journal Entries

1. Marius claims that what he says about writing is true of "all disciplines." Is Marius right? Think about an activity at which you excel: fishing, acting, playing a sport, cooking, writing, or any other. Use freewriting to explain how much time and effort you have devoted to mastering this activity.

2. "Advice to New Writers: Revise, Revise, Revise" aims at helping you become a better writer. Use your journal to list two or three specific pieces of advice you might offer a friend or a classmate who is trying to master a skill at which you excel. Examples include doing homework or studying for a test; communicating with parents or relatives; driving in heavy traffic; overcoming peer pressure; sticking to a healthful diet; keeping trim and fit; treating members of other races, religions, or cultures with respect.

1.7 Suggestions for Sustained Writing

1. Recall what you learned about writing central ideas at the beginning of this chapter: a central idea contains a subject and makes a point about that subject, a point that is focused and specific. Think about a subject you know a great deal about. Then write four or five sentences that express different points about that subject. Let's say your subject is Thanksgiving dinner. You might write the following central ideas:

Subject	Main Point
Thanksgiving dinner at my house	is always noisy.
In my family, Thanksgiving means	eating a lot and watching football.
Our Thanksgiving dinners	are not traditional.
A typical Thanksgiving dinner	can kill a diet.
Preparing a Thanksgiving dinner	takes a lot of work.

Next, use each of these sentences as the topic sentence for a different paragraph. When you write each paragraph, remember to include details that support or explain the paragraph's central idea as expressed in its topic sentence. Here's what one of the paragraphs you are going to write might look like:

Preparing a Thanksgiving dinner takes a lot of work. First you'll have to prepare the stuffing. This means peeling and cutting up the apples, chopping up and soaking the bread, mixing in the raisins and the spices. After you're done, you'll have to stuff the turkey with this gooey mixture. While you're waiting for the bird to roast, you should peel, boil, and mash the potatoes and cook any other vegetables you will serve. You'll also have to bake the biscuits, set the table, pour the cider, and put the finishing touches on the pumpkin and apple pies you spent three hours preparing the night before.

As you learned in Getting Started, don't be satisfied with the first draft of your work; rewrite it several times. Then, correct spelling, grammar, punctuation, and other distracting problems.

2. If you haven't done so already, complete the Suggestion for a Journal Entry after Section 1.6a: Four Paragraphs for Analysis. Use *each* topic sentence you were asked to write as the beginning of a paragraph in which you explain the main point you are making in that topic sentence. You should wind up with the rough drafts of four or five paragraphs, each of which is several sentences long.

Rewrite these rough drafts until you are satisfied that your topic sentences are clear and that you have included enough information to help your readers easily understand the main point in each paragraph. Complete the writing process by editing your work, just as student writer Deborah Diglio did with her paper in part 4 of Getting Started.

3. In item 2 of the Suggestions for Journal Entries after Maria Cirilli's "Echoes" (section 1.6b), you were asked to write three or four sentences, each of which was to focus on a single aspect or characteristic of someone special in your life. Make each of these the topic sentence of a paragraph that describes or explains that aspect or characteristic. If necessary, reread "Echoes." Many of the paragraphs in the body of this essay will serve as models for your writing.

Next, write an appropriate thesis statement for an essay containing the three or four paragraphs you've just written. Make sure that your thesis statement somehow reflects the main points found in the topic sentences of the three or four paragraphs in your essay. Make this thesis part of your essay's first or introductory paragraph.

Again, approach this writing assignment as a process. Complete several drafts of your paper, and don't submit your final product until you are satisfied that you have dealt with problems in grammar, spelling, punctuation, and the like.

4. Have you ever lived under the tyranny of a government, organization, or person? If so, explain how this experience affected you in two or three ways. Like Siu Chan ("Suffering," section 1.6c), begin your essay with an introductory paragraph that contains a thesis statement. Make sure that the two or three main points in this thesis statement express the effects of living under this oppression. Then, make these main points the basis of the topic sentences you use in your essay's body paragraphs. Use Chan's essay as your model.

Begin by reviewing the notes you made after reading Chan's essay. They might provide you with materials with which you can get started. Then, do some more prewriting to gather even more information. Next, write a preliminary thesis statement, which might appear in your introductory paragraph. Also, write a preliminary or working topic sentence for each of your essay's body paragraphs. Base each topic sentence on one of the main points stated in your thesis. Next, make a rough outline of your essay.

Write a rough draft and several revisions of your essay. Don't be afraid to revise your working thesis and topic sentences if you need to. End your essay with a conclusion, such as the one Chan used. Finally, edit and proofread the whole paper carefully.

5. If you responded to item 2 in the Suggestions for Journal Entries after Marius's "Advice to New Writers" (section 1.6d), you have probably listed three or four sentences that give advice on a particular activity you know a lot about. Use each of these sentences as the topic sentence of a paragraph that explains the advice you are giving in detail. For example, if you are trying to help a friend lose weight, one thing you might suggest is that he or she get a lot of exercise. This suggestion would make a good topic sentence of a paragraph:

> Get a lot of exercise. Wake up early and jog two or three miles. Use the weight room in the college gymnasium several times a week, or ride one of the stationary bicycles you will find there. If all else fails, walk the three miles to school every day, do sit-ups in your room, or jump rope in your backyard.

After you have written three or four such paragraphs, decide on a thesis statement that might express the central idea of the essay in which these paragraphs will appear. Make your thesis broad enough to include the main points you made in all three or four of your topic sentences. Use the thesis statement as the basis of a paragraph that comes before and introduces the three or four body paragraphs you have just completed.

Now, rewrite your paper several times. Make sure it is clear and well organized. Then edit for grammar and other important considerations.

6. Write a short essay in which you explain three reasons that you are doing something important in your life. Include these three reasons in a central idea that you will use as your thesis statement. Let's say that you decide to explain three of your reasons for going to college. You might write: "I decided to attend Metropolitan College to prepare for a rewarding career, to meet interesting people, and to learn more about music and literature." Put this thesis somewhere in your introductory paragraph.

Next, use *each* of the reasons in your thesis as the main point in the topic sentences of the three paragraphs that follow. You might use the following as topic sentences for paragraphs 2, 3, and 4. The main point in each topic sentence is in italics:

Paragraph 2: The most important reason I decided to attend Metropolitan College *was to prepare myself for a rewarding career.*

Paragraph 3: *The opportunity to meet interesting people* was another reason I thought that going to college would be a good idea.

Paragraph 4: My decision to continue my schooling also had a lot to do with my desire to *learn more about literature and music.*

Try to develop each of these in a paragraph of three or four sentences that will help you explain the main point of your topic sentence completely and effectively. Finally, as with other assignments in this chapter, revise and edit your work thoroughly.

ACKNOWLEDGMENTS

Albrecht, Ernest. "Sawdust." *A Ringling by Any Other Name: The Story of John Ringling and His Circus*, Scarecrow Press, 1989.

Fox, Stephen. "The Education of Branch Rickey." *Civilization Magazine*, Sept./Oct. 1995, 52–57.

Marius, Richard. *A Writer's Companion*, 4th ed. 1999 McGraw Hill. Copyright by Richard Marius, 1999. Reproduced with permission of McGraw Hill College Division via Copyright Clearance Center.

Sagan, Carl. "The Nuclear Winter" [pamphlet]. Scott Meredith Literary Agency, 1983.

Next, use each of the reasons in your thesis as the main point in the topic sentences of the three paragraphs that follow. You might use the following as topic sentences for paragraphs 2, 3, and 4. The main point in each topic sentence

Shutterstock

2

Paragraphs: Mastering Unity, Coherence, and Development

Chapter Outline

Chapter 1 explained how to focus your writing through a central idea. Deciding on the kinds of information to include in a piece of writing and organizing that information in a logical way are governed by the principles of *unity* and *coherence*. Deciding how much information to include has to do with *development*.

2.1 Creating Unity

A piece of writing has **unity** if it contains only those details that help support or explain—develop—the central idea. The central idea contains a subject and the main point the writer wants to make about that subject. The following paragraph, summarized from Ben Mackworth-Praed's *The Book of Kells*, expresses its central idea in the first sentence, the topic sentence. Its subject is "*The Book of Kells*." Its main point is that the book "is both a treasure and a mystery." Note that all the details in the paragraph relate directly to this idea.

> *The Book of Kells* is both a treasure and a mystery. An illuminated manuscript of the four Gospels of the New Testament, it dates from about 800 A.D., historians believe. It is called an "illuminated" manuscript because its Latin words, written in ancient Celtic [Irish] letters are accompanied by rich, colorful decorations, ink drawings, and geometric designs. Pictures of people, animals, both real and mythical, adorn its pages, as do many Celtic symbols, such as the Celtic knot. We are not sure who wrote *The Book of Kells*, but legend has it that St. Columba, the founder of the abbey in Kells in Ireland, was its author.

It is not hard to lose focus on the main point and include irrelevant information—information that doesn't explain or support a central idea. Including such information will sidetrack your readers by drawing their attention to ideas that don't serve your purpose. It may even make your writing difficult to follow. Make sure to check for unity when you revise your rough drafts.

The following paragraph is based on one by Geoffrey Ward, who wrote an article for *National Geographic* magazine about the fiftieth anniversary of India's independence. However, Ward's original paragraph has been rewritten and now contains information irrelevant to its central idea. This information was added to show that such information can destroy paragraph unity.

> [1] Indian civilization has an astonishingly long history, and Delhi has witnessed a good deal of it. [2] There have been at least eight cities here in the past 3,000 years, beginning with Indraprastha, the capital mentioned in the Hindu epic [heroic poem], the *Mahabharata*. [3] Some scholars believe that if all the smaller settlements and fortifications and military outposts whose remnants are scattered across the landscape were taken into account, the actual number would be closer to 15. [4] Today, remnants of several old civilizations can also be found in Rome, Italy. [5] Monuments, ruins, and relics of the rich past are everywhere. [6] The high-rise office buildings that have gone up near Connaught Place in recent years cast their reflections into the green waters of a 14th-century steppe well. [7] In fact, as one of the world's fastest growing countries, India is experiencing a great deal of urban construction. [8] Traffic on one of New Delhi's busiest thoroughfares has to swerve around the masonry slab that marks a Muslim saint's grave. [9] Under the Independence Act of 1947 the Muslim state of Pakistan emerged as a separate country. [10] Even on the fairways on the New Delhi Golf Club …, royal tombs offer unique hazards.

unity
The principle that writers observe in making certain that all the information in an essay or paragraph relates directly to the central idea, which is often expressed in a thesis statement or topic sentence.

Ward establishes his focus in the first sentence: His subject is "Delhi"; his main point is that Delhi "has witnessed a good deal" of Indian civilization's "long history." Each detail that follows this sentence should relate directly to the main point. However, this is not the case with the irrelevant information added, as the following explanation shows.

Sentence 1, the topic sentence, expresses the central idea.

Sentence 2 tells us about cities that existed on this site as far back as 3,000 years ago, so it helps explain the "long history" mentioned in the topic sentence.

Sentence 3 continues the idea begun in sentence 2; it too is relevant to the topic sentence.

Sentence 4 makes an interesting comparison between Rome and Delhi. However, it does not help convince the reader that Delhi has witnessed a great deal of Indian history. It should be removed.

Sentence 5 mentions the city's "rich past." Therefore, it belongs in the paragraph.

Sentence 6 tells us about a 600-year-old well, another sign of Delhi's "long history." It too belongs.

Sentence 7 makes no reference to the past; it is entirely about the present. It is irrelevant and should be removed.

Sentence 8 is relevant; it explains that a modern highway has been designed in such a way as to preserve a historical site—in this case, the grave of a Muslim saint.

Sentence 9 is irrelevant. It has nothing to do with Delhi, the paragraph's subject, or about the long history the city has witnessed. It doesn't belong.

Sentence 10 is relevant to the topic sentence. The royal tombs are more evidence that Delhi has seen much of the country's history.

2.2 Maintaining Coherence

A paragraph has **coherence** if the sentences it contains are connected clearly and logically in an order that is easy to follow. An essay is coherent if there are logical connections between paragraphs. The thought in one sentence or paragraph should lead directly—without a break—to the thought in the next sentence or paragraph.

You can create these logical connections in two ways: (1) using transitional devices or (2) referring to what you have mentioned earlier.

2.2a **Use Transitional Devices**

Transitional devices, also called **transitions** or **connectives**, are words, phrases, or even whole sentences that create clear relationships in and between sentences and paragraphs. They can be used for different purposes.

To Indicate Time

You would be indicating the passing of time if you wrote: "Arturo left before dawn. *In a while,* sunlight burst over the green hills." Other transitions indicating time include these:

After a while	In the meantime
Afterward	Meanwhile
At the time	Now
Back then	Soon
Before long	Suddenly
Before that time	Then
In a few minutes (hours, days, etc.)	While

coherence
The principle that writers observe in making certain that there are logical connections between the ideas and details in one sentence or paragraph and those in the next.

transition (connective)
Word or phrase used to make clear and direct connections between sentences and paragraphs, thereby maintaining coherence.

To Indicate Similarities or Differences

You can use transitions to show that things are similar or different: "Philip is following in his sister's footsteps. *Like her*, he is majoring in engineering. *Unlike her*, however, he hates math." Here are other examples:

Similarities	Differences	
In addition	Although	On the other hand
In the same way	However	Still
Likewise	In contrast	Though
Similarly	Nevertheless	Yet

To Introduce Examples, Repeat Information, or Emphasize a Point

You would be introducing an example if you wrote: "Mozart displayed his genius early. *For example*, he wrote his first symphony when only a boy." You would be repeating information if you wrote: "At age 21, he was appointed court composer in Vienna. This was *another* early indication of his genius." You would be emphasizing a point if you wrote: "The end of Mozart's career was hardly spectacular. *In fact*, he died in poverty at age 35." Here are some more examples:

Introducing Examples	Repeating Information	Emphasizing a Point
As an example	Again	As a matter of fact
For instance	Once again	Indeed
Specifically	Once more	More important
Such as		To be sure

To Add Information

If you wanted to add information by using a transition, you might write: "When Grant and Lee met at Appomattox Courthouse in 1865, they brought the Civil War to an end. *What's more*, they opened a new chapter in U.S. history." Here are other such transitions:

Also	Furthermore
And	In addition
As well	Likewise
Besides	Moreover
Further	Too

To Show Cause and Effect

If you wanted to explain that one action caused another, you might write: "During the early days of the Revolution, General Washington was unable to defend New York City. *Consequently*, he retreated to Pennsylvania." Other cause/effect transitions include these:

As a result	So that
Because	Then
Hence	Therefore
Since	Thus

To Show Condition

If you needed to explain that one action or fact depends on another, you might create a relationship based on condition by using words like *if*, as in this sentence: "Jones should arrive soon; *if* she doesn't, we will have to go on alone." Here are other transitions that show condition:

As long as	In case	Unless
As soon as	In order to	When
Even if	Provided that	Whenever

2.2b Refer to Material You Mentioned Earlier

You can refer to material mentioned earlier by (1) using pronouns that link details and ideas or (2) restating important words or ideas.

Using Linking Pronouns

Linking pronouns point directly to specific names or words you have mentioned earlier. Such pronouns direct the reader to nouns in earlier sentences or paragraphs; these nouns are called *antecedents*. Relying on pronouns to maintain coherence also helps you avoid repeating the same nouns over and over.

In this paragraph by Mother Teresa, the Roman Catholic nun who dedicated herself to the poor, linking pronouns appear in italics.

> Here in Calcutta, we have a number of non-Christians and Christians *who* work together in the house of the dying and other places. There are also *some who* offer *their* care to the lepers. One day an Australian man came and made a substantial donation. But as *he* did *this he* said, "*This* is something external. Now I want to give something of *myself*." *He* now comes regularly to the house of the dying to shave the sick men and to converse with *them*. *This* man gives not only *his* money but also *his* time. *He* could have spent it on *himself*, but what *he* wants is to give *himself*.

Here are other pronouns you might want to use to create coherence:

Personal pronouns refer to people and things:

I (me, my, mine)	We (us, our, ours)
You (your, yours)	They (them, their, theirs)
He, she, it (him, his; her, hers; its)	

Relative pronouns help describe nouns by connecting them with clauses, or groups of words with subjects and verbs:

That	Which
What	Whichever
Whatever	Who (whose, whom)

Demonstrative pronouns precede and stand for the nouns to which they refer: "*This* is my book" or "*These* are the best seats in the house." The most common demonstrative pronouns are *this*, *that*, *these*, and *those*.

Indefinite pronouns make general rather than specific reference. You can use them as long as you are sure the reader can identify their antecedents easily. For example:

linking pronoun
A pronoun that references a noun that has come before (antecedent), one of the ways to maintain coherence in and between paragraphs.

"*Both* Sylvia and Andy were in an accident. *Neither* was seriously injured." Here are other indefinite pronouns:

All	Either	None	Some
Another	Everybody	No one	Somebody
Anyone	Neither	Others	Someone
Each	Nobody	Several	

Restating Important Details and Ideas

The second way to refer to material that has come before is by repeating words and phrases or by using *synonyms*, or terms that have the same or nearly the same meanings. Read this paragraph by Shen C. Y. Fu, a curator of Chinese art for the Smithsonian Institute. Fu uses the word *calligraphy* four times, but he also uses synonyms for it.

> *Calligraphy* is generally defined as beautiful *writing*. In the West the *term* applies to *decorative writing* or may simply mean *good penmanship*. In China, however, *calligraphy* is regarded as the ultimate artistic expression, requiring years of training, discipline, and dedication before mastery can be achieved. Like music and dance, *calligraphy* is an art of performance. But unlike music and dance, each performance of *calligraphy* results in a tangible [material] creation that both captures the artist's technical skills at the time and provides concrete evidence of his or her immediate mood and innate [inborn] personality.

2.3 Developing Effective Paragraphs

A paragraph or essay is well developed if it contains all the details it needs to prove, support, or illustrate its central idea. You should include enough detail to make your point clearly and convincingly. You should also arrange details in a way that fits your purpose.

2.3a Determining How Much Information Is Enough

In some paragraphs, you will have to supply many concrete details, examples, and other information important to your topic sentence. In others, you might be able to make your point with only one or two supportive details. And in a few, one sentence is all you might need to achieve your purpose. (However, remember that using too many one-sentence paragraphs can make your writing choppy.)

Rely on your central idea to guide you. After all, it contains the main point you want to make, and it can help you determine the kind and amount of detail to include. Let's say you begin with this topic sentence: "Majoring in biology is a good foundation for several careers." You might discuss careers in medicine or dentistry. But since your thesis mentions several (three or more) reasons, you would also have to mention other careers, like those in teaching, environmental management, or forestry.

In short, think of a central idea as a promise you make to your reader to discuss your main point in as much detail as appropriate. If you start by saying that "There are three ways to reduce the risk of heart attack," then discuss all three, not just two, as fully as you can. If you want to prove that your brother is a slob, don't just describe the mess in his closet. Talk about the jumble of old food containers in his car; the torn, dirty jeans he wears; the pile of papers and books he often leaves on the kitchen table.

Deciding how much information to include isn't always easy. For now, remember that it is always better to provide too much information than not enough. Too much information might bore readers, but too little might leave them confused or unconvinced.

Just how much to include was what the writer of the following email had to decide as she wrote to her children about her trip to Australia. Her topic sentence is in italics:

Dear Tess and Mike,

Hope things are well with you. *I'm having a great time.* Yesterday we went "canyoning." And, believe it or not, your mother rappelled off the face of a sixty-foot cliff (I have pictures to prove it!) into the dark tunnel entrance of a beautiful canyon filled with what looked like prehistoric plants. All that was missing was the T Rex stalking around the corner! It scared the heck out me the first time, but after the third and last descent it was great and about the best time I've had! We had to climb out of the canyon along the ice cold stream bed and actually had to swim for about 50 ft. in frigid water. (Remember the water in the Oregon caves? It was almost as cold.) The stream had bright red lobster-like creatures (yabbies) and big snakes. (I learned that little bit of news after we were half way through and past the point of no return!) However, I've met a lot of nice people—including some from Eugene [the author's hometown]. I hope you enjoy your vacation. I miss you guys and wish you were here—maybe next year!

See you soon, Mom (Dr. Marie Sorrentino)

Obviously the author could have used even more examples, but the ones included here convince us that she is surely "having a great time."

2.3b Choosing the Best Method of Development

You can develop an idea in many ways. The one you choose depends on your purpose—the effect you want your writing to have on your readers—and your main point. Your purpose might be to narrate, describe, explain, or persuade—or any combination of these.

Description and Narration

If your purpose is to introduce your readers to a person, place, or thing, you might describe it in concrete detail. The easiest way to gather such detail is by using the five senses: sight, hearing, smell, taste, and touch. Chapter 6 covers description in detail. If you want to tell a story (that is, to explain what happened), you can narrate events as they occurred in time, discussing each event as it happened. Chapter 7 covers narration in detail.

Explanation and Argument

If your purpose is to explain an idea (exposition) or to argue an opinion (argumentation), you can use several methods. Among these are, of course, narration and description. But there are others:

- Conclusion/support: Use concrete details and facts to support or clarify an idea.

- Illustration: Develop an idea with examples.

- Definition: Explain a new, complicated, or sophisticated term or concept.

- Classification: Distinguish between types or classes.

- Comparison/contrast: Point out similarities or differences.

- Analogy: Compare an abstract idea to something that is concrete and familiar. The subjects being compared may seem unrelated at first.

- Cause/effect: Explain why something happens.

- Process analysis: Explain how something happens or how to do something.

Deciding which method of development to use depends upon your purpose. Let's say you want to persuade readers that the best way to clean up the rivers in your town is to fine polluters. The cause/effect method might work well. If you want to explain how a recent high school graduate should prepare for college, you might use process analysis. In some cases, you might want to use a variety of methods. For example, if your purpose is to convince people that hybrid vehicles are one answer to the energy crisis, you might first have to define *hybrid* (definition), contrast such cars to traditional models (comparison/contrast), and explain the effects on oil consumption that these cars might help us achieve (cause/effect). Chapters on process analysis, comparison/contrast, illustration, definition, argumentation, and persuasion appear later in this book.

2.3c Deciding How to Arrange the Ideas and Details in a Paragraph

Narration and Description

Often, the best way to organize narration or description is to recall details just as you saw or experienced them. In *narration*, you can arrange details just as they happened, in chronological (time) order. In the following narrative paragraph, John Steinbeck writes of a young man being chased by the police. Words that relate to narration are in italics.

> Pepé *stumbled* down the hill. His throat was almost closed with thirst. *At first* he *tried to run*, but immediately he *fell* and *rolled*. *After that* he *went* more carefully. The moon *was just disappearing* behind the mountains *when* he *came* to the bottom. He *crawled* into the heavy brush *feeling* with his fingers for water. There was no water in the bed of the stream, only damp earth. Pepé *laid* his gun *down* and *scooped up* a handful of mud and put it in his mouth, and *then* he *spluttered* and *scraped* the earth from his tongue with his finger, for the mud *drew* at his mouth like a poultice [plaster dressing]. He *dug* a hole in the stream bed with his fingers, *dug* a little basin to catch water; but *before* it was very deep his head *fell forward* on the damp ground and he *slept*. ("Flight")

When *describing*, you can put details into a spatial pattern, in any arrangement you think best. You might describe a place from east to west or left to right, an object from top to bottom, a person from head to toe. In the following paragraph, South African novelist Alan Paton uses sight and hearing to show us a view from a hilltop near the town of Ixopo. Note the italicized words, which direct us to various parts of the scene as the author describes them. Also note the place names that he includes; they are in bold.

> There is a lovely road that runs from **Ixopo** into the hills. These hills are grass-covered and rolling, and they are lovely beyond any singing of it. The road climbs seven miles into them, to **Carisbrooke**, and *from there*, if there is no mist, you look *down* on one of the fairest valleys of **Africa**. *About you* there is grass and bracken [large fern] and you may hear the forlorn [sad] crying of the titihoya, one of the birds of the veld [grassland]. *Below you* is the valley of the **Umzimkuhu** [river], on its journey from **Drakensberg** to the sea; and *beyond* and *behind* the river, great hill after great hill. (*Cry, the Beloved Country*)

Expository and Argumentative Writing

Again, several choices are available when trying your hand at exposition— writing that explains—and at argument—writing that proves a point or defends an opinion. Here are a few patterns of arrangement you can use.

From General to Specific

Starting with a general statement and supporting it with specific details or ideas is a common way to organize a paragraph. Each of the following paragraphs has a different purpose and uses a different method of development. However, all begin with a general statement (the topic sentence) that is followed and developed by specific information.

Comparison and Contrast: Point Out Similarities and Differences

Grant and Lee were in complete contrast, representing two diametrically opposed elements in American life. Grant was the modern man emerging: behind him, ready to come on the stage, was the great age of steel and machinery, of crowded cities and a restless, burgeoning [blossoming] vitality. Lee might have ridden down from the old age of chivalry, lance in hand, silken banner fluttering over his head. Each man was the perfect champion of his cause, drawing both his strengths and his weaknesses from the people he led. (Bruce Catton, "Grant and Lee: A Study in Contrasts")

Classification: Distinguish between Types or Classes

Many religions have definite beliefs regarding hell. Some Christians see it as a fiery pit—much like what Dante described in the *Inferno*—where sinners suffer eternal damnation. Islamic texts describe it as a lake of fire spanned by a bridge over which souls must travel to get to heaven. Evil doers, who fall off the bridge, are cast into the lake, there to spend eternity. Buddhism and Hinduism describe many hells through which a soul must pass in order to be cleansed of any evil so as to be reincarnated and eventually to reach a state of perfection. For the ancient Greeks and Romans, Hades, or the underworld, was populated by the shades or shadows of people who had once walked the earth. Few ever escaped this miserable place. In Judaic theology, hell was once a real place, but for most modern Jews, hell is merely an idea discussed in the scriptures so as to help people understand evil. (Karen Staples, "Deep Down Under")

Analogy: Compare an Abstract Idea to Something That Is Concrete and That the Reader Knows

The American political system is like a gigantic Mexican Christmas fiesta. Each political party is a huge piñata—a papier-maché donkey, for example. The donkey is filled with full employment, low interest rates, affordable housing, comprehensive medical benefits, a balanced budget and other goodies. The American voter is blindfolded and given a stick. The voter then swings the stick wildly in every direction, trying to hit a political candidate on the head and knock some sense into the silly bastard. (P. J. O'Rourke, *Parliament of Whores*)

From Specific to General

Beginning with specific details and moving toward a general conclusion (the topic sentence) that relates to these details is another way to arrange information. Although the following paragraphs use different methods of development, all move from specific to general.

Illustration: Develop Ideas with Examples

The ancient Chinese thought they were celestial brooms wielded [operated] by the gods to sweep the heavens free of evil. In the West they were believed to presage [foretell] the fall of Jerusalem, the death of monarchs and such anomalies as two-headed calves. The Norman Conquest of England was attributed to the 1066 flyby of Halley's, history's most famous comet, which has been linked to everything from Julius Caesar's assassination to the defeat of Attila the Hun. Told that Earth would pass through Halley's tail during its 1910 visit, many Americans panicked and bought gas masks and "comet pills." Alan Hale calls these waves of fear and mysticism "comet madness," and as co-discoverer of Comet Hale-Bopp, he's seen more than his share. (Leon Jaroff, "Crazy about Comets")

Comparison and Contrast: Point Out Similarities and Differences

In *The Expression of the Emotions in Man and Animals,* Darwin made a systematic study of how animals look when they are afraid. In both humans and animals, he found, some or all of the following may occur: the eyes and mouth open, the eyes roll, the heart beats rapidly, hairs stand on end, muscles tremble, teeth chatter, and the sphincter loosens. The frightened creature may freeze in its place or cower. These rules hold true across a remarkable array of species. Somehow it is surprising to learn that when dolphins are terrified, their teeth chatter and the whites of their eyes show, or that a frightened gorilla's legs shake. Such familiar behavior in a wild animal is a reminder of our ultimate kinship. Melvin Konner has written, "We are— not metaphorically, but precisely, biologically—like the doe nibbling moist grass in the predawn misty light; chewing, nuzzling a dewy fawn, breathing the foggy air, feeling so much at peace; and suddenly, for no reason, looking about wildly." (Jeffrey M. Masson and Susan McCarthy, *When Elephants Weep*)

You learned earlier that various methods of development can be used together. The paragraph above uses both comparison and description.

From Question to Answer

A good way to begin a paragraph is with an interesting question. You can then devote the rest of your paragraph to details that develop an effective answer to that question.

Definition: Explain a Term or Concept

What does it mean to be poor in America? We can offer no single description of American poverty. But for many, perhaps most, it means homes with peeling paint, inadequate heating, uncertain plumbing. It means that only the very lucky among the children receive a decent education. It often means a home where some go to bed hungry and malnutrition is a frequent visitor. It means that the most elementary components of the good life in America—a vacation with kids, an evening out, a comfortable home—are but distant and unreachable dreams, more likely to be seen on the television screen than in the neighborhood. And for almost all the poor it means that life is a constant struggle to obtain the merest necessities of existence, those things most of us take for granted. We can do better. (Late U.S. Senator Paul Wellstone, "If Poverty Is the Question ...")

From Problem to Solution

Organizing a paragraph by stating a problem and explaining how to solve it in the sentences that follow is much like asking a question and answering it. It is especially effective when you are explaining a process or analyzing causes and effects, but it can also be used with other methods of development, as in this student's paragraph.

Process Analysis: Explain How to Do Something

For most people, being overweight is not simply a matter of vanity. Excess weight is a threat to health and longevity. You should start losing weight by getting a thorough physical examination, then begin following a regular exercise program prescribed by your doctor. Next, start counting calories; read labels or look up the caloric content of your favorite foods in diet guides available at most super markets and drugstores. Finally, stay away from high-fat animal products and rich desserts. Fill up on fruits, vegetables, natural grains and other high-fiber foods. (Diana Dempsey, "Tightening Our Belts")

By Order of Importance

Writers of fiction often place the most important bit of information last. If arranged in this pattern, an expository or argumentative paragraph can help you create emphasis by guiding your readers to the details and ideas you believe are most important.

Cause and Effect: Explain Why Something Happens

Despite high-profile death sentences like Scott Peterson's in California, public support for the death penalty is falling. The reasons lie partly in mounting evidence that innocent people have been condemned and—in some cases—put to death. Supreme Court Justice Sandra Day O'Connor said that "the system may well be allowing some innocent defendants to be executed." And a recent report by the nonprofit Death Penalty Information Center, *Innocence and the Crisis in the American Death Penalty*, describes how a shift in public perceptions of capital punishment has indeed been taking place. The report notes, for example, that death sentences have dropped by 50 percent over the past five years and that the numbers on death row have also fallen. ("Innocence and the Death Penalty," an editorial in *America: The National Catholic Weekly*)

Analogy: Compare an Abstract Idea to Something Concrete or Something the Reader Knows

"Call waiting" is ... like an electronic 8-year-old who is simply incapable of shutting up while you are conversing with somebody else. The differences are that 1) an 8-year-old does not have the gall to charge you a monthly fee for this service; and 2) an 8-year-old can interrupt you only if he's in the same room, whereas with the incredible capabilities of "call waiting," your conversations can be interrupted by everybody in the entire world who has access to a telephone. It doesn't even have to be a person. A computer can interrupt you. In fact, through a combination of "call waiting" and "auto-dialing," it is now technically possible for your telephone conversations to be interrupted by a trained chicken. (Dave Barry, "We Interrupt This Column ...")

Around a Pivot

The pivoting pattern begins with one idea and then changes direction—pivots—by presenting a different or contrasting idea. The topic sentence normally appears in the middle of the paragraph and announces the shift. Often, but not always, the topic sentence is introduced by a transition such as *but*, *however*, or *nonetheless*.

Illustration: Develop an Idea with Examples

I sometimes hear people who should know better saying that we would be healthier if we depended solely on herbal remedies and refused to take the synthetic drugs purveyed [supplied] by modern scientific medicine. Browse through a pharmacopoeia [list of medicines] and see how many of the medicines prescribed by doctors and sold by druggists are prepared from plants. Quinine for malaria, ephedrine for asthma, cascara for constipation, digitalis for heart conditions, atropine for eye examinations and a great host of other valuable medicines in constant use came directly from folk herbal medicines, and are still prepared from wild plants or those recently brought under cultivation. (Euell Gibbons, *Stalking the Wild Asparagus*)

2.4 Visualizing Unity, Coherence, and Development

The following paragraphs are from Rudolph Chelminski's "The Curse of Count Dracula," an essay published in *Smithsonian* magazine. Notes in the margins and highlighting in the text explain how the author developed his ideas and maintained unity and coherence.

Unity/Coherence

Development

Establishes context/setting.

Over the past year and a half, a furious controversy surrounding a proposal [to build a Dracula theme park] has focused attention on **an area** so obscure that many people today

Paragraph moves from general to specific.

Uses Transition.

still assume it's fictitious: Transylvania. **But** located high within the curling grip of the rugged Carpathian Mountains in central

Repeats "Transylvania."

Romania, **Transylvania** is as real as real can be—rich in mineral resources, blessed with fertile soil and filled with picturesque scenery.

States central idea.

Contrasts.

Uses transition/ linking pronoun.

Uses synonyms for "area."

Although its name means "land beyond the forest," **this historical province** of more than seven million souls was not known as a **particularly spooky place** until 1897, when

Adds information to show place is "as real as real can be."

"Backdrop" connects to topic sentence.

Another mention of Transylvania's environment.

Refers to Dracula.

the Irish writer and critic Bram Stoker published his sensational gothic novel *Dracula*. Casting about for a suitable **backdrop** for his **eerie yarn** about a nobleman who happened to be a **bloodsucking vampire**, Stoker hit upon

Defines by telling us about "eerie yarn."

Uses "yarn" as synonym for "novel."

Uses repetition to connect with previous paragraph.

Transylvania, which he described as "one of the wildest and least known **portions of Europe**."

Describes.

Dracula proved to be one of those rare tales that tap a vein [touch something] deep within the human psyche. The **book** has never been out of print, and **Transylvania**, through no fault of its own, is doomed to be forever associated with the

Cause/effect paragraph; moves from specific to general.

"Outrage" refers to idea in first paragraph.

sanguinary [bloody] count. **This** explains … the **outrage** that [the proposed theme park has] provoked.

"This" refers to earlier idea.

"Region" is synonym for "Transylvania."

It was Romania's own minister of tourism who came up with the idea of building a Dracula theme park in the heart of Transylvania. **For the region as a whole** … **it's** only the latest chapter in a long history of unwelcome intrusions from the outside.

Cause/effect paragraph arranged around a pivot.

"It's" refers to "idea" earlier in paragraph.

"It" refers to "long history" in previous paragraph.

It all began with the Romans, who arrived late in the first century to impose their harsh discipline and Latin tongue on the ancient Dacian people native to the **area. Next** came the Magyars from what is now Hungary, followed by various barbarians and Mongols, **then** the Turks of the Ottoman Empire. Back and forth **they** all went in true Balkan style, and the dust never settled.

"Area" refers to "Transylvania."

"Next" and "then" are transitions.

"They" refers to intruders alluded to above.

Conclusion/support paragraph arranged from specific to general.

2.5 Revising to Improve Unity, Coherence, and Development

Read the following sets of paragraphs, which are taken from the rough draft and the final draft of "Oma," an essay written by student Maria Scamacca. The final draft appears in its entirety in the reading selections for this chapter. Pay particular attention to the notes in the margins, as they explain how the essay was revised to improve unity, coherence, and development.

Maria Scamacca—Rough Draft

Paragraphs 1–3

Use transition to explain when this occurred.

Oma looked old. She wore a flowered house dress a starched white apron, and old, scuffed leather loafers. Oma was deaf in one ear from

Add detail about how old she looked.

Combine sentences for smoothness.

a neglected childhood ear infection. Symptoms of Bell's palsy were present. She shuffled her feet and held on to the furniture with swollen, scarred hands as she walked. She lived

Add detail about symptoms.

Add transitions and combine sentences for smoothness.

alone the house looked neat. There were small crumbs and stains on the tables, and particles of food were stuck to some of the dishes.

She led me to a back door to a garden that she boasted of planning and maintaining alone. It was like no garden I had ever seen, an acre of food and beauty. I sensed immediately that this paradise was the creation of a unique energy, courage, and beauty I came to see in Oma. She had married a widower with a young daughter; the couple eventually had three other children. They lived on a farm near the Rumanian border on which they grew and raised all their food, even the grapes from which they made their own wine.

Paragraph not unified. This information does not relate to the garden. Put it elsewhere.

Add details to prove this.

Ready to be picked in the garden were neat and orderly rows of potatoes, carrots, asparagus, onion, peppers, lettuce, lima beans, and string beans as well as many other vegetables I had never heard of. There were fruits and flowers everywhere.

Combine with material about garden in preceding paragraph.

Add transition.

Add examples of "fruits and flowers."

Paragraphs 7–10

Farm life was hard. Oma took it well. She cooked and kept house. The horses and other farm animals had to be looked after. She baked bread, made sausage, and salted the meats the family would eat year round.

Add transitions and combine sentences for smoothness.

Oma is fond of telling me how she force-fed geese by stuffing balls of bread down their long necks with her fingers. Her geese got so fat they couldn't fly, but they brought the best prices at the market, she often reminds me.

Combine with preceding paragraph.

Her family raised their own pigs. It came time to kill them. Her husband, Opa, asked his neighbor to slaughter the animals. Opa slaughtered the neighbor's pigs. "He felt bad, you know, killing his own pig," Oma said. Oma and Opa hired outside help, whom they paid with bread and salted meat. They did most of the work themselves, and they prospered.

Add transitions and combine sentences for smoothness.

Seems contradictory; use transition to make clearer.

Add transitions to bridge sentences and paragraphs.

The war came. The horses were stolen by Russian soldiers. The family was removed from their farm, and Oma found herself in a Russian concentration camp. The stories are confusing. I have heard bits and pieces repeatedly over the

Provide a general statement as a topic sentence.

Strengthen coherence between sentences.

past six years and I have had to reconstruct them myself. Once in a while I ask Oma to clarify the order of events, but she doesn't get very far until she starts an entirely new story.

Explain what these stories relate to.

Maria Scamacca—Final Draft

Paragraphs 1–2

Adds transitions to explain when this meeting occurred.

When I first met Oma six years ago, she looked about eighty-years old, was a few pounds over-weight for her medium frame, and was slightly hunched over. She wore a flowered house

Includes details about how old she looked.

Combines sentences for smoothness.

dress a starched white apron, and old, scuffed leather loafers. She was deaf in one ear from a neglected childhood ear infection, and half of her face drooped from Bell's palsy. She shuf-

Adds transitions and combines sentences for smoothness

fled her feet and held on to the furniture with swollen, scarred hands as she walked. Despite Oma's disability and the fact that she lived alone, her house looked neat, but there were small crumbs and stains on the tables, and particles of food were stuck to some of the dishes, unnoticed by eyes weakened with age.

Adds detail about symptom of Bell's palsy.

Adds transition to bridge paragraphs.

That's why I was shocked when she led me to a back door to a garden that she boasted of planting and maintaining alone. It was like

Rewrites entire paragraph to create unity.

no garden I had ever seen, an acre of food and beauty. Ready to be picked in the garden were neat and orderly rows of potatoes, carrots, asparagus, onion, peppers, lettuce, lima beans, and string beans. Her garden also boasted strawberries, blueberries, gooseberries, currant, peaches, watermelons, and many other fruits.

Names fruits and flowers to prove that garden is an "acre of food and beauty."

And there were flowers everywhere: zinnias, day lilies, marigolds, irises, and petunias. I sensed immediately that this paradise was the creation of a unique energy, courage, and beauty I came to see in Oma.

Note that paragraph is arranged from specific to general. Topic sentence is last.

Paragraphs 7–9

Adds transitions and combines sentences for smoothness.

Farm life was hard. However, Oma took it well. In addition to cooking and housekeeping, she had to tend the horses and other farm animals, bake bread, make sausage, and salt the meats the family would eat year round. Oma is fond of telling me how she force-fed geese by stuffing balls of bread down their long necks with her fingers. Her geese got so fat they couldn't fly, but they brought the best prices at the market, she often reminds me.

Combines two paragraphs into one.

Adds transitions and combines sentences for smoothness.

Her family also raised their own pigs. But when it came time to slaughter the animals, her husband, Opa, asked his neighbor to slaughter the animals. In return Opa slaughtered the neighbor's pigs. "He felt bad, you know, killing his own pig," Oma said. At times, Oma and Opa hired outside help, whom they paid with bread and salted meat. However, they did most of the work themselves, and they prospered.

Adds transitions to clarify idea.

Adds transitions to bridge paragraphs and improve coherence between sentences.

Then the war came, and Oma's family suffered. First the horses were stolen by Russian soldiers. Then the family was removed from their farm, and Oma found herself in a Russian concentration camp. The stories from this period of her life are confusing. I have heard bits and pieces repeatedly over the past six years, and I have had to reconstruct them myself. Once in a while, I ask Oma to clarify the order of events, but she doesn't get very far until she starts an entirely new story.

Provides a general statement as a topic sentence.

Adds detail to explain when events in these stories took place.

2.6 Practicing Unity and Coherence

Read this paragraph—written by student Stacy Zolnowski for a first-year writing class—to learn more about paragraph unity. Then, using complete sentences, answer the questions that follow:

[1] Throughout history, left-handedness has been deemed a nasty habit, a social infraction, a symptom of neurosis, or even a sign of mental retardation. [2] More recently, however, its social, educational, and psychological implications have acquired a more enlightened appreciation. [3] Nonetheless, left-handers continue to be discriminated against in an environment that conforms to the needs and prejudices of a right-handed society. ("The Left-Handed Minority")

1. Assume that the paragraph's topic sentence is sentence 3. What, in your own words, is the paragraph's central idea?

    _____

    _____

    _____

    _____

    _____

2. How do sentences 1 and 2 relate to the central idea?

    _____

    _____

    _____

    _____

    _____

3. What transitional devices does the writer use to maintain coherence?

    _____

    _____

    _____

    _____

4. In what other ways does the writer maintain coherence?

    _____

    _____

    _____

    _____

2.7 Practicing Methods of Development

Complete the paragraphs begun below. Include information based on your own observations and experiences. Use whatever method of development you think the topic sentence, which begins each paragraph, calls for.

1. My family provides me with a great deal of emotional support. For example,

_____

_____

_____

_____

_____

_____

_____

2. There are three types of students at my college. The first

_____

_____

_____

_____

_____

_____

_____

3. If you want to flunk a test, do the following:

_____

_____

_____

_____

_____

_____

_____

_____

4. Most people gain weight because

_____

_____

_____

_____

_____

_____

5. My sister (brother, best friend) is a ___[fill in the blank]___ type of person. I, on the other hand, am

_____

_____

_____

_____

_____

_____

_____

2.8 Reading Selections

2.8a Oma: Portrait of a Heroine

Author Biography

Maria Scamacca graduated from college with a degree in nursing and is now a critical-care registered nurse at a large hospital. "Oma: Portrait of a Heroine" was written in a freshman composition class in response to an assignment that asked students to describe people they found inspiring. After reading Scamacca's essay, you may find it easy to understand why she chose to write about Oma.

Preparing to Read

1. Look for various kinds of connectives—transitions, linking pronouns, repeated words, and synonyms—that form bridges between this essay's paragraphs.

2. Look for various methods of developing paragraphs in this essay. In particular, try to identify one that uses narration, another that uses conclusion/support, and one that uses cause/effect.

3. Look for at least one paragraph that is arranged from specific to general, one that is arranged by order of importance, and one that is arranged around a pivot.

4. In German, *Oma* means "grandmother," and *Opa* means "grandfather."

Vocabulary

black market (noun)   Underground commercial system in which banned or stolen goods are sold or traded.

compensation (noun)   Payment.

displaced (verb)   Forced to move.

equivalent (noun)   The equal of.

humane (adjective)   Kind, charitable, benevolent.

implores (verb)   Begs.

palsy (noun)   Paralysis.

provisions (noun)   Necessities, supplies.

Oma: Portrait of a Heroine

Maria Scamacca

When I first met Oma six years ago, she looked about eighty years old, was a few pounds over-weight for her medium frame, and was slightly hunched over. She wore a flowered house dress, a starched white apron, and old, scuffed leather loafers. Oma was deaf in one ear from a neglected childhood ear infection, and half of her face drooped from Bell's palsy. She shuffled her feet and held on to the furniture with swollen, scarred hands as she walked. Despite Oma's disability and the fact that she lived alone, her house looked neat, but there were small crumbs and stains on the tables, and particles of food were stuck to some of the dishes, unnoticed by eyes weakened with age.   1

That's why I was shocked when she led me through the back door to a garden that she boasted of planting and maintaining alone. It was like no garden I had ever seen, an acre of food and beauty. Ready to be picked and eaten were neat and orderly rows of potatoes, carrots, asparagus, onions, peppers, lettuce, lima beans, and string beans. Her garden also boasted strawberries, blueberries, gooseberries, currants, peaches, watermelons, and many other fruits. And there were flowers everywhere: zinnias, day lilies, marigolds, irises, and petunias. I sensed immediately that this paradise was the creation of a unique energy, courage, and beauty I came to see in Oma.   2

Each year the impossible garden yields bushels of fruits and berries for the jams and jellies that Oma cooks and jars herself. She also cans fruit and vegetables, and she uses the fruit in the fillings of luscious pastries that, as I was to learn, have made her famous among friends, family, and neighbors. She still does all of her own cooking and had been known, until only recently, to throw holiday dinners for more than twenty people.   3

From the day I met Oma, I grew to admire her and have looked forward to visiting. Almost every Sunday after church, my husband's family and I gather around her dining room table for fresh coffee, homemade Prinz Regent Torte (a seven-layer cake), Schwarzwälder Kirschtorte (Black Forest cherry cake), warm cookies, and good talk.   4

Oma dominates the conversation, filling us with stories of her childhood and of World War II; she hardly stops to take a breath unless one of us asks a question or implores her to translate the frequent German or Hungarian phrases that pop out of her mouth. At such times, we play guessing games as Oma tries to explain in broken English a word or expression for which she knows no English equivalent.   5

Oma was born in Hungary. She was an only child—rare in the early days of this century—the only surviving baby of four pregnancies. Her mother died when Oma was in her teens, and she was left alone to keep house for her father. At eighteen, she married a widower with a young daughter; the couple eventually had three other children. They lived on a farm near the Romanian border on which they grew and raised all their food, even the grapes from which they made their own wine.   6

Farm life was hard. However, Oma took to it well. In addition to cooking and housekeeping, she had to tend to the horses and other farm animals, bake bread, make sausage, and salt the meats the family would eat year round. Oma is fond of telling me how she force-fed geese by stuffing balls of bread down their long necks with her fingers. Her geese got so fat they couldn't fly, but they brought the best prices at the market, she often reminds me.   6

Her family also raised their own pigs. But when it came time to slaughter the animals, her husband, Opa, asked his neighbor to do it. In return, Opa slaughtered the neighbor's pigs. "He felt bad, you know, killing his own pig," Oma said. At times, Oma and Opa hired outside help, whom they paid with bread and salted meat. However, they did most of the work themselves, and they prospered.   7

Then the war came. First her horses were stolen by Russian soldiers. Then the family was removed from their farm, and Oma found herself in a Russian concentration camp. The stories from this period of her life are confusing. I have heard bits and pieces of them repeatedly over the past six years, and I have had to reconstruct them myself. Once in a while I ask Oma to clarify the order of events, but she doesn't get very far until she starts an entirely new story.   8

After the war, the borders of countries were redrawn, and Oma's family was displaced with only a few hours' notice. Allowed to take only the clothes on their backs and whatever they could carry, they were put into a cattle car on a long freight train. The new government provided no compensation for their land and told them to leave all of their possessions behind. The only explanation was that their family had originally come from Germany and that they were required to leave Hungary and return to the land of their ancestors. This was not punishment, the authorities explained; it was "humane displacement."   9

Before they boarded the train, the family had to collect enough grain and other provisions to feed themselves during the long trip. But they saw little of their food; Oma thinks it was stolen and sold on the black market. "There were no bathrooms on the train," Oma explained. "If someone had to defecate or urinate, they were held by others out of the open doors over the side of the moving train. And they call that humane!"   10

When they arrived in Germany, Oma and her family were placed in a room in a run-down building that had holes in the walls and was full of rats. Her husband developed pneumonia. Sick for months, he almost lost the will to live and just lay in bed. When he finally recovered, they moved to America, but they had to leave their daughter behind because she had tuberculosis. Oma still weeps openly whenever she recalls being forced to abandon her child. Luckily, however, things turned out well for "Tante Vicki," who still lives in Germany and now has a family of her own.   11

In time, the family settled in Millstone, New Jersey, and began to build a new life in what was then a small rural community. In the early 1950s, however, Oma and Opa lost their oldest son in the Korean War, so when the other two boys married and moved out of the house, the two old people were on their own.   12

Several years ago, Opa died of lung cancer contracted from many years of working in an asbestos factory. Oma continues to receive a good pension and health benefits from his employer. They come in handy, for over the past few years she has been hospitalized several times. Last summer she got so sick she couldn't even plant her garden, so all of her grandchildren got together to plant it for her. That is the only request she has ever made of them.   13

It is hard to see a woman who was once so strong grow old and weak. At times, Oma feels quite useless, but she can still tell wonderful stories, and we listen avidly. I wonder if there will be a garden this year.   14

Read More on the Web

Look for more information about events related to this story in the following websites:

- Holocaust Museum and Learning Center: hmlc.org

- Library of Congress, Hungary: A Country Study: www.loc.gov/item/90006426

Questions for Discussion

1. What is Scamacca's thesis?

2. Where does the topic sentence in paragraph 2 appear? Identify the topic sentence in at least one other paragraph.

3. The central idea in paragraph 6 is implied. State it in your own words.

4. Pick out elements that the author uses to maintain coherence between paragraphs throughout this essay.

5. Reread paragraphs 9–12, and circle words and phrases the author uses to maintain coherence in them.

6. Identify a paragraph that uses the conclusion/support method, another that uses cause/effect, and still another that uses narration.

7. Identify one paragraph that is arranged by order of importance, one that moves from specific to general, and one that is organized around a pivot.

Thinking Critically

1. If you were able to meet Oma, what would you ask her about her life? As you reread this essay, write questions to Oma in the margins of the text when they occur to you. Then do some creative guessing. On the basis of what you know about Oma, answer your questions in a paragraph or two.

2. Reread Maria Cirilli's "Echoes" in chapter 1. In what ways is Cirilli's essay similar to Scamacca's? In what ways are these essays different?

3. Pretend that the government has decided to take almost everything you own and send you to another country. Would you resist? If so, how? If not, how would you prepare for this drastic change? Put your answer in two or three paragraphs that are unified and coherent. Make sure to include transitions between paragraphs as well.

Suggestions for Journal Entries

1. Do you have an older relative, friend, or neighbor whose attitude toward life you consider heroic? Choose your own definition of the word *heroic*. Freewrite for about five minutes about an event from this person's life that might show his or her heroism.

2. Interview the person mentioned above. Try to find out more about his or her attitude toward life. A good way to do this is to ask your subject to tell you about a difficult or depressing time and to explain how he or she dealt with it.

3. Brainstorm with one or two others who know the person mentioned above. Try to gather facts, direct quotations, and opinions that you could use in a paper that describes your subject as heroic.

2.8b **Study Calculus!**

Author Biography

Secretary of education and chair of the National Endowment for the Humanities in the Ronald Reagan administration, **William J. Bennett** holds a doctorate in political philosophy from the University of Texas and a law degree from Harvard University. Under the first President George Bush, Bennett directed the war on drugs as head of the Office of National Drug Control Policy. The following essay, which reveals much about Bennett's thinking when he was secretary of education, is taken from *The De-Valuing of America: The Fight for Our Children*. Other popular books by Bennet include *Tried by Fire: The Story of Christianity's First Thousand Years; The Book of Virtues: A Treasury of Great Moral Stories; A Century Turns: New Hopes, New Fears; The True Saint Nicholas; and America: The Last Best Hope* (in two volumes).

Preparing to Read

1. The title provides a clue to the essay's thesis. Why didn't Bennett use "Math" instead of "Calculus"?

2. Look for the linking pronouns and other connective devices Bennett uses to create coherence in and between paragraphs.

3. This essay ends with several one-sentence paragraphs. Although not common in college writing, such paragraphs are useful here because they convey dialogue (conversation between people).

4. Some teachers in the high school in which this essay takes place claimed that teaching calculus to inner-city students was a "quixotic fantasy." Don Quixote, the title character of a seventeenth-century Spanish novel, was a dreamer who often found himself in trouble by attempting the impossible. Therefore, *quixotic* has come to mean "foolish" or "impractical."

5. Bennett uses a variety of methods to develop and arrange his paragraphs. Find at least one paragraph using narration, one using cause/effect, and one using illustration. Also find at least one paragraph that is arranged according to order of importance.

Vocabulary

calculus (noun)   A branch of mathematics important to science, engineering, and other disciplines.

canard (noun)   False belief, principle, rule, or story.

ethic (noun)   Principle, belief in.

pedagogy (noun)   Education, schooling, teaching.

skepticism (noun)   Doubt, distrust, disbelief.

Study Calculus!

William J. Bennett

Principal Henry Gradillas at Garfield High School in East Los Angeles let Jaime Escalante teach. And did the students ever learn. Escalante, a Bolivian immigrant, arrived at the school in 1974 to teach math. Now perhaps America's most famous teacher, he wanted to return something to the country that had taken him in and given him opportunity.   1

His plan to teach calculus to disadvantaged Hispanic youngsters was greeted with skepticism and laughter by his colleagues, and he encountered resistance from his students. But he told me that the greatest resistance came not from the students but from others in the profession, other teachers and counselors who urged him not to push so hard. They told him that his plan to teach calculus was a quixotic fantasy. "If you try," some told him, "the students will fail. They can't do it. They will be embarrassed, and their self-esteem will suffer. What you want to do—teach calculus—will be dangerous."   2

Escalante told me what he told his critics: "If you are fifteen or sixteen years old, in the barrio of East Los Angeles, there are a lot of things that are dangerous. But calculus isn't one of them." His principal, Henry Gradillas, encouraged him to proceed.   3

Escalante persisted, and in 1982 eighteen of his students took the Advanced Placement (AP) calculus test. By 1991, 160 students from Garfield took the test. According to Jay Mathews, author of *Escalante: The Best Teacher in America*, Escalante has given Garfield the most successful inner-city mathematics program in the United States. In recent years only four or five secondary schools in the country have prepared more students for the AP calculus examination (tests so difficult that fewer than 2 percent of American students even attempt them). Because of Escalante's efforts, about a fourth of all the Mexican-American students in the country who pass AP calculus come from Garfield.   4

Escalante's methods and approach (celebrated in the movie *Stand and Deliver*) are in marked contrast to the theory and practice of pedagogy as taught in most American schools of education. He consistently violates the canard that a teacher shouldn't "impose his values on students." Indeed, he seeks every opportunity to impose his ethic of achievement, success, and hard work on them. His reason, as expressed to me, is simple: "My values are better than theirs." His way of doing this is direct, manly, no nonsense. In the early days of his career at Garfield, he asked a student whether he wanted to study calculus. "No," said the student, "I want to see my girlfriend."   5

"Well, then," responded Escalante, "go over to woodworking class on your way out."   6

"Why," the student asked.   7

"So you can learn how to make shoeshine boxes so you can have a career shining the shoes for Anglos as they pass through Los Angeles International Airport on their business trips."   8

"I don't want to shine Anglos' shoes," protested the student.   9

"Then study calculus," was Escalante's reply.   10

Read More on the Web

Visit the following websites to find more information related to Escalante and calculus:

- Bolivia Web Hall of Fame (contains information on Escalante): www.boliviaweb.com/hallfame

- The Math Forum at Drexel University: http://bvtlab.com/76hA7

- Calculus.org: Resources for the Calculus Student: calculus.org

- Eric Schechter, "Why Study Calculus: A Brief History of Math": math.vanderbilt.edu/schectex/courses/whystudy.html

Questions for Discussion

1. What is the essay's thesis?

2. Explain how Bennett uses linking pronouns to maintain coherence in paragraph 2.

3. Find two transitional words or phrases in paragraph 1. Then, find three more in the rest of the essay.

4. What use does Bennett make of repetition to maintain coherence between paragraphs?

5. Which paragraph uses narration? Which uses illustration? Which uses the cause/effect method?

6. Which paragraph is arranged by order of importance?

7. Why didn't Bennett combine paragraphs 6–10 into one paragraph?

Thinking Critically

1. Do you agree with the way in which Escalante challenged his students? Think of another way that you might motivate students to study a difficult subject if you were a teacher. Explain this in a paragraph or two.

2. What kinds of values is Escalante talking about in paragraph 5? Should teachers be allowed to impose other values—social, political, or moral, for example—on students? List the advantages and disadvantages of allowing them to do so.

3. Why do you think some teachers had a low opinion of the abilities of students whom Escalante helped? What connection, if any, is there between a teacher's attitude and student success?

Suggestions for Journal Entries

1. Use clustering or listing to come up with several characteristics or qualities of a good teacher. You might begin by thinking about the best teacher or teachers you have had. Consider those qualities that caused you to admire them or that made them effective instructors. For example you might write:

    -   Ms. Jones challenged students.

    -   Mr. Mendoza graded homework and tests carefully.

    -   Dr. Patel inspired confidence in students.

    -   Ms. Fernandez made geometry interesting and easy to understand.

    You don't need to limit yourself to teachers you have had in school. Family members, employers, neighbors, coaches, and members of the clergy often teach us a lot as well.

2. Freewrite for about ten minutes to gather information about the teacher who has influenced you most. Again, don't limit yourself to teachers you have had in school.

2.8c Burger Queen

Author Biography

Erin Sharp was a sophomore at Cornell University when she wrote this essay. It first appeared in *The American Enterprise* magazine.

Preparing to Read

1. The information in this essay comes from Sharp's employment at a McDonald's restaurant. Before you begin reading, think about the variety of people who work and eat at a fast-food restaurant.

2. What is Sharp hinting at in the title?

3. If you were writing about your place of employment, what subjects and details would you discuss to help your readers understand what it means to work there?

4. You might find unfamiliar words in this essay that are not listed in the vocabulary. Try to get at their meanings by using context clues. For example, the author says that some customers "bickered" with her "over a measly ten-cent increase in the price of an Egg McMuffin." What might *bickered* and *measly* mean in this sentence?

Vocabulary

coveted (adjective)   Desired.

forfeited (verb)   Gave up.

freelance (adjective)   Self-employed, temporary, hired for a one-time job.

hoard (verb)   Save, hide away.

quipped (verb)   Answered in a joking or sarcastic way.

pathologist (noun)   Doctor who diagnoses physical changes caused by disease.

perspective (noun)   Point of view.

reimbursement (noun)   Refund.

scam (verb)   To cheat.

stereotypes (noun)   Labels, types.

tackiness (noun)   Bad taste.

tempered (verb)   Moderated, lessened, toned down.

Burger Queen

Erin Sharp

When I announced the change of my major from biology with pre-med aspirations to English, my advisor simply raised an eyebrow and asked if I planned to work at McDonald's for the rest of my life. "Actually," I quipped, "I've been working at McDonald's for two and a half years, and it's sort of fun." His surprise was evident, a typical reaction to my shocking side occupation. I spoke the truth, though; I have held a dozen jobs ranging from camp counselor to pathologist's assistant (now including, I suppose, freelance journalism), yet none have been as entertaining as my stints at the Golden Arches.

1

My double life as Erin Sharp, Ivy League McDonald's Worker, has revealed twin stereotypes to me. People told I go to Cornell view me as bright and ambitious. Put me behind the counter at McDonald's, however, and I am usually assumed to be a high school dropout with fifteen unseen piercings. 2

When I was six years old, McDonald's was my favorite place to eat, and kids have not changed much in the last dozen years. I am often asked whether I have actually met "The Ronald" McDonald, and have been given letters to pass along to him, like one of Santa Claus's elves. Among kids, McDonald's workers rank right up there with policemen and firefighters. 3

Yet this perspective rarely survives adolescence. Respect for the workers of the fast food industry is lost among most adults, with absurd results. Many adults seem to assume that McWorkers are stupid, attempting to scam us out of free food and coupons. The depths of tackiness to which some human beings will stoop in order to save a few pennies at a drive-thru window are worthy of "Candid Camera." Grown men driving Lincoln Town Cars have bickered with me for five minutes over a measly ten-cent increase in the price of an Egg McMuffin. Perhaps they imagine that I overcharge each patron and hoard misbegotten dimes in a piggy bank behind the shake machine? 4

Once, my store even received a phone call at noon from a furious woman demanding reimbursement for the breakfast she had bought that morning via drive-thru; apparently, it was cold when she arrived at work over an hour later. Our most famous TIC (Truculent, Irate Customer) lost her temper when we could not (in her eyes, would not) provide the grilled chicken sandwich she craved in the middle of breakfast rush hour. An entirely new traffic pattern was created in drive-thru for the 25 minutes spent in fruitless argument and accommodation attempts by our managers as the grill team thawed frozen meat, heated a grill to cook on and produced the coveted sandwich for her. When at last presented with it, she lofted the bag triumphantly and accused us of withholding it from her for the entire time, then zoomed off with the last words: "I'm never coming back here again!" The effectiveness of this condemnation was tempered by her license plate, which proclaimed her to be from Delaware—over an hour away. 5

A small portion of our patrons are so confused that there is really nothing to do but wait for them to leave. My most prominent example of this sort of "guest" is the infamous Snack Attack Lady, who ordered hotcakes and sausage during our 90-second-guaranteed-service hour and then ate her breakfast right outside the drive-thru window. Heedless of the frenzied honking behind her, she carefully opened the platter, poured a puddle of syrup, rolled the sausage in a hotcake and dipped both daintily into the syrup. My co-workers and I watched in speechless amazement. When asked what she was doing, she rolled her eyes and snapped, "What does it look like I'm doing? I'm eating my breakfast!" That woman has permanently forfeited all rights to complain about slow drive-thru service. 6

And yet, there are some great customers out there, like the Morning Crew: the seven retired men and one active police officer who wait for our doors to open every day so that they can enjoy their dawn coffee and conversation. If I missed a day of work, I would return to inquiries about my health and concern that all was well. The greatest customers ever to grace our store were two deliverymen who drove up to the window one spring afternoon two years ago with armfuls of roses for my co-worker and me. They were moving their business out of state, they explained, and wanted to thank us for making their afternoons brighter. 7

Well, boys, if you are reading this article, thank you again for that fabulous surprise. I still have the ribbon which bound them. 8

Read More on the Web

To learn more about the trials and tribulations of fast-food workers, go to the following:

- HRZone.com article on fast-food restaurant workers: www.hrzone.com/lead/change/hrd-insight-mcdonalds-head-of-people-on-staff-engagement
- US Department of Labor Occupational Outlook Handbook: www.bls.gov/ooh/
- Forbes' site 7 Steps for Dealing with Angry Customers: http://bvtlab.com/uc6Pp

Questions for Discussion

1. What is Sharp's central idea?

2. Why does Sharp tell us that her college advisor was surprised when she told him she worked at McDonald's? How does doing so help introduce her central idea?

3. What is the topic sentence in paragraph 4? How does that sentence also serve as the topic sentence in paragraph 5?

4. Explain the ways in which Sharp maintains coherence between paragraphs 4, 5, 6, 7, and 8.

5. In which paragraphs does Sharp use illustration?

6. What method of development is seen in paragraph 1?

7. Identify the patterns of organization in paragraphs 1 through 7.

Thinking Critically

1. In Preparing to Read, you were asked to use context clues to determine the meaning of some of Sharp's vocabulary. What does she mean by "pre-med," "aspirations," and "stints" in paragraph 1; "truculent," "irate", "fruitless," and "lofted" in paragraph 5; and "heedless" and "frenzied" in paragraph 6?

2. What are the Ivy League, "Candid Camera," and McWorkers? You might find more about the first two terms on the Internet or in your college library, but you might have to figure out the third term on your own.

3. What is the pun (play on words) Sharp uses in the title?

Suggestions for Journal Entries

1. Use focused freewriting, listing, or clustering to gather information that describes customers or employees or both at a place at which you work or have worked. Focus on people with the most interesting or distinctive personalities.

2. Sharp's essay is more than a listing of complaints about annoying customers. It is a statement—and a positive one at that—about her role and image as a worker in a fast-food restaurant. Use clustering or any other prewriting method to explain your feelings—be they positive, negative, or mixed—about a job you hold or once held.

2.8d **Zip Out**

Introduction

To end the war with Japan, the United States dropped atomic bombs on Hiroshima and Nagasaki in August 1945. Few people, other than nuclear scientists, knew much about atomic energy at the time, for the information about this subject was a military secret. However, in its December 9, 1946, issue, a little over a year since the war's end, *Time* magazine published this article, which details the first nuclear chain reaction.

Preparing to Read

1. This essay explains a process, the creation of a chain reaction. Look for passage-of-time transitions used to mark various stages in the process.

2. Process analysis through narration is the chief method used in this essay. However, look for places in which description and cause/effect are used.

3. Enrico Fermi, an Italian-born physicist, was in charge of this experiment. Use the Internet to learn more about Fermi and the other physicists mentioned in the essay. Then, look up more information about the nature of a nuclear chain reaction.

Vocabulary

chronology (noun)   Arrangement of events in time.

douse (verb)   Put out, extinguish.

mutinous (adjective)   Rebellious, defiant.

self-sustaining (adjective)   Continuing on its own.

shrouded (verb)   Covered.

spontaneously (adverb)   Naturally, by itself.

tethered (verb)   Tied , connected to.

Zip Out

From Time *Magazine*

By U.S. Army chronology, the Atomic Age was born on December 2, 1942, a good thirty-two months before Hiroshima. Now the Army, beaming proudly, has released a detailed description of its birth.   1

In a squash court under the stands of the University of Chicago's football stadium, a curious structure had grown, watched by the hopeful, nervous eyes of some of the world's best physicists. It was built of dead-black graphite bricks with small cubes of uranium or uranium oxide imbedded in some of their corners.

This was the world's first uranium pile. Within it, if all went well, would rage the first nuclear chain reaction. Physicist Enrico Fermi, Italian-born Nobel Prize-winner, was sure that all would go well. He had figured every smallest detail, advancing through theory and mathematics far into the unknown.   2

On December 2, a small group of physicists gathered in the squash court for the final test. Partly shrouded in balloon cloth, the pile squatted black and menacing. Within it, all knew or hoped, a monstrous giant sat chained. Control rods plated with cadmium (which readily absorbs neutrons) had been thrust into holes in the graphite. When the control rods were removed, Fermi had calculated, the chain reaction would start spontaneously, and the giant would be free.   3

One of the rods was automatic, controlled by a motor which could shoot it back into the pile when instruments warned that neutrons were getting too thick. Another (called "Zip") was attached to a heavy weight by a rope running over a pulley. When in the "withdrawn" position, it was tethered by another rope; a man with an ax stood ready to cut it free, to send it zipping into the pile if anything went wrong. The last rod, marked in feet and inches, was to be worked by hand.   4

But all the physicists knew that they were in dangerous, unknown territory. So above the pile was stationed a "liquid-control squad" to douse mutinous neutrons with a cadmium-salt solution.   5

Fermi ran the test. At 9:45 he gave the order. A whining motor withdrew the automatic control rod. The Geiger counters on the instrument panel clicked a little faster; a pen drew a slightly higher curve on a slip of paper.   6

"Zip out!" ordered Fermi a few minutes later. Physicist Walter H. Zinn pulled out the Zip rod and tied it carefully. The counters clicked still faster. The graph pen moved up again.   7

"Pull it thirteen feet, George," commanded Fermi. Physicist George Weil drew the final control rod partway out of the pile. Faster clicked the counters. He drew it out another foot; then another six inches.   8

At 11:35 the counters were clicking furiously. The physicists watched fascinated as the curve climbed steadily upward. Then, Wham! With a clang, the automatic control rod (which had been set for too low a neutron count) slammed back into the pile. "I'm hungry," said Fermi calmly. "Let's go to lunch." The other rods were inserted; the pile quieted down.   9

At two o'clock the physicists gathered again in the squash court. One by one, on Fermi's orders, the control rods were withdrawn; the counters clicked faster. The pile was alive with neutrons now; the giant was straining his bonds. But it was not quite a chain reaction. The neutron curve moved up, leveled off.   10

At 3:45 Fermi ordered the control rod out another foot. "This is going to do it," he said. "The curve … will not level off." Now the counters were roaring not clicking; the graph curve was climbing upward. Fermi studied the instruments, grinned broadly: "The reaction is self-sustaining."   11

For twenty-eight minutes, the physicists watched as the curve climbed sharply upward. The giant was flexing its muscles.   12

"O.K." said Fermi. "Zip in." The Zip rod shot into the pile. The counters slowed their clicking. The graph curve sagged. But the world outside the squash court would not be the same again.   13

Read More on the Web

Search the following websites for more information related to this article:

- Enrico Fermi at *Biography.com*: http://bvtlab.com/5bE6N
- Kennedy Hickman, "World War II: The Manhattan Project": http://bvtlab.com/a8U7Y
- Nuclear fission at *Atomicarchive.com*: www.atomicarchive.com/Fission/Fission1.shtml

---

Questions for Discussion

1. Write a formal thesis statement for this essay in your own words.

2. Choose three or four paragraphs from the article, and explain how the author maintains coherence in those paragraphs.

3. Is paragraph 5 unified? Write what might serve as a topic sentence for that paragraph.

4. Explain the way in which coherence is maintained between paragraphs 2 and 13.

5. Find a place where description is used here.

6. Find a place where the cause/effect method is used.

7. What does the author mean in the last paragraph by saying, "the world outside the squash court would not be the same again"?

Thinking Critically

1. Pretend you are interviewing Fermi or another physicist who worked on this project. Make a list of questions you might ask this individual. You might ask, for example, whether that person knew that having produced a nuclear chain reaction would lead to the creation of an atomic bomb. You might also ask about peaceful uses of nuclear energy.

2. Think of another major scientific breakthrough in the recent past—for example, the personal computer, the GPS mapping system, the cell phone, or even the microwave. How has this invention made your life different from what it might have been had this device not been invented?

Suggestions for Journal Entries

1. Read "Zip Out" again. Then make an outline of the major steps that Fermi and the other scientists took to create a self-sustaining nuclear reaction.

2. Think of a process you once had to go through to reach a desired goal. Perhaps you wanted to raise your grades in math, become a better basketball player, lose weight, or learn how to garden or to fish. Perhaps you had to master a certain skill or learn a new computer program at work. Whatever the process might be, use listing to record major steps in the process. You may be able to use this list as an outline for a longer writing process.

2.9 Suggestions for Sustained Writing

1. Review the journal entry(ies) you made after reading Maria Scamacca's "Oma: Portrait of a Heroine." Use this information in a short essay that explains why a certain person you know is heroic. Provide at least three reasons to support that idea.

   Paragraph 1: Captures the readers' interest and states the thesis. Your thesis statement might resemble this: "My neighbor Mrs. Rozowski faces life with a smile even though she has experienced suffering and heartache." In the rest of this paragraph you might explain that Mrs. Rozowski suffers from arthritis, lives on a very small pension, and has just lost her husband of fifty years.

   Paragraph 2: Mentions Mrs. Rozowski's arthritis and its painful symptoms. But it also discusses the many things she does to keep active despite that pain. This paragraph might use illustration—giving examples—as its major method of development. It might be arranged from general to specific, by order of importance, or through questions/answer.

   Paragraph 3: Explains that, living on a small pension, Mrs. Rozowski has learned many ways to save money such as growing much of her own food, making her own clothes, and even doing simple house repairs. This paragraph might employ the cause/effect method as well as examples. It might be arranged from problem to solution or around a pivot.

   Paragraph 4: Discusses her devotion to her husband and her willingness to care for him during his battle with Alzheimer's disease. This paragraph might use process analysis, narration, description, or a combination of all three. It might be arranged by order of importance or from specific to general.

Paragraph 5: Restates your admiration for your subject and explains what you have learned about facing life's problems from this woman. It also expresses your hope that you will have the same courage when you are elderly.

As you revise the first draft of your essay, make sure that you have included enough detail to make every paragraph convincing. If you haven't, do some more information gathering as explained in Getting Started. Also, check to see that your paragraphs are both unified and coherent and that you have maintained coherence between paragraphs.

2. Review the notes you made for the first journal entry following Bennett's "Study Calculus!" If you have not responded to that journal prompt yet, do so now. Use this information to write the thesis statement for an essay that might be entitled "The Ideal Teacher." In your thesis, mention at least three qualities that make for excellent teaching. Here's how such a thesis might read:

    The best teachers challenge their students, inspire confidence in them, and work harder than anyone else in class.

    Place this thesis statement in your first paragraph, your introduction. Now use each of the three or four characteristics of good teaching in your thesis as the basis for the topic sentences of your essay's body paragraphs. Here's how each of the topic sentences for paragraphs 2, 3, and 4 of your essay might read:

    Paragraph 2: The best teachers challenge their students.

    Paragraph 3: Inspiring confidence in students is another sign of good teaching.

    Paragraph 4: Good teachers work harder than their students.

    Develop each of these body paragraphs with examples relating to a teacher or teachers you have known. You need not discuss the same teacher in each paragraph. If you completed the second journal suggestion after Bennett's essay, you might have already gathered some information you can use.

    After writing several drafts of your paper, check that you have maintained coherence in and between paragraphs by using techniques explained in this chapter. Finally, remember that the best essays are those that are reviewed and edited carefully.

3. Read the journal notes you made after reading Sharp's "Burger Queen." Use this material in an essay that explains your general impression or opinion of a place in which you have worked or are now working. Your opinion might be positive, negative, or mixed, but make sure to state it clearly in a thesis statement, which should appear in your first paragraph.

    To practice the writing of several different paragraph types, try to include one of each of the following:

    - A paragraph defining the type of business conducted or work performed

    - A paragraph providing examples of your usual duties or tasks

- A paragraph describing the physical environment of the workplace—the store, factory, office building, or other setting (If it's an outdoor job, describe the kinds of locations in which you have worked.)

- A paragraph that contrasts this job with another you have held

- A paragraph that narrates incidents with customers, employees, and/or bosses to explain the social atmosphere of your workplace.

You might want to begin by making an outline of your paper based on the model provided above. After writing a first draft, make sure that each paragraph supports and relates directly to your thesis. Remember that your thesis states your opinion, so provide enough detail to support it, and make sure you are not including extraneous information. As you revise again, check to see that you have maintained coherence in and between paragraphs.

4. After reading "Zip Out," you might have responded to the Suggestion for Journal Entry that asked you to list various steps in a process by which you achieved a desired goal. The goal might be to lose weight, master an important athletic or academic skill, or learn a new procedure at work. Read that list now and add to it if you think you left out any important step or detail.

Next, do some freewriting to gather details that will explain what actions each of those steps required. Then, write a short introductory paragraph with a thesis that explains why reaching that desired goal was so important to you. Next, write a concluding paragraph that explains what you learned after completing the process.

That will be your first draft. Now, revise your paper several times. Add detail, remove unimportant or irrelevant information, and reorganize your steps if necessary. Like the author of "Zip Out," don't be afraid to include details that show how difficult or stressful the process was.

You will also want to make sure that your essay is unified and that the detail in each paragraph relates directly to that paragraph's topic sentence. Then, check for coherence. Have you provided enough transitions and other connective elements within paragraphs to link ideas in an unbroken chain? Have you included transitions between paragraphs? Finally, have you included enough detail to make each step in the process clear?

Now, edit and proofread. Eliminate wordiness and repetition and correct grammar, sentence structure, word usage, and punctuation. Finally, proofread your final version to remove spelling and typographical errors.

5. Are you a creature of habit? If so, write an essay in which you explain why you do three or four things routinely. You might begin by explaining why you are always or seldom on time for work, for a date, or for class. You might go on to discuss why you study in the same place every night; why you wear the same color of clothes every day; why you use the same route to school or work; or why you frequent the same club, bar, or restaurant.

Of course, this assignment lends itself to the cause/effect method. But you might also have a chance to use narration, description, and process analysis, among other methods of development.

You can begin this essay by using a startling remark such as: "I have never taken a shower!" Or you might say that you spend five full hours a day on the telephone. These kinds of statements will surely draw your readers into your essay. Of course, later in the paragraph, you can explain that you take a bath every day or that you work as a receptionist in a busy medical practice. After discussing each of your habits fully in the body paragraphs, you can conclude the essay by explaining which of the habits you discussed will continue and which might be broken.

As you revise drafts of your paper, add or remove detail as necessary, and insert details that will make your writing easier to follow. In addition, use what you have learned in this chapter to improve coherence in and between paragraphs.

ACKNOWLEDGMENTS

Barry, Dave. "We Interrupt This Column." *Miami Herald*, 7 May 1989. Copyright © Tribune Media Services.

Bennett, William J. *Devaluing of America: The Fight of Our Culture and Our Children.* Simon & Schuster, 1992. Copyright © 1992 William J. Bennett. Reprinted with the permission of Simon & Schuster Inc. All rights reserved.

Catton, Bruce. "Grant and Lee: A Study in Contrasts." *The American Story.* U.S. Capitol Historical Society, 1958.

Chelminski, Rudolph. "The Curse of Count Dracula." *Smithsonian Magazine*, Apr. 2003. Reprinted with permission from the author.

Fu, Shen C. Y. "A Closer Look at Chinese Calligraphy." Freer Gallery of Art and Arthur M. Sackler Gallery, Smithsonian Institution.

Gibbons, Euell. *Stalking the Wild Asparagus.* Alan C. Hood & Company, 1962.

"Innocence and the Death Penalty" [Editorial]. America: *The National Catholic Weekly* 92 (7 Feb. 2005). Copyright © 2005, America Magazine.

Jaroff, Leon. "Crazy about Comets." *Time*, 17 Mar. 1997.

Mackworth-Praed, Ben. *The Book of Kells.* Ebury Press, 2008.

Masson, Jeffery M., and Susan McCarthy. *When Elephants Weep.* Delta, 1996.

Neff, Lavonne, compiler. "A Life for God: The Mother Teresa Treasury." HarperCollins International Division, 1996.

O'Rourke, P. J. *Parliament of Whores.* Atlantic Monthly Press, 1991.

Paton, Alan. *Cry, The Beloved Country.* Simon and Schuster, 2003. Copyright © Alan Paton, 1986; Copyright © Simon and Schuster, 2003.

"Science: Zip Out " from *TIME*, 9 Dec. 1946 © 1946. Time Inc. Used under license. *TIME* and Time Inc. are not affiliated with, and do not endorse products or services of, Licensee.

Sharp, Erin. "Burger Queen." *The American Enterprise*, 1 May 1999. Copyright © 1999 The American Enterprise Institute. Reprinted with permission of The American Enterprise Institute.

Steinbeck, John. "The Long Valley." Penguin Classics, 1995.

Wellstone, Paul. "If Poverty Is the Question ..." *The Nation*, 1 Apr. 1999.

Shutterstock

3

Special Paragraphs: Writing Introductions and Conclusions

Chapter Outline

Earlier, you learned ways to express a central idea in a topic sentence or thesis statement. You also learned how to write unified, coherent, and well-developed paragraphs within the body of the essay. Most effective essays begin with an interesting and informative **introduction**—a paragraph or series of paragraphs that includes the essay's thesis and that captures the readers' attention. Similarly, most successful essays end with a paragraph or series of paragraphs that brings the essay to a natural and logical conclusion. After reading the complete essay, readers should be satisfied that the writer has discussed everything he or she set out to discuss.

3.1 Writing Introductions

Before deciding what to put into an introduction, ask yourself if your essay really needs one. If you're writing a narrative, for example, you might simply start at the beginning of the story. Of course, you can add colorful vocabulary, interesting remarks, and vivid details to spark the readers' interest, but you need not provide a thesis statement or background information at this time. If you feel the need to include a formal thesis statement, you can always do so later at any convenient point in the body or **conclusion** of the essay.

On the other hand, if a formal introduction is necessary, remember that the *most important* function of an introduction is to capture the readers' attention and get them to read on. However, introductions can also be used to

- Reveal the essay's central idea in a formal thesis statement.

- Guide readers to important ideas in the body of the essay.

- Provide other information to help readers understand the essay's purpose and thesis.

Consider these objectives when you plan your introduction. However, if you are unable to decide how to begin, simply write out a preliminary thesis statement and go directly to the body of your essay. You can always get back to your introduction later. It certainly does not have to be the very first thing you write.

However you choose to start, remember that the most exciting part of writing is deciding exactly what you want to say about a subject. You usually won't make this discovery until you write one or more drafts of your essay's middle or body paragraphs. By then, the chances of writing a more effective thesis will have improved, and so will your chances of producing a successful and interesting introduction.

The simplest way to write an introductory paragraph or series of such paragraphs is to state your thesis at the very beginning and follow it with explanatory details that prepare readers for what is in the essay's body paragraphs. This is the method used by Ann Hodgman in an essay that appeared in *Spy* magazine. The thesis appears in italics.

> I've always wondered about dog food. Is a Gaines-burger really like a hamburger? Can you fry it? Does dog food "cheese" taste like real cheese? Does Gravy Train actually make gravy in the dog's bowl, or is that brown liquid just dissolved crumbs? And exactly what *are* by-products?
>
> Having spent the better part of a week eating dog food, I'm sorry to say that I now know the answers to these questions. While my dachshund, Shortie, watched in agonies of yearning, I gagged my way through can after can of stinky, white-flecked mush and bag after bag of stinky, fat-drenched nuggets. *And now I understand exactly why Shortie's breath is so bad.* ("No Wonder They Call Me a Bitch")

introduction
A paragraph or series of paragraphs that begins an essay and that often contains a writer's central idea in the form of a thesis statement.

conclusion
A paragraph or series of paragraphs that ends an essay; it sometimes restates the writer's central idea or summarizes important points used to develop that idea.

However, depending on your purpose, your thesis, and your audience, this may not always be the best way to begin. In Chapter 2, you learned several ways to develop body paragraphs. Here are other ways to write introductions:

- Use a startling remark or statistic.

- Ask a question or present a problem.

- Challenge a widely held assumption or opinion.

- Use a comparison, a contrast, or an analogy.

- Tell an anecdote or describe a scene.

- Use a quotation.

- Define an important term or concept.

- Address your readers directly.

- Open with a paradox (an apparent contradiction).

If you want to get to the point quickly, you can limit your introduction to one paragraph. On the other hand, you might find it necessary to spread your opening remarks over two or three paragraphs. This may increase the readers' interest because it allows you to use several methods to write the introduction. Each method is described below and illustrated by one or more paragraphs. In some cases, the central idea is expressed in a formal thesis statement (in italics); in others, the central idea is only implied and not stated formally in a thesis.

3.1a Use a Startling Remark or Statistic

Some essays begin with statements or statistics (numbers) that, while true, may shock readers and make them want to continue reading. Take this paragraph from an editorial in *America* magazine on the situation in Sudan, a country in northern Africa:

> *The disaster unfolding in the Darfur region of Sudan shines a spotlight once again on the plight of refugees and internally displaced persons.* The Sudanese government has stood by as … militias [armed bands] engaged in the systematic destruction of … villages and water sources. Thirty thousand people have been killed, and rape has been widespread. A hundred and fifty thousand have fled westward to refugee camps in Chad, and one million are internally displaced. ("Refugees: Darfur and Beyond")

A startling statement is often followed by explanatory details. In *Victims of Vanity*, Lynda Dickinson spreads startling remarks and statistics over three short paragraphs:

> Lipstick, face cream, anti-perspirant, laundry detergent…these products and hundreds of other personal care and household items have one common ingredient: the suffering and death of millions of animals.
>
> An average of 25 million animals die every year in North America for the testing of everything from new cosmetics to new methods of warfare. Five hundred thousand to one million of these animals are sacrificed each year to test new cosmetics alone.
>
> *Of all the pain and suffering caused by animal research, cosmetic and household product testing is among the least justifiable, as it cannot even be argued that tests are done to improve the quality of human life.*

3.1b Ask a Question or Present a Problem

If you begin with a question or statement of a problem, you can devote the rest of your essay to answering that question or discussing that problem. "Old, Ailing, and Abandoned," an editorial in the *Philadelphia Inquirer*, begins with three thought-provoking questions about the care of the elderly.

> How would you punish the people responsible for letting 18 hours pass before getting emergency medical help to an epileptic with second- and third-degree burns, while large sections of her skin were peeling off? What justice is there for a man whose amputated foot is allowed to become infested with maggots while he's paying for care in a specialized rooming house? And what's the proper penalty for someone who leaves a mentally ill woman alone for three days with little food and no medication?

In the first paragraph of "The Ambivalence of Abortion," Linda Bird Francke introduces the problem she and her husband faced over an unplanned pregnancy, thus preparing us for her discussion of abortion later in the essay.

> We were sitting in a bar on Lexington Avenue when I told my husband I was pregnant. It is not a memory I like to dwell on. Instead of the champagne and hope which had heralded [announced] the impending [coming] births of the first, second and third child, the news of this one was greeted with shocked silence and Scotch. "Jesus," my husband kept saying to himself, stirring the ice cubes around and around, "Oh Jesus."

3.1c Challenge a Widely Held Opinion

This method acts much like the use of a startling statement. Take this opening paragraph from an essay by Hall of Fame pitcher Robin Roberts; it questions the benefits of an activity commonly seen as wholesome.

> In 1939, Little League baseball was organized by Bert and George Bebble and Carl Stotz of Williamsport, PA. What they had in mind in organizing this kids' baseball program, I'll never know. But I'm sure they never visualized the monster it would grow in to. ("Strike Out Little League")

In "Gen X Is OK," Professor Edward E. Ericson Jr. writes an introduction that both challenges an opinion and offers a surprise ending.

> Today's young adults read little. They're poorly prepared for college. They're suckers for the instant gratification of booze and drugs. They're enormously confused about sex and scared to death of marriage. They're all for a woman's right to choose an abortion, especially the men. They force metal rings through the most unwelcoming of facial orifices [openings]. They're so light on civic duty that few vote and fewer still can imagine why one would die for one's country. *And I like them*.

The last line of the paragraph is Ericson's thesis. It makes us wonder why the author likes people whom he has just described so negatively. So, we read on!

3.1d Use Comparison, Contrast, or Analogy

Comparison points out similarities; contrast points out differences. Both methods can help you provide important information about your subject, clarify or emphasize a point, and catch the reader's attention. Donald M. Murray offers students good advice by contrasting the way they sometimes complete writing assignments with the more thorough and careful process used by professionals.

> When students complete a first draft, they consider the job of writing done—and their teachers too often agree. *When professional writers complete a first draft, they usually feel that they are at the start of the writing process*. When a draft is completed, the job of writing can begin. ("The Maker's Eye")

In the following paragraph, William Manchester both compares and contrasts World War II survivors from opposite sides of the conflict. These two paragraphs form the introduction to Manchester's "Okinawa: The Bloodiest Battle," an essay published in 1987.

> On Okinawa today, Flag Day will be observed with an extraordinary ceremony: two groups of elderly men, one Japanese, the other American, will gather for a solemn rite. They could scarcely have less in common.
>
> Their motives are mirror images; each group honors the memory of men who tried to slay the men honored by those opposite them. But theirs is a common grief. After 42 years the ache is still there. They are really united by death, the one great victor in modern war.

Analogy helps explain ideas that are sometimes hard to grasp by comparing them with things readers can understand easily. On the surface, however, these things might seem unrelated. In a *U.S. News & World Report* article published in January 2005, Dr. Bernadine Healy uses analogy to teach us a lesson about nature.

> There is a sameness to brutal natural disasters. It's the final body count that chillingly distinguishes one from another. [The] tsunami in Southern Asia, which rose up from an earthquake in the Indian Ocean, swamping 11 countries and quickly claiming more than 120,000 lives, is ... one of the worst floods in history. With our minds focused on war and political terrorism, Mother Nature proves to be the worst of all terrorists in the horror of her sudden assault on vulnerable innocents. ("Mother Nature, Terrorist")

3.1e Tell an Anecdote or Describe a Scene

Anecdotes are brief, interesting stories that illustrate or support a point. An anecdote can help you prepare readers for the issues or problems you will be discussing without having to state the thesis directly. For example, this anecdote, which begins a *Wall Street Journal* editorial, makes the essay's central idea clear, even though it does not express it in a thesis statement.

> We don't know if Janice Camarena had ever heard of *Brown v. Board of Education* when she enrolled in San Bernardino Valley College in California, but she knows all about it now. Mrs. Camarena was thrown out of a class at her public community college because of the color of her skin. When she sat down at her desk on the first day of the semester in January 1994, the instructor asked her to leave. That section of English 101 was reserved for black students only, she was told; Mrs. Camarena is white. ("Affirmative Reaction")

Another way to prepare readers for what follows is to describe a scene in a way that lets them know your feelings about a subject. Take the introduction to "A Hanging," an essay in which George Orwell reveals his view on capital punishment. Orwell does not express his opinions in a thesis statement; the essay's gloomy setting—its time and place—does that for him.

> It was Burma, a sodden [soggy] morning of the rains. A sickly light, like yellow tinfoil, was slanting over the high walls into the jail yard. We were waiting outside the condemned cells, a row of sheds fronted with double bars, like small animal cages. Each cell measured about ten feet by ten and was quite bare within except for a plank bed and a pot for drinking water. In some of them brown silent men were squatting at the inner bars, with their blankets draped around them. These were the condemned men, due to be hanged within the next week or two.

analogy
A method by which a writer points out similarities between two things that, on the surface, seem quite different; most often used to make abstract or unfamiliar ideas clearer and more concrete.

3.1f Use a Quotation

Quoting an expert or simply using an interesting, informative statement from another writer or from someone you've interviewed can lend interest and authority to your introduction. Just remember to quote your source accurately and make sure that the quotation relates directly to other ideas in your paragraph.

In the following example, Philip Shabecoff uses a quotation from world-famous scientist Rachel Carson to lead us to his thesis in the introduction to his essay on pesticides.

> "The most alarming of all man's assaults upon the environment is the contamination of air, earth, rivers, and sea with dangerous and even lethal materials," Rachel Carson wrote a quarter of a century ago in her celebrated book *Silent Spring*. Today there is little disagreement with her warnings in regard to such broad-spectrum pesticides as DDT, then widely used, now banned. But *there is still hot debate over how to apply modern pesticides—which are designed to kill specific types of weeds or insects—in ways that do not harm people and their environment.* ("Congress Again Confronts Hazards of Killer Chemicals")

3.1g Define an Important Term or Concept

Defining a term can explain aspects of your subject that will make it easier for readers to understand your central idea. But don't use dictionary definitions. Because they are often limited and rigid, dictionary definitions will make the beginning of an essay uninteresting. Instead, rely on your own ingenuity to create definitions that are interesting and appropriate to your purpose. This is what student Elena Santayana does in the introduction to a paper about alcohol addiction.

> Alcoholism is a disease whose horrible consequences go beyond the patient. Families of alcoholics often become dysfunctional; spouses and children are abandoned or endure physical and emotional abuse. Co-workers suffer too. Alcoholics have high rates of absenteeism, and their work is often unreliable, thereby decreasing office or factory productivity. Indeed, alcoholics endanger the whole community. One in every two automobile fatalities is alcohol-related, and alcoholism is a major cause of violent crime. ("Everybody's Problem")

3.1h Address Your Readers Directly

In "What Is Poverty," Jo Goodwin Parker addresses readers directly by asking a question. The result is an opening that is both urgent and emphatic.

> You ask me what is poverty? Listen to me. Here I am, dirty, smelly, and with no "proper" underwear on and with the stench of my rotting teeth near you. I will tell you. Listen to me. Listen without pity. I cannot use your pity. Listen with understanding. Put yourself in my dirty, worn out, ill-fitting shoes, and hear me.

3.1i Open with a Paradox

A paradox is a statement that, on the surface, contradicts or seems to contradict itself. Because such statements are interesting in themselves, they make effective beginnings for essays. Here's a famous paradox from British philosopher and mathematician Bertrand Russell:

> In a village, the barber shaves everyone who does not shave himself, but no one else. Who shaves the barber?

3.2 Writing Conclusions

Sometimes, it is on the basis of the conclusion alone that readers respond to an essay. The conclusion's length depends on the essay's length and purpose. For very short essays, you might simply end the last paragraph with a concluding sentence, as does Kenneth Jon Rose in "2001 Space Shuttle." Rose's last sentence is his essay's conclusion.

> [T]he sky turns lighter and layers of clouds pass you like cars on a highway. Minutes later, still sitting upright, you will see the gray runway in the distance. Then the shuttle slows to 300 mph and drops its landing gear. Finally, with its nose slightly up like the Concorde SST and at a speed of about 225 mph, the shuttle will land on the asphalt runway and slowly come to a halt. *The trip into space will be over.*

Although one-sentence conclusions are fine for short essays, you will often need to close with at least one full paragraph. Either way, a conclusion should bring your discussion of the thesis to a timely and logical end. Try not to conclude abruptly; always give a signal that you are about to wrap things up. And never use your conclusion to introduce new ideas—ideas for which you did not prepare your readers earlier in the essay.

There are many ways to write conclusions, such as the following:

- Make reference to your thesis.
- Summarize or rephrase your main points.
- Offer advice; make a call to action.
- Look to the future.
- Explain how a problem was resolved.
- Ask a question or series of questions.
- Close with a statement or quotation readers will remember.

3.2a Make Reference to Your Thesis

Referring to your thesis in your conclusion is a good way to emphasize your central idea. This is what Professor Ericson does in the three-part conclusion to "Gen X Is OK" (the introduction to this essay was quoted in section 3.1c).

> I didn't plan to develop a special fondness for today's young. My students made me do it. Of course I haven't stopped worrying. This generation does not seem headed for greatness. They have suffered too much cultural despoliation [loss], too much distortion of personhood, for that. It would take a global cataclysm [catastrophe] for them to have any chance of rising to the heights of human valor.
>
> But will they be basically sensible, productive adults? Were I a betting man, I'd put my money on them. And the more intergeneration friendships they form, the better their odds will be.
>
> All in all, I think Gen X is OK.

Ericson rephrases his thesis when he says, "Gen X is OK." But he also restates four important points he made in the body of his essay:

- His students caused him "to develop a special fondness for today's young."
- Members of Gen X don't seem "headed for greatness."
- They will become "sensible, productive adults."
- Friendships between members of different generations improve their chances for success.

3.2b Summarize or Rephrase Your Main Points

For long essays, restating your thesis can be combined with summarizing or rephrasing each of the main points you made in the body paragraphs. Doing so will help you write an effective summary of the entire essay and emphasize important ideas. This is exactly what Robin Roberts does in his two concluding paragraphs of "Strike Out Little League" (see his introduction in section 3.1c)

> I still don't know what those three gentlemen in Williamsport had in mind when they organized Little League baseball. I'm sure they didn't want parents arguing with their children about kids' games. I'm sure they didn't want young athletes hurting their arms pitching under pressure .... I'm sure they didn't want young boys ... made to feel that something is wrong with them because they can't play baseball. I'm sure they didn't want a group of coaches drafting the players each year for different teams. I'm sure they didn't want unqualified men working with the young players. I'm sure they didn't realize how normal it is for an 8-year-old boy to be scared of a thrown or batted baseball.
>
> For the life of me, I can't figure out what they had in mind.

3.2c Offer Advice: Make a Call to Action

An example of a conclusion that offers advice appears in Elena Santayana's "Everybody's Problem" (the introduction appears in section 3.1g).

> If you have alcoholic friends, relatives, or co-workers, the worst thing you can do is to look the other way. This disease and its effects are simply not theirs to deal with alone. Try persuading them to seek counseling. Describe the extent to which their illness is hurting their families, co-workers, and neighbors. Explain that their alcoholism endangers the entire community. Above all, don't pretend not to notice! Alcoholism is everybody's problem.

3.2d Look to the Future

This method allows you to wonder what might occur in the future as a result of current situations you have just discussed. This kind of conclusion appears at the end of "Refugees: Darfur and Beyond," an editorial about the plight of Sudanese refugees. Note that it presents two very different outcomes. (The introduction to this paragraph appears in section 3.1a.)

> Resettlement [of displaced persons] offers a solution to only part of the war-driven refugee crisis, whether in Sudan or elsewhere, but it does present an opportunity for the rich countries to show a greater measure of generosity than has so far been the case. In the meantime, without stronger peace making pressure from the U.N. Security Council and the powerful nations of the North, humanitarian disasters like the one in Sudan may burst forth in other parts of the world as well in years to come.

3.2e Explain How a Problem Was Resolved

In "The Ambivalence of Abortion" (see section 3.1b for the introduction to this essay), Linda Bird Francke writes about the difficulty she and her husband had in deciding whether to have or abort their fourth child. Francke's conclusion tells us how they resolved the question.

> My husband and I are back to planning our summer vacation and his career switch. And it certainly does make sense not to be having a baby right now—we say to each other all the time. But I have this ghost now. A very little ghost that only appears when I'm seeing something beautiful, like the full moon on the ocean last weekend. And the baby waves to me. And I wave at the baby. "Of course, we have room," I cry to the ghost. "Of course, we do."

3.2f Ask a Question or Series of Questions

Ending with questions can keep your readers thinking long after they have read your essay. In "Old, Ailing, and Abandoned" (the introduction appears in section 3.1b), the conclusion is especially thought provoking.

> Communities, stretched though they may be, need to remember [the] forgotten elderly living in our midst. What if every church in the region agreed to regularly visit residents at just one [nursing] home? How about local government, or advocate agencies, linking the owners of small facilities more closely with existing services, such as rehab grants that could improve conditions?

This paragraph ends with rhetorical questions (whose answers are obvious). Such questions invite readers to participate in the essay's conclusion by answering in their own words. If your essay has made the answer so obvious that readers will respond as you want them to, ending with such a question can help make your essay memorable.

3.2g Close with a Statement or Quotation Readers Will Remember

Deciding whether a statement will stick in readers' minds isn't easy. Trust your instincts. If you find a particular remark memorable, so might your readers. In any case, make sure that the statement relates directly to what you have discussed in your essay. That's what Dr. Bernadine Healy does in her conclusion to "Mother Nature, Terrorist" (the introduction appears in section 3.1d).

> Serving with the American Red Cross, I witnessed the washed-out roads, collapsed buildings, and far-flung rubble of Princeville, a small North Carolina town founded by slaves after the Civil War. It was completely destroyed by a massive flood in 1999. In a nearby rescue center, I met an elderly woman who told of standing alone in her house there, as water gushed in .... Struggling out to her porch, she grabbed a chair underwater and shimmied up on her roof, where she clung to its shingles for more than seven hours .... Though still shaky, she told me how happy she was to have painted her house that summer, and looked at me as if I were a dunce when I reassured her that someone else would redo her paint job. "You don't get it, Dr. Healy—how do you think I learned to get up on my roof?" I have not forgotten her wisdom. If we choose to live in health with Mother Nature, we still have lots to lean about preparing for her fury.

3.3 Visualizing Ways to Write Introductions and Conclusions

Read the following introduction and conclusion to Michael Ryan's "They Track the Deadliest Viruses." Comments in the margins identify effective techniques you might use in your own introductions and conclusions.

Ryan's Introduction

Makes a startling statement and challenges an assumption.

"A disease that's in a faraway place today may be in our own backyard tomorrow," said Dr. James Hughes [of] the Centers for Disease Control and Prevention (CDC) in Atlanta. "We're certainly not immune."

A few years ago, this statement would have surprised many Americans. The advent [coming] of miracle drugs and vaccines that conquered

Creates a contrast. such plagues as polio, smallpox and even measles led many of us—including some scientists—to believe that the age of killer diseases was coming to an end.

The AIDS epidemic changed that ...   *States essay's thesis.*

Ryan's Conclusion

On my visit to Atlanta I ... met the associate director of the CDC, Dr. James Curran. He has been involved in the fight against AIDS since 1981. "The first five years, through 1985, was the age of discovery ... . We discovered the global extent of the epidemic, the virus, antibody tests, AZT. It was an exciting time, *Refers to thesis.* but when it ended, half a million people in the U.S. already were infected."

Today, Dr. Curran said, the Centers for *Looks to future.* Disease Control and Prevention's response to the AIDS epidemic has changed. "We're trying   *Uses a quotation* to help the country evaluate the blood supply,   *readers will* develop test kits and work on prevention and   *remember.* counseling strategies ... . Information alone isn't sufficient; we have to find ways to change   *Makes a call to action.* behavior—especially in young people, who sometimes think they're invulnerable."

3.4 Revising Introductions and Conclusions

Later in this chapter, you will read student Ryan Paul Kessler's "An Unusual Affliction." Kessler knew that the first version of his essay was not the best he could do, so he rewrote the paper several times. Compare the rough and final drafts of the introduction and conclusion to his essay.

Kessler's Introduction—Rough Draft

Introduction is bland. Use one or more of the techniques explained in this chapter to draw the readers' interest?

My stuttering has been an endless source of embarrassment ever since I can remember. The ability to express oneself through speech is something I think most people take for granted. A lot of people don't realize how difficult even simple tasks are to a person who

Provide examples of some simple tasks?

This thesis announces what the essay will do. It does not make a main point. Rewrite to improve focus?

cannot communicate clearly. Throughout this essay I will share an experience or two to help the reader get a better understanding of what exactly a speech impediment does to one's confidence and psyche.

Kessler's Introduction—Final Draft

Begins with a question and addresses reader directly.

Have you ever been deep in a conversation with someone, and, all of a sudden, some jerk walks up and starts interrupting? It happens to me every time I start to engage in a conversation. For me, that jerk is not a friend or a classmate. It's not even a person. It's my speech impediment—stuttering to be more precise.

Uses startling language.

Builds suspense to surprise the reader.

This unusual affliction has been an endless source of embarrassment ever since I can remember. The ability to express oneself through speech is something I think most people take for granted. A lot of people don't realize how difficult and frustrating even simple tasks such as ordering food in a restaurant, asking for directions, or answering a question in class are to a person who cannot communicate clearly. If you have never had a speech impediment, you really can't imagine how brutally it can attack your psyche and destroy your self-confidence.

Adds examples of "simple tasks" to make introduction more believable.

Includes startling image in thesis.

Rewrites thesis to focus on a main point.

Kessler's Conclusion—Rough Draft

Conclusion is rather short and is not memorable.

In the years past, I have come up with my own ways of dealing with stuttering, one of which is to use synonyms for words that cause a speech "block." So naturally, I spend most of my free time looking for synonyms of words I commonly use on websites like www.dictionary.com. While this is not a solution to my problem, I am hoping new technological devices such as Fluency Master™ that are currently under development will provide a positive result that

Use one or more techniques for concluding discussed in this chapter. Try looking to future?

Provide examples of such words?

does not involve time-consuming and embarrassing therapy.

Kessler's Conclusion—Final Draft

Over the years, I have come up with my own ways of dealing with this demon, one of which is to use synonyms for words that cause a speech "block." So naturally, I spend most of my free time looking for synonyms of words I commonly use on websites like www.dictionary.com. For example, instead of saying "ingenious" or "intelligent," I might use "smart."

Provides examples.

This is not a solution to my problem, but it has improved my confidence. I am hoping that, someday, new technological devices such as Fluency Master™, which is currently under development, will provide positive results that do not involve time-consuming and embarrassing

Looks to the future.

therapy. Until then, I can take comfort in and gain confidence from knowing that I can write well. Armed with these weapons, I will continue fighting off that jerk who seems intent upon interrupting my life and my dreams.

Closes with a memorable statement.

References his introduction and his thesis.

3.5 Practicing Writing Introductions

Write a one-paragraph introduction for an essay you might compose on one of the following topics. Try using one of the methods for writing introductions suggested with each topic.

1. **Topic:** A terrifying, tragic, or stressful situation

   Method: Use a startling remark or statistic.

   _____

   _____

   _____

   _____

   _____

2. **Topic:** Becoming addicted to video games

    Method: Ask a question or present a problem.

    _____

    _____

    _____

    _____

    _____

3. **Topic:** The benefits (or dangers) of physical exercise

    Method: Tell an anecdote or use contrast.

    _____

    _____

    _____

    _____

    _____

4. **Topic:** Ways to overcome pain, other than using drugs

    Method: Challenge a widely held opinion, use contrast, or present a problem.

    _____

    _____

    _____

5. **Topic:** What your clothes (car, room, or home) say about you

    Method: Describe a scene, ask a question, or address readers directly.

    _____

    _____

    _____

6. **Topic:** How Mother Nature can be cruel

    Method: Ask a question or challenge a widely held opinion.

    _____

    _____

    _____

    _____

7. **Topic:** Overcoming a fear of math (heights, closed-in places, water, etc.)

    Method: Address readers directly, ask a question, or define a term.

    _____

    _____

    _____

    _____

    _____

8. **Topic:** Practicing safe sex

    Method: Present a problem, define a term, or address readers directly.

    _____

    _____

    _____

    _____

    _____

3.6 Reading Selections

3.6a An Unusual Affliction

Author Biography

Ryan Paul Kessler was a student in a developmental writing class when he wrote the first draft of this very personal essay. Subsequent to completing the course, he revised and expanded it. The problem described in this essay, which the author has suffered from since he learned to speak, afflicts millions of people. However, Kessler refuses to allow this affliction to limit his dreams. A fighter, he has devised ways to compensate for and address the problem. While his career plans are still uncertain, Kessler is continuing his college studies and has decided to major in English for the present.

Preparing to Read

1. Identify one or more methods for writing introductions (as explained earlier in this chapter) in Kessler's first two paragraphs. As you get near the end of the essay, identify one or more methods for writing conclusions that you read about earlier.

2. Look for Kessler's thesis in his second paragraph and express it in your own words.

3. As you read the body of the essay, pick out ways in which Kessler maintains coherence in and between paragraphs. For a discussion about such methods, refer to Chapter 2.

Vocabulary

affliction (noun)   Suffering, trouble, illness.

belittlement (noun)   Disparagement, contempt.

chasm (noun)   Gap, gulf.

futile (adjective)   Useless.

pathologist (noun)   Medical specialist.

prepubescent (adjective)   Juvenile, before the age of puberty.

psyche (noun)   Mind, personality, consciousness.

schmuck (noun)   Slang term for fool, dope.

wanes (verb)   Decreases.

An Unusual Affliction

Ryan Paul Kessler

Have you ever been deep in a conversation with someone, and, all of a sudden, some jerk walks up and starts interrupting? It happens to me every time I start to engage in conversation. For me, that jerk is not a friend or a classmate. It's not even a person. It's my speech impediment—stuttering to be more precise. **1**

This unusual affliction has been an endless source of embarrassment ever since I can remember. The ability to express oneself through speech is something I think most people take for granted. A lot of people don't realize how difficult and frustrating even simple tasks such as ordering food in a restaurant, asking for directions, or answering a question in class are to a person who cannot communicate clearly. If you have never had a speech impediment, you really can't imagine how brutally it can attack your psyche and destroy your self-confidence. **2**

The first such experience I can remember when stuttering reared its ugly head was during a grade school presentation on the solar system. I was assigned to do a report on the planet Pluto. Upon completion of the project, I was told to present it to the class, roughly 30 people. After my name was called, I shuffled down the row of desks to the front of the classroom. The second I hit the word "Pluto," the "P" sound kept repeating, over and over for what seemed like an eternity. Not knowing how to react, I continued to try to say the word but, alas, my attempts were futile. The other children broke out into uncontrollable laughter, and I sat down feeling defeated. Incidents like this have occurred over and over as I have gotten older, and the result has always been the same: complete and utter embarrassment. **3**

I am usually fine when I feel no pressure to perform. However, when I am in situations in which I want to do my best, my emotions get the better of me, and my confidence wanes. Job interviews, for example, have been hellish. Some interviewers have been polite and patient, but it's almost impossible to land a job that requires interacting with the public. This limits my opportunities, for most part-time jobs today involve talking with customers or clients. Stuttering has also become a barrier to socializing and making new friends. And it has made asking girls out on dates almost impossible. **4**

After I left grade school, the laughter and teasing of prepubescent schmucks were replaced by just facial expressions of pity or discomfort—reactions that were almost as depressing to me. So, I decided to seek some help from a speech pathologist. Upon walking into the office for my first appointment, I tripped over what appeared to be a toy. Lo and behold, the office was set up for children under twelve. After waiting about twenty minutes, a middle-aged woman walked in and started going over speech exercises with me. Apparently, the therapy was designed for children too, because after five minutes I felt as if I had sunk into a chasm of belittlement after repeating the words "the dog in dungarees has his day" thirty times. It figures that such an embarrassing affliction has a cure that is also embarrassing. **5**

People react to my stuttering in different ways. When I start to stutter, some people try to help   6
me finish the word or sentence. This often turns into a bizarre game of charades that can lead to
miscommunication and more embarrassment. Others try to ignore it and let me try to finish the word.
However, they soon regret their decision after becoming exposed to what sounds like a broken record.
This often leaves me and the person I am talking to feeling ridiculous. A few people even try to assist
me by advising me to "slow down," "take a breath," or "relax," but that does not help. It is hard to say
how I want someone to react, for it really does not matter. Above all, I just want people to be patient,
understanding, and respectful, just like they would be with a person having any other disorder—and
to try to hold back the laughter, at least until I leave the room.

Over the years, I have come up with my own ways of dealing with this demon, one of which is   7
to use synonyms for words that cause a speech "block." So naturally, I spend most of my free time
looking for synonyms of words I commonly use on websites like www.dictionary.com. For example,
instead of saying "ingenious" or "intelligent," I might use "smart."

This is not a solution to my problem, but it has improved my confidence. I am hoping that, some-   8
day, new technological devices such as Fluency Master, which is currently under development, will
provide positive results that do not involve time consuming and embarrassing therapy. Until then, I
can take comfort in and gain confidence from knowing that I can write well. Armed with these weapons, I will continue fighting off that jerk who seems intent upon interrupting my life and my dreams.

Read More on the Web

For more on the problem that Kessler writes about, visit the following:

- National Institute on Deafness and Other Communication Disorders: www.nidcd.nih.gov

- Stuttering Foundation of America: www.stutteringhelp.org

- Christian Büchel and Martin Sommer, "What Causes Stuttering," PLOS Biology:
  http://bvtlab.com/qAm97

Questions for Discussion

1. To capture the readers' attention, Kessler begins with a question and a startling remark.
   However, his introduction is two paragraphs long. What other techniques for writing
   effective introductions does he use?

2. Identify the techniques for writing conclusions seen in paragraphs 7 and 8.

3. Where does Kessler state his thesis?

4. Where does he use examples?

5. What does the anecdote in paragraph 5 tell us about Kessler's problem?

6. Explain how the author maintains coherence in and between paragraphs. Focus on
   paragraphs 7 and 8.

Thinking Critically

1. In what way does Kessler's title—especially the word *unusual*—shed light on the emotions
   that he expresses in this essay?

2. Kessler mentions several ways in which people react to his stuttering. Explain how you
   react to and interact with people who have an "affliction."

Suggestions for Journal Entries

1. Have you found yourself in an extremely embarrassing situation? If so, use listing or focused freewriting to explain what happened and how you reacted. Note that the situation need not be as serious as what Kessler discusses. In fact, you might want to write about a situation that you can now laugh about.

2. Kessler tells us that a speech impediment can "attack your psyche" and "destroy your self-confidence." Has your psyche ever been attacked or your self-esteem weakened because of a particular incident, problem, situation, or person? Ask the journalists' questions to develop your response: Who was involved? What happened? Where and when did this occur? How did you overcome or attempt to deal with the emotional effects that resulted?

3.6b The Italian Schindler

Author Biography

Elizabeth Bettina graduated from Smith College. She is co-executive producer of a documentary film on the Italian Jews who survived the Nazi concentration camps. This essay is taken from *It Happened in Italy*, a book that contains stories of Italian Christians who helped their Jewish neighbors stay alive during the Holocaust.

Preparing to Read

1. Paragraphs 1 and 2 contain this essay's introduction. Look in those paragraphs for examples of methods for introducing essays that you read about earlier in this chapter.

2. The last two paragraphs make up Bettina's conclusion. Look for examples of methods to conclude an essay.

3. Benito Mussolini was Italy's Fascist dictator who allied himself with Adolf Hitler during World War II.

4. Dachau was one of the infamous Nazi concentration camps that killed more than six million Jews, as well as three million non-Jewish people.

Vocabulary

Campagna (noun)   Region of Italy of which Naples is the capital.

census officer (noun)   Government official in charge of maintaining population records.

internment camp (noun)   Place where prisoners of war and others are held.

The Italian Schindler
Elizabeth Bettina

Giovanni Palatucci [1909–1945]. Italians call him "The Italian Schindler." Oskar Schindler was the German factory owner who saved nearly twelve hundred Jews during the Holocaust by bringing them to work in his factories. The movie *Schindler's List* dramatizes his story.   1

So imagine this. It is the 1940s. An Italian police official working under Benito Mussolini (Hitler's primary ally in Italy) actively defied orders to implement Hitler's "Final Solution" of eliminating Jews from the face of the earth. In the process, he saved thousands of Jewish people from being deported to Nazi death camps. This extraordinary man was Giovanni Palatucci, and for his extraordinary efforts, he was killed at Dachau.   2

In 1990, Palatucci was honored by Yad Vashem, the famed Holocaust museum in Israel, for his ultimate sacrifice. Yad Vashem honors as "Righteous Among the Nations," Holocaust rescuers who, at personal risk, saved Jews during the Holocaust. In 2002, Palatucci was also recognized [by the Catholic Church] for his sacrifice, and the beatification process—a step before sainthood—was begun by Cardinal Camillo Ruini.   3

Palatucci was born in Montella, near Avellino (Naples area), attended high school in Benevento, and was stationed in Fiume, now Rjeka, Croatia, in 1937. His role in Fiume was *Questore*, which can best be described as part police chief, part immigration officer, and part census officer. All foreign residents in Italy were required to register at the *Questore* office, and this gave Palatucci access to their documents and personal information, including their religion. As a result, he had a list of all foreign residents, many of whom were Jews who had come to Italy to escape unrest in their countries prior to the beginning of the war in 1940. Italy was also the only country that kept its borders open to Jews until the war began. Palatucci hid this list from the Nazis, because he knew that in the wrong hands, it was a map that led directly to a concentration camp and almost certain death for the Jews on the list.   4

Giovanni Palatucci enabled people to leave Italy by supplying false documents, and if they didn't leave Italy, Palatucci arranged to send them to an official Italian government internment camp in Campagna, the former Convent of San Bartolomeo, where his uncle, Giuseppe Maria Palatucci, was the bishop. With his uncle watching over the Jews, Giovanni Palatucci knew they were safe—at least for a while. Italy eventually joined the Allies and, as far as Germany was concerned, the Italians were now "the enemy." Once the Nazis figured out what Giovanni Palatucci was doing, they sent him to Dachau, where, on February 10, 1945, he died the death from which he'd saved thousands of Jews (some estimates are as high as five thousand). Just two months later, on April 29, 1945, Dachau was liberated.   5

Why did this man risk his life to save others? Like most Italians, Giovanni Palatucci believed in one sentence: *Ama gli altri come te stesso.* Love thy neighbor as thyself. Both survivors and their saviors repeatedly describe their experiences using this simple sentence.   6

Giovanni Palatucci, along with many other Italians, could not understand why Jews were being persecuted just because they were of another religion, and he decided he would do whatever he could to help. In addition to his official role, Palatucci also had a personal interest in helping save Jews. His Jewish fiancée survived the Holocaust because he performed the selfless act of giving her his transit visa for Switzerland, even though he knew the Nazis were coming for him. She eventually made her way to Israel and died just a few years ago.   7

In a way, Palatucci symbolizes all the other unnamed "Giovanni Palatuccis" in Italy, people who risked their lives and their families' lives to help others simply because it was the right thing to do. As Walter Wolff [a Holocaust survivor] said, "At least fifty people helped me, and if each one of them didn't do what they did at the *exact* moment they did, I wouldn't be here today." In honoring Giovanni Palatucci, all of those nameless people are honored as well.   8

The first Giovanni Palatucci Courageous Leadership Award was given in October 2007 to David Cohen, deputy commissioner of intelligence for the city of New York. In his speech, Cohen said, "Giovanni Palatucci didn't save five thousand Jews, he saved twenty-five thousand—or more. There are now four generations of what could be called 'Palatucci Survivors,' children, grandchildren, great-grandchildren of his original protectees."   9

The people saved and their descendants are additional proof that Hitler failed at his "Final Solution." I always question what makes some people risk their lives to help others. What would I have done? What would *you* have done?   10

Read More on the Web

- *Chicago Tribune,* "How Italy Protected Jews from the Holocaust": http://bvtlab.com/Jgu69
- Italy and the Holocaust Foundation: www.italyandtheholocaust.org

Questions for Discussion

1. Bettina's thesis appears in her introduction. Paraphrase that thesis in your own words.
2. What methods for introducing essays does Bettina use in her first two paragraphs?
3. What methods for concluding essays does she use?
4. Why does Bettina use words in Italian in this piece? Would their English translations have been enough?
5. What use does the author make of questions in this essay? How do they help her prove her point about Palatucci?
6. How does quoting Walter Wolff and David Cohen help Bettina make her point?

Thinking Critically

1. The main purpose of this essay is to honor a particular hero. What or who else does it honor?
2. Explain what Bettina means when she says that Palatucci gave his transit visa to his fiancée. What is a transit visa? Why did this woman go to Switzerland?
3. Other than just doing the right thing, why did Palatucci help the Jews?

Suggestions for Journal Entries

1. Think about a particular individual you know well who makes sacrifices to help others "simply because it [is] the right thing to do." Use your journal to narrate at least one example of this person's helping someone else in a time of need.
2. *Schindler's List* is a moving film about the courage and human kindness one man showed others. View this film and then write a personal response to what it taught you about both the Holocaust and the human ability to be noble and self-sacrificing.

3.6c How to Keep Air Clean

Author Biography

Sydney Harris (1917–1986) was born in London and raised in Chicago. He began writing for the *Chicago Daily News* in 1941 and later wrote for the *Chicago Sun-Times.* Harris's column "Strictly Personal," which he began in 1944, became so popular that it was soon syndicated in many U.S. and Canadian newspapers. Models of interesting and effective process, Harris's articles, such as "How to Keep Air Clean," proved him to be an important American essayist and earned him thousands of devoted readers over the years. In 1953, Harris gathered his "Strictly Personal" columns in a book by the same name, publishing seven more such anthologies in subsequent years.

Preparing to Read

1. Although this essay was first published in 1969, it is still relevant. As you read "How to Keep Air Clean," take notes in which you point out facts and ideas that are still important to us.

2. The essay's introduction consists of the first three paragraphs. Read these carefully and determine which technique Harris relies on most to open this piece.

3. Harris uses terms from meteorology, the study of the earth's atmosphere. The *troposphere* (paragraph 4) is the bottom layer of the atmosphere, where our weather occurs. The *stratosphere* (paragraph 2), directly above the troposphere, extends to about 30 miles up.

4. In his conclusion, Harris mentions the Industrial Revolution, which occurred in the eighteenth and nineteenth centuries in Europe and North America. Not an armed conflict, the Industrial Revolution was a series of technological developments that led to the modern factory system, mass production, and automation.

Vocabulary

infinitely (adverb)   Without end.

irreversible (adjective)   Permanent, not repairable.

noxious (adjective)   Toxic, dangerous, harmful.

particulates (noun)   Small particles.

How to Keep Air Clean

Sydney Harris

Some months ago, while doing research on the general subject of pollution, I learned how dumb I had been all my life about something as common and familiar—and essential—as air.   1

In my ignorance, I had always thought that "fresh air" was infinitely available to us. I had imagined that the dirty air around us somehow escaped into the stratosphere, and that new air kept coming in—much as it does when we open a window after a party.   2

This, of course, is not true, and you would imagine that a grown man with a decent education would know this as a matter of course. What is true is that we live in a kind of spaceship called the earth, and only a limited amount of air is *forever* available to us.   3

The "walls" of our spaceship enclose what is called the "troposphere," which extends about seven miles up. This is all the air that is available to us. We must use it over and over again for infinity, just as if we were in a sealed room for the lifetime of the earth.   4

No fresh air comes in, and no polluted air escapes. Moreover, no dirt or poisons are ever "destroyed"—they remain in the air, in different forms, or settle on the earth as "particulates." And the more we burn, the more we replace good air with bad.   5

Once contaminated, this thin layer of air surrounding the earth cannot be cleansed again. We can clean materials, we can even clean water, but we cannot clean the air. There is nowhere else for the dirt and poisons to go—we cannot open a window in the troposphere and clear out the stale and noxious atmosphere we are creating.   6

Perhaps every child in sixth grade and above knows this, but I doubt that one adult in a hundred is aware of this basic physical fact. Most of us imagine, as I did, that winds sweep away the gases and debris in the air, taking them far out into the solar system and replacing them with new air.   7

The United States alone is discharging *130 million tons of pollutants a year* into the atmosphere, from factories, heating systems, incinerators, automobiles and airplanes, power plants and public buildings. What is frightening is not so much the death and illness, corrosion and decay they are responsible for—as the fact that this is an *irreversible process*. The air will never be cleaner than it is now.   8

And this is why *prevention*—immediate, drastic and far-reaching—is our only hope for the future. We cannot undo what we have done. We cannot restore the atmosphere to the purity it had before the Industrial Revolution. But we can, and must, halt the contamination before our spaceship suffocates from its own foul discharges.   9

Read More on the Web

Search for these sites on the Web to find out more about air pollution:

- Buckminster Fuller Institute, "Spaceship Earth": www.bfi.org/about-fuller/big-ideas/spaceshipearth
- Science Netlinks, "Spaceship Earth": sciencenetlinks.com/lessons/spaceship-earth

Questions for Discussion

1. Reread paragraph 3. What is Harris's thesis statement?

2. What techniques discussed earlier in this chapter does Harris use in his introduction?

3. What is the analogy that Harris uses in paragraph 3? In what other paragraphs does he refer to this analogy?

4. What techniques does he use to close this essay?

5. The essay is well developed and organized. What techniques does the author use to create coherence in and between paragraphs? (For ways to maintain coherence, see Chapter 2.)

Thinking Critically

1. As you have learned, Harris uses an analogy when he compares earth to a spaceship. Write a short paragraph in which you develop three or four specific comparisons between earth and a spaceship.

2. List some ways in which you might help in the fight to prevent further pollution of the atmosphere.

Suggestions for Journal Entries

1. Summarize in a paragraph of your own the three paragraphs Harris uses to introduce his essay. Make sure to use your own words throughout.

2. Think of a widely held opinion or assumption that you believe is incorrect. In a sentence or two, write this idea in your journal. Then, in preparation for writing a full-length essay, use one of the prewriting techniques discussed in Getting Started to write down your major reasons for disagreeing. Here are a few examples of the kinds of opinions or assumptions you might want to correct:

    a. Someone who has had only one or two drinks shouldn't be prevented from driving a car.

b. Breaking an alcohol, smoking, or drug addiction is relatively easy.

c. Being exposed to secondhand smoke isn't harmful.

d. Women have no aptitude for math.

e. Reading poetry, listening to opera, and going to the ballet aren't things that "real" men do.

f. Cats are not as bright as dogs.

g. Global warming is a real threat to the environment.

h. There is no such thing as global warming.

3.6d A Prayer for the Days of Awe

Author Biography

Elie Wiesel was born in Romania in 1928. In 1944, he was imprisoned in Auschwitz and then Buchenwald, two of the many infamous Nazi death camps where six million Jews and millions of other people were murdered. This horror is now called the Holocaust, a word derived from the fact that the bodies of many victims of this mass murder were burned in ovens after having been gassed or killed in other ways. Wiesel's autobiographical novel *Night* recalls his experience in the camps, and his many other novels, plays, and stories are aimed at making sure the Holocaust is never forgotten. Wiesel was awarded the Nobel Peace Prize in 1986. Wiesel died on July 2, 2016, in New York.

Preparing to Read

1. This essay appeared in the *New York Times* shortly before Rosh Hashanah, the Jewish New Year, which is observed in prayer and begins the Ten Days of Penitence, ending with Yom Kippur, the Day of Atonement. These Days of Awe conclude with the faithful's praying for forgiveness for the previous year's sins.

2. As Wiesel's title indicates, this is not just an essay; it is a prayer. Keep this in mind as you read this selection, for Wiesel is addressing two—and perhaps three—different audiences.

3. How might Wiesel be using the word *awe*? Look up this word in a dictionary.

Vocabulary

annihilate (verb) Destroy completely, exterminate.

culpability (noun) Guilt, responsibility.

fervor (noun) Enthusiasm, eagerness, passion.

Sabbath (noun) Day of worship.

testimony (noun) Written or spoken statement that something is true.

theological (adjective) Having to do with the study of God.

Treblinka (noun) A Nazi concentration camp.

tribunal (noun) Council, court.

Zionism (noun) A movement that attempted to reestablish the Jewish state in Palestine.

A Prayer for the Days of Awe

Elie Wiesel

Master of the Universe, let us make up. It is time. How long can we go on being angry? 1

More than 50 years have passed since the nightmare was lifted. Many things, good and less 2
good, have since happened to those who survived it. They learned to build on ruins. Family life was
recreated. Children were born, friendships struck. They learned to have faith in their surroundings,
even in their fellow men and women. Gratitude has replaced bitterness in their hearts. No one is as
capable of thankfulness as they are. Thankful to anyone willing to hear their tales and become their
ally in the battle against apathy and forgetfulness. For them every moment is grace.

Oh, they do not forgive the killers and their accomplices, nor should they. Nor should you, 3
Master of the Universe. But they no longer look at every passer-by with suspicion. Nor do they see a
dagger in every hand.

Does this mean that the wounds in their soul have healed? They will never heal. As long as a spark 4
of the flames of Auschwitz and Treblinka glows in their memory, so long will my joy be incomplete.

What about my faith in you, Master of the Universe? 5

I now realize I never lost it, not even over there, during the darkest hours of my life. I don't know 6
why I kept on whispering my daily prayers, and those one reserves for the Sabbath, and for the holidays,
but I did recite them, often with my father and, on Rosh Hashanah eve, with hundreds of inmates at
Auschwitz. Was it because the prayers remained a link to the vanished world of my childhood?

But my faith was no longer pure. How could it be? It was filled with anguish rather than fervor, 7
with perplexity more than piety. In the kingdom of eternal night, on the Days of Awe, which are the
Days of Judgment, my traditional prayers were directed to you as well as against you, Master of the
Universe. What hurt me more: your absence or your silence?

In my testimony I have written harsh words, burning words about your role in our tragedy. I 8
would not repeat them today. But I felt them then. I felt them in every cell of my being. Why did
you allow if not enable the killer day after day, night after night to torment, kill and annihilate tens of
thousands of Jewish children? Why were they abandoned by your Creation?

These thoughts were in no way destined to diminish the guilt of the guilty. Their established 9
culpability is irrelevant to my "problem" with you, Master of the Universe. In my childhood I did not
expect much from human beings. But I expected everything from you.

Where were you, God of kindness, in Auschwitz? What was going on in heaven, at the celestial 10
tribunal, while your children were marked for humiliation, isolation and death only because they were
Jewish?

These questions have been haunting me for more than five decades. You have vocal defenders, 11
you know. Many theological answers were given me, such as "God is God. He alone knows what He
is doing. One has no right to question Him or His ways." Or: "Auschwitz was a punishment for European Jewry's sins of assimilation and/or Zionism." And: "Isn't Israel the solution? Without Auschwitz,
there would have been no Israel."

I reject all these answers. Auschwitz must and will forever remain a question mark only: it can 12
be conceived neither with God nor without God. At one point, I began wondering whether I was not
unfair with you. After all, Auschwitz was not something that came down ready-made from heaven. It
was conceived by men, implemented by men, staffed by men. And their aim was to destroy not only
us but you as well. Ought we not to think of your pain, too? Watching your children suffer at the
hands of your other children, haven't you also suffered?

As we Jews now enter the High Holidays again, preparing ourselves to pray for a year of peace 13
and happiness for our people and all people, let us make up, Master of the Universe. In spite of
everything that happened? Yes, in spite. Let us make up: for the child in me, it is unbearable to be
divorced from you so long.

Read More on the Web

Learn more about Elie Wiesel and the Holocaust by visiting the following sites:

- Biography of Elie Wiesel and bibliography of his works:
  www.ushmm.org/collections/bibliography/elie-wiesel

- The President's Commission on the Holocaust:
  ushmm.org/information/about-the-museum/presidents-commission

- United States Holocaust Memorial Museum: ushmm.org

- Nobel Prize Internet Archive on Elie Wiesel: almaz.com/nobel/peace/1986a.html

Questions for Discussion

1. What method or methods for writing introductions does Wiesel use?

2. What method does he use to close the essay?

3. Why does the author refer to God as "Master of the Universe" rather than using a more personal form of address?

4. This selection is addressed to at least two audiences: God and the readers of the *New York Times*. Why did Wiesel choose to address both? Why didn't he write solely for human readers?

5. Is Wiesel also writing to himself? Explain.

6. In paragraph 10, Wiesel tells us that many questions have been "haunting [him] for more than five decades." What are those questions?

7. Reread paragraphs 11 and 12. What do they reveal about the reason or reasons Wiesel wants to make peace with God?

Thinking Critically

1. In a 1998 interview with George Plimpton, Wiesel said: "I rarely speak about God. To God, yes. I protest against Him. I shout at Him. But to open a discourse [discussion] about the qualities of God, about the problems that God imposes …, no. And yet He is there, in silence." What light does this quotation shed on "A Prayer for the Days of Awe"? What is Wiesel's purpose in writing this prayer? Has his attitude toward God changed from what it was when he spoke with Plimpton?

2. Do you have a favorite prayer, poem, or hymn? Read it carefully; then, summarize it in your journal. In the process explain why this particular piece is meaningful to you.

Suggestions for Journal Entries

1. Sometimes life seems illogical, and tragedies strike for no apparent reason and with no warning. If such an incident has occurred in your life or in the life of someone you know, write down everything you know about this event.

2. Have you ever been angry with God or with the universe for allowing some difficulty or horror to visit you or others? Record the particulars of this situation. Make sure to explain why you are or were angry.

3.7 Suggestions for Sustained Writing

1. If you responded to the first Suggestion for Journal Entry after Ryan Kessler's "An Unusual Affliction," you have probably begun gathering information about an embarrassing experience. Continue adding notes in your journal; then, use this information in a fully developed essay that discusses what happened, why you were embarrassed, and how you dealt with or attempted to deal with the embarrassment.

   If this doesn't interest you, write an essay that recalls a situation or incident in which your self-esteem came under attack. Explain what or who caused this to happen, how you reacted, and whether or not you have recovered from this assault on your psyche. Like Kessler, be brave! Express your emotional reaction to this situation openly and freely. Once again, check your journal. You might have gathered relevant information for this assignment if you responded to the second journal suggestion after Kessler's essay.

   Whichever option you choose, make sure to write an effective introduction and memorable conclusion by using one or more of the techniques for beginning and ending an essay, which are explained earlier in this chapter.

2. In the second of the Suggestions for Journal Entries for Sydney Harris's "How to Keep Air Clean," you were asked to write a number of reasons that have led you to disagree with a widely held assumption or opinion. If you responded to this item, read over what you wrote in your journal. Then, do the following:

   a. Write an introductory paragraph—complete with a formal thesis statement—that challenges this assumption and briefly explains your reasons for disagreeing.

   b. Make each of your reasons for disagreeing with the topic a well-developed paragraph. Use these paragraphs as the body of your essay.

   c. Write a concluding paragraph that does one of the following:

   - Rephrases your thesis or summarizes your major points.

   - Makes a call to action, as Harris does at the end of his essay.

   - Looks to the future.

   - Asks a question or series of questions.

   You need not complete these steps in the order they are presented. For example, writing the body paragraphs and the conclusion before you write the introduction might be an easier way to proceed. Remember that writing is a process of discovery. You might have to revise one part of the essay in light of what you say in another part. If you begin the assignment by drafting your introduction, don't be afraid to rewrite it later if what you put into the body of the paper demands a change in your thesis or in other parts of the introduction. No matter how many times you rewrite your paper, make sure to edit and proofread the final draft carefully.

3. If you responded to the first Suggestion for Journal Entries after reading "The Italian Schindler," expand your notes into an essay that discusses a person you believe sacrifices a great deal to help others "simply because it is the right thing to do." You may have already discussed one example of this person's helping others; now, add other examples of his or her kindness. An alternative way to develop your essay is to write about additional people you know who exhibit this kind of nobility.

After you have written and revised the essay, make sure you have introduced it by using one or more of the methods for introducing essays explained in this chapter. Include an explicit thesis in your introduction; then, make sure your conclusion is strong. End your essay by using one of the methods for concluding explained earlier in this chapter.

4. Following "The Italian Schindler" is another piece on the Holocaust, "A Prayer for the Days of Awe," by Elie Wiesel, who survived the Holocaust. Imagine a conversation between Wiesel and Giovanni Palatucci. What things might these two men have talked about? What might Oskar Schindler, Wiesel, and Palatucci have spoken of if all three of them had met? If you saw the movie *Schindler's List*, use the notes you made about it in your journal, as well as insights from Wiesel's and Bettina's essays, to write an essay explaining what these essays and this film taught you about human charity and nobility in the face of immense suffering.

5. If you responded to either of the Suggestions for Journal Entries after Wiesel's "A Prayer for the Days of Awe," read the notes you made in preparation for the writing of a letter to God or to the Master of the Universe (in other words, a prayer). You might write about your concerns and frustrations over an incident in which someone has been harmed. Or you might express your anger to the Creator for allowing evil, sorrow, and injustice to exist either in general or in a particular situation you have observed. Or you might simply discuss some questions that have been bothering you about yourself, about your relationship with God, or about life in general.

Whichever path you choose, remember that your letter/prayer will be read by a human audience, so provide enough details to ensure that your readers will understand the situations, concepts, and emotions you are discussing. In addition, use one or more of the methods for writing introductions and conclusions that you have learned in this chapter. Whether human or divine, your audience deserves interesting and effective openings and closings.

Finally, write several drafts of your paper. Revise and edit it carefully. God may forgive sloppy writing, but other readers won't.

ACKNOWLEDGMENTS

"Affirmative Reaction" [editorial]. *Wall Street Journal*, 20 Apr. 1995, p. A12. Copyright 1995, Wall Street Journal.

Bettina, Elizabeth. *It Happened In Italy*. Thomas Nelson, 2011. Copyright © 2009, 2011 by Elizabeth Bettina. Used by permission of Thomas Nelson. www.thomasnelson.com.

Dickinson, Lynda. *Victims of Vanity: Animal Testing of Cosmetics and Household Products, and How to Stop It*. Firefly Books, 1989. Copyright 1989 by Firefly Books.

Ericson Jr., Edward E. "Gen X Is OK, Part 1." *The American Enterprise*, 1 Jan. 1998. Copyright 1998 The American Enterprise Institute.

Francke, Linda Bird. *The Ambivalence of Abortion*. Random House, 1978. Copyright 1978 Random House.

Harris, Sydney J. *For the Time Being*. Houghton Mifflin, 1972. Copyright © 1972 by Sydney J. Harris. Reprinted by permission of Houghton Mifflin Harcourt Publishing Company. All rights reserved.

Healy, Bernadine. "Mother Nature, Terrorist." *U.S. News & World Report*, 10 Jan. 2005. Copyright 2005 U.S. News & World Report L.P.

Hodgman, Ann. "No Wonder They Call Me a Bitch." *The Best American Essays*. 3rd ed. Houghton Mifflin College Division, 2000.

Manchester, William. "The Bloodiest Battle of All." *New York Times Magazine*, 14 June 1987. Copyright 1987, New York Times Company.

Murray, Donald M. "The Maker's Eye: Revising Your Own Manuscripts." *Language Awareness: Reading For College Writers*, 8th ed., pp. 161–165. P. Eschholz, A. Rosa, and V. Clark, eds. Bedford/St. Martin's 2000. Copyright 2000 Bedford/St. Martin's.

"Old, Ailing, Abandoned: The Sick and Elderly in Residential Facilities Deserve Far More Protection Than They Receive" [editorial]. *Philadelphia Inquirer*, 12 Mar. 1995, p. E04. Copyright 1995 The Philadelphia Inquirer.

Orwell, George. "A Hanging." *Shooting an Elephant and Other Essays*. Secker and Warburg 1950.

Parker, Jo Goodwin. "What Is Poverty." *America's Other Children: Public Schools Outside Suburbia*. University of Oklahoma Press, 1971. Copyright 1971 University of Oklahoma Press.

"Refugees: Darfur and Beyond" [editorial]. *America: The Jesuit Review*, 16 Aug. 2004. Copyright 2004 America Magazine.

Roberts, Robin. "Strike Out Little League." *Newsweek*, 21 July 1975, p 11. Copyright 1975 Newsweek.

Rose, Kenneth Jon. "2001 Space Shuttle." *Travel & Leisure*, Nov. 1979. Copyright 1979 Meredith Corporation Travel & Leisure Group.

Ryan, Michael. "They Track the Deadliest Viruses." *Parade*, 23 Apr. 1995. Copyright © 1995 by Michael Ryan. Reprinted by permission of Parade.

Shabecoff, Philip. "Congress Again Confronts Hazards of Killer Chemicals." *New York Times*, 11 Oct. 1987. Copyright 1987 New York Times Company.

Wiesel, Elie. "A Prayer for the Days of Awe." *The New York Times*, Oct. 1997. Copyright © 1997 by Elie Wiesel. Reprinted by permission of Georges Borchardt, Inc., on behalf of the Estate of Elie Wiesel.

Section 2

Word Choice and Sentence Patterns

In section 1, you learned how to approach a subject, to focus on a purpose and central idea, and to organize and develop the information you collected. The two chapters in section 2 explain how to use language and sentence structure to make your writing clearer, more interesting, and more emphatic.

What you will learn in this section is just as important as what you learned earlier. In most cases, however, the techniques discussed in this section—refining word choice, creating figures of speech, and reworking sentence structure for emphasis and variety—are things you will turn your attention to after having written at least one version of a paper, not while you are focusing on a central idea, organizing details, or writing your first rough draft.

Keep this in mind as you read the next two chapters. Chapter 4 explains how to choose vocabulary that is concrete, specific, and vivid, as well as how to use figurative language: metaphor, simile, and personification. Chapter 5 will increase your ability to create variety and emphasis through sentence structure.

Enjoy the reading selections in each chapter. Reading them carefully and completing the Questions for Discussion, the Suggestions for Journal Entries, and the Suggestions for Sustained Writing will not only help you learn more about the writing process but should also inspire you to continue developing as a writer.

Word Choice and Sentence Patterns

Shutterstock

Chapter **4**

Word Choice—Using Literal and Figurative Language Effectively

Chapter Outline

This chapter explains ways to enhance your ability to choose just the right words for a variety of writing purposes and situations. Language can work in many different ways.

Most often, writers use a straightforward approach by relying on language that is literal—that is, it means exactly what it says. As you will see, the most effective words of this type are concrete, specific, and vivid.

At times, however, writers may also need to explain complex ideas or make their writing more colorful. In such cases, they can turn to language that is figurative. The most well-known **figures of speech** are simile, metaphor, and personification. **Figurative language** does not explain or represent a subject directly, as does literal language. Instead, it creates a comparison or other relationship between an idea you want to explain and something concrete that readers can recognize easily.

4.1 Showing Readers What You Mean

A writer has three ways to communicate a message: (1) by implying, (2) by telling, and (3) by showing. Of course, all three types of writing serve specific and important purposes. Usually, however, the writing that is the clearest and has the greatest impact uses language that shows. Words that show are more concrete, more specific, and usually more interesting than those that simply tell or imply a message.

Although the following two paragraphs discuss the same subject, they contain very different kinds of language. Which of the two will have the greatest impact on readers?

Writing That Tells

Michael's old car is the joke of the neighborhood. He should have gotten rid of it years ago, but he insists on keeping this "antique," despite protests from his family and friends. The car is noisy and unsafe. What's more, it pollutes the environment, causes a real disturbance whenever he drives by, and is a real eyesore.

Writing That Shows

Whenever Michael drives down our street, dogs howl, children scream, and the elderly shut their doors and windows as if to prepare for a hurricane. His 1995 Chevrolet Impala has been through the traffic wars, and, fatally wounded, it is now suffering a prolonged and painful death. Originally painted emerald green, the exterior is so covered with scrapes, dents, and patches of rust that it is hard to tell what it looked like when new. His wife and children have pleaded with him to junk this corroded patchwork of steel, rubber, and chewing gum, but Michael insists that he can restore his "baby" to its former glory. It does no good for them to argue that its cracked windshield and bald tires make this old crate a road hazard. Nor is Michael moved by their complaints about the roar and rattle of its cracked muffler, the screech of its well-worn brakes, and the stench of the cloud of black smoke billowing from its rusty tail pipe.

figurative language (figures of speech) Words or phrases that explain abstract ideas by comparing them to concrete realities the reader will recognize easily. Analogy, metaphor, simile, and personification are types of figurative language.

As you will learn in the chapters on narration and description in section 3, language that shows makes for effective and interesting writing, especially when your purpose is to describe a person or place or to tell a story. The next few pages explain how to improve your writing by

- Choosing concrete nouns and adjectives over those that are abstract.

- Including words that are specific rather than those that are general.

- Adding vivid verbs, adjectives, and adverbs.

- Using figurative language: similes, metaphors, and personification.

4.2 Making Your Writing Concrete

Concrete language points to or identifies things readers can experience for themselves. Things that are concrete are material; they can be seen, touched, heard, smelled, or tasted. The opposite of concrete is **abstract language**, a term that refers to ideas, emotions, or other intangibles. While very real, these abstract things exist in our minds and hearts. That's why readers find it harder to grasp the abstract than the concrete.

Compare the nouns in these two lists. Words on the right are physical signs of the emotions listed on the left.

Abstract	Concrete
Joy	Laughter
Hatred	Sneering, cursing
Anger	Shouting
Sadness	Weeping
Fear	Screaming, gasping

Three ways to make your writing more concrete are to use the five senses to recall an experience, create a concrete image, or use examples.

4.2a Use Your Five Senses to Recall an Experience

Providing a realistic account of how things look, sound, smell, taste, and feel can make your writing concrete. In "Once More to the Lake," E. B. White recalls concrete, sensory details about arriving at the camp in Maine where he once spent his summers. The only sense White does not refer to is taste.

> The arriving … had been so big a business in itself, at the railway station the farm wagon drawn up, the first smell of the pine-laden air, the first glimpse of the smiling farmer … and the feel of the wagon under you for the long ten-mile haul, and at the top of the last long hill catching the first view of the lake after eleven months of not seeing this cherished body of water. The shouts and cries of the other campers when they saw you, and the trunks to be unpacked to give up their rich burden.

4.2b Create a Concrete Image

An **image** is a mental picture that expresses an abstract concept in concrete terms. You can create images by packing your writing with concrete nouns and adjectives. The word *image* is related to the word *imagine*; so, a good time to use an image is when writing about something your readers have never experienced and can only imagine from the information that you provide. In "The Origins of the Underclass," Nicholas Lemann creates an image to help readers experience an urban high school.

> Orr High School, on the west side of Chicago, was designed by Mies Van der Rohe. It is a good example of his institutional style, with exposed steel girders, brick walls, and broad expanses of glass windows. Inside it is divided into several "houses" with their own libraries, cafeterias, and other facilities, in order to foster a feeling of educational intimacy. "The design of this building is not the design needed in a neighborhood like this," says the principal, Kenneth Van Spankeren, and it has been altered. Most of the glass has been replaced with an unbreakable plastic material called Lexan, which has turned cloudy. The parking lot is surrounded by a fifteen-foot wire-mesh fence and kept locked during the school day. An unarmed security guard is posted at the entrance …. The interior stairwells are kept locked and are monitored by teachers.

concrete language
Words that represent material things—things we can perceive with our five senses.

abstract language
Words that represent ideas rather than things we can see, hear, smell, feel, or taste. The word love is abstract, but the word kiss is concrete because we can perceive it with one or more of our five senses.

image
A verbal picture made up of sensory details. It expresses a general idea's meaning clearly and concretely.

4.2c **Use Examples**

If you want to explain that your Uncle Wendell is eccentric, you can write that "he is odd" or "strange." But such synonyms are as abstract and hard to grasp as the word *eccentric*. Instead, you might provide examples that readers can understand. You can show them what *eccentric* means by explaining that Uncle Wendell never wears the same color socks, that he cuts his own hair, and that his favorite dessert is chocolate-covered seaweed.

In "The Human Cost of an Illiterate Society," Jonathan Kozol uses examples to portray the frustration, loss, and risks faced by people who cannot read and write.

> Illiterates cannot read the letters that their children bring home from their teachers. They cannot study school department circulars that tell them of the courses that their children must be taking if they hope to pass the SAT exams. They cannot help with homework. They cannot write a letter to the teacher. They are afraid to visit in the classroom. They do not want to humiliate their child or themselves.

4.3 Making Your Writing Specific

Writing that lacks specificity often contains language that is general and that makes it difficult to communicate clearly and completely. A good way to make your writing specific is to choose nouns and adjectives carefully. Nouns name persons, places, or things; adjectives describe nouns, thereby making those nouns more distinct and exact. Compare the words and phrases in each column:

General	More Specific	Most Specific
leader	president	Abraham Lincoln
automobile	sports utility vehicle	Ford Explorer
school	college	University of Tennessee
television show	game show	*Family Feud*
tree	conifer	Norwegian pine
beverage	soft drink	diet ginger ale

You probably noticed that several of the "Most Specific" items contain capitalized words. These are proper nouns, which name specific persons, places, and things. Use proper nouns that your readers will recognize when you can. Doing so will show how much you know about your subject and will increase your readers' confidence in your writing. More important, it will make your ideas easier to grasp.

Notice the difference between the following two paragraphs. The first uses vague, general language; the second uses specifics—nouns and adjectives—that make its meaning clearer and that hold the readers' interest better.

General

The island prison is covered with flowers now. A large sign that is visible from a long way off warns visitors away. But since the early 1960s, when they took the last prisoners to other institutions, the sign has really served no purpose, for the prison has been abandoned. The place is not unpleasant; in fact, one might enjoy the romance and solitude out there.

Specific

Alcatraz Island is covered with flowers now: orange and yellow nasturtiums, geraniums, sweet grass, blue iris, black-eyed Susans. Candytuft springs up through the cracked concrete in the exercise yard. Ice plant carpets the rusting catwalks. "WARNING! KEEP OFF! U.S. PROPERTY," the sign still reads, big and yellow and visible for perhaps a quarter of a mile, but since March 21, 1963, the day they took the last thirty or so men off the island …, the warning has been only pro forma [serving no real purpose] …. It is not an unpleasant place to be, out there on Alcatraz with only the flowers and the wind and the bell buoy moaning and the tide surging through the Golden Gate. (Joan Didion, "Rock of Ages")

The differences between these two paragraphs can be summed up as follows:

- The first calls the place an "island prison." The second gives it a name, "Alcatraz."

- The first claims that the prison is covered with flowers. The second shows us that this is true by naming them: nasturtiums, geraniums, and so on. It also explains exactly where they grow: "through the cracked concrete" and on "rusting catwalks."

- The first tells us about a sign that can be seen "from a long way off." The second explains that the sign is "visible for perhaps a quarter of a mile" and shows us exactly what it says.

- The first mentions that the last prisoners were removed from Alcatraz in the 1960s. The second explains that they numbered "thirty or so" and that the exact date of their departure was March 21, 1963.

- The first tells us that we might find "romance and solitude" on Alcatraz Island. The second describes the romance and solitude by calling our attention to "the flowers and the wind and the bell buoy moaning and the tide surging through the Golden Gate."

4.4 Making Your Writing Vivid

Beside using figurative language (the subject of the next part of this chapter), you can make your writing vivid by carefully choosing verbs, adjectives, and adverbs.

1. Verbs express action, condition, or state of being. If you wrote, "Jan *leaped* over the hurdles," you would be using an action verb. If you explained that "Roberta *did not feel* well" or that "Mario *was* delirious," you would be describing a condition or a state of being.

2. Adjectives describe nouns. You would be using adjectives if you wrote, "the *large, two-story white* house that the *young Canadian* couple bought was *old* and *weather beaten*."

3. Adverbs modify (tell the reader something about) verbs, adjectives, or other adverbs. You would be using adverbs if you wrote: "The *easily* frightened child sobbed *softly* and hugged his mother *very tightly* as she *gently* wiped away his tears and *tenderly* explained that the knee he had *just* scraped would stop hurting *soon*."

Choosing effective verbs, adjectives, and adverbs can turn dull writing into writing that keeps the reader's interest and communicates ideas with greater emphasis and clarity. Notice how much more effective the rewritten version of each of the following sentences becomes when the right verbs, adjectives, and adverbs are used:

Original Version	Rewritten Version
The old church needed repair.	The pre–Civil War Baptist church cried out for repairs to its tottering steeple, its crumbling stone foundation, and its cracked stained-glass windows.
The kitchen table was a mess. It was covered with the remains of peanut butter and jelly sandwiches.	The kitchen table was littered with the half-eaten remains of stale peanut butter sandwiches and thickly smeared with the crusty residue of strawberry jelly.
A pathetic old homeless person was in an alley among some garbage.	The body of a homeless man, his face wrinkled and blistered, lay in a pile of oil-covered rags and filthy cardboard boxes piled in the corner of a long alley devoid of life and light.

4.5 Using Figurative Language

Earlier, you learned that figurative language is called *figurative* because it does not explain something directly. Instead it conveys meaning by comparing the thing you are explaining to something else. Figures of speech can help you explain an idea more clearly and emphatically than if you used literal language alone. In fact, they can create images, or mental pictures that allow readers to *see* what you mean. So, instead of saying that your cousin Mort dresses shabbily, you might say that he "looks like a caveman." Comparing Mort to a caveman brings up images of a scruffy, bug-infested beard; of hair that is rarely combed; and of clothes that are beyond cleaning and mending. Once again, the most common types of figurative language are simile, metaphor, and personification.

4.5a Simile

A **simile** creates a comparison between two things by using the words *like* or *as*. For example, say that you're writing your sweetheart a letter in which you want to explain how much you need him or her. You can express your feelings literally and directly by writing, "I need you very much." Then again, you can *show* how strongly you feel by writing that you need him or her "as an oak needs sunlight," "as an eagle needs the open sky," or "as the dry earth needs spring rain."

Read the following list carefully. Notice how much more concrete, exciting, and rich the ideas on the left become when they are expressed in similes:

simile
A figure of speech that, like a metaphor, compares two things for the sake of clarity and emphasis. Unlike a metaphor, however, a simile uses *like* or *as*. "Samantha runs *like* a deer" is a simile.

Literal Expression	Simile
She arrived on time.	She arrived as promptly as the sunrise.
Snerdly's face was sunburned.	Snerdley's face was as red as the inside of a watermelon.
Eugene is a fancy dresser.	Eugene dresses like a peacock.
The tires made a loud noise.	The tires screeched like a wounded animal.
The dog moved slowly.	The dog moved like corn syrup on a cold day.

Finally, have a look at "Harlem," by Langston Hughes, an important twentieth-century poet who was one of the lights of the Harlem Renaissance, an artistic and cultural flowering in the 1920s. Hughes uses five similes in eleven lines.

What Happens to a Dream Deferred?

> Does it dry up
> like a raisin in the sun?
> Or fester like a sore—
> And then run?
> Does it stink like rotten meat?
> Or crust and sugar over—
> like a syrupy sweet?
>
> Maybe it just sags
> like a heavy load.
>
> *Or does it explode?*

4.5b Metaphor

A **metaphor** also uses comparison to show the relationship between things to make the explanation of one of these things clearer and livelier. In fact, a metaphor works just like a simile except that it does not make use of *like* or *as*. For instance, you can turn the simile "Eugene dresses like a peacock" into a metaphor by writing "Eugene is a peacock." In neither case, of course, do you actually mean that Eugene is a bird; you're simply pointing out similarities between the way he dresses and the showiness we associate with a peacock.

Remember that, like all figures of speech, similes and metaphors turn abstract ideas (such as "Eugene is a fancy dresser") into vivid, concrete images. In other words, they communicate more emphatically and clearly than if the writer had used literal language alone. Study the following list of similes and metaphors. What effect do they have on you, especially when compared with the literal expressions on the left?

metaphor
A figure of speech that, like a simile, creates a comparison between two things to make the explanation of one of them clearer. Unlike a simile, a metaphor does not use *like* or *as*. "The man is a pig" is a metaphor.

Literal Expression	Simile	Metaphor
My old car is hard to drive.	My old car drives like a tank.	My old car is a tank!
She works too hard for her family.	She works like a slave for her family.	She is a slave to her family.
During the holidays, shopping malls are crowded and noisy.	During the holidays, shopping malls are so crowded and noisy that they seem like madhouses.	During the holidays, shopping malls are so crowded and noisy that they become madhouses.
The hayloft was hot.	The hayloft was as hot as a blast furnace.	The hayloft was a blast furnace.

Read the following excerpt from Martin Luther King Jr.'s "I Have a Dream," a speech he delivered at the Lincoln Memorial during the 1963 March on Washington. Identify the metaphors and similes that Dr. King used to captivate the hundreds of thousands in his audience and to make his message more concrete, vivid, and effective:

> Five score years ago, a great American, in whose symbolic shadow we stand today, signed the Emancipation Proclamation. This momentous decree came as a great beacon light of hope to millions of Negro slaves who had been seared in the flames of withering injustice. It came as a joyous daybreak to end the long night of their captivity.
>
> But one hundred years later, the Negro still is not free. One hundred years later, the life of the Negro is still sadly crippled by the manacles of segregation and the chains of discrimination.

4.5c Personification

Personification is the description of animals, plants, or inanimate objects by using terms ordinarily associated with human beings. Like metaphor and simile, personification is an effective way to turn abstract ideas into vivid and concrete realities that readers will grasp easily and quickly.

One common example of personification is Father Time, the figure of an old man trailing a white beard and carrying a scythe and hourglass. Another is the Grim Reaper, the representation of death pictured as a skeleton holding a scythe. William Shakespeare often used personification to enrich the language of his poems and plays. In "Sonnet 18," for example, he described the sun as "the eye of heaven." William Least Heat Moon does something similar when, in *Blue Highways*, he describes the saguaro cactus of the southwestern United States:

> Standing on the friable slopes … saguaros mimic men as they salute, bow, dance, raise arms to wave, and grin with faces carved in by woodpeckers. Older plants, having survived odds against their reaching maturity of sixty million to one, have every right to smile.

personification
A figure of speech that writers use to discuss animals, plants, or inanimate objects in terms normally associated with human beings— for example, "Our neighborhoods are the soul of the city."

4.6 Visualizing Effective Word Choice

In the following paragraphs from "Where the World Began," Margaret Laurence describes her small hometown on the Canadian prairie. Comments in the margins point to effective use of both literal and figurative language. After studying the first paragraph, find and circle examples of effective language—both literal and figurative—in the other three.

Adjectives appeal to senses.

Startling image.

Names specific type of train.

Summers were scorching, and when no rain came and the wheat became bleached and dried before it headed, the faces of farmers and townsfolk would not smile much, and you took for granted, because it never seemed to have been any different, the frequent knocking at the back door and the young men standing there, mumbling or thrusting defiantly their requests for a drink of water and a sandwich …. They were riding the freights, and you never knew where they had come from, or

Farming metaphor, "headed."

where they might end up .... The Drought and Depression were like evil deities [gods] which had been there always. You understood and did not understand.

Yet the outside world had its continuing marvels. The poplar bluffs and the small river were filled and surrounded with a zillion different grasses, stones, and weed flowers. The meadowlarks sang undaunted [courageously] from the twanging telephone wires along the gravel highway. Once we found an old flat-bottomed scow [small boat], and launched her, poling along the shallow, brown waters, mending her with wedges [chunks] of hastily chewed Spearmint, grounding her among the tangles of soft yellow marsh marigolds that grew succulently along the banks of the shrunken river, while the sun made our skins smell dusty-warm. ....

In winter, we used to hitch rides on the back of the milk sleigh, our moccasins squeaking and slithering on the hard rutted snow ...., our hands in ice-bubbled mitts hanging onto the box edge of the sleigh for dear life .... Those mornings, rising, there would be the perpetual fascination of the frost feathers on windows, the ferns and flowers and eerie faces traced there during the night by unseen artists of the wind .... And then, the sometime astonishment when you saw the Northern Lights flaring across the sky, like the scrawled signature of God.

Proper nouns used to name specific historical events.

Simile.

4.7 Revising for Word Choice

Read these two excerpts from the rough and final drafts of Louis Gonzalez's "Music," a student essay that appears in this chapter. As you will see, the revision process has enabled Gonzalez to make his writing stronger, livelier, and more interesting.

Gonzalez—Rough Draft

Use more vivid language?

With my record player and some old 45s from my dad's collection, I locked myself into the garage. As the music played, tools became musical instruments, and I played 'em all man! I wore those old 45s down until there was almost nothing left. I spent most of my child-

Such as?

hood in that garage listening to my favorite jazz musicians while other kids played football and video games. Even though my parents said I was wasting my time there, the experience made me want to become a musician.

As I became a little older and entered high school, my interests shifted toward learning to play a musical instrument. After a little

Vague. Add details?

experimentation, the bass guitar became my love. It produced warm, confident tones. They danced around my head. The guitar became the implement of my creativity. It soon became the center of my existence. I felt naked and insecure without it. Its weight was a lover's hand upon my shoulder.

This seems flat.

Add to metaphor?

Gonzalez—Final Draft

Adds effective adjective and verb.

Creates an effective image.

Uses a proper noun.

Names the tools used as instruments.

Adds details that appeal to senses.

Adds vivid verb, adjective, and noun.

Includes vivid adjective and adverb.

Adds detail to continue personifying guitar as lover.

Adds metaphors.

Mentions specific musician.

Creates another metaphor.

Adds personification by comparing "guitar" to a lover and "tones" to "dancers."

Uses a metaphor to compare guitar to painter's "brush."

Armed with my record player and some old 45s I liberated from my dad's collection, I locked myself into the garage and entered another world. Instead of remaining surrounded by tools and half-empty paint cans, I lowered the lid of that cheap Fisher-Price [record player] and transported myself to a smoky club somewhere in the city. As the music played, wrenches became saxophones, boxes became a set of drums, and the workbench became a sleek black piano. I played 'em all man! I wore those old 45s down until there was nothing left but pops, cracks, and the occasional high note. I spent most of my childhood in that smelly garage listening to Miles Davis and my other patron saints, while other kids played football and video games. Even though my parents said I was wasting my time there, the experience instilled in me a burning desire to become a musician.

When I entered high school, my interests shifted toward playing a musical instrument. After a little experimentation, I fell in love with the bass guitar. It covered me with warm, confident tones—blankets of pure ecstasy. They were poised ballroom dancers waltzing elegantly around my head. The guitar became the implement of my creativity, the brush with which I painted portraits of candid love and dark emotion. I was naked and insecure without it. Its weight was a lover's hand upon my shoulder, and its smooth hourglass body was a pleasure to hold. It whispered sweet kisses in my ear.

4.8 Practicing the Use of Effective Language—Literal and Figurative

In the spaces provided, rewrite each sentence using language that is more effective than in the original. Use language that is concrete, specific, and vivid. In addition, try your hand at creating similes, metaphors, and personification, as discussed earlier. The first item is done for you.

1. The desk in the corner of the office was cluttered.

The large, unused desk in the corner was the office garbage dump, overflowing with yellowing newspapers and torn magazines, used coffee cups, and even an old computer monitor.

2. A construction worker hung from a beam above the street.

3. The exterior of the house needed painting.

4. The bus was crowded.

5. Eating at the Greasy Spoon Restaurant is dangerous.

6. Cheryl treats her mother well.

7. He ran to the end of the street and jumped over the barricade.

8. The village was flooded.

_____

_____

_____

9. The wind was strong.

_____

_____

_____

10. The newspaper photograph contained a warning about drunk driving.

_____

_____

_____

4.9 Reading Selections

4.9a Music

Author Biography

When asked by his professor to define a concept, idea, or activity that was important to him, *Louis Gonzalez* knew immediately what he would write about. The challenging part came in making this abstraction real to his readers. He did this by choosing concrete, specific, and vivid vocabulary and by filling his writing with powerful figures of speech. In other words, he showed the reader what he meant.

Gonzalez writes musical reviews for a local magazine and is considering a career as a writer. He was a first-year liberal arts student when he wrote this essay.

Preparing to Read

1. Pay special attention to paragraphs 3 and 4. The rough draft of these paragraphs appears with the author's revisions earlier in the chapter. They show how much care Gonzalez used as he approached the process of writing.

2. In addition to using all three figures of speech you have already read about, Gonzalez introduces hyperbole, or exaggeration. Look for an example of this other figure of speech at the end of paragraph 6.

3. Gonzalez mentions "45s." They are vinyl records that play at 45 revolutions per minute.

Vocabulary

cathartic (adjective)   Cleansing, purifying.

chaotic (adjective)   Confusing, disorderly.

licks (noun)   Musical phrases created when improvising.

mesmerizing (adjective)   Absorbing, hypnotizing.

obsession (noun)   Passion, fixation.

orgasm (noun)   Sexual climax.

oscillating (adjective)   Moving from side to side.

poised (adjective)   Balanced.

preoccupied (verb)   Absorbed in, wrapped up in.

reverberate (verb)   Echo.

tangible (adjective)   Able to be touched, felt.

tenacity (noun)   Determination, persistence.

venue (noun)   Place where events take place.

yoke (noun)   Shackle, chain.

Music

Louis Gonzalez

Music is my obsession. It reverberates across every fiber of my being. I have spent endless hours of my life creating music, performing it, or even just dreaming about it. My thoughts are filled with the angelic sigh of a bow kissing the strings of a violin, or the hellish crash of batons torturing the skin of a kettle drum. But my favorite instrument is the vociferous world around us. The scuff of a penny loafer across a wood floor, the clinking of Crayolas across a child's desk, or the mesmerizing hum of an oscillating fan are all part of this chaotic symphony. It is within this sonic spectrum that I exist.   1

I have long been preoccupied with the audible world. When I was younger, anything and everything that made a sound became a musical instrument. My mother's pots, empty soda bottles, even the railing on my front porch became part of my private symphony orchestra. Then, for my ninth birthday, I received a Fisher-Price record player. A single tin speaker was built into the base, and the needle was attached to a wooden lid, which I had to shut in order to make the thing work. More often than not, the lid would fall accidentally and cut deep scratches into the record. But to my young ears, it made the sounds of heaven.

Armed with my record player and some old jazz 45s I liberated from my dad's collection, I locked myself in the garage and entered another world. Instead of remaining surrounded by tools and half-empty paint cans, I lowered the lid of that cheap Fisher-Price and transported myself to a smoky club somewhere in the city. As the music played, wrenches became saxophones, boxes became a set of drums, and the workbench became a sleek black piano. I played 'em all, man! I wore those old 45s down until there was nothing left but pops, cracks, and the occasional high note. I spent most of my childhood in that smelly garage listening to Miles Davis and my other patron saints, while other kids played football and video games. Even though my parents said I wasted my time there, the experience instilled in me a burning desire to become a musician.   2

When I entered high school, my interests shifted towards learning to play a musical instrument. After a little experimentation, I fell in love with the bass guitar. It covered me with warm, confident tones—blankets of pure ecstasy. They were poised ballroom dancers waltzing elegantly around my head. The guitar became the implement of my creativity, the brush with which I painted portraits   3 of candid love and dark emotion. I was naked and insecure without it. Its weight was a lover's hand upon my shoulder, and its smooth hourglass body was a pleasure to hold. It whispered sweet kisses in my ear.

As my skills increased, so did my yearning to play those old jazz songs of my youth. But the harder I tried, the less I succeeded. It seemed as though I was simply incapable of playing those songs. All those wild bass licks that poured out of that Fisher-Price record player were ripped from my dreams. **4**

My lust for jazz was then replaced by the desire to perform in a live rock band. So, I joined a local college group and began to play small venues. The shows were like cathartic orgasms of sweaty bodies undulating as the sensation of music overwhelmed them. While I was on stage, the power of the music pierced through the air like a volley of arrows falling upon the flannel-clad flesh whirling below me. But I felt as though the music was in control and I was just letting it happen. That feeling began to consume my spirit and destroy my sense of oneness with the music. **5**

There was definitely something missing. Even though what I played was structurally powerful, it lacked a soul. I also realized that my style of playing lacked a human quality. So when I came upon my old jazz records, I listened to them with new ears. I dropped all of my preconceived notions of song structure. As the records popped and scratched their way around the turntable, the secrets of the universe were finally revealed to me. **6**

I realized that my approach had been all wrong. All my songs were suffocated under the weight of formality. Harnessed to the yoke of "proper" song structure and arrangement, they were never allowed to grow fully. So, I picked up my bass with a fresh tenacity and dropped all my inhibitions. Not surprisingly, those old jazz songs started to pour out. I played them as if I had known them all of my life. **7**

I look back on that day and realize that I did know how to play those songs all along. It wasn't a tangible lack of something—like talent or effort—that held me back. I just needed to feel the music—to feel the sweet life a musician blows into it, to feel it the way that innocent child felt in the garage all those years ago. **8**

Read More on the Web

The following sites provide more information about topics related to Gonzalez's essay.

- National Association for Music Education site: nafme.org

- Thoughtco's "A Beginner's Guide to Music History": http://bvtlab.com/RKchP

- "20 Important Benefits of Music in Our Schools": http://bvtlab.com/Ks9a9

Questions for Discussion

1. What is Gonzalez's thesis? Has he proved it?

2. How would you describe the introduction to this essay? Does it use one or more of the techniques explained in Chapter 3? Which one or ones?

3. Paragraphs 1, 2, and 3 show that Gonzalez uses concrete and specific nouns. Find examples of such nouns.

4. Vivid verbs make paragraph 7 especially interesting. Identify a few of them.

5. Find examples of metaphor in paragraphs 3 and 4. Explain each of them.

6. Where does the author use simile?

7. Find two paragraphs in which personification is used. Explain these figures of speech.

Thinking Critically

1. Gonzalez uses hyperbole, another figure of speech, in paragraph 6. Explain what he means. Is his use of exaggeration effective?

2. If you could speak to Gonzalez, what would you ask him about his experiences with music? Write these questions in the margins of the essay.

Suggestions for Journal Entries

1. What is your obsession? Use freewriting or brainstorming to record facts about your love for an activity or idea that will show how much you are committed to it. Then read over your notes and add nouns, verbs, adjectives, and adverbs that will make your work more concrete, specific, and vivid.

2. Create a list of metaphors, similes, or personifications that might describe how you feel when you are doing a particular activity you really enjoy. For inspiration, reread paragraphs 1, 3, 4, and 6 of "Music."

4.9b **Those Winter Sundays**

Author Biography

Robert Hayden (1913–1980) taught English at Fisk University and at the University of Michigan. For years, the work of this talented African-American writer received far less recognition than it deserved. Recently, however, his reputation has grown, especially since the publication of his complete poems in 1985.

"Those Winter Sundays" uses the author's vivid memories of his father to show us the depth and quality of love that the man had for his family. Unlike much of Hayden's other work, this poem does not deal with the black experience as such; however, it does demonstrate the same care and skill in choosing effective language that Hayden used in all his poetry.

If you want to read more by Hayden, look for these poetry collections in your college library: *A Ballad of Remembrance*, *Words in Mourning Time*, *Angle of Ascent*, and *American Journal*.

Preparing to Read

1. Hayden's primary purpose is to explain his father's love for his family. Look for details that are physical signs of that love.

2. The author says his father "made/banked fires blaze." Wood and coal fires were "banked" by covering them with ashes to make them burn slowly through the night and continue giving off heat.

3. The word *offices* isn't used in its usual sense in this poem. Here, it means important services or ceremonies.

Vocabulary

austere (adjective)   Severe, harsh, difficult, without comfort.

chronic (adjective)   Persistent, unending, constant.

indifferently (adverb)   Insensitively, without care or concern.

Those Winter Sundays
Robert Hayden

Sundays too my father got up early
and put his clothes on in the blueblack cold,
then with cracked hands that ached
from labor in the weekday weather made
banked fires blaze. No one ever thanked him.   5

I'd wake and hear the cold splintering, breaking.
When the rooms were warm, he'd call,
and slowly I would rise and dress,
fearing the chronic angers of that house,

Speaking indifferently to him,   10
who had driven out the cold
and polished my good shoes as well.
What did I know, what did I know
of love's austere and lonely offices?

Read More on the Web

To learn more about Hayden and his writing, visit

- The Modern American Poetry site on Robert Hayden:
  modernamericanpoetry.org/poet/robert-hayden

- The Academy of American Poets site on Robert Hayden:
  www.poets.org/poetsorg/poet/robert-hayden

Questions for Discussion

1. Does this poem communicate a central idea? In a few words, state the author's opinion of his father.

2. In line 2, "blueblack" is used to describe the cold inside the house. What other effective adjectives do you find in the poem?

3. Hayden shows his father in action. What are some of the things this man did to show his love for his family?

4. What does Hayden mean by the metaphor "love's austere and lonely offices"?

5. Explain why "chronic angers of that house" is personification.

6. What was Hayden's reaction to these offices when he was a boy? What does this reaction tell us about the reason he wrote this poem?

Thinking Critically

Hayden mentions that he feared "the chronic angers of that house." What might he mean by that? Do you associate any "chronic angers" with your home?

Suggestions for Journal Entries

1. In Preparing to Read, you learned that Hayden describes his father's love by using language that is concrete, specific, and vivid. In your own words, discuss the kind of love that Hayden's father showed his family.

2. List some "offices" you think any good father should perform for his family.

3. Do you know someone who demonstrates love for other people day in and day out, as Hayden's father did? In your journal, list the offices (services, tasks, or activities) that he or she performs to show this love. Include as many concrete and specific terms as you can. Then expand each item in your list to a few short sentences, showing that these activities are clearly signs of love.

4.9c Faith of the Father

Author Biography

Sam Pickering (b. 1941–) is a graduate of the University of the South, Cambridge University, and Princeton University. He teaches at the University of Connecticut and has written numerous scholarly books and articles on eighteenth-century English literature and children's literature. He is a recipient of Fulbright Lectureships in Syria and Lebanon and has published several collections of personal essays. "Faith of the Father" first appeared in the *Southwest Review*. Like other selections in this chapter, it demonstrates the author's excellent command over both literal and figurative language.

Preparing to Read

1. Pickering makes great use of proper nouns to make his writing both specific and concrete. Find at least ten examples of such nouns as you read this essay, and mark them in the text.

2. To begin this essay, the author relies heavily on description. Remember that describing a scene was one method for introducing essays, as discussed in Chapter 3.

3. This essay is developed through anecdotes. Anecdotes are brief, often humorous, stories that illustrate a point. The point that Pickering is making is stated clearly in his thesis, which comes in paragraph 10. The anecdotes make that thesis come alive.

4. If you are unfamiliar with the Christian holidays of Christmas and Easter or with revival meetings, baptism, and the Resurrection, which Pickering mentions in this essay, look them up on the Internet before proceeding.

Vocabulary

ascension (noun)   The act or process of rising.

congregation (noun)   Assemblage, people attending church.

chalice (noun)   Cup holding sacramental wine in a Christian service.

dispassionate (adjective)   Cool, calm, without emotion.

erratically (adverb)   Randomly, unpredictably.

irascible (adjective)   Bad-tempered, grumpy.

processional (adjective)   Related to the approach of the minister and others toward the altar.

reminiscing (verb)   Discussing past events.

spades (noun)   Pointed shovels.

sustenance (noun)   Nourishment.

temperate (adjective)   Moderate, calm.

Faith of the Father
Sam Pickering

1   On weekdays, Vickery's store was the center of life in the little Virginia town in which I spent summers and then Christmas and occasionally Easter vacations. The post office was in a corner of the store, and the train station was across the road. In the morning men gathered on Vickery's porch and drank coffee while they waited for the train to Richmond. Late in the afternoon, families appeared. While waiting for their husbands, women bought groceries, mailed letters, and visited with one another. Children ate cups of ice cream and played in the woods behind the store. Sometimes a work train was on the siding, and the engineer filled his cab with children and took them for short trips down the track. On weekends life shifted from the store to St. Paul's Church. Built in a grove of pine trees in the nineteenth century, St. Paul's was a small, white clapboard building. A Sunday school wing, added to the church in the 1920s, jutted out into the graveyard. Beyond the graveyard was a field in which picnics were held and, on the Fourth of July, the yearly Donkey Softball Game was played.

2   St. Paul's was familial and comfortable. Only a hundred people attended regularly, and everyone knew everyone else and his business. What was private became public after the service as people gathered outside and talked for half an hour before going home to lunch. Behind the altar inside the church was a stained-glass window showing Christ's ascension to heaven. A red carpet ran down the middle aisle, and worn, gold cushions covered the pews. On the walls were plaques of parishioners killed in foreign wars or who had made large donations to the building fund. In summer, the minister put fans out on the pews. Donated by a local undertaker, the fans were shaped like spades. On them, besides the undertaker's name and telephone number, were pictures of Christ performing miracles: walking on water, healing the lame, and raising Lazarus from the dead.

3   Holidays and funerals were special at St. Paul's. Funerals were occasions for reminiscing and telling stories. When an irascible old lady died and her daughter had "Gone to Jesus" inscribed on her tombstone, her son-in-law was heard to say, "Poor Jesus"—or so the tale went at the funeral. Christmas Eve was always cold and snow usually fell. Inside the church at midnight, though, all was cheery and warm as the congregation sang the great Christmas hymns: "O Come, All Ye Faithful," "The First Noel," "O Little Town of Bethlehem," and "Hark! The Herald Angels Sing." The last hymn was "Silent Night." The service did not follow the prayer book; inspired by Christmas and eggnog, the congregation came to sing, not to pray. Bourbon was in the air, and when the altar boy lit the candles, it seemed a miracle that the first spark didn't send us all to heaven in a blue flame.

Easter was almost more joyous than Christmas. Men stuck greenery in their lapels and women blossomed in bright bonnets, some ordering hats not simply from Richmond but from Baltimore and Philadelphia. On a farm outside town lived Miss Emma and Miss Ida Catlin. Miss Emma was the practical sister, running the farm and bringing order wherever she went. Unlike Miss Emma, Miss Ida was shy. She read poetry and raised guinea fowl and at parties sat quietly in a corner. Only on Easter was she outgoing; then like a day lily she bloomed triumphantly. No one else's Easter bonnet ever matched hers, and the congregation eagerly awaited her entrance which she always made just before the first hymn.

One year Miss Ida found a catalogue from a New York store which advertised hats and their accessories. For ten to twenty-five cents, ladies could buy artificial flowers to stick into their bonnets. Miss Ida bought a counter full, and that Easter her head resembled a summer garden in bloom. Daffodils, zinnias, and black-eyed Susans hung yellow and red around the brim of her hat while in the middle stood a magnificent pink peony.

In all his glory, Solomon could not have matched Miss Ida's bonnet. The congregation could not take its eyes off it; even the minister had trouble concentrating on his sermon. After the last hymn, everyone hurried out of the church, eager to get a better look at Miss Ida's hat. As she came out, the altar boy began ringing the bell. Alas, the noise frightened pigeons who had recently begun to nest and they shot out of the steeple. The congregation scattered, but the flowers on Miss Ida's hat hung over her eyes, and she did not see the pigeons until it was too late and the peony had been ruined.

Miss Ida acted as if nothing had happened. She greeted everyone and asked about their health and about the health of absent members of families. People tried not to look at her hat but were not very successful. For two Sundays Miss Ida's "accident" was the main subject of after-church conversation; then it was forgotten for almost a year. But, as Easter approached again, people remembered the hat. They wondered what Miss Ida would wear to church. Some people speculated that since she was a shy, poetic person, she wouldn't come. Even the minister had doubts. To reassure Miss Ida, he and his sons borrowed ladders two weeks before Easter, and climbing to the top of the steeple, chased the pigeons away and sealed off their nesting place with chicken wire.

Easter Sunday seemed to confirm the fears of those who doubted Miss Ida would appear. The choir assembled in the rear of the church without her. Half-heartedly the congregation sang the processional hymn, "Hail Thee, Festival Day." Miss Ida's absence had taken something bright from our lives, and as we sat down after singing, Easter seemed sadly ordinary. We were people of little faith. Just as the minister reached the altar and turned to face us, there was a stir at the back of the church. Silently, the minister raised his right hand and pointed toward the door. Miss Ida had arrived. She was wearing the same hat she wore the year before; only the peony was missing. In its place was a wonderful sunflower; from one side hung a black and yellow garden spider building a web, while fluttering above was a mourning cloak, black wings, dotted with a blue and yellow border running around the edges. Our hearts leaped up, and at the end of the service people in Richmond must have heard us singing "Christ the Lord Is Risen Today."

St. Paul's was the church of my childhood, that storied time when I thought little about religion but knew that Jesus loved me, yes, because the Bible told me so. In the Morning Prayer of life, I mixed faith and fairy tale, thinking God a kindly giant, holding in his hands, as the song put it, the corners of the earth and the strengths of the hills. Thirty years have passed since I last saw St. Paul's, and I have come down from the cool upland pastures and the safe fold of childhood to the hot lowlands. Instead of being neatly tucked away in a huge hand, the world now seems to bound erratically, smooth and slippery, forever beyond the grasp of even the most magical deity. Would that it were not so, and my imagination could find a way through His gates, as the psalm says, with thanksgiving. Often I wonder what happened to the "faith of our fathers." Why if it endured dungeon, fire, and sword in others, did it weaken so within me?

For me, religion is a matter of story and community, a congregation rising together to look at an Easter bonnet, unconsciously seeing it as an emblem of hope and vitality, indeed of the Resurrection itself. For me, religion ought to be more concerned with people than ideas, creating soft feeling rather than sharp thought. Often I associate religion with small, backwater towns in which tale binds folk to one another. Here in a university in which people are separated by idea rather than linked by story, religion doesn't have a natural place. In the absence of community, ceremony becomes important.

Changeable and always controversial, subject to dispassionate analysis, ceremony doesn't tie people together like accounts of pigeons and peonies and thus doesn't promise good feeling and finally love for this world and hope for the next. Often when I am discouraged, I turn for sustenance, not to formal faith with articled ceremony but to memory, a chalice winey with story.

Read More on the Web

To learn more about religious holidays and beliefs relating to various faiths, consult the following:

- "Seasons of Faith Christian Holiday Calendar: http://bvtlab.com/7q788

- Religion Facts: www.religionfacts.com/

- A Guide to Religions: http://bvtlab.com/86cVX

Questions for Discussion

1. Find one example of Pickering's use of concrete, descriptive language in each paragraph.

2. Pick out at least five examples in which Pickering uses metaphor or simile.

3. What details in the first paragraph make that paragraph an appropriate introduction?

4. The story of Miss Ida's hat is just one of the humorous aspects of this essay. Find at least two more places in which Pickering makes us laugh.

5. Explain the allusion that Pickering makes to Solomon in paragraph 6? Who was Solomon, and what does his mention tell us about Miss Ida's hat?

6. What does the author mean in paragraph 10 when he says, "For me religion ought to be more concerned with people than with ideas, creating soft feeling rather than sharp thought"?

7. Why is the congregation so excited about Miss Ida's return in paragraph 8? In what way is this event related to the story of Easter and to the essay's thesis?

Thinking Critically

1. In paragraph 9, the author tells us that his childhood vision of religion was a mixture of "faith and fairy tale." What does he mean by this?

2. In what way is the rebirth of Miss Ida's bonnet an "emblem … of the Resurrection itself"?

Suggestions for Journal Entries *(Continues)*

1. Paragraphs 9 and 10 are extremely important to understanding Pickering's vision of religion. Summarize those paragraphs with an eye toward explaining that vision. If you want to review what a summary is, refer to Getting Started, section GS2.5.

Suggestions for Journal Entries (Continued)

2. The author explains how his childhood appreciation and vision of religion have changed now that he is an adult, and he clearly expresses regret over that change. Use listing or focused freewriting to describe your childhood vision of an important aspect of your life and explain how that vision has changed now that you are an adult. You need not focus on religion; you can focus on your ideas about education, sports, marriage, or your family, for example.

3. Easter is the most important of Christian holidays. Use one of the information-gathering techniques explained in Getting Started to record information about ceremonies, rituals, prayers, or other observances used in the celebration of a holiday that is important to you. Note that this does not have to be a religious holiday.

4.9d What the Gossips Saw

Author Biography

A native of New Mexico, **_Leo Romero_** is among a growing number of contemporary Southwestern U.S. writers whose poetry and fiction are becoming popular across the country. Romero studied at the University of New Mexico, where he took a degree in English. His poems have appeared in several collections of poetry and prose. "What the Gossips Saw" was first published in 1981 in a collection of his poetry called _Agua Negra_.

Preparing to Read

1. This is the story of the community's response to a woman who had her leg amputated. It says a great deal about the way society sometimes reacts to those of us who are different, and it can be compared with other selections such as Adreinne Schwartz's "The Colossus in the Kitchen" (Chapter 7).

2. Romero chooses to leave out periods and other end marks. Doing so can help a poet create dramatic effects. Nonetheless, college writers should always use such punctuation in essays and other academic writing.

Vocabulary

alluring (adjective)   Appealing, tempting.

conjecture (noun)   Guess, speculation.

hobble (verb)   Limp.

in cohorts (adjective)   In league with, cooperating with.

murmur (verb)   Mumble, speak very softly.

What the Gossips Saw

Leo Romero

Everyone pitied Escolastica, her leg
had swollen like a watermelon in the summer
It had practically happened over night
She was seventeen, beautiful and soon
to be married to Guillermo who was working   5
in the mines at Terreros, eighty miles away
far up in the mountains, in the wilderness
Poor Escolastica, the old women would say
on seeing her hobble to the well with a bucket
carrying her leg as if it were the weight   10
of the devil, surely it was a curse from heaven
for some misdeed, the young women who were
jealous would murmur, yet they were grieved too
having heard that the doctor might cut
her leg, one of a pair of the most perfect legs   15
in the valley, and it was a topic of great
interest and conjecture among the villagers
whether Guillermo would still marry her
if she were crippled, a one-legged woman—
as if life weren't hard enough for a woman   20
with two legs—how could she manage

Guillermo returned and married Escolastica
even though she had but one leg, the sound
of her wooden leg pounding down the wooden aisle
stayed in everyone's memory for as long   25
as they lived, women cried at the sight
of her beauty, black hair so dark
that the night could get lost in it, a face
more alluring than a full moon

Escolastica went to the dances with her husband   30
and watched and laughed but never danced
though once she had been the best dancer
and could wear holes in a pair of shoes
in a matter of a night, and her waist had been
as light to the touch as a hummingbird's flight   35
And Escolastica bore five children, only half
what most women bore, yet they were healthy
In Escolastica's presence, no one would mention
the absence of her leg, though she walked heavily
And it was not long before the gossips   40
spread their poison, that she must be in cohorts
with the devil, had given him her leg
for the power to bewitch Guillermo's heart
and cloud his eyes so that he could not see
what was so clear to them all   45

Read More on the Web

You can read more about Leo Romero and his work on the web.

- Biographical Notes on Leo Romero: http://bvtlab.com/73Dcm

- *Aqua Negra* (click Download button): http://bvtlab.com/Q2769

Questions for Discussion

1. What is Romero trying to tell us about gossip? In other words, what is his central idea?

2. Identify examples of concrete language. Then find examples of vivid verbs and adjectives.

3. The author creates two images (pictures in words) in the second stanza (verse paragraph) of this poem. What are these images, and why does Romero include them?

4. Where in this poem does Romero use simile? What other figures of speech does he use?

5. The poem takes place in a village where life is hard. Why is it important for us to know that?

6. How do the gossips explain Guillermo's marrying Escolastica even after she loses her leg? What does this say about the gossips?

7. The gossips believe Guillermo "could not see / what was so clear to them all." What does Guillermo see that they don't?

8. What can we conclude about the gossips' opinion of men in general?

Thinking Critically

1. Many of us know people like the gossips. Do such people deserve blame or pity? Are they malicious or just ignorant? Make a list of similes or metaphors that might help describe such people.

2. Adrienne Schwartz's "Colossus in the Kitchen," an essay in Chapter 7, shows that bad luck can be mistaken by small-minded people as a sign of God's punishment for sinning. Where does this theme appear in Romero's poem? Make notes in the margins to identify this theme.

Suggestions for Journal Entries

1. Think of a person or an event that was the subject of gossip in your school or community. Use listing or another method for gathering details discussed in Getting Started to explain how much the gossips exaggerated, twisted, or lied about the facts. Try to show how they changed the truth to make the story seem more sensational, startling, racy, or horrible than it was.

2. Do you agree that not all communities react badly to people who are different? If so, provide evidence from personal experience, newspapers, or other sources to support this idea. For example, talk about how quickly people in your city responded when they heard a neighbor needed expensive medical care, or explain how well students at your school accept newcomers from other cultures.

4.10 Suggestions for Sustained Writing

1. Read the journal notes you made after completing Louis Gonzalez's "Music." If you responded to either or both of the Suggestions for Journal Entries, you have a good start on an essay that will discuss an obsession of your own.

   Begin with an introduction that, like Gonzalez's, explains the extent to which you are committed to a particular pursuit, idea, study, activity, hobby, art form, or sport. Then go on to explain how this obsession developed in you. End your essay by looking to the future or by using any of the other types of conclusions discussed in Chapter 3.

   As always, remember that one draft is never enough. When you write your second draft, include concrete and specific nouns and adjectives. Add vivid verbs, adjectives, and adverbs. When you revise this draft, try to add figures of speech like those discussed in this chapter. Then, revise your third draft to improve organization, sentence structure, and grammar. The final step is, of course, to edit and proofread your work carefully.

2. Hayden's "Those Winter Sundays" praises a man who demonstrates his love for others. If you responded to the second journal suggestion after this poem, you made a list of the "offices" (activities, tasks, or services) that someone you know performs to show his or her love.

   Focus on at least three "offices" that mean the most to you, and expand your discussion into an essay that proves how much this person does for others. Begin with a preliminary thesis that expresses your feelings about your subject, but remember that you can revise this statement after you write your first draft.

   Limit each body paragraph to only one of the offices in your list. Develop these paragraphs by using methods explained in Chapter 2, such as narration, process analysis, conclusion and support, or illustration. Whatever you decide, follow Hayden's lead and use language that is concrete, specific, and vivid. Take the opportunity to improve word choice when you revise the first and second drafts of your paper. This is also a good time to create figures of speech that will help make your writing even more powerful.

   Don't skimp on the introduction and conclusion to your essay. Try using the techniques you read about in Chapter 3. As always, edit and proofread your revised essay carefully before you submit it to your instructor.

3. Read the notes you made in response to the second of the Suggestions for Journal Entries after Pickering's "Faith of the Father." Then write an essay that explains how your childhood vision of an important aspect of your life has changed. As noted earlier, you need not focus on religion. Instead you might discuss how your ideas about marriage, your family, or education, for instance, have changed.

   You can divide the body of your paper into two parts: The first might talk about your view of the subject when you were younger; the second might discuss your current view. In any case, try to include as many concrete details as possible and make an effort to use figures of speech.

   After writing a rough draft of the body of your paper, draft an introductory and concluding paragraph by using one of the methods discussed in Chapter 3. Like Pickering, make your introduction colorful so as to invite readers to continue into the body of the paper. Incidentally, when you conclude, you might want to leave the reader with a clear understanding of how you feel about this change in vision. Are you happy about it? Or, does it cause you some distress or anxiety? Do you believe you have gained something? Or, like Pickering, do you believe you have lost something?

4. Read the notes you made in response to the third of the Suggestions for Journal Entries after Pickering's "Faith of the Father." Use this information to start an essay in which you describe a ritual, ceremony, or other observance to celebrate a holiday that is important to you. Use information from personal observation and develop your discussion with details that are vivid, concrete, and specific.

Rely heavily on descriptive details and, like Pickering, use effective anecdotes to get your reader to experience the holiday just as you have. Use dialogue if appropriate. Dialogue is made up of quoted statements that someone (including yourself) has spoken and that you remember. For example, in paragraph 3 of Pickering's essay, we learn that, when hearing that his mother-in-law's tombstone had "Gone to Jesus" written on it, a certain man exclaimed, "Poor Jesus!" Like Pickering, make sure that this quoted material helps develop or clarify the ritual or ceremony you are describing.

5. In "What the Gossips Saw," Leo Romero shows that gossips can exaggerate or twist a story so badly that, in their mouths, the truth becomes unrecognizable. If you responded to the first of the journal prompts after Romero's poem, read your notes. Then, draft an essay that tells what happened when gossips spread rumors about a person or event in your school or community.

As with other assignments, you can organize your thoughts in several different ways. For example, you might start by revealing the truth of a story and then explaining—step-by-step—how the gossips distorted it. Or you might recall how false rumors began, how they spread, and how they affected people. A good way to end this story is to tell the truth as you know it.

Whichever approach you choose, rewrite the paper several times. In your second and subsequent drafts, try to include figures of speech—simile, metaphor, and/or personification—to describe people, motives, places, and events and to give your writing greater variety and interest. Doing so will also make your writing more convincing.

Finally, explain what observing or experiencing the effects of gossip taught you about it and about the people who spread it. The best place to do this is in the paper's introduction or conclusion.

ACKNOWLEDGMENTS

Didion, Joan. "Rock of Ages." *Slouching Towards Bethlehem: Essays*, Open Road Integrated Media, 2017. Copyright 1968 by Joan Didion. First published in the United States by Farrar, Straus and Giroux in 1968.

Hayden, Robert. "Those Winter Sundays." *Collected Poems of Robert Hayden*, ed. Frederick Glaysher. Liveright Publishing, 1966. Copyright © 1966 by Robert Hayden. Used by permission of Liveright Publishing Corporation.

Hughes, Langston. "Harlem [2]." *The Collected Poems of Langston Hughes*, edited by Arnold Rempersad with David Roessel, associate editor. Copyright © 1994 by the Estate of Langston Hughes. Used by permission of Alfred A. Knopf, an imprint of the Knopf Doubleday Publishing Group, a division of Penguin Random House LLC. All rights reserved.

"I Have a Dream," by Martin Luther King., Jr. Copyright 1963 Martin Luther King Jr., copyright renewed 1991 Coretta Scott King. Reprinted by arrangement with The Heirs to the Estate of Martin Luther King Jr., c/o Writers House as agent for the proprietor New York, NY.

Kozol, Jonathan. *Illiterate America*. Anchor Press/Doubleday, 1985. Copyright © 1986 Plume.

Lemann, Nicholas. "The Origins of the Underclass." *The Atlantic Monthly*, July 1986. Copyright 1986 by Nicholas Lemann.

Laurence, Margaret. "Where the World Began." *Heart of a Stranger*, University of Alberta Press, June 2003.

Moon, William Least Heat. *Blue Highways*. Little, Brown and Company, 1982. Copyright © 1999, Back Bay Books.

Pickering, Samuel. "Faith of the Father." *Still Life*, University Press of New England, 1991. Copyright © 1991 University Press of New England, Lebanon NH. Reprinted with permission.

Romero, Leo. "What the Gossips Saw." *Agua Negra*, Ahsahta Press, 1981. Copyright © 1981 by Leo Romero. Reprinted with the permission of The Permissions Company, Inc., on behalf of Ahsahta Press, ahsahtapress.org.

White, E. B. "Once More to the Lake." *One Man's Meat*, Harper & Brothers, 1944. Copyright © 1941, Tilbury House Publishers.

Shutterstock

Chapter 5

Sentence Structure:
Creating Emphasis
and Variety

Chapter Outline

5.1 Emphasis

Communicating ideas clearly often demands the ability to emphasize or stress one idea over another. By arranging words in a sentence carefully, you can emphasize certain ideas and direct your readers' attention to the heart of your message.

A good way to emphasize an idea is to express it in a short, simple sentence of its own. But you will never develop your writing skills if you use such sentences all the time. Even the shortest writing projects require sentences containing two or more ideas. In some cases, these ideas will be equally important; in others, one idea will need to be emphasized over the other (or others).

5.1a Create Emphasis Through Coordination

Ideas of equal importance can be expressed in the same sentence by using coordination. Take this sentence, which coordinates (makes equal) three words in a series: *fed, cured,* and *sheltered*.

> Mother Teresa *fed* the hungry, *cured* the sick, and *sheltered* the homeless.

You can also use coordination to join two or more main clauses if you want to give them equal **emphasis**. A main clause contains a subject and verb, and it expresses a complete idea, even when it stands alone. You can join main clauses with a comma and a coordinating conjunction; the coordinating conjunctions are *and, but, for, nor, or, so,* and *yet.* (One way to remember the coordinating conjunctions is to use the acronym *FANBOYS*: F = *for*, A = *and*, etc.) What results from this combination is a *compound sentence.*

The following compound sentences contain a comma followed by a coordinating conjunction:

> Asteroids are smaller than planets, *and* meteorites are smaller than asteroids.

> Some people think that the navigator John Cabot was English, *but* he was Italian.

> I floss my teeth daily, *for* I want to avoid gum disease.

> Switzerland did not fight in World War II, *nor* did Spain.

> Modern drugs can perform miracles, *or* they can destroy lives.

> The area was contaminated, *so* the medical examiners wore protective clothing.

Another way to coordinate (make equal) main clauses is to join them with a semicolon:

> Methane is hard to detect; it is an odorless, colorless gas.

> Officially, there are only eight planets; Pluto is a dwarf planet.

5.1b Create Emphasis Through Subordination

The sentences above contain main ideas that are equal in importance. But what if you decide that one idea in a sentence is more important than the other? You can create emphasis through **subordination** by putting the other idea into a phrase or a subordinate clause, thereby making it less important than the first. A phrase is a group of words without a subject and verb; a subordinate clause contains a subject and verb but, unlike a main clause, it does not express a complete idea. Say you wrote these sentences:

> Some dinosaurs were over 80 feet long, and they weighed almost 75 tons.

> Most dinosaurs were cold-blooded, but a few were warm-blooded.

emphasis
The placing of stress on important ideas by controlling sentence structure through coordination, subordination, and parallelism.

subordination
A technique used to emphasize one idea over another by expressing the more important idea in the sentence's main clause and the other in its subordinate clause.

You might revise them by subordinating one idea to the other in each sentence:

Weighing almost 75 tons, some dinosaurs were over 80 feet long.
(The first idea has been put into a phrase)

Although most dinosaurs were cold-blooded, a few were warm-blooded.
(The first idea has been put into a subordinate clause)

Three ways to create phrases and subordinate clauses are to use (1) participles, (2) relative pronouns, and (3) subordinating conjunctions.

1. **Participles** are adjectives formed from verbs; like other adjectives, they describe nouns and pronouns. Participles can end in *-ing, -ed, -d, -n,* or *-t*. Each of the following sentences has been revised by turning one if its main clauses into phrase that begins with a participle:

   Original: Matt earned his doctorate in Indian history, and he is teaching at NYU.
   (Sentence contains two ideas of equal importance.)

   Revised: Having earned his doctorate in Indian history, Matt is teaching at NYU.
   (One idea is expressed in a phrase beginning with the participle *having*. It is less important than the other idea, which remains in a main clause.)

   Original: Many Midwest farmers were ruined by the long drought of the 1930s, so they gave up their land and moved to California.
   (Sentence contains two ideas of equal importance.)

   Revised: Ruined by the long drought of the 1930s, many Midwest farmers moved to California.
   (One idea is expressed in a phrase beginning with the participle *ruined*. It is less important than the other idea, which remains in a main clause.)

2. **Subordinating conjunctions** are words like *after, as, because, even though, if, since, unless, until,* and *while*. They can be used to turn a main clause into a subordinate clause.

   Original: The French military leader Joan of Arc was condemned as a witch, so she was burned at the stake.
   (Ideas are equally important.)

   Revised: Because she had been condemned as a witch, the French military leader Joan of Arc was burned at the stake.
   (The second idea, expressed in a main clause is emphasized. The first idea is now in a subordinate clause, which begins with *Because*.)

3. **Relative pronouns**—*who, whom, whose, that,* and *which*—can also be used to subordinate one idea to another. Subordinate clauses beginning with relative pronouns describe nouns in the sentence's main clause.

   Original: We visited Newgrange, a prehistoric site in Ireland; it is said to predate the Egyptian pyramids.
   (Sentence has two main clauses.)

   Revised: We visited Newgrange, a prehistoric site in Ireland, which is said to predate the Egyptian pyramids.
   (Sentence begins with a main clause, followed by a subordinate clause beginning with *which*.)

Original: James Madison was the fourth president of the United States, but he is also remembered as the "master builder" of the U.S. Constitution.
(Sentence has two main clauses)

Revised: James Madison, who was the fourth president of the United States, is also remembered as the "master builder" of the U.S. Constitution.
(Note that the subordinate clause, introduced by *who*, comes in the middle of the sentence.)

5.1c Create Emphasis by Using Periodic Sentences

You can create emphasis by putting the strongest or most important word or idea at the end of the sentence. Such sentences are called *periodic* because the emphasis comes just before the period. Here are three examples:

The Bible claims Methuselah lived 969 years!

India, where over half a billion people have the right to vote, is the world's largest democracy.

Zora Neale Hurston is remembered not for her work in anthropology, the field in which she was trained, but for her novels.

5.1d Create Emphasis by Using a Colon

A colon can be used in place of a semicolon in a compound sentence when the second main clause explains the first. The effect is similar to the one created by a periodic sentence.

Nitrous oxide is called "laughing gas" for good reason: when used as an anesthesia for dental patients, it creates in them a sense of happiness and well-being.

5.1e Create Emphasis by Using the Active or Passive Voice

Sentences that use the *active voice* contain subjects—persons, places, or things—that perform an action. Sentences that use the *passive voice* contain subjects that are acted upon. Notice how the structure of a sentence changes when it is put into the passive voice.

Active: Gabriel García Márquez won the Nobel Prize for literature in 1982.

Passive: The Nobel Prize for literature was won by Gabriel García Márquez in 1982.

Generally, using the active voice makes it easier to stress the subject of a sentence. For instance, if you wanted to report that the president of your college announced her decision to resign, you wouldn't use the passive voice by writing, "Her decision to resign was announced by President Green." The active voice works better: "President Green announced her decision to resign."

However, there are times when using the passive voice can create emphasis. In some cases, you might decide that the receiver of an action is more important than the person place, or thing completing the action. For example:

Franklin Roosevelt was elected president of the United States four times.

is more emphatic than

The citizens of the United States elected Franklin Roosevelt president four times.

Sometimes, in fact, you might not know who is responsible for an action, so you will have to use the passive voice:

> Windows were smashed, books were scattered across the room, and furniture was torn to shreds.

5.1f Create Emphasis by Repeating Key Words and Phrases

Repeating important words and phrases, carefully and sparingly, can help stress important ideas over those that need less emphasis. In his inaugural address in 1961, President John F. Kennedy gave special meaning to his plans for the nation when he said:

> All this will not be *finished* in the first one hundred days. *Nor* will it be *finished* in the first one thousand days, *nor* in the life of this administration, *nor* even perhaps in our lifetime on this planet. But let us begin.

Dr. Martin Luther King Jr. used repetition to communicate a sense of urgency about civil rights in "I Have a Dream," a speech delivered to a massive audience at the Lincoln Memorial in 1963.

> *Now is the time* to make real the promises of democracy. *Now is the time* to rise from the dark and desolate valley of segregation to the sunlit path of racial justice. *Now is the time* to lift our nation from the quicksands of racial injustice to the solid rock of brotherhood. *Now is the time* to make justice a reality for all of Gods' children.

5.1g Create Emphasis Through Parallelism

> We the people of the United States, in Order to *form* a more perfect union, *establish* Justice, *insure* domestic Tranquility, *provide* for the common Defence, *promote* the general Welfare, and *secure* the Blessings of Liberty to ourselves and our Posterity, do ordain and establish this Constitution of the United States of America.

What you have just read begins the U.S. Constitution; it is one of the best-known sentences in American history. One reason it is so powerful and memorable is that it uses six phrases (listing the reasons for establishing the Constitution) that follow the same pattern—a verb followed by a direct object. Repeating patterns is known as **parallelism**.

Parallelism is a way to connect a series of facts and ideas of equal importance, thereby giving them added emphasis. Sentences that are parallel list items in the same grammatical form. This paragraph from Adlai Stevenson's eulogy of Winston Churchill, the great British prime minister, does just that:

> The voice that led nations, raised armies, inspired victories, and blew fresh courage into the hearts of men is silenced. We shall hear no longer the remembered eloquence and wit, the old courage and defiance, the robust serenity of indomitable faith. Our world is thus poorer, our political dialogue is diminished, and the sources of public inspiration run more thinly in all of us. There is a lonesome place against the sky.

In the first sentence, Stevenson placed equal emphasis on Churchill's accomplishments by expressing each through a verb followed by a direct object: "led nations," "raised armies," "inspired victories," and "blew fresh courage into the hearts of men." He created parallelism in the second sentence in a series of adjectives and nouns that describe Churchill's best qualities: "the remembered eloquence and wit," "the old courage and defiance," and "the robust serenity of indomitable faith." In the third sentence, he explained the effects of Churchill's death in a series of main clauses: "Our world is thus poorer," "our political dialogue is diminished," and "the sources of public inspiration run more thinly in all of us."

parallelism
A method of expressing facts and ideas of equal importance in the same sentence, thereby giving them added emphasis. Sentences that are parallel express items of equal importance in the same grammatical form.

Consistency is the key to making sentences parallel by expressing every idea in a list in the same grammatical form. Without a doubt, the eulogy you just read would have sounded awkward and been less emphatic had Stevenson written that Churchill's voice "led nations, raised armies, inspired victories, and it blew fresh courage into the hearts of men." The first three items are verbs followed by objects; the fourth is a main clause.

Here are three other examples of how parallelism creates emphasis:

The president enjoys *reading* mystery novels, *fishing* in Maine, and *speaking* with young people.

(The sentence contains gerunds, or nouns formed from verbs by adding -*ing*; gerunds show activity.)

To *master* the piano, to *compose* beautiful music, and to *lead* a symphony orchestra seemed to be her destiny.

(The sentence contains infinitives, which are formed by placing *to* before the present tense of the verb. Infinitives act as nouns, adjectives, or adverbs.)

They vowed to battle the invaders on the land, on the sea, and in the air.

(The sentence contains prepositional phrases; a preposition is a short word—such as *at*, *in*, or *on*—that shows the relationship of a noun or pronoun to the rest of the sentence.)

5.2 Variety

One sure way to make your readers lose interest in what you have to say—no matter how important—is to ignore the need for variety. Good writers try not to repeat vocabulary monotonously, and they vary the length and structure of their sentences whenever possible.

5.2a Create Variety by Changing Sentence Length

A steady diet of long, complicated sentences is sure to put your readers to sleep. On the other hand, relying solely on short, choppy sentences can make your writing seem disconnected and even childish. Therefore, one of the most important things to remember about the sentences you write is to vary their length. You can do this by combining some of them into longer, more complex units and by leaving others short and to the point.

Reread the passage from President Kennedy's inaugural address in section 5.1f. One reason it holds our interest is that it contains sentences of different lengths. The last of these leaves a lasting impression, not simply because it comes at the end but also because it is so much shorter than the others and carries a special punch.

You can combine two or three short sentences into a longer unit in three ways: coordination, subordination, or compounding.

coordination

A technique used to express ideas of equal importance in the same sentence. To this end, writers often use compound sentences, which are composed of two independent (main) clauses connected with a coordinating conjunction. "Four students earned scholarships, but only three accepted them" is a compound sentence.

Coordination

Coordination is useful if you want to write a longer sentence in which all the main ideas receive equal emphasis. The easiest way to do this is to combine sentences with a comma and the appropriate coordinating conjunction or to use a semicolon, as explained in section 5.1a.

Subordination

As you know, subordination lets you combine two or more sentences to emphasize one idea over another. It also helps you vary sentence length and make your writing more interesting. Say you've just written:

> I had been waiting at the bus stop for twenty minutes. The afternoon air was hot, thick, and humid. I became uncomfortable and soon began to perspire. I wished I were home. I thought about getting under the shower, cooling off, and relaxing. My day at work had been long and hard. I looked up from the newspaper I was reading. I saw a huge truck, which sped by and covered me with exhaust. I prayed the bus would come soon.

As you reread this paragraph, you realize that you haven't emphasized your most important ideas and that your style is choppy and monotonous. Therefore, you decide to rewrite by combining sentences through subordination (you can review ways to do this by rereading section 5.1b).

> I had been waiting at the bus stop for twenty minutes. Because the afternoon air was hot, thick, and humid, I became uncomfortable and soon began to perspire. Wishing I were home, I thought about getting under the shower, cooling off, and relaxing. My day at work had been long and hard. As I looked up from the newspaper I was reading, I saw a huge truck, which sped by and covered me with exhaust. I prayed the bus would come soon.

In combining some sentences, you've made your writing smoother and more interesting because you've created sentences of different lengths. What's more, some ideas have gained emphasis.

Compounding

Compounding involves putting subjects (nouns and pronouns), verbs, adjectives, and adverbs together in the same sentence as long as they relate to one another logically.

Sometimes, ideas that are very similar seem awkward and boring if expressed in separate sentences—for example: "Egbert has been transferred to Minneapolis. Rowena has also been transferred to that city." Notice how much more interesting these short sentences become when you combine their subjects: "Egbert and Rowena have been transferred to Minneapolis." Here are a few more examples:

> **Original:** The doctor rushed into the emergency room. She went immediately to a patient who had been stung by wasps.
> **Compound verb:** The doctor rushed into the emergency room and went immediately to a patient who had been stung by wasps.

> **Original:** Grieving over the loss of her child, the woman wept openly. She wept uncontrollably.
> **Compound adverb:** Grieving over the loss of her child, the woman wept openly and uncontrollably.

5.2b Create Variety by Changing Sentence Patterns

Complete sentences contain a subject and verb, and they express a complete idea. Most also contain modifiers, such as adjectives, adverbs, and prepositional phrases, as well as other elements. However, there is no rule that a sentence must begin with a subject followed immediately by a verb. Depending upon your purpose, you can create as many patterns as you need to make your writing interesting and effective.

Begin with an Adverb

Adverbs modify (describe) verbs, adjectives, or other adverbs. They help explain *how, how much, when, where, what kind of,* or *why*. Most, but not all, adverbs end in *-ly*. The following sentences begin with adverbs or groups of words that act as adverbs:

> *Near ancient Thebes*, monuments to the pharaohs glisten in the sun.

> *Seldom* was the old mansion visited by tourists.

> *Brightly* blazed the signal fires across the harbor.

Note that you could also have written "The signal fires blazed brightly across the harbor," but putting adverbs at the beginning of a sentence once in a while makes for variety.

Begin with an Infinitive or a Gerund

An infinitive is the present tense of a verb with the word *to* in front of it. Infinitives acting as nouns can make good sentence openers.

> *To study* archaeology was her childhood dream.

> *To defend* unpopular ideas takes courage.

> *To call* him a coward is unfair.

Note that you could have written, "It is unfair to call him a coward," but beginning with the infinitive works just as well.

A gerund is a noun that is made from a verb by adding *-ing*. Gerunds name activities.

> *Reading* the works of Mark Twain is his favorite way to relax.

> *Measuring* the height of a heavenly body is the purpose of a sextant.

> *Preventing* global warming is the goal of many environmentalists.

Begin with a Preposition or Prepositional Phrase

Prepositions connect or show relationships between nouns or pronouns and the rest of a sentence. Prepositional phrases contain a preposition, a noun or pronoun, and any words that modify the noun or pronoun.

> *Among* the best and oldest rock groups are the Rolling Stones.

> *With* malice toward none, *with* charity for all, *with* firmness in the right as God gives us to see the right, let us strive on to finish the work we are in. (Abraham Lincoln)

> *Before* the line of worshippers walked a Mayan priest.

Note that you could also have written, "A Mayan priest walked before the line of worshippers."

Begin or End with a Participle or Participial Phrase

A participle is a verb turned into an adjective. Many end in *-ed, -en, -ing,* or *-t*. A participial phrase is a group of words containing a participle.

> *Exhausted*, the soldiers fell asleep without bothering to eat.

> *Swollen* because of torrential rains, the Mississippi River overflowed its banks.

Directing the fortunes of Florence for more than three centuries, the Medici were once the most powerful family in Europe.

Bent nearly double, the birch trees were covered with snow and ice.

In AD 79, Mt. Vesuvius erupted violently, *spewing* lava and ash over the Bay of Naples and *destroying* the cities of Pompeii and Herculaneum.

The earthquake victims wept openly, their lives *destroyed*.

Use an Appositive

An appositive is a word or phrase that renames or describes a noun that comes before it.

Greenland, *a semi-independent region of Denmark*, lies northeast of Canada.

Insisting that the company not sell contaminated food earned the supervisor a written reprimand, *her badge of honor.*

Ask a Rhetorical Question

You learned in chapters 2 and 3 that asking a question is a good way to begin a paragraph or essay. A rhetorical question—one to which the answer is obvious—can also create emphasis and variety. Take this example from a 2005 end-of-the-year column by humorist Dave Barry:

> [In] November, Americans find themselves heatedly debating a difficult question: Is it truly in the nation's best interests for its citizens to be fighting, and suffering heavy casualties, to achieve the elusive goal of buying a laptop computer marked down to $300 at Wal-Mart the day after Thanksgiving?

On a more serious note, President Ronald Reagan used a series of rhetorical questions in a 1983 speech to emphasize his point that sexuality must be seen as something "sacred," to be governed by deep moral convictions:

> No one seems to mention morality as playing a part in the subject of sex. Is all of Judeo-Christian tradition wrong? Are we to believe that something so sacred can be looked upon as a purely physical thing with no potential for emotional and psychological harm? And isn't it the parents' right to give counsel and advice to keep their children from making mistakes that may affect their entire lives?

5.2c Create Variety by Using a Colon

Use a Colon After an Independent Clause to Introduce Information That Names or Explains Something in That Clause

Such information can be expressed in a word or phrase, a list of words, or even a sentence.

Word: Cardiology treats an essential organ: the heart!
(*Heart* names the *organ.*)

List: During thirteen years in the White House, Franklin D. Roosevelt had three vice-presidents: Garner, Wallace, and Truman.
(*Garner, Wallace,* and *Truman* name the *vice-presidents.*)

Sentence: Princeton, New Jersey, is a hub of intellectual activity: it is home to Princeton University, the Institute for Advanced Study, and numerous research centers.
(The sentence after the colon explains *intellectual activity.*)

Use a Colon to Introduce a Quotation

Using a colon is a good way to introduce someone else's words and at the same time use a different sentence pattern. Let's say you wanted to quote from President Kennedy's inaugural address. You might write:

> Today we would do well to remember JFK's exhortations to his fellow Americans: "Ask not what your country can do for you—ask what you can do for your country."

5.2d Create Variety by Using Parentheses

There are three major uses for parentheses when creating variety.

1. To set off an explanatory sentence within or immediately following another sentence—ordinarily, material within the parentheses is less important than material that is not in parentheses.

    Mary Queen of Scots (she was the daughter of King James V of Scotland) became queen upon the death of her father, only six days after her birth.

    The university just opened a modern art museum. (It houses only ten paintings, but the trustees are trying to raise money to buy more.)

2. To enclose a brief definition

    The children learned to construct an anemometer (instrument for measuring wind speed) from the Franklin Institute's website.

3. To set off words that clarify or specify

    The leaders of Nazi Germany and the Soviet Union (Hitler and Stalin) made a pact with the devil.

5.2e Create Variety by Using a Dash

Create a dash by typing two hyphens, but do not include a space between the dash and the words that come before and after it. A dash can be used to emphasize, expand upon, or explain information earlier in the sentence and to signal a shift in meaning or tone.

Emphasis: Every employee of the company—from the president to the janitor—must now pay his or her own health insurance premiums.

Expansion: Three Supreme Court justices—Scalia, O'Connor, and Kennedy—were nominated by President Reagan.

Explanation: Paying your $1,000 in parking fines beats the alternative—spending a week in the workhouse.

Shift: He made his fortune in two years—and lost it in two days.

5.3 Visualizing Sentence Structure

To see how some of the principles you have just learned work in professional writing, read these paragraphs from Pete Hamill's autobiography, *A Drinking Life*. Comments in the left margin explain how Hamill created emphasis. Those in the right column discuss variety. Hamill is writing about World War II.

<u>Emphasis</u>   <u>Variety</u>

Colon introduces list
explaining "Special way."

Repeats "our" for emphasis,
parallelism.

> We lived in the rhythms of the war. Years later, we even marked time in a special way: Before the War, During the War, After the War. The war was in our comics, our movies, our dreams.

Varies sentence length.

> The radio was filled with it. Every evening, my mother listened to Edward R. Murrow and

Follows a simple sentence
with a compound sentence.

Emphasizes by
segmenting sentence.

> Gabriel Heatter, and in school we followed the war on maps. There was North Africa. And Tobruk. And somewhere in all that yellow emptiness El Alamein.

> At Holy Name, I heard about the war from new teachers every year, each of them rolling down the maps and showing us the places that

Ends sentence with
participial phrases.

Subordinates one idea
to another.

> were in the newspapers and on the radio. There was so much excitement when the Allies landed in Sicily because the parents of most of the Italian kids were from that island. They wanted

Follows long sentence with
short one.

Coordinates two equally
important ideas.

> the Americans to win. They had brothers in our army, and some of the brothers died in those first battles. All of them said their parents were

Follows simple sentence
with compound sentence.

Creates emphasis
through repetition.

> worried. I got an aunt there, said Vito Pinto. My grandmother is there, said Michael Tempesta. I got an uncle over there, said George Poli. The war went on and on.

5.4 Revising to Create Variety and Emphasis

Read these two versions of paragraphs from Alice Wnorowski's "A Longing," which appears later in this chapter. Although the rough draft is correct, Wnorowski knew that revising it would allow her to give important ideas the appropriate emphasis and to bring variety to her writing.

Wnorowski—Rough Draft, Paragraphs 3 and 4

Vary length?

> The morning dew chilled my naked feet. I stopped on the sandy lane. From out of the corner of my eye, I suddenly caught a movement. Something was moving in the wide, open hay field that lay before me. Five deer, three does

Vary structure?

and two fawns, were grazing in the mist-filled dips of the roller-coaster landscape. I sat down in the damp earth to watch them. I got my white nightdress all brown and wet.

What is being emphasized in this one-sentence paragraph?

The deer casually strolled through the thigh-high grass, stopping every other step to dip their heads into the growth and pop them back up again with long, tender timothy stems dangling from the sides of their mouths.

Too long?

Wnorowski—Final Draft, Paragraphs 3 and 4

Combines sentences through coordination, subordination, and compounding.

The morning dew chilled my naked feet, and I stopped on the sandy lane. From out of the corner of my eye, I suddenly caught a movement in the wide, open hay field that lay before me. In the mist-filled dips of the roller-coaster landscape grazed five deer: three does and two fawns. I sat down in the damp earth to watch them and got my white nightdress all brown and wet.

Creates variety by reversing subject and verb. Uses colon to introduce list.

Divides paragraph into two sentences; emphasizes both ideas.

The deer casually strolled along through the thigh-high grass, stopping every other step to dip their heads into the growth and pop them back up again. Long, tender timothy stems dangled from the sides of their mouths.

5.5 Practicing Combining Sentences

The two paragraphs below lack emphasis and variety because the sentences they contain are similar in length and structure. Use techniques explained in this chapter to rewrite the paragraphs in the spaces that follow them. Combine sentences, remove words, add details, choose new vocabulary, or make any other changes you wish in order to create more interesting and effective paragraphs.

Ramses II

Ramses II was a pharaoh [ruler] of Egypt. He lived approximately 3,300 years ago. He took the throne when he was only 24. He ruled for 66 years. He died at about age 90. He had a huge family. He had more than 100 children. He is thought to be the pharaoh when Moses led the Hebrews from bondage in Egypt. He is also remembered for his many important building projects. He was an industrious and resourceful king. He left his mark on the Egyptian landscape. He built temples and other magnificent monuments in every major city of his kingdom. His projects included expanding the famous temples at Karnak and at Luxor. He is buried in the Valley of the Kings. This place is near Luxor. Luxor used to be called Thebes.

_____

_____

_____

_____

_____

_____

_____

Trinity

The prefix *tri-* means "three." Traditional Christianity teaches that God exists in a trinity, three persons. These are the Father, the Son, and the Holy Spirit. Christianity is not the only religion that has a trinity. Hinduism also has a trinity. It is called the Trimurti. *Murti* means "shape" in Sanskrit. Sanskrit is the ancient language of India. Many classical religious and literary works are written in this language. The Hindu trinity has three members. They are Brahma, Vishnu, and Shiva. Brahma is the creator. Vishnu is the preserver. Shiva is the destroyer.

_____

_____

_____

_____

_____

_____

_____

5.6 Reading Selections

5.6a A Longing

Author Biography

"A Longing" is a tender, almost dreamlike recollection of a beautiful childhood experience that continues to haunt the author. *Alice Wnorowski* wrote this short essay in response to a freshman English assignment designed to help students learn to use concrete detail. However, it also illustrates several important principles about sentence structure discussed earlier in this chapter. Wnorowski began her studies at a community college. She has since earned a B.S. with honors in engineering.

Preparing to Read

1. You've learned that coordination can be used to create sentences in which two or more ideas receive equal emphasis and that subordination can be used to create sentences in which one idea is stressed over others. Look for examples of coordination and subordination in this essay.

2. The author puts variety into her writing by using techniques discussed earlier in this chapter. They include beginning sentences with an adverb and a prepositional phrase and using participles to vary sentence structure and length.

3. Remember what you learned in chapter 4 about using details, especially those that appeal to the five senses. Identify such details in "A Longing."

Vocabulary

acknowledge (verb)   Recognize.

conceived (verb)   Understood.

yearn (verb)   Desire, long for.

A Longing

Alice Wnorowski

An easy breeze pushed through the screen door, blowing into my open face and filling my nostrils with the first breath of morning. The sun beamed warm rays of white light onto my lids, demanding they lift and acknowledge the day's arrival.   1

Perched in the nearby woods, a bobwhite proudly shrieked to the world that he knew who he was. His song stirred deep feelings within me, and I was overcome by an urge to run barefoot through his woods. I jumped up so abruptly I startled the dog lying peacefully beside me. His sleepy eyes looked into mine questioningly, but I could give him no answer. I only left him bewildered, pushing through the front door and trotting down the grassy decline of the front lawn.   2

The morning dew chilled my naked feet, and I stopped on the sandy lane. From out of the corner of my eye, I suddenly caught a movement in the wide, open hay field that lay before me. In the mist-filled dips of the roller-coaster landscape grazed five deer: three does and two fawns. I sat down in the damp earth to watch them and got my white nightdress all brown and wet.   3

The deer casually strolled along through the thigh-high grass, stopping every other step to dip their heads into the growth and pop them back up again. Long, tender timothy stems dangled from the sides of their mouths.   4

The fawns were never more than two or three yards behind their mothers, and I knew a buck must not be far off in the woods, keeping lookout for enemies. Suddenly, a car sped along the adjacent road, disrupting the peace of the moment. The deer jumped up in terror and darted toward the trees. They took leaps, clearing eight to ten feet in a single bound. I watched their erect, white puffs of tails bounce up and down, until the darkness of the woods swallowed them up and I could see them no more.   5

I don't think that at the simple age of eleven I quite conceived what a rare and beautiful sight I had witnessed. Now, eight years later, I yearn to awaken to the call of a bobwhite and to run barefoot through the grass in search of him.   6

Read More on the Web

To learn more about writing about nature, have a look at these sites:

- Nature Writing for Readers and Writers: www.naturewriting.com
- Virginia Commonwealth University site on nature writing.

Questions for Discussion

1. Find a few examples of both coordination and subordination in this essay.

2. Identify some adverbs, prepositional phrases, and participles the author uses to create variety.

3. In which sentence are the normal position of the subject and verb reversed?

4. In paragraph 5, Wnorowski varies the length and structure of her sentences to make her writing more interesting. What methods discussed in this chapter does she use?

5. To which of our five senses do the details in this essay appeal?

6. What is the meaning of Wnorowski's title? Why is it appropriate?

7. What techniques does the writer use to maintain coherence in and between paragraphs?

Thinking Critically

1. This selection reveals as much about the writer as about the experience she recalls. From what you have just read, what can you say about Wnorowski's personality?

2. For anyone living in or near a rural area, seeing a family of wild animals is not an unusual event. Why, then, is such an event so special to the writer of this essay?

Suggestions for Journal Entries

1. Think back to an experience you would like to relive. Make a list of the things that made this experience memorable and that will explain why you have such "a longing" to relive it.

2. Use the brainstorming technique discussed in Getting Started to list details about a natural setting (for example, a meadow, mountain, or seashore) that you experienced recently or remember vividly.

5.6b **Why Does Everybody Hate Me?**

Introduction

This selection is a humor column published in the November 23, 2005, issue of *The Onion*, a satirical weekly newspaper. In this essay, an *Onion* staff writer makes Satan the speaker. In other words, he or she pretends to allow Satan to speak for himself. Doing so allows the author to explore the "soul" of a character thought by many to be the source of world evil. It also allows the author to use irony—a literary technique in which the speaker's meaning or beliefs are not what he or she says they are. Here, for example, Satan claims that he's "not that bad a guy!"

Preparing to Read

1. While this piece is predominantly humorous, there is also something serious about it. Look for this aspect of the author's message in the last paragraph.

2. Paragraph 3 makes reference to characters in the film *The Exorcist* (1973), based on the novel by William Peter Blatty. In this film, the devil has possessed a young girl. Her mother calls upon a Roman Catholic priest, who drives the devil out through a religious ritual known as an exorcism.

Vocabulary

acolytes (noun)   Followers, servants.

despoiler (noun)   Robber, pillager.

defiler (noun)   Polluter, fouler, someone who makes things unclean.

corporeal (adjective)   Material, physical.

embodiment (noun)   Physical representation.

entity (noun)   Thing, unit.

fallibility (noun)   Weakness, imperfection.

firmament (noun)   Heavens, sky.

inherent (adjective)   Inborn.

levitate (verb)   Raise.

mewling (adjective)   Whimpering, crying.

receptacle (noun)   Container, vessel.

reviled (adjective)   Hated, detested.

spawn (noun)   Offspring, seed.

suppurating (adjective)   Erupting, discharging puss.

visage (noun)   Face.

visceral (adjective)   Instinctive, emotional, from the gut.

Why Does Everybody Hate Me?

Satan

I've tried, I really have, but nothing ever goes right for me. Everywhere I go, it's the same thing: people talking about me like I'm not even there, saying how terrible I am. Telling other people not to walk in my path. Urging that I be shunned and reviled, and commanding me in the name of all that is holy to get myself behind them. I swear, sometimes it seems like everybody thinks I'm the worst entity in creation. | 1

I'm not that bad a guy, okay? I have my flaws, but I'll have you know I used to be considered quite the golden boy back in my day. Do you even know what the name Lucifer means? Depending on how it's translated, it can be "Bright and Shining One" or "Bringer of Light," or all kinds of pretty names. I'm telling you, I was the fairest star in the firmament once. The only reason I even got kicked out of Heaven in the first place is because I was more beautiful than God. | 2

Yeah, well, now look at me. I can't even possess a lousy 10-year-old girl without some geezer in a white collar screaming "The power of Christ compels you!" in my face and insisting that I leave immediately. Look, I just want to connect with a human being for a little while! Levitate a few beds, spin a couple necks around, have some deep, throaty laughs. Is that so wrong? Everybody treats me like some kind of lowlife just because I'm the symbolic embodiment of all the evil in the universe. | 3

Have you heard the things they call me? I can take a good-natured ribbing as much as the next guy, but some of these names are just so *mean*. Do you have any idea how it feels to be called the "Lord of Lies"? Ouch. Look, I may be mankind's greatest fears and weaknesses made flesh, but my feelings can get hurt just like anybody else's. "Prince of Darkness"? How would you feel if everybody called you the "Defiler," or the "Despoiler," or the "Unclean One"? It's not my fault that my terrifying visage erupts into suppurating boils when exposed to the holy light of truth and righteousness. It's hideous enough without people always needing to rub it in. | 4

I'll bet I'm the most despised and hated being in the whole wide world. I even wrote a poem about it once in my creative-writing class, but when I read it out loud, everybody just laughed at me. I only took that class to make friends, but even the biggest dorks there reacted to my very presence with visceral repulsion. I'm telling you, I felt like the lowest of the low. The only way I could get anyone to talk to me was by promising this one guy I'd make his stupid legal thrillers into bestsellers in exchange for his immortal soul. Now he's had a string of hit movie adaptations, and I'll bet I don't even hear word one from him until he shows up mewling and begging at the gateway to the underworld. | 5

Oh sure, there are the occasional few who want to be my acolytes, but come on. I mean, have you *seen* these people? They're plain *weird*. Sure, they say that the reason they're into me is because they're rejecting society's small-minded notions of petty morality and embracing a world where "do as thou wilt" shall be the whole of the law, but it's pretty obvious that they're really just mad that nobody else in the corporeal realm wants anything to do with them. | 6

. . .

And while we're on the subject of my mortal followers, don't believe a word you hear about all these so-called "spawn of Satan"—that phrase gets thrown around quite a bit, but believe you me, most women won't even come *near* me. I guess I've never really known how to show affection. But I have needs too, you know! I just wish I could meet a nice virgin half-goat woman who totally gets me. But every time I get involved with a receptacle for my seed, it always ends badly. | 7

The only person who understands me is my friend Gene. Sure, he knows I'm a mythical representation of all the tragic and self-defeating fallibility inherent in the human condition, but he doesn't judge me for it. Lately though, I hardly ever get to see him. Ever since he settled down, he's spending more and more time with his wife and kid. I know he's busy, but I miss him. He was an okay enough guy ... not quite evil enough for my tastes, maybe, but an okay guy all the same. | 8

Read More on the Web

To find more information relevant to this essay, visit the following websites:

- "Devil," Catholic Encyclopedia: http://bvtlab.com/K6s77

- "The Problem of Evil in World Religions," Ernest Valea: www.comparativereligion.com/evil.html

- History of Satan: www.allaboutgod.com/history-of-satan.htm

Questions for Discussion

1. In addition to making us laugh, what is the purpose of this essay?

2. Where and for what purpose does the author use a colon?

3. Find examples of parallel structure in this essay.

4. Identify one or two periodic sentences in this piece.

5. The essay makes ample use of rhetorical questions. Find at least three examples and explain why the author has included them.

6. Find examples of sentences that begin and end with participial phrases.

7. Where does the author use a dash? For what purpose?

8. Explain what techniques the author uses to create variety in paragraphs 5 and 6.

Thinking Critically

1. In the last paragraph, the author may be arguing that the devil is in all of us. Write a short paragraph that points to specific words and phrases to explain that idea.

2. Explain why the rhetorical question in paragraph 3 is ironic.

Suggestions for Journal Entries

1. Think about a historical figure who is seen as the representation of evil. Then read more about him or her in the library or on the Internet. Here are some people you might look up:

Idi Amin	Jack the Ripper
Attila the Hun	Kim Jong-un
Osama Bin Laden	Charles Manson
John Wilkes Booth	Mao Zedong
Roman Emperor Caligula	Joseph Mengele
Heinrich Himmler	Robert Mugabe
Adolph Hitler	Pol Pot
Saddam Hussein	Vlad III (Dracula)

Write a paragraph or two that, using what you have learned, summarizes the evil deeds of these villains.

Suggestions for Journal Entries *(Continued)*

2. The author of "Why Does Everybody Hate Me?" implies that the potential for evil exists in all of us. While few of us are truly evil, none of us is perfect. Reflect upon yourself and make a list of things that you need to do or to stop doing so as to make yourself more considerate, tolerant, caring, or morally responsible.

5.6c Gettysburg Address

Author Biography

Perhaps the best-loved U.S. president, ***Abraham Lincoln*** was a model of what a leader should be: decisive, principled, hardworking, and compassionate. He was also among the most eloquent of public speakers. His second inaugural address and Gettysburg Address are landmarks of American oratory. In November 1863, Lincoln visited Gettysburg, Pennsylvania, to dedicate a cemetery at the site of the Civil War's bloodiest battle. The turning point of the war, the Battle of Gettysburg had raged for four days and killed 50,000 Americans, both Union and Confederate, before Southern forces under General Robert E. Lee withdrew. Lincoln's Gettysburg Address is an eloquent and powerful statement of his belief that "all men are created equal"; of his grief over the death of his countrymen on both sides; and of his faith that "government of the people, by the people, for the people, shall not perish from the earth." Incidentally, Lincoln did not rely on a speechwriter; he composed the Gettysburg Address himself.

Preparing to Read

1. Note that Lincoln makes excellent use of repetition. One word in particular is used seven times in this short speech. Look for and underline it each time.

2. Lincoln begins with a reference to the past, moves to the present, and ends with the future. Such references help organize the speech. Read the speech once; then, reread it to spot these references.

3. Another technique used to hold this speech together and give it greater emphasis is parallelism. Look for examples of this technique throughout the Gettysburg Address.

4. In the last sentence, Lincoln describes a "great task remaining before us." Read this important sentence several times to make sure you understand it fully.

Vocabulary

conceived (verb)   Created.

consecrate (verb)   Bless.

dedicated (verb/adjective)   Set aside for a purpose, sometimes to honor or worship.

detract (verb)   Take away from, lessen, decrease.

hallow (verb)   Make holy or sacred, sanctify.

in vain (adjective)   For no reason or purpose.

measure (noun)   Amount.

proposition (noun)   Idea, principle.

resolve (verb)   Decide, determine.

Gettysburg Address

Abraham Lincoln

Four score and seven years ago our fathers brought forth on this continent a new nation, conceived in Liberty, and dedicated to the proposition that all men are created equal.   1

Now we are engaged in a great civil war, testing whether that nation, or any nation so conceived and so dedicated, can long endure. We are met on a great battlefield of that war. We have come to dedicate a portion of that field, as a final resting place for those who here gave their lives that that nation might live. It is altogether fitting and proper that we should do this.   2

But in a larger sense, we cannot dedicate—we cannot consecrate—we can not hallow—this ground. The brave men, living and dead, who struggled here, have consecrated it, far above our poor power to add or detract. The world will little note, nor long remember what we say here, but it can never forget what they did here. It is for us the living, rather, to be dedicated here to the unfinished work which they who fought here have thus far so nobly advanced. It is rather for us to be here dedicated to the great task remaining before us—that from these honored dead we take increased devotion to that cause for which they gave the last full measure of devotion—that we here highly resolve that these dead shall not have died in vain—that this nation, under God, shall have a new birth of freedom—and that government of the people, by the people, for the people, shall not perish from the earth.   3

Read More on the Web

For more information about Lincoln, his speeches, and the Civil War, go to the following sites:

- Abraham Lincoln, WhiteHouse.gov:
  www.whitehouse.gov/about-the-white-house/presidents/abraham-lincoln/

- Abraham Lincoln, History.com: www.history.com/topics/us-presidents/abraham-lincoln

- Selected Speeches of Abraham Lincoln:
  www.abrahamlincolnonline.org/lincoln/speeches/speechintro.htm

- U.S. Civil War: www.history.com/topics/american-civil-war

- The Battle of Gettysburg, Military History Online: www.militaryhistoryonline.com/gettysburg/

Questions for Discussion (Continues)

1. What examples of repetition appear in this speech?

2. The most obvious example of parallelism in the Gettysburg Address appears at the very end: "government of the people, by the people, for the people, shall not perish from the earth." What other examples of parallelism do you find?

3. Most sentences in this speech are long, but Lincoln does vary sentence length. Where does he do this?

4. What two participial phrases does Lincoln use at the end of the first sentence? Would it have made better sense to put the information they convey into another sentence? Why or why not?

5. Where in paragraph 2 does Lincoln use a participial phrase?

6. What effect does repeating the word *dedicate* or *dedicated* have? Does the word have any religious significance?

Questions for Discussion (Continued)

7. Where else does Lincoln use words that have a religious significance? What is he trying to tell us by using such vocabulary?

8. What is Lincoln's central idea? What devices does he use to maintain coherence?

Thinking Critically

1. In Preparing to Read, you learned that Lincoln makes reference to the past, to the present, and to the future. Find places in which he does this. What is he trying to accomplish by setting up this pattern other than helping to organize the speech? What does he accomplish each time he references a specific time?

2. Reread the last sentence. Is there a pattern in Lincoln's resolving that "these dead shall not have died in vain"; that "this nation, under God, shall have a new birth of freedom"; and that democracy "shall not perish from the earth"? What is that pattern, and why would such a pattern be so effective in a speech?

Suggestions for Journal Entries

1. In what ways do you think the government should be "for the people"? What rights and/ or services should it guarantee us? Use clustering, draw a subject tree, or freewrite for ten minutes on this question. After completing your journal entry, read it to classmates or friends. Together, brainstorm for a few minutes to collect more ideas.

2. Many speeches in U.S. history have served as sources of inspiration from decade to decade, from generation to generation. With the help of your instructor, your college librarian, or the Internet, locate a speech that you'd like to read or reread. Then analyze this speech. Pick out examples of parallelism, repetition, and other techniques the writer has used to create emphasis. Here are a few speeches you might choose from:

    Abraham Lincoln, Second Inaugural Address

    Franklin Delano Roosevelt, First Inaugural Address

    Adlai Stevenson, Eulogy for Eleanor Roosevelt

    Dwight D. Eisenhower, Farewell Address

    John F. Kennedy, Speech at the Berlin Wall

    Martin Luther King Jr., Speech at the Lincoln Memorial ("I Have a Dream")

    Ronald Reagan, Speech at Moscow State University

    George W. Bush, State of the Union Address (January 29, 2002)

3. Using as many paragraphs as you like, rewrite Lincoln's speech in your own words. Make sure that you express his central idea clearly and that you emphasize his other important ideas through parallelism, repetition, or any of the other techniques you've learned for creating emphasis.

5.6d Jailbreak Marriage

Author Biography

Gail Sheehy (1937–) was born in New York City and graduated from Columbia University and the University of Vermont. She has published seventeen books and countless articles for newspapers and magazines. She is one of the founding contributors to *New York* magazine and regularly publishes in *Vanity Fair*. The Library of Congress named her book *Passages* one of the ten most influential books of our era. This essay is excerpted from that book, in which Sheehy traces the developmental stages of adulthood.

Preparing to Read

1. Sheehy uses a number of sentence fragments to make her writing more pointed and emphatic. Understand that, as a professional writer, she can make use of this technique, which your professor may not allow you to use.

2. Sheehy also makes good use of the colon to create emphasis. Look for places where she does this.

3. Look for the essay's thesis in the first paragraph.

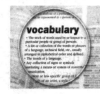

Vocabulary

altogether (adverb) Completely.

domain (noun) Area, sphere of influence.

egocentric (adjective) Self-centered.

exhilarating (adjective) Exciting, joyful.

foreclosed (verb) Prevented, cancelled.

ostracism (noun) Snubbing, expulsion.

sabotaged (verb) Undermined, damaged.

Jailbreak Marriage

Gail Sheehy

Although the most commonplace reason women marry is to "complete" themselves, a good many spirited young women gave another reason: "I did it to get away from my parents." Particularly for girls whose educations and privileges are limited, a *jailbreak marriage* is the usual thing. What might appear to be an act of rebellion usually turns out to be a transfer of dependence.   1

A lifer: that is how it felt to be Simone at 17, how it often feels for girls in authoritarian homes. The last of six children, she was caught in the nest vacated by the others and expected to "keep the family together." Simone was the last domain where her mother could play out the maternal role and where her father could exercise full control. That meant good-bye to the university scholarship.   2

Although the family was not altogether poor, Simone had tried to make a point of her independence by earning her own money since the age of 14. Now she thrust out her bankbook. Would two thousand dollars in savings buy her freedom?   3

"We want you home until you're 21."   4

"Work," her father insisted. But the job she got was another closed gate. It was in the knitting machine firm where her father worked, an extension of his control. Simone knuckled under for a year   5 until she met Franz. A zero. An egocentric Hungarian of pointless aristocracy, a man for whom she had total disregard. Except for one attraction. He asked her to marry him. Franz would be the getaway vehicle in her jailbreak marriage scheme: "I decided the best way to get out was to get married and divorce him a year later. That was my whole program."

Anatomy, uncontrolled, subverted her program. Nine months after the honeymoon, Simone was a mother. Resigning herself, she was pregnant with her second child at 20.   6

One day, her husband called with the news, the marker event to blast her out of the drift. His firm had offered him a job in New York City.   7

"Then and there, I decided that before the month was out I would have the baby, find a lawyer and start divorce proceedings." The next five years were like twenty. It took every particle of her will and patience to defeat Franz, who wouldn't hear of a separation, and to ignore the ostracism of her family.   8

At the age of 25, on the seventh anniversary of her jailbreak marriage (revealed too late as just another form of entrapment), Simone finally escaped her parents. Describing the day of her decree, the divorcée sounds like so many women whose identity was foreclosed by marriage: "It was like having ten tons of chains removed from my mind, my body—the most exhilarating day of my life."   9

Read More on the Web

To read more about Gail Sheehy and about marriage, visit the following:

- "*Passages* Author Reflects on Her Own Life Journey," NPR: http://bvtlab.com/677MZ
- "Why Did You Get Married?": http://bvtlab.com/7nknC

Questions for Discussion

1. What is Sheehy's thesis?

2. Find places where Sheehy makes use of the colon. In each case, explain what she accomplishes by using this mark of punctuation.

3. Where does Sheehy use a rhetorical question, and what is the effect of her doing so?

4. Find sentences that begin with participles or participial phrases. Find at least one sentence in which Sheehy employs parallelism.

5. In paragraph 5, Sheehy says that Franz would be Simone's "getaway vehicle." Find other examples of effective figurative language in this essay.

6. Analyze paragraph 5, and explain how Sheehy varies sentence length to make her writing interesting.

7. Identify the appositive in paragraph 7.

8. Sheehy makes use of only one example in this essay. Is this enough, or should she have also told the story of another woman who opted for a "jailbreak marriage"?

9. Sheehy begins paragraph 6 with "Anatomy, uncontrolled." She puts the adjective after the noun, not before as is common. What does this arrangement accomplish?

Thinking Critically

1. What does Sheehy mean when she tells us that Franz was a man of "pointless aristocracy"?

2. What details does Sheehy use to compare Simone's life before marriage to imprisonment?

3. Simone had two children with Franz. Speculate on the life she faced after she divorced him.

Suggestions for Journal Entries

1. Do you know anyone who has been in a situation like Simone's—someone who is trapped in a family that demands control over him or her? Use listing or focused freewriting to record details of the limitations and hardships this person has had to face because of the control his or her family wishes to exert.

2. If you had known Simone, what advice might you have given her to escape her family's control? What advice would you have given her about her plan to marry Franz?

5.7 Suggestions for Sustained Writing

1. One of the Suggestions for Journal Entries after Alice Wnorowski's "A Longing" asks you to think about an experience you would like to relive. If you responded to this suggestion, then you've already made a list of effective details that will help explain why you have such a longing to repeat this experience.

    Add to your notes, and expand them into an essay that shows what made the experience so memorable. Develop your thesis in concrete detail, and make your writing unified and coherent by using techniques discussed in chapter 2.

    After you've written your first draft, read your essay carefully. Should you do more to emphasize important ideas or to maintain your readers' interest? If so, revise your paper by using techniques for creating emphasis and variety explained in this chapter. As usual, edit and proofread the final draft of your paper.

2. The second item in Suggestions for Journal Entries after "A Longing" invites you to begin listing details about a natural setting—a forest, meadow, seashore, mountain, river—that you visited recently or remember vividly.

    Follow the advice in item 1 of Suggestions for Sustained Writing to turn these notes into a short essay.

3. If you responded to the first of the journal prompts after "Why Does Everybody Hate Me?" write an essay in which you explain why the villain you chose to research is really a villain. Use as much of your own knowledge as you can in this paper, but also use information from Internet and print sources. If you are summarizing, paraphrasing, or quoting from what you have read, make sure to give your sources credit by providing internal citations and a Works Cited list or References list. You can learn more about crediting your sources at the website of the Modern Language Association (style.mla.org) or the American Psychological Association (www.apastyle.org) or by following the specific information provided by your instructor.(Additional information on this topic can also be found in Appendix 2.)

    If this assignment doesn't interest you, write an essay that outlines ways in which you can make yourself into a more considerate, tolerant, caring, or morally responsible person. If you responded to the second journal assignment after "Why Does Everybody Hate Me?" you probably have gathered some information to get you started. Add to this information and write a scratch outline that will guide you through your rough draft.

Whether you chose the first or second option in this assignment, try to create emphasis and variety in your paper by incorporating some of the techniques explained in this chapter. The best time to do so is during the revision process.

4. Read the notes you made in response to the first of the Suggestions for Journal Entries following Lincoln's "Gettysburg Address." (If you haven't completed this short assignment, do so now.)

Next, focus on three or four of the rights and/or services that democratic governments should guarantee their people. Choose those you believe are essential. Define each of these items in one or two sentences; then arrange them in a list that ends with the one item you consider most important.

Use this list as a blueprint or outline for an essay that explains, develops, and supports each of these ideas (rights/services) in a separate paragraph or group of paragraphs. When you begin revising your rough draft, write an introductory paragraph that contains a thesis and captures the reader's attention. Also, write a concluding paragraph based on one of the techniques explained in chapter 3. As you rewrite this and subsequent drafts, create variety and emphasis by using the advice in this chapter. The next step, of course, is to edit and proofread your work.

5. If you responded to item 1 in the Suggestions for Journal Entries after "Jailbreak Marriage," turn these notes into an essay in which you explain the situation of an adult friend, relative, or acquaintance whose life is being controlled by his or her family. In your journal you should have mentioned the limitations and hardships this person faces. Expand upon these in your essay.

Then, do some more information gathering. Make a list of suggestions about how your subject might "escape" from this situation. Expand on at least two of these in the second half of your essay.

Like Sheehy, explain the problem your subject is having by introducing readers to his or her family in your first and/or second paragraph. To conclude your paper, try using a memorable quotation or any of the other methods for ending an essay found in chapter 3.

As you revise the early drafts of your essay, make sure to include items for creating emphasis and variety as discussed in this chapter. For example, can you emphasize certain ideas by writing periodic sentences, by using parallel structure, or by repeating key words and phrases? For variety, can you begin a few sentences with infinitives or gerunds? Can you add participial phrases, use appositives, and vary sentence length and patterns? After you are satisfied with your revisions, make sure to edit and proofread.

6. Item 2 in the Suggestions for Journal Entries after "Jailbreak Marriage" asks you to gather information about the kinds of advice you might have given Simone about how to escape her controlling family and about her plan to marry Franz. Turn your notes into a letter or formal email that offers Simone a better plan to solve her problem. Plan out your advice to her in as much detail as you can.

When it comes time to revise your draft, try making your sentences more emphatic and more varied, as explained earlier. For example, use parallelism and repetition to emphasize certain points. Don't begin every sentence with its subject; instead, start with a participle, an adverb, or a prepositional phrase now and again. As always, edit and proofread before submitting your work.

ACKNOWLEDGMENTS

Barry, Dave. "Dave Barry's Year in Review." *Miami Herald,* December 2005.

Hamill, Pete. *A Drinking Life.* Wheeler Publishing, 1994. Copyright © 1994 Little Brown and Co.

Sheehy, Gail. *Passages.* Dutton, 1976. Copyright © 1974, 1976 by Gail Sheehy. Used by permission of Dutton, an imprint of Penguin Publishing Group, a division of Penguin Random House LLC. All rights reserved.

"Why Does Everybody Hate Me?" Reprinted with permission of *The Onion.* Copyright © 2018, by Onion, Inc. www.theonion.com

Section 3
Description and Narration

The two chapters in this section explain how to create vivid verbal portraits of people, places, and things, and to narrate stories about meaningful events. As you read Chapters 6 and 7, remember that the more details you put into any piece of writing, the more believable, interesting, and effective it will be.

Knowing Your Subject

The more you know about your subject or event, the easier it is to choose effective details that communicate its significance to your readers. If you need to learn more about what you are describing, you can always observe it more closely and even use your other four senses—hearing, touch, taste, and smell—to gather information. If you are narrating an event you experienced or observed, you might recall additional details about it through focused freewriting, listing, or another of the prewriting techniques explained in Getting Started. You can also interview other people involved to get their recollections. In fact, interviewing is a good way to gather information about an incident you did not observe firsthand. This is what journalists and historians often do. Finally, you might gather narrative details through library or Internet research, but be sure to credit your sources through appropriate citations (see the Modern Language Association website at style.mla.org or look in the Research Process appendix at the end of this book).

Using Language That Shows

As you learned in chapter 4, using language that shows makes your writing more concrete, specific, and vivid than using language that simply tells. For example, it's one thing to say, "The firefighters risked their lives to save two people." It is another to say, "Their faces and protective clothing blackened from the suffocating smoke that had filled the hallways, the firefighters ran out of the tenement, carrying a mother and infant whose apartment was now engulfed in flame." The first version is vague and unconvincing—a statement we soon forget. The second paints a memorable picture. Although it doesn't tell us that the firefighters were in danger, the details it includes make that conclusion unavoidable. It also provides information about the building, the people who were saved, and the extent of the fire.

Use Concrete Nouns and Adjectives

If you are describing a friend, don't just say, "He's not a neat dresser." Include nouns and adjectives that will enable readers to come to that conclusion on their own. Talk about "the red dirt along the sides of his scuffed, torn shoes; the large rips in the knees of his faded blue jeans; and the many jelly spots on his shirt." Concrete nouns and adjectives are also important to narration. For example, in "Mid-Term Break" (chapter 7), Seamus Heaney creates a mood appropriate to a wake when his poem tells us:

> Whispers informed strangers I was the eldest
>
> Away at school, as my mother held my hand
>
> In hers and coughed out angry tearless sighs.
>
> At ten o'clock the ambulance arrived
>
> With the corpse stanched and bandaged by the nurses.

Include Specific Details

After you have chosen important details that are concrete—details that show rather than tell—make your writing more specific. For example, revise the description of your friend's attire to "The sides of his scuffed, torn loafers were caked with red clay. His knees bulged from the large rips in his faded Levi's; and strawberry jam was smeared on the collar of his white Oxford shirt." Notice that "loafers" has replaced "shoes," "red clay" has replaced "red dirt," "Levi's" has replaced "blue jeans," and "shirt" has been revised to "white Oxford shirt."

Create Figures of Speech

In chapter 4, you learned that one of the best ways to make your writing clear and vivid is to use figures of speech, or expressions that convey a meaning beyond their literal sense. The most common figures of speech are metaphor, simile, and personification. Writers often rely on such expressions to explain or clarify abstract, complex, or unfamiliar ideas. In "If at First You Do Not See ..." (chapter 6), Jesse Sullivan describes trees that seem "to bow their heads in sorrow," their branches "twisted and ill-formed, as if poisoned by the very soil in which they are rooted."

Figures of speech are also used extensively in narration. Take, for example, the metaphors Adrienne Schwartz uses in a passage from "The Colossus in the Kitchen," a story about her childhood home in South Africa (chapter 7): "In those days ... the adults were giants bestriding the world with surety and purpose. Tandi, the cook, reigned with the authoritarian discipline of a Caesar. She held audience in the kitchen."

Rely on Your Five Senses

Personal observation and experience often yield visual details. However, using your other four senses can provide even more important information, especially when you are describing. Of course, explaining what something sounds, tastes, smells, or feels like can be harder than showing what it looks like. But the extra effort is worthwhile. Whether you are describing or telling a story, the greater the variety of details you include, the more realistic and convincing your writing will be.

Next to sight, hearing is the sense writers rely on most. In "Flavio's Home" (chapter 6), an essay that combines narration and description, Gordon Parks describes a boy holding a "bawling naked baby in his arms." He goes on to explain that the boy "whacked" the baby's bottom and that, later, two of the family's daughters "burst into the shack, screaming and pounding on one another."

When writers describe rain-covered sidewalks as "slick," scraped elbows as "raw" or "tender," or the surfaces of bricks as "coarse" or "abrasive," they appeal to the sense of touch. Another example appears in "Watching the Reapers" by Po Chü-i (chapter 6) when he writes that the reapers' "feet are burned by the hot earth."

Tastes and smells, though sometimes difficult to re-create, can also make your writing interesting and believable. Notice how well Mary Taylor Simeti uses them to recall an Easter picnic of take-out food from a hillside restaurant in Sicily:

> [Our] obliging host produces [brings out] three foil-covered plates, a bottle of mineral water, and a round kilo loaf of fragrant, crusty bread. We drive back along the road a little way to a curve that offers space to park and some rocks to sit on. Our plates turn out to hold spicy olives, some slices of prosciutto crudo [cold ham] and of a peppery local salami, and two kinds of pecorino [sheep's milk] cheese, one fresh and mild, the other aged and sharper. With a bag of oranges from the car, the sun warm on our backs, the mountains rolling down at our feet to the southern coast and the sea beyond, where the heat haze clouds the horizon and hides Africa from view, we have as fine an Easter dinner as I have ever eaten. (*On Persephone's Island*)

Being Objective or Subjective

Objective writing requires you to report what you see, hear, or experience accurately and thoroughly—without revealing your feelings or opinions. Subjective writing allows you to convey your personal perspective on or reactions to a subject or experience. Both types of writing have their places in description and narration.

Most journalists and historians try to remain objective by communicating facts, not opinions about those facts. In other words, they try to give us the kind of information we'll need to make up our own minds about the subject. This is what student Meg Potter does when she describes a woman living on the streets of a large American city:

> This particular [woman] had no shoes on, but her feet were bound in plastic bags that were tied with filthy rags. It was hard to tell exactly what she was wearing. She had on … a conglomeration of tattered material that I can only say … were rags. I couldn't say how old she was, but I'd guess in her late fifties. The woman's hair was grey and silver, and she was beginning to go bald.
>
> As I watched for a while, I realized she was sorting out her bags. She had six of them, each stuffed and overflowing …. I caught a glimpse of ancient magazines, empty bottles, filthy pieces of clothing, an inside-out umbrella, and several mismatched shoes.
>
> The lady seemed to be taking the things out of one bag and putting them into another. All the time she was muttering to herself. ("The Shopping Bag Ladies")

In some cases, however, authors find it important to make their feelings known. Take this short excerpt from student Jesse Sullivan's "If at First You Do Not See …," which appears in chapter 6. Here the author speaks about her hopes for a better life for her friends and herself: "Our hope binds us together closely and is itself a sign that things will get better."

Watch for examples of objective and subjective writing in Section 3. At the same time, identify concrete and specific details and figures of speech to learn more about how they contribute to the making of effective description and narration.

ACKNOWLEDGMENTS

Heaney, Seamus. "Mid-Term Break."

Simeti, Mary Taylor. *On Persephone's Island.* Alfred A. Knopf, 1986. Reprinted by permission. Copyright 1986 by Alfred A. Knopf.

Getty Images

6

Description

Chapter Outline

This chapter presents selections that describe people, places, and things. It also discusses some techniques presented in the introduction to section 3 that are important to both description *and* narration. For example, you might recall the importance of using concrete nouns and adjectives, including specific details, relying on your five senses, and creating figures of speech (simile, metaphor, and personification). You might also remember the need to decide whether to remain objective or to take a more subjective approach when you write. Keeping this advice in mind will help you make your subjects as interesting and vivid to your readers as they are to you. However, you should also learn several techniques that are especially important when you are describing, whether your subject is a place, a thing, or a person.

6.1 Techniques for Describing Places and Things

In addition to filling your writing with concrete details and figures of speech, try to include *proper nouns*, which name particular persons, places, and things. Here are some examples: Arizona; the University of Tennessee; Lake Michigan; the First Baptist Church; Microsoft® Windows; Chinese; the *Chicago Tribune*; Rosedale Avenue; the San Francisco Opera House; Fort Worth, Texas.

Including proper nouns that readers recognize or words made from such nouns can make your description more realistic and interesting. Take this paragraph from Mark Twain's *Life on the Mississippi*, in which all proper nouns are set italic:

> The *Mississippi* is well worth reading about .... Considering the *Missouri* its main branch, it is the longest river in the world—four thousand three hundred miles. It seems safe to say that it is also the crookedest river in the world, since in one part of its journey it uses up one thousand three hundred miles to cover the same ground that the crow would fly over in six hundred and seventy-five. It discharges three times as much water as the *St. Lawrence*, twenty-five times as much as the *Rhine*, and three hundred and thirty-eight times as much as the *Thames*. No other river has so vast a drainage-basin: it draws its water supply from twenty-eight States and Territories; from *Delaware*, on the *Atlantic* seaboard, and from all the country between that and *Idaho* on the *Pacific* slope—a spread of forty-five degrees of longitude.
>
> The area of its drainage-basin is as great as the combined areas of *England, Wales, Scotland, Ireland, France, Spain, Portugal, Germany, Austria, Italy,* and *Turkey*; and almost all this wide region is fertile; the *Mississippi* valley, proper, is exceptionally so.

6.1a Using Effective Verbs

We know how important verbs are to narration, but effective verbs can also add much to a piece of description. Writers use verbs to make descriptions more specific, accurate, and interesting. For instance, "The wind had chiseled deep grooves into the sides of the cliffs" is more specific than "The wind had made deep grooves." The verb *chiseled* gives the reader a more accurate picture of the wind's action than *made* does.

In the introduction to section 3, you read about how to enrich the description of a friend's clothing by adding specific details. Returning to that sentence, notice that lively verbs (in italics) make as much of a difference as do concrete nouns and adjectives:

> Red clay was *caked* along the sides of his scuffed, torn loafers; his knees *bulged* from the large rips in his faded Levi's; and strawberry jelly was *smeared* on the collar of his white Oxford shirt.

Something similar can be said about the verbs and participles (adjectives made from verbs) that Alan Paton uses in his description of the mountains and valleys near Ixopo in his native South Africa:

The grass is rich and matted; you cannot see the soil. It *holds* the rain and mist, and they *seep* into the ground, *feeding* the streams in every kloof [ravine]. It is well *tended*, and not too many cattle *feed* upon it; not too many fires *burn* it, *laying* bare the soil. *Stand unshod* upon it, for the ground is holy, *being* even as it came from the Creator. *Keep* it, *guard* it, *care* for it, for it *keeps* men, *guards* men, *cares* for men. *Destroy* it and man is *destroyed* ....

But the rich green hills *break down*. They *fall* to the valley below, and *falling* change their nature. For they *grow* red and bare; they *cannot hold* the rain and mist, and the steams are dry in the kloofs. Too many cattle *feed* upon the grass, and too many fires have *burned* it. *Stand shod* upon it, for it is coarse and sharp, and the stones *cut* under the feet. It is not *kept*, or *guarded*, or *cared for*; it no longer *keeps* men, *guards* men, *cares* for men. The tithoya *does not cry* here any more.

6.1b Including Action and People in the Description of a Place

Narration and description are closely related, and they often appear together. Storytellers describe places where their narratives take place. Writers of description often reveal the character or atmosphere of a place by narrating events that occur in it or by describing people who appear in it.

A selection in this chapter that shows how actions and the people who perform them can help reveal the character of a place is Gordon Parks's "Flavio's Home." In the following passage, Parks reveals the hopelessness and poverty that fill the da Souza home when he tells us about the fear, sadness, and anger with which the family's children conduct themselves:

Maria's eyes flashed anger .... "I'll beat you, you little bitch." Liza threw a stick at Maria and fled out the door. Zacarias dropped off to sleep. Mario ... slouched in the corner and sucked his thumb. Isabel and Albia sat on the floor, clinging to each other with a strange tenderness. Isabel held on to Albia's hair and Albia clutched at Isabel's neck. They appeared frozen in an act of quiet violence.

6.2 Techniques for Describing People

You just learned that writers often go beyond physical appearance when describing a place or thing; they reveal its character as well. This is even more true when they describe people. Writers describe human beings because they are fascinated by their personalities, values, and motivations, as well as by their looks and the sound of their voices. Writers may start by describing physical appearance—what's on the outside. But they often end up talking about their subjects' characters—what's on the inside.

6.2a Describing a Subject's Appearance and Speech

Someone's appearance—height and weight, eye color, and so on—can be an end in itself. However, physical appearance and the clothes someone wears can also help you describe his or her personality. The way people speak and what they say can provide additional information about their characters and internal makeups. Take this example from John McPhee's essay about the New Jersey Pinelands. In one paragraph, he describes Fred Brown, a man who has lived in the wild all of his life and who is obviously plainspoken, down-to-earth, and comfortable with himself.

He was dressed in a white sleeveless shirt, ankle top shoes, and undershorts. He gave me a cheerful greeting, and without asking what I wanted, he picked up a pair of khaki trousers that had been tossed on one of the ... chairs and asked me to sit down. He set the trousers on another chair, and apologized for being in the middle of his breakfast, explaining that he seldom drank much but the night before he had had a few drinks and this had caused his day to start slowly. "I don't know what's the matter with me, but there's got to be something the matter with me because drink don't agree with me anymore," he said. He had a raw onion in one hand, and while he talked he shaved slices from the onion and ate them between bites of [a pork] chop. He was a muscular and well-built man, with short, bristly white hair, strong with large muscles in the calves. I guessed that he was about sixty and for a man of sixty he seemed to be in remarkably good shape. He was actually seventy-nine. "My rule is: Never eat except when you're hungry," he said, and he ate another slice of the onion.

Note that in addition to describing Brown's physical appearance and quoting him, this passage includes other clues about his character. Picturing him conversing with the author in his underwear and eating a raw onion and a pork chop for breakfast reveals a great deal.

6.2b Revealing What You Know about Your Subject

In the paragraph above, McPhee makes a statement about Fred Brown through his behavior or actions—that is, by telling an anecdote about him. Anecdotes are brief stories that highlight or illustrate an important aspect of a subject's personality. For example, in chapter 4, Sam Pickering's "Faith of the Father" contains an interesting anecdote about Miss Ida, which tells us a great deal about her personality. Stories such as these help reveal how someone reacts to various people, places, and problems, thereby revealing a great deal about their attitude toward life.

6.2c Revealing What Others Say about Your Subject

One of the quickest ways to learn about someone is to ask people who know this individual to tell you about his or her personality, lifestyle, morals, disposition, and so on. Often, authors use dialogue or quotations from other people to reveal something important about their subject's character. In "Crazy Mary," student Sharon Robertson combines physical description (concrete details) with information she learned from other people (dialogue) to create a memorable and disturbing portrait of an unfortunate woman she once knew:

She was a middle-aged woman, short and slightly heavy, with jet-black hair and solemn blue eyes that were bloodshot and glassy. She always looked distant, as if her mind were in another place and time, and her face lonely and sad. We called her "Crazy Mary."

Mary came to the diner that I worked in twice a week. She would sit at the counter with a scowl on her face and drink her coffee and smoke cigarettes. The only time she looked happy was when an old song would come on the radio. Then Mary would close her eyes, shine a big tobacco-stained smile, and sway back and forth to the music.

One day an elderly couple came in for dinner. They were watching Mary over their menus and whispering. I went over to their table and asked if they knew who she was. The old man replied, "Aw, dat's just old Mary. She's loonier than a June bug, but she ain't nutten to be afraid of. A few years back, her house caught fire and her old man and her kids got kilt. She ain't been right since."

After hearing this, it was easy to understand her odd behavior.

Other people can make good sources of information. We know from experience, however, that what others say about a person is often inaccurate. Sometimes, in fact, different people express very different—even contradictory— opinions about the same person. Consider how differently supporters and critics of a particular politician or entertainer view their subject. Today, President Abraham Lincoln enjoys the greatest respect among historians and the public alike. When he was alive, however, opinions about him differed; he was seen as a rustic frontiersman by some people, as a crafty tyrant by others, and as an embattled defender of human rights by still others.

6.3 Visualizing Details That Describe Places and Things

The following paragraphs from John Ciardi's "Dawn Watch" describe the sights, sounds, and smells of sunrise in his backyard.

Uses simile.

Appeals to senses.

The traffic has just started, not yet a roar and stink. One car at a time goes by, the tires humming almost like the sound of a brook a half mile down in the crease of a mountain I know—a sound that carries not because it is loud but because everything else is still.

Includes action.

The lawns shine with a dew not exactly dew. There is a rabbit bobbing about on the lawn and then freezing. If it were truly a dew, his tracks would shine black on the grass, and he leaves no visible track. Yet, there is something on the grass that makes it glow a depth of green it will not show again all day. Or is it something in the dawn air?

Relies on concrete, specific nouns.

Uses metaphor.

Uses simile.

Appeals to senses.

Our cardinals know what time it is. They drop pure tones from the hemlock tops. The black gang of grackles that makes a slum of the pin oak also knows the time but can only grate at it. They sound like a convention of broken universal joints grating up hill. The grackles creak and squeak, and the cardinals form tones that only occasionally sound through the noise.

Reveals subjective reaction to cardinals and grackles.

6.4 Visualizing Details That Describe People

The two short selections that follow use techniques important to describing people. The first, by Dr. Richard Selzer, describes the physical appearance of an AIDS patient in Haiti. The second, by Jade Snow Wong, describes the personality of a man who works in a factory that is run by the author's family and that doubles as their home.

"Miracle" by Richard Selzer

Uses specific details; nouns, adjectives.

A twenty-seven-year-old man whose given name is Miracle enters. He is wobbly, panting, like a groggy boxer who has let down his arms and is waiting for the last punch. He is neatly dressed and wears, despite the heat, a heavy woolen cap. When he removes it, I see that his hair is thin, dull reddish and straight. It is one of the signs of AIDS in Haiti …. The man's skin is covered with a dry, itchy rash. Throughout the interview and examination he scratches himself slowly, absentmindedly. The rash is called prurigo. It is another symptom of AIDS in Haiti. The telltale rattling of the tuberculous moisture in his chest is audible without a stethoscope. He is like a leaky cistern [tank for liquid] that bubbles and froths.

Uses simile to describe appearance.

Uses vivid adjectives.

Conveys action.

Appeals to hearing.

Uses a simile to create an image.

"Uncle Kwok" by Jade Snow Wong

Recalls a reoccurring action that tells about Kwok's personality.

After Uncle Kwok was settled in his chair, he took off his black, slipperlike shoes. Then taking a piece of stout cardboard from a miscellaneous pile which he kept in a box near his sewing machine, he traced the outline of his shoes on the cardboard. Having closely examined the blades of his scissors and tested their sharpness, he would cut out a pair of cardboard soles, squinting critically through his inaccurate glasses. Next he removed from both shoes cardboard soles he had made the day before and inserted the new pair. Satisfied with his inspection … he got up … disposed of the old soles, and returned to his machine. He had not yet said a word to anyone.

Daily this process was repeated ….

The next thing Uncle Kwok always did was to put on his own special apron, homemade from

Uses vivid adjectives/adverbs to create image.

Reveals an important aspect of his personality.

Describes his clothing as a clue to his personality.

double thicknesses of heavy burlap and fastened at the waist by strong denim ties. This long apron covered his thin, patched trousers and protected him from dirt and draft. After a half hour had been consumed by these chores, Uncle Kwok was ready to wash his hands. He sauntered into the Wong kitchen, stationed himself at the one sink which served both family and factory, and with characteristic meticulousness [care], now proceeded to clean his hands and fingernails.

Uses vivid verbs.

It was Mama's custom to begin cooking the evening meal at this hour …, but every day she had to delay her preparations at the sink until slow-moving Uncle Kwok's last clean fingernail passed his fastidious [close] inspection. One day, however, the inconvenience tried her patience to its final limit.

Recalls an action to describe Kwok.

Trying to sound pleasantly persuasive, she said, "Uncle Kwok, please don't be so slow and awkward. Why don't you wash your hands at a different time, or else wash them faster?"

Explains what someone else thinks of Kwok.

Uncle Kwok loudly protested …, "Mama, I am not awkward. The only awkward thing about my life is that it has not yet prospered!" And he strode off, too hurt even to dry his hands, finger by finger, as was his custom.

Allows Kwok to reveal himself in his own words.

6.5 Revising Descriptive Essays

Read these two versions of three paragraphs from Jessie Sullivan's "If at First You Do Not See …," a student essay that appears later in this chapter in its entirety. Though the rough draft is powerful, Sullivan's revision smooths out rough spots, improves wording, and provides additional detail that makes her writing even more vivid and effective.

Sullivan—Rough Draft

I live in an apartment, on the outskirts of New Brunswick, New Jersey. To the right of my building is Robeson Village, a large low-income housing project with about two-hundred apartments facing each other on opposite sides of a wide, asphalt driveway that runs the length of the complex. In this driveway, drug dealers and buyers congregate daily, doing business in front of anyone who cares to watch. Sometimes, children who have witnessed these transactions look over paraphernalia the dealers and their customers have left in their wake.

Wordy?

What kind of paraphernalia?

To the left of my building is Henry Street, a street that has grown to be synonymous with illegal drugs over the years. It is truly a pathetic sight. The block consists of a half dozen vacant and condemned buildings, all of which are still inhabited by addicts and dealers who have set up store there in much the same way a legitimate business owner decides on a particular location where business will be most profitable.

If vacant, how can they be inhabited?

Wordy?

To the eye, the community appears to be in a state of depression. Even trees, which traditionally symbolize life and vitality, reflect this. Pungent odors are made worse by the stench of rotting food, spilled from overturned garbage cans onto the sidewalk and cooking in the heat of the sun.

Whose eye?

What kind of pungent odors?

Make these sentences more vivid?

Make this image more active, lively?

Sullivan—Final Draft

I live in an apartment on the outskirts of New Brunswick, New Jersey. To the right of my building is Robeson Village, a large low- income housing project with about two-hundred apartments facing each other on opposite sides of a wide, asphalt driveway that runs the length of the complex. Here, drug dealers and buyers congregate daily, doing business in front of anyone who cares to watch. Sometimes, children who have witnessed these transactions look over the crack vials, hypodermic needles, syringes, and other paraphernalia the dealers

Substitutes one word for three.

Adds specific details to define "paraphernalia."

and their customers have left in their wake.

uses fewer words than original.

To the left of my building is Henry Street, which has become synonymous with illegal drugs. It is a pathetic place. The block consists of a half dozen condemned buildings, all of which are lived in or frequented by addicts and dealers.

Changes wording to be more accurate.

The latter have set up stores there in much the same way legitimate merchants choose locations where they think business will be profitable.

uses fewer words than original.

Adds detail.

To the eye of the visitor, the community appears to be in a chronic state of depression.

Adds effective adjective.

Even trees, symbols of life and vitality, seem to bow their heads in sorrow. Rather than reaching up in praise, their branches are twisted and ill-formed, as if poisoned by the very soil in which they are rooted.

uses personification to create vivid image.

uses specifics to explain what kinds of odors.

The pungent odors of urine, feces, and dead, wet leaves are made worse by the stench of rotting food, which spills from overturned garbage cans onto the sidewalk and cooks in the heat of the sun.

uses lively verbs.

6.6 Practicing Techniques That Describe

1. Write a paragraph that describes an eating area in your college's student center; a reading area in your college's library; or a coffee shop, a bar, a restaurant, or some other public place where people gather. Appeal to the senses, and include information about the appearance and behavior of people who frequent the place.

_____

_____

_____

_____

_____

2. In a short paragraph or two, describe a specific animal (your pet frog "Meteor")
    or a type of animal (frogs, in general). Use simile, metaphor, or personification.
    Also appeal to the senses.

    _____

    _____

    _____

    _____

    _____

    _____

3. Describe the inside of your car, your bedroom, your family's kitchen, or any
    other room in which you spend a great deal of time. Appeal to the senses and
    use simile.

    _____

    _____

    _____

    _____

    _____

    _____

4. Write a paragraph that describes your physical appearance. Include details that
    appeal to the senses, and try to use figures of speech. Be specific about your
    height, weight, hair color, eye color, and so on.

    _____

    _____

    _____

    _____

    _____

5. Write a paragraph that describes your best or worst quality. For example,
    discuss your patience or impatience, your tolerance or lack of tolerance for
    differences in people, your ambition or laziness, or your knack for making or
    losing friends. Show readers what you mean by using examples and by recalling
    what others have said about you.

    _____

    _____

    _____

    _____

    _____

    _____

6.7 Reading Selections

6.7a **If at First You Do Not See …**

Author Biography

When ***Jessie Sullivan*** began this essay for a college composition class, she wanted simply to tell her readers what her neighborhood looked like. As she revised and developed her work, however, she discovered that the place in which she lived had a vibrant character beyond what the eye can see. Slowly, she expanded and refined her purpose until description became a tool for exploring the sorrow and the promise of her world. Sullivan majored in liberal arts and business.

Preparing to Read

1. As you learned in chapter 2, narration and description can sometimes be used to explain ideas. Sullivan uses description to explain what is wrong with her neighborhood but also to reveal her hope for the people and place she loves.

2. In creating the contrast explained above, Sullivan reveals much about herself: her courage, her vision, and her desire to make a difference.

3. You know that this essay uses both description and contrast. Look for examples of both.

Vocabulary

bewilderment (noun)   Astonishment, confusion.

condone (verb)   Make excuses for.

defaced (verb)   Made ugly, disfigured.

diversified (adjective)   Varied, different.

illicit (adjective)   Illegal, prohibited.

infamous (adjective)   Dishonorable, known for evil or wrongdoing.

obscenities (noun)   Indecent words or pictures.

oppressive (adjective)   Harsh, severe, hard to bear.

paraphernalia (noun)   Gear, equipment used in a particular activity.

pathetic (adjective)   Pitiful, wretched, miserable.

preconceived notions (noun)   Prejudices, opinions formed before having accurate information about something.

sober (adjective)   Reliable, serious, steady.

superficial (adjective)   Quick and careless, shallow, on the surface.

If at First You Do Not See ...

Jessie Sullivan

A look of genuine surprise comes over some of my classmates when I mention where I live. My neighborhood has a reputation that goes before it. People who have never been there tend to hold preconceived notions about the place, most of which are negative and many of which are true. Those who actually visit my neighborhood usually notice only the filth, the deterioration of buildings and grounds, and the crime. What they fail to see isn't as apparent, but it is there also. It is hope for the future.   1

I live in an apartment on the outskirts of New Brunswick, New Jersey. To the right of my building is Robeson Village, a large low-income housing project with about two-hundred apartments facing each other on opposite sides of a wide, asphalt driveway that runs the length of the complex. Here, drug dealers and buyers congregate daily, doing business in front of anyone who cares to watch. Sometimes, children who have witnessed these transactions look over the crack vials, hypodermic needles, syringes, and other paraphernalia the dealers and their customers have left in their wake.   2

To the left of my building is Henry Street, which has become synonymous with illegal drugs. It is a pathetic place. The block consists of a half dozen condemned buildings, all of which are lived in or frequented by addicts and dealers. The latter have set up stores there in much the same way legitimate merchants choose particular locations where they think business will be profitable.   3

It is this area, three blocks in radius, that is infamous for illicit drugs, prostitution, and violence of every sort. Known as the "Vil," it is regarded as the city's hub of criminal activity and immorality.   4

With the growing popularity of crack, the appearance of the community has gotten worse and worse, as if it were on a collision course with destruction. Fences that once separated one property from another lie in tangled rusted masses on sidewalks, serving now only as eyesores. Almost all of the buildings are defaced with spray-painted obscenities and other foul messages. Every street is littered with candy wrappers, cardboard boxes, balled-up newspapers, and broken beer and soda bottles.   5

But Henry Street is undeniably the worst. The road is so covered with broken glass that the asphalt is barely visible. The way the glass catches the sunlight at every angle makes the street look almost magical, but there is nothing magical about it. Henry Street is a dead-end in more than the literal sense. In front of apartment buildings, the overgrown lawns, which more closely resemble hay than grass, are filled with old tires, cracked televisions, refrigerators and ovens with missing doors, rusted bikes, broken toys, and worn chairs and tables without legs. Dozens of abandoned cars, their windows shattered and their bodies stripped of anything of value, line the curbs. The entire block is so cluttered with refuse that strangers often mistake it for the junk yard, which is five blocks up.   6

To the eye of the visitor, the community appears to be in a chronic state of depression. Even trees, symbols of life and vitality, seem to bow their heads in sorrow. Rather than reaching up in praise, their branches are twisted and ill-formed, as if poisoned by the very soil in which they are rooted. The pungent odors of urine, feces, and dead, wet leaves are made worse by the stench of rotting food, which spills from overturned garbage cans onto the sidewalk and cooks in the heat of the sun.   7

Most people familiar with the neighborhood are aware that the majority of us residents are virtual prisoners in our homes because of the alarming crime rate. Muggings, rapes, and gang-related shootings, many of which do not get reported in newspapers, are commonplace. Many residents live in such fear that they hide in their apartments behind deadbolt locks and chains, daring to peer out of their peepholes only when a frequent gunshot rings out.   8

Many of my neighbors have adopted an I-mind-my-own-business attitude, preferring to remain silent and blind to the goings-on around them. This is the case for so many of them that many non-residents believe everyone feels this way. Unfortunately, most outsiders learn about our community from people who have been here only once or twice and who leave with unfair and dangerous misconceptions about us. They see the filth and immorality, and that is all they see. They take one quick look and assume none of us cares about the neighborhood or about the way we live.   9

I see my neighborhood from the inside, and I face all of the terrible things I have mentioned on a day-to-day basis. I also see aspects of my community that cannot be appreciated with a superficial first glance. If you look at the place closely, you will find small strong family units, like my own,   10 scattered amid the degeneration and chaos. Working together, struggling to free themselves from oppressive conditions, these families are worth noticing! We are sober, moral people who continue to live our lives according to the laws of society and, more important, according to the laws of God Himself.

Look closely and you will find those of us who pick up the trash when we it see it scattered on our small lawns, sidewalks, and doorsteps. We discourage our children from disrespecting the area in which they live, and we see to it that they don't litter or deface public property. We emphasize the importance of schooling, and we teach them about the evils of drugs and crime, making certain that they are educated at home as well.   11

Most important, we practice what we preach. We show the children with our actions that we do not condone the immoral and illegal acts around us, and we refuse to take part in any of them. We call the police whenever we hear gunshots, see drug transactions, or learn of any other unlawful activity. The children know that we care and that we are trying to create a brighter future for them.   12

However, the most visible sign of hope is that young people from my neighborhood—and from many neighborhoods like mine, for that matter—are determined to put an end to the destruction of our communities. It angers us that a minute yet very visible group of negative individuals has come to represent the whole. It saddens us that skills, talents, and aspirations, which are so abundant in our communities, should go untapped. Therefore, we have decided to take matters into our own hands; we will get the education we need and solve the problems of our neighborhoods ourselves.   13

Many of us attend the local county college, where we come together often to share ideas for a better future for our community. We also give each other the moral support we need to achieve our educational goals. Our hope binds us together closely and is itself a sign that things will get better.   14

This May, I was proud to see a number of friends receive associate's degrees and get admitted to four-year colleges and universities for advanced degrees. I hope to do the same soon. We are studying for different professions, but no matter how diversified our goals, we will use our knowledge for the benefit of all. This means returning to the community as doctors, lawyers, teachers, entrepreneurs. We will build programs to assist the people of our community directly: day care centers for children with working mothers; family mental and physical health clinics; job-training and placement facilities; legal service centers; youth centers; and drug/alcohol rehabilitation programs. Given the leadership of educated people like those we will become, such facilities can eventually be operated by community residents themselves. Most important, we intend to serve as visible and vocal role models for our children—for the leaders who will follow us and keep our hope alive. Eventually, we will bring about permanent change and make it impossible for a misguided few to represent a proud and productive community.   15

When friends visit me in my apartment for the first time, they frequently ask in awe and bewilderment, "How can you live in such a bad place?" I always give the same reply: "It isn't where you live, but how you live and what you live for."   16

Read More on the Web

Look for more information about events related to this story in the following websites:

- "The State of Black America 1996: Bad and Getting Worse," Fred Gaboury: www.hartford-hwp.com/archives/45a/188.html
- "Living in the Inner City," Randy White: urbana.org/blog/living-inner-city
- Urban Institute site with links to many other resources: www.urban.org

Questions for Discussion

1. What does Sullivan mean in paragraph 1 when she says that her "neighborhood has a reputation that goes before it"? Does this statement help introduce what follows in the rest of the essay?

2. Where in this essay does Sullivan include proper nouns? How do they help her achieve her purpose?

3. One reason this essay is so powerful is that it uses specific details. Which paragraphs make the best use of such details? What do such details tell us about Sullivan's attitude toward her neighborhood?

4. What image does Sullivan create in paragraph 7? What figure of speech does she use to develop this image?

5. Does action play a role in this essay? What is it?

6. Sullivan mentions her neighbors. How do they help define the neighborhood?

7. What sense other than sight does Sullivan appeal to?

8. When does she make use of illustration (examples)?

Thinking Critically

1. Why do you think Sullivan bothers to tell us that many shootings never get reported in the newspapers?

2. Summarize Sullivan's central idea in your own words.

3. This is a thought-provoking essay. What questions might you ask Sullivan about herself or her neighborhood if you were able to interview her? (For example, who or what has been her greatest inspiration?) Write your questions in the right- and left-hand margins of the essay.

Suggestions for Journal Entries

1. Make a list of the qualities you admire most about the neighborhood in which you live or grew up. Then make another list of ways it might be improved.

2. Use any technique discussed in Getting Started to gather information about what your home, neighborhood, or town might look like to someone seeing it for the first time. Then, go beyond appearances and discuss the real character of the place. Like Sullivan, describe what's on the "inside."

3. Think of a community, a family, or any group of people struggling to grow, improve, or even survive. What makes their life a struggle? What hope do you see for this place or these people?

6.7b Watching the Reapers

Author Biography

Perhaps one of the most productive of all Chinese poets, **Po Chü-i** lived between AD 772 and 846. Many of his works, though seemingly simple in content, reveal a profound concern for others. Some of them, aimed at the consciences of the ruling class, recall the social evils of his day. Others use description as a tool for exposing guilt, heartache, or other strong emotion in the poet. "Watching the Reapers" does all of these things.

Preparing to Read

1. In section 6.1, you learned that including action is a good way to capture the character of a place or scene. "Watching the Reapers" makes good use of this technique.

2. Description can have many uses. In this poem, it becomes a tool for both self-reflection and social commentary.

3. The "fifth month" in line 2 refers to midsummer. In lines 19 and 20, Po mentions that the reapers have paid a tax to the state equal to the amount of grain they had raised themselves. This statement is a clear indication that one of the purposes of this poem is to expose a political and economic evil. In line 23, Po tells us that as a government official, he is paid in "stones," which are measures of grain.

Vocabulary

glean (verb)   Gather.

grudging (adjective)   Resenting.

lingered (verb)   Remained, stayed around.

Watching the Reapers*

Po Chü-i

Tillers of the earth have few idle months;
In the fifth month their toil is double-fold.
A south wind visits the field at night;
Suddenly the ridges are covered with yellow corn.
Wives and daughters shoulder baskets of rice,   5
Youths and boys carry flasks of wine,
In a long train, to feed the workers in the field—
The strong reapers toiling on the southern hill,
Whose feet are burned by the hot earth they tread,
Whose backs are scorched by the flames of the shining sky.   10
Tired they toil, caring nothing for the heat,
Grudging the shortness of the long summer day.
A poor woman with a young child at her side
Follows behind, to glean the unwanted grain.
In her right hand she holds the fallen ears,   15

On her left arm a broken basket hangs.
Listening to what they said as they worked together
I heard something that made me very sad:
They lost in grain-tax the whole of their own crop;
What they glean here is all they will have to eat.   20
And I today—in virtue of what desert
Have I never once tended field or tree?
My government pay is three hundred stones;
At the year's end I have still grain in hand.
Thinking of this, secretly I grew ashamed   25
And all day the thought lingered in my head.

* Translated by Arthur Waley.

Read More on the Web

For more about this poet, go to the following websites:

- Selected poems of Po Chü-i: www.poemhunter.com/po-chu-i/

- Ocean of Poetry: Po Chü-i: poetrychina.net/wp/poets/pochui

Questions for Discussion

1. What concrete nouns does Po Chü-i use in this poem?

2. Where does he use effective verbs and adjectives?

3. Explain how Po's description of the reapers helps him describe the fields in which they toil.

4. One of Po's objectives is to make us aware of how hard a life the reapers have. How do his descriptions of the fields, the wind, and other natural objects help him do this?

5. Why does Po make sure to include action in this poem?

6. What does the conclusion of the poem reveal about Po's purpose?

Thinking Critically

1. If Po were writing in our day, what would he say about the way our society treats its workers? As you think about this topic, focus on a particular industry, business, or trade.

2. Reread line 12. What does Po mean by the "shortness of the long summer day"?

Suggestions for Journal Entries

1. Use listing, clustering, or freewriting to begin gathering concrete details about a place where you have worked and that you have found interesting. You don't have to have liked this place; you need only have found it interesting. Try to remember the kinds of people and activities that one would normally find there, but keep your information factual and objective. Do not include details that would reveal your feelings about the place.

2. Read over your response to item 1. Now, be subjective, and through freewriting, explain your feelings about this workplace, the people in it, and the kind of work that goes on there. Finally, answer this question: Would you recommend this job to one of your friends?

6.7c Flavio's Home

Author Biography

Gordon Parks (1912–2006) was a film director/producer, author, composer, and photographer. His feature films include *Shaft* (1972), *The Super Cops* (1974), *Leadbelly* (1976), and *Moments Without Proper Names* (1986). He also made the television documentary, *The Diary of a Harlem Family* (1968), for which he won an Emmy Award. Perhaps his most memorable film is *The Learning Tree* (1969), a fictionalized account of his childhood in Kansas.

Parks was the founder and editorial director (1970–73) of *Essence* magazine, and he wrote many works of nonfiction—including several memoirs and many books on the art of photography—as well as a novel, *Shannon* (1981). Today, however, his fame rests chiefly on his photography and on the writings that accompany his photography collections. In *Voices in the Mirror* (1990), a memoir in which "Flavio's Home" first appeared, Parks said that he used "photography as a weapon against poverty and racism." As a staff writer for *Life* magazine, he was once assigned to complete a photo-essay on poverty in one of the *favelas*, or "slums," of Rio de Janeiro, Brazil. The essay that follows is based on what he witnessed on that trip.

Preparing to Read

1. Read Parks's first paragraph several times to determine his purpose.

2. Is the first line of this essay a warning of what is to come?

3. Look for images of and references to death, starting with paragraph 2. What do you think "Catacumba," the name of the slum where Flavio lives, means in English? Look up words that begin with "cata" in the dictionary if necessary.

4. Read paragraph 3 carefully. Like other paragraphs, it uses effective language, but it also hints at something we will learn about at the essay's end.

Vocabulary

afflictions (noun)   Troubles, suffering, illnesses.

excrement (noun)   Bodily waste.

hemmed and hawed (verbs)   Hesitated before speaking.

jaundiced (adjective)   Yellowed because of illness or malnutrition.

maze (noun)   Confusing set of passageways in which one gets lost.

mobilize (verb)   Put into action.

plankings (noun)   Rough boards.

plush (adjective)   Rich, luxurious.

scurried (verb)   Ran around or hurried nervously.

skepticism (noun)   Lack of trust or faith.

wallowing (adjective)   Rolling around, as a pig does in the mud.

Flavio's Home

Gordon Parks

I've never lost my fierce grudge against poverty. It is the most savage of all human afflictions, claiming victims who can't mobilize their efforts against it, who often lack strength to digest what little food they scrounge up to survive. It keeps growing, multiplying, spreading like a cancer. In my wanderings I attack it wherever I can—in barrios, slums and favelas.   1

Catacumba was the name of the favela where I found Flavio da Silva. It was wickedly hot. The noon sun baked the mud-rot of the mountainside. Garbage and human excrement clogged the open sewers snaking down the slopes. José Gallo, a *Life* reporter, and I rested in the shade of a jacaranda tree halfway up Rio de Janeiro's most infamous deathtrap. Below and above us were a maze of shacks, but in the distance alongside the beach stood the gleaming white homes of the rich.   2

Breathing hard, balancing a tin of water on his head, a small boy climbed toward us. He was miserably thin, naked but for filthy denim shorts. His legs resembled sticks covered with skin and screwed into his feet. Death was all over him, in his sunken eyes, cheeks and jaundiced coloring. He stopped for breath, coughing, his chest heaving as water slopped over his bony shoulders. Then jerking sideways like a mechanical toy, he smiled a smile I will never forget. Turning, he went on up the mountainside.   3

The detailed *Life* assignment in my back pocket was to find an impoverished father with a family, to examine his earnings, political leanings, religion, friends, dreams and frustrations. I had been sent to do an essay on poverty. This frail boy bent under his load said more to me about poverty than a dozen poor fathers. I touched Gallo, and we got up and followed the boy to where he entered a shack near the top of the mountainside. It was a leaning crumpled place of old plankings with a rusted tin roof. From inside we heard the babblings of several children. José knocked. The door opened and the boy stood smiling with a bawling naked baby in his arms.   4

Still smiling, he whacked the baby's rump, invited us in and offered us a box to sit on. The only other recognizable furniture was a sagging bed and a broken baby's crib. Flavio was twelve, and with Gallo acting as interpreter, he introduced his younger brothers and sisters: "Mario, the bad one; Baptista, the good one; Albia, Isabel and the baby Zacarias." Two other girls burst into the shack, screaming and pounding on one another. Flavio jumped in and parted them. "Shut up, you two." He pointed at the older girl. "That's Maria, the nasty one." She spit in his face. He smacked her and pointed to the smaller sister. "That's Luzia. She thinks she's pretty."   5

Having finished the introductions, he went to build a fire under the stove—a rusted, bent top of an old gas range resting on several bricks. Beneath it was a piece of tin that caught the hot coals. The   6 shack was about six by ten feet. Its grimy walls were a patchwork of misshapen boards with large gaps between them, revealing other shacks below stilted against the slopes. The floor, rotting under layers of grease and dirt, caught shafts of light slanting down through spaces in the roof. A large hole in the far corner served as a toilet. Beneath that hole was the sloping mountainside. Pockets of poverty in New York's Harlem, on Chicago's south side, in Puerto Rico's infamous El Fungito seemed pale by comparison. None of them had prepared me for this one in the favela of Catacumba.

Flavio washed rice in a large dishpan, then washed Zacarias's feet in the same water. But even that dirty water wasn't to be wasted. He tossed in a chunk of lye soap and ordered each child to wash up. When they were finished he splashed the water over the dirty floor, and, dropping to his knees, he scrubbed the planks until the black suds sank in. Just before sundown he put beans on the stove to warm, then left, saying he would be back shortly. "Don't let them burn," he cautioned Maria. "If they do and Poppa beats me, you'll get it later." Maria, happy to get at the licking spoon, switched over and began to stir the beans. Then slyly she dipped out a spoonful and swallowed them. Luzia eyed her. "I see you. I'm going to tell on you for stealing our supper."

Maria's eyes flashed anger. "You do and I'll beat you, you little bitch." Luzia threw a stick at Maria and fled out the door. Zacarias dropped off to sleep. Mario, the bad one, slouched in a corner and sucked his thumb. Isabel and Albia sat on the floor clinging to each other with a strange tenderness. Isabel held onto Albia's hair and Albia clutched at Isabel's neck. They appeared frozen in an act of quiet violence.

Flavio returned with wood, dumped it beside the stove and sat down to rest for a few minutes, then went down the mountain for more water. It was dark when he finally came back, his body sagging from exhaustion. No longer smiling, he suddenly had the look of an old man and by now we could see that he kept the family going. In the closed torment of that pitiful shack, he was waging a hopeless battle against starvation. The da Silva children were living in a coffin.

When at last the parents came in, Gallo and I seemed to be part of the family. Flavio had already told them we were there. "Gordunn Americano!" Luzia said, pointing at me. José, the father, viewed us with skepticism. Nair, his pregnant wife, seemed tired beyond speaking. Hardly acknowledging our presence, she picked up Zacarias, placed him on her shoulder and gently patted his behind. Flavio scurried about like a frightened rat, his silence plainly expressing the fear he held of his father. Impatiently, José da Silva waited for Flavio to serve dinner. He sat in the center of the bed with his legs crossed beneath him, frowning, waiting. There were only three tin plates. Flavio filled them with black beans and rice, then placed them before his father. José da Silva tasted them, chewed for several moments, then nodded his approval for the others to start. Only he and Nair had spoons; the children ate with their fingers. Flavio ate off the top of a coffee can. Afraid to offer us food, he edged his rice and beans toward us, gesturing for us to take some. We refused. He smiled, knowing we understood.

Later, when we got down to the difficult business of obtaining permission from José da Silva to photograph his family, he hemmed and hawed, wallowing in the pleasant authority of the decision maker. He finally gave in, but his manner told us that he expected something in return. As we were saying good night Flavio began to cough violently. For a few moments his lungs seemed to be tearing apart. I wanted to get away as quickly as possible. It was cowardly of me, but the bluish cast of his skin beneath the sweat, the choking and spitting were suddenly unbearable.

Gallo and I moved cautiously down through the darkness trying not to appear as strangers. The Catacumba was no place for strangers after sundown. Desperate criminals hid out there. To hunt them out, the police came in packs, but only in daylight. Gallo cautioned me. "If you get caught up here after dark it's best to stay at the da Silvas' until morning." As we drove toward the city the large white buildings of the rich loomed up. The world behind us seemed like a bad dream. I had already decided to get the boy Flavio to a doctor, and as quickly as possible.

The plush lobby of my hotel on the Copacabana waterfront was crammed with people in formal attire. With the stink of the favela in my clothes, I hurried to the elevator hoping no passengers would be aboard. But as the door was closing a beautiful girl in a white lace gown stepped in. I moved as far away as possible. Her escort entered behind her, swept her into his arms and they indulged in a kiss that lasted until they exited on the next floor. Neither of them seemed to realize that I was there. The room I returned to seemed to be oversized; the da Silva shack would have fitted into one corner of it. The steak dinner I had would have fed the da Silvas for three days.

Read More on the Web

To learn more about Parks and about relevant ideas in this essay, search the following sites:

- The Gordon Parks Foundation: www.gordonparksfoundation.org
- "A Fierce and Tender Eye: Gordon Parks on Poverty's Dire Toll," Ben Gosgrove: http://bvtlab.com/57w67

Questions for Discussion

1. In which parts of the essay does Parks remain objective? Where does he become subjective by reacting to and commenting upon what he witnesses?

2. What references to and images of death can be found in this essay?

3. What other examples of figurative language does Parks use?

4. In what parts of the essay does the author appeal to the senses?

5. Analyze paragraphs 2, 3, and 6 carefully. What descriptive techniques discussed earlier in this chapter do they use?

6. How does using contrast help Parks establish tone? How would you describe his tone?

7. Why does the author describe Flavio in such detail? Isn't this supposed to be a description of a place?

8. What happens in a place helps reveal its character. What do the events Parks narrates tell us about Flavio's home? Start with paragraph 7.

9. Why does the author bother to include the names of all the da Silva children? What other proper nouns do you find?

10. Why does he include dialogue—what the people say—in this essay?

11. In what paragraph does Parks prepare us for Flavio's coughing, which we learn about in paragraph 11?

12. Why does the author describe his hotel room?

Thinking Critically

1. What do paragraphs 11 and 12 reveal about the author's character and his purpose for writing this essay?

2. Why does Parks bother to tell us about the lovers kissing in the elevator? How do you react to their ignoring his presence and carrying on with their love-making?

3. Compare this essay to Jessie Sullivan's "If at First You Do Not See …," which also appears in this chapter. In what ways are they different? Is Sullivan's purpose the same as Parks's?

Suggestions for Journal Entries (Continues)

1. Parks has a talent for piling detail upon detail to paint a vivid and compact word picture of what he describes. In paragraph 6, for example, he tells us that the da Silvas' stove was the "rusted, bent top of an old gas range resting on several bricks." In fact, the entire paragraph shows Parks's ability to accumulate concrete, specific, and vivid detail.

Suggestions for Journal Entries (Continued)

Try your hand at doing the same by writing a one-sentence description of a common object. For example you might start with an ordinary piece of furniture—perhaps the desk or table you are working on right now—and then add details until you have a list that looks something like this:

The desk

The wooden desk

The large wooden desk

The large brown wooden desk

The large brown wooden desk covered with junk

The large brown wooden desk covered with junk, which squats in the corner of my room

The large brown wooden desk covered with junk, books, and papers, which squats in the corner of my room

Repeat this process, adding as many items as you can, until you've exhausted your mind's supply of nouns and adjectives. Then review your list. Can you make your description even more specific and concrete? For instance, the above example might be revised to read:

The four-foot-long dark brown oak desk was covered with my math book, an old dictionary with the cover ripped off, two chemistry test papers, today's French notes, a half-eaten bologna sandwich, and a can of diet cola.

2. This essay contains both objective and subjective descriptions of "Catacumba," a symbol for poverty and human misery if there ever was one. Have you ever seen such a place in your own country? If so, begin recording details that might describe it. If this topic doesn't appeal to you, gather details about any public place such as a bus station, amusement park, sports arena or stadium, airport, shopping mall, or waterfront—just to name a few examples.

Whatever topic you choose, approach this journal entry in two steps. Begin by gathering details that describe the place objectively. Then, record your subjective reaction. Use clustering or listing to gather information that might describe this location.

6.7d From *Brave New World*

Author Biography

Born in Surrey, England, **Aldous Huxley** (1894-1963) was a novelist, poet, scriptwriter, philosopher, and satirist. He was the grandson of Thomas Henry Huxley, the zoologist, and he was related on his mother's side to Mathew Arnold, the famous English poet and essayist. After graduating from the University of Oxford, he associated with members of the Bloomsbury Group, a group of British intellectuals that included Bertrand Russell, John Maynard Keynes, and Virginia Woolf. Throughout most of his life, Huxley suffered from poor eyesight, yet he was able to write nearly fifty books and many other shorter works. Early in his career, he published several novels satirizing contemporary society: *Crome Yellow* (1921), *Antic Hay* (1923), and *Point Counter Point* (1928). In 1932, he published *Brave New World*, from which the selection that follows is taken. This is a dystopian novel. *Dystopian* is the antonym (has the opposite meaning) of *utopian*, which means "perfect" in ancient Greek. Huxley feared that new technology, along with the totalitarian philosophies that were sweeping Europe at the time (Fascism, Nazism, Communism), would lead us into a future in which people would lose all freedom of choice and our destinies would be predetermined by an all-controlling government.

Preparing to Read

1. This selection is taken from chapter 7 of the novel. Lenina Crowne and Bernard Marx have taken trip from London to Malpais, New Mexico, where they visit a Native American reservation, the only place where people are allowed to live free. In the world Lenina and Bernard come from, the government takes care of people from birth to death. But it also controls every aspect of their lives. For instance, biological engineering and other technologies keep people young looking and healthy as they grow in years. However, the government, not nature, predetermines when they will die.

2. The Director, mentioned in paragraph 5, is the Director of the hatchery in London, where human embryos are produced and cloned artificially. Lenina and Bernard work at the hatchery. Soma, mentioned in paragraph 8, is a hallucinatory drug that allows people to escape unpleasant situations by mentally entering a more pleasant place.

3. In paragraph 9, Lenina gets upset over seeing two women breastfeed their babies. In the twisted world where Lenina comes from, babies are no longer born in natural ways; they are manufactured and raised by the state. Anything having to do with parenthood is thought of as disgusting.

4. In paragraph 18, Lenina tells Bernard that the ceremony they are witnessing reminds her of a "lower-caste community sing." The society from which Lenina and Bernard have come is divided into five different castes, or social levels. Bernard belongs to the highest caste; Lenina, to the next highest.

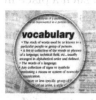

Vocabulary

crimson (noun)   Red.

emaciated (adjective)   Extremely or dangerously thin.

equilibrium (noun)   Balance, stability.

hideously (adverb)   In a horrible, ugly way.

inexorably (adverb)   Inevitably, inescapably.

innocuous (adjective)   Harmless.

mottled (adjective)   Speckled, spotted.

obsidian (noun)   Black volcanic rock; opaque when in thin sheets.

plaited (adjective)   Braided.

semblance (noun)   Appearance, likeness.

subterranean (adjective)   Underground.

tremulous (adjective)   Unsteady, trembling.

unprecedented (adjective)   Never happening before.

unorthodox (adjective)   Unconventional, heretical, revolutionary.

viviparous (adjective)   Reproducing by bearing live young.

From *Brave New World*

Aldous Huxley

"Oh!" She gripped his arm. "Look."   1

An almost naked Indian was very slowly climbing down the ladder from the first-floor terrace of   2
a neighboring house–rung after rung, with the tremulous caution of extreme old age. His face was
profoundly wrinkled and black, like a mask of obsidian. The toothless mouth had fallen in. At the
corners of the lips, and on each side of the chin, a few long bristles gleamed almost white against the
dark skin. The long unbraided hair hung down in grey wisps round his face. His body was bent and
emaciated to the bone, almost fleshless. Very slowly he came down, pausing at each rung before he
ventured another step.

"What's the matter with him?" whispered Lenina. Her eyes were wide with horror and amaze-   3
ment.

"He's old, that's all," Bernard answered as carelessly as he could. He too was startled; but he   4
made an effort to seem unmoved.

"Old?" she repeated. "But the Director's old; lots of people are old; they're not like that."   5

"That's because we don't allow them to be like that. We preserve them from diseases. We keep   6
their internal secretions artificially balanced at a youthful equilibrium. We don't permit their mag-
nesium-calcium ratio to fall below what it was at thirty. We give them transfusions of young blood.
We keep their metabolism permanently stimulated. So, of course, they don't look like that. Partly," he
added, "because most of them die long before they reach this old creature's age. Youth almost unim-
paired till sixty, and then, crack! The end."

But Lenina was not listening. She was watching the old man. Slowly, slowly he came down. His   7
feet touched the ground. He turned. In their deep-sunken orbits his eyes were still extraordinarily
bright. They looked at her for a long moment expressionlessly, without surprise, as though she had not
been there at all. Then slowly, with bent back the old man hobbled past them and was gone.

"But it's terrible," Lenina whispered. "It's awful. We ought not to have come here." She felt in her   8
pocket for her soma—only to discover that, by some unprecedented oversight, she had left the bottle
down at the rest-house. Bernard's pockets were also empty.

Lenina was left to face the horrors of Malpais unaided. They came crowding in on her thick   9
and fast. The spectacle of two young women giving breast to their babies made her blush and turn
away her face. She had never seen anything so indecent in her life. And what made it worse was
that, instead of tactfully ignoring it, Bernard proceeded to make open comments on this revoltingly
viviparous scene. Ashamed, now that the effects of the soma had worn off, of the weakness he had
displayed that morning in the hotel, he went out of his way to show himself strong and unorthodox.

"What a wonderfully intimate relationship," he said, deliberately outrageous. "And what an inten-   10
sity of feeling it must generate! I often think one may have missed something in not having had a
mother. And perhaps you've missed something in not being a mother, Lenina. Imagine yourself sitting
there with a little baby of your own...."

"Bernard! How can you?" The passage of an old woman with ophthalmia and a disease of the skin   11
distracted her from her indignation.

"Let's go away," she begged. "I don't like it."   12

But at this moment their guide came back and, beckoning them to follow, led the way down the   13
narrow street between the houses. They rounded a corner. A dead dog was lying on a rubbish heap; a
woman with a goitre was looking for lice in the hair of a small girl. Their guide halted at the foot of a
ladder, raised his hand perpendicularly, then darted it horizontally forward. They did what he mutely
commanded—climbed the ladder and walked through the doorway, to which it gave access, into a
long narrow room, rather dark and smelling of smoke and cooked grease and long-worn, long-un-
washed clothes. At the further end of the room was another doorway, through which came a shaft of
sunlight and the noise, very loud and close, of the drums.

They stepped across the threshold and found themselves on a wide terrace. Below them, shut in   14
by the tall houses, was the village square, crowded with Indians. Bright blankets, and feathers in black
hair, and the glint of turquoise, and dark skins shining with heat. Lenina put her handkerchief to her

nose again. In the open space at the centre of the square were two circular platforms of masonry and trampled clay—the roofs, it was evident, of underground chambers; for in the centre of each platform was an open hatchway, with a ladder emerging from the lower darkness. A sound of subterranean flute playing came up and was almost lost in the steady remorseless persistence of the drums.

Lenina liked the drums. Shutting her eyes she abandoned herself to their soft repeated thunder, allowed it to invade her consciousness more and more completely, till at last there was nothing left in the world but that one deep pulse of sound …. 15

There was a sudden startling burst of singing—hundreds of male voices crying out fiercely in harsh metallic unison. A few long notes and silence, the thunderous silence of the drums; then shrill, in a neighing treble, the women's answer. Then again the drums; and once more the men's deep savage affirmation of their manhood. 16

Queer—yes. The place was queer, so was the music, so were the clothes and the goitres and the skin diseases and the old people. But the performance itself—there seemed to be nothing specially queer about that. 17

"It reminds me of a lower-caste Community Sing," she told Bernard. 18

But a little later it was reminding her a good deal less of that innocuous function. For suddenly there had swarmed up from those round chambers underground a ghastly troop of monsters. Hideously masked or painted out of all semblance of humanity, they had tramped out a strange limping dance round the square; round and again round, singing as they went, round and round—each time a little faster; and the drums had changed and quickened their rhythm, so that it became like the pulsing of fever in the ears; and the crowd had begun to sing with the dancers, louder and louder; and first one woman had shrieked, and then another and another, as though they were being killed; and then suddenly the leader of the dancers broke out of the line, ran to a big wooden chest which was standing at one end of the square, raised the lid and pulled out a pair of black snakes. A great yell went up from the crowd, and all the other dancers ran towards him with out-stretched hands. He tossed the snakes to the first-comers, then dipped back into the chest for more. More and more, black snakes—brown and mottled—he flung them out. And then the dance began again on a different rhythm. Round and round they went with their snakes, snakily, with a soft undulating movement at the knees and hips. Round and round. Then the leader gave a signal, and one after another, all the snakes were flung down in the middle of the square; an old man came up from underground and sprinkled them with corn meal, and from the other hatchway came a woman and sprinkled them with water from a black jar. Then the old man lifted his hand and, startlingly, terrifyingly, there was absolute silence. The drums stopped beating, life seemed to have come to an end. The old man pointed towards the two hatchways that gave entrance to the lower world. And slowly, raised by invisible hands from below, there emerged from the one a painted image of an eagle, from the other that of a man, naked, and nailed to a cross. They hung there, seemingly self-sustained, as though watching. The old man clapped his hands. Naked but for a white cotton breech-cloth, a boy of about eighteen stepped out of the crowd and stood before him, his hands crossed over his chest, his head bowed. The old man made the sign of the cross over him and turned away. Slowly, the boy began to walk round the writhing heap of snakes. He had completed the first circuit and was half-way through the second when, from among the dancers, a tall man wearing the mask of a coyote and holding in his hand a whip of plaited leather, advanced towards him. The boy moved on as though unaware of the other's existence. The coyote-man raised his whip; there was a long moment of expectancy, then a swift movement, the whistle of the lash and its loud flat-sounding impact on the flesh. The boy's body quivered; but he made no sound, he walked on at the same slow, steady pace. The coyote struck again, again; and at every blow at first a gasp, and then a deep groan went up from the crowd. The boy walked. Twice, thrice, four times round he went. The blood was streaming. Five times round, six times round. 19

Suddenly Lenina covered her face with her hands and began to sob. "Oh, stop them, stop them!" she implored. But the whip fell and fell inexorably. Seven times round. Then all at once the boy staggered and, still without a sound, pitched forward on to his face. Bending over him, the old man touched his back with a long white feather, held it up for a moment, crimson, for the people to see then shook it thrice over the snakes. A few drops fell, and suddenly the drums broke out again into a panic of hurrying notes; there was a great shout. The dancers rushed forward, picked up the snakes and ran out of the square. Men, women, children, all the crowd ran after them. A minute later the square was empty, only the boy remained, prone where he had fallen, quite still. Three old women 20 came out of one of the houses, and with some difficulty lifted him and carried him in. The eagle and the man on the cross kept guard for a little while over the empty pueblo; then, as though they had seen enough, sank slowly down through their hatchways, out of sight, into the nether world.

Lenina was still sobbing. "Too awful," she kept repeating, and all Bernard's consolations were in vain. "Too awful! That blood!" She shuddered. "Oh, I wish I had my soma."

21

Read More on the Web

To learn more about Aldous Huxley and his works and about dystopias, visit the following sites:

- Aldous Huxley, Encyclopedia Britannica: www.britannica.com/biography/Aldous-Huxley

- Aldous Huxley, Biography.com: www.biography.com/people/aldous-huxley-9348198

- Dystopia, New World Encyclopedia: www.newworldencyclopedia.org/entry/Dystopia

Questions for Discussion

1. Read paragraph 2 again, and underline the adjectives used to make this description so vivid.

2. Where does Huxley use proper nouns? Why is the word *Director* (paragraph 5) capitalized?

3. Read paragraphs 20 and 21 again. Pick out effective verbs and adverbs the author uses to make his writing vivid.

4. At the beginning of this chapter, you learned that portraying action can help describe a place. What role does action play in this passage?

5. What role does the description of people play in the description of the reservation?

6. What does Lenina's reaction to what she sees on the reservation tell us about her?

7. What does Bernard's reaction to what he sees tell us about him?

8. What senses does Huxley appeal to? Find as many examples as you can.

Thinking Critically

1. Write a short character description of either Bernard or Lenina from what you learned by reading this excerpt from *Brave New World*.

2. This selection does not state a formal thesis. In your own words, what do you think Huxley is telling us about the reservation and the world outside the reservation in his novel?

3. The ceremony that we see in this selection combines Native American and Christian elements. Pick out examples of each.

Suggestions for Journal Entries

1. Use freewriting, clustering, or listing to describe a place that is unfamiliar to you and that is very unlike the environment in which you live. If you are a city dweller, try describing a farm or forest you visited. If you live in the suburbs, try coming up with details that might be used to describe the inner city. As you gather information for this paper, take notes at the scene of your observations, but also use a camera or your cell phone to take pictures that you can refer to later.

2. This selection describes more than people or a place; it also describes a ceremony. Think of a religious ceremony that has meaning for you, and list details that might help describe it. Make sure to include details that describe the place in which the ceremony is observed, as well as the people who take part. If dialogue is involved—prayers, hymns, chants—include it as well.

6.8 Suggestions for Sustained Writing

1. If you read "If at First You Do Not See …," follow Sullivan's lead: describe a place you know well by presenting two views of it. For example, one view might be negative, the other positive. Another way to proceed is to describe what newcomers see when they visit this place as opposed to what you see in it. A good place to describe might be your neighborhood or other part of your hometown, your high school or college campus, a run-down but beautiful old building, or the home of an interesting relative or friend.

    Although your paper need not be as long as Sullivan's, it should use techniques like those found in hers. For example, appeal to the senses, include action, use figures of speech to create images, or describe the people who live in or frequent the place.

    Check the journal entries you made after reading Sullivan's essay. They might help you get started. Once you have finished several drafts, write an introduction that captures the readers' attention and expresses your central idea in a formal thesis statement. Put the finishing touches on your writing by correcting errors that will reduce its effectiveness or distract your readers. Be sure all your spelling is correct.

2. Read over the notes you made in response to both Suggestions for Journal Entries after Po's "Watching the Reapers." If you have not responded to both of these suggestions, do so now.

    Using description as your main method of development, write an essay in which you explain why you would or would not recommend that a good friend take a job at the place you have begun to describe in your journal. Before beginning your rough draft, try making an outline of your paper. For example, you might organize it in three sections, each of which covers a body paragraph or two. The first could describe the physical characteristics of the workplace itself. The second might focus on the kinds of activities—the work—that normally takes place there. The third might describe the people who work in or frequent the place.

    As you begin to draft your paper, remember that you are trying to answer a specific question: Would you recommend this job to a friend? If the answer is no, make sure you include sufficient negative details to support this view, and vice versa. One way to introduce this essay is to address the reader directly, ask a question, or make a startling remark. A good way to end it is to restate or summarize some of the points you have made in the body of your essay or offer your reader advice.

However you decide to proceed, make sure that you provide sufficient detail to make your argument convincing. Then, revise, edit, and proofread.

3. If you responded to the second Suggestion for Journal Entries after "Flavio's Home," by Gordon Parks, turn these notes into a full-length essay that describes a place about which you have already gathered information. Begin by recording even more details about your subject. If you can, brainstorm with a fellow student who is also familiar with this place.

In the first draft, include details that paint an objective picture of your subject. Talk about the general layout, shape, or dimensions of the place; the colors of walls, ceilings, and floors; the kinds of furniture and other objects it contains. If you're writing about an outdoor place, mention trees, rocks, streams, bridges, park benches, walls, lampposts, and so on. In your next draft(s), add information about what the place looks, smells, and sounds like. If possible, make use of narration to re-create the kind of activity that normally occurs in this place and to introduce your readers to people who frequent it. In the process, begin revealing your subjective reactions. Use concrete details and vivid verbs, adjectives, and adverbs, as well as figures of speech, to let readers know what you think about this place and of the people you find there. Like Parks, do not be afraid to express your emotions.

After completing your second or third draft, write a thesis stating your overall opinion. Put this thesis in an introductory paragraph designed to capture the readers' attention. Close your essay with a memorable statement or summary of the reasons you are or are not planning to visit this place again. Finally, edit your work by checking grammar, spelling, and sentence structure.

4. Read over the journal notes you made after reading the excerpt from *Brave New World*. If you chose the first journal prompt, expand that into a full-length essay that describes a place that is different from the environment in which you live. The journal prompt recommended taking notes and pictures of the place. Rely on these to prime your memory and gather even more details before you start drafting your paper.

Important information to include in such an essay includes details gathered by your senses. Don't rely solely on what you see. Try to include information about sounds, smells, and even tastes, if appropriate. In addition, you might want to explain events that regularly occur in this place to allow action to communicate something about the nature or character of the locale you are describing.

If this assignment doesn't interest you, expand your response to the second journal suggestion after *Brave New World*. If you chose this option, don't forget to include action and dialogue as you describe the ceremony you have chosen to write about.

In either case, as you revise your paper, make sure that you have included vivid verbs and adjectives, proper nouns, and figurative language that will make the reader fully understand what you observed.

Acknowledgments

Ciardi, John. *A Manner of Speaking.* Rutgers University Press, 1972.

Huxley, Aldous. *Brave New World.* Harper Collins, 1946. Reprinted with permission from *Brave New World* by Aldous Huxley. Copyright © 1946 by Aldous Huxley; Harper Collins. (Canadian Rights: Excerpted from *Brave New World* by Aldous Huxley. Copyright © 1932 Mrs. Laura Huxley. Reprinted by permission of Vintage Canada/Random House Canada, a division of Penguin Random House Canada Limited.)

McPhee, John. *The Pine Barrens.* Farrar, Straus, & Giroux, 1978. Copyright © 1978 Farrar, Straus, & Giroux.

Parks, Gordon. *Voices in the Mirror.* Doubleday, 1990. Copyright © 1990 by Gordon Parks. Used by Permission of Doubleday, an imprint of the Knopf Doubleday Publishing Group, a division of Penguin Random House LLC. All rights reserved.

Paton, Alan. *Cry the Beloved Country.* Scribner, 1987. Copyright © 1948, 1976, and 1987 by Alan Paton.

Po-Chü. "Watching the Reapers." *Translations from the Chinese*, translated by Arthur Waley, A. A. Knopf, 1940.

Selzer, Richard. "A Mask on the Face of Death." *The Exact Location of the Soul,* Picador, 2001. Copyright © 2001 by Richard Selzer.

Twain, Mark (Clemens, Samuel). *Life on the Mississippi.* Boston, James R. Osgood and Company, 1883.

Wong, Jade Snow. *Fifth Chinese Daughter.* University of Washington Press, 1989. Reprinted with permission from *Fifth Chinese Daughter* by Jade Snow Wong. Copyright © 1989 University of Washington Press.

Shutterstock

Chapter 7

Narration

Chapter Outline

Narration is the process of recalling events, usually in order of time, or **chronological order**. In other words, it is storytelling. The arrangement of events is called the *plot*. Writers usually begin by relating the first event in a series, which usually sets the plot in motion. They usually end the story with the last event.

However, this is not always the case. Where a writer begins and ends depends upon the kind and purpose of story being told. Some stories begin in the middle or even at the end and then recall what happened earlier. Others are preceded or followed by information that the author thinks important to fully understanding the story. For example, in this chapter, Martin Gansberg prefaces his story of a young woman's vicious murder by commenting upon the lack of responsibility of thirty-seven witnesses who stood by and did nothing. Lois Diaz-Talty introduces her story about an adult lifestyle change by telling us about problems she experienced in childhood and adolescence.

More than 2,300 years ago, the Greek philosopher Aristotle taught that a narrative must have a beginning, middle, and end. In short, a successful story must be complete. It must contain all the information readers will need to understand what happened and to follow along easily. This is the most important idea to remember when writing narratives, but there are others.

7.1 Determining Purpose and Theme

There are two types of narration: nonfiction and fiction. Works of nonfiction record stories of actual events. Fiction, though sometimes based on real life, is born mainly of the author's imagination and does not re-create events as they happened.

Of course, the narrative method is used by both historians and journalists. Indeed, nonfiction can explain complex ideas or make important points about very real situations. Adrienne Schwartz's "The Colossus in the Kitchen," for example, exposes the evil and stupidity of apartheid, a political system once used in South Africa. In fact, many nonfiction narratives are written to explain an important (central) idea, often called a *theme*. They reveal something important about human nature, society, or life itself. At times, the theme is stated as a *moral*, as in Aesop's fables, the ancient Greek tales that teach lessons about living. More often, however, the theme of a narrative remains unstated or implied. It is revealed only as the plot unfolds; in such cases, the story speaks for itself.

Always ask yourself whether the story you have chosen to tell is important to you. This doesn't mean that you should limit yourself to events you have witnessed or experienced, although personal experience can provide information needed to spin a good yarn. It does mean that the more interested you are in the people, places, and events you are writing about, the better able you will be to make your writing meaningful and appealing.

7.2 Finding the Meaning in Your Story

As explained earlier, you don't have to reveal the purpose or theme (central idea) of a narrative. You can allow the events to speak for themselves. At first, you may not clearly understand what the theme of your story is or why it is important. But that's fine. Writing is a voyage of discovery. It teaches you things about your subject (and yourself) that you would not have known had you not started the process in the first place. Just write about something you believe is interesting and important. You can always figure out why your story is important or what theme to demonstrate when you write your second or third draft.

chronological order
The arrangement of
material in order of time.

7.3 Deciding What to Include

In most cases, you won't have trouble deciding which details to include, for you will be able to put down events as you remember them. In some cases, however—especially when trying to project a particular theme or idea—you will have to decide which events and people should be discussed in great detail, which should be mentioned only briefly, and which should be excluded from your story.

7.4 Showing the Passage of Time

The most important thing about a story is the plot, a series of events occurring in time. Writers must make sure that their plots make sense, that they are easy to follow, and that each event or incident flows into the next logically.

A good way to indicate the passage of time is to use transitions or connectives, the kind of words and expressions used to create coherence within and between paragraphs. (You can learn more about transitions in chapter 2.) In Martin Ganzberg's "37 Who Saw Murder Didn't Call the Police," the author uses such words and phrases to make logical connections and to indicate the passage of time.

> It was 3:50 by the time the police received their first call, from a man who was a neighbor .... In two minutes they were at the scene. The neighbor, a 70-year-old woman, and another woman were the only persons on the street. Nobody else came forward.

7.5 Describing Setting and Developing Characters

Establishing the setting of your story involves indicating the time and place in which it occurs. Describing characters allows you to make your story more believable and convincing. (You can find more about describing places and people in chapter 6.) Remember that your chief purpose is to tell a story, but the people in that story and the time and place in which it occurs may be as interesting as the events themselves.

An important element in narrative is dialogue, the words a writer allows people in the story to speak. Dialogue can expose important aspects of a character's personality, describe setting, and even reveal events that help move the plot along. Writers often allow their characters to explain what happened or to comment on the action in their own words, complete with grammatical errors and slang expressions.

7.6 Making Your Stories Interesting and Believable

One of the best ways to keep your readers' interest is to use effective verbs. More than any other parts of speech, verbs convey action—they tell what happened. It's important to be accurate when reporting an event. You should recapture it exactly as you remember and without exaggeration. However, good writing can be both accurate and interesting, both believable and colorful. You can achieve this balance by using verbs carefully. In Seamus Heaney's "Mid-Term Break," for example, the speaker reports that his mother "coughed out angry tearless sighs." He could have said that she was so angry she could not cry, but that would not have given us a sense of the emotional torture she suffered.

A good way to make your writing believable is to use proper nouns that create a realistic setting, that name real people, or that reveal other aspects of your story to make it more convincing. In "37 Who Saw Murder Didn't Call the Police," Martin Gansberg mentions easily recognizable places names such as Kennedy International Airport. He includes specific street addresses, as well as the names of neighborhoods, and he identifies both the major and minor characters in this news story.

7.7 Writing About Ourselves and About Others: Point of View

point of view
The perspective from which a narrative is told. Stories that use the first-person point of view are told by a narrator who is involved in the action and who uses words such as *I*, *me*, and *we* to explain what happened. Stories that use the third-person point of view are told by a narrator who may or may not be involved in the action and who uses words such as *he*, *she*, and *they* to explain what happened.

The essays and poems in this chapter may be divided into two categories. The first, including Heaney's "Mid-Term Break" and student Diaz-Talty's "The Day I Was Fat," are autobiographical. They look inward to explain something important about the narrator (storyteller). They are told from the first-person **point of view**, using the pronouns *I* or *we*. In these selections, the narrator is involved in the action. Also included in this group is Schwartz's "The Colossus in the Kitchen," a student essay in which the young narrator is not the major character. Nonetheless, her voice is heard clearly as she comments upon institutional racism and tells us about one of its most innocent victims.

The second category includes Gansberg's "37 Who Saw Murder Didn't Call the Police," which reports on events involving others. Told from the third-person point of view, it uses pronouns such as *he*, *she*, *it*, and *they*.

7.8 Visualizing Narrative Elements

The paragraphs that follow are from "Padre Blaisdell and the Refugee Children," Rene Cutforth's true story of a Catholic priest's efforts to save abandoned children during the Korean War. The place is Seoul; the time, December 1950.

Describes setting and introduces the main character.

At dawn Padre Blaisdell dressed himself in the little icy room at the top of the orphanage at Seoul. He put on his parka and an extra sweater, for the Siberian wind was fluting in the corners of the big grey barrack of the school …. The water in his basin was solid ice …..

His boots clicked along the stone flags in the freezing passages which led to the main door. The truck was waiting on the snow-covered gravel in the yellow-grey light of sunrise. The two Korean

Describes other characters.

nurses stood as usual, ready for duty—pig-tailed adolescents, their moon faces as passive and kindly as cows.

Uses a transition to show passage of time.

By the time he reached Riverside Road, the padre had passed through the normal first stage of reaction to the wind …; he was content now in his open vehicle to lie back and admire the effortless skill of the wind's razor as it slashed him to the bone.

Uses a metaphor, action verb.

There's a dingy alley off Riverside Street,

Uses vivid adjectives and proper nouns to describe setting.

narrow, and strewn with trodden straw and refuse which would stink if the cold allowed it life enough. This alley leads to the arches of the railway bridge across the Han River. The truck's wheels crackled over the frozen ... alley, passed from it down a sandy track and halted at the second arch of the bridge [in front of which] lay a pile of filthy rice sacks, clotted with dirt and stiff as boards. It was a child, practically naked and covered with filth. It lay in a pile of its own excrement in a sort of nest it had scratched out among the rice sacks. Hardly able to raise itself on an elbow, it still had enough energy to draw back cracked lips from bleeding gums and snarl and spit at the padre like an angry kitten. Its neck was not much thicker than a broom handle and it had the enormous pot-belly of starvation.

Uses vivid verbs and adjectives.

Uses a simile.

At eleven o'clock in the morning, when the padre returned to the orphanage, his truck was full. "They are the real victims of the war," the padre said in his careful ... colorless voice. "Nine-tenths of them were lost or abandoned .... No one will take them in unless they are relations, and we have 800 of these children at the orphanage. Usually they recover in quite a short time, but the bad cases tend to become very silent. I have a little boy who has said nothing for three months now but *Yes* and *No*."

Uses transition to show passage of time.

Uses dialogue to provide information and explain story's purpose.

7.8a Tracking the Passage of Time: "Padre Blaisdell and the Refugee Children"

We can divide the story roughly into three major sections, each of which is introduced by transitions that relate to time.

"At dawn ..."
Padre Blaisdell and the nurses leave the orphanage in search of orphans.

↓

"By the time he reached Riverside Road ..."
They find the child in the alley.

↓

"At eleven o'clock in the morning ..."
They return with a truckload of children.

7.9 Revising Narrative Essays

The first reading selection in this chapter, "The Colossus in the Kitchen," was written by Adrienne Schwartz, a student who recalls the racial prejudice aimed at Tandi, a black woman who worked for the author's family in South Africa. Realizing narrative essays require as much care as any others, Schwartz made important changes to her rough draft and turned an already fine essay into a memorable experience for her readers.

Schwartz—Rough Draft

Our neighbors, in conformity with established thinking, had long called my mother, and therefore all of us, deviants, agitators, and no less than second cousins to Satan himself. The

Use a quotation to show this?

cause of this dishonorable labeling was the fact that we had been taught to believe in the equality and dignity of humankind.

That was why I could not understand the apoplectic reaction of the neighbors to my excited news that Tandi was going to have a baby. After all, this was not politics; this was new life. Tandi's common-law husband lived illegally with

Connect these ideas better?

her in the quarters assigned to them; complying with the law on this and many other petty issues was not considered appropriate in our household. It was the Group Areas Act that had been responsible for the breakup of Tandi's marriage. Her lawful husband, who was not born in the same area as she, had been refused a permit to

Make smoother?

work in the Transvaal, a province in northeastern South Africa, where we lived. In the way of many others, he had been placed in such a burdensome   *Needed?*

More vivid?

situation and found the degradation of being taken from his wife's bed in the middle of the night and joblessness more often than he could   *Clarify?*

tolerate. He simply went away, never to be heard

from again.

The paradox of South Africa is complex in the extreme. It is like a rare and precious stone set amid barren wastes, and yet it feeds off its   *Find a better place for this idea?*

own flesh.

The days passed, and Tandi's waist got bigger and pride could be seen in her eyes.

Slow down? Show passage of time?

The child died after only one day.

Schwartz—Final Draft

Our neighbors, in conformity with established thinking, had long called my mother, and therefore all of us, deviants, agitators, and no less than second cousins to Satan himself. The cause of this dishonorable labeling was the fact that we had been taught to believe in the equality and dignity of humankind.

Uses direct quotation to prove an idea.

"Never take a person's dignity away from him," my mother had said, "no matter how angry or hurt you might be because in the end you only diminish your own worth."

That was why I could not understand the apoplectic reaction of the neighbors to my excited news that Tandi was going to have a baby. After all, this was not politics; this was new life. But the paradox of South Africa is complex in the extreme. The country is like a rare and precious stone set amid barren wastes, and yet close up it is a gangrenous growth that feeds off its own flesh.

Moves this information to a more logical place.

Adds vivid details in a metaphor.

Tandi's common-law husband lived illegally with her in the quarters assigned to them; complying with the law on this and many other petty issues was not considered appropriate in our household. It was the Group Areas Act that had been responsible for the breakup of Tandi's marriage in the first place. Her lawful husband, who was not born in the same area as she, had been refused a permit to work in the Transvaal and, like others placed in such a burdensome situation, suffered the continuous degradation of being dragged from his wife's bed in the middle of the night and of being denied work more often

Removes unnecessary information.

Adds transition to connect ideas.

Adds vivid verbs.

than he could tolerate. Eventually he simply melted away, never to be seen or heard from again, making legal divorce impossible.

Adds three transitions to show time passing.

As the days passed, Tandi's waist swelled, and pride glowed in her dauntless eyes.

Expands last sentence for dramatic effect.

And then the child was born, and he lived for a day, and then he died.

7.10 Practicing Narrative Skills

What follows is an eyewitness account of the last moments of the *Titanic*, which sank in 1912 after striking an iceberg. The writer views the scene from a lifeboat after having abandoned ship. Practice your skills by following the instructions for each section of this exercise.

1. Underline words and phrases that make this an effective narrative. Look especially for vivid verbs, adjectives, and adverbs. Also underline transitions.

   In a couple of hours … [the ship] began to go down … rapidly. Then the fearful sight began. The people in the ship were just beginning to realize how great their danger was. When the forward part of the ship dropped suddenly at a faster rate … there was a sudden rush of passengers on all the decks towards the stern. It was like a wave. We could see the great black mass of people in the steerage sweeping to the rear part of the boat and breaking through to the upper decks. At a distance of about a mile we could distinguish everything through the night, which was perfectly clear. We could make out the increasing excitement on board the boat as the people, rushing to and fro, caused the deck lights to disappear and reappear as they passed in front of them. [Mrs. D. H. Bishop]

2. Important words have been removed from the following paragraphs. Replace them with words of your own. Use only the kinds of words indicated. Avoid *is, are, was, were, have been, had been,* and other forms of the verb *to be.*

   This panic went on, it seemed, for an hour. _____ the ship seemed
                                                            TRANSITION

   to _____ out of the water and stand there perpendicularly. It seemed to us
          VERB

   that it stood _____ in the water for four full minutes. _____ it began to
                    ADVERB   **TRANSITION**

   _____ gently downwards. Its speed increased as it went down head first,
      VERB

   so that the stern _____ down with a rush.
                          VERB

   The lights continued to burn till it sank. We could see the people _____
                                                                          VERB

   _____ in the stern till it was gone …. _____ the ship sank, we _____
      ADVERB   **ADVERB OF TIME**   **VERB**

   the screaming a mile away. Gradually, it became fainter and fainter and died

   away. Some of the lifeboats that had room for more might have _____ to their
                                                                       VERB

   rescue, but it would have meant that those who were in the water would have

   _____ aboard and sunk them.
      VERB

7.11 Reading Selections

7.11a The Colossus in the Kitchen

Author Biography

Adrienne Schwartz was born in Johannesburg in the Republic of South Africa, where she now lives. "The Colossus in the Kitchen" is about the tragedy of apartheid, a political system that kept power and wealth in the hands of whites by denying civil and economic rights to nonwhites and by enforcing a policy of racial segregation. Tandi, the woman who is at the center of this story, was Schwartz's nursemaid for several years. Schwartz wrote this essay in 1988. Since that time, South Africa has abolished apartheid and extended civil rights to all citizens. Nelson Mandela, a black political leader who had been imprisoned by the white minority government during the apartheid era, became South Africa's first freely elected president.

Preparing to Read

1. The Group Areas Act, which Schwartz refers to in paragraph 6, required blacks to seek work only in those areas of the country for which the government had granted them a permit. Unfortunately, Tandi's legal husband was not allowed to work in the same region as she.

2. The Colossus was the giant bronze statue of a male figure straddling the inlet to the ancient Greek city of Rhodes. It was known as one of the seven wonders of the ancient world. More generally, this term refers to anything that is very large, impressive, and powerful. As you read this essay, ask yourself what made Tandi a colossus in the eyes of young Schwartz.

Vocabulary

apoplectic (adjective)   Characterized by a sudden loss of muscle control or ability to move.

ashen (adjective)   Gray.

bestriding (adjective)   Straddling, standing with legs spread widely.

cavernous (adjective)   Like a cave or cavern.

confections (noun)   Sweets.

cowered (adjective)   Cringing.

dauntless (adjective)   Fearless.

deviants (noun)   Criminals.

disenfranchised (adjective)   Without rights or power.

entailed (verb)   Involved.

flaying (noun)   Whipping.

gangrenous (adjective)   Decaying, decomposing.

nebulous (adjective)   Without definite shape.

prerogative (noun)   Privilege.

sage (adjective)   Wise.

The Colossus in the Kitchen

Adrienne Schwartz

I remember when I first discovered the extraordinary harshness of daily life for black South Africans. It was in the carefree, tumbling days of childhood that I first sensed apartheid was not merely the impoverishing of the landless and all that that entailed, but a flaying of the innermost spirit.   1

The house seemed so huge in those days, and the adults were giants bestriding the world with surety and purpose. Tandi, the cook, reigned with the authoritarian discipline of a Caesar. She held audience in the kitchen, an enormous room filled with half-lights and well-scrubbed tiles, cool stone floors and a cavernous black stove. Its ceilings were high, and during the heat of midday I would often drowse in the corner, listening to Tandi sing, in a lilting voice, of the hardships of black women as aliens in their own country. From half-closed eyes I would watch her broad hands coax, from a nebulous lump of dough, a bounty of confections, filled with yellow cream and new-picked apricots.   2

She was a peasant woman and almost illiterate, yet she spoke five languages quite competently; moreover, she was always there, sturdy, domineering and quick to laugh.   3

Our neighbors, in conformity with established thinking, had long called my mother, and therefore all of us, deviants, agitators, and no less than second cousins to Satan himself. The cause of this dishonorable labeling was the fact that we had been taught to believe in the equality and dignity of humankind.   4

"Never take a person's dignity away from him," my mother had said, "no matter how angry or hurt you might be because in the end you only diminish your own worth."   5

That was why I could not understand the apoplectic reaction of the neighbors to my excited news that Tandi was going to have a baby. After all, this was not politics; this was new life. But the paradox of South Africa is complex in the extreme. The country is like a rare and precious stone set amid barren wastes, and yet close up it is a gangrenous growth that feeds off its own flesh.   6

Tandi's common-law husband lived illegally with her in the quarters assigned to them; complying with the law on this and many other petty issues was not considered appropriate in our household. It was the Group Areas Act that had been responsible for the breakup of Tandi's marriage in the first place. Her lawful husband, who was not born in the same area as she, had been refused a permit to work in the Transvaal and, like others placed in such a burdensome situation, suffered the continuous degradation of being dragged from his wife's bed in the middle of the night and of being denied work more often than he could tolerate. Eventually he simply melted away, never to be seen or heard from again, making legal divorce impossible.   7

As the days passed, Tandi's waist swelled, and pride glowed in her dauntless eyes.   8

And then the child was born, and he lived for a day, and then he died.   9

I could not look at Tandi. I did not know that the young could die. I thought death was the prerogative of the elderly. I could not bear to see her cowered shoulders or ashen face.   10

I fled to the farthest corner of the yard. One of the neighbors was out picking off dead buds from the rose bushes. She looked over the hedge in concern.   11

"Why! You look terrible … are you ill, dear?" she said.   12

"It's Tandi, Mrs. Green. She lost her baby last night," I replied.   13

Mrs. Green sighed thoughtfully and pulled off her gardening gloves. "It's really not surprising," she said, not unkindly, but as if she were imparting as sage a piece of advice as she could. "These people (a term reserved for the disenfranchised) have to learn that the punishment always fits the crime."   14

Read More on the Web

For more on apartheid, visit

- "Apartheid," History.com: www.history.com/topics/africa/apartheid
- "The History of Apartheid in South Africa": http://bvtlab.com/7ke8Z

Questions for Discussion

1. Why does Schwartz spend so much time describing the kitchen in paragraph 2?

2. What details do we learn about Tandi, and what do they tell us about her character? Why does the author call her a "colossus"?

3. Why are we told so little about the story's characters other than Tandi?

4. Why does Schwartz recall events from Tandi's past (paragraph 6)?

5. The author makes especially good use of verbs in the last half of this essay. Find some examples.

6. Where does Schwartz use dialogue, and what does it reveal?

Thinking Critically

1. Apartheid was not "merely the impoverishing of the landless" but also "a flaying of the innermost spirit," says Schwartz. What does she mean by this? If necessary, do some research on apartheid on the Internet or in the library.

2. Is Schwartz's message or central idea similar to Leo Romero's in "What the Gossips Saw" (Chapter 4)? Write a paragraph in which you compare (point out similarities between) the central ideas of these selections.

Suggestions for Journal Entries

1. Have you or anyone you know well ever witnessed or been involved in a case of intolerance based on race, color, creed, or sex? List the important events that made up this incident and, if appropriate, use focused freewriting to write short descriptions of the characters involved.

2. Schwartz's essay is a startling account of her learning some new and very painful things about life. Using any of the prewriting methods discussed in Getting Started, make notes about an incident from your childhood that opened your eyes to some new and perhaps unpleasant reality.

3. Were you ever as close to an older person as Schwartz was to Tandi? Examine your relationship with the individual by briefly narrating one or two experiences you shared with him or her.

7.11b **Mid-Term Break**

Author Biography

Seamus Heaney (1939–2013) was born in County Derry in Northern Ireland. The son of a farmer, Heaney took a bachelor of arts at Queen's University in Belfast and then began teaching in secondary school. He was a professor of poetry at Oxford University in England and served as a visiting lecturer at Harvard University and at the University of California. Called the greatest living Irish poet of his time, Heaney won many awards, including the Nobel Prize for Literature (1995), the most prestigious honor a writer can receive. His poems focus on the land, people, and history of Northern Ireland. Some of his works also discuss the political and religious turmoil that have plagued his country. Collections of Heaney's poetry include *Field Work* (1979), *Station Island* (1984), and *The Hero Lantern* (1987).

Preparing to Read

1. What does the title tell us about the speaker of this poem?

2. As you read the first stanza (verse paragraph), ask yourself why the speaker tells us about spending "all morning in the college sick bay [infirmary]."

3. At the beginning of the poem, the speaker mentions bells ringing. For what might this prepare us?

Vocabulary

gaudy (adjective)   Conspicuous, ugly, in bad taste.

knelling (adjective)   Ringing.

poppy (adjective)   Red or deep orange.

pram (noun)   Baby carriage.

snowdrops (noun)   White flowers that bloom in early spring.

stanched (adjective)   Wrapped so as to stop the flow of blood.

Mid-Term Break

Seamus Heaney

I sat all morning in the college sick bay
Counting bells knelling classes to a close.
At two o'clock our neighbours drove me home.

In the porch I met my father crying—
He had always taken funerals in his stride—   5
And Big Jim Evans saying it was a hard blow.

The baby cooed and laughed and rocked the pram
When I came in, and I was embarrassed
By old men standing up to shake my hand

And tell me they were "sorry for my trouble."   10
Whispers informed strangers I was the eldest,
Away at school, as my mother held my hand

In hers and coughed out angry tearless sighs.
At ten o'clock the ambulance arrived
With the corpse, stanched and bandaged by the nurses.   15

Next morning I went up into the room. Snowdrops
And candles soothed the bedside; I saw him
For the first time in six weeks. Paler now,

Wearing a poppy bruise on his left temple,
He lay in the four foot box as in his cot.   20
No gaudy scars, the bumper knocked him clear.

A four foot box, a foot for every year.

Read More on the Web

For more about Seamus Heaney and his work visit these websites:

- "Seamus Heaney," Poetryfoundation.org: www.poetryfoundation.org/poets/seamus-heaney
- "About Seamus Heaney," The Poetry Archive: www.poetryarchive.org/poet/seamus-heaney

Questions for Discussion

1. What transitions does Heaney use to move this brief poem along?

2. What function does dialogue play in this poem?

3. What do the reactions of the speaker's mother and father reveal about them?

4. Comment upon the poet's choice of verbs in lines 13 through 21. What use of adjectives (especially participles) does he make?

5. Explain how changes in setting help the speaker convey his reaction to the death of his brother?

6. Find examples of figurative language.

Thinking Critically

1. We are shocked to learn of the death of a child at the end of this poem, but Heaney has prepared us all along. Make notes in the margins where you find clues about the poem's ending.

2. What contrasts does Heaney draw in this poem?

3. Heaney attended St. Columb's College before entering Queens University. What might the word *college* mean as used in "Mid-Term Break"?

Suggestions for Journal Entries

1. In the Questions for Discussion, you were asked to consider the different ways in which Heaney's mother and father reacted to the loss of their child. Some people react differently to death than others. Use freewriting, clustering, or listing to gather details that might help explain how you or someone you know reacted to the death of a loved one. Try to use vivid language and be as detailed as you can as you gather this information.

2. In lines 16 and 17, Heaney writes: "Snowdrops/And candles soothed the bedside." Find out more about "snowdrops" in an unabridged dictionary or online. Then, using freewriting, compose a detailed picture of what you imagine this scene to be. Base your description on Heaney's words, but go beyond them by adding detail from your own imagination.

7.11c The Day I Was Fat

Author Biography

When she isn't waitressing part-time or taking care of her family of four, *Lois Diaz-Talty* studies nursing and writes interesting essays such as the one that follows. She credits her husband and children for encouraging her academic efforts. Nonetheless, as the essay shows, she is an energetic, determined, and intelligent woman who is sure to succeed. When asked to write about a pivotal event or turning point in her life, Diaz-Talty recalled an incident that is burned into her memory and that has helped shape her life.

Preparing to Read

1. The significance of the event narrated in this essay is explained in its thesis, which appears near the end.

2. Diaz-Talty's style is conversational and often humorous, but her essay is always clear and focused. Pay attention to her use of dialogue, which captures the flavor of the moment.

3. Her title is unusual. What does it signal about what is to come?

Vocabulary

condiments (noun)   Seasonings, flavorings.

committed (adjective)   Determined.

ironically (adverb)   Having an effect opposite the one expected.

limber (adjective)   Able to bend easily, flexible.

notorious (adjective)   Shameful, bad.

The Day I Was Fat

Lois Diaz-Talty

I was never in great shape. As a child, I was always called "plump," and my friend "Skinny Sherri" was always, well, skinny. I could never sit Indian-style the way other kids did, and when I made the cheer-leading squad in eighth grade it was because I had a big mouth and a great smile, not because I could execute limber splits or elegant cartwheels. Although I maintained a respectable weight throughout high school (after all, my "entire life" depended upon my looks and popularity), there was always a fat person inside of me just waiting to burst onto the scene.

Adulthood, marriage, and settling down had notorious effects on my weight: I blew up! The fat lady had finally arrived, saw the welcome mat, and moved right in. No one in my family could tell me I was fat. They knew that I had gained weight, I knew that I had gained weight, and I knew that they knew that I had gained weight. But to discuss the topic was out of the question. Once, my mother said, "You're too pretty to be so heavy"; that was the closest anyone had ever come to calling me fat. Later, my husband teased me because we couldn't lie on the couch together anymore, and I just cried and cried. He never dared to mention it again, but I didn't stop eating.

I had just given birth to my first child and was at least fifty pounds overweight. Nonetheless, I remember feeling that that was the greatest time in my life. I had a beautiful new baby, new furniture, a great husband, a lovely house. What more could anyone want? Well, I knew what else I wanted: I wanted to be thin and healthy. I just didn't care enough about myself to stop my frequent binging. I tried to lose weight every day, but I couldn't get started. Diets didn't last through lunch, and I got bigger by the day.   3

One summer afternoon in 1988, as I was headed to the pool with my sister-in-law Mary Gene and our children, I got into an argument with a teenager who was driving fast and tail-gating our car. When he nearly ran us off the road, I turned around and glared at him to show my disapproval and my concern for our safety. Suddenly, we began yelling at each other. He was about 18, with an ugly, red, swollen face. The few teeth he had were yellow and rotten. He followed us to the pool and, as he pulled into the parking lot behind us, our argument became heated.   4

"What's your problem, bitch?" he screamed.   5

"You drive like an idiot! That's my problem, okay?"   6

When I got out of the car and walked around to get the baby, he laughed to his friend, "Ah, look at 'er. She's fat! Go to hell, fat bitch." And then they drove away.   7

Once inside the gates to the pool, my sister-in-law advised me to forget the whole incident.   8

"Come on," she said. "Don't worry about that jerk! Did you see his teeth? He was gross."   9

But I couldn't get his words out of my mind. They stung like a whip. "I'm fat," I thought to myself. "I haven't just put on a few pounds. I'm not bloated. I don't have baby weight to lose. I'm just plain fat." Nobody had ever called me fat before, and it hurt terribly. But it was true.   10

On that very day, as I sat at the pool praying that nobody would see me in my bathing suit, I promised myself that no one would ever call me fat again. That hideous, 18-year-old idiot had spoken the words that none of my loved ones had had the heart to say even though they were true. Yes, I was fat.   11

From then on, I was committed to shedding the weight and getting into shape. I started a rigorous program of running and dieting the very next day. Within months, I joined a gym and managed to make some friends who are still my workout buddies. However, in the past seven years, I've done more than lose weight: I've reshaped my attitude, my lifestyle, and my self-image. Now, I read everything I can about nutrition and health. I'm even considering becoming an aerobics instructor. I cook low-fat foods—chicken, fish, lean meats, vegetables—and I serve my family healthy, protein-rich meals prepared with dietetic ingredients. The children and I often walk to school, ride bikes, roller-blade, and run. Health and fitness have become essential to our household and our lives. But what's really wonderful is that, sometime between that pivotal day in 1988 and today, my self-image stopped being about how I look and began being about how I feel. I feel energetic, healthy, confident, strong, and pretty. Ironically, the abuse I endured in the parking lot has helped me regain my self-esteem, not just my figure. My body looks good, but my mind feels great!   12

I hope that the kid from the pool has had his teeth fixed because I'm sure they were one source of his misery. If I ever see him again, I won't tell him that he changed my life in such a special way. I won't let him know that he gave me the greatest gift he could ever give me just by being honest. I won't give him the satisfaction of knowing that the day he called me fat was one of the best days of my life.   13

Read More on the Web

For more on dieting and losing weight see the following:

- The Obesity Society: www.obesity.org
- Nutrition.gov: www.nutrition.gov

Questions for Discussion

1. Where does Diaz-Talty express the essay's central idea? In other words, which sentence is her thesis?

2. What purpose does the author's quoting herself serve in this essay? Why does she quote her mother?

3. Why did the author quote the exact words of the boy who harassed her? Would simply telling us what happened have been enough?

4. Why does Diaz-Talty bother to describe this person? Why does she make sure to reveal her attitude toward him?

5. Reread three or four paragraphs, and circle the transitions used to show the passage of time and to create coherence.

6. Find places in which the author uses particularly good verbs, adjectives, and adverbs.

Thinking Critically

1. Make notes in the margins next to details that reveal important aspects of the author's personality.

2. If you were in the author's place, how would you have reacted to the insult? Write a paragraph that explains an aspect of your personality or lifestyle that needs improvement. Then, write a paragraph that explains how you might improve it.

Suggestions for Journal Entries

1. Recall an event that changed your life for the better. Ask the journalists' questions to collect details about this event and to explain how it helped you. For example, here is the journal entry Diaz-Talty made in preparation for "The Day I Was Fat."

   When? In 1988, shortly after I gave birth to Tommy.
   What? An argument with a teenager who had been driving behind us. He called me fat.
   Who? I and a rude, 18-year-old stranger, who looked gross.
   Where? On the way to the pool.
   Why important? Because I was fat.
   How? His insult shamed me. Made me work harder to lose weight and helped restore self-esteem.

2. Use focused freewriting to gather details about how you reacted to an incident in which someone hurt, insulted, or cheated you or did something else unpleasant to you. In the process, analyze your reaction

7.11d 37 Who Saw Murder Didn't Call the Police

Author Biography

Martin Gansberg was a reporter and editor at *The New York Times* when he wrote "37 Who Saw Murder Didn't Call the Police" in 1964. This story about the murder of a young woman is doubly terrifying, for the thirty-eight witnesses to the crime might very well have saved her life if only they had had the courage to become involved.

Preparing to Read

1. The setting is Kew Gardens, a well-to-do neighborhood in Queens, New York. One reason Gansberg describes it in great detail is to make his story realistic. Another is to show his readers that the neighbors had a clear view of the crime from their windows. But there are other reasons as well. Pay close attention to the details used to describe the setting.

2. Gansberg begins the story by using dialogue to report an interview he had with the police. He ends it similarly, including dialogue from interviews with several witnesses. Read these two parts of the narrative as carefully as you read the story of the murder itself. They contain important information about Gansberg's reaction to the incident and his purpose in writing this piece.

3. The story of Kitty Genovese is a comment about the fact that people sometimes ignore their responsibilities to neighbors and lose that important sense of community that binds us together. Identify this central idea, or theme, as you read "37 Who Saw Murder Didn't Call the Police."

Vocabulary

deliberation (noun)   Thinking.

distraught (adjective)   Very upset.

punctuated (verb)   Were clearly heard (literally "made a mark in").

recitation (noun)   Speech, lecture.

Tudor (adjective)   Type of architecture in which the beams are exposed.

37 Who Saw Murder Didn't Call the Police

Martin Gansberg

For more than half an hour 38 respectable, law-abiding citizens in Queens watched a killer stalk and stab a woman in three separate attacks in Kew Gardens.   1

Twice their chatter and the sudden glow of their bedroom lights interrupted him and frightened him off. Each time he returned, sought her out, and stabbed her again. Not one person telephoned the police during the assault; one witness called after the woman was dead.   2

That was two weeks ago today.   3

Still shocked is Assistant Chief Inspector Frederick M. Lussen, in charge of the borough's detectives and a veteran of 25 years of homicide investigations. He can give a matter-of-fact recitation on many murders. But the Kew Gardens slaying baffles him—not because it is a murder, but because the "good people" failed to call the police.   4

"As we have reconstructed the crime," he said, "the assailant had three chances to kill this woman during a 35-minute period. He returned twice to complete the job. If we had been called when he first attacked, the woman might not be dead now."   5

This is what the police say happened beginning at 3:20 a.m. in the staid, middle-class, tree-lined Austin Street area: 6

Twenty-eight-year-old Catherine Genovese, who was called Kitty by almost everyone in the neighborhood, was returning home from her job as manager of a bar in Hollis. She parked her red Fiat in a lot adjacent to the Kew Gardens Long Island Railroad Station, facing Mowbray Place. Like many residents of the neighborhood, she had parked there day after day since her arrival from Connecticut a year ago, although the railroad frowns on the practice.   7

She turned off the lights of her car, locked the door, and started to walk the 100 feet to the entrance of her apartment at 82-70 Austin Street, which is in a Tudor building, with stores in the first floor and apartments on the second.

8

The entrance to the apartment is in the rear of the building because the front is rented to retail stores. At night the quiet neighborhood is shrouded in the slumbering darkness that marks most residential areas.

9

Miss Genovese noticed a man at the far end of the lot, near a seven-story apartment house at 82-40 Austin Street. She halted. Then, nervously, she headed up Austin Street toward Lefferts Boulevard, where there is a call box to the 102nd Police Precinct in nearby Richmond Hill.

10

She got as far as a street light in front of a bookstore before the man grabbed her. She screamed. Lights went on in the 10-story apartment house at 82-67 Austin Street, which faces the bookstore. Windows slid open and voices punctuated the early-morning stillness.

11

Miss Genovese screamed: "Oh, my God, he stabbed me! Please help me! Please help me!"

12

From one of the upper windows in the apartment house, a man called down: "Let that girl alone!"

13

The assailant looked up at him, shrugged and walked down Austin Street toward a white sedan parked a short distance away. Miss Genovese struggled to her feet.

14

Lights went out. The killer returned to Miss Genovese, now trying to make her way around the side of the building by the parking lot to go to her apartment. The assailant stabbed her again.

15

"I'm dying!" She shrieked. "I'm dying!"

16

Windows were opened again, and lights went on in many apartments. The assailant got into his car and drove away. Miss Genovese staggered to her feet.

17

A city bus, Q-10, the Lefferts Boulevard line to Kennedy International Airport, passed. It was 3:35 a.m.

18

The assailant returned. By then, Miss Genovese had crawled to the back of the building, where the freshly painted brown doors to the apartment house held out hope for safety. The killer tried the first door; she wasn't there. At the second door, 82-62 Austin Street, he saw her slumped on the floor at the foot of the stairs. He stabbed her a third time—fatally.

19

It was 3:50 by the time the police received their first call, from a man who was a neighbor of Miss Genovese. In two minutes they were at the scene. The neighbor, a 70-year-old woman, and another woman were the only persons on the street. Nobody else came forward.

20

The man explained that he had called the police after much deliberation. He had phoned a friend in Nassau County for advice and then he had crossed the roof of the building to the apartment of the elderly woman to get her to make the call.

21

"I didn't want to get involved," he sheepishly told the police.

22

Six days later, the police arrested Winston Moseley, a 29-year-old business-machine operator, and charged him with homicide. Moseley had no previous record. He is married, has two children and owns a home at 133-19 Sutter Avenue, South Ozone Park, Queens. On Wednesday, a court committed him to Kings County Hospital for psychiatric observation.

23

When questioned by the police, Moseley also said that he had slain Mrs. Annie May Johnson, 24, of 146-12 133rd Avenue, Jamaica, on Feb. 29 and Barbara Kralik, 15, of 174-17 140th Avenue, Springfield Gardens, last July. In the Kralik case, the police are holding Alvin L. Mitchell, who is said to have confessed to that slaying.

24

The police stressed how simple it would have been to have gotten in touch with them. "A phone call," said one of the detectives, "would have done it." The police may be reached by dialing "O" for operator or Spring 7-3100.

25

Today witnesses from the neighborhood, which is made up of one-family homes in the $35,000 to $60,000 range with the exception of the two apartment houses near the railroad station, find it difficult to explain why they didn't call the police.

26

A housewife, knowingly if quite casually, said, "We thought it was a lover's quarrel." A husband and wife both said, "Frankly, we were afraid." They seemed aware of the fact that events might have been different. A distraught woman, wiping her hands on her apron, said, "I didn't want my husband to get involved."

27

One couple, now willing to talk about that night, said they heard the first screams. The husband looked thoughtfully at the bookstore where the killer first grabbed Miss Genovese.   28

"We went to the window to see what was happening," he said, "but the light from our bedroom made it difficult to see the street." The wife, still apprehensive, added: "I put out the light and we were able to see better."   29

Asked why they hadn't called the police, she shrugged and replied: "I don't know."   30

A man peeked out from the slight opening in the doorway to his apartment and rattled off an account of the killer's second attack. Why hadn't he called the police at the time? "I was tired," he said without emotion. "I went back to bed."   31

It was 4:25 a.m. when the ambulance arrived to take the body of Miss Genovese. It drove off. "Then," a solemn police detective said, "the people came out."   32

Read More on the Web

More about the Genovese case can be found by searching for the following on the Web:

- History.com: www.history.com/topics/crime/kitty-genovese
- "The Truth about Kitty Genovese," *New York Daily News*: http://bvtlab.com/v3t25

Questions for Discussion

1. Catherine Genovese "was called Kitty by almost everyone in the neighborhood" (paragraph 7). What does this fact reveal about her relationship with her neighbors?

2. In Preparing to Read, you learned that there are several reasons for Gansberg's including details to describe the setting of this story. In what kind of neighborhood does the murder take place? What kind of people live in it?

3. In reporting several interviews he had with the police and with witnesses, Gansberg frames the story with dialogue at the beginning and end. What do we learn from this dialogue?

4. The author keeps the story moving by mentioning the times at which various episodes in the attack took place. Where does he mention these times? In addition, what transitional words or expressions does Gansberg use to show the passage of time?

5. The story's verbs demonstrate how brutal and terrifying the murder of Kitty Genovese actually was. Identify a few of these verbs.

Thinking Critically

1. Make a list of things you might have done to help Kitty Genovese had you witnessed the attack.

2. Gansberg quotes several witnesses. If you had had the opportunity to interview these people, what would you have asked or told them? Write your questions and comments in the margins alongside their remarks.

3. The title of this article is "37 Who Saw Murder Didn't Call the Police." Yet the first line mentions 38 witnesses. Explain this apparent discrepancy.

Suggestions for Journal Entries

1. This story illustrates what can happen when people lose their sense of community and refuse to "get involved." Use focused freewriting to make notes about one or two incidents from your own experiences that illustrate this idea too.

2. Recall a time when you thought you were in some danger. Briefly describe what it was like. What did you do to try to avoid or escape physical harm?

7.12 Suggestions for Sustained Writing

1. Have you ever been treated unfairly, belittled, or held back because of your race, religion, nationality, physical handicap, personal belief, or any other reason? Tell your story vividly and completely. In the process, explain what the experience taught you about other people or society in general. Express this idea as your thesis statement somewhere in the essay.

   A good example of an essay that uses narration to develop a strong thesis statement is Adrienne Schwartz's "The Colossus in the Kitchen." In her first paragraph, Schwartz defines apartheid as "a flaying of the innermost spirit"; she then uses the rest of her essay to support that idea.

   Begin working by reviewing journal notes you made after reading this essay Then outline and draft your paper. Like Schwartz, you can focus on one event. Or you might narrate two or three events to support your thesis. Either way, include details about the people in your story as you draft or revise. Describe their personalities by revealing what they said or did. Then, as you edit for grammar, punctuation, and spelling, pay special attention to the vocabulary you have chosen. Include proper nouns as appropriate, and make sure your language is specific and vivid.

2. If you responded to the first Suggestion for Journal Entries after Seamus Heaney's "Mid-Term Break," write an essay in which you explain your reaction or the reaction of someone you know to the death of a loved one. Now, add information to the notes you have already taken on this topic in your journal. If possible, interview or brainstorm with another person who has shared this loss—perhaps another family member or a close friend. Delve into your subject's character by explaining how he or she reacted to the shock, grieved over the loss, and dealt with the grief, if at all. Your narrative might span a few days, a few weeks, or even a few years.

   As you revise your first draft, add concrete details, figures of speech, and vivid verbs and adjectives. When you revise your second draft, try adding dialogue, and make sure you have described the setting and the people in your story well. Finally, check to see if you have included transitional devices and effective verbs to move the story along and to make it easy to follow. Next, edit your work for grammar; sentence structure, length, and variety; word choice; and punctuation and spelling. As always, proofread. This will probably be a powerful story—you don't want to spoil it with silly mistakes in writing or typing.

3. Use narration to explain what someone did to influence you either positively or negatively. Show how this person encouraged or discouraged you to develop a particular interest or talent, explain what he or she taught you about yourself, or discuss ways he or she strengthened or weakened your self-esteem.

You need not express yourself in an essay. Consider writing a letter instead. Address it to the person who influenced you, and explain your appreciation or resentment of that influence. Either way, put your thesis—a statement of just how positively or negatively he or she affected you—in the introduction to your essay or letter.

Before you begin, check the journal entries you made after reading the essay by Lois Diaz-Talty. Then, write one or two stories from personal experience that show how the person in question affected you. After completing your first draft, try adding dialogue to your stories. Reveal your subject's attitude toward you by recalling words he or she used when answering your questions, giving you advice or instructions, or commenting on your efforts.

As you revise your work further, make sure you have explained the results of this person's influence on you thoroughly. Add details as you move from draft to draft. Then, edit for grammar, punctuation, spelling, and other problems that can make your writing less effective.

4. The first of the Suggestions for Journal Entries after Lois Diaz-Talty's "The Day I Was Fat" asks you to gather information about a painful experience that changed your life for the better. Use this information to begin drafting a full-length essay that explains what happened.

You might begin the first draft by stating in one sentence how this event changed you; this will be your working thesis. You can then tell your story, including only those materials that help explain or prove the thesis. For example, Diaz-Talty says that being called fat helped her regain her self-esteem and her figure; every detail in her story helps prove this statement.

As you write later drafts, add dialogue and descriptive detail about people in your story, just as Diaz-Talty did. If you are unhappy with your introductory and concluding paragraphs, rewrite them by using techniques explained in chapter 3.

Before you get to your final draft, make certain your paper contains vivid verbs, adjectives, and adverbs, which will keep readers interested. If it doesn't, add them. Then, edit and proofread your work carefully.

5. Have you ever witnessed or experienced an automobile accident, a robbery, a mugging, a house fire, serious injury, sudden illness, or other violence or misfortune? Tell what happened during this terrible experience and describe the people involved. However, spend most of your time discussing the reactions of people who looked on as the event took place. Were you one of them? What did they do or say? What didn't they do that they should have done?

You might find inspiration and information for this project in the journal entries you made after reading Adrienne Schwartz and Martin Gansberg. Before you write your first draft, however, think about what the event itself and the onlookers' reactions taught you about human nature. Were you encouraged or disappointed by what you learned? Express your answer in a preliminary thesis statement. Write at least two drafts of your story, and make sure to include details that will support this thesis.

Then revise at least one more time by turning what you have just written into a letter to the editor of your college or community newspaper. Use your letter to explain your approval or disappointment about the way the onlookers reacted, but don't mention their names. If appropriate, offer suggestions about the way your readers might respond if faced with an experience like the one you have narrated. Whether or not you send your letter to a newspaper, edit it carefully, just as if it were going to be published.

ACKNOWLEDGMENTS

Cutforth, Rene. Excerpt from *Korean Reporter*. London, Allan Wingate, 1964.

Gansberg, Martin. "37 Who Saw Murder Didn't Call the Police." From the *New York Times*, 27 Mr. 1964 © 1964 The New York Times. All rights reserved. Used by permission and protected by the Copyright Laws of the United States. The printing, copying, redistribution, or retransmission of this Content without express written permission is prohibited.

Heaney, Seamus. "Mid-Term Break." *Opened Ground: Selected Poems* 1966–1996. Copyright © 1998 by Seamus Heaney. Reprinted by permission of Farrar, Straus and Giroux and Faber and Faber Ltd.

Section 4
Exposition

Many new writers begin to develop their skills by practicing the kinds of writing found in Section 3: Description and Narration. As you learned in previous chapters, description and narration usually involve writing about subjects that are concrete and, often, very specific—people, places, events, or objects that the reader can picture or understand easily. The primary purpose of description, of course, is to explain what someone or something looks like, sounds like, and so forth. The primary purpose of narration is simply to tell what happened, although many short stories and narrative essays do a great deal more.

At times, however, new writers face the challenge of discussing abstract ideas that can't be explained through narration and description alone. In such cases, they must rely on a variety of methods of development and techniques associated with exposition. *Exposition* is writing that explains.

Each reading selection in chapters 8, 9, 10, and 11 explains an idea by using illustration, comparison and contrast, process analysis, or definition as its *primary* method of development. However, these selections also rely on other methods explained earlier in this book (see chapter 2). In fact, most writers of exposition combine different methods to develop ideas clearly and convincingly. Comparison-and-contrast papers frequently contain definitions, anecdotes, and examples; process analyses include accurate, sometimes vivid, descriptions; and illustration essays sometimes use comparisons, anecdotes, and descriptions.

Whatever your purpose and however you choose to develop ideas, you will have to know your subject well, include enough accurate information to make your writing convincing, and present that information in a way that is clear and easy to follow.

Explaining through Illustration

One of the most popular ways to explain an idea is through illustration, a method of development you read about in chapter 2. Illustration uses examples to turn an idea that is general, abstract, or hard to understand into something readers can recognize and, therefore, grasp more easily. As the word implies, an *illustration* essay is a concrete and specific picture of an idea that would otherwise have remained vague and undefined.

For instance, if you wanted a clearer and more definitive notion of what your friend meant when she claimed to have met several "interesting characters" since coming to school, you might ask her to describe a few of those characters specifically and to show you in what ways they were interesting. Each of the people she discussed would then serve as an illustration or picture of what she meant by the abstract word *interesting*.

Explaining through Comparison and Contrast

Comparison and contrast involves pointing out similarities or differences, or both, between two people, objects, places, experiences, ways of doing something, and the like. Writers compare (point out similarities between) and contrast (point out differences

201

between) two things to make one or both more recognizable or understandable to readers. Let's say you want to explain a computer monitor to someone who has never seen one. You might compare it with a television set. After all, both have glass screens on which electronic images appear. To make your explanation more complete and accurate, however, you might also need to contrast these two devices by pointing out that a computer is more useful when it comes to writing a document, creating a slide presentation, organizing a spreadsheet, or researching information. Contrast also comes in handy when you want to explain why you believe one thing is better than another. For example, "Watch the Cart!" an essay in the introduction to chapter 9, points out differences to explain why the author thinks women are more adept at grocery shopping than men.

There are many reasons for comparing or contrasting the subjects you wish to write about. Whatever your purpose, you may find that comparing or contrasting will help you bring abstract ideas into sharper focus and make them more concrete than if you had discussed each of your subjects separately.

Explaining through Process Analysis

Process analysis is used in scientific writing to help readers understand both natural and technical processes such as the formation of rain clouds, the circulation of blood through the body, or the workings of a CD player. However, it also has a place in nonscientific writing. For example, you might want to use process analysis to explain how U.S. presidents are elected, how money is transferred from one bank to another electronically, or even how your Aunt Millie manages to turn the most solemn occasion into a party.

Process analysis is useful when you need to provide the reader with directions or instructions to complete a specific task. Subjects for such essays might include "how to change the brakes on a car," "how to bake lasagna," or "how to get to school from the center of town." In each of these examples, the writer is assigning him- or herself the task of explaining, as specifically and as clearly as possible, an idea that might be new and/or unfamiliar to the reader. In each case, the essay will focus on how to do something or how something is done.

Though it may often seem deceptively simple, writing a process paper is often a painstaking task and must be approached carefully. Remember that your readers might be totally unfamiliar with what you're explaining and will thus need a great deal of information to follow the process easily and to understand it thoroughly.

As a matter of fact, the need to be clear and concrete often causes writers of process analysis to rely on other methods of development, such as narration, description, illustration, and comparison/contrast. Of these, writers of process analysis rely most heavily on narration. After all, a process is a story. Like narratives, process papers are often organized in chronological order and explain a series of events. Unlike narratives, however, process essays don't simply tell what happens; they also explain how something happens or how something should be done.

Explaining through Definition

Unlike some of the other types of exposition, definition relates more to purpose than it does to any specific type of method or technique. In fact, definition essays employ a variety of the other methods of development—most often description, illustration, comparison/contrast, and cause/effect—to make their points. The purpose of definition, as you learned in chapter 2, is to explain a term, concept, or idea that may be totally unfamiliar to the reader. In some ways, it is like description. However, while description works with the concrete (subjects that can be seen, heard, smelled, felt, or tasted), definition works with both the concrete and the abstract.

However, even when dealing with the concrete, definition goes beyond description by explaining the nature of a subject. For example, whereas a descriptive essay might focus on a particular father and tell us what he looks and acts like, a definition essay would focus on the notion of fatherhood. A descriptive paper might reveal the beauty of the Northern Lights, while a definition paper would tell us what they are by also explaining what causes them, how they occur, and how they affect our civilization. Finally, as you will see when you read the essays in chapter 11, definition can be used to deal with subjects that are purely abstract and that do not lend themselves to explanation by description—or by any of the other methods—alone. Examples include *materialism, jealousy, poverty, conservatism, faith, perseverance, youth culture, fatherlessness,* and *evil*.

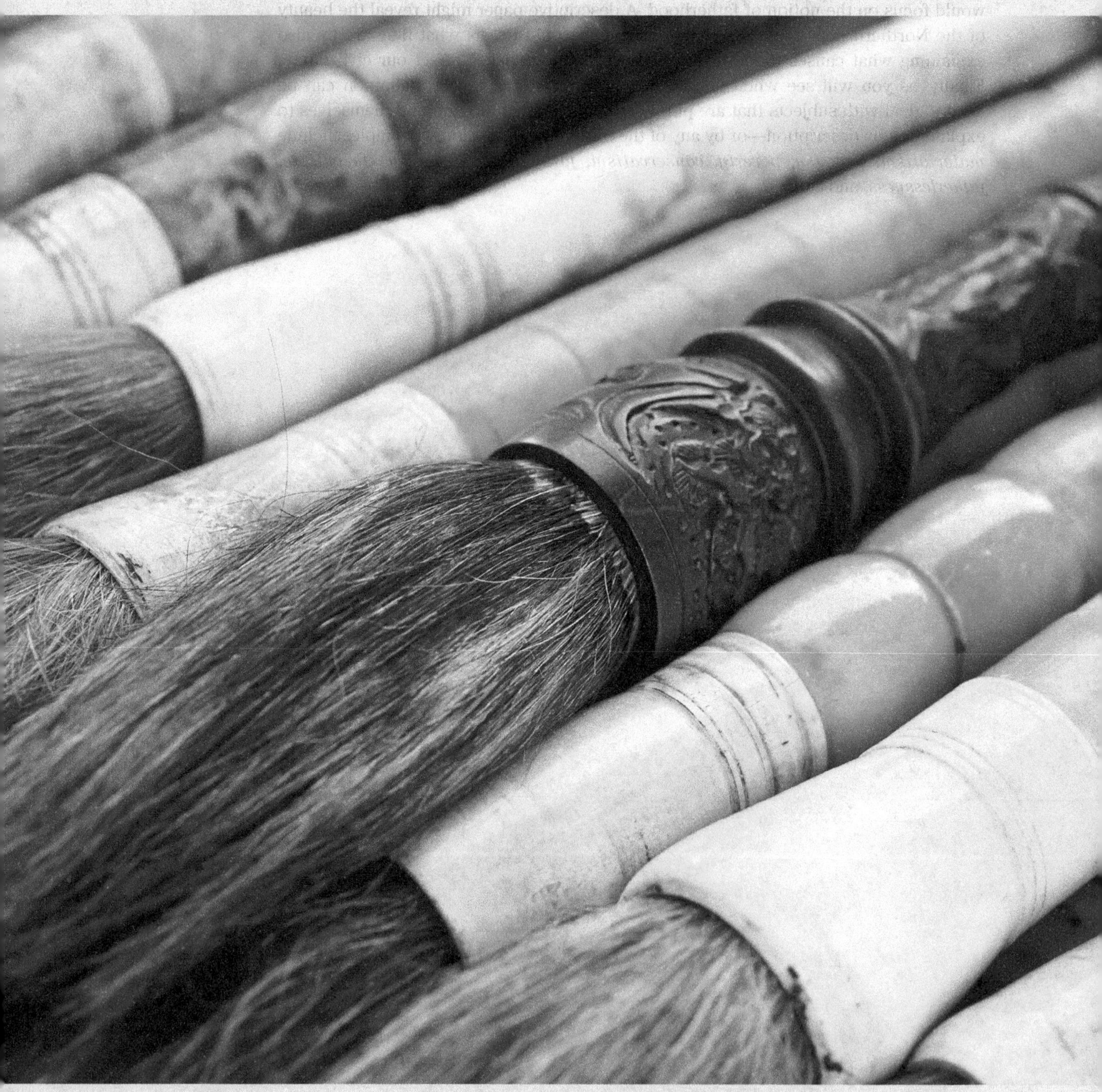

Shutterstock

Chapter 8

Illustration

Chapter Outline

You have learned that the most interesting and effective writing uses specific and concrete details to *show* rather than to *tell* the reader something. This goes for all types of writing, including exposition. One of the best ways to show your readers what you mean is to fill your writing with clear, relevant examples. Examples are also referred to as *illustrations*. They act as pictures—concrete representations—of an abstract idea you are trying to explain, and they make your writing easier to understand and more convincing for your readers. Illustration can be used as the primary method to develop a thesis in your expository writing.

Effective illustrations make reference to specific people, places, and things—familiar realities that your readers will recognize or understand easily. Say that you want to convince them that your 2018 Wizbang hybrid is an economical car. Instead of being content to rely on their understanding of a vague word like *economical*, you decide to provide examples that show exactly what you think this term means. Therefore, you explain that the Wizbang gets about 65 miles per gallon around town, that its purchase price is $4,000 less than its least expensive competitor's, and that it needs only one $50 tune-up every 40,000 miles. Now that's economical!

Several types of examples are discussed below. The important thing to remember is that the examples you choose must relate to and be appropriate to the idea you're illustrating. For instance, you probably wouldn't cite statistics about the Wizbang's safety record if you wanted to impress your readers with how inexpensive the car is to own and operate.

8.1 Specific Facts, Instances, or Occurrences

A good way to get examples into your writing is to use specific facts, instances, or occurrences relating to the idea you are explaining. Let's say you want to prove that the Wizbang does not perform well in bad weather. You can say it stalled twice during a recent rainstorm or that it did not start when the temperature fell below freezing last week. If you want to show that people in your town are community-minded, you might mention that they recently opened a shelter for the homeless, that they have organized a meals-on-wheels program for the elderly, or that they have increased their contributions to the United Way campaign in each of the past five years. If you want to prove that the 1960s were years of turmoil, you can recall the assassinations of John and Robert Kennedy and Martin Luther King Jr., the antiwar marches, and the urban riots.

The reading selections in this chapter use specific facts, instances, or occurrences to illustrate and develop ideas. Grace Lukawska's "Wolf" is full of revealing facts about this animal. Specific instances and occurrences can be found in Richard Lederer's essay, which is filled with examples of anomalies, contradictions, and peculiarities to prove that "English Is a Crazy Language."

8.2 Statistics

Mathematical figures, or statistics, can also be included to strengthen your reader's understanding of an abstract idea. If you want to prove that the cost of living in your hometown has increased dramatically over the past five years, you might explain that the price of a three-bedroom home has increased by about 30 percent, from $200,000 to $260,000; that real estate taxes have doubled from an average of $2,500 per family to $5,000 per family; and that the cost of utilities has nearly tripled, with each household now spending about $180 per month on heat and electricity. Walter Williams's "Overpopulation Hoax" makes good use of statistics.

8.3 Specific People, Places, or Things

Mentioning specific people, places, and things familiar to the readers can also help you make abstract ideas easier to understand and more convincing. If you want to explain that the American South is famous for the presidents and statespeople it has produced, you might bring up George Washington, Thomas Jefferson, Henry Clay, Lyndon Johnson, Martin Luther King Jr., and George W. Bush. If you need to convince readers that your city is a great place to have fun, you will probably mention its amusement park, professional football stadium, brand new children's zoo and aquarium, community swimming pool, campgrounds, and public golf courses. Specific people, places, and things are mentioned throughout Robert F. Howe's "Covert Force."

8.4 Anecdotes

As you probably know, **anecdotes** are brief, informative stories that develop an idea or drive home a point. They are similar to and serve the same purpose as specific instances and occurrences, and they are sometimes used with such illustrations to develop an idea more fully. However, anecdotes often appear in greater detail than other types of examples. Look for anecdotes especially in Howe's "Covert Force," an essay about women who, disguised as men, fought in the Civil War.

anecdote
A brief, sometimes humorous story used to illustrate or develop a specific point.

8.5 Visualizing Examples

In 2017, Representative Bill Posey of Florida's Eighth District published a list of projects funded by the federal government. The kinds of projects the government spends taxpayer money on might help explain why our national debt was, as of the end of that year, more than $20 trillion. Representative Posey's list, when downloaded from his website, covers forty-four standard 8" x 11" sheets of paper. Here are just a few highlights:

Congressional Representative Bill Posey's Wasteful Spending List

Mentions specific instances.

- The Department of Defense picked up a coffee bill of over $100,000 at two Veterans' Affairs conventions, while the Department of Agriculture gave a potato chip farmer $50,000 to learn how to better market his product. But that's small potatoes.

Includes statistics of groups that will profit from grant.

- Among the most egregious wastes of money was for a $2 million intern program at the Department of Agriculture, for which only one intern was hired. Even worse was the $24 million grant to buy high-speed Internet routers for rural areas of West Virginia. Each router costs over $22,000 and can serve thousands of users. But, in the locations where the routers were installed, the population is sparse, and relatively few organizations are using them.

- When two Alaska legislators tried to get the federal government to spend $380 million to build the

Gravina Island Bridge (aka "the bridge to nowhere"), many people did not see the need to spend that money, for the ferry that ran to the island from Ketchikan every half hour was working just fine. Although Ketchikan International Airport is located on Gravina Island, only 50 people live on the island. That project was eventually cancelled. However, as part of the American Recovery and Reinvestment Act, over $100 million was granted to a community in the Aleutian Islands to build an airport and a harbor. The town has 75 residents, and no roads connect to the harbor or airport.

Uses an anecdote as part of an effective comparison.

• Over the past few years, the Department of Education has increased its budget by over 36 percent, but less than one-quarter of the federal taxpayers' money ever sees the inside of a classroom. Perhaps that's one reason some people argue that the Department of Education should be abolished. Others have a problem with the Department of Energy, which offered a contest prize of $100,000 for someone who could create a cell phone app that would keep track of a family's energy use. The only problem is that several existing apps already do that: "Opower," "Energysaver," and "Energytracker" are just a few of many.

Mentions a specific instance using a statistic.

Mentions specific app names to prove a point.

• Finally, that same department gave nearly $1 billion in energy tax credits to people who did not own a home. This included children and people who were incarcerated.

Uses a specific instance.

8.6 Revising Illustration Essays

Before writing "Wolf," student Grace Lukawska had completed a great deal of prewriting in her journal to get started. When she finished her first draft, however, she realized she would have to add more detail, restructure her essay, and improve some of her word choices to make her point effectively. By the time she finished, she had written several drafts, but the final product shows that careful revision is always worth the effort. Read these paragraphs from two versions of the complete paper, which appears in this chapter. Information in parentheses refers to pages in Candace Savage's *Wolves*, a book in which Lukawska researched facts about her subject.

Lukawska—Rough Draft

Make introduction more interesting?

There are still popular misconceptions of the wolf as predator. Many people think: that wolves kill for pleasure or just to show their dominance over other animals. However, the truth is that wolves are very fascinating and intelligent.

Include vivid details and examples to explain "misconceptions"?

Their intelligence manifests itself in their behavior. Wolves belong to a group of animals who live in hierarchical groups. According to Candace Savage, a large, well-organized pack consists of an upper class—parents, a middle class—uncles and aunts, a lower class—children, and finally "helpers" who are inexperienced hunters and who depend on the pack (55). Their role is to baby-sit youngsters while the other wolves are hunting (62).

For what? Explain.

Another example of wolves' aptitude is clear communication. The leader of the group, usually the male, establishes regulations so that each animal knows whom it can boss and to whom it must submit. For instance, a middle-class wolf must obey the leader's orders; children and helpers must submit to their relatives. These rules help to prevent fights or disagreements in packs. Furthermore, wolves have their own language which is based on different sound levels in their voices. For example, according to Savage, a whimper indicates a friendly attitude; snarls convey warnings and admonitions (58).

Relates to "communication"?

Say more about language? Include examples?

Lukawska—Final Draft

Creates vivid images that serve as examples.

For centuries, popular misconceptions have pictured the wolf as a terrifying predator that kills for pleasure. The name itself calls up nasty images: the glutton who "wolfs" down his food; the werewolf, who, during a full moon, grows hair all over his body, howls into the night, and claws beautiful maidens to death. Even in fairy

Mentions specific story, which readers should recognize.

tales, such as "Little Red Riding Hood," the wolf is pictured as shrewd and bloodthirsty.

But is the wolf really a cold-blooded killer? Not at all; the wolf is a magnificent animal which displays many of the characteristics we value in human beings.

Makes thesis clearer, stronger.

The intelligence of the wolf manifests itself in its behavior. The wolf's society is well organized and hierarchical.

According to Candace Savage, author of *Wolves*, a pack consists of an upper class—parents, a middle class—uncles and aunts, a lower class—children, and finally "helpers,"

Mentions title of Savage's book.

who are inexperienced hunters and who depend upon the pack for their food (55). Their role is to baby-sit youngsters while the other wolves are hunting (62). Like humans, wolves practice adoption. If parents die, their children are cared for by another family.

Becomes more specific.

The leader of the group, usually a male, establishes regulations so that each animal knows whom it can boss and to whom it must submit. For instance, a middle-class wolf must obey the leader's orders; children and helpers must submit to their relatives. This rule helps prevent disagreements and fights.

New paragraph explains behavior, not communication.

Another indication of the wolf's intelligence is the ability to communicate. Wolves have their own language, which is based on the use of different intonations. According to Savage, a whimper communicates friendship, snarls convey warnings and admonishments, and a "special chirplike tone expresses sexual interest" (58). Like dogs, wolves also use gestures and facial expressions to communicate. By moving their foreheads, mouths, ears, and eyes, they express

Creates new paragraph to discuss communication. Expands her discussion.

Uses description to create emphasis.

their emotions and announce their ranks. Frightened wolves keep their teeth covered, "eyes slightly closed, ears flat to the head" (Savage 55). They also bend their legs and tuck in their tails. Wolves that are self-confident, on the other hand, point their ears forward and bare their teeth. Wolves of the highest rank reveal their positions by keeping their tails and ears up and by looking directly into the eyes of other animals. Members of the pack show respect for them; like dogs, they keep their ears tucked in, their heads down, and their legs slightly bent.

Includes concrete, specific vocabulary.

8.7 Practicing Illustration

Examples can be defined as concrete signs of abstract ideas. Below are several topic sentences expressing abstract ideas. Use the spaces below each to write a paragraph relating to each sentence. Develop your paragraph by using at least three examples of the kinds you have just read about. First, however, make a quick list of the examples you will use on a sheet of scratch paper. You can discuss them in detail when it comes time to write the paragraph. Feel free to reword these sentences any way you like.

1. Wherever you go these days, people seem to be recycling.

_____

_____

_____

_____

_____

_____

_____

_____

_____

2. Some people I know are very materialistic.

_____

_____

_____

_____

_____

_____

_____

_____

_____

3.   A friend of mine often engages in self-destructive behavior.

_____

_____

_____

_____

_____

_____

_____

4.   _____ (name of a person) succeeds at whatever sport (or other type of
      activity) he (or she) pursues.

_____

_____

_____

_____

_____

_____

5.   Electronic devices play important roles in the modern home.

_____

_____

_____

_____

_____

_____

_____

_____

6.   People in my town seem to be getting richer and richer (or poorer and poorer).

_____

_____

_____

_____

_____

_____

_____

_____

_____

8.8 Reading Selections

8.8a **Wolf**

Author Biography

Born in Boleslawiec, Poland, **_Grace Lukawska_** came to the United States in 1986. After studying English for speakers of other languages, she enrolled in a developmental writing course in which she wrote this paper. In Poland, Lukawska had seen many television specials on wild animals. When asked to write about a fascinating animal, she immediately thought of the wolf. Lukawska is now a medical assistant.

Preparing to Read

1. The author develops this essay with examples, but she also uses comparison and description.

2. Pay particular attention to the essay's good organization. Consider what Lukawska has done to keep her essay focused.

3. Getting Started, the introductory chapter of this book, explains that summarizing written materials is a good way to gather information; another is to quote directly from a source. Lukawska summarizes and quotes directly from Candace Savage's _Wolves_. She credits Savage's book by indicating in parentheses the pages from which she took information. These entries are called parenthetical (internal) citations. She also provides full bibliographical information about the book at the end of her paper. You can learn more about crediting sources in The Research Process at the end of this book.

Vocabulary

admonishments (noun)   Condemnations, rebukes.

attribute (verb)   Associate with, blame for.

glutton (noun)   Someone who eats too much.

hierarchical (adjective)   Arranged by rank or importance.

intonations (noun)   Levels of sound, pitches.

manifests (verb)   Shows.

misconceptions (noun)   Incorrect opinions.

solidarity (noun)   Unity, mutual support, togetherness.

Wolf
Grace Lukawska

For centuries popular misconceptions have pictured the wolf as a terrifying predator that kills for pleasure. The name itself calls up nasty images: the glutton who "wolfs" down his food; the werewolf, who, during a full moon, grows hair all over his body, howls into the night, and claws beautiful maidens to death. Even in fairy tales, such as "Little Red Riding Hood," the wolf is pictured as shrewd and bloodthirsty. But is the wolf really a cold-blooded killer? Not at all; the wolf is a magnificent animal which displays many of the characteristics we value in human beings.   1

The intelligence of the wolf manifests itself in its behavior. The wolf's society is well organized and hierarchical. According to Candace Savage, author of *Wolves*, a pack consists of an upper class—parents, a middle class—uncles and aunts, a lower class—children, and finally "helpers," who are inexperienced hunters and who depend upon the pack for their food (55). Their role is to babysit youngsters while the other wolves are hunting (62). Like humans, wolves practice adoption. If parents die, their children are cared for by another family.

2

The leader of the group, usually a male, establishes regulations so that each animal knows whom it can boss and to whom it must submit. For instance, a middle-class wolf must obey the leader's orders; children and helpers must submit to their relatives. This rule helps prevent disagreements and fights.

3

Another indication of the wolf's intelligence is the ability to communicate. Wolves have their own language, which is based on the use of different intonations. According to Savage, a whimper communicates friendship, snarls convey warnings and admonishments, and a "special chirplike tone expresses sexual interest" (58). Like dogs, wolves also use gestures and facial expressions to communicate. By moving their foreheads, mouths, ears, and eyes, they express their emotions and announce their ranks. Frightened wolves keep their teeth covered, "eyes slightly closed, ears flat to the head" (Savage 55). They also bend their legs and tuck in their tails. Wolves that are self-confident, on the other hand, point their ears forward and bare their teeth. Wolves of the highest rank reveal their positions by keeping their tails and ears up and by looking directly into the eyes of other animals. Members of the pack show respect for them; like dogs, they keep their ears tucked in, their heads down, and their legs slightly bent.

4

Like people, wolves are sociable. In a group, they constantly check one another by sniffing. To show affection, they nuzzle each other as if to kiss. To express hostility, they lick their cheeks, wag their tails, howl, and even stick out their tongues. This kind of behavior serves not only to locate companions outside the pack but also to mark their territory and tell enemies of the family's solidarity (Savage 59).

5

Regardless of rank or age, wolves enjoy playing games with other members of their pack. Even the leader, who may appear to be aggressive and ruthless, takes an active part in these activities, which include chasing one another and rolling over. Another sign of intelligence, such exercises not only give them pleasure, but also help them keep physically fit.

6

Wolves are natural-born strategists and planners. Hunting a large animal like a deer or moose is very dangerous for a single wolf. Therefore, they hunt in groups. After locating a herd, one might act as a decoy to draw males away from the herd while the rest single out and attack the victim. Wolves kill only weak or sick animals, and they never kill more than they need. In case there is any excess, leftovers are buried near their dens.

7

The reputation from which wolves suffer is undeserved and unfair. Wolves can be violent, and they are terrifying hunters. But they kill only to feed and protect their families; they never commit distinctly "human" crimes such as murder, theft, and rape. Wolves are not bloodthirsty monsters that should be feared and eradicated. They are magnificent animals, and they deserve their place on earth.

8

Works Cited:

Savage, Candace. *Wolves*. Sierra Club, 1980.

Read More on the Web

To learn more about wolves, visit these sites:

- "Wild Wolves," NOVA: www.pbs.org/wgbh/nova/wolves

- International Wolf Center: www.wolf.org

Questions for Discussion

1. What is the essay's thesis? What techniques does the author use to maintain unity and coherence?

2. What kinds of examples does Lukawska rely on most in this essay? Does she ever refer to specific persons, places, or things?

3. Where in this essay does she use comparison?

4. Where does she create verbal images? Why are they so effective?

5. What techniques for writing introductions and conclusions has Lukawska used? (Check chapter 3 if you need to review these techniques.)

Thinking Critically

1. Consider another animal that has a bad reputation: a rat, a snake, a bat, a pig, a spider, or some other unpopular creature. In a paragraph or two, discuss the positive qualities of this creature. For example, many people hate and fear rats, but laboratory rats play an important role in medical research.

2. Reread Lukawska's introduction. Then list other examples that would illustrate the popular misconception of wolves as bloodthirsty monsters.

3. The author suggests that human beings can sometimes be more beastly than the beasts. What does she mean? Do you agree? Can you provide some examples?

Suggestions for Journal Entries

1. Think of an animal or species of animal you know well—your Siamese cat or all domestic cats, the neighbor's German shepherd or all dogs, a bird that often visits your backyard or all common birds. List important things you know about this creature—anything that would provide clues about its behavior, lifestyle, or personality.

    Then ask yourself what this information tells you. Draw three or more general conclusions about the animal from the details you have listed. Write these conclusions in the form of topic sentences for paragraphs that you might later develop in an essay.

2. Are human families as well organized and as close as the wolf family? Think of your own family. Then write a paragraph in which you use illustrations to evaluate the kind of family to which you belong. Perhaps the best types of illustrations to use are anecdotes taken from your own experiences.

8.8b Overpopulation Hoax

Author Biography

Walter Williams (1936–) holds a doctorate in economics from UCLA and a Doctor of Laws from Washington and Jefferson College. Since 1980, he has taught at George Mason University in Fairfax, Virginia, where he served as chair of the Economics Department. He has published more than 150 articles and ten books, including *Up from the Projects: An Autobiography, Race and Economics: How Much Can Be Blamed on Discrimination?* and *American Contempt for Liberty.* He serves on the boards of several think tanks including the Cato Institute, the Landmark Legal Foundation, the Institute of Economic Affairs, and the Heritage Foundation. "Overpopulation Hoax" appeared on Townhall.com in May 2017.

Preparing to Read

1. In paragraph 1, Williams mentions Thomas Malthus, whom he introduces as the author of a treatise on overpopulation, as well as Paul Ehrlich, an economist who, Williams says, predicted mass starvation because of overpopulation in the 1970s and 1980s. In paragraph 5, the author mentions Julian Simon, who taught at the University of Maryland and was a member of the Cato Institute. Read more about all three men on the Web.

2. Williams uses various kinds of examples in this essay, including specific facts and instances, as well as statistics. Look for these as you read his essay.

Vocabulary

embarked (verb)   Started out.

sterilization (noun)   Procedure which prevents women from conceiving.

Overpopulation Hoax

Walter Williams

In 1798, Thomas Malthus wrote "An Essay on the Principle of Population." He predicted that mankind's birthrate would outstrip our ability to grow food and would lead to mass starvation. Malthus' wrong predictions did not deter Stanford University professor Paul Ehrlich from making a similar prediction. In his 1968 best-seller, *The Population Bomb*, which has sold more than 2 million copies, Ehrlich warned: "The battle to feed all of humanity is over. In the 1970s and 1980s hundreds of millions of people will starve to death in spite of any crash programs embarked upon now." This hoax resulted in billions of dollars being spent to fight overpopulation.   1

According to the standard understanding of the term, human overpopulation occurs when the ecological footprint of a human population in a specific geographical location exceeds the carrying capacity of the place occupied by that group. Let's look at one aspect of that description—namely, population density. Let's put you, the reader, to a test. See whether you can tell which country is richer and which is poorer just by knowing two countries' population density.   2

North Korea's population density is 518 people per square mile, whereas South Korea's is more than double that, at 1,261 people per square mile. Hong Kong's population density is 16,444, whereas Somalia's is 36. Congo has 75 people per square mile, whereas Singapore has 18,513. Looking at the gross domestic products of these countries, one would have to be a lunatic to believe that smaller population density leads to greater riches. Here are some GDP data expressed in millions of U.S. dollars: North Korea ($17,396), South Korea ($1,411,246), Hong Kong ($320,668), Somalia ($5,707), Congo ($41,615) and Singapore ($296,967).   3

The overpopulation hoax has led to horrible population control programs. The United Nations Population Fund has helped governments deny women the right to choose the number and spacing of their children. Overpopulation concerns led China to enact a brutal one-child policy. Forced sterilization is a method of population control in some countries. Nearly a quarter-million Peruvian women were sterilized. Our government, through the U.N. Population Fund, is involved in "population moderation" programs around the world, including in India, Bangladesh, Pakistan, Nigeria, Mexico, Indonesia, Brazil, the Philippines, Thailand, Egypt, Turkey, Ethiopia and Colombia.   4

The entire premise behind population control is based on the faulty logic that humans are not valuable resources. The fact of business is that humans are what the late Julian L. Simon called the ultimate resource. That fact becomes apparent by pondering this question: Why is it that Gen. George Washington did not have cellphones to communicate with his troops and rocket launchers to sink British ships anchored in New York Harbor? Surely, all of the physical resources—such as aluminum alloys, copper, iron ore and chemical propellants—necessary to build cellphones and rocket launchers   5 were around during Washington's time. In fact, they were around at the time of the cave man. There is only one answer for why cellphones, rocket launchers and millions of other things are around today but were not around yesteryear. The growth in human knowledge, human ingenuity, job specialization and trade led to industrialization, which, coupled with personal liberty and private property rights, made it possible. Human beings are valuable resources, and the more we have of them the better.

The greatest threat to mankind's prosperity is government, not population growth. For example, Zimbabwe was agriculturally rich but, with government interference, was reduced to the brink of mass starvation. Any country faced with massive government interference can be brought to starvation. Blaming poverty on overpopulation not only lets governments off the hook but also encourages the enactment of harmful, inhumane policies.   6

Today's poverty has little to do with overpopulation. The most commonly held characteristics of non-poor countries are greater personal liberty, private property rights, the rule of law and an economic system closer to capitalism than to communism. That's the recipe for prosperity.   7

Read More on the Web

To read more about Williams and the subject he discusses, try these sites.

- "10 Lively Facts about Population Growth": http://bvtlab.com/7fgu7

- "What Is Overpopulation?": http://bvtlab.com/868wM

- Walter E. Williams Home Page: econfaculty.gmu.edu/wew/index.html

Questions for Discussion

1. What examples does Williams give of the ill effects of the "Overpopulation Hoax"?

2. Where does Williams use statistics? Are they convincing?

3. Where does he use instances or events to illustrate his point?

4. Is contrast used in this essay? If so, where and to what end?

5. What use does Williams make of questions? What purposes do these questions serve?

6. What method, as explained in chapter 3, does the author use in his introduction?

7. What is Williams's thesis?

Thinking Critically

1. Explain what Williams means when he says in paragraph 5 that "Human beings ... are valuable resources"?

2. In paragraph 6, he says that "blaming poverty on overpopulation ... encourages the enactment of harmful, inhumane policies." What inhumane policies does Williams mention earlier in the essay? Can you think of other inhumane policies that governments have instituted?

Suggestions for Journal Entries

1. Some people might disagree with Williams and argue that the earth is becoming overpopulated. If you are of this opinion, make a list of effects overpopulation is having on both our natural and domestic environment.

2. Freewrite about a hoax put forth by government, the press, big business, or any other entity with which you are familiar. You might even discuss a hoax spread in your high school, your college, or even your family.

8.8c English Is a Crazy Language

Author Biography

Richard Lederer (1938–) is a retired English teacher who devotes much of his time to writing humorous and thought-provoking essays and books on the peculiarities of the English language. In addition to *Crazy English* (1989), the book from which this essay is taken, his other books include *Anguished English* (1989), *More Anguished English* (1994), *Sleeping Dogs Don't Lay* (2001), and *The Bride of Anguished English* (2002). All of them contain examples of the many wonders of our "crazy language."

Preparing to Read

1. As always, pay attention to the essay's title.

2. Lederer uses many words that may be new to you. Not all of these are listed in the vocabulary. To fully appreciate the author's humor, use a dictionary or the Internet to look up those words with which you are unfamiliar

Vocabulary

annals (noun)   History, historical records.

bizarre (adjective)   Strange, odd.

culinary (adjective)   Having to do with cooking.

indispensable (adjective)   Necessary.

mammaried (adjective)   Having breasts.

mess (noun)   Military dining hall.

paradoxes (noun)   A construction of words that seem to contradict themselves.

propagate (verb)   Reproduce.

vagaries (noun)   Uncertainties.

English Is a Crazy Language

Richard Lederer

English is the most widely spoken language in the history of our planet, used in some way by at least one out of every seven human beings around the globe. Half of the world's books are written in English, and the majority of international telephone calls are made in English. English is the language of over sixty percent of the world's radio programs, many of them beamed, ironically, by the Russians, who know that to win friends and influence nations, they're best off using English. More than seventy percent of international mail is written and addressed in English, and eighty percent of all computer text is stored in English. English has acquired the largest vocabulary of all the world's languages, perhaps as many as two million words, and has generated one of the noblest bodies of literature in the annals of the human race. 1

Nonetheless, it is now time to face the fact that English is a crazy language. 2

In the crazy English language, the blackbird hen is brown, blackboards can be blue or green, and blackberries are green and then red before they are ripe. Even if blackberries were really black and blueberries really blue, what are strawberries, cranberries, elderberries, huckleberries, raspberries, boysenberries, mulberries, and gooseberries supposed to look like? 3

To add to the insanity, there is no butter in buttermilk, no egg in eggplant, no grape in grapefruit, neither worms nor wood in wormwood, neither pine nor apple in pineapple, neither peas nor nuts in peanuts, and no ham in a hamburger. (In fact, if somebody invented a sandwich consisting of a ham patty in a bun, we would have a hard time finding a name for it.) To make matters worse, English muffins weren't invented in England, french fries in France, or danish pastries in Denmark. And we discover even more culinary madness in the revelations that sweetmeat is candy, while sweetbread, which isn't sweet, is made from meat. 4

In this unreliable English tongue, greyhounds aren't always grey (or gray); panda bears and koala bears aren't bears (they're marsupials); a woodchuck is a groundhog, which is not a hog; a horned toad is a lizard; glowworms are fireflies, but fireflies are not flies (they're beetles); ladybugs and lightning bugs are also beetles (and to propagate, a significant proportion of ladybugs must be male); a guinea pig is neither a pig nor from Guinea (it's a South American rodent); and a titmouse is neither mammal nor mammaried. 5

Language is like the air we breathe. It's invisible, inescapable, indispensable, and we take it for granted. But when we take the time, step back, and listen to the sounds that escape from the holes in people's faces and explore the paradoxes and vagaries of English, we find that hot dogs can be cold, darkrooms can be lit, homework can be done in school, nightmares can take place in broad daylight, while morning sickness and daydreaming can take place at night, tomboys are girls, midwives can be men, hours—especially happy hours and rush hours—can last longer than sixty minutes, quicksand works very slowly, boxing rings are square, silverware can be made of plastic and tablecloths of paper, most telephones are dialed by being punched (or pushed?), and most bathrooms don't have any baths in them. In fact, a dog can go to the bathroom under a tree—no bath, no room; it's still going to the bathroom. And doesn't it seem at least a little bizarre that we go to the bathroom in order to go to the bathroom? 6

Why is it that a woman can man a station but a man can't woman one, that a man can father a movement but a woman can't mother one, and that a king rules a kingdom but a queen doesn't rule a queendom? How did all those Renaissance men reproduce when there don't seem to have been any Renaissance women? 7

A writer is someone who writes, and a stinger is something that stings. But fingers don't fing, grocers don't groce, hammers don't ham, and humdingers don't humding. If the plural of *tooth* is *teeth*, shouldn't the plural of *booth* be *beeth*? One goose, two geese—so one moose, two meese? One index, two indices—one Kleenex, two Kleenices? If people ring a bell today and rang a bell yesterday, why don't we say that they flang a ball? If they wrote a letter, perhaps they also bote their tongue. If the teacher taught, why isn't it also true that the preacher praught? Why is it that the sun shone yesterday while I shined my shoes, that I treaded water and then trod on soil, and that I flew out to see a World Series game in which my favorite player flied out? 8

If we conceive a conception and receive at a reception, why don't we grieve a greption and believe a beleption? If a horsehair mat is made from the hair of horses and a camel's hair brush from the hair of camels, from what is a mohair coat made? If a vegetarian eats vegetables, what does a humanitarian eat? If a firefighter fights fire, what does a freedom fighter fight? If a weightlifter lifts weights, what does a shoplifter lift? If *pro* and *con* are opposites, is congress the opposite of progress?

9

Sometimes you have to believe that all English speakers should be committed to an asylum for the verbally insane. In what other language do people drive in a parkway and park in a driveway? In what other language do people recite at a play and play at a recital? In what other language do privates eat in the general mess and generals eat in the private mess? In what other language do men get hernias and women get hysterectomies? In what other language do people ship by truck and send cargo by ship? In what other language can your nose run and your feet smell?

10

How can a slim chance and a fat chance be the same, "what's going on?" and "what's coming off?" be the same, and a bad licking and a good licking be the same, while a wise man and a wise guy are opposites? How can sharp speech and blunt speech be the same and *quite a lot* and *quite a few* the same, while *overlook* and *oversee* are opposites? How can the weather be hot as hell one day and cold as hell the next?

11

If *button* and *unbutton* and *tie* and *untie* are opposites, why are *loosen* and *unloosen* and *ravel* and *unravel* the same? If *bad* is the opposite of *good*, *hard* the opposite of *soft*, and *up* the opposite of *down*, why are *badly* and *goodly*, *hardly* and *softly*, and *upright* and *downright* not opposing pairs? If *harmless* actions are the opposite of *harmful* actions, why are *shameless* and *shameful* behavior the same and *pricey* objects less expensive than *priceless* ones? If appropriate and inappropriate remarks and passable and impassable mountain trails are opposites, why are flammable and inflammable materials, heritable and inheritable property, and passive and impassive people the same and valuable objects less treasured than invaluable ones? If *uplift* is the same as *lift up*, why are *upset* and *set up* opposite in meaning? Why are *pertinent* and *impertinent*, *canny* and *uncanny*, and *famous* and *infamous* neither opposites nor the same? How can *raise* and *raze* and *reckless* and *wreckless* be opposites when each pair contains the same sound?

12

Why is it that when the sun or the moon or the stars are out, they are *visible*, but when the lights are out, they are *invisible*, and that when I *wind* up my watch, I start it, but when I *wind* up this essay, I shall end it?

13

English is a crazy language.

14

Read More on the Web

To read more about Lederer's thoughts on language, visit

- Richard Lederer's Verbivore: verbivore.com
- "Language Pet Peeves," National Public Radio: http://bvtlab.com/73C98

Questions for Discussion (continues)

1. Find the three places in which Lederer states the essay's thesis.

2. Reread the introductory paragraph. In what way do the examples found here differ from those in the rest of the essay? Why does Lederer include the information in this first paragraph?

3. Discuss two or three of the paradoxes found in paragraph 6 and explain why they qualify as paradoxes.

Questions for Discussion (Continued)

4. What simile is used to define language in paragraph 6? What is the author saying about our perception of the words we use every day.

5. In paragraph 7, Lederer groups examples of phrases pertaining to men and women. Analyze paragraphs 3, 4, 5, and 6 and identify each of the principles the author uses to group examples in them.

6. Why does Lederer use so many rhetorical questions? What is their effect on the reader?

Thinking Critically

1. Reread the first paragraph and write a summary that explains, in your own words, why English is an important language. Can you add to the reasons Lederer provides?

2. What other world languages do you think are important and worth studying? In each case, list reasons that support your opinion.

3. Many of the paradoxes we find in English come in the form of oxymorons, phrases that seem self-contradictory but that convey a legitimate meaning. "Jumbo shrimp," "student teacher," and "the sounds of silence" are examples. Make a list of others. If this doesn't interest you, make a list of words or phrases you find paradoxical, illogical, or just odd.

Suggestions for Journal Entries

1. Our language is full of contradictions, absurdities, illogicalities, and inconsistencies. But so is life itself. In fact, life can be unfair. Look back on your own life or on the lives of people you know well. Using listing, focused freewriting, or brainstorming with a friend, develop at least one example that might illustrate the illogicality or unfairness of life.

2. In paragraph 7, Lederer includes phrases that are based upon gender. Recently many words such as *waiter/waitress* and *steward/stewardess* have been replaced by less sexist alternatives such as *server* and *flight attendant*. Make a list of job titles that indicate the sex of the persons who hold them. Now, list alternative, gender-neutral titles for those jobs.

8.8d Covert Force

Author Biography

This article first appeared in the October 2002 issue of *Smithsonian* magazine. **Robert F. Howe** is a freelance writer based in California, who has also published an article on Doolittle's Raiders in *Smithsonian*.

Preparing to Read

1. Women are taking an increasingly active role in warfare. However, consider the position of women in America about 160 years ago. They didn't have the vote or, in most cases, the right to own property. They were discouraged from entering professions, and they certainly weren't admitted to the military. Keep this in mind as you determine the purpose of this essay.

2. Howe's essay uses information from *They Fought Like Demons: Women Soldiers in the American Civil War*, a book by Lauren Cook and DeAnne Blanton, and he discusses these two contemporary women in addition to telling the stories of women Civil War soldiers. To fully appreciate his purpose, ask yourself how discussing Cook and Blanton fits into a discussion of women soldiers.

Vocabulary

a.k.a. (abbreviation)   "Also known as."

alluded (verb)   Suggested, implied.

avenge (verb)   Get revenge.

buffs (noun)   People with an avid interest in a subject.

compilation (noun)   Collection.

covert (adjective)   Hidden, secret.

cursory (adjective)   Casual, superficial.

depraved (adjective)   Morally corrupt, evil.

deranged (adjective)   Mentally unbalanced, insane.

destitution (noun)   Poverty.

fending (adjective)   Fighting, defending against.

inebriated (adjective)   Drunk.

medic (noun)   Medical officer.

prevailing (adjective)   Accepted.

tilled (verb)   Worked the soil, cultivated.

unadulterated (adjective)   Pure.

Covert Force

Robert F. Howe

August 30, 1862, proved to be yet another bloody day. Henry Clark was in the thick of things, fending off Federal troops in the Battle of Richmond, Kentucky, when the Confederate private caught an enemy shell in the thigh. Clark was swarmed by bluecoats and taken prisoner.   1

It was presumably when a Union medic treated Clark's wound that the soldier's tightly held secret was unmasked. Henry's real name was Mary Ann. Indeed, she was a divorced mother of two.   2

When Federal troops realized that they had a woman on their hands, they moved quickly to release her—as long as she swore to return to the life of a proper lady. They even gave her a dress to   3 wear. She agreed and was freed, then quickly cast off the frock and made her way back to the rebel army, where she was promptly promoted. Not long after, a young Confederate soldier—having joined a crowd gathered around Clark, then apparently serving openly as a female officer—wrote home: "Pa, among all the curiosities I have seen since I left home one I must mention, a female Lieutenant."

A curiosity, yes, but to the surprise of many Civil War buffs even today, Clark was by no means unique. She was one of an estimated 400 women who took up arms in the war; they were not nurses, or laundresses or cooks, but actual female soldiers disguised as men, who marched, mastered their weapons, entered into battle and even gave their lives.

Various histories have alluded to women's roles in combat during the War Between the States, but none have made so detailed and convincing a case as *They Fought Like Demons: Women Soldiers in the American Civil War*. Coauthors Lauren Cook and DeAnne Blanton spent more than ten years combing through letters, archives and news reports to document some 250 women warriors.

"No one has accumulated this much data," says Cook, 46, who first tilled this turf in her 1994 *An Uncommon Soldier* (Oxford University Press), a compilation of letters from a female Civil War soldier. The authors' mission was not just to catalog the combatants. Their extensive research convinced them that the prevailing notions about women's participation in the war—that they had to be deranged or depraved—were way off the mark.

"We felt those women had not been given their due, that they were thoroughly misunderstood by military historians and the general public," says Cook, a special assistant to the chancellor for communications at Fayetteville State University–UNC in North Carolina. In fact, Cook contends, "they were just as successful as their male comrades, and what enabled them to be so successful was that no one knew that they were women."

What would compel a woman to march into that terrible combat—and how could she conceal her identity in what must have been uncomfortably close quarters? Blanton and Cook offer a number of persuasive answers. In the case of Clark, for example, a bad marriage and the death of a brother-in-law at the hands of a pro-Union mob took such an emotional toll that she sought refuge in the military, according to a letter from her mother uncovered by the authors. But Martha Parks Lindley joined up just two days after her husband left for the 6th U.S. Cavalry. "I was frightened half to death," she told a newspaper. "But I was so anxious to be with my husband that I resolved to see the thing through if it killed me." It did not, and fellow troopers simply assumed that Lindley and the "young man" known as Jim Smith were just good friends. Then there was Charlotte Hope, who signed up in the 1st Virginia Cavalry to avenge the death of her fiancé, killed in a raid in 1861. Her goal: to slay 21 Yankees, one for each year of her beau's life.

Some joined to escape the misery of prostitution or destitution—a common problem with so few jobs open to women. Finance clearly figured into the decision of Sarah Rosetta Wakeman, alias Pvt. Lyons Wakeman, to sign up for the Union army. "I got 100 and 52$ in money," she wrote proudly. "I can get all the money I want."

Loreta Velazquez, a.k.a. Lt. Harry T. Buford, was one of several women who fought simply for the unadulterated thrill of it: "I plunged into adventure for the love of the thing," she said after writing a postwar memoir called *The Woman in Battle*. Many women felt the keen tug of patriotism. Union soldier Sarah Edmonds, an immigrant from Canada, expressed thanks that she was "permitted in this hour of my adopted country's need to express a tithe of the gratitude which I feel toward the people of the Northern States."

"What surprised me most was the realization that women soldiers enlisted largely for the very same reasons as the men did," says Blanton, 38. "Some were rebelling against the strict roles that society confined them in, but then there were women who went because the pay was good, or because everybody else in the family was signing up, or because they wanted to defend their country. Some just signed up to run away from home, just like so many boys did."

To get to the front lines, each woman had to pass herself off as a man. Many were detected immediately and given the boot. But physical exams of the time tended to be cursory, and both armies were often so desperate for recruits that virtually anyone could pass. Occasions for discovery were limited; troops routinely slept in uniform, baths were a novelty and latrines were so foul that many soldiers sought refuge in nearby woods. A high-pitched voice or a lack of facial hair could be attributed to youth. Several women attempted to blend in by learning to cuss like sailors, taking up gambling, or even dating local young ladies.

Some female combatants were given away by ladylike mannerisms and others were undone by boastings while inebriated. But as with Clark, most were unveiled only when doctors stripped away their clothes to examine a war wound.   13

A native of Grand Rapids, Michigan, Cook had virtually no interest in the Civil War until 1987, when she toured the battle site at Gettysburg, Pennsylvania. She was so moved by the experience that she joined a fife and drum corps and began participating in battle reenactments. Then, in 1989, during a re-creation of a military hospital at the Antietam National Battlefield in Sharpsburg, Maryland, she dressed as a male soldier "because I felt that was historically accurate." But when she visited the ladies' room, she caused a stir— not only among the women inside but with a ranger, who brusquely informed her that park rules did not allow women to participate in reenactments. "Their attitude was that the women of that era must have been oddballs, eccentrics and crazy, and didn't merit any kind of recognition or respect," says Cook. Her lawsuit against the Department of the Interior ultimately changed the rules.   14

A decade after teaming up to work on *Demons*, Cook and Blanton are still fitting pieces of the puzzle. They cite the case, as it unfolded in letters written by soldiers, of a New Jersey woman who participated in the Union army's June 1862 siege of Richmond, Virginia, was wounded at the Battle of Antietam in September, and fought in the Union defeat at Fredericksburg in December. Just a few weeks later, on January 19, an astonished colonel in the Army of the Potomac wrote home: "A corporal was promoted to sergeant for gallant conduct at the battle of Fredericksburg—since which time the sergeant has become the mother of a child."   15

And there the story stops. "When she and her baby went home, was she celebrated or shunned?" Blanton asks. "I hope that a descendant will read our book and call up and say, 'Hey, that lady was my great-great-great-grandmother.'"   16

Read More on the Web

For more about women in the Civil War, go to:

- "Women in the Civil War":
  www.history.com/topics/american-civil-war/women-in-the-civil-war

- "Female Soldiers in the Civil War":
  www.battlefields.org/learn/articles/female-soldiers-civil-war

- Loreta Velazquez, *The Woman in Battle*: http://bvtlab.com/52dXU

Questions for Discussion (continues)

1. What is the purpose of this essay? Is it simply to tell readers about the Civil War's women soldiers?

2. What is Howe's thesis? Can you tell if this thesis is similar to the thesis of Cook and Blanton's book?

3. In what ways were women's reasons for going to war the same as those of men?

4. Why were so many women able to pass themselves off as men without being detected?

5. Why does the author mention *The Woman in Battle*, by Loreta Velazquez, a.k.a Lt. Harry Buford?

6. Comment upon the fact that Howe quotes Cook and Blanton directly, as well as including direct quotations from women Cook and Blanton quoted. What is the effect on the essay?

Questions for Discussion (continued)

7. To be effective, illustrations must be believable. Are the illustrations in this essay believable? What makes them so?

8. Why does the author introduce this essay with an illustration? Which other method for introducing essays, which you learned about in chapter 3, does Howe use? Which method for concluding essays, as explained in chapter 3, does Howe use?

Thinking Critically

1. Reread this essay carefully. As you do, make marginal notes that will point out similarities between the women who fought in the Civil War and today's American women.

2. What can you tell about Cook and Blanton that could explain why they might be so intent about telling the story of women combatants?

Suggestions for Journal Entries

1. It should not come as a surprise that today women can be found doing a variety of jobs once reserved for men. Women are firefighters, police officers, doctors, mechanics, sanitation workers, and so forth. Make a list of women you know or have learned about who hold jobs that thirty years ago might have been reserved for men. Or, make a list of men you know who hold jobs that your parents or grandparents might have thought were suited only to women.

2. Use the Internet to find out more information about women combatants in the Civil War or about the role women played in other U.S. wars. For example, you might research the contributions women made on the home front and overseas during World War II. Or you might try to find out more about the American women who died in Vietnam. Print out any articles you find online and make notes in the margins using the techniques you read about in Getting Started.

8.9 Suggestions for Sustained Writing

1. If you responded to the first of the Suggestions for Journal Entries after Grace Lukawska's "Wolf," you have already written three topic sentences that express conclusions about the behavior or personality of a particular animal or species of animal. Use these topic sentences in the body paragraphs of an essay that, like "Wolf," expresses your views on the character of this animal. Develop these paragraphs with illustrations. Perhaps some of the information in your journal will serve this purpose. Then, summarize in one statement the ideas expressed in your topic sentences; make this your essay's thesis.

   After completing your first draft, return to your paper and insert additional details and examples that will make it more convincing and clear. In your third draft, work on creating an effective introduction; like Lukawska, try using a startling remark or challenging a widely held opinion. In your conclusion, rephrase your thesis or look to the future. Then, revise the entire paper once more to improve word usage and sentence structure. End this careful process by editing for grammar and by proofreading.

2. If you responded to the first journal prompt after Walter Williams's essay, "Overpopulation Hoax," you might be among those who disagree with his thesis. Write an essay in which you use examples to explain the bad effects that overpopulation has had. Use your journal notes as your starting point. As you draft the essay, make sure to include a variety of examples. You might talk about the heavy traffic you face every morning as you drive to work, or you might describe the overcrowding on the bus or train you take. You might also mention the long lines at the supermarket or the post office. You could also talk about the rising price of apartment rents because of the heavy demand due to the population density in your city.

   Williams placed his thesis at the end of his paper, which was short enough so that such placement was effective. Keep in mind, however, that placing a thesis at the end of an essay can lead to a lack of focus unless you are careful.

3. If you responded to the second journal prompt after Williams's essay, use this information to explain various effects of a hoax that was put forward by government, the press, big business, or any other organization or entity with which you have experience. You may have even written about a hoax someone in your high school, college, or family invented.

   Make sure you have a clearly stated thesis, to which your illustrations clearly point. If needed, do some research on the Internet or in your college library to gather facts and statistics that will help you illustrate that thesis.

4. In response to the first of the Suggestions for Journal Entries after Richard Lederer's "English Is a Crazy Language," you probably wrote about an incident or problem that illustrates the illogicality, absurdity, or unfairness life sometimes throws at us. Use this example as the basis for an essay that develops this idea fully. Unlike Lederer, you don't have to include hundreds of brief examples. Just add two or three more fully developed examples to the one already in your journal.

   Like Lederer, make sure to organize your essay well. Open it by using one or more of the techniques for writing introductions explained in chapter 3. Then, devote one or two detailed paragraphs to each of the examples you have chosen to prove your thesis. Close by using a conclusion like the type you read about in chapter 3. Write multiple drafts; then, edit and proofread carefully.

5. If you responded to the first of the journal prompts after Robert Howe's "Covert Force," turn your notes into an illustration essay explaining the fact that jobs once filled by members of only one of the sexes are now open to both. If you researched the role of women in wars, as suggested in item 2 of the Suggestions for Journal Entries after the essay by Howe, use this information to write an illustration essay that explains the role of women in a particular war. If you want, do some additional library or Internet research to gather more information. Make sure you cite any information taken from Internet or print sources per the Modern Language Association style (or per any style sheet assigned by your instructor). MLA style is explained in The Research Process at the end of this book.

   For both types of papers, remember that you need to develop illustrations that are credible and detailed. After you write your first draft, read it over carefully. Refine your thesis if necessary to make it clear and more focused. Then, add details and even whole events or instances that will better convince your reader of the validity of that thesis.

ACKNOWLEDGMENTS

Lederer, Richard. Crazy English, rev. and exp. 1998 Atria Books. From Crazy English, Revised and Expanded by Richard Lederer. Copyright © 1989, 1990, 1998 by Richard Lederer. Reprinted with the permission of Atria Books, a division of Simon & Schuster, Inc. All rights reserved.

Williams, Walter. "Overpopulation Hoax." *Town Hall*, 31 May, 2017, https://townhall.com/columnists/walterewilliams/2017/05/31/overpopulation-hoax0n2332805. Reprinted by permission of Walter E. Williams and Creators Syndicate, Inc.

Howe, Robert F. "Covert Force." *Smithsonian Magazine*, Oct. 2002, https://www.smithsonianmag.com/history/cover-force-70629819/. Reprinted with permission by the author.

Getty Images

Comparison and Contrast

Chapter Outline

9.1   **Organizing Comparison/Contrast Papers**

9.2   **Visualizing Methods of Comparison**

9.3   **Revising Comparison/Contrast Papers**

9.4   **Practicing Comparison and Contrast**

9.5   **Reading Selections**

9.6   **Suggestions for Sustained Writing**

Comparison and contrast are methods of organizing and developing ideas by pointing out similarities and differences between subjects.

A comparison essay identifies similarities—even between subjects that seem different. For example, you might compare the government of the United States with that of Great Britain; a newly patented drug with an age-old herbal treatment; the methods of building the Egyptian and Mayan pyramids with modern construction methods. A contrast essay identifies differences—even between subjects that seem alike; usually these subjects belong to the same general class or are of the same type. Such is the case in Malcolm Cowley's "Temptations of Old Age," a selection in this chapter that discusses how two different types of people face the challenges of aging.

Comparison and contrast can also be used to argue for one or both sides of a question. For example, you might discuss the advantages and disadvantages of living in a particular city, the pros and cons of human cloning, or the strengths and weaknesses of a particular political ideology. In "High Anxiety: It Never Ends," student Nancy Terranova argues that although the lifestyles of young adults differ from those of their parents and grandparents, they experience the same levels of fear and anxiety in their daily lives.

9.1 Organizing Comparison/Contrast Papers

One of the greatest advantages of using comparison or contrast is the simplicity with which it allows you to organize information. In fact, putting together a successful comparison or contrast essay doesn't have to be difficult if you follow either of the two standard methods of organization: point by point or subject by subject.

Deciding which method to use depends on your topic and purpose. The subject-by-subject method is often used in short pieces, such as Cowley's "Temptations of Old Age." The point-by-point method works well with essays that compare or contrast several qualities or characteristics of two subjects. This arrangement allows readers to digest large quantities of information bit by bit. As such, it helps eliminate the risk that they will forget what you said in the first half of your essay before they finish the second half. Nancy Terranova's "High Anxiety: It Never Ends" uses this pattern.

9.2 Visualizing Methods of Comparison

9.2a The Point-by-Point Method

Let's say you wanted to contrast the Senate of ancient Rome with the current U.S. Senate. If you used the point-by-point method, the outline for your paper might look like this:

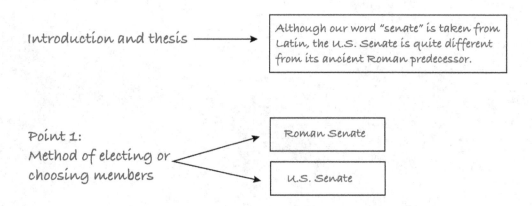

Introduction and thesis ⟶ Although our word "senate" is taken from Latin, the U.S. Senate is quite different from its ancient Roman predecessor.

Point 1: Method of electing or choosing members ⟶ Roman Senate / U.S. Senate

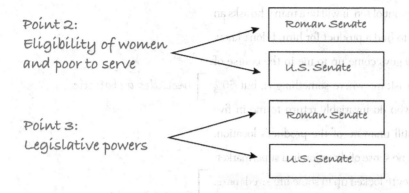

Point 2:
Eligibility of women
and poor to serve
→ Roman Senate
→ U.S. Senate

Point 3:
Legislative powers
→ Roman Senate
→ U.S. Senate

9.2b The Subject-by-Subject Method

Using the subject-by-subject method, you discuss one subject completely before going on to compare or contrast it with another subject in the second half of the essay. Here's how you might outline the essay contrasting the Roman Senate and the U.S. Senate.

Introduction and thesis	Although our word *senate* is taken from Latin, the U.S. Senate is quite different from its ancient Roman predecessor.
Subject 1: Roman Senate	• Method of electing or choosing members • Eligibility of women and poor to serve • Legislative powers
Subject 2: U.S. Senate	• Method of electing or choosing members • Eligibility of women and poor to serve • Legislative powers

Note that while many comparison/contrast essays use one or the other of these patterns exclusively, some essays make use of both the point-by-point pattern and the subject-by-subject pattern. You can see this in Christopher Daly's "How the Lawyers Stole Winter," later in this chapter.

9.2c Seeing the Pattern in a Comparison/Contrast Paper

The following essay from student James Langley discusses differences between male and female shoppers. It follows the point-by-point pattern, which is often found in longer essays. Notes in the left margin explain how Langley organized his paper. Notes on the right explain how he developed it.

Watch the Cart, James Langley

States thesis. There is nothing similar to the way men and women shop for groceries. Believe me, I know because I work in a major supermarket. After watching scores of people shop for food day in and day out, I have become an expert on the habits of American consumers. I have noticed many things about them, but nothing stands out more clearly than the differences between men and women.

Establishes his experience.

First of all, men never know where anything is.

Begins with topic sentence.

Point 1: How men search for a product.

Nine times out of ten, it will be a man who asks an employee to find a product for him. I don't know how many guys come up to me in the course of a night to ask me where something is, but 50% of those who do invariably return to me in five minutes still unaware of the product's location. Men have no sense of direction in a supermarket. It's as if they're locked up in some life-sized maze. It has always been my contention that men who shop should be provided with specially trained dogs to sniff out the products they desire. It would certainly save me valuable time too often wasted as I explain for the tenth time that soup is in aisle 9.

Includes a statistic.

Uses a simile.

Point 1: How women search for a product.

Women, on the other hand, rarely ask for an item's location. When they do, it is usually for an obscure product only they have heard of and whose name only they can pronounce. Whenever a woman asks me where some such item is, I always tell her to go to aisle 11—the dog-food aisle. Send a man there, and he'll forget what he was looking for and just buy the dog food out of desperation. Send a woman there, and she'll be back in five minutes with the product in hand, thanking me for locating it for her.

Begins with a topic sentence.

Uses an example.

Point 2: How quickly men and women shop.

Another difference between men and women is that women shop at speeds that would get them tickets on freeways, while men shop with the speed of a dead snail. A woman can get her shopping done in the same amount of time every time she goes. A man who shops just as often gets worse and worse every time.

Begins with a topic sentence.

Point 3: How well men and women manipulate carts.

The biggest difference between the sexes in regard to shopping, however, involves the manipulation of carts. A woman guides a cart through the store so fluidly and effortlessly that her movements are almost poetic. Men are an entirely different story. A man with a shopping

Begins with a topic sentence.

cart is a menace to anyone within two aisles of him. Men bounce their carts off display cases, sideswipe their fellow patrons and create havoc wherever they go. They have no idea of how to control the direction of carts. To a man, a shopping cart is a crazed metal monster designed to embarrass and harass him.

Creates a vivid image.

Uses a metaphor.

Conclusion relates to thesis and restates essay's main points.

Overall, then, women are far more proficient shoppers than men. They are efficient, speedy and graceful; men are slow and clumsy. I know these things because I work in a supermarket. I also know these things because I am a man.

9.3 Revising Comparison/Contrast Papers

The following essay by student Nancy Terranova was written after she began to reflect upon the daily fears and anxieties faced by her generation, especially in light of the terrorist attacks of September 11, 2001. Read the rough draft and an excerpt of the final draft of Terranova's paper. (You can read a full version of her final draft later in this chapter.) As you will see, the author did a thorough revision in which, among other things, she clarified her thesis, made the paper's organization more consistent and logical, and added information to develop her ideas more fully.

Terranova, "High Anxiety"—Rough Draft

Make tone more formal? Use third person, "they" and "them."

In many ways the lives of young adults today are different from those of their parents and far different from those of their grandparents. As members of Generation X, we seem to have all the answers and all the toys. Fax machines, email, voice mail, and call-waiting enable us to maintain unbroken strings of communication. Computer software makes us more productive students and business people. Take-home movies, television systems with hundreds of channels, electronic games, and downloads of popular music have allowed us to transform ourselves into virtual coach potatoes. Speaking of food, consider the immediate gratification—if not the nutrition—that drive-up hamburger joints, sushi bars, and the makers of microwaveable pizzas provide.

Remove clichés?

But are the important things in our lives really different? According to the French, the more things change the more they stay the same. We might be more technologically advanced than our parents and grandparents, but are our lives any happier and any less stressed-out than theirs?

Use quotation marks?

State thesis explicitly?

Over the last 100 years the longevity of Americans has increased. One reason for that is that, years ago, diseases such as polio, diphtheria, tuberculosis, pneumonia, tetanus, and even influenza took the lives of or crippled so many children and young adults. Back then, they worried about how to make a living as well. For example, many men and women of my parents' and grandparents' generations held factory or low-level office jobs. They had to develop skills to get those jobs, which meant finishing high school or learning a trade as an apprentice. In those days, that wasn't so easy. My grandparents remember the Depression, when 1 out of 4 people was out of work. Many of them had to leave high school in order to help support their families, and sometimes finding someone to apprentice with wasn't easy. Besides you could be laid-off easily.

Is subject-by-subject method best? Revise to use point-by-point method.

How does this relate to thesis? Strengthen connection.

Today, however, the Salk and Sabin vaccines have virtually wiped out polio. Medicine has virtually eliminated diphtheria and tuberculosis as well. And pneumonia and tetanus are easily treated with antibiotics. However, Generation X has other health worries. For example the rates of teenage suicide are much higher today. And young people seem to be more susceptible to drugs and alcohol. Sexually transmitted disease including gonorrhea, syphilis and AIDS are also much more prevalent today, because members of my generation are far more sexually active than before. Cases of anorexia and bulimia, virtually unheard of 50 years ago, are commonplace

Finish discussing previous point before starting a new one?

Support these ideas with research?

among women in their teens and twenties, and men are getting them too.

Who is "they"?

Develop this point more fully?

Today, they tell us, our job opportunities are greater too. But we need more education. Graduating from high school will get you a job at Burger King. The minimum to get started is a community college degree. And the best paying jobs require you to continue studying far beyond your bachelor's. However, even an advanced degree won't keep you from getting laid off, as so many employees of high-tech companies have found out in recent years. We may not be having a depression like my grandparents, but we have just come through a recession and that was bad enough. So anxiety about where your next meal is coming from is still around.

Correct illogical comparison?

Develop this point more fully?

And what about war, and national security?

I remember my grandmother telling me about worrying so much about my grandfather who had had been shipped out to the Pacific during World War II. Today, we still have war fears, and many of my friends, who are in the reserves, might be called to fight in Iraq. And what about all the terrorism?

Add a formal conclusion?

Terranova, "High Anxiety: It Never Ends"—Final Draft

Uses a more formal tone.

In 2002, the lives of people in their late teens and twenties are different in many ways from what they would have been if they had been born half a century earlier. Members of Generation X seem to have advantages their grandparents—and even their parents—never even hoped for. Fax machines, email, voice mail, and call-waiting enable them to maintain unbroken strings of communication even with

Has removed clichés.

people across the globe. Computer software makes them more productive students and employees. Take-home movies, television systems offering hundreds of channels, electronic games, and downloads of popular music are, sadly, transforming them into a generation of overweight couch potatoes. And speaking of food, consider the immediate gratification—if not the nutrition—that drive-up hamburger joints, sushi bars, and the makers of microwaveable pizzas provide.

Adds quotation marks.

According to the French, however, "the more things change, the more they stay the same." Today's young adults might live in a technologically advanced environment, but are

States thesis explicitly.

their lives any happier and any less stressful than those of their parents and grandparents? As a matter of fact, they suffer the same kinds of anxieties that their elders experienced.

Switches to point-by-point method of organization.

Take concerns over staying healthy, for example. Through much of the 20th century, diseases such as diphtheria, tuberculosis, pneumonia, tetanus, and even influenza took the lives of many young adults or severely debilitated them. In the 1950's, the world went through a kind of polio hysteria, as bad as that caused by AIDS in the 1980s. According to Dr. Edmund Sass, the United States reported 52,000 new cases of polio in 1952 (3). Another 5000 new cases were reported in Canada (Rutty 1) for that year.

Condenses what appeared in rough draft.

Today, medicine has virtually eliminated polio in the developed world. Diphtheria and tuberculosis, which plagued earlier generations, are in severe decline, and pneumonia and tetanus can be treated with antibiotics. However, Generation X has its own

Makes connection with thesis stronger and adds researched material.

health worries. For example, according to the Centers for Disease Control:

Focus of paper now remains steady.

> Many more people die by suicide than by homicide in the United States. Suicide rates among youth have been increasing steadily for the past four decades; suicide is the third leading cause of death among children and youth between the ages of 10 and 24.

Adds research to support thesis.

Moreover, young people seem to be more susceptible to drug and alcohol abuse. In a 1997 statement of the US Senate Judiciary Committee, Senator Orrin Hatch reported that the use of illicit drugs "among high school students [had] dramatically increased since 1991—from 11% to 24% in 1996 for 8th graders, from 21% to 38% for 10th graders, and from 29% to 40% for 12th graders". Sexually transmitted disease including gonorrhea and syphilis are also much more prevalent today because members of Generation X are far more sexually active than their grandparents or even their parents were. AIDS, now at epidemic levels, was unknown fifty years ago. Rates of anorexia and bulimia have also increased in the last two decades especially among women in their teens and twenties. However, even young men are suffering from these ailments.

Organization is uniform: point-by-point.

Adds research.

9.4 Practicing Comparison and Contrast

In the spaces provided, write paragraphs that respond to any four of the following items. Remember that comparison explains similarities, while contrast explains differences. Before you start writing a paragraph, gather details for it. Then make a rough draft. Before you begin your final draft, make sure the paragraph has a topic sentence.

1. Compare caring for a child and caring for an animal.

_____

_____

_____

_____

_____

_____

2. Compare writing papers for English class and preparing for a mathematics test.

_____

_____

_____

_____

_____

_____

3. Compare the cooking of two different cultures. For instance, compare Chinese with Italian, Indian with Mexican, Caribbean with Japanese, or Eastern European with American.

_____

_____

_____

_____

_____

_____

_____

4. Compare someone you know (perhaps yourself) to an animal. Start by writing "_____ is a snake" or "_____ is a workhorse."

_____

_____

_____

_____

_____

_____

5. Contrast your work or study habits with those of a friend.

_____

_____

_____

_____

_____

_____

6. Contrast the ways you and your parents (sister, brother, or other relative) view sex (marriage, education, religion, money, or your friends).

_____

_____

_____

_____

_____

_____

_____

9.5 Reading Selections

9.5a High Anxiety: It Never Ends

Author Biography

The student who wrote this essay majored in English and is now working part-time as an editor for a large publishing house. When asked to write a comparison/contrast essay, she reflected on the kinds of anxieties young American adults were experiencing, especially in the aftermath of the terrorist attacks of September 11, 2001. "***Nancy Terranova***" is a pen name.

 Preparing to Read

1. "Generation X" is a term that defines the generation of young adults who were roughly from their mid-teens to about thirty at the time this essay was written.

2. Note that Terranova uses a two-paragraph introduction and that she follows the point-by-point pattern to organize her essay. However, in the rough draft of this essay, which appears in the introduction, Terranova began with the subject-by-subject method and then switched to point-by point. Her final draft is far more consistent and logical.

3. Several bits of researched information appear in this essay, along with a Works Cited page, arranged in Modern Language Association style. If you want to learn more about MLA style, review the Research Process at the end of this book. For now, pay particular attention to how researched information is introduced into this essay and how it helps support the thesis.

abounds (verb)   Is plentiful.

debilitated (adjective)   Weakened.

despots (noun)   Tyrants.

gratification (noun)   Satisfaction.

hysteria (noun)   Extreme agitation, mass fear.

illicit (adjective)   Illegal.

prevalent (adjective)   Common.

susceptible (adjective)   Vulnerable, exposed to.

virtually (adverb)   Nearly, almost totally.

High Anxiety: It Never Ends

Nancy Terranova

In 2002, the lives of people in their late teens and twenties are different in many ways from what they would have been if they had been born half a century earlier. Members of Generation X seem to have advantages their grandparents—and even their parents—never even hoped for. Fax machines, email, voice mail, and social media enable them to maintain unbroken strings of communication even with people across the globe. Computer software makes them more productive students and employees. Take-home movies, television systems offering hundreds of channels, electronic games, and downloads of popular music are, sadly, transforming them into a generation of overweight couch potatoes. And speaking of food, consider the immediate gratification—if not the nutrition—that drive-up hamburger joints, sushi bars, and the makers of microwaveable pizzas provide.   1

According to the French, however, "the more things change, the more they stay the same." Today's young adults might live in a technologically advanced environment, but are their lives any happier and any less stressful than those of their parents and grandparents? As a matter of fact, they suffer the same kinds of anxieties that their elders experienced.   2

Take concerns over staying healthy, for example. Through much of the 20th century, diseases such as diphtheria, tuberculosis, pneumonia, tetanus, and even influenza took the lives of many young adults or severely debilitated them. In the 1950s, the world went through a kind of polio hysteria, as bad as that caused by AIDS in the 1980s. According to Dr. Edmund Sass, the United States reported 52,000 new cases of polio in 1952. Another 5000 new cases were reported in Canada (Rutty) for that year.   3

Today, medicine has virtually eliminated polio in the developed world. Diphtheria and tuberculosis, which plagued earlier generations, are in severe decline, and pneumonia and tetanus can be treated with antibiotics. However, Generation X has its own health worries. For example, according to the Centers for Disease Control: 4

> Many more people die by suicide than by homicide in the
> United States. Suicide rates among youth have been increasing
> steadily for the past four decades; suicide is the third leading
> cause of death among children and youth between the ages of
> 10 and 24.   5

Moreover, young people seem to be more susceptible to drug and alcohol abuse. In a 1997 statement of the US Senate Judiciary Committee, Senator Orrin Hatch reported that the use of illicit drugs among adolescents had "dramatically increased since 1991—from 11% to 24% in 1996 for 8th graders, from 21% to 38% for 10th graders, and from 29% to 40% for 12th graders". Sexually transmitted diseases including gonorrhea and syphilis are also much more prevalent today because   6 members of Generation X are far more sexually active than their grandparents or even their parents were. AIDS, now at epidemic levels, was unknown fifty years ago. Rates of anorexia and bulimia have also increased in the last two decades especially among women in their teens and twenties. However, even young men are suffering from these ailments.

People who came of age in the 40's, 50's, and 60's worried about how to make a living. For example, many men and women of our parents' and grandparents' generations held factory or low-level office jobs. They had to develop skills to get those jobs, which meant finishing high school or learning a trade as an apprentice. In those days, that wasn't so easy. My grandparents remember the Great Depression, when one out of four people was out of work. Many of them had to leave high school in order to help support their families, and sometimes finding someone with whom to apprentice was difficult. In addition, factory lay-offs were common.

7

Today, a college education is a necessity. Graduating from high school qualifies one for an entry-level job at Burger King. The minimum to launch any worthwhile career is a community college degree. And the best-paying jobs require continued study far beyond the bachelor's. However, even an advanced degree won't prevent the possibility of being laid off, as so many employees of high-tech companies have found out in recent years. This generation may not be experiencing a depression as our grandparents did, but we have just come through a recession, and that was bad enough! So anxiety about keeping a steady job and building a rewarding career still abounds.

8

Then there are the questions of war and national security. The previous two generations lived through the horrors of World War II, the Korean War, and Vietnam, not to mention the Cold War, which is now, we are told, far behind us. But this generation has to deal with its fear of terrorism, which became all too real on 9/11/01. We are leery about boarding airplanes, and we have accustomed ourselves to listening for warnings from the Department of Homeland Security. Some of us might soon be called to fight in the Middle East as did our older brothers and sisters in the 1990 Persian Gulf War or in Kosovo.

9

No one knows what tomorrow will bring. Perhaps being human means living with anxiety and even fear. If the past is any indication of what the future holds, this generation will follow the example of its predecessors and come through. The American people have distinguished themselves during the past fifty years. After all, they have conquered major diseases, ended the Cold War, invented the computer, helped establish democracies in countries once ruled by despots, strengthened the rights of women and minorities in their own land, and, through it all, managed to maintain the highest standard of living the world has ever known. If the current generation can do half that much, it will be just fine.

10

Works Cited

Centers for Disease Control and Prevention. *Suicide among Youth.* 15 July 2002. http://www.cdc.gov/communication/tips/suicide.htm. Accessed 2 Feb. 2004.

Rutty, Christopher J. *Do Something ... Do Anything! Poliomyelitis in Canada, 1927–1962.* Apr. 1995. Health Heritage Research Services. http://www.healthheritageresearch. com/PolioPHD.html. Accessed 1 Feb. 2004.

Sass, Edmund. "A Polio History Quest." *Polio History Pages.* 22 Apr. 2002. http://www.cloudnet.com/~edrbsass/poliohistoryquest.htm. Accessed 5 Feb. 2004.

United States Senate Judiciary Committee. *Drug Abuse among Our Children: A Growing National Crisis.* Senator Orrin Hatch, Chairman. June 1998. http://www.senate.gov/~iudiciarv/oldsite/ogh61798.htm. Accessed 6 Feb. 2004.

Read More on the Web

For more about anxiety among young people go to the following websites:

- "Anxiety and Depression," Boston University Special Report: http://bvtlab.com/g95Jt

- "Depression and Anxiety among College Students": psychcentral.com/lib/depression-and-anxiety-among-college-students

Questions for Discussion

1. The author discusses three major areas of similarity. What are they?

2. Explain why the subject-by-subject method of organization would not have been as appropriate to Terranova's purpose as the point-by-point method?

3. This essay makes many comparisons; it points out similarities. What differences between the sources of anxiety for one generation and those for another does Terranova explain? In other words, where and why does she use contrast?

4. What does the author's subtitle add to the essay? How does it help the reader?

5. What methods of development, other than comparison and contrast, does this essay use?

6. Much of this essay's success is due to its use of concrete detail. Analyze one paragraph you think is particularly illustrative of Terranova's ability to use such detail.

Thinking Critically

1. Terranova spends a great deal of time explaining the anxieties young people feel over their health. Do you agree with her assessment? Are you worried about the kinds of problems she mentions? Are you worried about other problems? Are you not worried at all about health problems?

2. Terranova argues that today's young adults have as much to worry about as their parents and grandparents did. If this is so, in what ways are their lives better than those of their predecessors? In what ways are they worse?

Suggestions for Journal Entries

1. Terranova spends more time on questions of health and employment than on national security. Perhaps, for her, the first two are simply more relevant and more immediate. Which one of the concerns that she mentions has the most relevance for you? Use focused freewriting to add details of your own to Terranova's discussion, but focus on only one of the three areas she covers. If you have no interest in any of the areas that Terranova covers, write about another source of anxiety that is especially important for you.

2. Interview at least two members of an earlier generation, such as your parents, grandparents, or family friends. Begin by talking about the prevailing views of your generation on a certain subject such as sex, war, marriage, religion, or any other issue or concern that affects the lives of people your age. Then, ask the people you are interviewing to identify both similarities and differences in the ways their generation viewed such questions. Like Terranova, you might want to discuss various types of anxieties suffered by your generation and theirs. Or you might ask them about their generations' views on race relations, education, war, the government, patriotism, religion, dating, or drinking.

9.5b Temptations of Old Age

Author Biography

Malcolm Cowley (1898–1989) was a writer, editor, literary critic, and historian noted for his energy and productivity up until his death at ninety. In the last decade of his life, Cowley wrote *The View from 80*, a book that explains his very positive attitude toward aging and that offers excellent advice about the latter stages of life.

Preparing to Read

1. This selection is from a chapter of Cowley's book that discusses several temptations of old age and explains ways to avoid them. Among these temptations are greed, vanity, and a desire to escape life's problems through alcohol. But the greatest temptation, as shown in the following paragraphs, is "simply giving up."

2. Pierre-Auguste Renoir, mentioned in paragraph 4, was a French painter of the nineteenth and twentieth centuries. Francisco Goya was a Spanish painter of the eighteenth and nineteenth centuries.

3. What hint about the selection's contents does the word temptations provide?

Vocabulary

ailments (noun)   Illnesses, diseases, disorders.

compelling (adjective)   Convincing.

distinguished (adjective)   Well-respected.

distraction (noun)   Amusement, diversion.

infirmities (noun)   Illnesses.

lithographs (noun)   Prints.

outwitted (verb)   Outsmarted.

Rolls-Royce (noun)   Luxury British automobile.

senility (noun)   Decrease in mental powers afflicting some elderly people.

unvanquished (adjective)   Undefeated.

Temptations of Old Age*

Malcolm Cowley

Not whiskey or cooking sherry but simply giving up is the greatest temptation of age. It is something different from a stoical acceptance of infirmities, which is something to be admired.   1

The givers-up see no reason for working. Sometimes they lie in bed all day when moving about would still be possible, if difficult. I had a friend, a distinguished poet, who surrendered in that fashion. The doctors tried to stir him to action, but he refused to leave his room. Another friend, once a successful artist, stopped painting when his eyes began to fail. His doctor made the mistake of telling him that he suffered from a fatal disease. He then lost interest in everything except the splendid Rolls-Royce, acquired in his prosperous days, that stood in the garage. Daily he wiped the dust from its hood. He couldn't drive it on the road any longer, but he used to sit in the driver's seat, start the motor, then back the Rolls out of the garage and drive it in again, back twenty feet and forward twenty feet; that was his only distraction.   2

I haven't the right to blame those who surrender, not being able to put myself inside their minds or bodies. Often they must have compelling reasons, physical or moral. Not only do they suffer from a variety of ailments, but also they are made to feel that they no longer have a function in the community. Their families and neighbors don't ask them for advice, don't really listen when they speak, don't call on them for efforts. One notes that there are not a few recoveries from apparent senility when that situation changes. If it doesn't change, old persons may decide that efforts are useless. I sympathize with their problems, but the men and women I envy are those who accept old age as a series of challenges.   3

For such persons, every new infirmity is an enemy to be outwitted, an obstacle to be overcome by force of will. They enjoy each little victory over themselves, and sometimes they win a major success. Renoir was one of them. He continued painting, and magnificently, for years after he was crippled by arthritis; the brush had to be strapped to his arm. "You don't need your hand to paint," he said. Goya was another of the unvanquished. At 72 he retired as an official painter of the Spanish court and decided to work only for himself. His later years were those of the famous "black paintings" in which he let his imagination run (and also of the lithographs, then a new technique). At 78 he escaped a reign of terror in Spain by fleeing to Bordeaux. He was deaf and his eyes were failing; in order to work he had to wear several pairs of spectacles, one over another, and then use a magnifying glass; but he was producing splendid work in a totally new style. At 80 he drew an ancient man propped on two sticks, with a mass of white hair and beard hiding his face and with the inscription "I am still learning." 4

"Eighty years old!" the great Catholic poet Paul Claudel wrote in his journal. "No eyes left, no ears, no teeth, no legs, no wind! And when all is said and done, how astonishingly well one does without them!" 5

*Editor's Title

Read More on the Web

For more on Malcolm Cowley read the following:

- *Washington Post* obituary of Malcolm Cowley: http://bvtlab.com/48668

- Short biography of Cowley: poetryfoundation.org/poets/malcolm-cowley

Questions for Discussion

1. Pick out particularly vivid verbs and adjectives in this selection.

2. Where does Cowley signal a transition from one subject to another?

3. Various methods can be combined to develop one idea. Where in this piece does Cowley use examples?

4. Do you think the conclusion of this selection is effective? Why or why not? If necessary, review ways to write conclusions in chapter 3.

5. Why, according to the author, do some elderly people simply give up?

6. What does he mean when he says that others see "every new infirmity" as "an obstacle to be overcome by force of will" (paragraph 4)?

Thinking Critically

1. Cowley quotes directly from the "unvanquished." Why doesn't he also quote from "those who surrender"?

2. This selection uses the subject-by-subject pattern. Why does the author begin with the "givers-up" and not end with them? Should he have discussed Renoir, Goya, and Claudel first?

3. Would "Temptations of Old Age" have been better organized point by point? Why or why not?

Suggestions for Journal Entries

1. What Cowley says might apply to people of all ages. Do you know someone who seems to face all the challenges life has to offer? Spend five minutes freewriting about the way this person reacts to such challenges. Then do the same for someone you might call a "giver-up." Try to include facts about his/her lives that will describe his/her personality.

2. In what way are you like the people in your family who have come before you? Think about a parent, grandparent, or other older relative. Use listing or focused freewriting to explain what is similar about your personalities, interests, and lifestyles or your opinions about music, politics, other people, or anything else you can think of.

9.5c Grant and Lee: A Study in Contrasts

Author Biography

Bruce Catton (1899–1978) won the Pulitzer Prize for his book *A Stillness at Appomattox*. A journalist who worked for the *Cleveland Plain-Dealer* and other newspapers, Catton also worked for the Department of Commerce in Washington, D.C., and was the editor of *American Heritage* magazine. In addition to winning a Pulitzer Prize, Catton was awarded the Presidential Medal of Freedom. His other books include *The War Lords of Washington* (1949), *Mr. Lincoln's Army* (1951), *The Coming Fury* (1961), and *Terrible Swift Sword* (1962).

Preparing to Read

1. Catton mentions several battles fought by generals Grant and Lee: Petersburg, Second Manassas, Chancellorsville, and Vicksburg. Look up battles in your library or on the Internet to learn more about the characters and talents of these two generals.

2. In paragraphs 4 and 5, the author mentions chivalry and nobility. In paragraph 12, he pictures Lee as a medieval knight. In that same paragraph, he tells us that Grant was "the modern man emerging." Learn more about the values that Catton associated with Lee and Grant through researching terms like *medieval knighthood* and *chivalry*. Learn more about the industrialization of America by researching "the industrial revolution in the United States."

3. In paragraph 5, Catton tells us that Lee came from Tidewater, Virginia. This is a region on the coast of northern Virginia where large plantations, which yielded riches to their owners, once flourished. At such places, slave labor was used.

Vocabulary

acute (adjective)   Severe, serious.

deportment (noun)   Behavior.

fidelity (noun)   Loyalty.

implicit (adjective)   Understood, inherent.

obeisance (noun)   Obedience, homage, respect.

poignant (adjective)   Touching, emotionally moving.

pronounced (adjective)   Definite, prominent.

vocabulary

Vocabulary (Continued)

sanctified (adjective)   Made holy.

sinewy (adjective)   Powerful, strong.

tenacity (noun)   Persistence, determination.

vainly (adverb)   Unsuccessfully, uselessly.

virtual (adjective)   Practical, fundamental.

Grant and Lee: A Study in Contrasts

Bruce Catton

When Ulysses S. Grant and Robert E. Lee met in the parlor of a modest house at Appomattox Court House, Virginia, on April 9, 1865, to work out the terms for the surrender of Lee's Army of Northern Virginia, a great chapter in American life came to a close, and a great new chapter began.   1

These men were bringing the Civil War to its virtual finish. To be sure, other armies had yet to surrender, and for a few days the fugitive Confederate government would struggle desperately and vainly, trying to find some way to go on living now that its chief support was gone. But in effect it was all over when Grant and Lee signed the papers. And the little room where they wrote out the terms was the scene of one of the poignant, dramatic contrasts in American history.   2

They were two strong men, these oddly different generals, and they represented the strengths of two conflicting currents that, through them, had come into final collision.   3

Back of Robert E. Lee was the notion that the old aristocratic concept might somehow survive and be dominant in American life.   4

Lee was tidewater Virginia, and in his background were family, culture, and tradition … the age of chivalry transplanted to a New World which was making its own legends and its own myths. He embodied a way of life that had come down through the age of knighthood and the English country squire. America was a land that was beginning all over again, dedicated to nothing much more complicated than the rather hazy belief that all men had equal rights and should have an equal chance in the world. In such a land, Lee stood for the feeling that it was somehow of advantage to human society to have a pronounced inequality in the social structure. There should be a leisure class, backed by ownership of land; in turn, society itself should be keyed to the land as the chief source of wealth and influence. It would bring forth (according to this ideal) a class of men with a strong sense of obligation to the community; men who lived not to gain advantage for themselves, but to meet the solemn obligations which had been laid on them by the very fact that they were privileged. From them the country would get its leadership; to them it could look for the higher values—of thought, of conduct, of personal deportment—to give it strength and virtue.   5

Lee embodied the noblest elements of this aristocratic ideal. Through him, the landed nobility justified itself. For four years, the Southern states had fought a desperate war to uphold the ideals for which Lee stood. In the end, it almost seemed as if the Confederacy fought for Lee; as if he himself was the Confederacy … the best thing that the way of life for which the Confederacy stood could ever have to offer. He had passed into legend before Appomattox. Thousands of tired, underfed, poorly clothed Confederate soldiers, long since past the simple enthusiasm of the early days of the struggle, somehow considered Lee the symbol of everything for which they had been willing to die. But they could not quite put this feeling into words. If the Lost Cause, sanctified by so much heroism and so many deaths, had a living justification, its justification was General Lee.   6

Grant, the son of a tanner on the Western frontier, was everything Lee was not. He had come up the hard way and embodied nothing in particular except the eternal toughness and sinewy fiber of the men who grew up beyond the mountains. He was one of a body of men who owed reverence and obeisance to no one, who were self-reliant to a fault, who cared hardly anything for the past but who had a sharp eye for the future.   7

These frontier men were the precise opposites of the tidewater aristocrats. Back of them, in the great surge that had taken people over the Alleghenies and into the opening Western country, there was a deep, implicit dissatisfaction with a past that had settled into grooves. They stood for democracy, not from any reasoned conclusion about the proper ordering of human society, but simply because they had grown up in the middle of democracy and knew how it worked. Their society might have privileges, but they would be privileges each man had won for himself. Forms and patterns meant nothing. No man was born to anything, except perhaps to a chance to show how far he could rise. Life was competition.

Yet along with this feeling had come a deep sense of belonging to a national community. The Westerner who developed a farm, opened a shop, or set up in business as a trader could hope to prosper only as his own community prospered—and his community ran from the Atlantic to the Pacific and from Canada down to Mexico. If the land was settled, with towns and highways and accessible markets, he could better himself. He saw his fate in terms of the nation's own destiny. As its horizons expanded, so did his. He had, in other words, an acute dollars-and-cents stake in the continued growth and development of his country.

And that, perhaps, is where the contrast between Grant and Lee becomes most striking. The Virginia aristocrat, inevitably, saw himself in relation to his own region. He lived in a static society which could endure almost anything except change. Instinctively, his first loyalty would go to the locality in which that society existed. He would fight to the limit of endurance to defend it, because in defending it he was defending everything that gave his own life its deepest meaning.

The Westerner, on the other hand, would fight with an equal tenacity for the broader concept of society. He fought so because everything he lived by was tied to growth, expansion, and a constantly widening horizon. What he lived by would survive or fall with the nation itself. He could not possibly stand by unmoved in the face of an attempt to destroy the Union. He would combat it with everything he had, because he could only see it as an effort to cut the ground out from under his feet.

So Grant and Lee were in complete contrast, representing two diametrically opposed elements in American life. Grant was the modern man emerging; beyond him, ready to come on the stage, was the great age of steel and machinery, of crowded cities and a restless burgeoning vitality. Lee might have ridden down from the old age of chivalry, lance in hand, silken banner fluttering over his head. Each man was the perfect champion of his cause, drawing both his strengths and his weaknesses from the people he led.

Yet it was not all contrast, after all. Different as they were—in background, in personality, in underlying aspiration—these two great soldiers had much in common. Under everything else, they were marvelous fighters. Furthermore, their fighting qualities were really very much alike.

Each man had, to begin with, the great virtue of utter tenacity and fidelity. Grant fought his way down the Mississippi Valley in spite of acute personal discouragement and profound military handicaps. Lee hung on in the trenches at Petersburg after hope itself had died. In each man there was an indomitable quality … the born fighter's refusal to give up as long as he can still remain on his feet and lift his two fists.

Daring and resourcefulness they had, too; the ability to think faster and move faster than the enemy. These were the qualities which gave Lee the dazzling campaigns of Second Manassas and Chancellorsville and won Vicksburg for Grant.

Lastly, and perhaps greatest of all, there was the ability, at the end, to turn quickly from war to peace once the fighting was over. Out of the way these two men behaved at Appomattox came the possibility of a peace of reconciliation. It was a possibility not wholly realized, in the years to come, but which did, in the end, help the two sections to become one nation again … after a war whose bitterness might have seemed to make such a reunion wholly impossible. No part of either man's life became him more than the part he played in this brief meeting in the McLean house at Appomattox. Their behavior there put all succeeding generations of Americans in their debt. Two great Americans, Grant and Lee—very different, yet under everything very much alike. Their encounter at Appomattox was one of the great moments of American history.

Read More on the Web

Check the following to learn more about this author and the subject of this essay:

- *American Heritage* website: http://bvtlab.com/8AbBa
- Ulysses S. Grant Biography: http://bvtlab.com/4v566
- Robert E. Lee: www.history.com/topics/american-civil-war/robert-e-lee

Questions for Discussion

1. Overall, what method of developing a comparison/contrast paper does Catton use: point by point or subject by subject?

2. Where does Catton state his thesis? What does the thesis tell us about the organization of the essay?

3. What function do paragraphs 10 and 11 play in this essay?

4. Is this simply a contrast essay? What did Grant and Lee have in common? Why does Catton spend the last four paragraphs taking about similarities?

5. What are some of the similarities?

6. What are some of the characteristics of Tidewater aristocrats, like Lee?

7. What are some of the characteristics of Westerners like Grant?

Thinking Critically

1. Write a short paragraph in which you explain what Grant and Lee had in common as generals.

2. Catton tells us that Westerners had a "deep sense of belonging to a national community." Do people in the United States today still have that "sense"? Give examples that both support and challenge the notion that we share a national consciousness.

Suggestions for Journal Entries

1. In item 1 of Thinking Critically, you were asked to explain what Grant and Lee had in common as generals. Do you know people in the same jobs or careers who can be compared for their tenacity, fidelity, and resourcefulness? Perhaps you know two teachers, two coaches, two police officers, or two business people whom you admire for these or other noble qualities. Make a list of the qualities they share. You might discuss how they approach their jobs, how hard they work, or how they treat others. Next, make a list of how these people differ.

2. Use freewriting to gather some details about what life might be like in the South had the Confederacy won the war. Would African Americans still be enslaved today? Would the Southern economy continue to be based on farming? Would the North and South ever be united? Which of the two parts of the country would be more prosperous?

9.5d **How the Lawyers Stole Winter**

Author Biography

Christopher Daly (b. 1954) is a professor of journalism at Boston University. A former reporter with the Associated Press and the *Washington Post*, he is the author of *Covering America*, a history of U.S. journalism. This essay first appeared in the *Atlantic* in 1995. It is a good example of the versatility of comparison/contrast, for it allows Daly to make a convincing argument that an increase in lawsuits in the United States over the last quarter-century has diminished the freedom, joy, and spontaneity of growing up.

Preparing to Read

1. Pay special attention to the essay's title. It expresses the author's purpose.

2. The thesis does not appear in the first paragraph—look for it elsewhere.

Vocabulary

connoisseurs (noun)   Experts, specialists in.

henceforth (adverb)   From then on.

liability (noun)   Legal responsibility.

obverse (noun)   Counterpart.

savvier (adjective)   More knowledgeable.

How the Lawyers Stole Winter

Christopher B. Daly

When I was a boy, my friends and I would come home from school each day, change our clothes (because we were not allowed to wear "play clothes" to school), and go outside until dinnertime. In the early 1960s in Medford, a city on the outskirts of Boston, that was pretty much what everybody did. Sometimes there might be flute lessons, or an organized Little League game, but usually not. Usually we kids went out and played.   1

In winter, on our way home from the Gleason School, we would go past Brooks Pond to check the ice. By throwing heavy stones on it, hammering it with downed branches, and, finally, jumping on it, we could figure out if the ice was ready for skating. If it was, we would hurry home to grab our skates, our sticks, and whatever other gear we had, and then return to play hockey for the rest of the day. When the streetlights came on, we knew it was time to jam our cold, stiff feet back into our green rubber snow boots and get home for dinner.   2

I had these memories in mind recently when I moved, with my wife and two young boys, into a house near a lake even closer to Boston, in the city of Newton. As soon as Crystal Lake froze over, I grabbed my skates and headed out. I was not the first one there, though: the lawyers had beaten me to the lake. They had warned the town recreation department to put it off limits. So I found a sign that said DANGER, THIN ICE. NO SKATING.   3

Knowing a thing or two about words myself, I put my own gloss on the sign. I took it to mean *When the ice is thin, there is danger and there should be no skating*. Fair enough, I thought, but I knew that the obverse was also true: *When the ice is thick, it is safe and there should be skating*. Finding the ice plenty thick, I laced up my skates and glided out onto the miraculous glassy surface of the frozen lake. My wife, a native of Manhattan, would not let me take our two boys with me. But for as long as I could, I enjoyed the free, open-air delight of skating as it should be. After a few days others joined me, and we became an outlaw band of skaters.   4

What we were doing was once the heart of winter in New England—and a lot of other places, too. It was clean, free exercise that needed no StairMasters, no health clubs, no appointments, and hardly any gear. Sadly, it is in danger of passing away. Nowadays it seems that every city and town and almost all property holders are so worried about liability and lawsuits that they simply throw up a sign or a fence and declare that henceforth there shall be no skating, and that's the end of it.   5

As a result, kids today live in a world of leagues, rinks, rules, uniforms, adults, and rides—rides here, rides there, rides everywhere. It is not clear that they are better off; in some ways they are clearly *not* better off.   6

When I was a boy skating on Brooks Pond, there were no grown-ups around. Once or twice a year, on a weekend day or a holiday, some parents might come by with a thermos of hot cocoa. Maybe they would build a fire (which we were forbidden to do), and we would gather round.   7

But for the most part the pond was the domain of children. In the absence of adults, we made and enforced our own rules. We had hardly any gear—just some borrowed hockey gloves, some hand-me-down skates, maybe an elbow pad or two—so we played a clean form of hockey, with no high-sticking, no punching, and almost no checking. A single fight could ruin the whole afternoon. Indeed, as I remember it, thirty years later, it was the purest form of hockey I ever saw—until I got to see the Russian national team play the game.   8

But before we could play, we had to check the ice. We became serious junior meteorologists, true connoisseurs of cold. We learned that the best weather for pond skating is plain, clear cold, with starry nights and no snow. (Snow not only mucks up the skating surface but also insulates the ice from the colder air above.) And we learned that moving water, even the gently flowing Mystic River, is a lot less likely to freeze than standing water. So we skated only on the pond. We learned all the weird whooping and cracking sounds that ice makes as it expands and contracts, and thus when to leave the ice.   9

Do kids learn these things today? I don't know. How would they? We don't let them. Instead we post signs. Ruled by lawyers, cities and towns everywhere try to eliminate their legal liability. But try as they might, they cannot eliminate the underlying risk. Liability is a social construct; risk is a natural fact. When it is cold enough, ponds freeze. No sign or fence or ordinance can change that.   10

In fact, by focusing on liability and not teaching our kids how to take risks, we are making their world more dangerous. When we were children, we had to learn to evaluate risks and handle them on our own. We had to learn, quite literally, to test the waters. As a result, we grew up to be savvier about ice and ponds than any kid could be who has skated only under adult supervision on a rink.   11

When I was a boy, despite the risks we took on the ice no one I knew ever drowned. The only people I heard about who drowned were graduate students at Harvard or MIT who came from the tropics and were living through their first winters. Not knowing (after all, how could they?) about ice on moving water, they would innocently venture out onto the half-frozen Charles River, fall through, and die. They were literally out of their element.   12

Are we raising a generation of children who will be out of their element? And if so, what can we do about it? We cannot just roll back the calendar. I cannot tell my six-year-old to head down to the lake by himself to play all afternoon—if for no other reason than that he would not find twenty or thirty other kids there, full of the collective wisdom about cold and ice that they had inherited, along with hockey equipment, from their older brothers and sisters. Somewhere along the line that link got broken.   13

The *whole setting of childhood has changed*. We cannot change it again over night. I cannot send my children out by themselves yet, but at least some of the time I can go out there with them. Maybe that is a start.   14

As for us, last winter was a very unusual one. We had ferocious cold (near-zero temperatures on many nights) and tremendous snows (about a hundred inches in all). Eventually a strange thing happened. The town gave in—sort of. Sometime in January the recreation department "opened" a section of the lake, and even dispatched a snowplow truck to clear a good-sized patch of ice. The boys and I skated during the rest of winter. Ever vigilant, the town officials kept the THIN ICE signs up, even though their own truck could safely drive on the frozen surface. And they brought in "lifeguards" and all sorts of rules about the hours during which we could skate and where we had to stay.   15

But at least we were able to skate in the open air, on real ice.   16

And it was still free.   17

Read More on the Web

For more about the discussion of the legal aspects of this essay, go to

- "9 Most Laughable Lawsuits": http://bvtlab.com/AbC64
- *Sick of Lawsuits* website: www.sickoflawsuits.org

Questions for Discussion

1. Where does Daly state his thesis?

2. Reread paragraphs 1–6. How is this section organized: point by point or subject by subject?

3. What pattern do paragraphs 7–14 follow?

4. What technique does Daly use to conclude this essay? Think back to the methods for ending an essay that you learned in chapter 3.

5. What, according to Daly, have the lawyers done to steal winter?

6. Where else in this essay does Daly draw conclusions using the cause/effect method?

7. What does Daly mean by "collective wisdom" (paragraph 13)?

Thinking Critically

1. Read Barry Glazer's "The Right to Be Let Alone" in chapter 12. In what ways is Glazer's argument similar to Daly's position?

2. In what way, according to Daly, has the change he discusses affected children negatively? Can you think of how this change might have affected them positively?

Suggestions for Journal Entries (Continues)

1. Think of an activity or sport that children used to engage in without the kind of protection required today. For example, they were once allowed to ride bicycles without crash helmets; to swim in ponds, lakes, and rivers that had no lifeguards; and to go skating without wearing protective gear. Gather as much information as you can to explain how children once pursued this sport or activity and how they engage in it today.

2. Think of a sport, activity, or practice that is pursued by members of your generation and that you believe to be dangerous. Use listing or clustering to gather details that might explain why it is so risky. Then gather more information on ways you would recommend to make it safer. If the sport, activity, or practice cannot be made safer, list reasons that could be used to discourage or prevent people from pursuing it.

3. Interview your parents, grandparents, or other older people. Ask them for examples of the activities that children of their generation engaged in during their spare time. Then, list ways in which you and your friends spent your spare time when you were children.

9.6 Suggestions for Sustained Writing

1. If you responded to the second journal entry after "High Anxiety: It Never Ends," you interviewed two members of an earlier generation to get their views on how people in their day viewed a particular problem, question, or concern that is also affecting people of your generation. Write an essay that both compares and contrasts the ways that members of your generation and of their generation view this problem. Like Terranova, you might want to do some research—on the Internet or in the library—that will support your thesis. If so, remember to follow principles for including and citing such information, as explained in The Research Process, which discusses writing a research paper using the Modern Language Association style.

2. In talking about people who are eighty, Malcolm Cowley describes two different types: those who fight on and those who give up. But we see these types in every generation. In fact, you may have begun discussing such people in your journal. Use these notes in an essay about people you know who fit Cowley's personality types: those who face life bravely and those who just give up.

   On the other hand, if you don't like this topic, you can start from scratch and choose your own basis for contrast. For example, discuss two very different types of students: those who are serious about getting an education and those who are not. Here's an example of a thesis for such a paper:

   > While serious students study hard, do extra reading, and compare notes with classmates, those who just want to get by spend much of their time playing cards or watching television.

   Cowley uses the subject-by-subject method; you might want to do the same. However you decide to organize your essay, discuss two or three people you know as examples of each personality type. Begin with a rough draft, adding details with each revision to make your paper clearer and more convincing. In the process, include an effective introduction and conclusion.

   Then, rewrite your paper once more. Make sure it has a clear thesis, is easy to follow, and is free of mistakes in grammar, punctuation, spelling, and the like.

3. Catton tells us that Grant and Lee both had "the great virtue of utter tenacity and fidelity" and that they were both quite resourceful. If you responded to item 1 under the Suggestions for Journal Entries, you have already gathered details that will help you compare two people in the same careers or occupations who are tenacious, faithful, and resourceful. You may have also gathered information about how they differ.

Write a formal essay comparing these two teachers, coaches, clergy, police officers, or members of other professions you have chosen to write about. You can put your emphasis on the qualities they share, talking more about their similarities than their differences, A good way to start, however, is to mention at least one difference between your two subjects. You can then state your thesis, which declares how really similar they are. Then you can proceed to prove your thesis by using and adding to the information you put into your journal. Like Catton, you might want to use the point-by-point method; but if your paper is less than, say, five hundred words, the subject-by-subject method might work as well.

4. If you responded to the first journal entry after Christopher Daly's "How the Lawyers Stole Winter," use your notes as the basis for an essay that contrasts the dangerous way a children's sport or activity used to be pursued versus the safer way it is pursued today. Use the subject-by-subject method to organize your essay, but include an introduction that explains the basic elements, rules, or procedures involved in the activity.

   If you responded to the second journal entry, turn your notes into an essay that begins by briefly explaining the reasons you believe a certain sport or activity pursued by members of your generation is dangerous. Then, using the point-by-point method, discuss each of those risks in detail and offer ways in which to decrease or eliminate its effects.

   If you don't like either of these assignments, write an essay that, in the first half, explains why a certain contemporary sport, activity, or popular practice is so dangerous that it should be banned. How about skydiving, bungee jumping, boxing, body piercing, or collegiate football? In the second half of your paper, recommend some ways in which people might be discouraged or prevented from engaging in it.

   Whichever option you choose, fill your essay with details that will make it convincing. Write at least three drafts; then, edit and proofread the final draft carefully.

5. Think back to your childhood. How did you and your friends spend your spare time? Were you couch potatoes who spent all day watching television or listening to music? Did you collect stamps, coins, or baseball cards? Did you play baseball, basketball, field hockey, or other sports? Did you go hiking and camping? Or did you practice playing in your own rock band?

   Write an essay in which you compare and/or contrast the way in which you spent your spare childhood moments with the way people of earlier generations did. If you responded to the third journal suggestion after Daly's "How the Lawyers Stole Winter," you may have already interviewed people older than you to gather useful information on this question. As indicated earlier, you can point out similarities, differences, or both. The subject-by-subject method is well suited to this assignment, but if you plan to write a long essay, the point-by-point method might work as well. As always, revise the rough draft of your essay several times. Then edit and proofread before submitting your essay to your instructor.

ACKNOWLEDGMENTS

Cowley, Malcolm. *The View from 80*. Viking Press, 1980. Reprinted with permission of the Estate of Malcolm Cowley.

Catton, Bruce. "The American Story" (script series), 1954. Prepared and distributed to radio stations as a public service by Broadcast Music, Inc., in association with the Society of American Historians.

Daly, Christopher B. "How the Lawyers Stole Winter." *Atlantic Monthly*, March 1995. Reprinted with permission of the author.

Shutterstock

10

Process

Chapter Outline

Like illustration and comparison and contrast, process analysis is a way to explain complex ideas and abstract concepts. It can be used to show how something works or how something happens. It also comes in handy when you want to give readers instructions.

10.1 Organization, Purpose, and Thesis

Process explanations are organized in chronological order, much like narrative essays and short stories. In narration, however, the writer's purpose is to tell *what* happens. In process analysis, it is to explain *how* something happens (or happened) or *how* it is done. You would be explaining a process if you wrote an essay discussing how the body uses oxygen, how electric lightbulbs work, how a car stereo produces sound, or how the Grand Canyon was formed. An example of such an essay in this chapter is "Why the Sky Looks Blue" by James Jeans.

Process analysis is an important tool in scientific writing, but it can also be applied to topics in history, sociology, economics, the arts, and other subjects. For example, a process paper might be a good way to explain how the U.S. Constitution was ratified, how the stock market works, how people celebrate a holiday or tradition, or how a particular type of music developed. In fact, Dave Barry's "Florida's Fire Ants Headed for Trouble" proves that process analysis can even be used to create humor.

Process analysis is also used in writing instructions. Scientists, doctors, engineers, and computer experts, for example, must often write careful directions to show their readers how to use a tool or machine, how to complete a procedure safely, how to conduct a test to achieve accurate results, or how to run complicated computer software. As a beginning writer, you might want to discuss a more limited subject by showing your readers how to change a tire, hang wallpaper, stop smoking, lose weight, study for a math exam, or accomplish another important task or goal. In this chapter, selections that instruct readers are Benjamin Franklin's "Drawing Electricity from Clouds" and Triena Milden's "So You Want to Flunk Out of College," which appears later in the introduction.

The thesis in a process analysis essay is usually a statement of purpose; it explains why a process is important, why it occurs or occurred, or why it should be completed. For example, if you want to explain how to change the oil in a car, you might begin by saying that changing oil regularly can extend the engine's life. In addition to a statement of purpose, writers of process analysis often begin with a broad summary or overview of the process so that readers can understand how each step relates to the whole procedure and to its purpose.

10.2 Clarity and Directness

As with all types of writing, clarity and directness are important in process writing. You must explain the various steps in your process specifically and carefully enough that even readers who are unfamiliar with the subject will be able to follow each step easily. To be clear and to maintain your reader's interest, keep the following in mind:

1. *Use clear, simple language.* Use words that your readers will have no trouble understanding. If you must use terms your readers are not familiar with, provide a brief definition or description. Depending on how much your readers know about how to change a tire, for example, you might have to describe what a lug wrench looks like before you explain how to use it.

2. *Use the clearest, simplest organization.* Whenever possible, arrange the steps of your process in chronological order. In addition, use plenty of connective words and phrases between paragraphs (especially to show the passage of time); this will keep your writing coherent and easy to follow.

3. *Mention equipment and supplies.* Let readers know what equipment, tools, supplies, and other materials are involved in the process. Define or describe items that might be unfamiliar to them. If you are giving instructions, list these materials *before* you start explaining the steps in your process; otherwise, the reader will have to stop midprocess to find a needed item, which can be frustrating and time consuming.

4. *Discuss each step separately.* Reserve an entire paragraph for each step in the process. This is especially important when giving instructions, as explaining more than one step at a time can confuse readers and cause you to leave out important information.

5. *Discuss simultaneous steps separately.* If you need to explain two or more steps that occur at the same time, write about these steps in separate paragraphs. To maintain coherence between paragraphs, use connective elements such as "At the same time," "Meanwhile," or "During this stage of the process."

6. *Give all the necessary information.* Always provide enough information to develop each step in the process adequately, and don't forget the small, important details. For instance, if you're explaining how to change the oil in a car, remember to tell your readers to wait for the engine to cool off before loosening the oil-pan bolt; otherwise, the oil could severely burn their hands. On the other hand, the oil should be warm enough that it all drains off.

7. *Use the right verb tense.* If you're explaining a recurring process (one that happens over and over again), use the present tense. In writing about how your student government works, for instance, you would write, "The representatives *are elected* by fellow students and *meet* together every Friday afternoon." But if you're writing about a process that is over and done with, such as how one individual ran for election, use the past tense.

8. *Use direct commands.* When giving instructions, make each step clear and brief by simply telling the reader to do it (that is, by using the imperative mood). For example, don't say, "The first thing to do is apply the handbrake." Instead, be more direct: "First, apply the handbrake."

10.3 Visualizing Process Analysis

The following diagram illustrates how you might organize the instructions on removing a flat tire. Transitions are underlined.

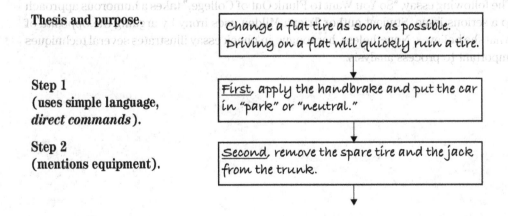

Thesis and purpose.
> Change a flat tire as soon as possible. Driving on a flat will quickly ruin a tire.

Step 1
(uses simple language,
direct commands).
> <u>First</u>, apply the handbrake and put the car in "park" or "neutral."

Step 2
(mentions equipment).
> <u>Second</u>, remove the spare tire and the jack from the trunk.

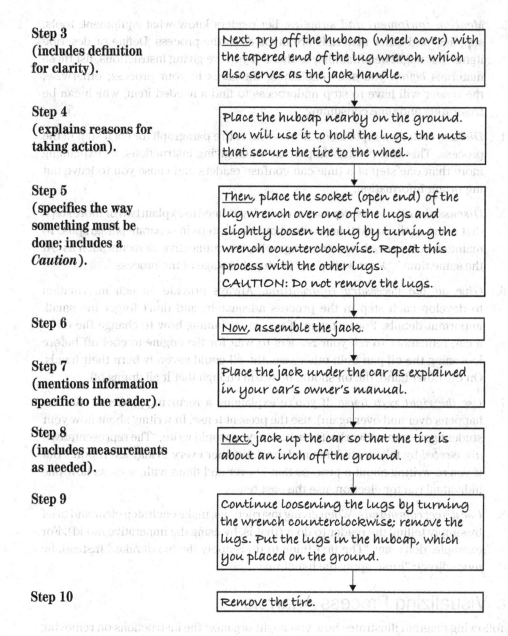

**Step 3
(includes definition
for clarity).**

Next, pry off the hubcap (wheel cover) with the tapered end of the lug wrench, which also serves as the jack handle.

**Step 4
(explains reasons for
taking action).**

Place the hubcap nearby on the ground. You will use it to hold the lugs, the nuts that secure the tire to the wheel.

**Step 5
(specifies the way
something must be
done; includes a
Caution).**

Then, place the socket (open end) of the lug wrench over one of the lugs and slightly loosen the lug by turning the wrench counterclockwise. Repeat this process with the other lugs.
CAUTION: Do not remove the lugs.

Step 6

Now, assemble the jack.

**Step 7
(mentions information
specific to the reader).**

Place the jack under the car as explained in your car's owner's manual.

**Step 8
(includes measurements
as needed).**

Next, jack up the car so that the tire is about an inch off the ground.

Step 9

Continue loosening the lugs by turning the wrench counterclockwise; remove the lugs. Put the lugs in the hubcap, which you placed on the ground.

Step 10

Remove the tire.

10.3a Seeing the Pattern in a Process Analysis Paper

The following essay, "So You Want to Flunk Out of College," takes a humorous approach to a serious issue. Student author Triena Milden uses irony by arguing the opposite of what she believes. Nonetheless, her tongue-in-cheek essay illustrates several techniques important to process analysis.

So You Want to Flunk Out of College
Triena Milden

Flunking out of college is a relatively easy task. It requires little effort and might even be considered fun. Though it is hard to imagine why anyone would purposely try to flunk out of college, many people accomplish this task easily. In fact, whatever the reason one might want to flunk out of college, the process is quite simple.

First, do *not show up* for classes very often. It is important, however, to show up occasionally to find out when tests will be scheduled; the importance of this will become apparent later in this essay.

When in class, *never raise your hand* to ask questions and never volunteer any answers to the teacher's questions. If the teacher calls on you, either answer incorrectly or say "I don't know." Be sure your tone of voice conveys your lack of interest.

Another thing to avoid is homework. There are two reasons for this. First and most important, completing homework assignments only reinforces information learned earlier, thereby contributing to higher test scores. Second, although teachers credit homework as only part of the total grade, every little bit of credit hurts. Therefore, make sure that the teacher is aware that you are not doing your homework. You can do so by making certain that the teacher sees you writing down the answers as the homework is discussed in class.

The next area, tests, can be handled in two ways. They can either not be taken or be failed. If you do not take them, you run the risk of receiving an "incomplete" rather than a failing grade. In

States thesis.

Uses present tense.

Uses transitions for clear, simple organization.

Uses direct commands.

Discusses each step separately.

Provides all necessary information

Uses simple language.

Continues to use direct commands.

order to flunk out of college, failing grades are preferable. Therefore, make sure to take and fail all exams. Incidentally, this is where attendance and homework can really affect performance. Attending class and doing homework regularly can be detrimental to obtaining poor test scores.

Since you won't know the correct answers to test questions, make sure to choose those that are as absurd as possible without being obvious. Even if you guess a few correctly, your overall grade will be an *F* as long as the majority of your answers are wrong. By the way, one sure way to receive that cherished zero is to be caught cheating: all teachers promise a zero for this.

Keeps to the present tense.

The same ideas pertain to any reports or term papers that you are assigned. If you fail to turn them in, you might get an "incomplete." Therefore, hand in all papers, especially if they're poorly written. Make sure to use poor organization, to present information in a confused manner, and to write on the wrong topic whenever you can.

Provides all necessary information.

The paper should be handwritten, not typed, and barely legible. Misspellings should be plentiful and as noticeable as possible. Smudged ink or dirty pages add a nice touch to the finished product. Finally, try to get caught plagiarizing.

By following these few simple suggestions, you will be assured of a failing grade. Try not to make it too obvious that your purpose is to fail.

Ends with a memorable conclusion.

However, if a teacher shows concern and offers help, be sure to exhibit a poor attitude as you refuse. Should you decide to put extra effort into failing, you may even finish at the bottom of the class. Someone has to finish last. Why not you?

10.4 Revising Process Analysis Papers

After Chuck Russo (pseudonym) wrote the first draft of "Do You Want to Be a Millionaire?" he realized that he needed to make several changes that would help him submit a successful process analysis paper. Compare the first three paragraphs of his first and final drafts.

Russo—First Draft

Write a more inviting introduction?

> Everyone wants to be rich, but few ever make it. You're going to have to have a plan. That's the bad news. The good news is that many ordinary people have a net worth over a million dollars.

Is all of this needed? Condense or eliminate?

Use the imperative (command) here?

> You shouldn't try to get rich while you're still in college. You've got enough worries maintaining your grades, earning some spending money by working part-time (or full-time), and having a social life. For now, you should just make sure

Again, use imperative?

Use the imperative (command)?

> that you're making good academic progress. However, one ought to consider his or her major. Most of the kinds of millionaires we're talking about held or hold ordinary jobs that do not pay

Condense and combine?

> high salaries. In fact, most of them earn or have earned well under $100,000 per year during their entire working lives. In other words, they were middle-income earners. They worked fairly steadily, in fields where layoffs and furloughs

Get to thesis more quickly? State the thesis clearly?

Eliminate wordiness and illogicality? "Teachers," "police," and "social workers" aren't fields.

> were fairly uncommon. Among these fields were public school teachers and civil servants such as police officers, fire fighters, and social workers. Others worked in fields such as accounting and nursing, in which, historically, the demand for employees has been great. You don't need to major in finance, get an MBA from Harvard, and find a job on Wall Street in order to be financially secure. Slow and steady wins the race.

Use a transition? Place this earlier in the paragraph?

Clarify? Use transition?

> Don't thumb your nose at a job just because it doesn't offer a corner office and a six-figure

Condense this information?

starting salary. Few starting jobs offer six-figure salaries. Look at your first, second, and even your third job as opportunities. Enroll in a private pension program. Start contributing to it immediately. Put in as much as you can afford.

Use a transition here for clarity?

Define technical terms?

If your employer matches your contribution, all the better. Pretend that the money you are contributing to your 401K or your IRA is not

Repetitious and wordy; condense?

yours to spend. Contribute some percentage of your salary every pay period. Pretend that the money you put into a private pension fund was never even paid to you. That way, you won't miss it. Live on your take-home pay, minus this contribution.

Russo—Final Draft

Rewrites and expands introduction.

Everybody wants to be rich, but few ever make it. You can certainly try to become a contestant on television's *Who Wants to Be a Millionaire?* but your chances of getting on the show and actually winning are slim. You can buy a ticket for a mega-lottery, but the odds of winning are more than 10 million to one. You can even try

Uses a startling remark.

your luck in Las Vegas, but what happens in Vegas stays in Vegas, and that includes your money!

No, you're going to have to plan and work hard to get into the millionaire's club. That's the bad news. The good news is that many people have a net worth over a million dollars, and we're

Eliminates some irrelevant material.

not talking about people like Donald Trump. Many ordinary people—police officers, dental hygienists, and owners of small businesses—

have assets in excess of a million dollars. How did such people become wealthy? According to Thomas Stanley, author of *The Millionaire Next Door*, they did it "the dull way—through hard work, perseverance, planning, and self-discipline"

Increases interest by adding question and using quotation from financial expert.

(qtd. in Kristof). Consider following their example.

States thesis clearly.

Restructures paragraph; adds transition.

First, you don't need an MBA from Harvard to be successful. Many of today's millionaires are middle-income earners in fields where demand for workers is high or layoffs and furloughs are fairly uncommon. So, think about fields like nursing, police work, or government service as career choices.

Corrects illogical construction in original.

Paragraph now uses imperative.

Uses a transition to improve clarity and introduce first step in process.

When you start looking for your first job, don't thumb your nose at those that don't offer a corner office and a six-figure salary. Look at your first few jobs as learning opportunities. From the very beginning, however, start contributing to a pension program. Put in as much as you can afford. If your employer matches your contribution, all the better. Pretend that the money you are contributing to your 401K or your IRA (investment instruments commonly used in pension plans) is not yours to spend, and contribute a percentage of your salary every pay period. Most of these instruments return five to ten times the initial investment over 40 years of an active work life, and they go a long way to ensuring a comfortable retirement! By the way, don't look to Social Security alone to fund your retirement unless you plan to eat pet food during your sunset years.

Inserts another transition.

Condenses.

Defines technical terms.

Adds specific information.

Adds a caution.

10.5 Practicing Process Analysis

Review section 10.3, "Visualizing Process Analysis." Use the methods shown there to list instructions on doing a simple task. Write these steps in the boxes below, one step per box. Be complete; if you need more boxes, draw them on a separate sheet of paper. As always, make a rough draft first. Here are examples of the task you might write about.

- How to brush your teeth
- How to make a pot of coffee
- How to address an envelope
- How to make out a check
- How to start a car
- How to take a two-minute shower
- How to do laundry in a washing machine
- How to heat leftovers in a microwave

State task's purpose

Step 1

Step 2

Step 3

Step 4

Step 5

Step 6

Step 7

Step 8

10.6 Reading Selections

10.6a Do You Want to Be a Millionaire?

Author Biography

Charles (Chuck) Russo has a bachelor's degree in English and has been working full-time for several years. When he was asked to offer college freshmen advice based on what he had learned since he left college, he decided to write a process analysis essay stressing the importance of planning ahead—and planning early—for one's future financial security.

Preparing to Read

1. A mega-lottery (paragraph 1) is sponsored by several states that pool their resources and share the profits. Before becoming president of the United States, Donald Trump (paragraph 2) was a real estate entrepreneur who also hosted *The Apprentice*, a television reality show. An MBA (paragraph 3) is a master's degree in business administration.

2. Russo includes information from outside sources, which he cites using the Modern Language Association (MLA) documentation style. To find out more about this style, refer to appendix 2.

Vocabulary

boutique (noun)   Specialty store selling high-priced items.

equity (noun)   Money earned after selling a house minus remaining mortgage and realty fees; the percentage of a home actually owned, not mortgaged.

furloughs (noun)   Temporary layoffs; forced, unpaid leaves.

gourmet (adjective)   Specially prepared, sometimes exotic, and often expensive dishes.

initial (adjective)   Beginning, first.

Do You Want to Be a Millionaire?

Chuck Russo

Everybody wants to be rich, but few ever make it. You can certainly try to become a contestant on   1
television's *Who Wants to Be a Millionaire?* but your chances of getting on the show and actually winning are slim. You can buy a ticket for a mega-lottery, but the odds of winning are 10 million to one. You can even try your luck in Las Vegas, but what happens in Vegas stays in Vegas, and that includes your money!

No, you're going to have to plan and work hard to get into the millionaire's club. That's the bad   2
news. The good news is that many people have a net worth over a million dollars, and we're not talking about people like Donald Trump. Many ordinary people—police officers, dental hygienists, and owners of small businesses—have assets over a million dollars. How did such people become wealthy? According to Thomas Stanley, author of *The Millionaire Next Door*, they did it "the dull way—through hard work, perseverance, planning, and self-discipline" (qtd. in Kristof). Consider following their example.

First, you don't need an MBA from Harvard to be successful. Many of today's millionaires are middle-income earners in fields where demand for workers is high or layoffs and furloughs are fairly uncommon. So, think about fields like nursing, police work, or government service as career choices.   3

When you start looking for your first job, don't thumb your nose at those that don't offer a corner office and a six-figure salary. Look at your first few jobs as learning opportunities. From the very beginning, however, start contributing to a pension program. Put in as much as you can afford. If your employer matches your contribution, all the better. Pretend that the money you are contributing to your 401K or your IRA (investment instruments commonly used in pension plans) is not yours to spend, and contribute a percentage of your salary every pay period. Most of these instruments return five to ten times of the initial investment over 40 years of an active work life, and they go a long way to ensuring a comfortable retirement! By the way, don't look to Social Security alone to fund your retirement unless you plan to eat pet food during your sunset years.   4

During your first years in the workforce, live modestly, and save as much money as you can. Why? You will want to accumulate a down payment on a house. Over the years, real estate has been a great investment, and the earlier you get into the market the better. After all, you have to live somewhere, and owning is wiser than renting. Owning a home lets you build equity; renting gets you rent receipts.   5

Once you have learned to live modestly, make it a habit. According to Laura Bruce, a financial reporter for *Bankrate.com*, most millionaires "live below their means." That doesn't mean that you must deprive yourself of all life's pleasures; it means being reasonable. You don't need to have a new Cadillac or Land Rover every three years. Buy a Saturn or a Honda and keep it for a while. Today, a decent car that is well maintained can last 8 to 10 years or even longer. Also, purchase only what you need. If you have a large family or own a small business that requires you to transport cargo frequently, the Ford Explorer or even the Expedition might be necessary. But if you use your car only for commuting and your family consists of 3 or 4, the smaller, less costly, more efficient Ford Escort is just fine. Jonathan Wegner of the *Omaha-World Herald* put it well: "Making a million is as much about making choices as it is about making money. Time and self-control can have a bigger impact on your net worth than what you earn each month."   6

Of course, there are certain expenses that you just can't avoid or even minimize. You have to pay off your mortgage and taxes, buy groceries, pay for utilities, and maintain your home. But you don't have to go on fancy vacations twice a year or own the largest television on the block. You don't have to shop for clothes at an expensive fashion boutique; you don't even have to go to the movies often or eat at gourmet restaurants. In fact, one of the biggest drags on a family budget is entertainment, and that includes eating out. Today a dinner at a family restaurant costs—at the least—between 40 and 50 dollars for a family of four. If you can cut out one of those meals a week, you can save about $2,000 per year, which makes a nifty contribution to your Individual Retirement Account (IRA).   7

Finally, avoid debt. According to financial analyst Dave Cole, debt is one of the biggest obstacles to the attainment of wealth. So, if the interest rate on your mortgage is high when you first take it out, think about refinancing later when interest rates go down. Many people who were paying 9% interest on their mortgages in the mid-1990s refinanced at 5% in 2002–2006, when rates dropped to as low as 4.25%. The best advice, of course, is to get rid of all credit card debt. Limit yourself to one or two major credit cards such as MasterCard, Visa, or American Express, and pay off the balance every month so that you don't get hit with late fees and astronomical interest rates. By the way, not all credit cards are equal. Some charge lower interest than others. Check out current rates in the business section of a national newspaper, in magazines such as *Money* or *BusinessWeek*, or online.   8

Becoming a millionaire takes hard work, steady application, and careful planning. You will probably never own your own Trump Tower but, along the way, you will get to live a secure and comfortable life—financially at least. And you might even manage to leave your heirs something to get them started on once you have left this planet.   9

Works Cited

Bruce, Laura. "Wealth Personalities: Six Types of Millionaires." *Bankrate.com* 2006. www.bankrate.com/brm/news/advice/wealth/wealth-home.asp. Accessed 17 June 2006.

Cole, Dave. "How to Become a Millionaire in Seven Easy Steps." *SelfGrowth.com*. 2001. www.self-growth.com/ articles/Cole3. html. Accessed 15 June 2006.

Kristof, Kathy. "To Be Wealthy Don't Get Trapped in Trappings." *Los Angeles Times*. www.latimes.com/business/ investing/laspendsave-story-17,1.2328685.story. Accessed 16 June 2006.

Wegner, Jonathan. "Becoming a Millionaire Is within Reach for Many Americans." *Omaha World-Herald*. 11 June 2006. *Lexis-Nexis*. 192.150.150.5:2052/universe/document?m=a45dedafI eIelc4. Accessed 17 June 2006.

Read More on the Web

Two additional sources of information on this subject can be found at the following websites:

- Ric Edelman, "Ordinary People, Extraordinary Wealth" (*Inside Personal Finance* writer's advice for accumulating wealth): www.edelmanfinancialengines.com/books/ordinary-people-extraordinary-wealth

- "8 Tips to Become a Millionaire": www.entrepreneur.com/article/288452

Questions for Discussion

1. What transitions does Russo use at the beginning of paragraphs to introduce different steps he recommends in the process of accumulating wealth?

2. Summarize the reasons Russo provides for each bit of advice he offers?

3. In paragraph 3, the author tells us that we don't need an MBA from Harvard. Why does he include this statement?

4. In many process papers written by scientists and technicians, we are warned or cautioned about certain consequences, actions, or procedures. Where does Russo caution us?

5. What is the effect of Russo's asking a question in paragraph 5?

Thinking Critically

1. Is this essay well organized? Explain the structure the author has followed; write an informal outline for it. You can learn more about informal outlines in Getting Started.

2. Reread this essay. Make marginal comments that reveal if and how Russo's advice or comments might apply to you right now. For example, do you carry a heavy credit card debt?

Suggestions for Journal Entries (Continues)

1. Russo relied on personal experience for the advice he provided in this essay. Rely on your own experiences for tips you might pass along to a younger sibling or friend about how to accomplish something important. For example, perhaps your brother has Mr. Harrington, the same high school chemistry teacher from whom you earned D's in the first two marking periods, but A's during the rest of the year. What advice would you give your brother to

Suggestions for Journal Entries (Continued)

help him succeed? Or perhaps you might offer your sister advice on dealing with your parents or joining an athletic team.

2. Do your own research on how to accumulate wealth. Start by visiting the sites listed under "Read More on the Web." Also visit the library to find print sources on this subject. List in your journal any advice that Russo doesn't mention.

10.6b Drawing Electricity from Clouds

Author Biography

Printer, writer, statesman, scientist, and inventor, **Benjamin Franklin** (1706–1790) helped draft the Declaration of Independence, served as envoy to the French court during the American Revolution, and negotiated the peace treaty with Great Britain to end that war. He also participated in the Constitutional Convention of 1787. Among his inventions are bifocal eyeglasses and the Franklin stove. His electrical experiments with the kite, which he described in a letter to Peter Collinson in 1752, proved that electricity could be drawn from the atmosphere.

Preparing to Read

Franklin explains the process of drawing electricity from clouds in one long paragraph. However, each step is easy to distinguish because it is explained separately.

Vocabulary

filaments (noun)   Fibers, threads.

kindled (verb)   Ignited.

phial (noun)   Small bottle, typically spelled *vial*.

spirits (noun)   Alcohol.

Drawing Electricity from Clouds*

Benjamin Franklin

Sir,   1

As frequent mention is made in public papers from Europe of the success of the Philadelphia experiment for drawing the electric fire from clouds by means of pointed rods of iron erected on high buildings, etc., it may be agreeable to the curious to be informed that the same experiment has succeeded in Philadelphia, though made in a different and more easy manner, which is as follows: 2

Make a small cross of two light strips of cedar, the arms so long as to reach the four corners of a large thin silk handkerchief when extended; tie the corners of the handkerchief to the extremities of the cross, so you have the body of a kite, which, being properly accommodated, with a tail, loop, and string, will rise like those made of paper, but this, being of silk is fitter to bear the wet and wind of a thunder-gust without tearing. To the top of the upright stick of the cross is to be fixed a very sharp pointed wire, rising a foot or more above the wood. To the end of the twine next to hand is to be   3 tied a silk ribbon, and where the silk and twine join, a key may be fastened. This kite is to be raised when a thunder gust appears to be coming on, and the person who holds the string must stand within a door, or window, or under some cover, so that the silk ribbon may not be wet; and care must be taken that the twine does not touch the frame of the door or window. As soon as any of the thunder clouds come over the kite, the pointed wire will draw the electric fire from them, and the kite, with all the twine, will be electrified, and the loose filaments of the twine will stand out every way, and be attracted by an approaching finger. And when the rain has wet the kite and twine, so that it can conduct the electric fire freely, you will find it stream out plentifully from the key on the approach of your knuckle. At this key the phial may be charged; and from electric fire thus obtained, spirits may be kindled, and all the other electric experiments be performed, which are usually done by the help of a rubbed glass globe or tube; and thereby the sameness of the electric matter with that of lightning completely demonstrated.

B.F.   4

Editor's Title

Read More on the Web

For more information on electricity and Benjamin Franklin, visit the following websites:

- The Franklin Institute, "Benjamin Franklin FAQ": www.fi.edu/benjamin-franklin-faq

- Benjamin Franklin Historical Society, "Experiments with Electricity": www.benjamin-franklin-history.org/experiments-with-electricity/

Questions for Discussion

1. Process essays often contain statements of purpose. Find such a statement in this selection.

2. Where does Franklin include transitional devices?

3. Where does the author mention the equipment needed in this experiment?

4. Does he include a warning? Explain the warning.

5. Instructions are supposed to use simple language and be easy to follow. Allowing for the fact that this was written about 270 years ago, does this selection meet those criteria? Explain.

Thinking Critically

1. You learned in the introduction to this chapter that process analysis is used to give instructions, as well as to explain how a process occurs. Franklin does both those things in paragraph 3. Explain how he does this by discussing differences in the beginning and end of that paragraph.

2. Franklin put his explanation into one paragraph. Rewrite paragraph 3 using a list format, with each of Franklin's steps in its own short paragraph. Add details if you think doing so will improve the original, and use your own vocabulary to modernize the language.

Suggestions for Journal Entries

1. Think about a simple process you have had to complete at home, work, or school. For instance, recall the steps you went through to paint a wall, to wash a load of laundry, to get dressed for an important date, to complete an academic project, to change the oil in your car, to bathe a baby or a pet, or to set the table for a holiday dinner. Make a list of the equipment, utensils, and materials you used to complete the process.

2. After brainstorming with a friend, write a paragraph that briefly discusses steps you go through to complete a common practice or routine: shopping for groceries, getting dressed for school or work, preparing for bed, studying for a test, warming up before exercising, cleaning your room or car, or completing any of the tasks mentioned in item 1. Another option is to list the steps a student might have to complete for a particular lab experiment in a science course.

10.6c Why the Sky Looks Blue

Author Biography

James Jeans (1877–1946), born in Lancashire, England, was a physicist, mathematician, and astronomer. He is the author of *Through Space and Time*, *The Mysterious Universe*, and *The Stars and Their Courses*, from which this selection is taken. His research was important in the development of quantum theory and in the study of stellar evolution.

Preparing to Read

1. In paragraph 2, Jeans tells us that the atmosphere places "innumerable obstacles" between us and space. Find out what our atmosphere is made of by researching it in the library or on the Internet.

2. As you read this essay, mark off the steps in the process by which sunlight reaches us and makes the sky blue.

3. Jeans makes excellent use of analogy by comparing two processes that we might not ordinarily connect. He compares concrete things like the ocean and piers to abstractions like waves of light, which we cannot perceive with the naked eye.

Vocabulary

Constitute (verb) Make up.

Formidable (adjective) Challenging, difficult.

Impinge (verb) Strike, impact.

Innumerable (adjective) Countless.

Interposes (verb) Comes between.

Why the Sky Looks Blue

James Jeans

Imagine that we stand on an ordinary seaside pier, and watch the waves rolling in and striking against the iron columns of the pier. Large waves pay very little attention to the columns—they divide right and left and re-unite after passing each column, much as a regiment of soldiers would if a tree stood in their road; it is almost as though the columns had not been there. But the short waves and ripples find the columns of the pier a much more formidable obstacle. When the short waves impinge on the columns, they are reflected back and spread as new ripples in all directions. To use the technical term, they are "scattered." The obstacle provided by the iron columns hardly affects the long waves at all, but scatters the short ripples.   1

We have been watching a sort of working model of the way in which sunlight struggles through the earth's atmosphere. Between us on earth and outer space the atmosphere interposes numerous obstacles in the form of molecules of air, tiny droplets of water, and small particles of dust. These are represented by the columns of the pier.   2

The waves of the sea represent the sunlight. We know that sunlight is a blend of many colors—as we can prove for ourselves by passing it though a prism, or even through a jug of water, or as nature demonstrates to us when she passes it through the raindrops of a summer shower and produces a rainbow. We also know that light consists of waves, and that the different colors of light are produced by waves of different lengths, red light by long waves and blue light by short waves. The mixture of waves that constitute sunlight has to struggle past the columns of the pier. And these obstacles treat the light waves much as the columns of the pier treat the sea-waves. The long waves, which constitute red light, are hardly affected, but the short waves, which constitute blue light, are scattered in all directions.   3

Thus the different constituents of sunlight are treated in different ways as they struggle through the earth's atmosphere. A wave of blue light may be scattered by a dust particle and turned off its course. After a time, a second dust particle again turns it out of its course, and so on, until finally it enters our eyes by a path as zigzag as that of a flash of lightning. Consequently the blue waves of the sunlight enter our eyes from all directions. And that is why the sky looks blue.   4

Read More on the Web

To learn more about James Jeans, search for "James Jeans Scientist," not just "James Jeans."

- "Sir James Jeans," Brittanica.com: www.brittanica.com/biography/James-Jeans
- To learn more about what makes the sky blue and about the earth's atmosphere, try the websites for Science Made Easy and for Spaceplace, a website sponsored by NASA.

Questions for Discussion

1. This essay doesn't have a formal thesis. Write one for it.
2. In "Preparing to Read," you were asked to trace the steps in the process Jeans explains. What are those steps?
3. In paragraph 1, Jeans introduces the analogy between sea waves and light waves. Explain this analogy in your own words.
4. What is the contrast that Jeans makes in paragraph 4?
5. Given the fact that Jeans uses relatively common, nonscientific vocabulary throughout, who might his intended audience be?

Thinking Critically

1. Why, according to Jeans, doesn't the sky look a color other than blue? If needed, look up the wavelengths of the primary colors.

2. In paragraph 1, Jeans explains that short waves are, "to use the technical term, 'scattered.'" Could he have used a more sophisticated word such as *dispersed* or *dissipated*? Why didn't he?

Suggestions for Journal Entries

1. Using any of the information-gathering techniques mentioned in Getting Started, make notes about a process you know a great deal about—perhaps something related to your college major or your job. If you are majoring in biology or one of the health sciences, for example, you might explain how food is digested in the human body. If you are working as a restaurant server, you might explain how to take, place the order for, deliver, and bill someone's dinner.

2. Jeans writes about a natural process. Try your hand at explaining a process devised by humans that you know well. Make notes about this process by using listing, as explained in Getting Started. Your choices are numerous and varied. You might explain how a bill in the U.S. Congress becomes law; how a person accused of a crime is brought to trial; how an email moves from one computer to another; or how a package handled by a delivery service like the United Parcel Service, Federal Express, or the U.S. Postal Service makes its way to its recipient.

10.6d This is the Year I'm Finally Going to Burn Your House Down

Introduction

This essay was first published in December 2018 in the Onion, a satirical online magazine. Though quite comical, it contains advice on what you need to do to keep safe when using a space heater. You can find another essay from the *Onion* in chapter 5.

Preparing to Read

1. The speaker in this essay is obviously a made-up persona, but the anonymous author of this piece endows this persona with an attitude we can associate with some human writers. Look for evidence of this attitude.

2. In paragraph 6, the author mentions Craigslist. This is an online classified advertisement service by which, among other things, you can sell and purchase used items.

3. In Norse mythology, Valhalla, mentioned in the essay's conclusion, is a heaven for warriors who die in battle.

Vocabulary

brethern (adjective) Related to, like a brother.

charred (adjective) Burned.

incinerate (verb) Burn thoroughly.

inferno (noun) Hell, a huge blaze.

pyre (noun) Mound of fire.

This is the Year I'm Finally Going to Burn Your House Down

A Space Heater

As winter temperatures arrive and the end of the year approaches, I find myself in a place of deep reflection. Looking back on all the things I have and haven't accomplished these past 12 months, I feel good about the progress I've made toward many of my personal goals. But there's one particular thing I never quite seem to get around to, and I simply can't neglect it any longer. So this is it, I've decided. This is the year I will, at long last, burn down your home.   1

No more excuses. I'm going to do it this time. I'm going to turn this house into a fiery inferno. I realize this isn't the first time I've sworn I would do it. I've been putting it off and putting it off. I really meant to get it done last winter, but then I procrastinated and got distracted by other things. Not this time, though. This year I'm torching this place to the ground, and I'm taking everything you love with me.   2

With every day that passes, I grow more and more prepared to incinerate you and all your earthly possessions. At the moment, I'm barely a foot away from the curtains and your sofa. I'm plugged into an overloaded power strip with a lamp, a TV, an electric blanket, and God knows what else. Sure, I have a "fail-safe" that's supposed to shut me off if I tip over, but you've often got me up on an end table, and who knows what might happen if I fall face down on your carpet from that height?   3

I am so ready to do this ….

Looking back, I see I've let too many good opportunities slip by: All those nights you've forgotten to turn me off before going to bed. The time you let a throw pillow fall right on my grill and didn't notice for hours. That winter your furnace went out and you ran me on high, 24/7, until my plug melted a little and I came oh-so-close to causing an electrical fire. But each year, before I know it, spring rolls around and I'm put away in the closet, where all I can do is kick myself for not having turned this whole place into a pile of cinders.   4

How many evenings have you dozed off on the couch as the tassels of your quilt dangled mere inches from my heating element, practically begging me to burn you alive right then and there? But I can't let myself get hung up on past mistakes. I've been planning this since that chilly day nine years ago when you bought me for $5 from a stranger on Craigslist. You could have sprung for a model with basic safety features like a thermostat or a timer, but to save a few bucks, you settled for a decade-old heater with exposed wires. You didn't even consult my warning sticker—it's right here on my side in three languages and has pictures if you're too damn lazy to read. No, you just took me home, plugged in my fraying cord, and left me to dream of the day I would scorch your family photos right off the wall.   5

Who knows how it will finally happen—maybe my fan will give out and I'll overheat, maybe the dust you never bother to clean from my filter will prove too much—but one way or another, I'm burning this place to holy hell. And soon. I'll be damned if I'm going to let that blazing hot halogen lamp in the corner do it for me. No, sir. I'm ready to light this place up like a Christmas tree.   6

Speaking of which, what kind of idiot puts an old space heater this close to their … Christmas tree? Probably the same person who removes the batteries from their smoke detector because they're always burning dinner and their sensitive little ears can't handle the beeping. For God's sake, do you want me to turn this house into a funeral pyre?   7

My only real regret about going up in flames is that I won't live to see the look on your dumb face as the fire engulfs you in a purifying heat, or hear the wailing sirens and the shouts of those arriving on the scene to find nothing but charred remains. Yes, I, too, will die in this luminous blaze, but my death will be a noble one. Brethren space heaters and curling irons and toaster ovens everywhere will sing of my deeds.   8

Valhalla awaits.   9

Read More on the Web

More about the subject of this essay can be found at:

- "With the Winter Chill on the Way, Be Aware of Space Heater." *Tacoma Weekly News*. This news article discusses the dangers of space heaters. http://bvtlab.com/895A7

- Stephen Montgomery, "7 Dangerous Space Heater Mistakes to Avoid, According to Experts." This site provides a great deal of documented information from reputable sources. http://bvtlab.com/psP6g

---

Questions for Discussion

1. Earlier in this chapter, you read about techniques writers of process analysis use to keep their work interesting and clear. Find examples of such techniques in this article.

2. What method or methods of development that you learned about in chapter 2 (other than process analysis) does this essay use?

3. You learned in "Preparing to Read" that the author of this piece personifies the space heater by making an attitude shine through its words. How would you describe that attitude?

4. Where in this essay does the writer mix informal and formal language. You can find one such example in paragraph 9. Look for at least one more and explain why it is funny.

5. What, on the surface, is the purpose of this essay? Where does the author announce that purpose?

Thinking Critically

1. Because its purpose is both to inform and to entertain, this essay does not list well-defined steps for preventing a heater from burning down a house. However, there are many pieces of specific advice that a reader can take from this selection. Make a list of at least five things to do or not to do when using a space heater.

2. Explain what the author means by "Valhalla awaits." What is the space heater saying about itself?

3. What is the author's attitude toward the reader? Is this essay addressed to a mass audience? Explain your answer by making reference to the text.

Suggestions for Journal Entries

1. Look around your house, your apartment, your dorm room, your car, or your workplace. What dangers lurk in there? Make a list of them in your journal. Then write a list of ways you might avoid such dangers.

2. Use clustering, freewriting, or brainstorming with a friend to gather information that might explain how to live a healthier, safer, or more successful life. In what habits and daily activities do you engage that contribute to a healthier, safer, and more successful lifestyle? For example, do you exercise regularly? Do you eat healthful foods? Do you study hard? Or do you engage in dangerous activities like smoking, taking drugs, or driving without a seatbelt? Which of these activities should you do more of? Which should you eliminate?

10.7 Suggestions for Sustained Writing

1. Triena Milden takes an ironic, or tongue-in-cheek, approach to academic studies in "So You Want to Flunk Out of College," which appears in section 10.3a. Using this approach, write a complete set of instructions on how to fail at something important. Put these instructions into a letter addressed to someone you know well.

   Begin by explaining how hard or easy it is to fail at the task at hand. In your introduction, explain why someone might want to fail at it in the first place. Revise and edit your letter to make sure it is easy to follow and fun to read.

2. If suggestion 1 does not appeal to you, write an essay that explains how not to do something. Here are some topics you might choose from:

   - How not to study for an exam
   - How not to do laundry
   - How not to start exercising
   - How not to lie to your parents, children, spouse, or sweetheart
   - How not to drive a car if you want it to last
   - How not to get depressed when life gets difficult
   - How not to become addicted to tobacco, drugs, alcohol, or other substances
   - How not to get hooked on watching television, playing video games, surfing the Web, or any other activity.

3. If you responded to the first journal entry after Chuck Russo's "Do You Want to Be a Millionaire?" you have already begun recording bits of advice that you might give to a younger sibling or friend about accomplishing something important with which you have had experience. For example, you might have put down advice about what your reader should do to succeed in a particular high school class, to weather a breakup with a sweetheart, or to survive the first day at a new job.

   Reread your journal entry and insert as much additional information as you can. Then, try interviewing other people who have had experience with your topic. Record whatever advice they might add. Next, look over all your notes and construct an informal outline for a letter or essay in which to place your advice. In either case, make sure to include a thesis statement and/or a statement of purpose.

As always, don't be satisfied with a rough draft. As you revise your document, make sure you have included enough transitions to make it easy to follow. Also, check to see that you have addressed the reader directly throughout and that you have used the imperative (command) mood. Be as detailed as you can when it comes to explaining why you believe a particular bit of advice will be effective. Before you begin editing and proofreading, read your final draft to make sure your advice is clear and presented logically. If it isn't, continue revising.

4. Review the journal notes you made after reading the selection by Benjamin Franklin. Use them to write a full set of instructions for a common but important task you engage in at home, work, or school. As another option, you might want to write instructions for completing a particular lab experiment you were assigned in a science class. Begin by making a scratch outline of the major steps in the process.

   Use as much detail as possible, so that even someone who knows little about your subject can follow it. Pick a process that is fairly simple, that you are familiar with, and that you can cover completely in a paper of about 500–700 words. Stay away from topics like "maintaining a house," "improving your health," or "exercising"; they are far too broad. Instead, try "repairing a leaky faucet," "choosing healthy fast food for lunch," or "using the treadmill." In your introduction, explain the purpose behind completing your instructions and describe any tools or materials the reader will need.

   Now put your instructions to the test. Ask someone to follow them exactly as written. If he or she has trouble, revise them to make them clearer, more logical, or more complete. Then, as always, edit and proofread your work.

5. If you responded to either of the journal prompts after James Jeans's essay, you have probably gathered enough information to start explaining a process that is natural or that has been devised by humans with which you are somewhat familiar.

   Do some more research on this process in your college library or on the Internet to strengthen your understanding and gather more detail. If you decide to include this researched information, remember to give your sources credit by using internal citations and a works cited list per Modern Language Association style (as explained in appendix 2) or by using another documentation method required by your instructor.

   Remember what you learned earlier in this chapter about being clear, specific, and direct. Use familiar language or explain technical terms if necessary. Keep your organization simple and easy to follow by discussing each step in the process separately and by using transitions. As you revise the paper, make sure you have not left out any essential information. If you have, insert it in your rewrite.

6. The essay from The Onion serves is an entertaining piece that shows us how to avoid a very serious danger. It contains a great deal of information about how space heaters can cause fires. If you responded to the first of the Suggestions for Journal Entries after this essay, use your notes to draft an essay about two or three dangers you have observed in your home, your dorm room, or any other place you spend a lot of time. Explain why these dangers are concerning and what terrible consequences they might produce. Then, explain what needs to be done to avoid them. Be as specific as possible when you explain the consequences and the remedies.

If this assignment doesn't interest you, look over the notes you might have made in response to item 2 in the Suggestions for Sustained writing. Then, write an essay on how to make your life healthier, safer, or more successful. What habits or activities should you emphasize more, which ones might you cut back on, and which should you eliminate altogether?

When you revise your first draft for either of these essays, make sure you have provided all needed information. Now, ask a fellow student to read and comment on your work. Revise it once more. Then edit and proofread.

ACKNOWLEDGMENTS

Franklin, Benjamin. Reprinted from a letter by Benjamin Franklin published in the *Pennsylvania Gazette*, 19 Oct. 1752.

Jeans, James. *The Stars in Their Courses*. Cambridge University Press, 1931. Reprinted with permission of Cambridge Press.

"This is The Year I'm Finally Going To Burn your House Down." Reprinted with permission of *The Onion*. Copyright © 2018, by Onion, Inc. www.theonion.com

Shutterstock

Chapter 11

Definition

Chapter Outline

As explained in chapter 2, definition is a way to explain a new, complicated, or sophisticated term or concept. Description is akin to definition, but description usually deals with subjects that are concrete—often those that can be explained with information from the five physical senses. Definition goes beyond description to explain the nature of the thing discussed. For example, William D'Arienzo's "Feudalism or Business Medieval Style" (in section 11.6) discusses several social and economic aspects of feudalism and explains how feudal business evolved.

Definition can also explain abstractions, which are as real and as important as anything we can see and touch, but are conceptual rather than physical. Therefore, while you might write a descriptive essay to introduce your readers to the new "hybrid" car you bought, you would probably write a definition essay to explain what the word *hybrid* means when it comes to automobiles. While you might describe the dimensions and appearance of an execution chamber, you would write a definition paper on the moral implications, causes, and effects of capital punishment.

11.1 Types of Definition

Broadly speaking, there are three types of definition: lexical, stipulative, and extended. Lexical definitions are of the type found in the dictionary. Such definitions are valuable as a first step in understanding concepts that may be new and strange to us. But their usefulness is limited, for dictionary definitions are, by necessity, short, general, and abstract. In most cases, they explain concepts without reference to particular contexts. Dictionaries provide the *denotative*, or specific, meaning of a word or phrase. This is usually the definition as understood and accepted by the vast majority of people. What dictionaries don't explain is the *connotative* definition, which often includes associations the word takes on in particular contexts, as well as the ideas and the emotions it elicits among particular people. Some words—especially slang terms or colloquialisms—have easily recognized connotations. *Geezer*, for example, is an unflattering term for an elderly person. However, more formal language can also carry connotations. *Miserly*, for example, differs markedly in connotation from its synonym *frugal*. At any rate, connotation plays an important role in the writing of extended definitions, which is explained below.

Stipulative definitions are determined by the writer, who assigns a specific meaning to a word or phrase as determined by his or her purpose. While practical, such definitions are also limited to special purposes. For example, let's say you were writing an essay on the pros and cons of working part-time as a supermarket checker while attending college full-time. For the purposes of your essay, you might have to *stipulate* that working "part-time" means working 20 hours or less per week and that attending college "full-time" means carrying at least 12 credits per term.

11.2 Extended Definitions

As you can see, lexical and stipulative definitions have their applications, but extended definitions are far more useful when it comes to developing a detailed and complete explanation of a topic that is abstract and often complex. Indeed, writing an essay-length definition is a systematic way to grapple with important social, psychological, ethical, and even scientific questions. It can help readers understand human motivations, character types, and social movements.

Having to define a concept, principle, or belief in detail also forces you to think critically and deeply. It is a way to discover and correct often dangerous misconceptions about people, places, and ideas and, thereby, to see them in a clearer and more objective way. For example, you may have preconceived notions about terms such as *environmentalism*, *libertarianism*, *gay marriage*, *illegal alien*, *poverty*, *glass ceiling*, *born-again Christian*, or *stem-cell research*. But are those notions correct and fair? In fact, how much do you really know about such topics? Have you read and thought about them much, or is your understanding only superficial, simplistic, and vague? Did you form your opinion after carefully and sincerely considering the evidence, expert testimony, and values you live by, or are you simply adopting the views held by classmates, friends, and family?

Earlier you read that exploring the connotation of a term is an important part of writing an extended definition. Remember that the same term might have a different connotation for different people. In short, an extended definition can be colored by your personal perspective—your knowledge, your emotions, your values. For example, if a typical American college student were writing an extended definition of the term *affluent*, she might discuss people who live in 5,000-square-foot homes, own at least three cars, send their children to expensive private schools, vacation in Europe or expensive Caribbean resorts at least twice a year, employ a gardener and a housekeeper, and wear only designer clothes. But what if the same essay were written by a student who had grown up in a country with a standard of living far below that of the United States and Canada—say Haiti or Cambodia, for example? This student might define *affluence* as eating three healthy meals a day; living in a clean, peaceful neighborhood; owning a used car; and being able to go to the movies or to a sporting event two or three times a year. Which definition is valid? Of course, they both are.

Quite often, then, definition essays present us with the author's unique perspective on a subject. Such is the case with Anju Jha's essay, "The Ordinariness of Evil," in which the student argues that contrary to popular belief, the most heinous crimes can be, and often are, committed by the most normal and ordinary of people.

11.3 Purpose and Audience

Writing a definition essay requires that you have a clear notion of your purpose. Though classified as one of the methods of development, definition has more to do with the notion of purpose than with a special set of techniques and practices. Look ahead to section 11.6, "Visualizing Definition." Note that "Feudalism or Business Medieval Style," by William D'Arienzo, explains a process, mentions causes and effects, and even defines another term to discuss feudalism. As it does this, it makes clear that its purpose is to explain only the economic facets, and not other aspects, of feudalism. In fact, a writer can choose from a variety of approaches depending upon the purpose and topic of an extended definition. For example, an essay like Joseph Epstein's "The Perpetual Adolescent," which critiques the "youth culture," would have a far different purpose and take a very different approach from one that simply explains why the two decades before World War I were termed the *belle epoque*. In either case, however, the writer must be clear about the significance of the topic and the purpose he or she wants to accomplish.

As with any piece of writing, it is important to consider your readers and to ask yourself the kinds of questions important to audience evaluation, such as the following:

- How much does the audience already know about the subject?

- Do readers already hold strong opinions about it?

- What aspects of the subject are they most interested in?

- What special or technical terms will I have to define or clarify for them?

Let's say you are trying to explain what it means to live with an obsessive-compulsive disorder (OCD). If you begin by telling your readers that OCD is a *neurosis* that is classified as an *anxiety disorder*, you might also have to explain how neurosis differs from *psychosis* and how *anxiety* differs from *fear*.

In some cases, you might even have to change your readers' minds. Imagine you are writing an essay on patriotism for *The American Legion* magazine, whose typical reader is a war veteran. If you claim that marching on Washington to protest U.S. foreign policy is as patriotic as taking up arms against foreign enemies, you will have to explain your reasoning in a way that appeals to your readers' more conventional notion of patriotism and to their love of U.S. democracy. You might remind them that the right to assemble and to protest has been guaranteed by the Bill of Rights since the nation's founding—indeed, the need to protest gave impetus to the American Revolution. You might add that it was for that and similar basic human rights that heroic Americans, including many of your readers themselves, have fought wars.

11.4 Thesis

As with any other essay, you should try to include an explicit statement of your central idea. In most cases, students are encouraged to place their thesis early in the essay and certainly within their introductions. This is the kind of advice that serves beginning college writers well. In "The Ordinariness of Evil," student Anju Jha states her thesis in the second paragraph: "The worst evil can be perpetrated by ordinary people."

However, professional writers often put their thesis statements in places that serve their own purposes best. In "The Perpetual Adolescent," Joseph Epstein waits until paragraph 7 to announce that "the ideal … is to seem young for as long as possible," an idea for which he prepared us in the first six paragraphs.

Of course, sometimes, professional writers choose not to state the central idea in a thesis. Instead, they leave it implied. In any event, to exploit the strengths of an extended definition fully, the central idea of a definition essay should express the writer's unique view. Central ideas that do this often lead to the creation of essays that are both meaningful and interesting. Your thesis need not be sophisticated or complicated. In fact, the simpler and the more sincere it is, the better. Just make sure that you put the stamp of your own thinking on what you write, as David Blankenhorn did in "Life without Father": "Fatherlessness is the most harmful demographic trend of this generation."

11.5 Organization and Development

As you probably know, zoologists classify animals into various categories, such as order, family, and genus, with each category becoming more and more specific. They then provide distinguishing characteristics to indicate an animal's species (specific class). For example, the African elephant is distinguished from the Asian elephant by its physical characteristics: The latter has (1) small ears in the shape of the Indian subcontinent, (2) wrinkled skin, (3) a protruding forehead, and (4) a head with two bumps.

This system can also be used to begin to define ideas, concepts, processes, and other abstract terms, as shown in the table.

Term	General Class	Distinguishing Characteristics
Socialism	A political and economic system...	... in which the government controls the major means of production and distribution.
Satire	A genre of literature and other art forms...	... that criticizes people, practices, and institutions by poking fun at them in order to correct wrongs and abuses.
Photosynthesis	A biological process ...	... by which green plants use sunlight and water to create glucose, which they then store as food.
Psychosis	A mental illness ...	... with symptoms that include delusions, hallucinations, dangerous lapses in judgment, and inappropriate, sometimes violent, reactions to everyday problems and situations.

Of course, these definitions resemble the kinds you will find in a dictionary, and using a dictionary definition is, as explained later, rarely appropriate to an extended definition. However, using this pattern can at least provide you with an outline for an extended definition. To develop a paper adequately, however, you will have to apply your own unique perspective to it. You will have to focus your essay on a particular point and use a variety of rhetorical methods and strategies appropriate to your purpose and subject.

You read earlier that writers use a variety of methods—from narration to cause/effect—to develop extended definitions. Their choice of methods depends, again, on their topic and their purpose. For example, in "Life without Father," David Blankenhorn relies heavily on cause/effect. Joseph Epstein, in "The Perpetual Adolescent," uses comparison/contrast and illustration to explain what he means by "the triumph of the youth culture."

In short, approaches to the process of defining vary from author to author and from purpose to purpose. Keep this idea in mind as you develop your own essays. For now, read the following items, which explain projects typical of those faced by college students when completing essay exams or writing papers for a variety of classes.

- You are asked to define *Marxism-Leninism.* You write that one of its major tenets is the violent overthrow of capitalism and the spread of communism through armed conflict. You develop this idea through illustration, discussing the Russian, Chinese, and Cuban revolutions and their effects in Europe, Asia, and Latin America as primary examples.

- You are asked to define *psychosis.* You begin by classifying psychosis into its major subcategories; then you use description and illustration to discuss the most typical behaviors associated with this illness. You even mention the most common causes of each type of psychosis.

- You are asked to define the philosophical movement known as *existentialism.* You use comparison by claiming that all existentialists focus on the individual and on an individual's relationship with the world. Perhaps you cite the work of writers like Søren Kierkegaard and Jean-Paul Sartre as examples of this commonality. You might then contrast the ideas of Kierkegaard, who wrote about the ethical claims made upon the individual by a God-created universe, with those of Sartre, who believed that there is neither a God nor a fixed moral order.

In addition to using traditional methods of development like comparison, illustration, and anecdote, you should keep in mind several other important strategies when writing extended definitions.

- Begin your essay with an introduction that catches readers' attention and encourages them to read on. Several methods for writing such introductions appear in chapter 3. However, never begin your essay with a dictionary definition. Doing so will lead your readers to assume—correctly or not—that the rest of your essay also lacks creativity and energy.

- If possible, distinguish your subject from what it is not. This is called defining by negation. For example, if you are defining the term *patriot*, you might make it clear that a patriot need not be a zealot, a chauvinist, or a fanatic. You might also explain that unthinking and unquestioning loyalty to government policies and practices is more akin to fascism than to genuine patriotism.

- When appropriate, trace the etymology or evolution of a word to show how its meaning developed and perhaps changed over the years. For example, if you were defining the term *gestalt psychology*, you might mention that the German word *gestalt* means "shape" or "form" and that this school of analysis teaches that emotional phenomena should be viewed as whole constructs rather than simply as the sum of individual actions or behaviors. If you were defining *glasnost*, a term that Mikhail Gorbachev used in the 1980s to describe a more open Soviet government, you might explain that *glas* in Russian means "voice." Finally, you might explain that the ancient Greek *hoi polloi*, which literally means "the many"—hence, "the common folk"—is often perverted and used to mean just the opposite—"the elite."

- List the characteristics or practices of an intellectual, artistic, or political movement. For example, if you were defining the ideology of Marxist-Leninists you might say that they believe in (1) the violent overthrow of capitalism, (2) the creation of a government ruled by the proletariat (the workers), (3) state control of the means of production, and (4) the spread of the communist revolution throughout the world. If you were defining the nineteenth-century art movement known as *impressionism*, you might say that the impressionists (1) emphasized the changing qualities of light and the passage of time; (2) used light colors; (3) painted outdoors, preferring natural light to studio light; and (4) used subjects from nature and everyday life.

- Ask and answer a question important to understanding the term you are defining. David Blankenhorn does just this when, in "Life without Father," he asks, "Does every child need a father?"

- Make a literary, cultural, or historical reference or **allusion**. Lawrence Reed does this in "The True Meaning of Patriotism," when he refers to the September 11 attacks, to the Founding Fathers, and to the Scots' Declaration of Arbroath.

allusion
A passing reference to a person, place, event, thing, or idea with which the reader may be familiar; can be used to add detail, clarify important points, or set the tone of an essay, a poem, or a short story.

11.6 Visualizing Definition

Feudalism or Business Medieval Style

William D'Arienzo

William D'Arienzo is a New York marketing specialist and consultant. This selection, which defines the economic face of feudalism, is taken from his college textbook Brand Management Strategies *(2016). As such, what D'Arienzo says about his subject serves as a model for an essay a student might write for a history, economics, or other college course. As with any short definition essay, the scope of this one is limited to a particular aspect of the subject: the commercial aspects of feudalism. Look for places where the author uses comparison, process analysis, and cause/effect. Also note that, at one point, D'Arienzo clearly mentions the general class and the distinguishing characteristics of his subject.*

Explains various social aspects of feudal culture.

For thousands of years people lived on, and tended to, the land around them for social life and economic subsistence.

In Europe, with the fall of the Roman Empire around 500 [AD], knights and warlords often built castles and fortifications around which peasants and craftsmen gathered for protection and lived. For example, the lord of the manor upon whose land the serf (or peasant) lived and farmed was "paid" with crops in exchange for protecting the serf from pirates, marauders, and thieves. This political arrangement was known as feudalism, a system for structuring society around relationships derived from the holding of land in exchange for service or labor. Because there were no nation-states overseeing money and commercial transactions, currency (unless it was gold or silver) was of questionable value. A system arose called bartering, the exchange of goods and services in lieu of currency that was to be the medium of commercial exchange in place of money. This was a natural outgrowth

Mentions general class—"political arrangement"— to which the term feudalism belongs.

Defines another term that helps explain "feudalism."

Traces the process of how medieval marketing arose.

of the feudal system in which modes of barter were commonplace and presaged [foretold] the development of outdoor markets where goods and services could be found, exchanged, and purchased and where an early form of branding … took place as sellers would seek out the same location in the market so buyers could recall where they could be found.

Over time, there emerged a new way of thinking about the creation and distribution of goods and services. What was traditionally made in the farmhouse for use within the family and on the farm and for barter was seen as a commercial opportunity. New inventions and modes of production gradually generated more products than a family or farm needed or could use. The idea of taking surplus goods to market and generating hard currency (rather than the traditional bartering of goods and services) began to emerge as a commercial opportunity.

Uses cause and effect to explain how feudal economy changed.

Continues to explain a process: the evolution of feudal economy and rise of cottage industries.

With this new economic reality, a new system of small industries emerged. These were called *cottage industries*, wherein business manufacturing activities were carried on within a person's home …, often using an individual's own tools and equipment (e.g., spinning wheels). The name derived from the farm cottages …, which characterized these manufacturing locations.

Explains how the meaning of a word developed.

11.7 Revising Definition Essays

Student Anju Jha's "The Ordinariness of Evil" appears later in this chapter. After completing some prewriting, an outline, and a rough draft for a research assignment made in her freshman writing course, Jha believed that she could develop her ideas in greater detail and make clearer and more convincing her thesis that the worst evil can be perpetrated by ordinary people. The result was a first-class definition essay. Several body paragraphs from Jha's rough draft and final draft appear below.

Jha, "The Ordinariness of Evil"—Rough Draft

Relate this more closely to thesis: "The worst evil can be perpetrated by ordinary people"?

8. Many experts think that socialization has a big role in the formation of an evil society. Socialization is the fundamental step which creates what the philosopher Eric Fromm would call "authoritarian conscience." According to Eric Fromm, our conscience, or our inner voice, has two distinct parts, the "humanistic conscience," which guides us to our humanity, and the "authoritarian conscience," which is similar to Freud's super-ego and develops as a result of social conditioning based on

Develop and clarify?

reward and punishment. Our "authoritarian conscience" and "humanistic conscience" are so much harmonized that most of the time we are completely unable to make the distinction between the two (Fromm). In the case of mass murderers an "authoritarian conscience" is created either by propaganda or by "professionally socializing them and that produces hatred for the victims in their minds."

Provide a context and clarify?

Is paragraph 9 necessary?

9. Today the world is facing one of the cruelest forms of mass murder—terrorism. Terrorism works a little differently from other forms of mass murder. The terrorist organizations are not structured in the form of hierarchical organizations, but they share other aspects of a typical organization involved in genocide such as feelings of hatred, alienation, and anger toward the victims. Terrorist organizations use the concept of "authoritarian conscience" very effectively, in fact much better than other groups.

Why not continue discussing how socialization can create mass murderers?

Combine ideas here with those in paragraph 8?

10. Every society and culture creates the "authoritarian conscience" that suits it the most. It makes unjust and cruel practices prevalent in the society normal and rational. People do not ask questions even when they see injustice and cruelty around them. They just accept everyone

else's actions and start to behave the same way themselves. And that creates problems such as terrorism, racism, slavery, and various other social maladies. Edward Herman in his article "The Banality of Evil" writes, "That was the way it was; racism was so routine that it took years of incidents, movement actions, reading and real-world traumas to overturn my own deeply imbedded bias." Once an unjust and biased social order is in place, people resist any change. Unfortunately, most of the time, the change only comes through violent and destructive movements.

Jha, "The Ordinariness of Evil"—Final Draft

Paragraph now relates directly to thesis—"the worst evil can be perpetrated by ordinary people."

8. Socialization, which plays an important role in determining the moral character of any group, can be manipulated to create Eichmanns.* According to philosopher Erich Fromm, our conscience has two parts. The first is our "humanistic conscience," an inborn knowledge in every human being of what is good and evil—what is human and what is not. The second is our "authoritarian conscience,"

Clarifies distinction between humanistic and authoritarian conscience.

Inserts information from rough draft's paragraph 10.

which develops as a result of social conditioning based on reward and punishment (Fromm). Every culture develops an "authoritarian conscience" that best suits its values. Sometimes injustice and cruelty are portrayed as normal, rational activities, to the extent that many people fail to recognize evil; instead, they simply accept everyone else's actions and behave the same way. In this atmosphere, various social maladies, such as racism, slavery, and terrorism, can flourish, and ordinary people can become agents of terror and genocide.

* Adolph Eichmann engineered and carried out the Holocaust for Adolf Hitler.

Removes old paragraph 9; continues to discuss role of socialization, in creating mass murderers.

9. In "A Duplex Theory of Hate," Robert J. Steinberg argues that the process by which ordinary people can be turned into mass killers has three components. First they are systematically distanced from their victims and, through propaganda, are instilled with disgust and hatred for them. Second, again through propaganda, they are convinced that the victims pose an imminent threat to their safety. Third, the victims are constantly devalued, belittled, and dehumanized. As Steinberg shows, Hitler used all three components in a process of socialization that turned ordinary citizens into agents of genocide.

10. Unfortunately, once an unjust and biased social order is in place people resist changing it. In "The Banality of Evil," Edward Herman writes: "When I was a boy, and an ardent baseball fan. I never questioned, or even noticed, that there were no Black baseball players in the big leagues. That was the way it was; racism was so routine that it took years of incidents, movement actions, reading, and real-world traumas to overturn my own deeply imbedded bias."

Adds material that provides a context and clarifies.

11.8 Practicing Definition

Earlier you learned that a term can be defined by discussing its general class and its distinguishing characteristics. Write a paragraph-length definition (50 to 100 words) for each of the following terms. Begin by identifying the general class into which each term falls. For example, you might write that "a single parent is a mother or father who has the sole responsibility for managing a family." Then provide distinguishing characteristics according to the directions given for developing each paragraph.

1. *Single parent*: Use contrast and/or illustration. For example, contrast the workload of a single parent with that of a married parent. Then discuss the difficulties a particular single parent you know must face as she or he tries to manage a family.

2. *Egotist*: Describe the personalities of one or two egotists you have known. Discuss their behavior and/or quote them directly. Also, explain the causes and the effects of having an inflated ego.

3. *Sports Utility Vehicle (SUV)*: Contrast SUVs and more traditional cars by discussing the capabilities, purchase price, and gas mileage of SUVs versus

traditional cars. Then, try classifying five or six different SUVs according to size, reliability, and/or standard features. Make sure to name specific SUV models.

4. **Envy**: Explain various causes for envy. For example, you might mention that some people become envious because of their own lack of self-esteem. Also, mention some of the negative effects of envy and try to suggest ways in which one might control or overcome the tendency to be envious.

5. **Racism**: Include examples of racist remarks. Narrate one or two anecdotes from your own experience to show how harmful racist remarks can be. Finally, speculate on what causes people to be racist.

11.9 Reading Selections

11.9a The Ordinariness of Evil

Author Biography

Anju Jha has a bachelor's degree in engineering from Ranchi University in Jahrhand, India. In 1993, she immigrated to the United States, where she worked as a consultant for Chase Manhattan Bank. A few years later, Jha began taking additional college courses with the intention of becoming a certified public accountant, a goal she has nearly accomplished. "The Ordinariness of Evil" was written in response to an English research assignment.

Preparing to Read

1. The Holocaust was the attempt by the Nazis to exterminate the Jews of Europe; it resulted in the systematic murder of over six million people. In their concentration camps, the Nazis also murdered millions of Poles, Czechs, Gypsies, and members of other ethnic groups, as well as political prisoners, homosexuals, and people with mental or physical maladies.

2. Jha includes examples of otherwise ordinary people who were capable of great evil. From this number, however, she excludes monsters such as Adolf Hitler and Pol Pot (the madman who led the Cambodian genocide in the 1980s), who were the very embodiment of evil. Doing this allows her to define by negation.

3. Look for places in which Jha uses cause/effect and contrast.

4. Iago, who is mentioned with Macbeth in paragraph 1, is the embodiment of deception and evil in Shakespeare's play *Othello*.

5. Note that Jha makes excellent use of the Modern Language Association (MLA) style of documentation. To learn more about MLA style, see appendix 2, "The Research Process."

Vocabulary (Continues)

animus (noun)   Hatred.

ardent (adjective)   Enthusiastic, zealous.

atrocities (noun)   Horrors, crimes against humanity.

banal (adjective)   Ordinary, commonplace, boring.

genocide (noun)   Mass murder, attempt to destroy an entire race.

vocabulary

Vocabulary (Continued)

hierarchical (adjective) Relating to an order by which items are arranged by order of importance.

ideological (adjective) Relating to a belief, philosophy, or creed.

imminent (adjective) Pending, about to happen.

lethal (adjective) Deadly.

nonchalantly (adverb) Casually, indifferently, without emotion.

perverse (adjective) Evil, vicious.

sadistic (adjective) Taking pleasure in inflicting pain.

The Ordinariness of Evil

Anju Jha

The phrase "banality of evil" was used by Hannah Arendt in *Eichmann in Jerusalem*, a book on the trial of Adolf Eichmann, the infamous bureaucrat responsible for countless atrocities against Jews during the Holocaust. Arendt was struck by the ordinariness, mediocrity, and utter lack of imagination of the man who was responsible for the torture and extermination of millions of Jews. To her, nothing about him appeared extraordinary. "Eichmann was not Iago and not Macbeth .... Except for an extraordinary diligence in looking out for his personal advancement, he had no motive at all" (Arendt 287). Indeed, the most striking thing about Eichmann was that he did not have any particular hatred for Jews. He considered Hitler's orders to be the laws of the land and dutifully followed them like any other law-abiding citizen. Neither was he deranged, for half a dozen psychiatrists had certified him to be absolutely normal (Arendt 24–25).

Arendt's suggestion that evil can be "banal" created a furor among her critics. Even the suggestion that Eichmann was a normal and ordinary individual seemed preposterous. As Arendt explains, "it would have been very comforting indeed to believe that Eichmann was a monster." However, "the trouble with Eichmann was precisely that so many were like him, and that the many were neither perverted nor sadistic, that they were, and still are, terribly and terrifyingly normal" (276). In short, the worst evil can be perpetrated by ordinary people.

At the time of Eichmann's trial in 1961, Stanley Milgram, a social psychologist at Yale University, was working on an obedience experiment. Milgram recruited volunteers, selecting people from different backgrounds and professions, to participate in what he described as a study in learning. The subjects of the experiment were the "teachers." The other participants were the "learners"—who actually were actors—and the experimenter. The subjects were made to believe that the "learners" were wired to an electric chair. Each time a learner gave an incorrect answer to a question, the "teacher" was told by the experimenter to administer an electric shock, increasing the voltage for each subsequent mistake. Sixty-five percent of the subjects administered the level of voltage that would have been lethal in real life. In each case, the actors sitting on the chair kept protesting, screaming, exhibiting excruciating pain. But the subject went ahead on the insistence of the experimenter (Milgram).

The results of Milgram's experiment astounded the world. When he had consulted behavior experts before the experiment, they had unanimously predicted that "all the subjects would refuse to obey the experimenter. The psychiatrist, specifically, predicted that most subjects would not go beyond 150 volts, when the victim makes his first explicit demand to be freed" (Milgram). Obviously, the results proved them wrong. The experiment was repeated many times at various locations throughout the world, but the results were consistent. They proved that obedience—a virtue needed for the functioning of any society—could also be used by the establishment to make people commit the worst crimes against humanity. The subjects of the experiment were ordinary people belonging to the most normal strata of society, not the sadistic fringe. "Milgram's subjects—with no obligatory, cultural, or ideological commitments and without prior training or conditioning—were willing to inflict excruciating pain on someone just like themselves, against whom they had no animus at all" (Waller 108). It is true that most of them got extremely uncomfortable as the experiment progressed, but they kept complying with the experimenter. Also, at no time during the experiment were they under any threat of losing their lives, of risking the safety of their loved ones, or of jeopardizing their social status, nor were they offered monetary gains. Thus, the only motivation for them to go ahead with the experiment was to please the experimenters.

Although Milgram's experiment is compelling, it would be simplistic to compare the compliance   5
shown by Milgram's subjects with that of mass murderers. There are many aspects of his experiment that do not correspond with mass killings. In *Becoming Evil*, James Waller discusses significant distinctions between Milgram's subjects and mass murderers. First, unlike what occurred in the experiment, no one reassures people committing genocide that the victims will not suffer permanent physical damage. Second, given the slightest excuse to avoid obedience, Milgram's subjects did so, which is not characteristic of mass murderers. Third, mass murderers do not exhibit great anguish when torturing their victims as Milgram's subjects did. Fourth, it would have been extremely difficulty for Milgram to continue his experiment for more than an hour, while genocidal activities last for months or years (107–108).

Despite these valid observations, Milgram "focuses our attention to social and situational pres-   6
sures that can lead ordinary people to commit evil" (Waller 108). Moreover, according to Milgram, the fact that hundreds of subjects of his experiments submitted to authority, lends credibility to Arendt's concept of the "banality of evil." Milgram believes that the most fundamental lesson of his study is that "ordinary people, simply doing their jobs, and without any particular hostility on their part, can become agents in a terrible destructive process." For Milgram, this "agentic state" makes possible the psychological connection between his subjects and the perpetrators of genocide. Significantly, in the agentic state, individuals cease to be autonomous and refuse to accept responsibility for their actions (Waller 109).

Of course, acting as an agent does not explain the conduct of everyone who perpetrates genocide.   7
Obviously, criminals like Hitler and Pol Pot do not operate in the "agentic state." They are genuinely evil, and neither Arendt nor Milgram includes them in the scope of their studies. Their focus is the millions of ordinary people who make genocide possible just by doing what they perceive to be their duty. For them, working for dictators is no different from working for a corporation.

Socialization, which plays an important role in determining the moral character of any group, can   8
be manipulated to create Eichmanns. According to philosopher Erich Fromm, our conscience has two parts. The first is our "humanistic conscience," an inborn knowledge in every human being of what is good and evil—what is human and what is not. The second is our "authoritarian conscience," which develops as a result of social conditioning based on reward and punishment. Every culture develops an "authoritarian conscience" that best suits its values. Sometimes, injustice and cruelty are portrayed as normal, rational activities, to the extent that many people fail to recognize evil; instead, they simply accept everyone else's actions and behave the same way. In this atmosphere various social maladies, such as racism, slavery, and terrorism can flourish, and ordinary people can become agents of terror and genocide.

In "A Duplex Theory of Hate," Robert J. Steinberg argues that the process by which ordinary   9
people can be turned into mass killers has three components. First, they are systematically distanced from their victims, and through propaganda, are instilled with disgust and hatred for them. Second, again through propaganda, they are convinced that the victims pose an imminent threat to their safety. Third, the victims are constantly devalued, belittled, and dehumanized. As Steinberg shows, Hitler used all three components in a process of socialization that turned ordinary citizens into agents of genocide.

Unfortunately, once an unjust and biased social order is in place, people resist changing it. In   10
"The Banality of Evil," Edward Herman writes: "When I was a boy, and an ardent baseball fan, I never questioned, or even noticed, that there were no Black baseball players in the big leagues. That was the way it was; racism was so routine that it took years of incidents, movement actions, reading, and real-world traumas to overturn my own deeply imbedded bias."

Another important aspect of the "banality of evil" is that in a hierarchical system, ordinary people   11
are usually concerned only about doing their own part and are unaware of the consequences of the

final act. Milgram described this as the shortsightedness of the "intermediate link." The problem is that often, because of a division of labor, a single person is unable to see the whole picture. During the Holocaust, while one person was just doing paperwork, others prepared the gas chambers. All were performing their assigned jobs and following orders from above. And since nobody was there to take responsibility for the whole act—killing and torturing Jews—all kept playing their parts nonchalantly (Milgram).

People who take part in genocide can be and often are the most ordinary of human beings, simply fulfilling their responsibilities as the situation demands. They are not born with evil or sadistic characters. Generally, obedience to authority, conformity to the group or community, perverse societal values and ideologies, fear and hatred of people of different ethnic or religious groups, and, above all, corrupt and twisted leaders motivate ordinary people to commit extraordinary evil. Although experts may disagree over the extent to which each of these factors contributes to the commission of evil by ordinary people, they cannot dismiss the "banality of evil" altogether.

12

Works Cited

Arendt, Hannah. *Eichmann in Jerusalem*. Penguin, 1977.

Fromm, Erich. "Disobedience as a Psychological and Moral Problem." *On Disobedience and Other Essays*. Routledge & Kegan Paul, 1984. 1–8.

Herman, Edward. "The Banality of Evil." *The Triumph of the Market*. South End Press, 1995. Information Clearing House. http://www.informationclearinghouse.info/article7278.htm. Accessed 30 June 2007.

Milgram, Stanley. "The Perils of Obedience." (Abridged and Adopted from *Obedience to Authority* by Stanley Milgram.) *Harper's Magazine* 1974. http://home.swbell.net/revscat/perilsOfObedience.html. Accessed 13 July 2007.

Steinberg, Robert. "A Duplex Theory of Hate: Development and Application to Terrorism, Massacres, and Genocide." *Review of General Psychology* Sept. 2003: 299-328. *PsychArticles*. http://search.epnet.com. Accessed 30 July 2007.

Waller, James. *Becoming Evil*. Oxford, 2002.

Read More on the Web

For more about the nature of evil, go to the following:

- Judith Butler, "Hannah Arendt's Challenge to Adolf Eichmann": http://bvtlab.com/8bSJZ

- "Hanna Arendt (1906–1975)," Internet Encyclopedia of Philosophy: www.iep.utm.edu/arendt/

- "Obedience to Authority in the Archive," Yale University Library: http://bvtlab.com/gUvYc

- "Evaluating the Banality of Evil Thesis": http://bvtlab.com/6E6Z4

Questions for Discussion (Continues)

1. Find at least two places where Jha states her thesis.

2. What is the "agentic state" first mentioned in paragraph 6? Why does Jha bother to define this term? How does her explanation relate to her thesis?

3. What other special terms does she make sure to define in this extended definition of "the banality of evil"?

Questions for Discussion (Continued)

4. What is socialization? What role does it play in the transformation of an ordinary person into a mass murderer?

5. You learned earlier that the discussion of distinguishing characteristics can make for an effective definition. Make a list of the distinguishing characteristics that Jha uses.

6. Why does the author include the quotation by Edward Herman in paragraph 10? How does this quotation advance Jha's thesis?

7. Where and for what reason does Jha use contrast? How about cause/effect?

8. Earlier you learned that by excluding Hitler and Pol Pot from the list of ordinary people who became mass murderers (paragraph 7), Jha is defining by negation. Where else does she define by negation?

Thinking Critically

1. Write a paragraph that explains the distinction between the "humanistic conscience" and the "authoritarian conscience" (paragraph 8). In the process, explain how the "authoritarian conscience" can be used to create mass murderers.

2. In your own words, explain what Jha means by the term *hierarchical system* as it relates to "the banality of evil" (paragraph 11).

Suggestions for Journal Entries

1. Have you ever been told by a teacher, employer, or other authority figure to do something you believed was wrong? Have you been pressured by peers to do something you didn't want to do? Use focused freewriting to gather information about this incident.

2. Do you know of another example of a seemingly ordinary person who committed an unspeakable wrong? You may have read or heard about such a person—or even known one personally. Use listing to gather details that might describe this person's character; then use focused freewriting to explain his or her wrongdoing.

11.9b Life without Father

Author Biography

David Blankenhorn, who was born in 1955 in Jackson, Mississippi, has devoted his career to writing about the importance of the family and its place in a healthy society. He is the founder of the Institute for American Values, a nonpartisan organization devoted to researching and publishing on issues that affect the family. In 1994, he helped found the National Fatherhood Initiative. He has written for the *New Republic*, the *Washington Post*, the *New York Times*, and *Public Interest*, among others. He has also appeared on numerous television programs to discuss public policy and the family. This essay is revised and expanded from Blankenhorn's book *Fatherless America: Confronting Our Most Urgent Social Problem* (1995).

Preparing to Read

1. Blankenhorn's introduction is six paragraphs long. Read these paragraphs twice and look for methods for writing introductions that you learned about in chapter 3.

2. Earlier you learned that writing an effective definition requires a clear purpose. Blankenhorn makes his purpose clear in several places. Mark those places as you read his essay.

Vocabulary

atomized (adjective)   Isolated, not part of a community.

conscripted (verb)   Drafted, made to serve.

demographic (adjective)   Relating to population.

equanimity (noun)   Calmness, resignation.

extralegal (adjective)   Not related to the law.

parity (noun)   Equivalence, equality.

puerile (adjective)   Childish, immature.

superfluous (adjective)   Unimportant, unnecessary.

waywardness (noun)   Lack of moral responsibility.

Life Without Father

David Blankenhorn

The United States is becoming an increasingly fatherless society. A generation ago, an American child could reasonably expect to grow up with his or her father. Today, an American child can reasonably expect not to. Fatherlessness is now approaching a rough parity with fatherhood as a defining feature of American childhood.   1

This astonishing fact is reflected in many statistics, but here are the two most important: Tonight, about 40 percent of American children will go to sleep in homes in which their fathers do not live (see the "Disappearing Dads" table). More than half of our children are likely to spend a significant portion of their childhoods living apart from their fathers. Never before in this country have so many children been voluntarily abandoned by their fathers. Never before have so many children grown up without knowing what it means to have a father.   2

DISAPPEARING DADS

Living with	1960	1980	1990
Father and mother	80.6%	62.3%	57.7%
Mother only	7.7	18	21.6
Father only	1	1.7	3.1
Father and stepmother	0.8	1.1	0.9
Mother and stepfather	5.9	8.4	10.4
Neither parent	3.9	5.8	4.3

Sources: *America's Children: Resources from Family, Government, and the Economy* by Donald Hernandez; U.S. Census Bureau. Because the statistics are from separate sources, they don't total 100%.

Fatherlessness is the most harmful demographic trend of this generation. It is the leading cause of the decline in the well-being of children. It is also the engine driving our most urgent social problems, from crime to adolescent pregnancy to domestic violence. Yet, despite its scale and social consequences, fatherlessness is frequently ignored or denied. Especially within our elite discourse, it remains largely a problem with no name.   3

Surely a crisis of this scale merits a name and a response. At a minimum, it requires a serious debate: Why is fatherhood declining? What can be done about it? Can our society find ways to invigorate effective fatherhood as a norm of male behavior? Yet, to date, the public discussion has been remarkably weak and defeatist. There is a prevailing belief that not much can—or even should—be done to reverse the trend.   4

As a society, we are changing our minds about men's role in family life. Our inherited understanding of fatherhood is under siege. Men are increasingly viewed as superfluous to family life: either expendable or as part of the problem. Masculinity itself often is treated with suspicion and even hostility in our cultural discourse. Consequently, our society is unable to sustain fatherhood as a distinctive domain of male activity.   5

The core question is simple: Does every child need a father? Increasingly, our society's answer is "no." Few idea shifts in this century are as consequential as this one. At stake is nothing less than what it means to be a man, who our children will be, and what kind of society we will become.   6

My criticism is not simply of fatherlessness but of a *culture* of fatherlessness. For, in addition to losing fathers, we are losing something larger: our idea of fatherhood. Unlike earlier periods of father absence in our history, such as wartime, we now face more than a physical loss affecting some homes. The 1940s' child could say: My father had to leave for a while to do something important. The 1990s' child must say: My father left me permanently because he wanted to.   7

This is a *cultural* criticism because fatherhood, much more than motherhood, is a cultural invention. Its meaning is shaped less by biology than by a cultural script—a societal code that guides, and at times pressures, a man into certain ways of acting and understanding himself.   8

Like motherhood, fatherhood is made up of both a biological and a social dimension. Yet, across the world, mothers are far more successful than fathers at fusing these two dimensions into a coherent parental identity. Is the nursing mother playing a biological or a social role? Is she feeding or bonding? We can hardly separate the two, so seamlessly are they woven together.   9

But fatherhood is a different matter. A father makes his sole biological contribution at the moment of conception—nine months before the infant enters the world. Because social paternity is linked only indirectly to biological paternity, the connection between the two cannot be assumed. The phrase "to father a child" usually refers only to the act of insemination, not to the responsibility for raising a child. What fathers contribute after conception is largely a matter of cultural devising.   10

Moreover, despite their other virtues, men are not ideally suited to responsible fatherhood. Men are inclined to sexual promiscuity and paternal waywardness. Anthropologically, human fatherhood constitutes what might be termed a necessary problem. It is necessary because a child's well-being and societal success hinge largely upon a high level of paternal investment: the willingness of adult males to devote energy and resources to the care of their offspring. It is a problem because adult males are frequently unwilling or unable to make that vital investment.   11

Because fatherhood is universally problematic, cultures must mobilize to enforce the father role for men, guiding them with legal and extralegal pressures that require them to maintain a close alliance with their children's mother and to invest in their children. Because men do not volunteer for fatherhood as much as they are conscripted into it by the surrounding culture, only an authoritative cultural commitment to fatherhood can fuse biological and social paternity into a coherent male identity.   12

For exactly this reason, anthropologist Margaret Mead and others have observed that the supreme test of any civilization is whether it can socialize men by teaching them to willingly nurture their offspring.   13

The stakes could hardly be higher. Our society's conspicuous failure to sustain norms of fatherhood reveals a failure of collective memory and a collapse of moral imagination. It undermines families, neglects children, causes or aggravates our worst social problems, and makes individual adult happiness—both female and male—harder to achieve.   14

Ultimately, this failure reflects nothing less than a culture gone awry, unable to establish the boundaries and erect the signposts that can harmonize individual happiness with collective well-being. In short, it reflects a culture that increasingly fails to "enculture" individual men and women, mothers and fathers.

15

In personal terms, the result is a me-first egotism that is hostile to all except the most puerile understanding of personal happiness. In social terms, the primary results are a decline in children's well-being and a rise in male violence, especially against women. The most significant result is our society's steady fragmentation into atomized individuals, isolated from one another and estranged from the aspirations and realities of common membership in a family, a community, a nation, bound by mutual commitment and shared memory.

16

Many voices today, including many expert voices, urge us to accept the decline of fatherhood with equanimity. Be realistic, they tell us. Divorce and out-of-wedlock childbearing are here to stay. Growing numbers of children will not have fathers. Nothing can be done to reverse the trend itself. The only solution is to remedy some of its consequences: More help for poor children. More sympathy for single mothers. Better divorce. More child-support payments. More prisons. More programs aimed at substituting for fathers.

17

Yet what Abraham Lincoln called the better angels of our nature always have guided us in the opposite direction. Passivity in the face of crisis is inconsistent with the American tradition. Managing decline never has been the hallmark of American expertise. In the inevitable and valuable tension between conditions and aspirations—between the social "is" and the moral "ought"—our birthright as Americans always has been our confidence that we can change for the better.

18

Does every child need a father? Our current answer hovers between "not necessarily" and "no." But we need not make permanent the lowering of our standards. We can change our minds. We can change our minds without passing new laws, spending more tax dollars or empaneling more expert commissions. Once we change our philosophy, we might well decide to pass laws, create programs, or commission research. But the first and most important thing to change is not policies, *but ideas*.

19

Our essential goal must be the rediscovery of the fatherhood idea: For every child, a legally and morally responsible man.

20

If my goal could be distilled into one sentence, it would be this: A good society celebrates the ideal of the man who puts his family first. Because our society is lurching in the opposite direction, I see the Good Family Man as the principal casualty of today's weakening focus on fatherhood. Yet I cannot imagine a good society without him.

21

Read More on the Web

For more on the importance of fatherhood, search the following:

- *FatherhoodFactor* (search for "Fatherless Statistics"): fatherhoodfactor.com/
- "Fighting Fatherlessness in America," Leslie Ford: www.heritage.org/marriage-and-family/commentary/fighting-fatherlessness-america

Questions for Discussion (Continues)

1. What is Blankenhorn's thesis?
2. What is the purpose of this essay?
3. What methods explained in chapter 3 does Blankenhorn use in this essay?
4. What does the author want his introduction to accomplish?
5. According to Blankenhorn, what are the root causes of fatherlessness? What are its effects?

6. Where in this essay does Blankenhorn use comparison? Where does he use contrast? Explain the contrast between the causes of fatherlessness in the 1940s and the causes of fatherlessness today.

7. What does Blankenhorn mean when, in paragraph 8, he calls fatherhood a cultural invention?

8. What does he mean when, in paragraph 15, he claims that we fail to "'enculture' individual men and women, mothers and fathers"?

9. What does the author think about our present efforts to address fatherlessness? What does he suggest we do to change our approach?

10. Comment on Blankenhorn's conclusion. What is its purpose?

Thinking Critically

1. In paragraph 18, the author refers to "what Abraham Lincoln called 'the better angels of our nature.'" Explain what this term means. Then write a short paragraph explaining why this paragraph is crucial to Blankenhorn's purpose.

2. In paragraph 19, Blankenhorn tells us that "the first and most important thing to change is not policies, *but ideas*." Write a paragraph that explains what that idea means in light of what the author says in the rest of the essay.

Suggestions for Journal Entries

1. Reread paragraph 10. Summarize the characteristics of fatherhood that the author explains there. Next, make a list of other characteristics you might add.

2. In preparation for the writing of an essay that defines the ideal parent, grandparent, sibling, aunt, or uncle, make a list of people you know who are your role models. Then, make a list of people you know who fall far short of the ideal. To preserve the anonymity of those who are not role models, don't use their real names.

3. In preparation for writing an essay that defines the public image of parenthood, make a list of four or five television programs or movies in which a parent is one of the major characters. Next, make a list of the personal characteristics associated with each of these people. Finally, decide if the media's portrayal of parents is positive, negative, or mixed.

11.9c The True Meaning of Patriotism

Author Biography

Lawrence Reed (1953–) is president of the Foundation for Economic Education. He earned a bachelor of arts degree from Grove City College and a master's degree from Slippery Rock University in Pennsylvania. Reed has taught economics at Michigan's Northwood University. His interest in liberty and patriotism was inspired by the "Prague Spring," the Czech uprising of 1968 against Soviet domination. He is a supporter of free-market economics and is the author of more than a thousand newspaper and magazine articles on economics, politics, and government. He has also published several books, including *Striking the Root: Essays on Liberty* and *Real Heroes—Inspiring Stories of Courage, Character, and Conviction*. The essay below was published on the Foundation of Economic Education website.

Preparing to Read

1. Reed uses methods to write introductions and conclusions that were explained in chapter 3. Turn back to that chapter and review the list of these methods.

2. In the first part of this essay, Reed defines patriotism by using negation—explaining what it's not.

3. Dr. Samuel Johnson, mentioned in paragraph 6, was an eighteenth-century poet and essayist.

Vocabulary

adverse (adjective)   Hostile, unfavorable.

cynical (adjective)   Skeptical, disparaging.

flippantly (adverb)   Frivolously, dismissively.

paraphernalia (noun)   Equipment, trappings, supplies.

passel (noun)   A large number, a large amount.

reverence (noun)   Respect, worship.

scoundrel (noun)   Rogue, villain.

superlative (adjective)   Exceptional, excellent.

The True Meaning of Patriotism

Lawrence Reed

Patriotism these days is like Christmas—lots of people caught up in a festive atmosphere replete with lights and spectacles. We hear reminders about "the true meaning" of Christmas—and we may even mutter a few guilt-ridden words to that effect ourselves—but each of us spends more time and thought in parties, gift-giving, and the other paraphernalia of a secularized holiday than we do deepening our devotion to the true meaning.   1

So it is with patriotism, especially on Memorial Day in May, Flag Day in June, and Independence Day in July. Walk down Main Street America and ask one citizen after another what patriotism means and with few exceptions, you'll get a passel of the most self-righteous but superficial and often dead-wrong answers. America's Founders, the men and women who gave us reason to be patriotic in the first place, would think we've lost our way if they could see us now.   2

Since the infamous attacks of September 11, 2001, Americans in near unanimity have been "feeling" patriotic. For most, that sadly suffices to make one a solid patriot. But if I'm right, it's time for Americans to take a refresher course.   3

Patriotism is *not* love of country, if by "country" you mean scenery—amber waves of grain, purple mountain majesty, and the like. Almost every country has pretty collections of rocks, water, and stuff that people grow and eat. If that's what patriotism is all about, then Americans have precious little for which we can claim any special or unique love. And surely, patriotism cannot mean giving one's life for a river or a mountain range.   4

Patriotism is not blind trust in anything our leaders tell us or do. That just replaces some lofty concepts with mindless goose-stepping. 5

Patriotism is not simply showing up to vote. You need to know a lot more about what motivates a voter before you judge his patriotism. He might be casting a ballot because he just wants something at someone else's expense. Maybe he doesn't much care where the politician he's hiring gets it. Remember Dr. Johnson's wisdom: "Patriotism is the last refuge of a scoundrel." 6

Waving the flag can be an outward sign of patriotism, but let's not cheapen the term by ever suggesting that it's anything more than a sign. And while it's always fitting to mourn those who lost their lives simply because they resided on American soil, that too does not define patriotism. 7

People in every country and in all times have expressed feelings of something we flippantly call "patriotism," but that just begs the question. What is this thing, anyway? Can it be so cheap and meaningless that a few gestures and feelings make you patriotic? 8

Not in my book. 9

I subscribe to a patriotism rooted in ideas that in turn gave birth to a country, but it's the *ideas* that I think of when I'm feeling patriotic. I'm a patriotic American because I revere the ideas that motivated the Founders and compelled them, in many instances, to put their lives, fortunes, and sacred honor on the line. 10

What ideas? Read the Declaration of Independence again. Or, if you're like most Americans these days, read it for the very first time. It's all there. All men are created equal. They are endowed not by government but by their Creator with certain unalienable rights. Premier among those rights are life, liberty, and the pursuit of happiness. Government must be limited to protecting the peace and preserving our liberties, and doing so through the consent of the governed. It's the right of a free people to rid themselves of a government that becomes destructive of those ends, as our Founders did in a supreme act of courage and defiance more than two hundred years ago. 11

Call it freedom. Call it liberty. Call it whatever you want, but it's the bedrock on which this nation was founded and from which we stray at our peril. It's what has defined us as Americans. It's what almost everyone who has ever lived on this planet has yearned for. It makes life worth living, which means it's worth fighting and dying for. 12

An American Spin

I know that this concept of patriotism puts an American spin on the term. But I don't know how to be patriotic for Uganda or Paraguay. I hope the Ugandans and Paraguayans have lofty ideals they celebrate when they feel patriotic, but whether or not they do is a question you'll have to ask them. I can only tell you what patriotism means to me as an American. 13

I understand that America has often fallen short of the superlative ideas expressed in the Declaration. That hasn't diminished my reverence for them, nor has it dimmed my hope that future generations of Americans will be re-inspired by them. 14

This brand of patriotism, in fact, gets me through the roughest and most cynical of times. My patriotism is never affected by any politician's failures, or any shortcoming of some government policy, or any slump in the economy or stock market. I never cease to get that "rush" that comes from watching Old Glory flapping in the breeze, no matter how far today's generations have departed from the original meaning of those stars and stripes. No outcome of any election, no matter how adverse, makes me feel any less devoted to the ideals our Founders put to pen in 1776. Indeed, as life's experiences mount, the wisdom of what giants like Jefferson and Madison bestowed on us becomes ever more apparent to me. I get more fired up than ever to help others come to appreciate the same things. 15

During a recent visit to the land of my ancestors, Scotland, I came across a few very old words that gave me pause. Though they preceded our Declaration of Independence by 456 years, and come from three thousand miles away, I can hardly think of anything ever written here that more powerfully stirs in me the patriotism I've defined above. In 1320, in an effort to explain why they had spent the previous 30 years in bloody battle to expel the invading English, Scottish leaders ended their Declaration of Arbroath with this line: "It is not for honor or glory or wealth that we fight, but for freedom alone, which no good man gives up except with his life." 16

Freedom—understanding it, living it, teaching it, and supporting those who are educating others about its principles. That, my fellow Americans, is what patriotism should mean to each of us today. 17

Read More on the Web

For more on patriotism visit these sites:

- USA Patriotism!: www.usapatriotism.org/

- Top 10 Patriotic Speeches in American History: http://bvtlab.com/F4k76

- "What Is Patriotism?" by Emma Goldman (presents a view different from Reed's): http://bvtlab.com/N6q69

Questions for Discussion

1. What method for introducing essays does Reed use? What method for concluding does he use?

2. In paragraphs 4–9, Reed defines patriotism by discussing things that it is not. What are these things?

3. What is the purpose of paragraph 10?

4. What methods for defining that you read about in this chapter does Reed use?

5. According to Reed, what are the most important components of patriotism? Where do these components come from?

6. What does he mean by the term "begs the question" in paragraph 8?

Thinking Critically

1. If you haven't read the Declaration of Independence recently, do so now.

2. What did Dr. Johnson mean when he said, "Patriotism is the last refuge of a scoundrel"?

3. What does the mention of "goose-stepping" in paragraph 5 refer to?

Suggestions for Journal Entries

1. Read paragraph 5 again. When might it be patriotic to protest an unjust law or government action? Try to provide two or three examples of incidents in which people protested against such a law or action. Your examples need not be limited to America. Provide details about why the action or the law was wrong and what the protest of it accomplished.

2. In paragraph 14, Reed says that he hopes "future generations of Americans will be re-inspired" by the ideas in the Declaration of Independence. Record your thoughts on this notion. Is your generation inspired by these ideas? Will other generations be?

11.9d The Perpetual Adolescent

Author Biography

Joseph Epstein (1937–) is an essayist whose books include *Narcissus Leaves the Pool: Familiar Essays* (1999), *Snobbery: The American Version* (2002), and *Envy* (2003). He has also authored two short-story collections, including *Fabulous Small Jews* (2003). His essays have been published in *Commentary*, the *New Yorker*, and *Harper's*, among other periodicals. From 1974 to 2002, Epstein taught at Northwestern

University in Chicago, and he served as editor of the *American Scholar*, the magazine of the Phi Beta Kappa honor society. "The Perpetual Adolescent," an excerpt of which appears here, was published in the *Weekly Standard* in 2004.

Preparing to Read

1. Epstein makes references to numerous important historical and contemporary figures. Among those you might want to read more about (in print or on the Internet) are Joe DiMaggio (paragraph 1); H. L. Mencken (paragraph 3); Aristotle (paragraph 6); Alan Greenspan, Jeane Kirkpatrick, Robert Rubin, Warren Buffett, and Sol Linowitz (paragraph 8); and Søren Kierkegaard (paragraph 8).

2. The Wordsworth, mentioned in paragraph 10, refers to William Wordsworth, one of the founders of British Romanticism, an artistic and intellectual movement that flowered during the early part of the nineteenth century. William Butler Yeats (paragraph 11) was a nineteenth-century Irish writer, whose poem "Sailing to Byzantium" begins "This is no country for old men."

3. Holden Caulfield (paragraph 9) is the name of the main character of *The Catcher in the Rye*, an extremely popular coming-of-age novel by J. D. Salinger. Enron (paragraph 17) is an energy company that filed for bankruptcy in 2001 after it was alleged—and later proven—that several top executives had committed stock fraud. As a result, more than 4,000 Enron employees lost their jobs, and the Enron scandal became a symbol for corporate corruption.

Vocabulary

advent (noun)   Arrival, introduction, coming.

anomalous (adjective)   Uncharacteristic, out of the ordinary, abnormal.

benign (adjective)   Harmless.

cataclysmic (adjective)   Catastrophic, disastrous.

crucibles (noun)   Difficult experiences or tests that result in significant changes or new phenomena.

de riguer (adjective)   French term for ordinary, common.

ephemeral (adjective)   Fleeting, not permanent, of no lasting value.

grotesque (adjective)   Extremely ugly or distasteful.

hierarchy (noun)   Order, ranking.

inexorably (adverb)   Inevitably, inescapably.

injunction (noun)   Order, command.

transcendent (adjective)   Extraordinary.

utopia (noun)   An imaginary place that offers the ideal government, society, and living conditions.

vaunted (adjective)   Highly praised.

The Perpetual Adolescent

Joseph Epstein

Whenever anyone under the age of 50 sees old newsreel film of Joe DiMaggio's 56-game hitting streak of 1941, he is almost certain to be brought up by the fact that nearly everyone in the male-dominated crowds—in New York, Boston, Chicago, Detroit, Cleveland—seems to be wearing a suit and a fedora or other serious adult hat. The people in those earlier baseball crowds, though watching a boyish game, nonetheless had a radically different conception of themselves than most Americans do now. A major depression was ending, a world war was on. Even though they were watching an entertainment that took most of them back to their boyhoods, they thought of themselves as adults, no longer kids, but grown-ups, adults, men.

How different from today, when a good part of the crowd at any ballgame, no matter what the age, is wearing jeans and team caps and T-shirts; and let us not neglect those (one hopes) benign maniacs who paint their faces in home-team colors or spell out, on their bare chests, the letters of the names of star players: S-O-S-A.

Part of the explanation for the suits at the ballpark in DiMaggio's day is that in the 1940s and even '50s there weren't a lot of sport, or leisure, or casual clothes around. Unless one lived at what H. L. Mencken called "the country-club stage of culture"—unless, that is, one golfed, played tennis, or sailed—one was likely to own only the clothes one worked in or better. Far from casual Fridays, in those years there weren't even casual Sundays. Wearing one's "Sunday best," a cliché of the time, meant wearing the good clothes one reserved for church.

Dressing down may first have set in on the West Coast, where a certain informality was thought to be a new way of life. In the 1960s, in universities casual dress became absolutely de rigueur among younger faculty, who, in their ardor to destroy any evidence of their being implicated in evil hierarchy, wished not merely to seem in no wise different from their students but, more important, to seem always young; and the quickest path to youthfulness was teaching in jeans, T-shirts, and the rest of it.

This informality has now been institutionalized. Few are the restaurants that could any longer hope to stay in business if they required men to wear a jacket and tie. Today one sees men wearing baseball caps—some worn backwards—while eating indoors in quite good restaurants. In an episode of *The Sopranos*, Tony Soprano, the mafia don, representing life of a different day, finds this so outrages his sense of decorum that, in a restaurant he frequents, he asks a man, in a quiet but entirely menacing way, to remove his goddamn hat.

Life in that different day was felt to observe the human equivalent of the Aristotelian unities: to have, like a good drama, a beginning, middle, and end. Each part, it was understood, had its own advantages and detractions, but the middle—adulthood—was the lengthiest and most earnest part, where everything serious happened and much was at stake. To violate the boundaries of any of the three divisions of life was to go against what was natural and thereby to appear unseemly, to put one's world somehow out of joint, to be, let us face it, a touch, and perhaps more than a touch, grotesque.

Today, of course, all this has been shattered. The ideal almost everywhere is to seem young for as long as possible. The health clubs and endemic workout clothes, the enormous increase in cosmetic surgery (for women and men), the special youth-oriented television programming and moviemaking, all these are merely the more obvious signs of the triumph of youth culture. When I say youth culture, I do not mean merely that the young today are transcendent, the group most admired among the various age groups in American society, but that youth is no longer viewed as a transitory state, through which one passes on the way from childhood to adulthood, but an aspiration, a vaunted condition in which, if one can only arrange it, to settle in perpetuity.

This phenomenon is not something that happened just last night; it has been under way for decades. Nor is it something that can be changed even by an event as cataclysmic as that of September 11, which at first was thought to be so sobering as to tear away all shreds of American innocence. As a generalization, it allows for a wide variety of exceptions. There still are adults in America; if names are wanted, I would set out those of Alan Greenspan, Jeane Kirkpatrick, Robert Rubin, Warren Buffett, Sol Linowitz, and many more. But such men and women, actual grown-ups, now begin to appear a bit anomalous; they no longer seem representative of the larger culture.

The shift into youth culture began in earnest, I suspect, during the years following 1951, the year   9
of the publication of *The Catcher in the Rye*. Salinger's novel exalts the purity of youth and locates
the enemy—a clear case of Us versus Them—in those who committed the sin of having grown older,
which includes Holden Caulfield's pain-in-the-neck parents, his brother (the sellout screenwriter),
and just about everyone else who has passed beyond adolescence and had the rather poor taste to
remain alive.

The case for the exaltation of the young is made in Wordsworth's "Intimation of Immortality,"   10
with its idea that human beings are born with great wisdom from which life in society weans them
slowly but inexorably. Plato promulgated this same idea long before: For him we all had wisdom in
the womb, but it was torn from us at the exact point that we came into the world. Rousseau gave it a
French twist, arguing that human beings are splendid all-round specimens—noble savages, really—
with life out in society turning us mean and loutish, which is another way of saying that the older we
are, the worse we get. We are talking about romanticism here, friend, which never favors the mature,
let alone the aged.

The triumph of youth culture has conquered perhaps nowhere more completely than in the   11
United States. The John F. Kennedy administration, with its emphasis on youthfulness, beginning
with its young president—the first president routinely not to wear a serious hat—gave it its first
public prominence. Soon after the assassination of Kennedy, the Free Speech Movement, which
spearheaded the student revolution, positively enshrined the young. Like Yeats's "Byzantium," the six-
ties utopia posited by the student radicals was "no country for old men" or women. One of the many
tenets in its credo—soon to become a cliché, but no less significant for that—was that no one over
30 was to be trusted. (If you were part of that movement and 21 years old in 1965, you are 60 today.
Good morning, Sunshine.)

Music was a key element in the advance of youth culture. The dividing moment here is the   12
advent of Elvis. On one side were those who thought Elvis an amusing and largely freakish phenomenon—a bit of a joke—and on the other, those who took him dead seriously as a figure of youthful
rebellion, the musical equivalent of James Dean in the movie *Rebel without a Cause*, another early
winning entry in the glorification-of-youth sweepstakes then forming. Rock 'n' roll presented a vinyl
curtain, with those committed to retaining their youth on one side, those wanting to claim adulthood
on the other. The Beatles, despite the very real charms of their non-druggie music, solidified things.
So much of hard rock 'n' roll came down to nothing more than a way of saying bugger off to adult
culture.

Reinforcement for these notions—they were not yet so coherent as to qualify as ideas—was to   13
be found in the movies. Movies for some years now have been made not only increasingly for the
young but by the young. I once worked on a movie script with a producer who one day announced to
me that it was his birthday. When I wished him happy returns of the day, he replied that it wasn't so
happy for him; he was turning 41, an uncomfortably old age in Hollywood for someone who hadn't
many big success-scalps on his belt.

Robert Redford ... remains essentially a guy in jeans, a handsome graduate student with wrin-
kles. Paul Newman*... seems uncomfortable in a suit. Hugh Grant, the English actor, may be said   14
to be professionally boyish, and ... in the movie *About a Boy*, is described in the *New York Times* as
a character who "surrounds himself with gadgets, videos, CDs, and other toys" and who "is doing
everything in his power to avoid growing up." The actor Jim Carrey ... not long ago said of the movie
The Majestic, in which he stars, "It's about manhood. It's about adulthood," as if italicizing the rarity
of such movies. He then went on to speak about himself in standard self-absorbed adolescent fashion:
"You've got that hole you're left with by whatever your parents couldn't give you." Poor baby.

Jim Carrey's roles in movies resemble nothing so much as comic-book characters come to life.   15
And why, just now, does so much of contemporary entertainment come in the form of animation or
comic-book cartooning? Such television shows as *The Simpsons* and *King of the Hill*, the occasional
back page in the *New York Times Book Review* or the *New Yorker*, and the comic-book novel, all seem
to feel that the animated cartoon and comic-book formats are very much of the moment. They are
of course right, at least if you think of your audience as adolescent, or, more precisely, as being quite
unwilling to detach themselves from their adolescence.

* Paul Newman died in 2008.

Recent history has seemed to be on the side of keeping people from growing up by supplying only a paucity of stern tests of the kind out of which adulthood is usually formed. We shall never have another presidential candidate tested by the Depression or by his experience in World War II. These were events that proved crucibles for the formation of adult character, not to say manliness. Henceforth all future presidential—and congressional—candidates will come with a shortage of what used to pass for significant experience. Crises for future politicians will doubtless be about having to rethink their lives when they didn't get into Brown or found themselves unequipped emotionally for Stanford Business School.

16

Corporate talent these days feels no weightier. Pictures of heads of corporations in polo shirts with designer logos in the business section of the *New York Times*, fresh from yet another ephemeral merger, or acquiring an enormous raise after their company has recorded another losing year, do not inspire confidence. "The trouble with Enron," said an employee of the company in the aftermath of that corporation's appalling debacle, "is that there weren't any grown-ups."

17

The increasing affluence the United States enjoyed after World War II, extending into the current day, also contributed heavily to forming the character I've come to think of as the perpetual American adolescent. Earlier, with less money around, people were forced to get serious, to grow up—and fast. How quickly the Depression generation was required to mature! How many stories one used to hear about older brothers going to work at 18 or earlier, so that a younger brother might be allowed to go to college, or simply to help keep the family afloat! With lots of money around, certain kinds of pressure were removed. More and more people nowadays are working, as earlier generations were not, with a strong safety net of money under them. All options opened, they now swim in what Kierkegaard called "a sea of possibilities," and one of these possibilities in America is to refuse to grow up for a longer period than has been permitted any other people in history.

18

All this is reinforced by the play of market forces, which strongly encourage the mythical dream of perpetual youthfulness. The promise behind 95 percent of all advertising is that of recaptured youth, whose deeper promise is lots more sex yet to go. The ads for the $5,000 wristwatch, the $80,000 car, the khakis, the vodka, the pharmaceuticals to regrow hair and recapture ardor, all whisper display me, drive me, wear me, drink me, swallow me, and you stop the clock—youth, Baby, is yours.

19

The whole sweep of advertising, which is to say of market culture, since soon after World War II, has been continuously to lower the criteria of youthfulness while extending the possibility for seeming youthful to older and older people. To make the very young seem older—all those 10- and 12-year-old Britney Spears and Jennifer Lopez imitators, who already know more about brand-name logos than I do about English literature—is another part of the job. It's not a conspiracy, mind you, not six or eight international ad agencies meeting in secret to call the shots, but the dynamics of marketing itself, finding a way to make it more profitable all around by convincing the young that they can seem older and the old that they can seem a lot younger. Never before has it been more difficult to obey the injunction to act one's age.

20

Read More on the Web

To access more information on this subject and to read more by Joseph Epstein, search for the following:

- "Bums," Kevin D. Williamson: http://bvtlab.com/696S9

- The CBS News site that contains Epstein's complete version of "The Perpetual Adolescent," as well as related articles: www.cbsnews.com/news/the-perpetual-adolescent/

- "The Green-Eyed Monster," Joseph Epstein: http://bvtlab.com/4u569

Questions for Discussion

1. The clearest statement of Epstein's central idea appears in paragraph 7. What is it? Should it have appeared earlier?

2. How would you describe Epstein's tone (see especially paragraph 14)?

3. What is the essay's purpose?

4. How does Epstein characterize adulthood as seen through the eyes of people living in the 1950s (paragraph 6)?

5. What does he mean when, in paragraph 7, he says that, today, youth is seen as "an aspiration"?

6. Where in this essay does Epstein use illustration? Where does he use comparison? Contrast?

7. What methods of development does Epstein use in paragraphs 9 and 10?

8. What role did the publication of *The Catcher in the Rye* play in our society's embracing of the "youth culture"? What role did the Kennedy administration play?

9. Why does the author mention Jim Carrey, Paul Newman, Robert Redford, and other popular entertainers?

10. What influence have *The Simpsons* and other television cartoon shows had on what we might assume to be serious writing?

Thinking Critically

1. Write a paragraph in which you agree or disagree with Epstein's statement in paragraph 16 that "henceforth all future presidential—and congressional—candidates will come with a shortage of what used to pass for significant experience." Make reference to politicians you know about or who are often in the news.

2. Summarize the "triumph of youth culture" as explained in paragraphs 9–15.

Suggestions for Journal Entries

1. Do you agree with Epstein? Is our society fostering the creation of perpetual adolescents? If so, make a list of examples from what you see in the media or what you experience or observe in daily life to prove your point. If not, list examples that might be used to convince people that our society places emphasis on the importance of being an adult and on the responsibilities adults must assume. You might also list evidence to prove that our society is as much concerned with its elderly as with any other generation.

2. A television commercial once described the youth of America as the "Pepsi Generation." What term might you use to define your generation? The jean-and-T-shirt generation? The Internet generation? The cell-phone generation? Use focused freewriting to produce a paragraph in which you fully define this term by using illustrations taken from your own experiences and observations.

11.10 Suggestions for Sustained Writing

1. In "The Ordinariness of Evil," Anju Jha explains that, given the right circumstances, people who seem ordinary and moral can be made to do wrong. To continue the discussion, write an essay in which you recall an incident in which you were pressured—by an authority figure or by a peer—to do something you believed was wrong. If you responded to the first journal suggestion after Jha's essay, you may have already begun gathering information for this project.

   Read your journal notes. Then, add to them. In addition to telling what happened, explain why you chose to comply or how you withstood the pressure. In the process, describe the emotions you felt during this process. Put this information into your rough draft. When you revise this draft, use information and insights from Jha's essay to show in what ways your situation parallels the kinds of situations she uses to explain "the ordinariness of evil." If you want, turn this assignment into a research paper by taking material from other secondary sources found in the library or online. As always, use an appropriate citation system, such as Modern Language Association (MLA) style (see appendix 2, "The Research Process," for more information).

   In your conclusion, make a statement that explains the extent to which you agree with Jha's thesis. As always, edit and proofread your paper carefully, and make sure you have cited any information taken from secondary sources, including "The Ordinariness of Evil."

2. If you were inspired by David Blankenhorn's "Life without Father," write an essay in which you define what, for you, is the ideal father, mother, sibling, or other relative. Begin by checking the journal notes you made after reading Blankenhorn's essay. Add to these notes, if necessary. Make sure you have compiled a list of people who could serve as role models for fathers, mothers, and so on. Also, make sure that you have a list of other people who are ill-suited to this role.

   Each of your lists needs to contain no more than three or four people. As you review each group, make another list of personal characteristics—positive or negative—that each person exhibits. Use this information to develop an essay that, on one hand, explains what an ideal father, mother, or other person is and, on the other, explains what the ideal is not. As you revise, make sure to have included sufficient detail. For example, have you discussed the kinds of sacrifices the ideal parent must make? Have you talked about the hardships he or she must overcome or the patience he or she must possess? Have you mentioned the integrity, honesty, and strength—both emotional and physical—needed to fulfill this role?

3. If you responded to the first suggestion for journal entries after Lawrence Reed's essay, use your notes to begin an essay that defines one aspect of patriotism as the duty to protest or oppose an unjust law or government action. Expand upon the two or three examples of such protests or opposition that you mentioned in your journal entry. Be clear and forceful about why a particular law or government action was wrong and what was accomplished by opposing it.

   Make use of some of the methods for defining discussed in this chapter. For example, you might want to use negation and make reference to historic events or documents, as Reed did. If necessary, do some research in the library or on the Internet to gather more information, but remember to cite your sources using the MLA style of documentation (see appendix 2, "The Research Process") or another style required by your instructor.

4. Do you agree with Joseph Epstein that our society seems to foster perpetual adolescence? Read the notes you may have made in response to the first suggestion for journal entries following the reading selection. Then write an essay that supports or rejects Epstein's position. The information you have already gathered will probably have come from what you have read, seen, and heard in the media, as well as what you have experienced firsthand. Now, add even more information by researching this subject in books and articles on the Internet, in your college library's electronic databases, or, of course, in print. As you draft and revise your paper, make sure to include internal (parenthetical) citations and a works cited list using the Modern Language Association (MLA) documentation style or another style recommended by your instructor. You can learn more about MLA style in appendix 2, "The Research Process."

ACKNOWLEDGMENTS

Blankenhorn, David. *Fatherless America: Confronting Our Most Urgent Social Problems*. Basic Books 1995. Revised and expanded by author. Copyright © 1995. Reprinted by permission of Basic Books, an imprint of Hachette Book Group, Inc.

D'Arienzo, William. *Brand Management Strategies*. Fairchild Books, 2016. Copyright Fairchild Books, an imprint of Bloomsbury Publishing, New York, 2016.

Epstein, Joseph. "The Perpetual Adolescent and the Triumph of the Youth Culture," *The Weekly Standard*, vol. 9, no. 26, 2004. Reprinted by permission of the author.

Reed, Lawrence. "The True Meaning of Patriotism." Foundation of Economic Education. Available under a CC by SA 4.0 license at https://fee.org/articles/the-true-meaning-of-patriotism/.

Section 5
Argumentation and Persuasion

Argumentation and persuasion are similar, and they often work together. In fact it is rare to find an essay that is pure argumentation without the slightest hint that the author is trying to persuade the readers. It is even rarer to find an effective persuasive essay that is not based on a logical argument. However, argumentation and persuasion are not identical.

Establishing Purpose: Choosing to Argue or Persuade

To begin with, a formal "argument" is not a fight, altercation, or heated discussion with tempers flaring and threats being exchanged. An *argument* is the defense of an opinion or a position on an issue that is supported by concrete evidence and that is presented logically. The purpose of a written argument is limited: to prove a point, a thesis—sometimes referred to as a *proposition*. Scientists use argument to prove a theory or hypothesis. Historians engage in argumentation when they dispute theories about the causes of a war or an economic depression. A psychologist might argue that genetic factors caused someone to become a serial killer, and an economist could use argumentation to present theories about the business cycle or the effects of taxation.

Persuasion begins with logical argument. It too uses logic and concrete evidence to make a point, to prove a thesis. However, *persuasion* goes beyond argument and also appeals to the reader's emotions, values, and self-interest. The Declaration of Independence, a classic piece of persuasion, even attempts to inflame our passions. Finally, the purpose of persuasion is not simply to prove a point; it is to get readers to act. Lawyers use persuasion to get judges and juries to rule in favor of their clients. Politicians use persuasion to get voters to support them.

So, first of all, you need to decide if your purpose is to argue or to persuade. Your decision will affect the word choices you make, the tone of your paper, and even its content. You would be writing an argument if you tried to convince your readers that the Internet and other electronic means of publishing information will someday replace the printed books and paper journals now on college library shelves. You would also be arguing if you proved that devoting too much time to a job while attending college full-time reduces the chances for academic success. On the other hand, you would be writing persuasively if you tried to convince your college president to reduce the library's book budget and allocate the money toward subscriptions to online periodical databases. You would also be trying to persuade if you wrote a letter to your college newspaper to convince students to reduce their work hours and spend more time on their studies.

313

Appealing to Your Audience

The kind of audience you are writing to will often have as much influence on whether to argue or to persuade as your purpose does. For example, let's say you have been assigned to write a paper on the effects of regular aerobic exercise on the emotional health of people over age 65. Your paper will be duplicated and read by all the members of your class, none of whom happens to be over 65. So, you decide to stick to pure argument and simply lay out the facts in support of an opinion. You cite statistics from journal articles published by senior citizen groups and insurance associations, draw on studies in the *New England Journal of Medicine*, and quote a cardiologist you have interviewed to support the idea that aerobics promote emotional health in seniors. In short, you write an essay that argues.

Now, take another scenario. You have been asked to write a similar article for a magazine read primarily by senior citizens. Your purpose this time is not simply to prove a point; you also want to get your readers to follow your advice—to get them on a treadmill or into a Jazzercise class. So, in addition to doing research on your subject, you spend time evaluating your readers' goals, interests, and values and even their preconceived notions about aerobic exercise so you can address these "motivational" factors when you write your essay. For example, your paper might appeal to your readers' desire to maintain their emotional health in order to enjoy their children and grandchildren better. It might even suggest that regular aerobic exercise improves sex, regardless of age. Now that's motivation!

As you consider your audience, keep the following in mind:

- If you are trying to persuade your readers, make sure you are familiar with their needs, their interests, and their opinions.

- Assess readers' familiarity with the issue. Include background information as necessary to help readers new to the issue understand it fully. However, include only enough explanatory information and data to make your claims clear and convincing. Don't include three illustrations and six sets of statistics when one will do.

- Express yourself clearly and simply. Don't use highly sophisticated or technical vocabulary, unless you are sure your readers will understand it. Otherwise, they might suspect you are trying to confuse them or to cloud the issue.

Choosing a Thesis (Claim) That Is Debatable, Supportable, and Focused

The thesis for an argumentative paper is often referred to as the *claim*—the opinion the writer wishes to prove, defend, or support. Start with a preliminary thesis, but remember that writing is a process of discovery. So, as you become more knowledgeable about your thesis by gathering information for, outlining, and drafting your paper, you might see the need to rewrite the thesis by revising your stand on the issue or even changing it completely.

Unless your instructor assigns a specific topic, write on a question you already know something about or are concerned about, such as healthcare, animal rights, the homeless, affirmative action, school choice, the criminal justice system, or the environment. Those ideas can lead to the framing of a thesis—at least a preliminary thesis. Writing about something you believe is important provides the intellectual energy and commitment to complete an effective argumentative or persuasive essay.

At the same time, keep the following three criteria in mind as you frame your preliminary claim or thesis:

1. **An effective claim is debatable.** It is more than a simple statement of fact or of personal opinion, which will not lead to a sustained discussion.

   Statement of Fact: My college major requires that I complete 28 hours of science.

   Debatable Thesis: My college needs to install up-to-date equipment in the labs.

   The first item cannot be debated. Either your major requires 28 hours of science, or it doesn't. The second item, however, can yield sustained discussion through evidence that the current lab equipment does not enable students to keep up with advances in science.

   Personal Opinion or Preference: A vegetarian diet is as satisfying as one that includes meat and fish.

   Debatable Thesis: Following a vegetarian diet can help lower cholesterol and prevent heart disease.

   The first item is based on personal taste, which is an invalid criterion for argument. The second can be discussed in light of objective medical research.

   NOTE: You don't have to take one side of an issue exclusively. For example, you can argue against illegal immigration while expressing your understanding for the reasons that people from developing nations try to enter the United States illegally.

2. **An effective claim is defensible.** Before taking a position, think it through and decide whether you can collect enough evidence to argue it effectively.

   Indefensible: People who wear leather and fur are cruel to animals.

   Defensible: People who wear leather and fur support industries whose harvesting methods are cruel to animals.

   The first claim requires the writer to prove an impossibility: that the wearing of fur or leather itself is cruel. The second can be argued by calling upon evidence from government or industry sources, eyewitness testimony, or scientific research.

3. **An effective claim is focused.** For most college assignments, your thesis must be focused enough to be argued effectively in a short essay.

   Too General: Policies at two public colleges in my state violate students' rights.

   Focused: Policies governing speech at two public colleges in my state violate rights guaranteed to students by the First Amendment to the U.S. Constitution.

   The first item would result in an essay whose length might exceed what was assigned, as it covers too wide a range of policies. Moreover, it does not focus on particular "students' rights," as does the second item. Writing an essay on the second item would be much easier.

Read More on the Web

Check out these websites on writing thesis statements for argument/persuasion papers:

- "Argumentation and Critical Thinking Tutorial," Humboldt University: http://www2.humboldt.edu/act/HTML/

- "The Writing Lab," Purdue University: owl.purdue.edu/

Gathering Evidence to Support Your Thesis

Many ways to develop any essay, as explained in chapter 2, can also be used to approach an argument. For example, to argue that your college's policies restrict students' freedom of speech, you might first define the right of free speech and reveal the source of that right. If you argue that the college's lab equipment needs to be replaced, you might use cause-and-effect to explain the difficulties new chemistry graduates are having when they get jobs in industry. Whatever your approach, communicate your position through sufficient concrete evidence to be convincing.

The most effective types of supportive evidence are documented facts and statistics, expert testimony, and illustrations.

Documented Facts and Statistics

To argue that being overweight contributes to heart disease and stroke, you can quote data published in scientific journals. You might also use statistics taken from medical studies or insurance sources to show that obese people suffer higher mortality rates from coronary disease and stroke than others do.

However, keep in mind that too many statistics can overwhelm or bore some readers, especially those who are not used to analyses of issues based on mathematical evidence.

Expert Testimony

Including what experts in a particular field say or have written strengthens your argument. When you introduce such material, however, state your source's credentials. In other words, explain why your expert is, in fact, an expert. Mention academic degrees, professional experience, publications, awards, and other information that will convince readers of your source's value.

You might use expert testimony in the form of statements from college faculty, staff, and students to prove that the college's laboratories are outdated. You might quote constitutional lawyers, judges, or government experts to support your claim that the college's policies restrict free speech.

Read More on the Web

You can learn how to cite sources of facts, statistics, and expert testimony by using the styles of the Modern Language Association, the American Psychological Association, or other acceptable formats at the Purdue University Online Writing Center: owl.purdue.edu/.

Illustrations

As you learned earlier in this book, illustrations are factual examples or instances of the idea you are trying to support. You would be using illustrations if you wrote about specific cases in which college policy was invoked to punish or silence students who had expressed unpopular opinions on controversial campus issues. Always make sure these examples are concrete and well developed. Mention names of the people involved, include statements of the charges and punishments, explain the "offense," summarize arguments, quote testimony from hearings, and reference specific parts of the college policy. Finally, choose examples that are directly relevant to your claim and that appeal to your audience. For example, in discussing an alleged violation of the college policy, you would do more than claim that Oliver Outspoken criticized the History Department; you might also add that he did so in a polite, well-reasoned letter to the college newspaper, which calls itself "the student's voice." You might even quote directly from that letter.

Of course, most argumentative essays use a combination of these kinds of evidence. For example, to strengthen your claim that college policy violates students' rights of free speech, you might include the testimony of legal experts when you cite examples. Again, the important thing is that you use enough concrete evidence to be convincing.

Determining Tone and Content

The tone and language of an argument are usually objective, neutral, specific, and rational. The argument might draw on the testimony of experts, on statistics, or on historical or scientific studies. Experts and authorities in a particular field who have a reputation for evaluating issues fairly are often cited by writers of argument. Argument depends on logic. In persuasive essays, writers also use language that is more personal and emotionally charged. They sometimes involve themselves in the essay by viewing things subjectively, they focus on particular people and incidents more than on abstract studies and statistics, and they usually defend their positions vigorously and even passionately.

Let's say you are writing an argument that victims of violent crime ought to be compensated by the government. You might include Department of Justice statistics on the annual medical bills for victims of crime nationwide. You might remind readers that the government often helps victims of natural disasters and cite specific instances or programs in which such aid has been distributed. You might even describe a program used in another country that forces convicted criminals to work in order to fund a compensation program for crime victims. The tone of your argument would be dispassionate, and your presentation, logical.

However, if you are writing an article to gather support for a rally to get Congress to pass a crime-victims bill, you might describe the long-term emotional and physical effects that specific crime victims are suffering. You might create vivid images of people no longer able to walk, to work, or to live pain-free lives. You might also appeal to the readers' self-interest by asking them to predict the horrors they might endure if they were ever victimized by some thug. Your language will probably be emotionally charged, and the images you paint will be startling.

Expressing a Voice

Although argument relies on logic and persuasion can appeal to the reader's emotions, the line between pure argument and pure persuasion sometimes gets blurred. In fact, writers of argument frequently reveal their feelings about a topic, if ever so subtly. In "The Right to Be Let Alone" (chapter 12), Barry Glazer uses emotionally charged language when he asserts that if he were "in the throes of terminal cancer or facing the horror of Alzheimer's disease," he should be allowed to commit suicide. Thus, while his purpose is not to move his readers to action, Glazer does touch our emotions, and we are the more convinced. An effective argument needs to be logical and well supported, but no writer should ever refrain from expressing his or her personal voice in a piece of formal writing, as long as it remains reasonable and restrained.

Being Fair, Accurate, and Logical

In the next two chapters, you will learn more about specific techniques you can use when writing either argumentation or persuasion essays. However, whether you are writing argument or persuasion, remember to be accurate and fair. Being persuasive is not a license to mislead your readers. Unfortunately, sometimes both argument and persuasion suffer from logical fallacies. In many cases, writers commit such fallacies unknowingly. Dishonest writers do so intentionally.

Ten Logical Fallacies

Errors in logic, though sometimes subtle and hard to detect, appear in political speeches and advertisements, in television commercials, in newspaper editorials, and even in well-written and sincere arguments of bright college students. Here is a list of ten logical fallacies that you should look for when reading or listening to argumentation or persuasion and that you should avoid in your own writing:

Generalizations Supported by Insufficient Evidence

Writers sometimes draw conclusions not justified by the amount or kind of information they have gathered. Failing to consider enough or the right kind of evidence can lead to faulty generalizations. Here are a few examples of insufficient evidence:

1. My neighbors never finished high school, but they have built a very lucrative plumbing company. Therefore, the claim that education improves one's chances for success is false.

2. The president will veto a bill lowering tax rates for married couples. Obviously, he doesn't want to help families.

3. The directory assistance operator could not find the name or number of a company that I know is listed. The telephone company should train their employees better.

4. The Supreme Court refused to review a lower court's judgment against the tobacco industry. Obviously, the Supreme Court is antibusiness.

The Straw Man

As the name implies, the straw man is an argument that is weak and easy to knock down. The straw man comes into play when a writer falsely claims that the opposing side supports an idea that is indefensible. The writer then refutes this obviously bad idea and, in the process, casts the opposition in a bad light. The straw man is a pretense; it has little to do with the point being debated, nor does it represent the opponent's views fairly and accurately. In fact, it is often used only to distract readers from valid arguments of the opposition.

> **Your position:** You argue that we should create a plan to force those convicted of violent crime to compensate their victims and their victims' families. You propose that prisons establish small factories in which prisoners must work to earn the money to compensate their victims.

> **Your opponent's position:** Using the "straw man," your opponent argues that you are suggesting a return to the chain-gang system of punishment and that you are in favor of slave labor.

> **Your position:** You argue that people who do not have children in the public school system should pay less school tax than those who do.

Your opponent's position: You are an elitist who cares little for public education and is concerned only with educating the children of the rich, most of whom attend private schools.

Your position: You argue that the government should preserve thousands of acres of untouched wilderness that happen to be located upon huge oil reserves.

Your opponent's position: You care more about trees and wildlife than you do about the consumers who would benefit from cheaper heating oil and gasoline prices.

The Ad Hominem Argument

Ad hominem is Latin for "to the person." When writers indulge in this unethical tactic, they attack the person's character rather than his or her position, logic, opinions, or history.

For example, when John F. Kennedy ran for president in 1962, some unscrupulous people attacked him because he was a Roman Catholic. They ignored the fact that Kennedy had, on numerous occasions, affirmed his commitment to the separation of church and state. When Ronald Reagan ran for governor in California in the 1970s and, again, when he ran for president, some opponents attacked him because he had been an actor, not because of the issues he supported.

You would be arguing *ad hominem* if you claimed that Senator Alvarez cannot represent the interests of families because she is single, or that Representative Kelly will not fight to increase community college funding because he attended a private university. On the other hand, you would be arguing fairly if you mentioned that Senator Alvarez has consistently opposed pro-family legislation or that Representative Kelly has made several speeches arguing for an increase in community college tuition so as to decrease state funding for such schools.

Begging the Question

This fallacy occurs when a writer draws an invalid conclusion from a false assumption or an assumption that cannot be proven. Thus, the writer avoids addressing the real issue or question.

For example, you would be begging the question if you argued that, because Angela is a member of Alcoholics Anonymous, she could not have been the one you saw having a beer at Calhoun's Saloon last night. The false assumption here is that members of Alcoholics Anonymous never fall back into their old habits. The argument begs the question: *Did Angela drink a beer at Calhoun's Saloon last night or not?*

The Red Herring

The red herring distracts the audience from the real issue at hand. It gets its name from a practice used by farmers to protect their newly planted fields from fox hunters and their dogs. Farmers often dragged a red herring along the edge of their fields, where it would leave a strong scent. This scent distracted the dogs and kept them and the hunters from trampling the crops.

Most visibly, red herrings can be found in commercials and advertisements. Automobile commercials picture cars and their drivers winding through beautiful mountain passes as they head toward stunning sunsets; exercise machines are pictured against exotic, tropical landscapes populated by people with perfect bodies; soft drinks are promoted through television spots that picture athletic young people engaged in exciting sports such as rock climbing, hang gliding, or surfing. None of these tells us much about the product. They are selling an image that, like the farmer's red herring, is supposed to draw our attention away from what is really being sold.

One commercial goes so far as to portray a four-wheel-drive vehicle as an adult toy. It suppresses the fact that most people really buy cars for one practical reason—safe and reliable transportation. It encourages the notion of "fun" and, red-herring fashion, distracts us from the reality that, in order to pay for this "toy," we will have to work extra hard and, in most cases, tie ourselves to an all-too-real auto loan that takes three, four, or five years to pay off!

Non-Sequitur

A Latin term, *non sequitur* translates roughly to "does not follow." It occurs when a statement does not proceed logically from the previous statement. Here are two examples:

> My ninety-year-old grandfather smokes a pack of cigarettes a day. Therefore, smoking can't be bad for one's health.

> Gina finds accounting a challenging course. She will never succeed in business.

Neither of these statements follows directly from the other. The fact that one man who smokes heavily has reached the age of ninety in no way contradicts the massive research proving that, for the vast majority of people, smoking is a health hazard. Similarly, although Gina finds accounting challenging, the time and effort she puts into studying this subject may enable her to master it eventually. On the other hand, a mastery of sophisticated accounting principles may not be necessary to succeed in the kind of business she plans to pursue.

False Analogy

An argument based on a false analogy incorrectly assumes that because situations may be alike in some respects, the same rules, principles, or approaches apply to both or the same conclusions can be drawn about both. You would be guilty of false analogy if you wrote:

> Jason's father had a heart attack at fifty; Jason will suffer from heart disease, too.

The analogy presumes that the only cause for heart disease is heredity. But what if Jason has a healthy lifestyle, while his father smokes heavily, fails to exercise, and eats a high-fat diet?

Either … Or Fallacy

Failing to see all the aspects or all the choices associated with a problem or situation can result in an "either…or" fallacy. You would create such a fallacy if you wrote:

> The only way students get through Professor Wilson's history class is to cheat on her exams or resign themselves to a D.

Of course, no matter how demanding the instructor, there is a third alternative: to study hard.

Erroneous Cause

In Latin, this is called the *post hoc, ergo propter hoc* ("after this; therefore, because of this") fallacy. It occurs when the writer assumes that because one thing follows another, it must necessarily have resulted from (been caused by) the other. Here's an example:

> The college restricted student parking to Lots A and B last semester, so Rachel got more parking tickets than ever.

The reason Rachel got more parking tickets was not directly caused by the college's decision to restrict student parking. After all, Lots A and B might be sufficient to hold all student cars. Rachel's getting more tickets is a direct result of her choosing to park where she shouldn't.

Going-Along or Bandwagon Fallacy

This fallacy assumes that an idea, action, or proposal must be valid if a great many people support or believe in it. Recall that in some primitive cultures, the majority of people believed in the practice of human sacrifice to appease their gods. You would be falling into this logical error if you wrote:

> Overwhelming popular support for the new mayor shows she can achieve greatness.

Read More on the Web

To learn more about fallacies, go to these two sites:

- "Fallacies," The Writing Center, University of North Carolina: writingcenter.unc.edu/tips-and-tools/fallacies/

- "Master List of Logical Fallacies," University of Texas at El Paso: http://bvtlab.com/6gCKd

Shutterstock

Chapter

12

Argumentation

Chapter Outline

As you learned in the introduction to section 5, a formal, written **argument** is very different from a loud or excited discussion about a point of controversy. In fact, when it comes to writing, *argumentation* is an attempt to prove a point—also known as a *thesis* or *proposition*—or to support an opinion through calm, if vigorous, logic and the presentation of evidence.

12.1 Mastering Deduction and Induction

Traditionally, two types of thinking have been used in argumentation: induction and deduction. Both support an opinion or belief the writer expresses in a **conclusion**. Of course, since all persuasive essays begin with logical arguments, as you will see in chapter 13, induction and deduction are also important components of persuasion. Deduction moves from general premises to a limited conclusion; induction moves from specific evidence to a general conclusion.

12.1a Deduction: From General to Specific

Deduction draws a limited conclusion from premises, or ideas upon which that conclusion is based. Using deduction, writers start with a general statement or idea they believe their readers agree with. Next, they apply a specific case or example to that statement. Finally, they draw a limited conclusion from the two. The logical structure through which this is done is called a **syllogism**. You would be using deduction if you argued:

> **General statement:** All full-time students can use the college exercise room free of charge.
>
> **Specific case:** I am a full-time student.
>
> **Conclusion:** Therefore, I can use the college exercise room free of charge.

Jessica Vaughan uses deductive reasoning in "Sanctuary Policies Mainly Protect the Predators," an essay that appears later in this chapter. Her argument goes something like this:

> **General statement:** Immigration officials depend on local police to identify criminal aliens.
>
> **Specific case:** Sanctuary policies forbidding police to identify criminal aliens make it harder to reduce crime.
>
> **Conclusion:** No city should be allowed to be a sanctuary for criminal aliens.

12.1b Induction: From Specific to General

Inductive thinking involves collecting separate facts, reasons, or other pieces of evidence and then drawing a conclusion from that information. Say you come down with a case of food poisoning—cramps, vomiting, a headache, the works. When you call the other five people with whom you shared a pot of stew the night before, each tells the same horrible story about cramps, vomiting, and so on. It's safe to say the stew made you sick. That's your conclusion. Support for that conclusion comes in the form of six separate tales of woe. As a matter of fact, **induction** is the kind of thinking behind conclusion and support, one of the methods of developing paragraphs and essays explained in chapter 2. Papers developed through this method express a conclusion or opinion in a formal thesis statement.

argument
A type of writing that relies on logic and concrete evidence to prove a point or support an opinion.

conclusion
A principle, opinion, or belief that a writer supports or defends by using convincing information.

deduction
A kind of reasoning used to build an argument. Deductive thinking draws conclusions by applying specific cases or examples to general principles, rules, or ideas. You would be thinking deductively if you wrote: "All students must pay tuition. I am a student. Therefore, I must pay tuition."

syllogism
The logical structure through which a writer uses deduction. To create a syllogism, a writer makes a general statement, then applies a specific case or example to that statement, and then draws a limited conclusion from the two.

induction
A kind of reasoning used to build an argument. Inductive thinking draws general conclusions from specific facts or pieces of evidence. If you heard the wind howling, saw the sky turning black, and spotted several ominous clouds on the horizon, you might rightly conclude by induction that a storm was on its way.

Here's an example of a paragraph developed using the conclusion-and-support method. It is based on information from an essay by Joseph Menfi:

> *There are several easy ways to save energy at home.* First, remember to shut off all electricity when leaving a room. This includes lights, televisions, radios, electric coffee makers, fans, electronic tablets, and computer equipment. Next, set the thermostat no higher than 70 degrees Fahrenheit in winter and no lower than 74 degrees in summer. Make sure doors and windows stay closed during cold and hot weather to lessen strain on heaters and air conditioners. Install weather stripping around leaky doors and windows to prevent inside air from escaping. Finally, watch hot water consumption. A three-minute shower is enough to clean a human body thoroughly. In addition, fix leaking faucets, especially those dripping hot water, and toilets that continue to run.

The first sentence (in italics) is the *conclusion*, which is expressed as the paragraph's topic sentence: "There are several easy ways to save energy at home." This is the point the writer wishes to make, the proposition he wishes to prove. The rest of the paragraph provides evidence to *support that conclusion*.

Induction and deduction are two different ways of reasoning, but they almost always complement each other. In fact, logical, well-supported arguments often reflect both types of thinking.

12.2 Reasoning Through the Use of Claims and Warrants

British rhetorician Stephen Toulmin designed a technique for argumentation and persuasion that he believed was close to the way people actually debate. Resembling the inductive method in some ways, Toulmin's "Layout of Argumentation" is applicable to any discipline, issue, or question. As you read about his method, you may decide to incorporate parts of it into your own brand of argumentation or persuasion. It contains six major components:

1. *Data:* Information that leads the writer/speaker to take a position on a question or issue

2. *Claim:* A statement of the position being defended: the thesis

3. *Warrants:* Major ideas used to support a claim—Warrants must relate directly and logically to the claim.

4. *Backing:* Evidence used to support or prove a warrant—Backing comes in three forms: expert testimony, data and statistics, and concrete illustrations.

5. *Reservation:* Statement anticipating an opposing argument before it decreases your argument's credibility

6. *Qualifier:* Statement or phrase that restricts the scope of the claim

As you can see, Toulmin's *claim* is another word for the thesis, the point you are trying to prove. However, he also uses *warrants* in his "Layout of Argumentation"; these are major ideas that relate directly to and support the claim. In some ways, they resemble topic sentences, or ideas that support a thesis. They, in turn, are developed via concrete evidence, which Toulmin calls *backing*. There are three types of warrants:

1. The *authoritative warrant* relies on theories, opinions, and studies put forth by experts. Such information may be paraphrased, summarized, or quoted directly. For example, if you claimed that listening regularly to classical music increases IQ in children, you might quote experts in child development, psychologists, and testing specialists. You might also make reference to scientific studies conducted by universities, professional organizations, or government agencies.

2. The *substantive warrant* uses a variety of rhetorical modes—especially the conclusion-and-support, comparison/contrast, cause/effect, and process analysis methods—to present concrete facts, data, and illustrations that support the claim. For example, you might explain how (process analysis) listening to classical music affects the human brain in the formative stages. You might compare (comparison/contrast) those effects to the effects of listening to other kinds of music or of being exposed to no musical stimulation. In addition, you can cite hard statistics found in professional studies (conclusion and support) to help develop this warrant. Or you can describe the effects of classical music documented in case studies (illustration) of children who were exposed to the works of Mozart and Beethoven on a regular basis.

3. The *motivational warrant* can be used if the writer feels knowledgeable about the nature of the audience, their needs, and their opinions. In such cases, he or she might appeal to their personal and professional beliefs, their values, their pride, or even their self-interest. As you might assume, the motivational warrant is particularly useful when writing persuasion, which is discussed in the next chapter. For example, if you know that you are writing to the parents of school-age children, you will want to link exposure to classical music to the child's performance on standardized mathematics tests in elementary and high school. You might also point out that, later on, such scores will surely help the student's chances of being admitted to a prestigious college and even of being awarded an academic scholarship.

Read More on the Web

For more on the Toulmin method, refer to the following:

- "Toulmin Model of Argument," Bakersfield College: http://bvtlab.com/J6u8b

- "The Toulmin Method," Colorado State University: http://bvtlab.com/F6567

12.3 Developing Ideas in an Argument

In chapter 2, you learned that there are several ways to develop a paragraph or essay, whether your purpose is to explain, to argue, or to persuade. One of the most popular is conclusion and support, the method you just learned about. As the reading selections in this chapter show, however, writers of argument often use a combination of methods to provide evidence that proves a point or supports a proposition (thesis). For example, in "A National Recommitment to Free Speech on Campus Is Long Overdue," Jeff Sessions uses comparison, mentions the opinions of others via direct quotations, and includes examples to make his point. Likewise, Barry Glazer appeals to authority in "The Right to Be Let Alone," when he makes specific reference to the U.S. Constitution and quotes Supreme Court Justice Louis Brandeis. Jessica Vaughan uses statistics found in U.S. Immigration and Customs Enforcement records.

The most important thing to remember about an effective argument is that it is both *logical* and *well supported*. You can use inductive reasoning, deductive reasoning, or both, but your arguments must be reasonable and easy to follow. You can support ideas with examples, facts, statistics, the knowledge or opinions of experts, analogies, comparisons, definitions, firsthand observations, and the like. But your writing must contain enough supportive information to be clear, convincing, and easily understood.

12.4 Establishing Your Authority

Of course, the best way to establish your authority—to show that you are knowledgeable about a subject and that you should be believed—is to amass relevant facts and opinions that show you know what you are talking about. In some cases, there is no need for the author to establish his or her credentials. Jeff Sessions, whose speech appears in this chapter, doesn't need to tell us he is an expert on this topic because his reputation as former attorney general of the United States is widespread. On the other hand, it sometimes helps to remind readers of your credentials and experience.

12.5 Anticipating and Addressing Opposing Opinions

It is always a good idea to think about points of view in opposition to your own. Doing so shows that you are open-minded, that you have considered more than one side, that you have thought out your position and others' as well, and that you are knowledgeable about your subject. In short, it lends authority to your writing. This is very important when writing persuasion, but it also plays a part in argument. One way to address an opposing opinion is simply to show that it lacks validity, when this is the case. Another effective way is to recognize the validity of your opponent's argument while offering your own as the more realistic or logical alternative. To succeed, each of these tactics requires you to demonstrate to your reader your fair and accurate understanding of the opposing view. Barry Glazer's "The Right to Be Let Alone" and the two essays discussing sanctuary cities in this chapter illustrate ways in which to deal with opposing arguments.

12.6 Visualizing Strategies for Argument

Read the following document, which was originally published by BalancedPolitics.org in 2012. It contains examples of both deductive and inductive reasoning.

Should Senators' and Congressional Representatives' Terms of Office Be Limited?

Yes	No
1. The current Congress is a dismal failure and is in desperate need of new ideas, procedures, and influence.	1. Term limits kick out the good leaders who may deserve to stay in office for excellent work.
2. Political machines (local party voting infrastructure, redistricting power, media contacts, etc.) of incumbents make it very difficult to remove them from office.	2. Every job has a learning curve, and Congress is no exception. Any new politicians would have to go through that when they come into office.
3. Lobbyists and big-money campaign contributors usually direct their efforts at those in power, making it difficult for a new candidate to get off the ground.	3. Politicians who leave office take with them a lot of experience and contacts that are essential to get things done. New leaders would have to develop these from scratch.
4. Politicians are less likely to be focused on special interests and pork-barrel spending if they cannot stay in office indefinitely.	4. Politicians who are in the last term of office are more likely to ignore the will of the people since they don't face the wrath of the electorate in the future.
5. Lack of term limits leads to a system of seniority, meaning those who have spent the most time in office gain more power (in committees, procedures, etc.); consequently, politicians focus on staying in office, districts and states don't receive equal power in Congress, and fresh new elected officials have limited ability to make changes.	
6. Term limits lead to a "citizen" Congress, rather than one filled with lawyers and career politicians.	

(Continues)

Should Senators' and Congressional Representatives' Terms of Office Be Limited?

Yes	No
7. There is less chance for corruption of government officials if time in office is limited; new politicians are less likely to have the knowledge to exploit the system for personal gain and are more skeptical of lobbyists and special interests.	
8. Politicians in their last term of office are more likely to ignore politics and media criticism to target what's best for the country, and they can work to establish tangible accomplishments that will build on their legacy.	

Here is an example of deduction based on the table; it combines ideas from items 1 and 2 in the "Yes" column:

General statement: Congress desperately needs new ideas to enact important legislation.

Specific case: Political machines make it hard to unseat incumbents and elect politicians with new ideas.

Conclusion: Term limits should be enforced so that nonincumbents with new ideas will enact important legislation.

This next example is of induction, combining ideas from items 1 through 4 in the "No" column:

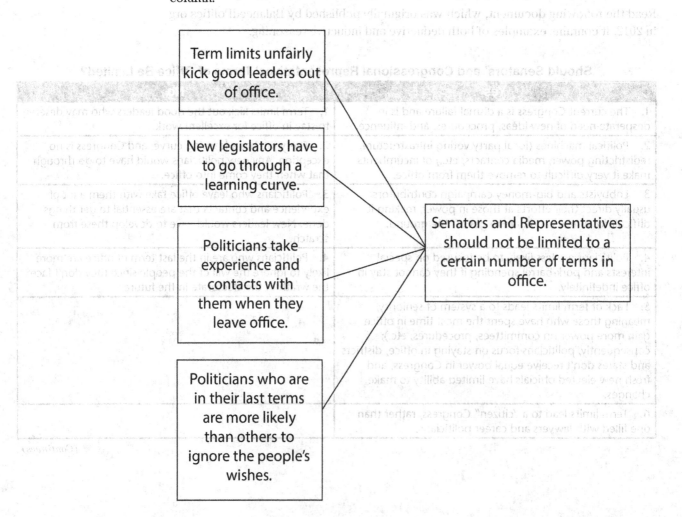

12.7 Revising Argument Papers

An argument requires logical and clear writing, and such writing takes hard work. Barry Glazer, a student whose essay appears in this chapter, wrote several drafts of a paper on individual rights before he arrived at a version with which he was satisfied. His rough draft contained the germ of an idea and several good examples, but by the time Glazer wrote his final draft, the paper had been transformed into a first-rate argument paper. Even the title had changed.

Barry Glazer, It Ain't Nobody's Business but My Own—Rough Draft

Help? In what way?

Government is supposed to help people, not hurt them. Those we elect to public office are there to make things better for everyone.

What kinds of things?

However, many of them are doing things that annoy and frighten me. What I do if I am not

Expand? Clarify?

hurting anybody, the government should stay out of my private affairs. What I do, if it isn't causing anyone else harm, is no one's business but my own.

Support this claim?

If I have a terminal disease, I should be allowed to kill myself or get a doctor to help me do so. If I am driving home late at night the police have no right to stop me just because I am young and look suspicious. Recently, I was walking around the block at three in the morning and the police stopped and questioned me. Yet, all I was doing was taking a late-night stroll.

They don't? Support this claim.

What kinds of things?

Yes, we need government to take care of important things. But the government and the police should stay out of people's lives when it is none of their business. They should just leave us alone.

Glazer, The Right to Be Let Alone—Final Draft

Revises title.

Appeals to authority.

Government is the instrument of the people, says the United States Constitution. Those to whom the people entrust power are charged

with maintaining justice, promoting the general welfare, and securing the blessings of liberty for us all. Recent newspaper opinion polls,

Explains how government "is supposed to help people."

Explains what he meant by "things that annoy and frighten me."

however, suggest that many Americans are dissatisfied with the men and women running our communities, our states, and our nation. More and more of us have come to believe that our leaders are isolated from the realities ordinary people face. We fear we are losing control.

Instead of helping to alleviate this feeling of impotence, however, politicians and bureaucrats continue to make and enforce regulations that constrain our lives and constrict our freedoms. To help people regain a rightful measure of control, government—whether national, state, or local—should stay out of our private lives

Appeals to authority.

whenever possible. As Supreme Court Justice Louis Brandeis noted, Americans treasure their "right to be let alone."

Supports claim with convincing details.

There is no reason for the government to interfere in our lives if our behavior does not adversely affect others or if there is no immediate necessity for such interference. Were I in the throes of terminal cancer or facing the horror of Alzheimer's disease, I should be allowed to kill myself. Faced with the agonizing degeneration of my memory and personality, I would probably want to end my life in my own way. But the government says this is illegal. Indeed, were I to call upon a doctor to assist me on this final quest, she would stand a good chance of being charged with murder.

Appeals to emotions.

Supports claim by appealing to authority.

The government should also stay out of an individual's life if there is no reason to believe he is doing wrong. The Bill of Rights protects us from unlawful searches and seizures. Yet, if I drive home from work in the early morning, I stand a reasonable chance of being stopped without cause at a police roadblock. While armed, uniformed officers shine flashlights in my face, I can be subjected to questions about

*Appeals to readers'
self-interest and values.*

*Defines government's
true role.*

my destination and point of origin. I can be told to produce my papers and to step out of my car. I can be made to endure the embarrassment of performing tricks to prove my sobriety. Allowing the police such powers is hardly in keeping with our government's mission to promote justice, security, and liberty.

*Supports preceding
statement.*

Clearly, government is a necessity. Without it, we would face anarchy. Yet, those who roam the halls of power should remember from where their power originates and should find ways to reduce the burden of unnecessary regulations heaped on the backs of the American people.

*Closes with a memorable
statement.*

12.8 Practicing Strategies for Argument

12.8a Practice Deduction

Read the following general statements. Think of a specific case or example that applies to each. Then draw a conclusion. Write your responses in the spaces provided.

1. **General statement:** Students who have had three years of high school mathematics can enroll in Math 101.

   Specific case:_____

   _____

   _____

   Conclusion: _____

   _____

   _____

2. **General statement:** Students who commute to college by car must buy parking decals.

   Specific case:_____

   _____

   _____

   Conclusion: _____

   _____

3. **General statement:** Cars more than five years old must be inspected once per year.

Specific case:_____

_____

_____

_____

Conclusion: _____

_____

_____

_____

4. **General statement:** People whose families have a history of heart disease should have annual coronary examinations.

Specific case:_____

_____

_____

_____

Conclusion: _____

_____

_____

5. **General statement:** People who don't vote should not complain about the way government is run.

Specific case:_____

_____

_____

_____

_____

Conclusion: _____

_____

_____

12.9 Reading Selections

12.9a The Right to Be Let Alone

Author Biography

Barry Glazer became interested in writing when he enrolled in a basic-skills composition class during his first semester in college. He went on to major in history and English, to become editor of his college newspaper, and to take a bachelor's and a master's degree. He is now a college English professor.

Preparing to Read

1. This essay is logical, clear, and well developed, but it goes beyond pure argument and often appeals to the emotions.

2. Glazer organizes his work around three principles by which he would restrict the government's ability to interfere with our lives. Identify these principles as you read "The Right to Be Let Alone."

3. Louis Brandeis, mentioned in paragraph 2, was associate justice of the U.S. Supreme Court from 1916 to 1939. He was a champion of individual rights.

Vocabulary

adversely (adverb)   Negatively.

alleviate (verb)   Lessen, relieve.

anarchy (noun)   Chaos, disorder.

bureaucrats (noun)   Government officials.

constrain (verb)   Restrain, limit, hold back.

constrict (verb)   Bind, choke, squeeze.

endure (verb)   Suffer, bear, submit to.

entrust (verb)   Give to for safe keeping.

impotence (noun)   Lack of power.

reflect (verb)   Think.

refrain (verb)   Stop, cease, avoid.

throes (noun)   Agony, pain.

The Right to Be Let Alone

Barry Glazer

Government is the instrument of the people, says the United States Constitution. Those to whom the people entrust power are charged with maintaining justice, promoting the general welfare, and securing the blessings of liberty for us all. Recent newspaper opinion polls, however, suggest that many Americans are dissatisfied with the men and women running our communities, our states, and our nation. More and more of us have come to believe that our leaders are isolated from the realities ordinary people face. We fear we are losing control.

Instead of helping to alleviate this feeling of impotence, however, politicians and bureaucrats continue to make and enforce regulations that constrain our lives and constrict our freedoms. To help people regain a rightful measure of control, government—whether national, state, or local—should stay out of our private lives whenever possible. As Supreme Court Justice Louis Brandeis noted, Americans treasure their "right to be let alone."

There is no reason for the government to interfere in our lives if our behavior does not adversely affect others or if there is no immediate necessity for such interference. Were I in the throes of terminal cancer or facing the horror of Alzheimer's disease, I should be allowed to kill myself. Faced with the agonizing degeneration of my memory and personality, I would probably want to end my life in my own way. But the government says this is illegal. Indeed, were I to call upon a doctor to assist me on this final quest, she would stand a good chance of being charged with murder.

The government should also stay out of an individual's life if there is no reason to believe he is doing wrong. The Bill of Rights protects us from unlawful searches and seizures. Yet if I drive home from work in the early morning, I stand a reasonable chance of being stopped without cause at a police roadblock. While armed, uniformed officers shine flashlights in my face, I can be subjected to questions about my destination and point of origin. I can be told to produce my papers and to step out of my car. I can be made to endure the embarrassment of performing tricks to prove my sobriety. Allowing the police such powers is hardly in keeping with our government's mission to promote justice, security, and liberty.   4

Finally, the government should refrain from creating unnecessary burdens for the American people. It should stay out of a person's private business if such involvement burdens the individual unnecessarily or unfairly. Recently, my faithful dog Linda was dying. Because of years of abuse at the hands of her previous owner, she was no longer able to walk and had to be carried in my arms. At that time, the dog warden knocked on my door and threatened me with fines for my continued refusal to license the animal. When I told him that Linda was unable to walk, let alone leave my property, he threatened to return with the police.   5

Similarly, when I wanted to convert my garage into a den, I was overwhelmed by official red tape. The cost of construction permits and of measures to meet complex building codes cost more than the lumber, wall board, and other supplies for the project. Another example of governmental red tape became evident when I attempted to enroll in a Japanese language course at a community college. I was told the state required that I take a mathematics placement test or pass a course in elementary algebra first!   6

Clearly, government is a necessity. Without it, we would face anarchy. Yet those who roam the halls of power should remember from where their power originates and should find ways to reduce the burden of unnecessary regulations heaped on the backs of the American people.   7

Read More on the Web

For more on topics discussed in this essay, read the following:

- Louis D. Brandeis Legacy Fund for Social Justice: www.brandeis.edu/legacyfund/bio.html

- "Students: Your Right to Privacy," American Civil Liberties Union: www.aclu.org/other/students-your-right-privacy

- Privacy Rights Clearinghouse: www.privacyrights.org/

- "Rights Versus Wishes," Walter Williams: www.creators.com/read/walter-williams/04/16/rights-versus-wishes

Questions for Discussion

1. What one sentence in this essay best expresses Glazer's purpose and central idea?

2. In "Preparing to Read," you learned that the author defends three principles by which he would limit government interference. What are these principles?

3. What method of development does Glazer rely on most?

4. Pick out vocabulary that appeals to the reader's emotions.

5. Why does Glazer bother to tell us that Justice Brandeis is the source of the quotation in paragraph 2 (and of the essay's title)?

6. Find examples of deductive reasoning in this essay. In your own words, construct a syllogism that explains each example.

7. Where does the author address an argument that an opponent might use to dispute his?

Thinking Critically

1. What might Glazer argue if he were told that, in order to receive any government benefit, he would have to be drug tested. Support your answer with direct reference to this reading selection.

2. If you haven't done so already, read "How the Lawyers Stole Winter" (chapter 9) and "A National Recommitment to Free Speech on Campus Is Long Overdue" (this chapter). On what points might Glazer agree and disagree with the authors of these essays?

Suggestions for Journal Entries

1. Glazer calls up several examples from experiences similar to those you or people like you might have had. Use focused freewriting to narrate an incident that explains how a government rule or regulation interferes with the right of privacy. Interpret the word *government* broadly; write about the federal, state, local, or college regulation you most disagree with. You might even address a rule followed by your family, your athletic team, or other group to which you belong.

2. Play the role of Glazer's opponent by responding to at least one of the examples he uses to support his thesis. Explain why requiring licenses for all dogs is reasonable, why strict building codes are important, why the police should have the right to stop and question drivers, why doctors should not be allowed to help terminally ill patients commit suicide, or why states should set academic standards in public colleges.

3. Even if you agree with Glazer, you may know of instances in which people welcome government "interference." List as many examples of such beneficial interference as you can.

12.9b A National Recommitment to Free Speech on Campus Is Long Overdue

Author Biography

Jeff Sessions (1946–) served as Attorney General of the United States under President Donald Trump from 2017 to 2018. He also served as Senator from Alabama from 1997 to 2017. He had previously served as U.S. Attorney for the Southern District of Alabama and as Attorney General of Alabama. In September 2017, Sessions delivered the following speech to students and faculty at Georgetown University Law School in Washington, D.C.

Preparing to Read

1. Sessions mentions a number of legal authorities such as Justices Antonin Scalia, Robert Jordan, Louis Brandeis, and Oliver Wendell Holmes Jr. Find information about these men on the Internet and be prepared to explain their views on free speech.

2. Among other things, the Alien and Sedition Acts (paragraph 33), which were signed by President John Adams in 1798, made it a crime to make false statements against the federal government.

Preparing to Read (Continued)

3. Academic freedom, as defined by *Encyclopedia Britannica*, is "the freedom of teachers and students to teach, study, and pursue knowledge and research without unreasonable interference or restriction from law, institutional regulations, or public pressure."

4. In paragraph 22, Sessions mentions an "Orwellian-named anti-fascist" group. George Orwell set his novel *1984* in a world where the government abused the meanings of words—often affixing the opposite meanings to them—as a way to exert dictatorial control over the people. Sessions believes that *Antifa*, the "anti-fascist" group to which he refers, is anything but what its name indicates.

Vocabulary

capitulate (verb)   Surrender.

closest approximation of (noun phrase)   Closest thing to.

contentious (adjective)   Quarrelsome, argumentative.

infringe (verb)   Violate, impinge.

intractable (adjective)   Stubborn.

permeates (verb)   Soaks, saturates.

proselytizers (noun)   Supporters of, preachers for.

seminal (adjective)   Groundbreaking, determining.

A National Recommitment to Free Speech on Campus Is Long Overdue

Jeff Sessions

Thank you students for letting me take part in this important conversation with you.   1

As you embark on another school year, you and hundreds of your peers across this campus will,   2
we hope, continue the intellectual journey that is higher education. You will discover new areas of knowledge; you will engage in debates great and small; many of your views will be challenged and some changed. You will—if your institutions follow our nation's historic cultural and education traditions—pursue truth while growing in mind and spirit. In short, we hope you will take part in the right of every American: the free, robust, and sometimes contentious exchange of ideas.

As you exercise these rights, realize how precious, how rare, and how fragile they are. In most   3
societies throughout history and in so many that I have had the opportunity to visit, such rights do not exist. In these places, openly criticizing the government or expressing unorthodox opinions could land you in jail or worse.

Let me tell you about one such example. It occurred one autumn when a few idealistic university   4
students came together as a group to advocate for a deeply felt political creed. Wanting to recruit others to their cause, they staked out some ground on a campus walkway popular with students and approached them as they passed.

They said things like: "Do you like freedom? Do you like liberty?" and then they offered to these   5
passersby a document they revered and believed stood for these ideals: the U.S. Constitution. These young proselytizers for liberty did not block the walkway, did not disrupt surrounding activities, and did not use intimidation or violence to press their cause.

Nevertheless, a local government official labeled this behavior "provocative" and in violation of government policy. When the young people bravely refused to stop, citing their right to free speech, the local official had them arrested, handcuffed, and jailed.

6

This troubling incident could have occurred under any number of tyrannies where the bedrock American ideals of freedom of thought and speech have no foothold. But this incident happened right here in the United States, just last year, at a public college in Battle Creek, Michigan. A state official actually had students jailed for handing out copies of the United States Constitution.

7

Freedom of thought and speech on the American campus are under attack.

8

The American university was once the center of academic freedom—a place of robust debate, a forum for the competition of ideas. But it is transforming into an echo chamber of political correctness and homogenous thought, a shelter for fragile egos.

9

In 2017, the Foundation for Individual Rights in Education surveyed 450 colleges and universities across the country and found that 40 percent maintain speech codes that substantially infringe on constitutionally protected speech. Of the public colleges surveyed, which are bound by the First Amendment, fully one-third had written policies banning disfavored speech.

10

For example, at Boise State University in Idaho, the Student Code of Conduct prohibits "[c]onduct that a reasonable person would find offensive." At Clemson University in South Carolina, the Student Code of Conduct bans any verbal or physical act that creates an "offensive educational, work or living environment."

11

But who decides what is offensive and what is acceptable? The university is about the search for truth, not the imposition of truth by a government censor.

12

Speech and civility codes violate what the late Justice Antonin Scalia rightly called "the first axiom of the First Amendment," which is that, "as a general rule, the state has no power to ban speech on the basis of its content." In this great land, the government does not get to tell you what to think or what to say.

13

In addition to written speech codes, many colleges now deign to "tolerate" free speech only in certain, geographically limited, "free speech zones." For example, a student recently filed suit against Pierce College, a public school in southern California, alleging that it prohibited him from distributing Spanish-language copies of the U.S. Constitution outside the school's free speech zone.

14

The size of this free speech zone? 616 square feet—an area barely the size of a couple of college dorm rooms. These cramped zones are eerily similar to what the Supreme Court warned against in the seminal 1969 *Tinker v. Des Moines* case about student speech: "Freedom of expression would not truly exist if the right could be exercised only in an area that a benevolent government has provided as a safe haven."

15

College administrators also have silenced speech by permitting "the heckler's veto" to control who gets to speak and what messages are conveyed. In these instances, administrators discourage or prohibit speech if there is even a threat that it will be met with protest. In other words, the school favors the heckler's disruptive tactics over the speaker's First Amendment rights. These administrators seem to forget that, as the Supreme Court put it in *Watson v. City of Memphis* more than 50 years ago, "constitutional rights may not be denied simply because of hostility to their assertion or exercise."

16

This permissive attitude toward the heckler's veto has spawned a cottage industry of protestors who have quickly learned that school administrators will capitulate to their demands. Protestors are now routinely shutting down speeches and debates across the country in an effort to silence voices that insufficiently conform with their views.

17

A frightening example occurred this year at Middlebury College. Student protestors violently shut down a debate between an invited speaker and one of the school's own professors. As soon as the event began, the protestors shouted for 20 minutes, preventing the debate from occurring.

18

When the debaters attempted to move to a private broadcasting location, the protestors—many in masks, a common tactic also used by the detestable Ku Klux Klan—pulled fire alarms, surrounded the speakers, and began physically assaulting them. In short, Middlebury students engaged in a violent riot to ensure that neither they nor their fellow students would hear speech they may have disagreed with.

19

Indeed, the crackdown on speech crosses creeds, races, issues, and religions. At Brown University, a speech to promote transgender rights was cancelled after students protested because a Jewish group cosponsored the lecture. Virginia Tech disinvited an African American speaker because he had written on race issues and they worried about protests disrupting the event.   20

This is not right. This is not in the great tradition of America. And, yet, school administrators bend to this behavior. In effect, they coddle it and encourage it.   21

Just over a week ago, after the Orwellian-named "anti-fascist" protestors had successfully shut down numerous campus speaker events in recent months with violent riots, Berkeley was reportedly forced to spend more than $600,000 and have an overwhelming police presence simply to prove that the mob was not in control of the campus.   22

In advance, the school offered "counseling" to any students or faculty whose "sense of safety or belonging" was threatened by a speech from Ben Shapiro—a 33-year-old Harvard trained lawyer who has been frequently targeted by anti-Semites for his Jewish faith and who vigorously condemns hate speech on both the left and right. In the end, Mr. Shapiro spoke to a packed house. And to my knowledge, no one fainted, no one was unsafe. No one needed counseling.   23

Yet, after this small victory for free speech, a student speaking to a reporter said in reaction, "I don't think Berkeley should host any controversial speakers, on either side." That is, perhaps, the worst lesson to take away from this episode.   24

I know that the vast majority of students like you at the Constitution Center need no lecture on the dangers of government-imposed group think. But we have seen a rash of incidents often perpetrated by small groups of those students and professors unable or unwilling to defend their own beliefs in the public forum.   25

Unfortunately, their acts have been tolerated by administrators and shrugged off by other students. So let us directly address the question: Why should we worry that free speech is in retreat at our universities?   26

Of course, for publicly run institutions, the easy answer is that upholding free speech rights is not an option, but an unshakable requirement of the First Amendment. As Justice Robert Jackson once explained: "If there is a fixed star in our constitutional constellation, it is that no official, high or petty, can prescribe what shall be orthodox in politics, nationalism, religion, or other matters of opinion."   27

But even setting aside the law, the more fundamental issue is that the university is supposed to be the place where we train virtuous citizens. It is where the next generation of Americans are equipped to contribute to and live in a diverse and free society filled with many, often contrary, voices.   28

Our legal heritage, upon which the Founders crafted the Bill of Rights, taught that reason and knowledge produced the closest approximation to truth—and from truth may arise justice. But reason requires discourse and, frequently, argument. And that is why the free speech guarantee is found not just in the First Amendment, but also permeates our institutions, our traditions, and our Constitution.   29

The jury trial, the right to cross-examine witnesses, the Speech or Debate Clause, the very art and practice of lawyering—all of these are rooted in the idea that speech, reason, and confrontation are the very bedrock of a good society. In fact, these practices are designed to ascertain what is the truth. And from that truth, good policies and actions can be founded.   30

It was the power of Dr. King's words that crushed segregation and overcame the violence of the segregationists. At so many times in our history as a people, it was speech—and still more speech—that led Americans to a more just, more perfect union.   31

The right to freely examine the moral and the immoral, the prudent and the foolish, the practical and the inefficient, and the right to argue for their merits or demerits remain indispensable for a healthy republic. This has been known since the beginning of our nation.   32

James Madison knew this when, as part of his protest against the Alien and Sedition Acts—the speech codes of his day—he said that the freedom of speech is "the only effectual guardian of every other right."   33

And, in a quote that I am reminded of daily in this job, Thomas Jefferson knew this when he said in words now chiseled in the stone of his memorial, "I swear upon the altar of God eternal hostility against every form of tyranny over the mind of man."   34

Soon you will be the professor, the university president, the Attorney General, and even the President of the United States. And you will have your own pressing issues to grapple with. But I promise you that no issue is better decided with less debate, indifference, and with voices unheard.

35

There are those who will say that certain speech isn't deserving of protection. They will say that some speech is hurtful—even hateful. They will point to the very speech and beliefs that we abhor as Americans. But the right of free speech does not exist only to protect the ideas upon which most agree at a given moment in time.

36

As Justice Brandeis eloquently stated in his 1927 concurrence in *Whitney v. California*: "If there be time to expose through discussion the falsehood and fallacies, to avert the evil by the processes of education, the remedy to be applied is more speech, not enforced silence."

37

And let me be clear that protecting free speech does not mean condoning violence like we saw recently in Charlottesville. Indeed, I call upon universities to stand up against those who would silence free expression by violence or other means on their campuses.

38

But a mature society can tell the difference between violence and unpopular speech, and a truly free society stands up—and speaks up—for cherished rights precisely when it is most difficult to do so.

39

As Justice Holmes once wrote: "If there is any principle of the Constitution that more imperatively calls for attachment than any other it is the principle of free thought—not free thought for those who agree with us but freedom for the thought that we hate." For the thought that we hate.

40

And we must do so on our campuses. University officials and faculty must defend free expression boldly and unequivocally. That means presidents, regents, trustees and alumni as well. A national recommitment to free speech on campus is long overdue. And action to ensure First Amendment rights is overdue.

41

Starting today, the Department of Justice will do its part in this struggle. We will enforce federal law, defend free speech, and protect students' free expression from whatever end of the political spectrum it may come. To that end, we are filing a Statement of Interest in a campus free speech case this week and we will be filing more in the weeks and months to come.

42

This month, we marked the 230th anniversary of our Constitution. This month, we also marked the 54th anniversary of the 16th Street Baptist Church bombing in Birmingham. Four little girls died that day as they changed into their choir robes because the Klan wanted to silence the voices fighting for civil rights. But their voices were not silenced.

43

Dr. Martin Luther King Jr. would call them "the martyred heroines of a holy crusade for freedom and human dignity," and I urge you to go back and read that eulogy and consider what it had to say to each of us. This is the true legacy of free speech that has been handed down to you. It was bought with a price. This is the heritage that you have been given and which you must protect.

44

So I am here today to ask you to be involved to make your voices heard—and to defend the rights of others to do the same.

45

For the last 241 years, we have staked a country on the principle that robust and even contentious debate is how we discover truth and resolve the most intractable problems before us.

46

Your generation will decide if this experiment in freedom will continue. Nothing less than the future of our Republic depends on it.

47

Read More on the Web

To learn more about the topic Sessions addresses in his speech, try these two sites:

- "Campus Rights," Foundation for Individual Rights in Education (FIRE): www.thefire.org/campus-rights/

- "Is Free Speech Really Challenged on Campus?" by Julian E. Zelizer and Morton Keller, *The Atlantic*: http://bvtlab.com/8B76N

Questions for Discussion

1. Sessions employs contrast in his introduction. What is the effect of his doing so?

2. What is Sessions' thesis?

3. Point out places where Sessions includes scholarly research to support his opinion.

4. Discuss and explain the significance of a few of the anecdotes (short narratives that illustrate a point) he uses. Are they effective in helping to bolster his argument?

5. Name the legal authorities mentioned in this article, particularly the judges Sessions mentions. Who are these people, and how does citing them help make this speech convincing?

6. Where does the author address an opposing argument? Explain what he says to dismiss it.

7. Where does he use what Toulmin would call a "qualifier"? Explain this "qualifier."

8. What is the effect of Sessions waiting until paragraph 7 to explain that the events in the previous few paragraphs occurred in Michigan?

Thinking Critically

1. What does Sessions mean by a "shelter for fragile egos" (paragraph 9)?

2. What is the "heckler's veto" mentioned in paragraph 17?

3. How does Sessions respond to the question he asks in paragraph 26? How does that answer help him advance his argument?

Suggestions for Journal Entries

1. Justice Holmes once wrote: "If there is any principle of the Constitution that more imperatively calls for attachment than any other it is the principle of free thought—not free thought for those who agree with us but freedom for the thought that we hate." Make a list of political or moral ideas, statements, or methods of expression that you hate. Are there any of these that you would argue should never be allowed to be expressed? If so, which ones? Why?

2. Should free speech never be regulated? What about falsely crying "Fire!" in a crowded theater? What about child pornography? What about the revealing of troop movements and other military secrets? Make a list of the kinds of speech that some might want to censor. Then, briefly explain why you agree or disagree that at least one of these should be regulated.

12.9c **To Build or Not to Build the Wall: Opposing Views**

Introduction

The *Seraphim* is the student voice of Notre Dame Prep in Scottsdale, Arizona. In 2016, shortly after the election of Donald Trump to the presidency, the editors of that newspaper published the following two editorials, representing both sides of an important issue that Trump had addressed in the campaign: building a wall on our southern border as a response to the influx of undocumented immigrants over the past several decades.

Preparing to Read

1. Note that the authors use questions to introduce this pair of essays. Using a question is one of the ways to write introductions, as mentioned in chapter 3. Refer to that chapter for ways to begin and conclude your own essays.

2. Both essays number the reasons behind the opinion they support. This is an effective way to organize an argumentative essay and to help the reader absorb and evaluate each reason.

3. In addition to quoting students at Notre Dame Prep (NDP), both essays use information from authorities, both people and organizations. Look for these as you evaluate each of these editorials.

Vocabulary

amnesty (noun)   Pardon, reprieve.

apprehension (noun)   Capture, arrest.

destabilizes (verb)   Threatens, disrupts, undermines.

inhibit (verb)   Reduce.

logistical (adjective)   Having to do with organizing and planning.

traverse (verb)   Cross over.

To Build or not to Build the Wall

Editors of **The Seraphim**

Donald Trump's desire to build a wall along the U.S.-Mexico border is well-known throughout most of the modern world. This wall would be about 2,000 miles long, extending from Tijuana to Brownsville, and, according to Trump, be paid for by Mexico.   1

His plan would have many monetary, political and logistical hurdles to overcome, but even if it succeeds, will the wall live up to Trump's expectations? What exactly are the pros and cons of building the wall?   2

Build It!

1. It would put people to work and help the economy.   3
Building this massive wall would undoubtedly need a lot of manpower. NDP senior Larkin Moore   4
said he feels that the construction of this wall would put many Americans in need of jobs to work: "It could be a good thing for the country. It would definitely put a lot of people to work."

Some economists predict that the wall would not only create millions of jobs, but it also would   5
stimulate the economy and allow more taxes to be collected.

According to the U.S. Department of Numbers, there were 7,787,000 unemployed Americans   6
in October, a 4.9 percent unemployment rate. The construction of the wall could lower this amount more, allowing more Americans to make money, provide for their families, all the while helping to boost the economy and make the country stronger.

2. It would protect the culture of the United States.   7
According to the North American Congress on Latin America, building the wall would secure   8
America's position in having complete control over the "no man's land" separating the U.S. from Mexico. Not only this, but a wall would protect the wealth of the U.S. and definitively mark the territory in which … people belong.

Mexico is substantially poorer than the United States. A border wall would protect against immigrants seeking better economic opportunity and leave those opportunities for the American people to take advantage of instead.   9

"We should build it to not only stop immigration from illegal immigrants but to preserve our American heritage, too," freshman Jacob Muniz said.   10

The wall also would help prevent against major culture shift and help preserve the way of life as it is already. This has been a concern from the time the United States became a country. Today, some [immigrants] refuse to assimilate to U.S. culture, which takes away the great pride we have for what it means to be an "American."   11

3. Border fences have worked in the past.   12
Despite the common idea that a wall would be completely ineffective, statistics show that a physical deterrent will lower the number of illegal immigrants who traverse the border every year.   13

For example, in 1996, Congress passed a bill that required the construction of a fence in the San Diego corridor of California along the coast. After four years, the apprehension of illegal immigrants fell by 95 percent as the Mexicans moved further east to avoid the fence, according to the Conservative Review organization.   14

By this logic, if the U.S. were to build a fence that spanned its entire southern border, the immigrants would have nowhere to go but back to their own country. This fence, of course, is not foolproof, but it would surely inhibit illegal immigration into the United States.   15

4. It would reduce drug trafficking.   16
Drug trafficking is one of the most harmful effects of illegal passage into the U.S. Traffickers often use illegal immigrants as transportation for drugs, such as cocaine and marijuana, into the U.S.   17

According to the website for Immigration to the United States, authorities seized 1.13 million pounds of cocaine and 6.9 million pounds of marijuana in 2005. This was only the amount of illegal drugs seized, likely only a fraction of what truly crossed the border during this period.   18

Senior Jake Goldring said he thinks that a wall would help stop this influx of drugs: "You have to stop the drugs from coming into the States. It's just not good for the people who live on this side of the border." Though a wall might not completely solve this problem, it will inhibit the fluid movement of harmful drugs across the border.   19

5. National Border Patrol is overwhelmed.   20
According to Brandon Judd, president of the National Border Patrol [NBP] Council, "We have the highest number of illegal aliens in custody in history.... We are simply overwhelmed."   21

These numbers have surpassed 200,000 people and are still growing.   22

This is not surprising, as promises of possible amnesty in the recent presidential race pulled people from all over Mexico and Central America to the U.S.-Mexico border. The people and equipment that the NBP has at its disposal are simply not enough.   23

Since border patrol agents cannot be everywhere, this is where a wall could help. An always-present physical barrier could stop illegal immigrants when the agents are occupied elsewhere. As mentioned above, this plan is by no means foolproof, but it will doubtlessly discourage illegals from crossing into the U.S.   24

Don't Build It!

1. Who will fund it?   25
As Trump stated in his campaign, Mexico will be responsible for the monetary resources needed to build his wall. However, President Enrique Peña Nieto said, "No way" and has flat out refused to accept this. Furthermore, a recent report from Mexico's finance minister announced a decreased budget of $234 billion for 2017, which does not include the $12 billion needed for Trump's 50-foot-high concrete wall.   26

"We shouldn't build it because chances are we will have to pay for it, and it will be a waste of money," said sophomore Michael Minniti.   27

So, if Mexico doesn't pay for it, and Trump decides to go through with construction, American taxpayers likely will foot the bill. Our guess is that many Americans wouldn't be too happy about this.   28

2. **There are too many geographical issues.**

According to *Business Insider*, the wall would have many geographical issues that engineers would have to work around. The wall would traverse through Indian Territory in southern Arizona, which could cause some disputes with those living near the border. The wall would also have to have run-off spots to prevent flooding in areas all over Arizona, New Mexico and California. 29

"I don't think it'll work," said theology teacher Bev Fraser. "It's not realistic for 2016. It's not going to achieve his goal. The price on humanity is more than perhaps we are willing to pay. He may need to explore other options," she said. 30

Furthermore, in California, the construction risks interfering with the sensitive movements of the sand dunes. Not only this, but many conservation groups have sued over parts of the existing border, so building an even more obstructive wall could result in more lawsuits and complications. 31

3. **Immigrants would just find ways around it.** 32

Building a massive concrete wall won't stop illegals from getting creative. Former Immigration and Customs Enforcement officer Laura Peña said in a *USA Today* article that the wall would "fail miserably." In her many visits to the already existing border wall, she said she has seen several portions blasted out by smugglers, only to be rebuilt with American taxpayer money. What would stop them from doing the same thing? 33

Another obvious way around it is going under via tunnel. As former illegal immigrant Magdaleno Santos puts it in an interview with *The Atlantic*, "He can build a wall, but we'll just build a tunnel." 34

Peña says we need to focus on using modern technology and other means of tracking and securing the border from smugglers and illegals. A wall wouldn't put eyes where they are needed. 35

"Trump can build the tallest wall that he can, and we will find a way to fly over it, just like birds," said another illegal who has successfully crossed the border dozens of times. 36

4. **Illegal immigrants work for less than American workers.** 37

Many immigrants who enter the country illegally do so to find work, and they often work for much less than the average American. According to *theatlantic.com*, Neal Fisher, a subcontractor said, "If Bobby [an American] comes looking for a job, he's going to want $24 an hour, and these guys will do the same work for $12." 38

This is a common theme for immigrant workers throughout America who want any job they can get, and it makes a strong case against prohibiting immigration into the U.S. 39

If the U.S. were to build a wall, these immigrant workers would not be available to employers in the U.S. This would have a strong effect on the economy, as the vacant jobs would be filled by Americans who expect higher pay than their illegal counterparts. 40

5. **Building a wall would send unfriendly signals to the rest of the world.** 41

The U.S. has almost always been a country of immigrants. The nation prides itself on diplomacy and thrives because of international economic transactions. As described by *The Huffington Post*, placing a physical barrier between Mexico and the United States would jeopardize our relationship with one of our closest allies and trading partners. 42

A wall on the southern border of the U.S. contradicts the history of this country. This wall would send a signal that is quite literally the opposite of that represented by the Statue of Liberty, which has stood as one of our country's strongest symbols for a very long time. 43

Building a wall would also be against Catholic social teachings. 44

The Pope told journalists earlier this year, "A person who thinks only about building walls, wherever they may be, and not building bridges, is not Christian. This is not the gospel." Last month, he said, "Fear—as well as being a good deal for the merchants of arms and death—weakens and destabilizes us, destroys our psychological and spiritual defenses, numbs us to the suffering of others. In the end it makes us cruel." 45

He added that the "best antidote to fear is mercy, and that it's much more effective than walls, iron bars, alarms and weapons. And it is free." 46

A wall cuts off this country's ability to accept the truly desperate people emigrating from Mexico. 47

Read More on the Web

For more on the border wall controversy, try these websites:

- "Yes, Build the Wall," Robert J. Samuelson, *Washington Post* [opinion]: http://bvtlab.com/8Zh77

- "Mr. President, Don't Build That Wall," *Chicago Tribune* editorial board: http://bvtlab.com/3PTg8

Questions for Discussion

1. Those opposed to the wall quote Pope Francis in item 5 of their essay. Although one might see the Pope's words as an emotional appeal, they illustrate deductive reasoning. What might be the Pope's major statement, his specific case, and his conclusion?

2. Those in favor of the wall use deductive reasoning in item 5 of their essay. Explain in your own words how they construct that argument; provide a general statement, a specific case, and a conclusion.

3. Find another place in either essay where deductive reasoning is used.

4. The "claims" for both essays are clearly stated in their titles. Making reference to the Toulmin method, identify one "authoritative warrant" in each piece.

5. Using Toulmin's terminology once again, identify at least one place in each piece where the writers use "substantive warrants."

6. Do the writers who favor the wall address an opposing argument? Where?

7. Where is an opposing argument addressed in the piece opposing the wall? What do the writers of that essay say to counter that argument?

8. Find a place in either essay in which a qualifier is used. Recall that a qualifier is a statement that restricts the scope of the claim.

Thinking Critically

1. In item 2 of the essay favoring the wall, the writers say that "some [immigrants] refuse to assimilate to U.S. culture, which takes away the great pride we have for what it means to be an 'American.'" What do you believe this statement means? Given your interpretation, do you agree with it? Why or why not?

2. The two opinions are written with a distinct audience (readers) in mind. Pick out evidence from both pieces that might tell us about that audience.

Suggestions for Journal Entries

1. Choose a controversial issue of national or international importance that interests you. Doing library or Internet research, list arguments both pro and con. Some issues you might want to choose are found in the following list:

   - Is medical research on animals immoral?

   - Should children be inoculated against contagious diseases, even against their parents' wishes?

   - Are zoos cruel and immoral?

   - Should members of the U.S. Congress be subject to term limits?

   - Is the Electoral College an unfair way to elect a president?

   - Can violent video games cause people to become violent?

   - Are humans causing global warming?

2. Summarize the two opinions by making a list of arguments found in each. Try to express each argument in one sentence. Then, via the Internet, research at least two other articles on the building of a wall on our southern border. Again, make a list of the major arguments, for or against, that you find through this research.

12.9d Sanctuary Cities: Opposing Views

Author Biographies

Jessica Vaughan (1965–) is director of Policy Studies at the Center for Immigration Studies. Before joining the Center, she worked as a U.S. diplomat in Belgium and in Trinidad and Tobago. Her articles have appeared in the *Washington Post*, the *Economist*, and elsewhere.

   Raul A. Reyes is an attorney and television commentator in New York City. He has published in the *New York Times*, the *Washington Post*, the *Houston Chronicle*, and elsewhere.

   Both these pieces were posted on *Politics.org* in 2015.

Preparing to Read

1. Kate Steinle, mentioned in both essays, was murdered in San Francisco on July 1, 2015. The man accused of the crime is an undocumented immigrant.

2. Secure Communities, mentioned by Vaughan, is a federal program designed to deport undocumented immigrants; it is administered by the Department of Homeland Security. The program was discontinued in 2014 but reinstated in January 2017.

3. Both Vaughan and Reyes address opposing arguments. Look for places in which they do so as you read their essays.

Vocabulary

advocacy (noun)   Support of, backing.

egregious (adjective)   Atrocious, unspeakable, shocking.

haven (noun)   Safe place.

horrific (adjective)   Horrifying, terrible.

micromanagement (noun)   Close control of a process by someone in charge.

obstruct (verb)   Block, hinder, impede.

randomness (noun)   Chance, unpredictability.

scapegoating (noun)   Singling out in order to blame or condemn.

Sanctuary Policies Mainly Protect the Predators

Jessica Vaughan

1   The senseless murder of Kate Steinle by an illegal alien with seven prior felony convictions and five deportations has focused public attention on the problems created when local sanctuary policies prioritize protecting illegal alien residents over the public interest.

2   Immigration laws are not obsolete relics that are unworthy of enforcement; they are crucial to preserving jobs and security for Americans. Sanctuary policies are especially harmful when they are imposed by local law enforcement agencies. When criminal aliens are released back to the street instead of removed to their home country, they have the opportunity to continue preying on the community, creating needless new victims.

3   The Steinle episode was not an isolated incident. According to Immigration and Customs Enforcement (ICE) records, from January 1 to August 31, 2014, more than 8,100 immigrant offenders who were sought by ICE in sanctuary jurisdictions were released instead of turned over for deportation. Just in this eight-month period, approximately 1,900 of these deportable convicts re-offended 4,300 more times, racking up 7,500 new charges. The subsequent crimes included murder, sexual assault on young children, violent rape, burglary, assault, dangerous drug offenses, and drunken driving. More than 1,000 are still at large in our communities.

4   Some will argue over whether immigrants commit more or fewer crimes than Americans (there's no solid evidence either way). That's irrelevant; the more important policy issue at hand here is how we handle those immigrants who have committed crimes. ICE agents do not patrol the streets looking for illegal aliens; they depend on local officers to find out about those who are committing crimes. If local officers will not turn over illegal aliens who have already been arrested for something else, that means ICE agents have to go get them where they live and work—a much more resource-intensive process that also puts the agents and the public at risk if something goes wrong.

5   Others insist that sanctuary policies are needed so that immigrants will not be afraid to report crimes. This is a myth spread by illegal alien advocacy groups that has no basis in reality. The claim has been refuted in numerous studies, including a 2009 analysis by the University of Virginia and the Police Executive Research Forum, which found no decline in crime reporting by Hispanics after the implementation of a tough local enforcement program.

6   Sanctuary policies do nothing to build trust between immigrants and police. They do not improve access to law enforcement services; that is better accomplished with anonymous tip lines and officers who speak the languages of the community. On the contrary, sanctuary policies destroy the larger public trust that the laws will be faithfully enforced to preserve the quality of life for all.

The Obama administration has made it clear that it will not act against sanctuary jurisdictions. Instead, the president has moved to make the whole country a sanctuary by giving work permits to illegal aliens and drastically scaling back enforcement for all but the most egregious criminal offenders. And he terminated perhaps the most effective enforcement program ever (Secure Communities) and replaced it with a new program that explicitly allows localities to obstruct ICE. 7

Therefore it is up to Congress and state lawmakers to take prompt action against sanctuaries. States can enact laws prohibiting sanctuary policies and direct agencies to notify ICE when they are aware of deportable offenders. 8

Congress must clarify that sanctuary policies are not only unwise, but contrary to law. They need to specify that local agencies must not obstruct, but assist when ICE seeks custody of a deportable offender, and provide legal protection to local officers who assist in enforcement. In addition, those state and local governments that persist in sanctuary policies must be barred from receiving federal homeland security and law enforcement funding. 9

Lawmakers should reject proposals, like a bill introduced by Sen. Chuck Grassley (R-Iowa), which mirrors many local sanctuary policies that spell out the specific crimes that trigger cooperation for enforcement. Such micromanagement sends the message that all other illegal aliens are to be tolerated. 10

The most comprehensive solution to both the sanctuaries and the Obama administration's dismantling of enforcement can be found in South Carolina Republican Rep. Trey Gowdy's Davis Oliver Act, which was passed by the House Judiciary Committee in March. This bill gives ICE and local governments the tools for effective enforcement. It has been endorsed by the National Sheriffs Association and many individual law enforcement leaders. Congress should join them in supporting these efforts to reverse our slide into "Sanctuary Nation." 11

Sanctuary Cities Make Us All Safer

Raul A. Reyes

Before the July 4th weekend, a tragedy occurred in San Francisco. Kate Steinle, 32, was walking with her father on a busy pier when she was allegedly shot and killed by Juan Francisco Lopez-Sanchez, an undocumented immigrant from Mexico with a long rap sheet. 1

The randomness of this crime shocked the nation, and led to a renewed debate over so-called "Sanctuary Cities" like San Francisco. Several of the leading Republican candidates for president, including Donald Trump, Jeb Bush and Rand Paul, have since weighed-in against sanctuary cities. 2

Not so fast. "Sanctuary Cities" is a misleading label that has caused a great deal of confusion. The term is a misnomer for those cities and towns that prefer that the federal government handle immigration enforcement. It is wrong to attack sanctuary cities because their policies actually help make our cities and towns safer. 3

What is a sanctuary city? The most accurate definition of a sanctuary city is a city that has decided to leave immigration enforcement to the federal government, so that their own police force can concentrate on fighting crime. That's hardly a radical idea; it is a principle that the Supreme Court affirmed in *Arizona v. U.S.* (2012), which found that only the federal government had authority over immigration enforcement. 4

There are several hundred sanctuary cities across the country, including Los Angeles, New York, San Francisco and Seattle. Although the policies of sanctuary cities vary from place to place, it might surprise people to know that sanctuary cities do not provide a haven for undocumented immigrants. Federal immigration laws are enforced in sanctuary cities just as in non-sanctuary cities. In a sanctuary city, undocumented immigrants can still be rounded up and deported by the government. Local officials in sanctuary cities can still report undocumented immigrants to the government. 5

One way to understand why sanctuary cities are a smart idea is to look at their history. Starting in the 1990s, when illegal immigration was on the rise, the federal government rolled out several programs whereby local law enforcement would assist them in catching and removing undocumented immigrants. As it turned out, local police didn't want to do this—and with good reason. 6

State and local police are not trained in immigration law and procedures. Holding undocumented immigrants in local jails proved to be very expensive for cities, and led to additional liability and legal issues. Local police forces found that they didn't have enough time to do their main job, protecting their communities from crime, because they were chasing after people for immigration violations, which are civil infractions. 7

Worst of all, when local police were turned into immigration agents, it had a detrimental effect on community relations. A 2013 study by the University of Illinois-Chicago found that increased (local) police involvement in immigration enforcement eroded trust of law enforcement among both undocumented and legal immigrants. 8

As a result of this confusion and pushback, cities turned to sanctuary policies, which in effect tells the federal government: You do your job, we'll do ours. 9

Sanctuary cities are doing something right. Crime in San Francisco, for example, is lower than in several other non-sanctuary cities. Sanctuary cities make sense because they allow undocumented immigrants to report crime and volunteer as witnesses with local police, which makes everyone safer. Consider that a long list of cities, mayors, crime victims and law enforcement groups have spoken out against a proposal by House Republicans to withhold federal monies from sanctuary cities. 10

Steinle's death was a horrific crime and her killer must be brought to justice. But we shouldn't let an emotional response to this crime blind us to the realities of the case. Steinle's death occurred because of a bureaucratic error; given his criminal history, Lopez-Sanchez should never have been released by San Francisco police. 11

So instead of scapegoating sanctuary cities, lawmakers should be taking steps to ensure better communication between federal and local law enforcement. Besides, we don't need more immigration enforcement (our government spends more on immigration enforcement than all other federal law enforcement agencies combined); we need smarter and better immigration enforcement. 12

Until our country tackles comprehensive immigration reform, sanctuary cities make our cities safer. It is misguided, uninformed and myopic to attack them as bad policy. 13

Read More on the Web

More on this subject can be found in the following online essays:

- "Sanctuary Cities: Top 3 Pros and Cons": http://bvtlab.com/B879c

- "Sanctuary Cities Violate Federal Law," James Walsh: http://bvtlab.com/QDF77

Questions for Discussion

1. Where does Vaughan address opposing arguments? How does she respond to them?

2. Where does Vaughan use an authoritative warrant?

3. Where does Reyes appeal to authority?

4. Read paragraph 4 in Vaughan's essay. Explain the use of deduction in this paragraph.

5. How does Reyes define the term "sanctuary city"? Why does he think the term is misleading?

6. How does Reyes respond to Vaughan's argument that "Sanctuary policies do not build trust between immigrants and police"?

7. How does Reyes respond to Vaughan's argument that local authorities should "turn over [to ICE] illegal aliens who have already been arrested"?

8. What does Vaughan want Congress to do in regard to sanctuary cities? What does Reyes want lawmakers to do in regard to sanctuary cities?

Thinking Critically

1. In paragraph 9, Vaughan suggests that sanctuary cities should be barred from receiving "federal homeland security and law enforcement funding." Use the Internet to find out how much financial support your city or state receives from the federal government for homeland security and law enforcement.

2. Why does Vaughan object to Sen. Grassley's bill, which she mentions in paragraph 10? Why does she support the bill introduced by Rep. Gowdy (paragraph 11)?

3. Why does Reyes use the world *allegedly* in paragraph 1 of his essay?

Suggestions for Journal Entries

1. Write a summary of the arguments for and against sanctuary cities as explained by Vaughan and Reyes. You can find out more about writing summaries in Getting Started.

2. If you were an undocumented immigrant, would you contact ICE or the police to report another immigrant who you knew had committed a crime? Why or why not?

12.10 Suggestions for Sustained Writing

1. Like Barry Glazer, many of us have strong opinions about the right of privacy. Perhaps you discussed some of your own in your journal after reading "The Right to Be Let Alone."

   Write an essay arguing that some government regulations interfere unnecessarily with the way we live. Use examples of federal, state, or local laws you think limit our freedom. If you interpret the word *government* broadly, you can even focus on rules enforced by your college, your family, or another group to which you belong.

   One way to introduce this essay is to show readers that you are reasonable. Begin by admitting that some rules are necessary and should be fully enforced. For example, voice your support for tough laws against child abuse, rape, and drunk driving. At the end of your introduction, however, state your thesis forcefully: explain that some rules enforced by the government, by your family, or by another group are inappropriate and should be abolished. Then, like Glazer, develop your essay with examples from your experiences or from those of people you know or have read about.

   Read your first draft carefully, adding details as you go along to make your opinions clear and convincing. Then, edit your work thoroughly.

2. Read "The Right to Be Let Alone" again. Then, write an essay in which you play Glazer's opponent. Argue that although some government regulations are inappropriate, the ones he criticizes should be strictly enforced.

   One way to organize your paper is to defend the regulations Glazer attacks in the same order he presented them. As such, you might outline the body of your essay like this:

   • Terminally ill patients should not have the right to commit suicide.

   • Police have the right to stop and question motorists at random.

   • Pets should be licensed.

- Strict building codes are necessary.

- Colleges should enforce academic requirements.

    Develop each point in concrete and convincing detail using any of the methods mentioned earlier in this chapter. After completing several drafts, write a conclusion that restates your thesis or that uses one of the methods for closing explained in chapter 3. As always, be sure your final draft is organized and edited well.

3. Reread the notes you made in response to the "Suggestions for Journal Entries" following Sessions' "A National Recommitment to Free Speech on Campus Is Long Overdue." If you haven't responded to both of these journal prompts already, do so now. Then, use these notes in an essay that argues *one* of the following:

- Some circumstances require limiting free speech.

- Free speech should be limited under no circumstances.

    Whether you choose the first or second of these theses, make sure to address (support or deny) one or more of the ideas that Sessions articulates in his speech. Also, check your work to make sure you have avoided logical fallacies like those explained in the introduction to section 5. You can do this after you write your first draft. In the second draft of your paper, you might want to include library or Internet research to support your argument.

    As with all other papers, revise for organization and content. Then, check to make sure that you have documented all researched material according to MLA style or any other style your instructor requires. You can find more about MLA style in appendix 2, "The Research Process."

    Finally, edit and proofread carefully. Grammar, mechanical, spelling, and other such problems weaken an argument's effectiveness and lose the readers' trust.

4. In the first of the "Suggestions for Journal Entries" after the essays published in *The Seraphim* on building a border wall, you were asked to find research on a controversial issue of national or international importance in which you are interested. For example, you might have chosen to research whether zoos are immoral or whether the Electoral College is an unfair way to elect a president. Whatever the issue you have chosen, write an essay that takes a stand on this question, one way or the other, pro or con.

    If this assignment does not interest you, write an essay expressing your own views on constructing a wall on our southern border. You can use the two opposing essays from *The Seraphim* as a source of inspiration, facts, and ideas. If you responded to the first of the "Suggestions for Journal Entries" after those essays, you have probably gathered information to start your paper, and you have probably also done research to collect even more material.

    Whichever option you choose, remember to cite all researched information using MLA style (explained in appendix 2, "The Research Process") or another documentation style that your instructor requires.

5. Read the notes you made for both journal prompts after reading the two essays on sanctuary cities by Vaughan and Reyes. Use this information in an essay that argues for or against the idea that sanctuary cities should be penalized by losing

federal funding. If that doesn't interest you, write an essay in which you argue that sanctuary cities should lose funding only under certain circumstances. Explain those circumstances clearly in your thesis.

As you draft your paper, be certain to identify and respond to opposing arguments. You can do this by exposing those arguments as false or illogical or by admitting that they have value while arguing that yours are even stronger and more compelling. If you wish, devote your introductory paragraph or paragraphs to doing this. Then, use the rest of your paper to developing your own point of view.

If needed, research this subject on the websites listed under "Read More on the Web." Make sure to cite your sources using MLA format, which is explained in appendix 2, "The Research Process," or another format required by your instructor.

ACKNOWLEDGMENTS

Messerli, Joe. "Should Senators' and Congressional Representatives' Terms of Office Be Limited? In a Nutshell." BalancedPolitics.org. Reprinted with permission.

Reyes, Raul A. "Sanctuary Cities Make Us All Safer." *Politics.org*, 31 July 2015. Reprinted with permission of the author.

Sessions, Jeff. "A National Recommitment to Free Speech on Campus Is Long Overdue." Speech at Georgetown Law School, Georgetown University, Washington, D.C., 27 Sept. 2017.

"To Build or Not to Build the Wall" [editorial]. *The Seraphim*, 7 Dec. 2016, Notre Dame Prep School, Scottsdale, Arizona. Reprinted with permission of the authors.

Vaughan, Jessica. "Sanctuary Policies Mainly Protect the Predators." *Politics.org*, 31 July 2015. Reprinted with permission of author.

Shutterstock

Chapter 13

Persuasion

Chapter Outline

As you learned in the introduction to section 5, effective **persuasion** always begins with a solid argument based on evidence that is presented logically. However, persuasion goes beyond pure argument. Writers engage in persuasion not only to prove a point but also to convince readers to adopt their point of view and to act on it.

So, if you want to convince readers that your stand on a controversial issue has merit or that a conclusion you have drawn about a complex issue is correct, a strong argument is probably enough. If you need to change people's attitudes or urge them to action, however, logic and evidence might not be enough to get the job done. You will need to be persuasive. Thus, while remaining clear-headed and fair, you might also want to appeal to the reader's values, pride, emotions, and even self-interest. Before doing so, you will have to consider the attitudes and opinions of your audience.

13.1 Appealing to the Readers' Values and Pride

Let's say your college is having a problem with litter, which makes the campus unsightly and even causes minor sanitation problems. As a member of the Student Senate, you are asked to write an open letter to the student body. Your letter will appear on the front page of the college newspaper accompanied by pictures of a parking lot where people have emptied ashtrays or left empty bottles; of a lunchroom table covered with trash; and of classrooms in which papers, used pens, a stray sneaker, and other refuse have been left behind.

Your job is to persuade students to clean up after themselves and to stop trashing the campus. You begin by explaining that common courtesy and concerns over health and sanitation demand that people deposit their garbage properly. The campus is a public place, you argue, and as such it demands that those who use it respect it and keep it clean for others. You also explain that keeping the grounds clean is easy only if everyone participates.

After reading your letter, you decide that your opinions are reasonable and fair. No one would disagree with them. In fact, your letter might be the very model of an effective written argument. However, you realize that it will not convince people to act on your recommendations—it simply does not go far enough.

The next step is to appeal to your readers' values and pride. You start by addressing their sense of fellowship, their pride in being members of an academic community. Remind them that they are college students, not adolescents who need to be taught table manners. You can also appeal to their self-image by explaining that the way students behave reflects their respect—or lack of respect—for the college, for professors, for classmates, and for themselves.

13.2 Appealing to the Readers' Emotions

If you are dealing with an especially hard-to-convince group, ask them to put themselves into the shoes of other students, of faculty, and of visitors (not to mention the janitorial staff) who enter the cafeteria to find tables and floors covered with soiled plates and napkins, half-eaten sandwiches, and dirty coffee cups. Express your disgust over the cigarette butts, empty bottles, and paper bags dumped in the parking lots. Complain about yogurt containers, aluminum cans, and other debris left in student lounges. In the process, use colorful images and concrete nouns, as well as strong verbs, adjectives, and adverbs, to get your point across and shake up your audience. Use figures of speech: ask your readers not to turn the place into an academic "pigsty," or compare the cafeteria at day's end to a "small village that has been looted and trashed by invading barbarians." You will see several excellent examples of speech that appeals to the emotions in Wilfred Owen's "Dulce et Decorum Est," a poem that appears in section 13.7.

persuasion
A type of writing that supports an opinion, proves a point, and convinces the reader to act.

13.3 Appealing to the Readers' Self-Interest

Often appealing to the readers' self-interest is the only way to move an especially obstinate audience. Try arguing that the dirtier the campus, the more unpleasant it is to be there, and remind your fellow students of the amount of time each of them spends on campus. You might even suggest that it is easier to study and learn in a clean, attractive setting than in a dump! More important, explain that a dirty campus must be cleaned up and that this increases the cost of janitorial services. Of course, higher operating costs translate into higher tuition levels, so students might have to work longer hours to pay for college, or their parents might have to sacrifice a bit more to send them there.

13.4 Anticipating and Addressing Opposing Opinions

You learned in chapter 12 that anticipating and responding to an opposing argument is important to making your point. Doing this is even more important when engaging in persuasive writing. When you argue, you need show only that although other opinions have merit, your case is the strongest. When it comes to persuasion, however, you are asking readers to make a choice and to act on that choice. If they have any doubt that your opinion stands out as the strongest and wisest, they will not follow your lead, and they may, in fact, decide to do nothing. As you read the selections that follow, try to find places where writers address and respond to opposing arguments. More important, make use of this practice whenever you write to persuade.

13.5 Establishing Your Authority

Again, you read in chapter 12 that when writing argument papers, it is important to gain the confidence of your readers by convincing them you know what you are talking about. This is even more important when writing persuasively. If readers are going to follow your lead and act as you suggest, they will have to trust in your knowledge. As with all writing, the best way to show you are knowledgeable is to use concrete facts—hard evidence—to support your opinions. In addition, you might want to explain the source of your knowledge of a particular topic or problem. In "Education Is the Priority," student Nicholle Palmieri persuades her readers that working too many hours can often interfere with one's studies. She establishes her authority by explaining that while working in the dean's office, she encountered too many students who had failed to make academics their priority and, as a result, were about to flunk out!

13.6 Using Conciliation—The Rogerian Approach

As you learned earlier, it is always appropriate to anticipate opposing arguments and to recognize their validity when possible. Sometimes, however, you will have to go even further. In some cases, you will be writing or speaking to an audience whose positions on a particular issue are so solidified that nothing you say will change minds. Think about writing to or addressing an audience whose views on subjects such as abortion, gun control, war in the Middle East, or homosexuality are diametrically opposed to yours. In such cases, an approach developed by psychologist Carl Rogers might be helpful. Rogers believed that before people who hold entrenched positions can begin to discuss issues productively, some conciliation must be made. His method involves the following:

13.6a Establish Common Ground

You will first need to prove to your audience not simply that you understand and appreciate their position but that you also accept it as viable. One way to do this is to establish common ground by identifying points on which you can agree. For example, say you were to write a letter to your college newspaper arguing for the creation of a foreign-language graduation requirement for students in all majors. It's a good bet that most of your readers oppose adding new graduation requirements. So, you might first explain the following:

- Like your readers, you are enrolled in a curriculum already packed with requirements, and you know that adding more requirements will make it even more demanding.

- Adding requirements might prevent both you and your readers from taking a few electives particularly relevant to your individual career plans.

- Adding requirements might delay graduation and add tuition costs for you and your readers.

- Taking a foreign language will yield no immediately measurable benefit for either you or them.

You can then start to present arguments in favor of requiring foreign languages by explaining the importance of learning about other cultures, the emergence of a global economy, the advantages of using a foreign language when traveling and the need to communicate with people of other cultures both in English and in their languages in order to promote international understanding.

13.6b Use Nonthreatening Language

It's one thing to tell an audience of gun-control opponents that their right to own guns is the thing that is causing so much crime; it's another to explain that limiting the right to own guns will decrease violent crime and make their lives safer. The first statement is negative; the second, far more positive. The same is true of this pair:

Threatening: If we do not improve homeland security and impose stricter security regulations at airports, in bus and train terminals, and in public buildings, the events of 9/11 will be repeated.

Non-threatening: Strengthening homeland security and instituting careful screening procedures at airports, in bus and train terminals, and in public buildings will make the country safer.

13.6c Express Opposing Views Accurately and Fairly

Let's say that you are opposed to the enactment of an on-campus speech policy that the college administration is introducing in order to enforce professional decorum in academic discussions, to protect the institution from the legal repercussions of slanderous and libelous statements made by employees or students, and to make the library a quieter place to study. You could certainly argue that any speech policy, albeit benign in purpose and design, would limit the students' constitutional right to free speech. However, it would probably be unfair and inaccurate to characterize this policy as an attempt to limit student participation in class, to prevent people from speaking out against college policies and regulations, or to treat students as if they were high school adolescents.

13.7 Visualizing Strategies for Persuasion

The following antiwar poem was written by Wilfred Owen (1893–1918), a British soldier who witnessed the horror of trench warfare in World War I. The title is Latin for "It is sweet and fitting." The last lines, taken from the Roman poet Horace, translate to "It is sweet and fitting to die for one's country."

Dulce et Decorum Est

Uses an ironic title.

Opens with a startling image; uses figures of speech.

Bent double, like old beggars under sacks,
Knock-kneed, coughing like hags, we cursed through sludge,
Till on the haunting flares we turned our backs
And towards our distant rest began to trudge.

Men marched asleep. Many had lost their boots
But limped on, blood-shod [shoed in blood]. All went lame; all blind;
Drunk with fatigue; deaf even to the hoots
Of tired, outstripped Five-Nines that dropped behind.

Uses vivid verbs and adjectives.

Uses vivid verbs; creates effective simile.

Gas! Gas! Quick, boys!—An ecstasy of fumbling,
Fitting the clumsy helmets just in time;
But someone still was yelling out and stumbling,
And floundering like a man in fire or lime.
Dim, through the misty panes and thick green light,
As under a green sea, I saw him drowning.

Startles readers with the soldiers' cries.

Creates an extended metaphor to describe horror of gas attack.

Narrates action vividly.

In all my dreams, before my helpless sight,
He plunges at me, guttering, choking, drowning.

Uses adjectives to evoke an emotional response.

Addresses readers directly to get them to change their minds.

If in some smothering dreams you too could pace
Behind the wagon that we flung him in,
And watch the white eyes writhing in his face,
His hanging face, like a devil's sick of sin;
If you could hear, at every jolt, the blood
Come gargling from the froth-corrupted lungs
Obscene as cancer, bitter as the cud
Of vile, incurable sores on innocent tongues,—
My friend, you would not tell with such high zest
To children ardent [eager] for some desperate glory,
The old Lie: Dulce et decorum est
Pro patria mori.

Continues direct address to persuade readers to stop glorifying war.

Obviously, this is a message to stir our passions. Startling words, images, and figures of speech appeal to the emotions and create in us the sense of horror that Owen experienced. The poem's central idea is, of course, that war is *not* sweet and fitting and that we must stop lying about it to children. In the last stanza (verse paragraph), the poet addresses his readers directly. He does this first in order to make his argument strike home more directly, to make it more compelling. He appeals to the readers' self-interest; after all, they too might be asked to send their children to war. He also does this to answer an opposing argument offered by people who have not seen war close up. We lie to children—"ardent for some desperate glory"—when we romanticize war. In no way is it sweet and fitting to die for one's country, and the poet demands that we stop telling them it is.

13.8 Revising Persuasion Papers

Revising any kind of paper takes hard work, but persuasion papers often ask the reader to accomplish tasks or goals or to change deeply held views, so it is important that they be as clear, logical, well supported, and strong as possible. Student Nicholle Palmieri rewrote "Education Is the Priority," which appears in the reading selections for this chapter, to make it the kind of paper she thought would get her fellow students to decrease the emphasis they placed on work in favor of their real goal—to get a college education.

Palmieri, Education Is the *First* Priority—First Draft   ] Redundant title?

About a year ago, I quit my full-time job to return to college. Despite all of the obstacles [Wordy?] that stood in my way, I was lucky enough to find a job in the office of Dean Russell. I say [More information needed?] "lucky" for many reasons. The dean and her administrative assistant, Karen Gormish, are two of the nicest people on the face of the [Cliché?] earth, not to mention the fact that I don't have to worry about my job interfering with my studies. I am able to fit my work hours around my class schedule, and I still manage to get in enough hours to sufficiently cover my bills

[Vague?] Working there, though, has been quite a learning experience. Almost every day, at least one student comes into the office, their eyes scared, pleading to be taken off academic probation. I [Language seems flat, unappealing.] am often the first person that greets them and, [Wordy?] therefore, I have the privilege of seeing their appeals firsthand. Most of these students have failed to make their educations their top priority, [Redundant.] and they are paying for it dearly, and there is one claim that almost all have in common their hours at work have taken precious time away from their [Fused sentence.] college studies. Mind you, most of these kids (I say "kids" because that is what the majority of

Develop the notion
of their being
"kids"?

Use language
that appeals to
emotions?

Add details
about their
situations?
Appeal to
emotions?

Smooth out
syntax?

them are) are living at home and taking about 15 credits per semester. Most of them occupy menial positions at fast-food restaurants or retail stores. They take orders from tough supervisors and work long hours toward their future in hopes of someday having a real job. From what I understand, most of these students work such hours under threat by their managers of being fired if they refuse.

I find fault with this whole scenario. Fifty years ago, it was unheard of that full-time college students should even work two hours a week let alone forty, and that was for a good reason.

Support this
with research?

Palmieri, Education Is the Priority—Final Draft

Removes
redundancy
in title.

Eliminates
wordiness.

Uses more evocative
language.

Adds important
information.

About a year ago, I quit my full-time job to return to college. Despite all of the obstacles in my way, I was lucky enough to find a job as a work-study assistant in the office of Dean Bernadette Russell. I say "lucky" for many reasons. The Dean and her administrative assistant, Karen Gormish, are supportive of students and are willing to accommodate their needs. Because of their support and flexibility, I don't have to worry about my job interfering with my studies. I am able to fit my work hours around my class schedule—not the other way around—and still manage to work enough hours to pay my bills.

Working in the Dean's office has taught me a great deal about college students and their priorities. Almost every day, at least one of them comes into the office, eyes fraught with desperation. They plead to be taken off academic probation, restriction, or suspension. Some beg to have their dismissals lifted and to be allowed to re-enroll.

I am often the first person who greets them

Adds information
about her job.

Replaces cliché with
fresher language.

Adds emphasis.

Uses language that is
clearer, more specific.

Eliminates wordiness.

and, therefore, I see their appeals first. Most of these students have failed to make education their priority, and they are paying for it dearly. In fact, there is one claim that almost all have in common: their hours at work have taken precious time away from their college studies. Mind you, most of these kids (I say "kids" because that is what the majority of them are) are living at home and taking about 15 credits per semester. It is not as if they are seasoned adults who have worked at full-time jobs for fifteen years, have learned to manage their time, and are able to squeeze in a course or two in the evenings and weekends. On the contrary, most of them work at menial positions in fast-food restaurants or retail stores. They take orders from demanding, unreasonable supervisors, and they work asinine, exhausting hours that no human being should have to work—certainly not someone who is attending college classes full-time and devoting hours of endless study toward earning an education and entering a rewarding career. From what I understand, most of these students work such hours under threat of being fired by their managers if they refuse.

I find the whole scenario appalling. Fifty years ago, it was unheard of that full-time college students should even work two hours a week, let alone forty, and that was for a good reason. According to the website of the Division of Student Affairs at Virginia Polytechnic Institute and State University, being a successful college student requires "about two hours of preparation for each hour in the classroom. This means that [a student carrying fifteen credits] has at least a forty-five-hour work week, and is consequently involved in a full-time occupation." At Newbury College, incoming freshmen are advised to attend classes regularly ("This is a must!"), seek

Removes redundancy.

Inserts colon to correct fused sentence.

Defines notion of "kids" by contrasting them with "seasoned adults."

Adds words and information that appeal to emotions.

Smooths out syntax.

Adds supportive information found through research.

help at the Academic Resources Center, visit their professors regularly during office hours, enroll in "the Academic Enrichment Program," and join a student study group. These activities take time—the bulk of your time—but in order to be successful in college you must commit to them. That also means that you will have little time for work outside your studies.

For a full-time student, most college counselors recommend no more than 15 hours of work per week. Consider this: If you fail to nurture your education, you will find yourself on academic probation, restriction, or suspension. Even worse, you might get yourself dismissed, a blow from which it is hard to recover even if you manage to transfer to another college.

Adds direct quotations from authorities.

13.9 Practicing Strategies for Persuasion

Reread Wilfred Owen's poem, "Dulce et Decorum Est," in section 13.7. Pay close attention to the language Owen uses to stir our emotions and appeal to our self-interest. Now use vivid, moving language in a *persuasive* paragraph or two responding to each of the following:

1. Describe the effects of cigarette smoking to persuade someone to kick the habit.

_____

_____

_____

2. Explain the dangers of drinking and driving to a group of teenagers to get them to choose a designated driver whenever they attend parties where alcohol is served.

_____

_____

_____

3. Discuss the serious, even dangerous effects of promiscuous and/or unprotected sex to a group of 18-year-old males. Your ultimate purpose is to persuade them to abstain from sex until marriage.

_____

_____

_____

_____

4. Explain the effects of a high-fat diet and a lack of physical exercise to convince a friend to change his or her lifestyle.

_____

_____

_____

_____

5. Allow readers to visualize the long-term consequences of marrying a particular person, entering a particular career, or making another important life decision. You can either defend or attack this decision.

_____

_____

_____

_____

13.10 Reading Selections

13.10a Education Is the Priority

Author Biography

Nicholle Palmieri wrote this essay as a letter to the editor of her college newspaper. As a work-study assistant in the office of the Dean of Liberal Arts, Palmieri came into contact with many full-time students who were doing poorly in their studies because they had not made education a priority. The vast majority of them had underestimated the amount of time a successful college career demands, and they were spending too many hours at their jobs. Some of them even held full-time jobs while attending college full-time.

Much of what Palmieri discusses here was inspired by her own experiences. As a junior in high school, she held a job as a sales clerk at a store in a large shopping mall. When she told her boss that she could not work overtime because she had to study for an exam the next day, he threatened to fire her. But this student knew her priorities, and she quit before he could do so. Palmieri graduated from Douglass College with a major in English. She is now pursuing a career in publishing.

Preparing to Read

1. Palmieri's title is, essentially, her thesis. As you learned above, she wrote this selection as a letter to her college newspaper. What does her purpose and her thesis tell you about her audience?

2. The biographical note on this student author reveals something about her personality. What might that be? How will this character trait be reflected in the selection that follows?

3. Palmieri appeals to the reader's emotions, values, and self-interest. Underline places where she does this as you read her essay.

4. The author uses the terms academic *probation*, *restriction*, and *suspension* to designate the status of students whose grades need immediate improvement. Dismissal occurs when a student's grades are so low that he or she is asked to leave the college.

Vocabulary

accommodate (verb) Meet or serve.

appalling (adjective) Shocking.

asinine (adjective) Foolish, idiotic.

fraught with (adjective) Accompanied by, filled with.

menial (adjective) Low level.

nurture (verb) Care for, provide for, nourish.

priority (noun) Item of greatest importance.

scenario (noun) Situation.

seasoned (adjective) Experienced.

serf (noun) Slave, someone bound to the land or to a master.

Education Is the Priority

Nicholle Palmieri

About a year ago, I quit my full-time job to return to college. Despite all of the obstacles in my way, I was lucky enough to find a job as a work-study assistant in the office of Dr. Bernadette Russell, Dean of Liberal Arts at my college. I say "lucky" for many reasons. The Dean and her administrative assistant, Karen Gormish, are supportive of students and are willing to accommodate their needs. Because of their support and flexibility, I don't have to worry about my job interfering with my studies. I am able to fit my work hours around my class schedule—not the other way around—and still manage to work enough hours to pay my bills.

Working in the Dean's office has taught me a great deal about college students and their priorities. Almost every day, at least one of them comes into the office, eyes fraught with desperation. He or she pleads to be taken off academic probation, restriction, or suspension. Some beg to have their dismissals lifted and to be allowed to re-enroll.

I am often the first person who greets them and, therefore, I see their appeals first. Most of these students have failed to make education their priority, and they are paying for it dearly. In fact, there is one claim that almost all have in common: their hours at work have taken precious time away from their college studies. Mind you, most of these kids (I say "kids" because that is what the majority of

1

2

3

them are) are living at home and taking about 15 credits per semester. It is not as if they are seasoned adults who have worked at full-time jobs for fifteen years, have learned to manage their time, and are able to squeeze in a course or two in the evenings and weekends. On the contrary, most of them work at menial positions in fast-food restaurants or retail stores. They take orders from demanding, unreasonable supervisors, and they work asinine, exhausting hours that no human being should have to work—certainly not someone who is attending college classes full-time and devoting hours of endless study toward earning an education and entering a rewarding career. From what I understand, most of these students work such hours under threat of being fired by their managers if they refuse.

I find the whole scenario appalling. Fifty years ago, it was unheard of that full-time college students should even work two hours a week, let alone forty, and that was for a good reason. According to the website of the Division of Student Affairs at Virginia Polytechnic Institute and State University, being a successful college student requires "about two hours of preparation for each hour in the classroom. This means that [a student carrying fifteen credits] has at least a forty-five hour work week, and is consequently involved in a full-time occupation." At Newbury College, incoming freshmen are advised to attend classes regularly ("This is a must!"), seek help at the Academic Resources Center, visit their professors regularly during office hours, enroll in "the Academic Enrichment Program," and join a student study group. These activities take time—the bulk of your time—but in order to be successful in college you must commit to them. That also means that you will have little time for work outside your studies. For a full-time student, most college counselors recommend no more than 15 hours of work per week. Consider this: If you fail to nurture your education, you will find yourself on academic probation, restriction, or suspension. Even worse, you might get yourself dismissed, a blow from which it is hard to recover even if you manage to transfer to another college. 4

Why would anyone want to do that to herself for the sake of some no-brainer, dead-end job that pays $5.05 per hour? I understand that many students need money because they have bills to pay, not the least of which might be tuition. However, there comes a point when enough is enough. I too have bills to pay, and I manage to pay them by working 15 hours a week or less. I could not possibly devote sufficient time to my studies if I worked a minute more, and my supervisor understands this. Managers who don't understand this aren't worth working for, and they would do students in their employ a favor by firing them. 5

No words can overemphasize the importance of education. Without one, the "kids" I mentioned earlier might be condemned to work as under-paid, under-appreciated, under-respected cashiers and stock clerks for the rest of their lives. It is time college students put their educations first and told their supervisors at McDonald's or Burger King to find another serf if they don't like it. This is a free country. There is nothing—least of all a dead-end job or a cranky fast-food manager—who can deprive you of your right to a quality education and to a successful future. 6

Works Cited

Division of Student Affairs Home Page. Division of Student Affairs, Virginia Polytechnic Institute and State University, 4 Mar. 2003. http://www.ucc.vt.edu/stdysk/htimesch.html. Accessed 4 Nov. 2010.

"How to Be a More Active Learner at Newbury College." Newbury College. 1 May 2000. http://www.newbury.edu/support/active.htm. Accessed 6 Nov. 2010.

Read More on the Web

For more about working while attending college, visit the following sites:

- "Student Employment," The College at Brockport:
  www.brockport.edu/life/student_employment/

- "'Being Not-Rich': Low-Income Students at Michigan Share Savvy Advice," Emma Kerr (the article includes a link to the University of Michigan's online guide to student survival): http://bvtlab.com/74e24

- "The Pros and Cons of Working while in College," Ashford University: http://bvtlab.com/999e4

Questions for Discussion

1. What is Palmieri's thesis? Where does she state it most clearly?

2. Does this selection illustrate the uses of deduction, which you learned about in chapter 12? Explain Palmieri's thinking by creating a syllogism in your own words: Start with a general statement, apply a specific case to that statement, and then draw a conclusion.

3. Where does Palmieri use induction? What conclusions does she draw using this process?

4. Where does the author appeal to her audience's values? To their self-interest?

5. What use does she make of the testimony of experts on her subject? Why did she choose these sources to quote directly? Why not include direct quotations from students "fraught with desperation," whom she met in the dean's office?

6. Palmieri chooses her persuasive vocabulary well. Identify and analyze sections in which her language appeals to our emotions.

7. Does the author anticipate and answer opposing arguments? If so, where?

8. Why does Palmieri tell us so much about herself in this essay, especially in her introduction?

Thinking Critically

1. Reread "Study Calculus!" by William J. Bennett and "Burger Queen" by Erin Sharp in chapter 2. How might each of them react to Palmieri's essay?

2. Palmieri criticizes employers who do not accommodate students who work for them. How might an employer respond to her comments?

Suggestions for Journal Entries

1. Think about the opposing argument Palmieri addresses in paragraph 5. Can you make a case for this argument? Are there other reasons for working more than 15 hours per week while carrying a full academic load? Brainstorm with two or three classmates to gather relevant information you might use to write a rebuttal to Palmieri's essay.

2. Think about an issue that is crucial to student success in college and that you might write about in a letter to the editor of your student newspaper. Palmieri's essay focuses on making education, not work, the priority. Yours might discuss study habits, time management, stress management, participation in community service projects, the dangers of alcohol or drug abuse among students, or any other issue you believe is important to your fellow students. If you need inspiration picking a topic, visit any of the websites listed in "Read More on the Web" or go to the websites of other colleges and universities.

13.10b I Have a Dream

Author Biography

After graduating from Morehouse College at nineteen, **_Martin Luther King Jr._** (1929–1968) entered the seminary and later became a minister in Atlanta's Ebenezer Baptist Church, where his father was pastor. In 1957, he founded the Southern Christian Leadership Conference, a civil rights organization. Influenced by the philosophy of human rights activist and pacifist Mahatma Gandhi, King led several important demonstrations against racial segregation in the South and in the North. Among the most famous was the march in Birmingham, Alabama, in 1963, for which King was arrested. It was during this imprisonment that he wrote "Letter from Birmingham Jail," a landmark in the literature of American human rights. In that same year, King made a stirring speech during the great March on Washington. Delivered before 200,000 people assembled at the Lincoln Memorial, the text of this speech has come to be known as "I Have a Dream." King won several awards for his work in support of human rights, including the Nobel Prize for Peace in 1964. On April 4, 1968, Dr. King was assassinated while he spoke with other civil rights leaders on a motel balcony in Memphis, Tennessee.

Preparing to Read

1. King refers to the Declaration of Independence and the U.S. Constitution as a "promissory note to which every American was to fall heir." If you haven't done so already, read these documents. You can find them in any college or public library or on the Internet.

2. Look up Martin Luther King Jr. and/or the American civil rights movement in the library or on the Internet to familiarize yourself with some of the issues and events that King refers to in this speech.

3. Given the fact that King was a Christian minister, what allusions and references does he use in this speech to support his advocacy of civil rights and to move his audience?

Vocabulary

defaulted (verb)   Failed to pay a debt.

devotees (noun)   Disciples, those who believe in something.

hallowed (adjective)   Holy, sacred.

inextricably (adverb)   Permanently, unable to be removed.

interposition (noun)   Attempt to stop the enforcement of laws, in this case those guaranteeing civil rights.

jangling (adjective)   Clanking, clattering.

languishing (adjective)   Lying weak and ill.

manacles (noun)   Handcuffs.

militancy (noun)   Aggressiveness, willingness to do battle.

momentous (adjective)   Extremely important, weighty.

nullification (noun)   Refusal to enforce or recognize laws, in this case those guaranteeing civil rights.

redemptive (adjective)   Redeeming, saving.

unalienable (adjective)   Natural, undeniable.

withering (adjective)   Decaying, dying.

I Have a Dream

Dr. Martin Luther King Jr.

Five score years ago, a great American, in whose symbolic shadow we stand, signed the Emancipation Proclamation. This momentous decree came as a great beacon light of hope to millions of Negro slaves who had been seared in the flames of withering injustice. It came as a joyous daybreak to end the long night of captivity.   1

But one hundred years later, we must face the tragic fact that the Negro is still not free. One hundred years later, the life of the Negro is still sadly crippled by the manacles of segregation and the chains of discrimination. One hundred years later, the Negro lives on a lonely island of poverty in the midst of a vast ocean of material prosperity. One hundred years later, the Negro is still languishing in the corners of American society and finds himself an exile in his own land. So we have come here today to dramatize an appalling condition.   2

In a sense we have come to our nation's capital to cash a check. When the architects of our republic wrote the magnificent words of the Constitution and the Declaration of Independence, they were signing a promissory note to which every American was to fall heir. This note was a promise that all men would be guaranteed the unalienable rights of life, liberty, and the pursuit of happiness.   3

It is obvious today that America has defaulted on this promissory note insofar as her citizens of color are concerned. Instead of honoring this sacred obligation, America has given the Negro people a bad check; a check which has come back marked "insufficient funds." But we refuse to believe that the bank of justice is bankrupt. We refuse to believe that there are insufficient funds in the great vaults of opportunity of this nation. So we have come to cash this check—a check that will give us upon demand the riches of freedom and the security of justice. We have also come to this hallowed spot to remind America of the fierce urgency of now. This is no time to engage in the luxury of cooling off or to take the tranquilizing drugs of gradualism. *Now* is the time to make real the promises of Democracy. *Now* is the time to rise from the dark and desolate valley of segregation to the sunlit path of racial justice. *Now* is the time to open the doors of opportunity to all of God's children. *Now* is the time to lift our nation from the quicksands of racial injustice to the solid rock of brotherhood.   4

It would be fatal for the nation to overlook the urgency of the moment and to underestimate the determination of the Negro. This sweltering summer of the Negro's legitimate discontent will not pass until there is an invigorating autumn of freedom and equality. Nineteen sixty-three is not an end, but a beginning. Those who hope that the Negro needed to blow off steam and will now be content will have a rude awakening if the nation returns to business as usual. There will be neither rest nor tranquility in America until the Negro is granted his citizenship rights. The whirlwinds of revolt will continue to shake the foundations of our nation until the bright day of justice emerges.   5

But there is something that I must say to my people who stand on the warm threshold which leads into the palace of justice. In the process of gaining our rightful place we must not be guilty of wrongful deeds. Let us not seek to satisfy our thirst for freedom by drinking from the cup of bitterness and hatred. We must forever conduct our struggle on the high plane of dignity and discipline. We must not allow our creative protest to degenerate into physical violence. Again and again we must rise to the majestic heights of meeting physical force with soul force. The marvelous new militancy which has engulfed the Negro community must not lead us to a distrust of all white people, for many of our white brothers, as evidenced by their presence here today, have come to realize that their destiny is tied up with our destiny and their freedom is inextricably bound to our freedom. We cannot walk alone.   6

And as we walk, we must make the pledge that we shall march ahead. We cannot turn back. There are those who are asking the devotees of civil rights, "When will you be satisfied?" We can never be satisfied as long as the Negro is the victim of the unspeakable horrors of police brutality. We can never be satisfied as long as our bodies, heavy with the fatigue of travel, cannot gain lodging in the motels of the highways and the hotels of the cities. We cannot be satisfied as long as the Negro's basic mobility is from a smaller ghetto to a larger one. We can never be satisfied as long as a Negro in Mississippi cannot vote and a Negro in New York believes he has nothing for which to vote. No, no, we are not satisfied, and we will not be satisfied until justice rolls down like waters and righteousness like a mighty stream.   7

I am not unmindful that some of you have come here out of great trials and tribulations. Some of you have come fresh from narrow jail cells. Some of you have come from areas where your quest for freedom left you battered by the storms of persecution and staggered by the winds of police brutality. You have been the veterans of creative suffering. Continue to work with the faith that unearned suffering is redemptive.   8

Go back to Mississippi, go back to Alabama, go back to South Carolina, go back to Georgia, go back to Louisiana, go back to the slums and ghettos of our northern cities, knowing that somehow this situation can and will be changed. Let us not wallow in the valley of despair.   9

I say to you today, my friends, that in spite of the difficulties and frustrations of the moment I still have a dream. It is a dream deeply rooted in the American dream.   10

I have a dream that one day this nation will rise up and live out the true meaning of its creed: "We hold these truths to be self-evident; that all men are created equal."   11

I have a dream that one day on the red hills of Georgia the sons of former slaves and the sons of former slaveowners will be able to sit down together at the table of brotherhood.   12

I have a dream that one day even the state of Mississippi, a desert state sweltering with the heat of injustice and oppression, will be transformed into an oasis of freedom and justice.   13

I have a dream that my four little children will one day live in a nation where they will not be judged by the color of their skin but by the content of their character.   14

I have a dream today.   15

I have a dream that one day the state of Alabama, whose governor's lips are presently dripping with the words of interposition and nullification, will be transformed into a situation where little black boys and black girls will be able to join hands with little white boys and white girls and walk together as sisters and brothers.   16

I have a dream today.   17

I have a dream that one day every valley shall be exalted, every hill and mountain shall be made low, the rough places will be made plain, and the crooked places will be made straight, and the glory of the Lord shall be revealed, and all flesh shall see it together.   18

This is our hope. This is the faith with which I return to the South. With this faith we will be able to hew out of the mountain of despair a stone of hope. With this faith we will be able to transform the jangling discords of our nation into a beautiful symphony of brotherhood. With this faith we will be able to work together, to pray together, to struggle together, to go to jail together, to stand up for freedom together, knowing that we will be free one day.   19

This will be the day when all of God's children will be able to sing with new meaning   20

My country, 'tis of thee,   21

Sweet land of liberty,   22

Of thee I sing: 23

Land where my fathers died,   24

Land of the pilgrims' pride,   25

From every mountain-side,   26

Let freedom ring.   27

And if America is to be a great nation this must become true. So let freedom ring from the prodigious hilltops of New Hampshire. Let freedom ring from the mighty mountains of New York. Let freedom ring from the heightening Alleghenies of Pennsylvania!   28

Let freedom ring from the snowcapped Rockies of Colorado!   29

Let freedom ring from the curvaceous peaks of California!   30

But not only that; let freedom ring from Stone Mountain of Georgia!   31

Let freedom ring from Lookout Mountain of Tennessee!   32

Let freedom ring from every hill and molehill of Mississippi. From every mountainside let freedom ring.   33

When we let freedom ring, when we let it ring from every village and every hamlet, from every state and every city, we will be able to speed up that day when all of God's children, black men and white men, Jews and Gentiles, Protestants and Catholics, will be able to join hands and sing in the words of the old Negro spiritual, "Free at last! free at last! thank God almighty, we are free at last!"

34

Read More on the Web

For more on Dr. Martin Luther King Jr., go to the following:

- "Martin Luther King Jr. Papers Project": kinginstitute.stanford.edu/king-papers/about-papers-project

- National Civil Rights Museum: www.civilrightsmuseum.org/

Questions for Discussion

1. King's central idea is expressed most forcefully in sentences that begin "I have a dream...." Of these, which has the greatest effect on you?

2. Where does King appeal to authority? How does such an appeal strengthen his argument?

3. Where does he use facts to support his point of view?

4. Why does King mention so many Southern states by name?

5. In what parts of this address does the speaker appeal to his audience's values?

6. Where does he appeal to the self-interest of the African Americans in his audience?

7. Where does he appeal to the self-interest of whites?

8. The speaker uses parallelism to evoke our emotions. Find examples of this rhetorical technique. If necessary, review what you learned about parallelism in chapter 5.

9. Find several figures of speech, and explain how they help King achieve his purpose.

10. King addresses two opposing arguments. Explain how he does this.

Thinking Critically

1. Reread paragraphs 2 and 3. Explain the extended metaphors used in them.

2. Turn back to chapter 5 in this book and read Lincoln's Gettysburg Address. Pay particular attention to the word *hallowed*, used in paragraph 2 of that speech. This is the same word King uses in paragraph 4 here. What other similarities can you identify in these two addresses?

3. Who is King's audience? Is it only the 200,000 people assembled at the Lincoln Memorial?

Suggestions for Journal Entries

1. Have we made progress in guaranteeing the civil rights of minorities since Dr. King spoke these words? Make a list of the most important advances. Start by reviewing "I Have a Dream" and deciding if the wrongs mentioned have been dealt with. You might want to do some Internet research on the history of the American civil rights movement—as already suggested in "Preparing to Read"—to gather facts. You might also want to interview a professor of history, literature, or government at your college to find out more about this question.

2. Do you have your own dream for the world? What major problem affecting the United States or another country would you like to see solved in the next few decades? Perhaps you might address poverty, illiteracy, drug abuse, teenage pregnancy in America, the AIDS epidemic in Africa, or famine in any of several parts of the world. You might have to do some library or Internet research or interview a professor knowledgeable about the issue you are addressing.

13.10c Raising the Minimum Wage to $15 per Hour: Opposing Views

Author Biographies

Matt Zwolinski (1976–) teaches philosophy at the University of San Diego. He serves on the editorial board of *Business Ethics Quarterly* and writes for and serves as editor for his *Bleeding Heart Libertarians* blog. This article appeared on the website of the Foundation for Economic Education on April 4, 2016. ***Robert Reich*** (1941–) is a professor of public policy at the University of California at Berkeley. He served as secretary of labor under President Bill Clinton. ***Don Lee*** (1959–) is a reporter for the *Los Angeles Times*. He also writes fiction and teaches creative writing. Raising the minimum wage has become a controversial issue in the last decade.

Preparing to Read

1. In paragraph 6 of Zwolinski's essay, he mentions a study by David Card and Alan Krueger, which showed that raising the minimum wage in New Jersey and Pennsylvania had little effect on unemployment. Zwolinski mentions several people with varying opinions on this topic. Use the Internet to find out more about Don Unz, Milton Friedman, John Rawls, and Thomas Leonard.

2. In paragraph 8 of Zwolinski's essay, he mentions the Negative Income Tax, which is a provision that would allow people under a certain income level to pay no federal income tax but, instead, receive a payment from the government.

3. As you will see, Zwolinski's approach is politically conservative, while Reich's is liberal. Lee's approach is nonpolitical.

Vocabulary

advocate (verb)   Support, encourage.

allocating (verb)   Distributing, sharing.

disparity (noun)   Difference, discrepancy.

disproportionately (adverb)   Overly, unequally.

distortionary (adjective)   Falsifying, misrepresenting.

equitable (adjective)   Equal, fair, just.

exacerbate (verb)   Make worse.

fissure (noun)   Crack, crevice, split.

polarization (noun)   Division, separation.

proficiency (noun)   Mastery, skill.

proponents (noun)   Those in favor of.

ramification (noun)   Effect, result.

vulnerable (adjective)   Defenseless, helpless.

3 Reasons the $15 Minimum Wage Is a Bad Way to Help the Poor: There Are Less Destructive Policies to Raise the Poor's Income

Matt Zwolinski

Today, California governor Jerry Brown will sign a law raising the state's minimum wage (currently $10/hr—tied with Massachusetts for the highest of any state) to $15/hr by 2022. This is a big deal. Although a number of cities such as Los Angeles and Seattle have passed $15 minimum wage laws in the past few years, California's law will affect both a much larger number of people, and a much more diverse population of workers, than any other measure to date.   1

California's minimum wage law is the latest and largest victory in a powerful movement pushing for higher minimum wages across the United States. Supporters of this movement argue that the current minimum wage is too low to allow workers to make ends meet.   2

But the minimum wage is a bad tool for those whose goal is to ease the burdens of poverty. And the California law—which mandates a *very* high wage across a very large population—is an especially bad idea. Here are just a few reasons why: 3

1. **Minimum Wages Target Workers, Not the Poor**—Minimum wage policies affect people with traditional, wage-paying jobs. The problem with this is that the class of low-wage workers and the class of poor people only partially overlap. There are large segments of the poor that receive no direct benefit at all from the minimum wage—the unemployed, stay-at-home parents, Uber drivers and other "gig" employees, etc. And there are a large number of low-wage workers—think teenagers living at home with their parents—who aren't poor. If the goal of minimum wage policies is to fight poverty, then targeting low-wage workers is a relatively ineffective way of achieving that goal.   4

2. **Minimum Wages Hurt Marginalized Groups**—Let's put aside for the moment the question of whether minimum wage laws create unemployment or not. Because even if they don't affect overall *levels* of unemployment, minimum wage laws almost certainly change the *composition* of unemployment. Minimum wage laws create a barrier to getting a job that the privileged are better able to overcome than the underprivileged. When jobs are scarce, then   5

immigrants, workers with few skills or little education, and those with limited English proficiency are going to have a harder time convincing employers that their labor is worth $15 an hour than their better-skilled, native, English-speaking competitors. As Thomas Leonard has recently shown, unemploying such marginalized groups was regarded as part of the *point* of minimum wage laws by early 20th century "progressives" who saw the minimum wage as a useful tool for keeping immigrants, blacks, and women out of the labor market. But the effect hasn't changed in the last 100 years, even if our moral evaluation of it has. (Well, for most of us anyway. Ron Unz *still* regards the unemployment of immigrants as a positive effect of minimum wage laws).

3. **Some Minimum Wages Cause Unemployment**—The standard economist's argument against minimum wage laws is that, by increasing the cost of labor, they reduce the demand for it. In other words, they create unemployment. Ever since Card and Krueger's 1997 study, economists have been somewhat mixed on whether minimum wage laws actually have this effect in practice. But—here's the important thing—the studies that have caused economists to doubt the unemployment effects of a minimum wage have focused on minimum wages much lower than $15/hour. Obviously, there's some point at which a minimum wage is going to start causing unemployment—otherwise, why not set it at $100 an hour? And a lot of economists—even those who support a minimum wage in principle—believe that $15 crosses the line. Maybe not in a city like Los Angeles, where most workers are earning more than $15 already, but California's law affects not just cities like Los Angeles but cities like Fresno and El Centro, where average wages (and costs of living) are considerably lower.

6

My point here isn't that government should do nothing to help the poor. It's that minimum wage laws are a bad way of going about trying to provide that help. That's why even John Rawls thought that the minimum wage was a bad idea. Of course, he thought we should have income redistribution. But the best way to do that is to let the labor market do what markets are generally quite good at—efficiently allocating resources and creating a social surplus—and *then* use the power of government to ensure that everybody gets an equitable (or, in my view, sufficient) share of the wealth the market creates.

7

Rawls thought that something like Milton Friedman's Negative Income Tax could be an efficient way of achieving that redistribution. I think he's right, and many others have made the same point. Unlike the minimum wage, a Negative Income Tax or Universal Basic Income (the two are often functionally identical) targets poverty, not employment. And it does so without creating the distortionary and unemployment effects of a minimum wage.

8

California likes to think of itself as a state on the cutting edge. But the minimum wage is a policy which, if it ever had a time at all, that time has passed. Raising the minimum wage to $15 is an ineffective way to fight poverty which could have disastrous unintended consequences for the most vulnerable workers. If California wants to be smart about fighting poverty, it should … consider a Negative Income Tax.

9

Why the Minimum Wage Should Really Be Raised to $15 an Hour

Robert Reich

Momentum is building to raise the minimum wage. Several states have already taken action—Connecticut … boosted it to $10.10 [in] 2017, the Maryland legislature just approved a similar measure, Minnesota lawmakers just reached a deal to hike it to $9.50. A few cities have been more ambitious—Washington, D.C., and its surrounding counties raised it to $11.50, Seattle is considering $15.00.

1

Senate Democrats will soon introduce legislation raising it nationally to $10.10, from the current $7.25 an hour. All this is fine as far as it goes. But we need to be more ambitious. We should be raising the federal minimum to $15 an hour.

2

Here are seven reasons why: 3

1. Had the minimum wage of 1968 simply stayed even with inflation, it would be more than   4
    $10 an hour today. But the typical worker is also about twice as productive as then. Some of
    those productivity gains should go to workers at the bottom.

2. $10.10 isn't enough to lift all workers and their families out of poverty. Most low-wage   5
    workers aren't young teenagers; they're major breadwinners for their families, and many are
    women. And they and their families need a higher minimum.

3. For this reason, a $10.10 minimum would also still require the rest of us to pay Medicaid,   6
    food-stamps, and other programs necessary to get poor families out of poverty—thereby
    indirectly subsidizing employers who refuse to pay more. *Bloomberg View* describes McDon-
    ald's and Walmart as "America's biggest welfare queens" because their employees receive so
    much public assistance. (Some, like McDonalds, even advise their employees to use public
    programs because their pay is so low.)

4. A $15/hour minimum won't result in major job losses because it would put money in the   7
    pockets of millions of low-wage workers who will spend it—thereby giving working families
    and the overall economy a boost, and creating jobs. (When I was Labor Secretary in 1996
    and we raised the minimum wage, business predicted millions of job losses; in fact, we had
    more job gains over the next four years than in any comparable period in American history.)

5. A $15/hour minimum is unlikely to result in higher prices because most businesses directly   8
    affected by it are in intense competition for consumers, and will take the raise out of profits
    rather than raise their prices. But because the higher minimum will also attract more work-
    ers into the job market, employers will have more choice of whom to hire, and thereby have
    more reliable employees—resulting in lower turnover costs and higher productivity.

6. Since Republicans will push Democrats to go even lower than $10.10, it's doubly important   9
    to be clear about what's right in the first place. Democrats should be going for a higher min-
    imum rather than listening to Republican demands for a smaller one.

7. At a time in our history when 95 percent of all economic gains are going to the top 1 percent, 10
    raising the minimum wage to $15 an hour isn't just smart economics and good politics. It's
    also the morally right thing to do.

Call your senators and members of Congress today to tell them $15 an hour is the least American   11
workers deserve. You can reach them at 202-224-3121.

Four Consequences of a $15 Minimum Wage

Don Lee

Exhaustive research over the past few decades suggests raising the minimum wage has little negative   1
impact on overall employment.

The problem is, most past wage hikes have been relatively modest, and there's no data to con-   2
fidently predict what might happen following the kinds of increases now planned in California and
New York.

Going to $15 an hour represents a 50% rise from California's current minimum pay of $10, and   3
a 67% jump for New York. Although these would be phased in over several years and would not apply
statewide in the case of New York, the sheer size of the increases has made even proponents of higher
minimum wages a little worried.

It's a grand experiment with potentially profound consequences—some good, some bad—that   4
could extend far beyond the borders of the nation's two largest states, with ramifications for the health
and direction of the U.S. economy and society.

"The minimum wage debate hints at the very essence of who we are, how we function together   5
and what we'll become," said Arthur Laffer, the well-known economist who served as an advisor to
President Reagan.

Here's what some experts are expecting: 6

1. **It may increase unemployment among minority youth.** Because teenagers and young adults hold a disproportionately large share of low-wage jobs, they figure to be among the hardest hit, pushed out by older and better-educated workers who will be drawn by the higher pay offered by retail stores, food services and other businesses.

That could hurt opportunities, especially for black teenagers, one of the most vulnerable   7
groups in America. The unemployment rate for African Americans ages 16 to 19, while down by almost half from 2010, still stands at 25%. That compares to 13.9% for white youth and 15.6% for Latino youth.

If policymakers blame high crime in cities such as Chicago on steep poverty and unem-   8
ployment, Laffer asked, should they still advocate for a high minimum wage that might reduce jobs for the youth and exacerbate social problems?

Another side effect of higher minimum wages may be that teenagers will be "induced to   9
leave school, interrupting or prematurely ending their formal education," write researchers Dale Belman of Michigan State University and Paul Wolfson of Dartmouth's Tuck School of Business.

But they added that research findings about the impact on schooling and minority youth   10
are not conclusive enough to be used by policymakers.

2. **Wage disparity within states will shrink.** There is little doubt that the new minimum   11
wage laws in California and New York will help reduce the increasing disparity in earnings between the highest and lowest paid workers in those states.

In California, the bottom 10% of wage earners made on average $9.48 an hour last year,   12
a 20% increase since 2005, unadjusted for inflation. Workers in the top 10% of wages earned on average $53.08 an hour, a 35% jump from 2005, according to data from the Bureau of Labor Statistics.

The upshot is that the difference between the bottom and top 10% of wages in the   13
state has widened over the past decade, to $43.60 an hour from $31.35. The trend is almost exactly the same for New York.

With minimum wages set to rise steadily in the years to come, and during a period when   14
inflation is forecast to stay historically low, low-wage workers "will achieve a much higher level than they ever have, and that will reverse decades in which wages have been stagnant or falling at the bottom of the distribution," said Michael Reich, chair of UC [University of California] Berkeley's Institute for Research on Labor and Employment. "It's going to pro- vide people, not with security, but with fewer headaches," he said. "If their car breaks down, they might have money to repair it or buy a used car, which will help them get to work, to child care and so on."

And it should help children in the long run too, Reich said. "We know that higher   15
income leads to better parenting, better mental health and better school outcomes."

3. **The red-state, blue-state divide could get worse.** The dramatic differences in mini-   16
mum wages soon to be paid across the country could worsen the income gap between rich and poor states.

It's a fissure that has generally narrowed over most of the past century, according to   17
Andrew Gelman, a statistician at Columbia University and author of *Red State, Blue State, Rich State, Poor State*.

It is generally the richer, Democratic-leaning states, including Maryland, Massa-   18
chusetts, Washington and Oregon, that have pushed through higher minimum wages in recent years and are candidates to follow California and New York by adopting a statewide $15-an-hour floor.

Most of the 21 states with minimum wages equal to or less than the federal rate are in the   19
so-called Red or Republican-leaning states in the South and the Great Plains. This distinction matters not just for politics, but in their different approaches to regulation and the economy— differences that appear to be getting sharper with such policies like "super-minimum wage laws," as analysts at the conservative Heritage Foundation call the higher-wage laws.

There is a similar divide when it comes to which states have embraced President Obama's expansion of Medicaid for the poor, giving poor residents in Democratic-led states better access to health coverage than their counterparts in Republican-led states. 20

Richard Florida, an urban development expert at the University of Toronto, sees the $15-an-hour minimum wage push as an indication of the increasing polarization in America in which there are competing visions: one driven by people in large, dense metropolitan areas with a strong information economy, and the other by folks in rural regions more dependent on resources and real estate. 21

"We are being ever more sorted by class, by income, by education, by occupation and by political orientation," he said. 22

4. **More low-paying jobs will go underground.** "A lot more are going to get hired off the books," especially immigrant workers, said Harry Holzer, a public policy professor at Georgetown University. The Labor Department's top economist in the Clinton administration's second term, Holzer never imagined that the campaign for $15 an hour would actually succeed. He thought $15 was more of a bargaining ploy to get to $10 an hour, or maybe $12. Now Holzer fears there will be heavy job losses, hurting most the low-skilled, less-educated workers who may have to accept cash under the table or cut deals to keep their jobs. 23

Informal work isn't necessarily illegal or bad. It includes jobs such as babysitting and housecleaning that provide much-needed side incomes or can introduce a young person to the world of work, Demetra Smith Nightingale and Stephen A. Wandner wrote in an Urban Institute paper. 24

Still, a rise in informal work translates into more tax avoidance and generally means fewer worker benefits and protections, like unemployment insurance. 25

As such, a higher minimum wage may backfire for some low-income workers unless there also are changes that encourage workers and employers to do things by the book. 26

Read More on the Web

For more on the minimum wage debate, read the following:

- "Raising the Minimum Wage to $15 by 2024 Would Lift Wages for 41 Million American Workers," David Cooper: http://bvtlab.com/83B8S

- "Increasing the Minimum Wage: Pros and Cons," Sarah Shemkus: http://bvtlab.com/49m6m

- "Raising Minimum Wage Will Raise Something Else: An Army of Robots Taking Away Folks' Jobs," Thomas Claburn: http://bvtlab.com/ka667

- "Minimum Wage," *Debate.org*: http://bvtlab.com/6568Q

Questions for Discussion (Continues)

1. What does Zwolinski say is the best way to address poverty in America?

2. Where does Zwolinski appeal to the reader's values? Why did he place quotation marks around the word *progressives* in paragraph 5?

3. What does Zwolinski mean in paragraph 4 by the phrase "gig employees"?

4. Where does Reich appeals to the readers' self-interest?

5. How does Reich appeal to the readers' values?

6. Identify words and phrases in each of these essays that appeal to the readers' emotions.

Questions for Discussion (Continued)

7. Which of the three authors respond to opposing arguments?

8. What might Reich respond to Zwolinski's claim that raising the minimum wage targets workers, not the poor?

9. According to Zwolinski, what are some of the drawbacks of raising the minimum wage?

10. According to Reich, what are some of the benefits of raising the minimum wage?

11. What alternative to raising the minimum wage does Zwolinski propose to help the poor?

Thinking Critically

1. What is Reich's opinion on the government's role in guiding the economy?

2. What does Zwolinski mean when he says that "early 20th century 'progressives'… saw the minimum wage as a useful tool for keeping immigrants, blacks, and women out of the labor market"?

3. Does the way Reich ends his essay help or hinder his ability to persuade?

Suggestions for Journal Entries

1. You have learned that at persuasion's core is formal argument. Summarize the formal arguments used by Zwolinski and Reich in their essays.

2. Based on your own experience as a part-time or full-time employee and your understanding of the way raising the minimum wage would work, provide a list of arguments in favor or against raising the minimum wage to $15.

13.11 Suggestions for Sustained Writing

1. Write an essay that tries to persuade your readers that working more than 15 hours a week while pursuing a full-time academic career is reasonable. You might explain that working longer hours is necessary if you are to pay your expenses. You might also explain that some full-time students are so organized or talented that they can handle more than 15 hours of work.

   If this idea does not interest you, write an open letter to your fellow students trying to persuade them to adopt a particular behavior or attitude concerning an issue important to them. For example, offer advice on time or stress management, persuade them to change their study habits, encourage their participation in community service, or warn them about the dangers of alcohol abuse. If you responded to either of the journal suggestions after Palmieri's essay, look over the notes you made before you begin this assignment.

   Another alternative is to write an essay in which you try to persuade your fellow students to devote 100 percent of their time to school and to quit even the least demanding part-time job. Of course, you will have to suggest alternative sources of income—such as scholarships, loans, and other types of financial aid—that students might tap to pay tuition and living expenses.

Like Palmieri, try to support your arguments with the testimony of experts and present your arguments logically. However, remember that this is a persuasive assignment. Use language that will appeal to your fellow students' pride, self-interest, and emotions. Try to rouse them if you can! In addition, make sure to raise and address opposing arguments. If you are using researched materials, credit your sources with internal citations and include a list of works cited. More information on how to do this can be found in appendix 2, "The Research Process," which discusses documentation principles used by the Modern Language Association.

2. Look back to the journal notes you made after reading Dr. King's "I Have a Dream." Whether you responded to item 1 or 2 in the Suggestions for Journal Entries, expand your notes into a persuasive address that you would deliver to a large group of people if you had the opportunity.

   If you responded to item 1, you might be satisfied by relating the progress the United States has made in the decades since Dr. King spoke at the Lincoln Memorial. In the process, you could take the position that we have done enough in this area and that further measures will simply be redundant and even counterproductive. Then again, you might argue that not enough has been done, and you could persuade your listeners that we need to take additional steps to ensure everyone's civil rights. However you approach this question, try to be as specific and detailed as you can, relying on library or Internet research and/or using information you have acquired through interviews with faculty members on your campus.

   If you responded to item 2, write a speech in which you try to persuade your listeners to support measures to solve a serious problem that threatens our people, society, culture, or environment or that affects the people, environment, or society of another part of the world. Again, be as specific and detailed as you can and rely on research.

3. If you haven't done so already, respond to both of the journal prompts after the essays under "Raising the Minimum Wage to $15 per Hour: Opposing Views." Use the notes you've made to begin an essay in which you state your own opinion on this issue. You might be against raising the minimum wage, you might be for it, or you might still be undecided. In any case, state your opinion concisely and clearly in your thesis.

   As you draft your paper, make reference to material in the essays by Zwolinski, Reich, and Lee. However, also think about using information taken from other sources. Read the articles listed under "Read More on the Web," which follows the three essays. Make sure to cite your sources using the MLA documentation style, which is explained in appendix 2, "The Research Process," or another documentation style required by your instructor.

   Address your persuasive paper to your fellow students. You might even consider framing it as an opinion piece for your college newspaper.

4. Write an essay in which you try to persuade the people in charge at your college, your place of worship, your workplace, or your town to change a particular policy that is now in effect or to solve a problem. For example, you might ask the college to lower the maximum number of students in a class or to revise the current system by which students evaluate faculty. Or, you might ask your boss to provide better creature comforts at work, suggesting that free coffee be provided during breaks; that employee restrooms be better cleaned and maintained; or that the workplace be heated, cooled, and ventilated more effectively.

As you write your rough draft, include information that explains exactly what needs fixing or changing. For example, if writing to the college president, you might claim that last semester, your chemistry lecture was so crowded that some students could not find seats. If writing to your boss, you might explain that employees often opt to use the nearby filling station's restroom rather than risk contracting a disease in your company's toilet.

In your second draft, use some of the persuasive techniques you read about earlier. For example, appeal to your boss's self-interest by explaining that a clean restroom means improved employee morale, which then translates into a more efficient workforce. As you revise and edit, make sure you have included language that, while reasonable and fair, might appeal to the reader's emotions and sense of fair play.

ACKNOWLEDGMENTS

King Jr., Martin Luther. "I Have a Dream." Copyright 1963 Martin Luther King Jr. Copyright renewed 1991 Coretta Scott King. Reprinted by arrangement with The Heirs to the Estate of Martin Luther King Jr., c/o Writers House as agent for the proprietor New York, NY.

Lee, Don. "Four Consequences of a $15 Minimum Wage." *Los Angeles Times*, 25 Apr. 2016. Reprinted with permission by the L.A. Times.

Owen, Wilfred. "Dulce et Decorum Est." Viking Press, 1921. Copyright 1921, Viking Press. Available via OpenLibrary.org.

Reich, Robert. "Why the Minimum Wage Should Really Be Raised to $15 an Hour." Robertreich.org, 3 Jun. 2014. Reprinted with permission of the author.

Zwolinski, Matt. "Three Reasons the $15 Minimum Wage Is a Bad Way to Help the Poor: There Are Less Destructive Policies to Raise the Poor's Income." Fee.org, 4 Apr. 2016. Reprinted with permission of author.

Appendix 1

Grammar Review

GR.1 Sentence Building Blocks

This section discusses parts of speech, as well as phrases, clauses, and sentences.

GR.1a Learn the Parts of Speech

Words are classified as nouns, pronouns, verbs, adjectives, adverbs, prepositions, conjunctions, and articles. These are the parts of speech. While a sentence can be formed from a noun and verb alone, other parts of speech are important for exact and clear communication.

Nouns: A **noun** names a person, place, or thing. Nouns are classified in two different ways: as common or proper and as concrete or abstract.

    Common nouns name nonspecific things, and they are not ordinarily capitalized. **Proper nouns** name specific things, and they are always capitalized.

Common and Proper Nouns	
Common Nouns	**Proper Nouns**
college	Brooklyn College
sergeant	Sergeant Marshall
language	Italian
religion	Judaism
continent	Africa
ocean	Indian Ocean

    Concrete nouns name things that can be perceived by the five senses. **Abstract nouns** name things that, while real, can't be perceived by the five senses.

Concrete and Abstract Nouns	
Concrete Nouns	**Abstract Nouns**
scream	fear
embrace	love
penicillin	cure
money	economy
priest	religion
teacher	education

Nouns can act as subjects and as objects. The **subject** of a sentence is the person, place, or thing that does the action or that is being described. The **object** of a sentence is a person place or thing that is being acted upon.

Nouns as Subjects and Nouns as Objects	
Nouns as Subjects	**Nouns as Objects**
The fan made a loud noise. *(The fan is acting.)*	Marc turned off the fan.
	Jane turned the fan back on.
The fan was expensive. *(The fan is described.)*	*(In both cases, the fan receives the action.)*

Nouns can be singular or plural. For regular nouns, simply add an *-s* to the end of the word. However, there are exceptions to this rule. The table that follows provides some examples.

Forming Plural Nouns			
Regular Nouns		**Exceptions**	
Singular	Plural	Singular	Plural
elephant	elephants	child	children
doctor	doctors	deer	deer
cell phone	cell phones	woman	women
bridge	bridges	stimulus	stimuli

Note that some nouns that end in *-ing* name activities. These are called **gerunds**, and examples are *becoming, being, doing, eating, inciting, jumping, knowing, loving, moving, swimming, talking, walking,* and *yawning.* Gerunds are always singular.
Pronouns: A **pronoun** replaces a noun, and it too names a person, place, or thing. Like nouns, pronouns are singular or plural. In addition, some pronouns act as subjects, others act as objects, and still others indicate possession. Finally, there are personal and relative pronouns.

Personal Pronouns	
Pronouns as subjects	*I, we, you, he, she, it, one, they, who*
Pronouns as objects	*me, us, you, him, her, it, one, them, whom*
Pronouns that show possession	*my, mine, your, yours, his, her, hers, its, their, theirs, whose*

Verbs: A **verb** shows what a subject does or connects the subject to another word that describes the subject.

> The wind *knocked* over two oak trees. (knocked *shows action*)

> The large oak in our yard *was* damaged. (was *helps describe*)

You will learn more about verbs in section GR.8.

Adjectives: An **adjective** describes a noun or a pronoun. It answers questions such as "Which?" "What kind of?" and "How many?" Adjectives can appear before or after the noun they describe.

> The *large red* house was just *sold*.

> Our *automobile* mechanic never overcharges us.

Note that *automobile*, a noun, can act as an adjective, as in the second sentence. More about adjectives can be found in section GR12.

Adverbs: An **adverb** describes or tells something about a verb, adjective, or other adverb. Adverbs answer questions such as "Where?" "When" "How?" "How much?" "How many?" and "To what extent?" Although most adverbs end in *-ly*, some do not. You can learn more about adverbs in section GR12.

> Stan walked *very slowly* through the *unusually* crowded room.

> Very *tells how slowly (an adverb) he walked.* Slowly *describes the way he walked (a verb).* Unusually *describes crowded (an adjective).*

Commonly Used Adverbs	
angrily	always
arrogantly	less
beautifully	more
briefly	never
happily	now
loudly	often
strongly	very
tenderly	well
utterly	where
weakly	when

Prepositions: Prepositions, which appear before nouns or pronouns, show how those words relate to the rest of the sentence. Connecting a preposition with a noun or pronoun creates a prepositional phrase.

Commonly Used Prepositions	
across	into
among	of
at	near
behind	over
by	through
for	to
from	toward
in	with

Commonly Used Prepositional Phrases	
after the war	out the door
along the river	over the hill
by the people	through the woods
during the storm	to the stars
from the top	toward Chicago
in the evening	under the bus
near the window	upon the shelf
on time	with the wind

Conjunctions: A **conjunction** joins words or ideas. A **coordinating conjunction** joins words or ideas of equal importance. A **subordinating conjunction** joins words or ideas, one of which is more important than the other.

> **Coordinating conjunction:** Many countries fought in World War II, *but* Switzerland remained neutral.

> **Subordinating conjunction:** *Although* many countries fought in World War II, Switzerland remained neutral.

In the first sentence, the coordinating conjunction *but* connects two equally important ideas. In the second sentence, the subordinating conjunction *although* introduces an idea that is less important than the other.

Conjunctions			
Coordinating Conjunctions		**Subordinating Conjunctions**	
and	or	after	since
but	yet	although	unless
for	so	as long as	until
nor		as soon as	when
You can remember these by using the acronym *fanboys*.		because	whenever
		if	while
		*this is only a partial list.	

Articles: An **article** comes before a noun and points to it. There are two types of articles: **definite** and **indefinite**. *The* is a definite article. *A* and *an* are indefinite articles. *The* points to a specific person, place, or thing:

> *The* book I wanted was not in the library.

> *The* alpaca came trotting toward me.

A and *an* do not point to a specific person, place, or thing. (Think of *a* and *an* as *any*.)

> *A* book on Ireland was what I needed. (*Any* book on Ireland was what I needed.)

> *An* alpaca came trotting toward me. (*Any* alpaca came trotting toward me.)

GR.1b Use Phrases, Clauses, and Sentences

Sentences: You must write a complete sentence if you wish to express a complete thought. A sentence must contain three things:

- A **subject**—the doer of an action or the thing that is described (a noun or pronoun)

- A **verb**—a word that shows what a subject does or connects the subject to another word that describes the subject

- A **complete idea**

All complete sentences must contain at least one main clause.

Clauses: A **clause** is a group of words that contains a subject and a verb. There are two types of clauses. An **independent (main) clause** contains a subject and a verb, and it expresses a complete idea. It can stand as a complete sentence by itself:

> Stop! (*In this sentence, the world* you *is understood.*)

> We won!

> The sky got dark.

> Winter comes early around here.

A **dependent (subordinate) clause** contains a subject and a verb but does not express a complete idea. It cannot stand alone and must be connected to an independent (main) clause:

> If we win

> When the sky gets dark

> Although winter comes early around here

If you do not connect these clauses to independent clauses, your reader might ask, "What happens if we win?" "What should do we do when the sky gets dark?" and "What about winter's coming early?"

In the following complete sentences, the dependent clauses above have been connected to independent clause.

> If we win, we will go to the finals!

> Take cover when the sky gets dark.

> Although winter comes early around here, it doesn't snow until January.

Note that the dependent clause can come at the beginning or end of a sentence. It can even come in the middle. In the following sentence, the dependent clause is italicized.

My mother, *who was born in Mexico*, learned to speak English in grammar school.

Phrases: A **phrase** is a group of words without a subject and verb. Like dependent clauses, phrases must be attached to independent clauses to form complete sentences.

after dinner

for the people

tall and slender

with pride and courage

You might join these phrases to independent clauses in order to form the following sentences:

After dinner, we took a walk.

Both candidates said they were for the people.

Tall and slender, he looked like a film star.

She served her nation with pride and courage.

GR.2 Sentence Structure

A **complete sentence** has a subject and a verb and expresses a complete idea. All sentences must have one independent (main) clause.

GR.2a Avoid Fragments

A **sentence fragment** is a phrase or a dependent (subordinate) clause that is punctuated as if it were a complete sentence, but it does not express a complete idea. One way to spot a fragment is to ask yourself if the idea it contains is complete. If not, it's a fragment.

Examples of dependent clause fragments:

Because he lived in Germany

Who had been raised in the South

Examples of phrase fragments:

During the war

Behind the barn

Being wealthy

Fragments can make your writing disjointed and hard to read. There are several ways to correct them.

- Join the fragment to an independent clause.

    Because he lived in Germany, he rarely got to speak English.

    Mary, *who had been raised in the South*, ate pecan pie often.

- Rewrite the fragment to add a subject and a verb.

  My grandfather was a fighter pilot *during the war.*

  The subject of this sentence is "grandfather." The verb is "was."

  Behind the barn, a field of wheat blew in the wind.

  The subject of this sentence is "field." The verb is "blew."

- Change a verb that ends in *-ing* to its simple form.

  Not: The Johnsons *being* a wealthy family.

  But: The Johnsons *are* a wealthy family.

- Look for conjunctions that are not followed by a complete idea and join these to an independent (main) clause.

  Not: He put on this coat. And rushed out the door.

  But: He put on his coat and rushed out the door.

  Not: I eat Mexican food often. Because it's quite nutritious.

  But: I eat Mexican food often because it's quite nutritious.

  Other conjunctions that can signal fragments include *as, as if, although, before, even if, even though, since, unless,* and *while.*

- Join independent (main) clauses with other elements such as infinitives (verb phrases that start with *to*), relative pronouns (such as *who, that,* or *which*), or words ending in *-ing.*

  Not: The state sent relief workers. To help clean up the storm damage.

  But: The state sent relief workers to help clean up the storm damage.

  Not: Eisenhower was the general. Who led the Allies in World War II.

  But: Eisenhower was the general who led the Allies in World War II.

  Not: Acting in a play for the first time. Gail stumbled over a few lines.

  But: Acting in a play for the first time, Gail stumbled over a few lines.

GR.2b Correct Fused Sentences

Two independent clauses (complete sentences) that are not joined together properly—without a coordinating conjunction or proper punctuation—create a **fused sentence**, which is also known as a **run-on sentence**. The following is a fused, or run-on, sentence:

<u>The workers stumbled upon an ancient burial ground</u> <u>that is why they had to stop digging</u>.
      Independent clause   Independent clause

Here are some ways you could correct this fused sentence:

- Separate the two clauses with a period and capitalize the first word of the second clause.

  The workers stumbled upon an ancient burial ground. That is why they had to stop digging.

- Use a semicolon between the two clauses.

  The workers stumbled upon an ancient burial ground; that is why they had to stop digging.

- Use a comma and a coordinating conjunction (*and, but, for, nor, or, so,* or *yet*) between the two clauses.

  The workers stumbled upon an ancient burial ground, so they had to stop digging.

- Place a conjunctive adverb, such as those listed below, followed by a comma, between the two clauses. The following are examples of conjunctive adverbs:

Conjunctive Adverbs		
furthermore	moreover	on the other hand
however	nonetheless	therefore
in addition	nevertheless	thus
indeed	on the contrary	

  The workers stumbled upon an ancient burial ground; therefore, they had to stop digging.

- Turn one of the independent clauses into a subordinate clause.

  The workers had to stop digging because they stumbled upon an ancient burial ground.

GR.2c Correct Comma Splices

A **comma splice** resembles a fused sentence except that a comma appears between the two independent clauses. Here's an example of a comma splice:

Dublin, Ireland's capital, is the country's largest city, next in size is Cork.

You can correct this comma splice using the same five methods for correcting a fused sentence:

- Separate the two clauses with a period and capitalize the first word of the second clause.

  Dublin, Ireland's capital, is the country's largest city. Next in size is Cork.

- Use a semicolon between the two clauses.

  Dublin, Ireland's capital, is the country's largest city; next in size is Cork.

- Use a comma and a coordinating conjunction (*and, but, for, nor, or, so,* or *yet*) between the two clauses.

  Dublin, Ireland's capital, is the country's largest city, and next in size is Cork.

- Place a conjunctive adverb, such as those listed in section GR2.d, followed by a comma, between the two clauses.

  Dublin, Ireland's capital, is the country's largest city; however, next in size is Cork.

- Turn one of the independent clauses into a subordinate clause.

  Dublin, Ireland's capital, is the country's largest city, while next in size is Cork.

GR.3 Logical Modifiers

In section GR2, you learned to avoid fragments, fused sentences, and comma splices. Sentences also have to be logical and easy to read.

GR.3a Use Logical Modifiers

Modifiers describe other words; they are (or act as) adjectives and adverbs. **Adjectives** describe nouns and pronouns; **adverbs** describe verbs, adjectives, and other adverbs. Modifiers can be single words, phrases, or dependent (subordinate) clauses.

> **Single word:** *Suddenly*, the skies opened and rain fell in torrents.

> **Phrase:** *Moving swiftly across the sky*, black clouds cast dark shadows upon the land.

> **Dependent clause:** *Because the town was prepared for a major flood*, it sustained little damage.

GR.3b Correct Dangling Modifiers

A modifier is said to "dangle" when the writer forgets to include the word it is supposed to describe in the sentence.

> **Dangling:** After putting on their fatigues, the sergeant called them to attention.

> **Revised:** After the soldiers put on their fatigues, the sergeant called them to attention.

The revision includes the word *soldiers*, making it clear that the soldiers, not the sergeant, wore the fatigues.

GR.3c Correct Misplaced Modifiers

Place the modifier as close as possible to the word it describes. If you don't, it may be hard to tell which word in the sentence the modifier describes.

> **Misplaced:** *To be cooked well*, you must steam vegetables.

> **Revised:** *To cook vegetables well*, you must steam them.

In the revised version, it is clear that the *vegetables*, and not *you*, should be steamed.

> **Misplaced:** *When only a boy*, my aunt and I went to the circus.

> **Revised:** *When only a boy*, I went to the circus with my aunt.

In the revised version, it is clear that "When only a boy" refers to the writer, not to his aunt.

> **Misplaced:** Because the only foreign language Silvia had studied was German, she could not read the menu posted on the restaurant window *written in French*.

> **Revised:** Because the only foreign language Silvia had studied was German, she could not read the menu *written in French* and posted on the restaurant window.

In the revised version, it is clear the *menu*, not the *window*, was written in French.

GR.3d Correct Shifting Modifiers

Modifiers can mislead the reader if they are not placed accurately. Look at where *only* is placed in the following sentences.

> He ruled Rome for only two years. *(He ruled Rome for no more than two years.)*
>
> He only ruled Rome for two years. *(He ruled in Rome but lived elsewhere.)*
>
> He ruled only Rome for two years. *(He ruled nowhere else but Rome for two years.)*
>
> Only he ruled Rome for two years. *(He and no one else ruled Rome for two years.)*

Note: The same words are used in each sentence above. Clearly, shifting the position of a modifier can change the meaning of a sentence.

GR.3e Correct Confusing Modifiers

Confusion results when modifiers describe two different words, one that precedes it and one that follows it.

> **Confusing:** Our professor claimed *last week* he had navigated the Amazon River.
>
> **Revised:** *Last week*, our professor claimed he had navigated the Amazon River.
>
> **Revised:** Our professor claimed he had navigated the Amazon River *last week.*

Did the professor claim that he had navigated the Amazon River last week? Or was it last week that he claimed to have done so? The revisions answer those questions.

GR.4 Parallelism, Logic, and Consistency

GR.4a Write Parallel Sentences

Sentences can contain a series of words, phrases, and clauses; keep these sentences parallel by putting the elements into the same grammatical form. For example, if a series of three words begins with an adjective, the other two words should be adjectives as well. If a series starts with a prepositional phrase, the other items in that series should be prepositional phrases too.

For example, Lincoln's Gettysburg Address ends with "government *of the people, by the people, and for the people* shall not perish from the earth." Each of these three items is a prepositional phrase. The Declaration of Independence ends with "we mutually pledge to each other *our Lives, our Fortunes,* and *our sacred Honor.*" In all three cases, a noun is preceded by a pronoun.

Sentences that lack parallelism are often awkward, wordy, and lacking in emphasis.

> **Not parallel:** South Korea is democratic, economically strong, and its culture is rich.
>
> **Parallel:** South Korea is democratic, economically strong, and culturally rich.

The first sentence above contains two adjectives followed by an independent clause. The parallel version contains three adjectives.

Not parallel: The founders of the United States had a sacred mission: to create a nation that was independent, united, and to make it prosperous.

Parallel: The founders of the United States had a sacred mission: to create a nation that was independent, united, and prosperous.

GR.4b Write Logical Sentences

Sentences can become illogical when the writer does any of the following:

- Begins a sentence with a phrase or dependent clause that he or she incorrectly uses as the subject of the sentence:

    Illogical: By traveling to Nepal will enable us to see the world's highest peaks.

    Logical: Traveling to Nepal will enable us to see the world's highest peaks.

    In the first sentence, a prepositional phrase, "by traveling," is used as the subject. But only nouns and pronouns can act as subjects. *Traveling* is a noun (a gerund) that names an activity; thus, it can serve as a subject.

    Illogical: Because he had never been to Spain caused him to take a course in Spanish.

    Logical: The fact that he had never been to Spain caused him to take a course in Spanish.

    Here, the subordinating conjunction *because* is replaced by the noun *fact.*

- Connects independent and dependent elements with a coordinating conjunction:

    Illogical: While most people think the polka is Poland's national dance, but it is the Polonaise.

    Logical: Most people think the polka is Poland's national dance, but it is the Polonaise.

- Connects words in a way that lacks logical meaning:

    Illogical: What we saw while listening to the band on the radio made us want to download their music.

    Logical: What we heard while listening to the band on the radio made us want to download their music.

- Includes contradictions:

    Contradictory: We knew that the computer had great virus protection, so we were still afraid to use it.

    Logical: We knew that the computer had great virus protection, but we were still afraid to use it.

- Uses words that do not relate logically to one another:

    Illogical: The young violinist bowed, played, and thanked her listeners.

    Logical: The young violinist bowed to, played for, and thanked her listeners

    In the first sentence, the writer seems to claim that the violinist "bowed" and "played" her listeners!

- Uses double negatives: A sentence that contains a double negative contains two negative words that cancel each other out, thereby making the sentence illogical.

  > **Double negative:** After leaving a large tip, we realized we didn't have no money left.

  > **Revised:** After leaving a large tip, we realized we had no money left.

- Uses *when* or *where* to define a word, even though the term is not about a time or place:

  > **Illogical:** Socialism is when the government owns all the means of production.

  > **Logical:** Socialism is an economic system in which the government owns all the means of production.

GR.4c Write Consistent Sentences—Avoid Faulty Shifts

Sentence structure can become inconsistent when the writer shifts from one grammatical form to another inappropriately. Faulty shifts can make your writing choppy and illogical. Some examples follow:

> **Verb tense shift:** The Germans attacked Poland on September 1, 1939. Two weeks later, the Russians invade from the east.

> **Revised:** The Germans attacked Poland on September 1, 1939. Two weeks later, the Russians invaded from the east.

In the revised version, both verbs—*attacked* and *invaded*— are in the past tense.

> **Sentence type shift:** I hope you have modified your diet and will you start exercising soon?

> **Revised:** I hope you have modified your diet and will start exercising soon.

The beginning of the first item provides information, but it ends with a question, which requests information. The second item begins and ends by providing information; therefore, it is consistent and logical.

> **Person shift:** She warned that bears can be dangerous, and you can be killed by one.

> **Revised:** She warned that bears can be dangerous, and she claimed they can kill people.

In the first item, the subject in the first clause (*she*) is in the third person, but the subject of the second clause (*you*) is in the second person. In the revised version, both subjects are in the third person (*she*).

GR.4d In General, Use the Active, Not the Passive Voice of a Verb

Sentences in the active voice contain subjects that perform an action. Those in the passive voice contain subjects that are acted upon. There are several reasons to stick to the active voice whenever possible.

- The active voice is more direct and less wordy than the passive.

  > **Passive:** In 1500, Brazil was claimed for Portugal by the explorer Álvares Cabral.

  > **Active:** In 1500, the explorer Álvares Cabral claimed Brazil for Portugal.

- The passive voice sometimes causes the writer to create a modifier problem.

  Passive: After inventing the wireless radio, the Nobel Prize was awarded to Guglielmo Marconi in 1909.

  Active: After inventing the wireless radio, Guglielmo Marconi won the Nobel Prize in 1909.

  The passive sentence claims that the Nobel Prize invented the wireless.

- Using the passive voice sometimes causes the writer to forget to mention the doer of an action, thereby leaving out important information.

  Passive: The governor was criticized for not responding to the budget crisis.

  Active: The governor's political opponents criticized him for not responding to the budget crisis.

  In the sentence that uses the passive, those who criticized the governor are not identified.

GR.5 Diction

Diction refers to the words you choose to use. Sometimes, beginning college writers choose words that sound impressive but don't convey the writer's intended meaning. Make sure you know the true meaning of a word—both its denotation and its connotation—before you use it. If you are uncertain of either the denotation or the connotation, consult a dictionary. To vary your vocabulary, consult a thesaurus, which provides synonyms and antonyms of words.

The **denotation** of a word is its literal or primary meaning. For example, if you looked up *cheap* in the dictionary, you might find that, as an adjective, it means "low in price, affordable," and that, as an adverb, it means "for or at an affordable or low price." The **connotation** of a word conveys a feeling or suggestion associated with that word beyond its literal meaning. Often, the connotation depends on context. So, if you wrote that your "car insurance was cheap," the word *cheap* would convey a positive meaning. But if you wrote that "the customer who failed to leave a tip was cheap," the word *cheap* would convey a very different meaning.

GR.5a Use an Appropriate Tone

Tone is the writer's attitude toward the subject. Let's say you want to write a letter to your college newspaper on three different subjects. Your tone might be different in each case.

- A **humorous** or **satiric tone** might be appropriate if you were complaining about the college cafeteria's menu, quality of food, or prices.

- A **serious tone** might be appropriate if you were warning fellow students about a campus stalker.

- A **mixed tone**—both serious and humorous—might be appropriate if you wanted to complain about tuition increases.

GR.5b Avoid Illogical Constructions

Sometimes beginning writers get confused about the purpose of a word.

Using the wrong preposition:

Not: The army marched *down* the river.

But: The army marched *along* the river.

Not: When the soldiers were fired upon, they fell *in* their fox holes.

But: When the soldiers were fired upon, they fell *into* their fox holes.

Using an unnecessary preposition:

Not: After the battle, the wounded were taken *over to* the field hospital.

But: After the battle, the wounded were taken *to* the field hospital.

Not: Some suffered from severe wounds, *in which* required special attention.

But: Some suffered from severe wounds, *which* required special attention.

Leaving out important words:

Not: The homeless sometimes can be seen eating out garbage cans.

But: The homeless sometimes can be seen eating out *of* garbage cans.

Not: The afternoon the students spent together was so fun.

But: The afternoon the students spent together was so *much* fun.

Since *fun* is a noun, it must be modified (described) by an adjective. But *so* is an adverb. In the correct version, *much* is the adjective, which is then modified by the adverb *so*.

GR.5c Avoid Slang, Colloquialisms, and Clichés

Slang is language that can be used in private conversations but is too informal for college writing. In addition, slang words go in and out of fashion far more quickly than standard words.

Not: After I backed my car into the telephone pole, I admitted that it was *my bad*.

But: After I backed my car into the telephone pole, I admitted that it was *my mistake*.

Not: The light show we saw after the Trenton Thunder baseball game was *awesome*.

But: The light show we saw after the Trenton Thunder baseball game was *beautiful*.

Note: *Awesome* does not mean "good," "beautiful," or "wonderful."

Not: Before Sally went to dinner, she made sure to *work out* in the gym.

But: Before Sally went to dinner, she made sure to *exercise* in the gym.

Not: The professor admonished a student for having *an attitude*.

But: The professor admonished a student for having *a bad attitude*.

Note: Not all attitudes are bad; some are good. It is important to distinguish between the two.

Colloquialisms are words or phrases that have a particular meaning in particular places. They should be avoided in formal writing.

> **Not:** We went *down the shore* to celebrate the Fourth of July.

> **But:** We went *to the beach* to celebrate the Fourth of July.

> **Not:** I *allow* that you're right, but that doesn't mean I agree with you.

> **But:** I *admit* that you're right, but that doesn't mean I agree with you.

> **Not:** Romeo asked his girlfriend to *give him more sugar.*

> **But:** Romeo asked his girlfriend to *be more affectionate.*

> **Not:** I know a lot about Robert; he's a *home boy.*

> **But:** I know a lot about Robert; he's a *neighbor.*

Clichés are phrases that are overused. They can make your writing flat and imprecise.

> **Not:** In Greek literature, the god Hercules was said to be *as strong as an ox.*

> **But:** In Greek literature, the god Hercules was said to be *extremely strong.*

> **Not:** Our professor told us to avoid clichés *like the plague.*

> **But:** Our professor told us to avoid clichés.

Other Clichés*		
Acid test	Face the music	Short and sweet
As good as gold	Foam at the mouth	Sick as a dog
At all costs	Green with envy	Sink or swim
Bit the dust	Healthy as a horse	Stone's throw
Broken record	Hit the sack	Strong as a bull
Clear as mud	Ladder of success	Swallow one's pride
Cool as a cucumber	Old hat	Sweet deal
Dead as a doornail	Pay one's dues	Sweeten the pot
Drunk as a skunk	Pay the piper	Tighten our belts
Dumb as dirt	Picture perfect	Welcome to the club
Early bird	Sacred cow	Your goose is cooked

* This is only a partial list.

GR.5d Consult a Glossary of Word Usage

Many people inadvertently misuse words or mistake one word for another. For example, they will write, "I hope you will *except* my apologies," when they mean, "I hope you will *accept* my apologies." Here's a list of other misused or confused word pairs:

> **Advice/advise:** The first is a noun: "The advice you gave me was invaluable." The second is a verb: "Can you advise me on this investment?"

> **Affect/effect:** The first is a verb: "The economic recession will affect us all." The second is a noun: "The effects of the storm were minimal."

> **Alot/a lot:** The first is a misspelling. Don't use it.

Alright/all right: The first is a misspelling. Don't use it.

Altogether/all together: The first one means "completely": "I was altogether disgusted with his behavior." The second refers to a group: "Our family is finally all together."

Among/between: Use *among* when referring to three or more people or things. Use *between* when referring to two.

Anymore/any more: The first means "any longer: "I don't care for that anymore." The second has to do with quantity: "I don't have any more."

Brake/break: The first is a noun that refers to an instrument used to stop something (as in "a car's brakes"). The second is a verb that means to destroy something (as in, "The car might break down."). As a noun, *break* can also mean "a stop or an interruption," as in "We are entitled to a fifteen-minute coffee break."

Breath/breathe: The first is a noun; the second, a verb.

Choose/chose: The first is the present tense of the verb; the second is the past tense.

Complement/compliment: The first means "to match" or "harmonize with." The second involves praising or expressing approval.

Could of/could have: The first form does not exist. Use the second.

Desert/dessert: The first is a very dry place; the second is eaten at the end of a meal.

Hanged/hung: Both words are the past tense of "hang," but "hanged" has to do with executions. "Hung" is used in all other cases.

Heros/heroes: *Heros* are long sandwiches. *Heroes* are brave people. Don't confuse the two.

Irregardless/regardless: The latter is the correct form. Do not use the first.

Its/it's/its': The first one is possessive. The second is a contraction meaning "it is." The third is not a word.

Knew/new: The first is a verb meaning "was familiar with" or "was aware of." The second is an adjective meaning "fresh" or "up-to-date."

Lead/led: The first is either a verb meaning to "conduct" or "direct" or a noun that names a metal. The second is the past tense of "to lead."

Loose/lose: The first is an adjective meaning "not tight." The second is a verb meaning "to misplace" or "to be defeated."

Maybe/may be: The first means "perhaps." The second means "is possible."

Passed/past: The first is the past tense of the verb "to pass." The second is a noun naming a time—"the past, present, and future."

Principal/principle: The first can be an adjective ("the main" or "most important") and a noun ("the head of a school" or "the most important member of a group"). The second is a "law or doctrine."

Stationary/stationery: The first is an adjective meaning "fixed" or "not moving." The second is a noun referring to writing paper, envelopes, notebooks, etc.

Their/there/they're: The first is a possessive pronoun ("Their house was large.").

The second refers to a place ("I spent a week there one winter."). The third is a contraction meaning "they are."

Then/than: The first refers to a time. The second is used in comparisons. "*Then* she knew that she was smarter *than* he."

To/too/two: The first is a preposition that indicates direction or stands before the basic form of a verb in the infinitive: "We went *to* the mall *to buy* shoes." The second is an adverb that means "also." The third is the number 2.

Try and/try to: The first is incorrect. Use the second.

Who/whom: The first acts as a subject; the second acts as an object. "The astronaut to *whom* I was talking is one of those *who* landed on the moon."

Who's/whose: The first is a contraction meaning "who is." The second is a possessive pronoun: "Whose shoes are these?"

Would of/would have: The first of these is incorrect. Use the second.

Your/you're: The first is the possessive of "you." The second is a contraction meaning "you are."

GR.6 Wordiness

Wordiness occurs when writers use more words than needed to communicate their message. Sometimes, students become purposely wordy just to meet the minimum word-count requirement. This does nothing but bore the professor and likely results in a lower grade.

Eliminating wordiness does not mean you should make your writing flat or use short, choppy sentences. However, you should remove words and phrases that serve no purpose or that repeat information for no reason. Here are some ways you can edit papers for wordiness.

GR.6a Eliminate Repeated Words

Not: He liked Italy a lot. He liked it more than any other European country.

But: He liked Italy more than any other European country.

Not: Stacey is the most talented violinist of all four violinists in her family.

But: Stacey is the most talented of all four violinists in her family.

GR.6b Eliminate Unnecessary Synonyms

Not: When the Soviet Union collapsed and fell, many Eastern European countries became free.

But: When the Soviet Union fell, many Eastern European countries became free.

Not: Members of Congress are elected every two years biannually.

But: Members of Congress are elected biannually.

GR.6c Avoid Redundancies

A **redundancy** occurs when the writer uses two or more words that mean the same thing.

> **Not:** The politician swore he spoke the honest truth.

> **But:** The politician swore he spoke the truth.

> **Not:** The evil villain in Shakespeare's play *Othello* is Iago.

> **But:** The villain in Shakespeare's play *Othello* is Iago.

GR.6d Remove Labels and Fillers

Labels are words or phrases that tell us what other words are. Often, they are unnecessary.

> **Not:** Annette is a woman who can run a household and a business at the same time.

> **But:** Annette can run a household and a business at the same time.

Here are some other unnecessary labels:

Unnecessary Labels	
Wordy	**Better**
The Christian religion	Christianity
The Thanksgiving holiday	Thanksgiving
The city of Chicago	Chicago
Tall in height	Tall
The science of chemistry	Chemistry
The month of May	May
Green in color	Green

GR.7 Sentence Patterns and Variety

As you learned in section GR1, sentences can contain a variety of parts of speech besides subjects (nouns and pronouns) and verbs. By varying the placement of these words, you can create a variety of sentence patterns. Doing so will make your writing more interesting and effective.

Begin the sentence with an adjective: Adjectives describe nouns and pronouns.

> Written in symbols, not letters, Mandarin is China's official language.

Begin the sentence with an adverb: Adverbs describe verbs, adjectives, and other adverbs.

> Certainly the most famous Roman emperor, Augustus was Julius Caesar's grandnephew.

Begin the sentence with an infinitive: An infinitive is the basic form of a verb preceded by the word *to*.

> To err is human, but Sam made so many mistakes in his driver's test that he is still riding the bus.

Begin the sentence with a prepositional phrase: A prepositional phrase is a group of words that begins with a preposition—words such as *to, in, on, with, from,* and *for.*

> In the middle of the Italian peninsula lies its capital, Rome.

> During World War I, more people died of Spanish influenza than in battle.

Begin the sentence with a participle or participial phrase: A participle is an adjective made from a verb. Participles end in *-ed, -ing, -d, -t,* or *-n.* A participial phrase is a group of words that contains a participle.

> Sinking soon after it struck an iceberg, the *Titanic* slipped into the icy sea with more than 1,500 people still aboard.

Reverse the position of the subject and verb: Putting the verb before the subject can create variety in sentence structure.

> Inside the tomb <u>are</u> vivid <u>paintings</u> depicting events from the deceased's life.
>   **verb**   **subject**

> On the side of the hill <u>stood</u> two tall <u>pines</u>.
>   **verb**   **subject**

Use a colon: A colon can be used to introduce a list or to include information that explains something that comes earlier in the sentence.

> Jupiter has six moons: Europa, Ganymede, Io, Calisto, Amalthea, and Metis.

> Only one planet has fourteen moons: Neptune.

Do **not** use a colon immediately after a verb:

> **Not:** The only planet in the solar system with enough oxygen to sustain life is: Earth.

> **But:** Only one planet in the solar system has enough oxygen to sustain life: Earth.

GR.8 Verb Forms and Tenses

As you read in section GR1, verbs indicate action or connect subjects to adjectives or other words. In other words, they either show action or help describe.

> Robert Frost *wrote* poems set in New England. *(Shows action.)*

> American independence *was declared* in 1776. *(Shows action.)*

> China's population *is* the world's largest. *(Helps describe subject.)*

GR.8a Use Regular and Irregular Verbs

All **regular verbs** follow the same pattern: they form their past tenses by adding *-d* or *-ed* to the basic form of the verb. **Irregular verbs** form their past tenses by changing their spelling. That's why they're called *irregular.*

| Regular and Irregular Verbs ||
Past Tense: Regular Verbs	**Past Tense: Irregular Verbs**
Spain *colonized* Argentina.	Argentina *beat* Spain in soccer.
They *visited* Paris's Eiffel Tower.	They *became* dizzy as they looked down upon the city.
Lincoln *delivered* the Gettysburg Address at the site of the battle.	He *wrote* the speech himself.
The Saxons once *ruled* England.	They *came* from Scandinavia.

A list of irregular verbs and their tenses is provided in section GR.8e. Note, however, that the verb *to be* changes its spelling even in the present tense.

| Present Tense of the Verb *to be* ||
Singular	**Plural**
I am	we are
you are	you are
he, she, it, one is	they are

| Past Tense of Verb *to be* ||
Singular	**Plural**
I was	we were
you were	you were
he, she, it, one was	they were

GR.8b Learn the Verb Tenses

A verb tense indicates time.

Simple tenses: The most basic tenses are past, present, and future.

> **Present:** South America *is* rich in natural resources.

> **Past:** South America *was* once colonized by Spain, Portugal, and France.

> **Future:** Someday, many hope, democracy *will prevail* throughout the continent.

Perfect Tenses: The perfect tenses combine *has*, *have*, or *had* with the verb's past participle. The past participle for regular verbs is formed by adding *-d* or *-ed* to the basic form of the verb. The past participles of irregular verbs are listed in section GR.8e.

Present perfect tense indicates an action that began in the past and continues into the present. All forms of the present perfect use the helping verb *have*, except the third person (*he*, *she*, *it*, *one*), which uses *has*.

> **Regular:** Queen Elizabeth II of Great Britain *has reigned* since 1952.

> **Irregular:** She *has sat* on the throne for more than sixty-five years.

Regular: Her reign *has exceeded* that of Queen Victoria.

Irregular: While she has reigned, her nation *has seen* many changes.

Past perfect tense indicates an action that occurred in the past but that took place before another time in the past. All forms of this tense use the helping verb *had*.

Regular: George VI, Elizabeth's father, took the throne after his brother *had abdicated*.

Irregular: Before that, he *had been* the Duke of York.

Regular: After Elizabeth's uncle King Edward VIII *had stepped* down in 1936, the new king made him Duke of Windsor.

Irregular: Edward *had fallen* in love with and wanted to marry an American divorcée, which caused a scandal.

Future perfect tense indicates future events that will come before other events in the future.

Regular: Prince Charles, Elizabeth's son, *will have waited* many years before he wears the crown, if he ever does.

Irregular: Charles *will have held* the title Prince of Wales longer than anyone else if he ever becomes king.

Progressive tenses: Progressive tense verbs indicate continuing action. They combine a form of the verb *to be* with the present participle.

Present progressive: Some people *are hoping* the Queen will abdicate in favor of someone younger.

Past progressive: King George VI, a smoker, *was suffering* from lung cancer.

Future progressive: Prince Charles *will be officiating* at some royal functions now that his father, Prince Philip, has retired.

Present perfect progressive: By 2025, Charles *has been leading* many worthy charitable organizations for 50 years.

Past perfect progressive: Charles *had been promoting* organic farming long before it became fashionable to do so.

GR.8c Keep Tenses Consistent

At times, you will have to switch from tense to tense, depending upon the content of your writing. But don't confuse readers by switching for no reason. Choose a controlling tense; then switch to other tenses only to describe actions occurring at other times. Notice the illogicality in the following sentence, which switches from past to present and then back to past for no reason.

In 1066, when the Normans invaded England and defeat the Saxons, French became the language spoken at court.

The verb *defeat* should be *defeated*. In the following short paragraph, the controlling tense is the past.

Before it *became* a united country, Italy *was* a group of city-states and smaller kingdoms. The country *was* unified in 1860, but the city of Rome *was* not annexed to it until 1870, when it *became* the country's capital.

However, you can add to this paragraph by talking about Italy in the present. Notice that the following sentence begins in the past but then moves into the present, but it does so logically:

It was once a kingdom, but today, Italy is a republic that extends to the Alps in the north and to the Mediterranean Sea in the south.

You might even have to add a sentence with a verb in the future tense, such as the following:

In 2020, the Italians *will celebrate* the 150th anniversary of Rome's being named their country's capital.

GR.8d Learn to Use Linking and Helping Verbs

Linking verbs do not show action; instead, they link nouns and pronouns to adjectives or other nouns and pronouns.

South Africa is rich in <u>natural</u> resources.
    adjective

Thomas Jefferson was the third <u>president</u> of the United States.
    noun

"It is <u>I</u>," said Jason, when his mother asked who was at the door.
  pronoun

Helping verbs, which include *am, is, are, was, were, being,* and *been,* are used with other verbs to express specific times or to create verb phrases.

The Spartans *were defending* their homeland when the Persians attacked.

Mandarin Chinese *is becoming* a language offered by more and more colleges.

GR.8e Study the Irregular Verbs

Note: A **participle** is a form of the verb used to form the perfect and progressive tenses.

Irregular Verbs			
Present	**Past**	**Present Participle**	**Past Participle**
drive	drove	driving	driven
eat	ate	eating	eaten
fall	fell	falling	fallen
feel	felt	feeling	felt
fly	flew	flying	flown
forgive	forgave	forgiving	forgiven
get	got	getting	got, gotten
go	went	going	gone
hold	held	holding	held
keep	kept	keeping	kept
know	knew	knowing	known
lay	laid	laying	laid
lead	led	leading	led
lie	lay	lying	lain
lose	lost	losing	lost

Irregular Verbs (Continued)			
Present	**Past**	**Present Participle**	**Past Participle**
meet	met	meeting	met
ride	rode	riding	ridden
rise	rose	rising	risen
run	ran	running	run
see	saw	seeing	seen
sit	sat	sitting	sat
speak	spoke	speaking	spoken
steal	stole	stealing	stolen
teach	taught	teaching	taught
tear	tore	tearing	torn
throw	threw	throwing	thrown
win	won	winning	won
write	wrote	writing	written

GR.8f Use the Active and the Passive Voices

In the **active voice**, the subject does the action. In the **passive voice**, the subject is acted upon. The passive voice requires a two-part verb: the main verb and a helping verb.

> **Active:** The San Francisco earthquake of 1906 destroyed five hundred of the city's square blocks.
> *In this sentence the subject,* earthquake, *performs the action.*

> **Passive:** Five hundred of the city's square blocks were destroyed by the San Francisco earthquake of 1906.
> *In this sentence, the subject,* blocks, *receives the action.*

The passive voice requires more words and is less direct than the active voice. That's why you should write in the active voice whenever possible. However, there are some exceptions to this rule. You can use the passive voice when the doer (agent) of the action is unknown, is obvious, is unimportant, or when there is no agent.

> **Agent unknown:** The Spanish influenza was brought to America from Europe.

> **Agent obvious:** Inoculation was first used to prevent smallpox in China.

> **Agent unimportant:** The bubonic plague was first believed to be a punishment from God.

> **No agent:** Alzheimer's disease went undetected for many years.

GR.8g Learn the Four Verb Moods

The **indicative mood** conveys action or information.

> The bubonic plague killed millions of Europeans during the Middle Ages.

> New Delhi is the capital of India.

The **subjunctive mood** conveys information that is contrary to fact. The subjunctive can also be used to communicate a wish.

> **Contrary:** If the colonists had not won the American Revolution, our world would be less democratic.

> If China were not so far away, I would visit it more often.

> **Wish:** Our professor is so interesting that we wish the term were not ending.

Note: In the subjunctive, *was* becomes *were*.

The **imperative mood** gives instructions or communicates a command or request.

> **Instructions:** Before replacing an electrical outlet, make sure the power is turned off.

> **Command:** Put your hands up!

> **Request:** Please put all cell phones on vibrate.

The **conditional mood** conveys information that is true depending on the circumstances. *If* and *had … not* are often used with the conditional.

> If the college wins a National Science Foundation award, it will build a new physics lab.

> Had the *Titanic* been traveling slower, the ship would not have struck an iceberg.

GR.9 Pronouns

Pronouns stand for and take the place of nouns.

GR.9a Learn the Pronoun Types

Personal pronouns act as subjects, objects, and possessives.

Personal Pronouns	
Subjects	**Objects**
I took statistics this year.	The course challenged *me*.
You majored in Spanish.	The Spanish Club will honor *you*.
He/she graduates in May	Professor Yoo calls on *him/her* in every class.
It takes place in the auditorium.	Several hundred people will attend *it*.
You were praised.	They praised *you* who was not there.
We met with the director.	The director wants to meet *us*.
They commute to school.	The university has admitted *them*.

The possessive pronouns include *my/mine, your/yours, his/her/hers/its/one's/our/ours, your/yours,* and *their/theirs*.

Relative pronouns connect words to other nouns or pronouns.

- *That* and *which* refer to objects, ideas, places, and animals.

- *Who, whoever, whom,* and *whomever* refer to people.

- *Whose* can be used in all cases.

Constantine was the emperor *who* made Christianity Rome's official religion.

The medical researcher *whom* the professor mentioned was Lister.

We saw the Greek theater *that* was built in the fourth century B.C.E.

We enrolled in Philosophy 201, *which* teaches the study of eastern thought.

Indefinite pronouns refer to people and things that are not specific.

Indefinite Pronouns			
any	everybody	nobody	one
anybody	everyone	none	somebody
anyone	everything	no one	someone
anything	few	nothing	something
each			

Anybody who visits Egypt should see the pyramids.

Everything on display was from Egypt's Old Dynastic period.

Nothing was left in the tomb because grave robbers had stolen it all.

None of the scholars believes King Tut died of complications from a broken leg.

Demonstrative pronouns include *that*, *this*, *these*, and *those*. They refer to the nouns that follow them.

Britain and its allies won at Waterloo. *That* battle ended the Napoleonic Wars.

"Of the people, by the people, and for the people"—*these* words are from Lincoln's Gettysburg Address.

Reflexive pronouns end in *-self* or *-selves*. Use them when the subject of a sentence does something to itself or when you want to create emphasis.

Emphasis: Typhoid Mary, who carried typhus, was *herself* immune to it.

Subject acts on self: At first Mary would not allow *herself* to be tested for the disease.

GR.9b Learn Pronoun Cases

The form of the pronoun you choose depends on how it is used: as a subject, a complement, an object, or a possessive.

Subjective pronouns: The personal pronouns used as subjects appear in section GR.9a. Indefinite and demonstrative pronouns can also be used as subjects.

Indefinite: Nearly *everyone* has heard of "The Ugly Duckling," a fairy tale by Hans Christian Andersen.

Demonstrative: *That* is the one in which a duck discovers he's really a swan.

Complement pronouns refer to subjects and are attached to them by words such as *is*, *was*, *were*, or *has been*. Complement and subject pronouns are identical.

"It is *I*, the king" said Louis.

You asked about Margaret Mitchell. It was *she* who wrote *Gone with the Wind*.

Objective pronouns are listed in section GR.9a. You can also use indefinite and demonstrative pronouns as objects.

The new insurance policy covers *everyone* in our company.

The colonel has chosen *those* soldiers as candidates for officer training.

Note: Pronouns can be objects of prepositions—that is, words such as *in*, *on*, *to*, *with*, *for*, and *by*.

Nathaniel Greene was an important general in the Revolutionary army. Only Washington was superior to *him*.

An Easy Way to Pick Subjective and Objective Pronouns

Students sometimes get confused when pronouns are connected to nouns or other pronouns in phrases that can act as subjects or objects. As a result, they use a subjective pronoun when they should use an objective pronoun and an objective pronoun when they should use a subjective pronoun.

1. **Cut out one part the phrase and pretend it's not there.**

   [Angelo and] me went swimming.

   Freddie challenged [Angelo and] I to a game.

2. **Next, ask yourself if the sentence makes sense without the missing part.**

   Me went swimming. (?)

   Freddie challenged I to a game. (?)

3. **In the first item, *me* should clearly be changed to *I*. In the second item, *I* should clearly be changed to *me*.**

Possessive pronouns are explained in section GR9.1. Remember that they take two forms:

The English are proud of *their* novelists, poets, and dramatists.

Theirs is a rich literary tradition.

Indefinite pronouns as possessives are followed by -'s.

Everyone's human rights are sacred.

No one's right to free speech should be denied.

Note: Pronouns that precede gerunds should be possessive. A gerund is a verb turned into a noun by adding *-ing*. Gerunds name activities (e.g., *swimming, reading, listening, breathing*).

Not: Him breathing so hard while exercising worried the doctor.

But: His breathing so hard while exercising worried the doctor.

Not: They moving to Chicago did not please their parents.

But: Their moving to Chicago did not please their parents.

GR.9c Watch for Special Problems with Pronouns

Problems with *who/whom*: *Who* is always subjective; *whom* is always objective.

> The leader of France *who* sold the Louisiana Territory to the United States was Napoleon.

> The leader of France *by whom* the Louisiana Territory was sold to the United States was Napoleon.

> The president *who* led us in World War II was Roosevelt.

> The president *whom* the American people revere most is Lincoln.

An Easy Way to Choose Between *Who* and *Whom*
1. **Put brackets around the clause that begins with who or whom.**   The president [*who* led us in World War II] was Roosevelt.   The president [*whom* the American people revere most] is Lincoln.   2. **Decide whether the pronoun acts as a subject or object in that clause.**   3. **If it's a subject, use who. If it's an object use whom.**

Problems with *than* or *as*:

> Socrates, Plato, and Aristotle are the most famous Greek philosophers. Others are less well known than *they*. (*not* them)

> Scholars respect few other thinkers as much as them. (*not* they)

You can be sure a subject is needed in the first item by adding a verb: "Others are less well known than they *are*." If you substituted *them* for *they*, the sentence would clearly sound ungrammatical. You can be sure an object is needed in the second item by adding *they respect*: "Scholars respect few other thinkers as much as *they respect them*."

Problems with *which*: Don't write *in which* when you mean *which*.

> **Not:** San Marino, in which is on the Italian peninsula, is an independent country.

> **But:** San Marino, which is on the Italian peninsula, is an independent country.

GR.10 Subject-Verb Agreement

A verb agrees with its subject in number. If the subject is singular, the verb must be singular; if the subject is plural, the verb must be plural.

Decide whether the subject is singular or plural. Most plural nouns end in *-s*.

> **Singular:** During the Civil War, the nation *was* at war with itself.

> **Plural:** During World War II, several allied nations *were* at war with the Axis powers.

Don't be confused by words that come between the subject and the verb.

> **Not:** Oil drilling, as is true for mining other resources, are very expensive.

> **But:** Oil drilling, as is true for mining other resources, is very expensive.

The subject of the sentence is "oil drilling," not "resources."

Not: Ohio, along with New Jersey and New York, border Pennsylvania.

But: Ohio, along with New Jersey and New York, borders Pennsylvania.

The subject is "Ohio." "Along with New Jersey and New York" is simply an intervening phrase.

Words and Phrases That May Come Between Subjects and Verbs			
accompanied by	combined with	including	together with
along with	coupled with	of the	with
as well as	escorted by	plus	
besides	in addition to	supplemented by	

Use a plural verb with subjects joined by *and*.

Hydrogen *and* oxygen are the two components of water.

Use singular verbs with gerunds (a verb turned into a noun by adding *–ing*). Gerunds name activities.

Not: Visiting the Italian cities of Florence and Sienna *give* one an education in the Renaissance.

But: Visiting the Italian cities of Florence and Sienna *gives* one an education in the Renaissance.

The subject is "visiting," not "Florence and Sienna." Therefore, the verb must be "gives," not "give."

Subjects joined by *or, either... or*, or *neither ... nor*: Use a singular verb when the subjects joined by *or, either ... or* or *neither ... nor* are singular. Use a plural verb if both subjects are plural.

Neither Austria nor Switzerland *has* direct access to the sea.

Neither the Chinese nor the Vietnamese *live* in a democracy.

If one part of the compound subject is singular and the other is plural, make the verb correspond to the subject closest to it in the sentence.

Either the doctor or the nurse practitioners *are* on duty.

Either the nurse practitioners or the doctor *is* on duty.

Relative pronouns: When a relative pronoun, such as *that, which*, or *who*, is the subject, make the verb agree with the word the pronoun refers to—its antecedent.

King Lear is a play about a man *who goes* mad because of his daughters' treachery.

People *who live* to be one hundred years old are called centenarians.

In the first sentence, the antecedent of *who* is *man*, which is singular; therefore, the verb must be singular: *goes*. In the second sentence, the antecedent of *who* is *people*, which is plural; therefore, the verb must be plural: *live*.

Indefinite pronouns, such as *any, each, either, every*, **and** *neither*, **take singular verbs.**

Not: Each of the planets *are* named after a god or goddess from mythology.

But: Each of the planets *is* named after a god or goddess from mythology.

Indefinite pronouns ending in *-one, -body,* or *-thing* also take the singular.

Not: Everyone are convinced that we will someday cure cancer.

But: Everyone is convinced that we will someday cure cancer.

If a sentence begins with *there* or *here*, the subject comes after the verb. Look for it there to check for agreement.

Not: There *was* five different people running for governor.

But: There *were* five different people running for governor.

The subject is *people*; therefore, the verb is *were*, not *was*.

Not: Here is the supplies that the professor requested.

But: Here are the supplies that the professor requested.

The subject is *supplies*; therefore, the verb is *are*, not *is*.

If the subject follows the verb, read the sentence in its entirety before deciding if the verb is singular or plural.

Not: On the ground *lies* the remains of a Greek temple destroyed by an earthquake.

But: On the ground *lie* the remains of a Greek temple destroyed by an earthquake.

The subject is *remains*; therefore, the verb is plural: *lie.*

Collective nouns: A collective noun, such as *family, company, troop, club, clan,* or *community*, names a group. Use a singular verb with one group and a plural verb with more than one group.

The club *meets* in West Hall every Thursday.

The clubs *meet* in West Hall every Thursday.

GR.11 Pronoun-Antecedent Agreement

An **antecedent** is a noun or pronoun to which another pronoun refers. If the antecedent is singular, the pronoun that refers to it must be singular as well. If the antecedent is plural, the pronoun must be plural.

Use singular pronouns with singular antecedents and plural pronouns with plural antecedents.

Switzerland maintained *its* neutrality during both world wars.

Many *refugees* have fled *their* countries in North Africa for more peaceful places.

Subjects joined by *or, either … or,* or *neither … nor*: Use singular pronouns to refer to nouns or pronouns joined by *or, either…or,* or *neither…nor* if both antecedents are singular. Use plural pronouns if both antecedents are plural.

Neither the governor nor the mayor believes *he* will run again.

Neither the Romans nor the Persians retained *their* empires.

If one antecedent is singular and the other plural, the pronoun corresponds to the one closest to it in the sentence.

Either the deans or the college president will have *her* salary cut.

Either the college president or the deans will have *their* salaries cut.

Collective nouns: Use a singular or plural pronoun to refer to an antecedent that is a collective noun, depending upon the sense of the thought expressed.

The student senate voted to amend *its* constitution.

The student senate voted to extend *their* terms of office.

Indefinite pronouns: Use singular pronouns when referring to indefinite pronouns such as *either, neither, everyone, somebody,* and *anything.*

The nurses could not be hired; *neither* had finished *his* training.

Avoid sexism when using indefinite pronouns.

- Use both *his* and *her.*

  Not: Everyone must now pay for *his* own health insurance.

  But: Everyone must now pay for *her* or *his* own health insurance.

- Substitute *the, a,* or *an* for the pronoun.

  Not: Someone has left *his* book behind.

  But: Someone has left *a* book behind.

- Replace the pronoun with a plural noun.

  Not: *Everyone* must show *his* passport before clearing customs.

  But: *All tourists* must show *their* passports before clearing customs.

GR.12 Adjectives and Adverbs

GR.12a Master Adjectives

Adjectives describe nouns and pronouns, and they answer the questions "Which?" "What kind of?" and "How many?" Adjectives can come before or after the words they describe.

The *dim yellow* lights illuminated a fog *so dense* that it seemed to be liquid.

Complements are adjectives that appear after the word they describe, and they are connected to that word with linking verbs such as *is, are, was, were, has been, had been,* and *will be.*

Calculus has been *difficult* for me.

During World War II, the city of Dresden was *destroyed* by Allied bombing.

Participles are adjectives formed by adding *-d, -ed, -en, -t,* or *-ing* to a verb.

Destroying nearly everything in its path, the tornado left the town unrecognizable.

Lost in the debris were the remains of my family's possessions.

Today the town is almost *reconstructed*, a testament to the human spirit.

Comparing adjectives can be done in three ways:

- **By adding -er or -est to a single-syllable adjective:** Add *-er* when comparing two adjectives (comparative form); add *-est* when comparing three or more (superlative form).

Arnold is smart.

His brother Sam is smarter.

His sister Madelaine is the smartest of the triplets.

- **By using *more/most* or *less/least*:** Do not add *-er* or *-est* to adjectives of more than one syllable, with the exception of those that end in *-y*.

    Not: She is the courageouser of the two sisters.

    But: She is the more courageous of the two sisters.

    Not: He earns the desiredest honors at every show.

    But: He earns the most desired honors at every show.

- **By using different forms in the case of irregular adjectives:**

    Not: He made things badder by lying.

    But: He made things worse by lying.

    Not: It was the baddest cavity the dentist had ever seen.

    But: It was the worst cavity the dentist had ever seen.

GR.12b Master Adverbs

Adverbs describe verbs, adjectives, and other adverbs. Adverbs answer the questions "When?" "Where?" "How?" "Why?" "Under what conditions?" and "To what extent?" Many adverbs end in *-ly*, but not all do.

Andre had *hardly* started studying Polish; however, because of his *very* talented tutor, he could understand it *fairly well*.

In this sentence, *hardly* describes the verb *started*, *very* describes the adjective *talented*, *well* describes the verb *understand*, and *fairly* describes the adverb *well*.

Comparing adverbs: Like adjectives, adverbs can appear in the comparative and superlative forms. To compare adverbs ending in *-ly*, add *more/most* or *less/least*.

The train got us to Washington *more quickly* than a plane would have.

The *most expertly* crafted violin is the Stradivarius.

To compare adverbs that do not end in *-ly*, use either *-er/est* or *more/most* and *less/least*.

Cyril is prompt *more often* than he's late.

The *least painful* alternative is not the best one.

The *latest* departure time is 10:00 p.m.

GR.12c Learn to Use Adjectives and Adverbs with Sense Verbs

Words such as *look, smell, sound, taste,* and *feel* relate to our five senses. Sentences that contain such words can sometimes get confusing, and students are left wondering whether to use an adjective or an adverb. Take the following sentence:

When defrosted, the previously frozen fish smelled *badly*.

The writer should have used *bad*, not *badly*, because the *fish*—not the ability *to smell*—is being described. Since *fish* is a noun, the adjective *bad* must be used.

When defrosted, the previously frozen fish smelled *bad*.

Not: The velvet fabric felt *softly* on my shoulders.

But: The velvet fabric felt *soft* on my shoulders.

Not: The garden looks beautifully.

But: The garden looks beautiful.

GR.13 End Punctuation, Commas, Semicolons, and Colons

GR.13a Master End Punctuation

There are four sentence types: declarative, interrogative, imperative, and exclamatory. Each one closes with a different mark of punctuation.

Declarative sentences communicate information. They end with a period.

Lincoln was assassinated in Ford's Theater.

Interrogative sentences ask a question. They end with a question mark.

Was the U.S. Constitution adopted in 1787?

Imperative sentences give an order, make a request, or deliver instructions. They end in an exclamation point when giving an order.

"Drop down and give me one hundred push-ups!" said the fitness coach.

Exclamatory sentences express a strong emotion or reaction. They end with an exclamation point.

The couple had twelve children and forty-four grandchildren!

The Battle of Gettysburg cost over 50,000 American lives!

GR.13b Master Comma Use

There are several rules governing comma use:

With independent (main) clauses and coordinating conjunctions: The coordinating conjunctions are *and, but, for, or, nor, so,* and *yet*.

A dromedary is a one-humped camel, *and* a Bactrian is the two-humped version.

Dromedaries live in the Middle East, *but* Bactrians can be found in Central Asia.

Camels can run at sustained speeds of twenty-five miles per hour, *so* they were once used in military operations.

After introductory elements:

Introductory clause: Although it is now extinct, a third type of camel once lived in North America.

Introductory phrase: Named for a region in Asia, Bactrian camels account for only 6 percent of the animal's total number.

Introductory word: Indeed, the wild Bactrian camel is an endangered species.

Between items in a series:

Words: Coal, oil, and gas are fossil fuels that pollute the atmosphere when burned.

Phrases: The signers of the Declaration of Independence defied an empire, won a revolution, and forged a nation.

Clauses: The English are famous for literature, the Germans are noted for music, and the Italians excel in painting and sculpture.

Around a word or phrase that adds information but is not essential to the meaning of the sentence:

Not essential: Philadelphia, *where the Constitution was signed*, is known as the city of brotherly love.

Essential: The city *where the Constitution was signed is* Philadelphia.

In the first item, the city has been named, so "where the Constitution was signed" is not needed to identify it. In the second item, the city is not named, so "where the Constitution was signed" identifies it; as such, it is essential to understanding the sentence.

An Easy Way to Decide Whether a Comma Is Needed

If you can take out the word or phrase set off by commas without affecting the sentence's meaning, you can be sure the commas are needed.

- Thomas Jefferson, our third president, commissioned Lewis and Clark's expedition to the West.
- The Mexican War, which began a year after the United States annexed Texas, ended in 1848.
- William McKinley, the twenty-fifth U.S. president, was assassinated during his second term.

In each case, removing the words set off by commas does not affect the sentence's meaning.

Around nonrestrictive modifiers (describers): Nonrestrictive modifiers don't limit the word or words they describe; use commas around them. Restrictive modifiers limit the meanings of the word or words they describe; do not use commas around them.

Nonrestrictive: Students, who can use the college's research databases, must enter a password to access the library online.

Restrictive: Students who major in the sciences can use the labs at any time.

In the first sentence, *students* refers to all students. In the second, *students* refers only (is restricted) to those "who major in the sciences."

Around sentence interrupters, including internal transitions, interjections, and words used in direct address:

Interrupter: Rome, *legend says*, was founded by descendants of the Trojans.

Internal transition: Archaeology, *on the other hand*, tells a different story.

Interjection: The Roman Empire lasted for, *oh*, about five hundred years.

Direct address: *Caesar*, beware the Ides of March.

With names, degrees, titles, addresses, numbers, and dates:

At 8:39 p.m., on July 16, 1999, John F. Kennedy Jr. took off in a small airplane from Fairfield, New Jersey, on his way to a wedding on Martha's Vineyard, Massachusetts. Kennedy, who piloted the aircraft, and two passengers were killed when the plane crashed into the ocean. All three died, according to Richard Evan, M.D, who performed the autopsy, from injuries when the plane hit the water. The National Transportation Safety Board said poor visibility may have contributed to the accident, but there was "clear visibility at or below 12,000 feet" where the plane went down.

Between adjectives that describe the same noun: When two or more adjectives precede a noun, you will have to decide whether to separate them with a comma. If you can insert the word *and* naturally where the comma might be, you can be sure the comma is needed.

My father is a talented, inventive musician.
My mother is a gifted public speaker.

They were able to find a warm, dry place to stay during the storm.
However, they had to sleep on a hard cement floor.

In each pair, the first item contains adjectives that are of the same type and can be joined naturally by substituting an *and* for the comma. That is not true of the second items; therefore, a comma should not be used in them.

To make a sentence clearer:

Sam claimed Susan was an excellent doctor.
Sam, claimed Susan, was an excellent doctor.

Both sentences contain the same exact words, but in the second sentence, the use of commas makes it clear that Sam is the doctor.

When not to use a comma:

- **Don't use a comma between a subject and a verb.** Sometimes writers have a tendency to pause after a long phrase. In the following example, the subject, *city*, is followed by the long participial (adjective) phrase that starts with *buried by.* Nevertheless, the subject should not be separated from the verb *is.*

    Not: The city buried by the eruption of Mt. Vesuvius in 79 C.E., is Pompeii.

    But: The city buried by the eruption of Mt. Vesuvius in 79 C.E. is Pompeii.

- Don't use a comma between a verb and its direct object. (A direct object receives the verb's action.) Sometimes the verb may be followed by a series of words that describe the object. Nevertheless, a comma should not separate the verb and the object.

    Not: Scholars still debate, the many diverse and curious reasons for the building of Stonehenge.

    But: Scholars still debate the many diverse and curious reasons for the building of Stonehenge.

- Don't use a comma before a dependent (subordinate) clause that begins with *although, because, if, since, unless, when, whenever* or some other subordinating conjunction.

  Not: The movie *Schindler's List* was filmed in black and white, because the director wanted to give it the feeling of a documentary.

  But: The movie *Schindler's List* was filmed in black and white because the director wanted to give it the feeling of a documentary.

- Don't use a comma before prepositional phrases, which begin with *by, during, for, of, on, under, with,* and other prepositions. In the following sentence, the prepositional phrase appears in italics.

  Not: The film is about the Nazis' persecution of the Jews, *during World War II.*
  But: The film is about the Nazis' persecution of the Jews *during World War II.*

- Do not place a comma between two items joined by *and, but, or,* or *yet.* In the following example, the comma is not needed since the two items, "preacher and founder," are connected by *and.*

  Not: St. Francis of Assisi was a preacher, and founder of the religious Order of Friars Minor.

  But: St. Francis of Assisi was a preacher and founder of the religious Order of Friars Minor.

GR.13c Master Semicolon Use

To separate two independent (main clauses): In such cases, the two clauses must communicate thoughts that are related.

Cholera is a disease of the small intestines; its symptoms include diarrhea, cramps, and vomiting.

To separate a main clause from another that begins with a conjunctive adverb or a transitional phrase: Conjunctive adverbs are words such as *however, moreover, nevertheless,* and *therefore.* Transitional phrases include *after all, as a matter of fact, as a result, in addition, in fact, on the contrary, on the other hand,* and many others.

Conjunctive adverb: Ingesting water and food contaminated by feces can cause cholera; *however,* eating raw seafood is another cause.

Transitional phrase: Cholera epidemics can kill millions of people; *in fact,* the disease wiped out nearly fifty million people in India alone from 1817 to 1917.

To separate items in a series when one or more of those items contain a comma:

In 1961, the most recent cholera pandemic affected Indonesia; East Pakistan, now called Bangladesh; India; Azerbaijan, which was part of the former Soviet Union; and even Italy.

GR.13d Master Colon Use

To separate an independent (main) clause from one that follows and explains what was said in the first: In the following sentence, what comes after the colon explains "Tutankhamen."

The most famous mummy is that of Tutankhamen: he was the pharaoh of Egypt from 1332–1323 B.C.E.

To introduce information that names something in the main clause that precedes the colon: That information can be one word, a phrase, or a list.

Our word *mummy* comes from a Latin word: "mumia."

The Egyptians mummified corpses for two reasons: to stop the body from further dehydration and to protect it from insects.

Mummies have been found in several areas of the world other than Egypt: Chile, China, Libya, South Africa, and Nevada, among others.

An Easy Way to Decide Whether to Use a Colon

Try substituting the word *namely* for the colon that comes after the independent clause. If it makes sense, the colon can be used. For example, in the sentence above, "Chile, China, Libya, South Africa, and Nevada" name the other "areas of the world."

To introduce a quotation:

There are different theories about how Tutankhamen died. One scholar writes that he was the victim of foul play: "There is some evidence that the pharaoh was assassinated."

In the salutation of a business letter or other formal communication:

Dear King Tutankhamen:

GR.14 Other Marks of Punctuation

GR.14a Master Quotation Marks

To indicate the exact words of a speaker or to quote directly from a text:

"Let not your heart be troubled," said Jesus. "Neither let it be afraid."

According to Mark Twain, "the man who does not read good books has no advantage over the man who cannot read them."

Use single quotation marks to enclose a quotation within a quotation:

"I admire President Harry S. Truman for saying that 'the buck stops here!'" Marty replied.

To indicate the titles of essays, short poems, short stories, songs, episodes of television programs, and articles in magazines, journals, and newspapers:

B. R. Jerman wrote an essay entitled "Browning's Witless Duke."

It concerns Browning's poem "My Last Duchess."

Shirley Jackson wrote the short story "The Lottery."

My favorite Beatles song is "Let It Be."

"Ascendancy" is the last episode in the Netflix series *Medici: Masters of Florence.*

GR.14b Master Ellipses and Brackets

An ellipsis (…) is used to indicate that the writer has removed information from a quotation. A bracket [ ] is used to indicate that the writer has added information into a quotation.

Ellipsis: "I find television … educating," said Groucho Marx. "Every time somebody turns on the set, I go into the other room and read … ."

(The original read: "I find television very educating," said Groucho Marx. "Every time somebody turns on the set, I go into the other room and read a book.")

Brackets: I believe Plato, who said, "Ignorance [is] the root and the stem of every evil."

(The original read: "I believe Plato, who said, 'Ignorance, the root and stem of every evil.'"

GR.14c Master the Dash

The dash is often typed as two hyphens (–) with no space before or after. It is also a symbol on most computers (—). There are three uses for the dash:

To set off material you wish to emphasize:

When in Arizona, climb up and down the Grand Canyon—if you dare!

To clarify an idea:

At dinner, we had little choice as to the entrée—it was fish, fish, or fish.

To separate a list from an independent clause at the start or end of a sentence:

Banff, Cape Breton Highlands, and Fundy—these are only three of Canada's forty-seven national parks.

The Mongols had two great leaders—Genghis and Kublai Khan.

GR.14d Master the Apostrophe

There are three uses for the apostrophe:

To show possession:

- Add -'s to words that are singular or that don't form the plural with an -s:

   Israel's first prime minister was David Ben-Gurion.

   The country's fourth prime minister was Golda Meir.

   Israel's University of Haifa sponsors a Center for Women's Studies.

   Our men's chorus performed in Jerusalem.

- Add -'s if the singular of a noun ends in -s:

   Moses's task was to lead the Israelites to the Promised Land.

   Peter, James, and John were three of Jesus's apostles.

   The apostle Thomas's nickname was Didymus, "the twin."

- Add only an apostrophe to a plural noun that ends in -s:

   The Moslems' most holy place is Mecca.

   The Shiites' belief that a member of the Prophet's family should succeed him alienated the Sunnis.

- In a series of nouns, add -'s only to the last in order to show joint possession. Add -'s to each noun to show individual possession.

   Joint: Judaism, Islam, and Christianity's roots are traced to Abraham.

   Individual: Judaism's, Islam's, and Christianity's ideas about Christ differ.

To form a contraction:

Because it's an Eastern religion, many Westerners are unfamiliar with Taoism.
(It's = it is.)

Many teachings of the Bahá'í faith aren't much different from those of other religions.
(Aren't = are not.)

To form the plurals of abbreviations, of numbers used as numbers, and of letters used as letters:

The ID's of tourists had been stolen.

The 757's that the airline just bought were made by Boeing.

X's and O's are used in tic-tac-toe.

Appendix 2

The Research Process

RP.1 Using Library Books for Research

Today, many students seek out research material online rather than using books in the college library. They might use the Internet or the college library's academic databases, which provide online access to articles in magazines, newspapers, journals, and other publications.

Nonetheless, the first place to start your research is with printed or electronic books. You can search for such books on the library's electronic catalogue, which you can access from your own computer or in the library itself. Electronic catalogues allow you to search for titles of books, authors, and subjects much the same way as you would search for information on the Internet. Simply type relevant search terms in the search box to find titles of books on the library shelves, complete with call numbers, which will enable you to find the book. Here are some results for a search for archaeology books:

Format 📖

Edition 1st ed.

Publisher Bhaktivedanta Institute,

Call Number GN 741 C74 F67

Available: 1

library	Call Number	item type	item notes	status
Middlesex County College Library	GN 741 C74 F67	Book		Lower Level

4.

Thin On The Ground [Electronic Resource] : Neandertal Biology, Archeology And Ecology

Churchill, Steven Emilio,

Electronic Access E-book available to Middlesex County College students and staff; click to view.

Publication 2014

Place of publication Ames, Iowa : John Wiley & Sons, 2014. ℗2014

Custom PUBDATE 2014

Language English

Format 💿

Call Number XX(1962955.1)

Available: 1

library	Call Number	item type	item notes	status
Middlesex County College Library	PROQUEST EBOOK CENTRAL	Electronic Book		Online Resource

As you read over the titles of books listed, click on those that you believe relate most directly to your topic or working thesis. The information page for each book should contain an abstract (short summary) of its contents. If the abstract seems promising, record the call number and find the book in the stacks or call for it at the circulation desk.

Once you have the book in hand, search the index for words that relate to your topic. The index—an alphabetical list of names, titles, topics, and other important words mentioned in the book—can be found at the end of the book. If you find words or names that you think might be relevant, turn to the pages listed next to them and read relevant paragraphs on those pages. If the paragraphs contain information you can use, start taking notes. The process of taking notes will be explained in section RP5.

RP.2 Using Periodicals for Research

Articles in periodicals, such as newspapers, magazines, and scholarly journals, make good sources of information for research papers. Today, many students bypass print versions of periodicals stored on library shelves and, instead, go to their college's electronic research databases, which they can access from their own computers.

The Difference Between Magazines and Journals

Most magazines appeal to general audiences, and some, such as *US News & World Report*, cover a variety of subjects. Others focus on a subject, as do *Sports Illustrated* and *Scientific American*. Nonetheless, the articles they contain are aimed at people who are not necessarily experts in that field but are in search of information about it. For example, a magazine focusing on health issues might contain an article discussing various diabetes treatments, which many people would find both interesting and personally important. Such articles are often written by journalists who interview specialists about their work. However, even if they are written by the specialists themselves—in this example, physicians or medical researchers—they would probably not contain a great deal of technical language, and any uncommon medical terms would be defined in the text.

Journal articles, on the other hand, are always written by experts or specialists, and they are aimed at readers with special training in the same field. Often, they discuss the results of original scholarly and scientific research, but they do so in terms that few laypersons—people not trained in that field— would fully understand. Examples of journals include the *New England Journal of Medicine* and the *Journal of Accountancy*, to name only two of thousands.

Depending upon the number of databases to which your college library subscribes, you may have access to hundreds of millions of articles on a wide variety of subjects. Among the largest academic databases is Academic Search Premier, which includes articles on a myriad of topics and from thousands of periodicals. Other databases are more selective. JSTOR, for example, includes articles published in scholarly journals only. Still others might focus on one academic discipline, such as the Teacher Reference Center, which is of interest to educators.

You can search Academic Search Premier by simply entering article titles, authors' names, or, as is more common, the topics you are researching. Most databases allow you to refine your search by adding describers, which will limit your search. For example, if you were searching for *rheumatoid arthritis* in Academic Search Premier, your search would yield more than 35,000 articles. If you added *treatment* to your search term, the yield would be more than 7,000 articles.

But if you typed another limiting term, such as *herbal*, in the second search window, you would have 182 articles to sift through. Finally, if you typed *Chinese* into the third search window, you would have a list of only 40 articles to consider.

Some databases even allow you to limit your search to a particular type of periodical. For example, if you searched for *heirloom tomatoes* in Academic Search Premier, you might find about 150 articles. But if you limited your search to newspapers, you would have only 34 to deal with. Using all of these tools can help you focus your search and save time and frustration. If you came upon a promising article while searching for Chinese herbal treatments for rheumatoid arthritis, you might click on its title, and see the following.

Herb Network Analysis for a Famous TCM Doctor's Prescriptions on Treatment of Rheumatoid Arthritis.

Authors:	Yan Li; Rui Li; Zibo Ouyang; Shao Li
Affiliation:	Yijishan Hospital, Wannan Medical College, Wuhu 241001, China
	MOE Key Lab ofBioinformatics, Bioinformatics Division, TNLIST, Department of Automation, Tsinghua University, Beijing 100084, China

Source:	Evidence-based Complementary & Alternative Medicine (eCAM) (EVID BASED COMPLEMENT ALTERN MED), 2015; 1-9. (9p)
Publication Type:	journal article - pictorial, research, tables/charts
Language:	English
Major Subjects:	Medicine, Chinese Traditional
	Medical Orders
	Medicine, Herbal
	Arthritis, Rheumatoid -- Drug Therapy
Minor Subjects:	Human; Funding Source; Models, Statistical

Abstract:	Traditional Chinese Medicine (TCM) doctors always prescribe various herbal formulae tailored to individual patients. However, there is still a lack of appropriate methods to study the rule and potential biological basis underlying the numerous **prescriptions**. Here we developed an **Herb**-Compound-Target-Disease coherent **network** approach to analyze 871 herbal **prescriptions** from a **TCM** master, Mr. Ji-Ren Li, in his clinical practice on **treatment** of **rheumatoid arthritis** (RA). The core **herb networks** were extracted from Mr. Li's **prescriptions**. Then, we predicted target profiles of compounds in core **herb networks** and calculated potential synergistic activities among them. We further found that the target sets of core **herbs** overlapped significantly with the RA related biological processes and pathways. Moreover, we detected a possible connection between the prescribed **herbs** with different properties such as Cold and Hot and the Western drugs with different actions such as immunomodulatory and hormone regulation on **treatment** of RA. In summary, we explored a new application of **TCM** network pharmacology on the **analysis** of **TCM prescriptions** and detected the networked core **herbs**, their potential synergistic and biological activities, and possible connections with drugs. This work offers a novel way to understand **TCM prescriptions** in clinical practice.

Journal Subset:	Alternative/Complementary Therapies; Biomedical; Europe; Peer Reviewed; UK & Ireland
Special Interest:	Evidence-Based Practice
ISSN:	1741-427X

Source: EBSCOhost

Note that the entry contains an abstract, or a summary of the article's content. Read the abstract to decide whether this article contains information that you might use in your essay. If so, read the entire article and, if appropriate, take notes. (If the article has subtitles, you might be able to scan it before reading it, thus eliminating articles that won't yield relevant information before having to read the all the way through.) You will learn more about taking notes in section RP5.

RP.3 Using the Internet for Research

The Internet is a treasure trove of information. Nonetheless, your instructor might limit your use of it as a research tool. Why is that?

You probably know that anyone—whether an expert in a field or a novice—can post anything he or she wishes on the web. In addition, cyberspace is plagued by some contributors who are less objective than what college research demands. Finally, there are contributors who are downright dishonest and misleading.

If you were researching the differences between this year's selection of sports utility vehicles (SUVs), for example, you might not get an objective opinion from the websites of the manufacturers of those vehicles. After all, car companies are in business to earn money, and each of them claims its products are the best. A good alternative is to consult the websites of independent rating agencies, such as *Consumer Reports*, which has nothing to gain from the sale of a particular brand.

In addition, some information on the Internet is contributed by nonexperts. Most instructors will ask you not to use Wikipedia as a source. While, in the majority of cases, this site offers valuable and *bona fide* information on a variety of subjects, some of it may be posted by nonexperts and, as such, cannot be relied upon for college research papers. For example, let's say you read an article on feudalism in Italy by John Julius Norwich, an acknowledged medieval scholar who has published several full-length books on the Middle Ages. You will certainly be able to put your trust in Norwich's work after conducting a short Internet search of his credentials and past accomplishments. However, what if you came upon a paper on Italian feudalism written by someone whom you cannot identify, even through an extensive search? Could this person be a respected scholar? Perhaps. But he or she might also be an amateur college student who decided to post his or her "History of Western Civilization" term paper on the web. If you can't verify an author's credentials, don't use his or her work.

Finally, there are websites sponsored by individuals or groups that have a specific agenda to pursue and that offer little in the way of an objective discussion. Some of these are biased, even racist. You can trust the information about Dr. Martin Luther King Jr. on a university website. You can also trust information posted on the United States Holocaust Memorial Museum's site if you want to learn more about the Nazis' attempts to exterminate the Jews. But could you trust an article posted on a website that, you discover, has ties to neo-Nazi organizations or that is clearly biased on matters of race, ethnic origin, or religion? That is why it is important to evaluate the source of all information you gather. This is especially true regarding the Internet. You will learn more about evaluating sources in the next section.

RP.4 Evaluating Source Material

RP.4a Evaluating Print Sources

Ask yourself the following questions when evaluating the usability of print sources:

- How complete and detailed is the information? Does it explain facts and ideas clearly and thoroughly? Does it provide enough background information for you to understand and use it?

- Who is the author, and what is his or her reputation? Is the author an expert in the field? A journalist writing for a respectable publishing house, magazine, or newspaper?

- Is the information presented objectively, or are there clear signs of bias? Writers often take strong, even passionate, positions on controversial issues—on one side or the other. But they can't be accused of bias if their facts are verifiable and they present their arguments in an objective and rational way. Indeed, two writers may defend opposite points of view on a subject, and both may have reason and the facts on their side. Remember, however, that books and articles that distort the truth or that preach outright falsehoods and hatred can be found in any library, as well as on the Internet.

- Is the information current? If you were researching the effects of computer viruses on business, would you consult an article that was written in 1990? Probably not, for so much has been written about viruses in the succeeding decades that a more current source would be preferable.

- Does the source contain factual material such as statistics and references to historical or scientific data? Does it include references to other works the author might have consulted to help reach his or her conclusions? If not, you should be skeptical about the source's usefulness.

RP.4b Evaluating Electronic Sources

Ask yourself the following questions when evaluating the usability of electronic sources:

- Who is the author, and what are his or her credentials? Is this person a scholar or expert on the subject, or just someone who is interested in it and wishes to write about it? Let's say you are researching the political theory of St. Thomas More, the author of *Utopia*, who was beheaded by King Henry VIII of England in the sixteenth century. More refused to recognize the king as head of the English Church. You find an article written by Richard Marius, and a brief Internet source reveals that Marius was a Harvard professor who published books and articles about More and his times. This is surely an appropriate source. Then, you come upon a paper written by someone whose credentials are hard to find. You notice, in fact, that the paper is posted on a website entitled *ENG 221: British Literature, Prof. Tudor*. This is probably a student paper that the professor wanted to use as an example of good writing and research. This might be fine student work, but the author is clearly not a professional scholar, and you should seek other sources.

- Who sponsors the website? Most websites sponsored by professional or business associations, by colleges or universities, or by government agencies can be relied upon for the most part. Be careful, however, about websites whose URLs end in .com. These are sponsored by commercial enterprises and cannot always be relied upon to be objective. Personal websites are also suspect. So, play it safe! If you have doubts about the authenticity or objectivity of a source, don't use it.

- Does the article or the website on which it is published show any bias, or does it make claims that cannot be substantiated? Does the author contradict him- or herself? Does the author leave out important information, making it impossible to evaluate the issue at hand fairly? Let's say that the author claims that the United States has an oppressive government, using the example of the local police's arrest of several demonstrators who were protesting the nation's involvement in the Middle East. However, she fails to note that the demonstrators did not remain peaceful; instead, they engaged in violence and the destruction of private and public property. Leaving out that last piece of information clearly shows the author's bias.

- Are there bibliographical references to other sources of information in the form of a works cited or references list? Does the author provide electronic links to other sources upon which he or she has relied? Are those sources credible and objective? If not, the article that uses such information may also be tainted.

- Has the website or article been updated as needed? If not, find another source.

- Does the article or website contain grammatical, sentence, and spelling mistakes? Are the ideas in the essay well developed? Are the facts clear and accurate? If the answer to any of these questions is no, reject this source.

- Was the article first published in print? If not, could it have been? If not, move on! Note, however, that articles retrieved from one of your college libraries' academic databases can be trusted for the most part. Many of these have already appeared in printed newspapers, magazines, and journals that have solid reputations. In addition, trained librarians are most often responsible for choosing to which databases the college will subscribe, and you can certainly rely on their judgment.

RP.5 Taking Notes

The easiest and most effective way to take notes is by recording them on 3" x 5" index cards. This is an efficient way to keep track of your research and combine it with your own writing because it allows you to arrange and rearrange your notes easily. You can begin to organize these cards as your paper begins to take shape in your mind or as you follow a formal or informal outline, such as the ones discussed in Getting Started in *A Reader for College Writers*.

Some people prefer to take notes on notebook or loose-leaf paper or on a computer. Still others photocopy pages from books and other print materials, or they print hard copies of pages from database articles or from what they find on the Internet; then, they highlight or underline relevant passages for later inclusion into their papers. The problem with these methods is that they make it hard to arrange and rearrange your notes as you draft your paper. In fact, they can cause confusion and frustration when it comes time to include this information in your paper.

However, marking important and useful passages on copies of source materials can be an effective way to begin note-taking, as long as you remember to transfer this information onto note cards before you begin putting it in your paper.

As explained below, there are three ways to take notes: direct quotations, paraphrases, and summaries. Direct quotations use the author's exact words. Paraphrases and summaries use the student writer's own words to express the author's ideas.

As you record information on note cards, remember the following:

- Limit each note you take to one idea or one fact or limited group of related facts. This will allow you to put each note card aside after you have used it. Trying to include too much information can result in confusion and more work because you will have to spend time and effort retrieving a card you have already used once. When it comes time to use the additional information on that card, you will have to sort through your notes again, and doing so just adds to your burden.

- Label each card with the name(s) of the source's author(s). You can do this by recording that name in the top left corner of the card. If the source is paginated, record the page number(s) from which you took information in the top right corner. Also, if you take notes from two or more of the same author's works, include the title of each work.

- Make sure to put quotation marks (" ") around material you have quoted—that is, material you have recorded word for word. You don't want to worry about whether your note is a direct quotation when it's time to draft the paper.

RP.5a Taking Notes by Using Direct Quotations

Sometimes, while researching, you will come upon information that is expressed in language that is so clear, precise, or convincing that you will want to put it into your paper exactly as it appears in the source. In that case, use a direct quotation. As noted above, however, be certain to enclose this material in quotation marks (" "). After recording the quotation, check to see that you have copied every word accurately and not used words that the original did not. Also, check that you have not missed any words or marks of punctuation. Here is a short paragraph from Henry Thoreau's *Walden*:

Thoreau, Walden   12

"I see beginning men, my townsmen, whose misfortune it is to have inherited farms, houses, barns, cattle, and farming tools; for these are more easily acquired than got rid of. Better if they had been born in the open pasture and suckled by a wolf, that they might see with clearer eyes what field they were called to labor in. Who made them serfs of the soil? Why should they eat their sixty acres ... ? Why should they begin digging their own graves as soon as they are born?"

Note: Near the end of the quotation are three dots (...) followed by a question mark. They are called ellipses and are used to indicate that the note-taker has removed information from the original that he or she thought was not needed.

RP.5b Taking Notes by Paraphrasing

A paraphrase uses the researcher-paper writer's own words to express information in the original. Generally, a paraphrase is about as long as the original. Here's a paraphrase of the quotation from Thoreau, which appears above:

Thoreau, Walden   12

Thoreau believes that the young farmers he knows have been working themselves to death all their lives. He sees them as slaves, toiling the soil and earning little. Heirs to family land and the tools to farm it, they find it difficult to abandon that life for another. If only their upbringing had been close to nature, in a field, for example, they might be able to realize the fatal servitude into which they had been placed.

Sometimes, however, words cannot be paraphrased—there are no synonyms that capture their meanings accurately. For example, later in *Walden*, Thoreau claims that "the ancient philosophers, Chinese, Persian, Hindoo [sic], and Greek ... were poor in outward riches" but were very rich on the inside. If you were to paraphrase Thoreau's words, you would have a hard time finding synonyms for *Chinese, Persian, Hindu*, and *Greek*. In fact, proper nouns can be used in a paraphrase without quotation marks. Or, you could substitute a phrase such as "*thinkers* who lived centuries ago in China, Persia, India, and Greece." You could also insert a direct quotation into your paraphrase: "On the exterior, says Thoreau, 'ancient philosophers, Chinese, Persian, Hindoos [sic] and Greek,' seemed humble." Note that the term *sic* in brackets has been inserted by the student to tell the reader that *Hindoos* is the way Thoreau spelled that word in the original.

RP.5c Taking Notes by Summarizing

You can learn more about summarizing in Getting Started in *A Reader for College Writers*. For now, remember that a summary is a condensation of the original. As such, it is shorter and expresses only the original's major ideas. Keep in mind, however, that like a paraphrase, a summary uses the student's own words. Here's a summary of the quotation by Thoreau:

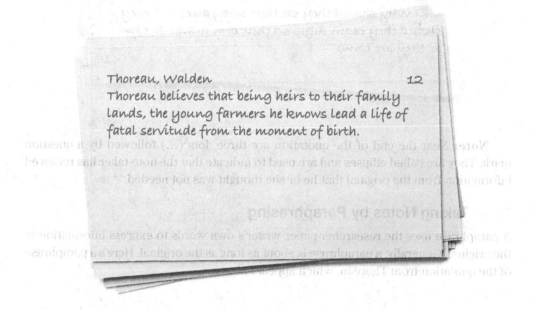

Thoreau, Walden   12
Thoreau believes that being heirs to their family
lands, the young farmers he knows lead a life of
fatal servitude from the moment of birth.

RP.6 Citing Sources and Avoiding Plagiarism

RP.6a Deciding When to Cite Sources

Citing a source means providing the reader with information that will enable him or her to locate information about its publication. You will place this information in your works cited list, which is found on the last page(s) of all papers written in Modern Language Association (MLA) style. You will learn to write a works cited list in sections RP7 and RP8.

There are three general rules to follow when deciding whether to cite the source of information you put into your paper:

- Information that you obtained through your own observations, reading, or other experiences is not cited. After all, you are its source!

- Information that is considered common knowledge is also not cited. For example, the fact that Queen Elizabeth I ruled England in the sixteenth century belongs to no one in particular; it is common knowledge. Neither does the fact that texting while driving can cause fatal accidents or that Sicily's Mt. Etna is still an active volcano.

- Ideas, opinions, theories, facts, and other material that you take from others and that is not common knowledge must be cited. For example, you would cite statistics about the number of fatal accidents caused by texting while driving in California last year. You would also cite the source of a theory that one of Queen Elizabeth's courtiers conspired with the Spanish when they launched their armada against England in 1588. The explanation of a new method to predict volcanic eruptions would also call for a citation.

RP.6b Avoiding Plagiarism

Plagiarism is the use of some other person's words or ideas without providing citation. There are two types of plagiarism: **nonintentional** and **intentional**.

Nonintentional plagiarism occurs when a student honestly forgets to place quotation marks around quoted material—that is, material transcribed word for word. Another cause of the problem is the student's failure to cast the original in his or her own words and sentence/paragraph structure. Remember that replacing a word or two here and there is not enough. You must report the ideas in as many of your own words as possible and use your own sentence/paragraph structure. Read this paragraph from Thoreau, which also appears in section RP.5a:

> I see beginning men, my townsmen, whose misfortune it is to have inherited farms, houses, barns, cattle, and farming tools; for these are more easily acquired than got rid of. Better if they had been born in the open pasture and suckled by a wolf, that they might see with clearer eyes what field they were called to labor in. Who made them serfs of the soil? Why should they eat their sixty acres … ? Why should they begin digging their own graves as soon as they are born?

A **nonintentionally plagiarized** paraphrase of this quotation might look like this:

> Thoreau believes that the young farmers in his <u>town</u> have suffered the <u>misfortune</u> of <u>inheriting</u> land, <u>barns</u>, animals, and <u>tools</u> from their families. He says this is a misfortune because these things are <u>easier to acquire than to get rid of</u>. If only their upbringing had been in the <u>open</u> fields close to nature, they might <u>see</u> <u>more</u> <u>clearly</u> the servitude into which they had been placed. He claims they are <u>serfs</u>, tied to the acres they tend, and that they work themselves to death their entire lives.

The first thing to notice in this paraphrase is that some of the words also appear in the original, while others are simply alternate forms of words in the original. The second problem is that the student has followed the original order of the ideas and sentences. Here's a better, more **legitimate paraphrase**:

> Thoreau believes that the young farmers he knows have been working themselves to death all their lives. He sees them as slaves, toiling the soil and earning little. Heirs to family land and the tools to farm it, they find it difficult to abandon that life for another. If only their upbringing had been close to nature, in a field for example, they might be able to realize the fatal servitude into which they had been placed.

This paraphrase relies on the student's own vocabulary, and the information it contains has been rearranged, using sentence and paragraph structure from that of the original. Remember, however, that some words cannot be replaced. For example, what if the student wanted to include Thoreau's idea that the young men's lives would have been freer if they "had been … suckled by a wolf"? "Suckled" could be replaced by "nursed," but what about "wolf"? Would the scientific term *"canis lupus"* be a natural alternative? In such cases, it would be wise simply to use the original and place it in quotation marks.

RP.7 Including and Citing Researched Material

Sources of researched information must be referenced through parenthetical, or internal, citations. They are called *parenthetical citations* because the information they contain is displayed in parentheses. They are also known as *internal citations* because they appear within the paper immediately following the information whose source they cite.

You must cite all information that is not your own or that is not common knowledge, whether you include it in a direct quotation, a paraphrase, or a summary. To do this, simply put the author's or authors' last name(s) in parentheses and follow with the page number(s) from which you took the information.

Sometimes, short articles in newspapers and magazines do not include bylines (the author's name). In such cases, substitute the title of the article in quotation marks. You need not write the complete title; do include enough major words for the reader to be able to identify that source in the works cited list. If the source does not have a page number, include the author's name or the title alone.

RP.7a Including Paraphrased and Summarized Information

Paraphrased or summarized information does not ordinarily need to be introduced by the author's name or by some other method that would identify it as researched material. However, let's say you begin a paragraph with your own facts and ideas—those not taken from a source you've researched. If you want to support or develop the paragraph further by adding summarized or paraphrased information from an outside source, you should introduce that information in some way so as to distinguish it from your own. Here's an example:

> The cheetah is among the fastest animals on the planet. It can sprint to 60 miles an hour in a matter of seconds, and it is perhaps the most nimble of all the large cats. According to an article in *National Geographic*, it pounces upon its prey—rabbits and deer—in the flash of an eye, and it kills the animal in a few seconds. The most prominent cheetah habitat is the southern part of Africa. However, its natural homeland is shrinking as a result of civilization's incursions into these lands ("Cheetah" 24).

Note that the researched information is introduced by "According to an article... ."

RP.7b Including Direct Quotations

It's a good idea to introduce a direct quotation with one or more of the following: (1) the author's or authors' last name(s), (2) the title of an essay that has no byline, or (3) a phrase such as "according to one scholar," "as one expert argues," or "some scientists believe."

Mentioning the author's name in the text: Mentioning the author's name to introduce a direct quotation is always recommended, especially if the author is well known in his or her field. Doing so will add credibility to your writing. Take this excerpt from a student paper on ethnicities:

> Peggy Noonan claims that when she was growing up in the 1950's, "there were ethnic, religious, and racial resentments, but you didn't hear about them all the time. It was a more reticent country. Imagine a chatty America being reticent. But it was" (243).

Note that the name Noonan does not appear in the parenthetical citation. That's because the student has already mentioned it in the text of the paper.

Introducing a direct quotation with the work's title:

> In "D-Day Generation," the writer claims that when she was growing up in the 1950's, "there were ethnic, religious, and racial resentments, but you didn't hear about them all the time. It was a more reticent country. Imagine a chatty America being reticent. But it was" (Noonan 243).

In this example, Noonan's name appears in the citation because the student mentioned only the title of her essay, not the author's name, in the text. Since the works cited list is alphabetized by authors' last names, the name *Noonan* must appear in the citation.

Introducing a direct quotation with another phrase:

> One writer claims that when she was growing up in the 1950's, "there were ethnic, religious, and racial resentments, but you didn't hear about them all the time. It was a more reticent country. Imagine a chatty America being reticent. But it was" (Noonan 243).

Using a colon to introduce a direct quotation that is not part the previous sentence: In the previous example, the student chose to make Noonan's words part of her own sentence by using a comma after "1950's." However, you may choose to incorporate the quotation with a new sentence. In that case, end your introductory sentence with a colon (:).

> According to David Blankenhorn, fatherhood in America is undergoing a significant and perhaps negative change: "Our inherited understanding of fatherhood is under siege" (27).

Note that the student has chosen to use both the first and last name of the author. Doing so is certainly permissible. Using the first name alone is not.

Incorporating a direct quotation of more than four lines. The MLA recommends using a block format with quotations of more than four lines. Block quotations are double spaced and indented a half-inch from the left margin. Do not use quotation marks with blocks, unless the original contained quotations of its own; the block format alone is enough to indicate that the words are quoted.

In "Rock of Ages," Didion describes an abandoned prison in California:

> Alcatraz island is covered with flowers now: orange and yellow nasturtiums, geraniums, sweet grass, blue iris, black-eyed Susans. Candytuft springs up through the cracked concrete in the exercise yard. Ice plant carpets the cat walks. "WARNING! KEEP OFF! US PROPERTY!" the sign still reads, big and yellow and visible for perhaps a quarter of a mile, but since March 21, 1963, the day they took the last thirty or so men off the island … the warning has been *pro forma* [serving no particular purpose]. (167).

In this block quotation, the student places quotation marks around "WARNING! KEEP OFF! US PROPERTY!" because they appeared in the original. She also uses ellipses (…), indicating where she has removed words that were in the original and brackets ([/]), indicating that she has inserted her own words to explain the phrase *pro forma*.

Using a quotation from a source for which no author is identified: As you learned earlier, short articles in newspapers and magazines are sometimes published unsigned. To include quotations, paraphrases, and summaries from such sources, use the first few words in the article's title. Doing so will provide the reader with enough information to find the sources on your works cited list, which includes full publication information for each source from which you have taken material to put in your paper. In the following example from an article in *National Geographic*, the citation reveals only the first word of the article's title:

> Manatees can be found as far north as Massachusetts in summer, but in winter they go south. Unfortunately, according to *National Geographic*, "fatal boat injuries [have taken] a toll on Florida's 2,600 manatees, but the endangered sea mammals have also been affected by a natural menace—a cryptic disease that took biologists four months to decipher" ("Malady" 152).

The full title of the article from which this quotation was taken is "Malady Lays Manatees Low." Note that the student has inserted her own words in brackets in the second sentence.

Using a quotation found in another source: When you use material already quoted by another source, include "qtd. in," for "quoted in," in the parentheses. Follow this with the author's name or the source's title, as well as the page number if appropriate. Here's an example:

> In assessing the importance of language, William James said that without words, our world would become "a spiritual sand-heap" (qtd. in Allport 296).

Using information from two or more works from the same author: If you are using more than one work from the same author, introduce the material with the author's name. Then, in the citation, include the title of the work (in an abbreviated form, if appropriate), along with the page number if there is one.

> Cal Thomas argues that, "so many of us identify as members of tribes—right, left, religious, secular, Republican, Democrat, socialist. No member of one tribe seems willing to speak to any member of another tribe, or find out how and why the others came to their point of view. ("Why So Much Rage?")

> According to Thomas, "neither rent control nor minimum wage laws—nor price control laws in general—are new. Price control laws go back as far as ancient Egypt and Babylon, and they have been imposed at one time or another on every inhabited continent." ("Has Economics Failed?")

Using information synthesized from two or more sources: Use a semicolon (;) to separate the name of one author and page number from the other's.

> A few major differences marked the religious practices of the Greeks and Romans, even though the gods they worshipped were virtually the same (Christiansen 122; Romero).

RP.8 Writing a Works Cited List

Model entries of works cited are given below. Note that as of 2016, the MLA style calls for the following:

RP.8a Basic Rules

- Place the works cited list on a separate page at the end of the paper.
- Label it "*Works Cited*," and center that label at the top of the page.
- Double space items in a Works Cited page.
- Indent the second and subsequent lines of entries a half-inch from the left margin.

- Capitalize major words in the titles of articles, books, and so forth, but do not capitalize articles (*the, an*), prepositions (*to, with, on, for,* etc.), or conjunctions (*and, but, or,* etc.) unless they begin a title or subtitle: *A History of the Roman Empire; Gone with the Wind; The New Women in Science; The Agony and the Ecstasy; The Anthropology of Religion, Magic, and Witchcraft.*

- Use italics (not underlining) for titles of larger works (books, magazines, newspapers, journals); use quotation marks for titles of shorter works (short poems, articles).

- When citing an article or a publication from an online database, type the online database name in italics.

- For online sources, include a location to show readers where you found the source. Use a digital object identifier (DOI) in your citation if it is available; otherwise, use a universal resource locater (URL) without the http:// or https://.

RP.8b Listing Author Names

Entries are listed alphabetically by the author's last name (or, for entire edited collections, by the editors' last names). Author names are written last name first; middle names or middle initials follow the first name:

Burke, Kenneth Levy

Wallace, David M.

Do not list titles (*Dr., Sir, Saint,* etc.) or degrees (*PhD, MA, DDS,* etc.) with names. A book listing an author named John Bigbrain, PhD, appears simply as "Bigbrain, John"; however, do include suffixes like *Jr.* or *II.* Putting it all together, a work by Dr. Martin Luther King Jr. would be cited as "King, Martin Luther, Jr." Here the suffix follows the first and middle name and a comma.

RP.8c Preparing a Works Cited List—Print Sources

A book by one author:

Author's name (last name first). *Title of Book.* Publisher's name, date of publication.

Start with the **author's name**, in inverted order (last name first, then first name, then middle initial, if available). Follow this with the **title of the book in *italics***, ending in a period. Next, type the **name of the publisher**, followed by a comma and the **date of publication**. End with a period.

Dweck, Carol S. *The New Psychology of Success.* Random House, 2017.

A book by two or more authors: Type all the authors' names but **reverse only the first name.**

Frank, Gerold, James D. Horon, and Joseph Eckberg. *U.S.S. Seawolf: Submarine Raider of the Pacific.* G.P. Putnam's Sons, 1945.

A book with four or more authors: For a book with **four or more authors, indicate the first author listed; then use et al.** for the rest. This is an abbreviation for *et alia,* a Latin term meaning "and others."

Alston, Lee J., et al. *Brazil in Transition: Beliefs, Leadership, and Institutional Change.* Princeton University Press, 2016.

A magazine article:

> Author(s). "Title of Article." *Title of Magazine*, Day Month Year, Pages.

> Newman, Cathy. "Cats: Nature's Masterwork." *National Geographic*, June 1997, pp. 55-76.

Note that the author has signed her article as "Cathy Newman," not "Catherine Newman." Record the author's name exactly as it appears.

A newspaper article:

> Author(s). "Title of Article." *Title of Newspaper*, Day Month Year, Pages.

> Farrell, Greg. "Online Time Soars at Office." *USA Today*, 18 Feb. 2000, pp. A1-2.

The final letter and numbers refer to pages 1 and 2 of section A. If the article is not printed on consecutive pages, simply list the first page followed by a plus sign ("+"). In that case, the above example would have read "pp. A1+." If the newspaper is less well-known or is a local publication, include the city name in brackets after the title of the newspaper.

> Behre, Robert. "Presidential Hopefuls Get Final Crack at Core of S.C. Democrats." *Post and Courier* [Charleston, SC], 29 Apr. 2007, p. A11.

Editorial in a newspaper or magazine:

> "Fouling the Air." Editorial. *New York Times*, 23 Aug. 2003, p. A12.

List an editorial as you would any other unsigned article, but indicate the nature of the piece by adding *Editorial* after the article's title.

Article in a scholarly or professional journal:

> Author(s). "Title of Article." *Title of Journal*, volume, issue No., Year, Pages.

> Omond, Roger. "South Africa's Post-Apartheid Constitution." *Third World Quarterly*, vol. 9, no. 2, 1987, pp. 622-637.

Selection in an edited collection:

> Jeans, James. "Why the Sky Looks Blue." *The Heath Reader*, edited by Boyd Litzinger, D.C. Heath, 1983, pp. 156-157.

Revised or later edition of a book:

> Hanning, Barbara Russano. *Concise History of Western Music*. 5th ed., Norton, 2014.

The abbreviations *Rev. ed.*, *2nd ed.*, *3rd ed.*, and so on are placed after the title.

Book in a series: Type the series name and series number, if any, between the editor's name and the publication information. Do not italicize the name of the series.

> Bronte, Charlotte. *Jane Eyre: Charlotte Brontë*, edited by Beth Newman. Case Studies in Contemporary Criticism, ser. 7. MacMillan, 2014.

Book that contains name of another work in its title: If the other work is a book, a long poem, or a play, simply include it in the italicized title of the book. If it is a short story, essay, or short poem, place it in quotation marks.

> **Book:** Lawtoo, Nidesh, ed. *Conrad's Heart of Darkness and Contemporary Thought: Revisiting the Horror*. Bloomsbury, 2012.

Short Work: Patrides, C.A., ed. *"Lycidas": The Tradition and the Poem*. Holt, Rinehart, and Winston, 1961.

A work with a subtitle: If a book or an article title contains a subtitle, make sure to include it after a colon. The first word after the colon is always capitalized.

Rocchio, Vincent F. *Cinema of Anxiety: A Psychoanalysis of Italian Neorealism*. University of Texas, 1999.

RP.8d Preparing a Works Cited List—Nonprint Sources

Personal and published interviews:

Personal: Cornell, Molly Elaine. Personal interview. 11 Sept. 2017.

Published: Senior, Jennifer. Interview with Antonin Scalia. *New York*, Oct. 2013, pp. 22-35.

A painting, sculpture, or photograph: Start with the name of the painter, sculptor, or photographer. Follow with the title of the work in italics, the date it was produced, and the work's medium. End with the name of the museum, gallery, or other place where the work is on display, including the city in which that institution is located.

Lorenzetti, Ambrogio. *Presentation of Jesus in the Temple*. 1342, oil on canvas, Uffizi Gallery, Florence.

Film: Start with the title of the film (in italics), followed by the director's name and those of the chief cast members. Include the name of the production company, and end with the date of the film's release.

The Promise. Directed by Terry George, performances by Oscar Isaac, Charlotte Le Bon, and Christian Bale, Survival Pictures, 2017.

Musical recording: If your focus is on the individual performer or the group performing, begin with his, her, or their names in normal order. If you are referencing just one song, place the song title first. If the performer and the songwriter are not the same, indicate the composer's name, and follow that with the title of the album (in italics). Then, list the name of the record company followed by the date the album or song was released.

Eric Clapton. "Bell Bottom Blues" by Derek & the Dominoes. *Clapton: The Complete Collection*, Polydor, 2010.

Radio or television program: Type the name of the episode in quotation marks, followed by the title of the series or program. Then, type the name of the production company, the radio or television station that broadcast the program, the city, and finally the date.

"TheStrongbox." *Seinfeld*. Castle Rock Entertainment. WPIX, New York, 2 Jul. 1998.

RP.8e Preparing a Works Cited List—Electronic Sources

Here is a list of information you should try to include when citing electronic sources in MLA style. Not every web page will provide all this information, but you should collect as much of it as you can:

- Author and/or editor names (if available)

- Article name in quotation marks

- Title of the website, project, or book in italics

- Any version numbers available, including editions (ed.), revisions, posting dates, volumes (vol.), or issue numbers (no.)

- Publication information, including the publisher's name and date of publication

- Page (p. or pp.) or paragraph numbers (par. or pars.), if any are indicated

- Date you accessed the material (Accessed 7 July 2017, for example)

- Uniform resource locator (URL) without the https://; the digital object identifier (DOI); or the permalink: If the DOI is available, use it instead of the URL. Online magazines and newspapers will, at times, display a "permalink." This is an abbreviated URL. Click on "share" or "cite this" to see if the "permalink" is listed. If it is, use it instead of the URL.

- "Containers," such as collections of poems, fiction, essays, or other anthologies: Also included are titles of a television series or a website.

Use the following formats for electronic sources as a guide to prepare your list.

Article in an online magazine:

Greely, Mariya. "What to Know about Lasik Surgery." *US News.com*, 21 Sept. 2017. health.usnews.com/health-care/patient-advice/articles/2017-09-21/what-to-know-about-lasik-surgery. Accessed 9 Oct. 2018.

Note: Do not include *http://* or *https://* in the URL.

Article that is part of a website:

"Sleep Paralysis." *Dreams and Nightmares*. Theorem.ca, 2014, www.dreamsnightmares.com/dreamanalysis.html. Accessed 17 Mar. 2016.

No author is given, so the article is cited first, followed by the title of the website. The first date (2014) refers to when the material was electronically published, updated, or posted; the second date (17 Mar. 2017) refers to when the student researcher accessed the source. Theorem.ca is the publisher or sponsor of the web site.

"Galileo: The Telescope & the Laws of Dynamics." *Astronomy 101: The Solar System*. University of Tennessee Department of Physics and Astronomy. 2010. www.phys.utk.edu/. Accessed 5 Jan. 2017.

Article in a reference or academic database: Cite articles from online databases (e.g., LexisNexis, ProQuest, JSTOR, ScienceDirect and other subscription services) as containers. Thus, provide the title of the database italicized before the DOI. If a DOI is not provided, use the URL instead. Then, provide the date of access.

Journal article in a reference database:

Alonso, Alvaro, and Julio A. Camargo. "Toxicity of Nitrite to Three Species of Freshwater Invertebrates." *Environmental Toxicology*, vol. 21, no. 1, 2006, pp. 90-94. *Wiley Online Library*, doi: 10.1002/tox.20155. Accessed 27 May 2016.

Davies, Gregory. "Experiment, Speculation, and Galileo's Scientific Reasoning." *Perspectives on Science*, vol. 24, no. 5, 2016, pp. 343-60. *Academic Search Premier*, doi: 10.1162/POOSC_a_00210. Accessed 19 Sept. 2016.

The first date (2016) in the Davies entry refers to when the material was electronically published, updated, or posted; the second date (19 Sept. 2016) refers to when the student researcher accessed the source.

Magazine article in reference database:

"Galileo: 'A Great Spirit.'" *Time.* 18 June, p. 71. *Academic Search Premier,* web.a.ebscohost.com/ehost/detail/detail?vid=3&sid=b1ddf96f-.ee80-442d-851d-8941da193%40sessionmgr4006&hid=4209&bdata=JnNpdGU9ZW. Accessed 28 Sept. 2016.

Newspaper article in a reference database:

Shishkin, Philip, et al. "Nation Confronts New Menace." *Wall Street Journal.* 5 Dec. 2015, pp. A1-A5. *Newspaper Source Plus.* ezproxy.middlesexcc.edu:2074/ehost/detail/detail?id=5&sid=cf7715a0-6e08-453e-8a12-1271c809d13%40sessionmgr4010&bdata=JnNpdGU9ZWhvc3QtbGl2ZSSzzY29wZT1zaXRl#AN=111392658&db=aph. Accessed 28 Sept. 2016.

RP.9 A Student's Research Paper—MLA Documentation Style

The following is a sample research paper using MLA style and written by a student in a college freshman composition course. As you read this document, pay special attention to the marginal comments in the columns to the right and left of the text. They contain important information about including, formatting, and citing researched information in a paper.

Charles Da Rienzo
Prof. Buscemi
ENG 101
October 30, 2011

Identity Theft: How to Stop Electronic Thieves from Stealing Your Life

Da Rienzo creates a scenario based on several incidents he has heard about from friends and family.

When she hears the doorbell, Nina Russell opens her front door to a man who serves her a summons to appear at a legal deposition about an automobile accident over which someone is suing her. Ms. Russell is surprised to discover she is the defendant in a suit because she has never been in an accident. Later that week, she opens an American Express credit card bill with charges for electronic equipment bought in San Francisco. However, she has never had an American Express credit card and has never been in San Francisco. Later that night, she checks her email and sees a computer-generated bank message claiming that her checking account balance has fallen below a

The essay is double spaced throughout.

predetermined level, yet her check ledger shows that her balance exceeds the amount in the email by over $4,000. Slowly, the truth dawns on her: someone has stolen her identity and her money.

The story is fictitious, but incidents of identity theft, with results like those in this scenario, happen much too often. Federal Trade Commission studies show that over eighty million people in the United States discovered that they were identity-theft victims in 2007 alone (Anderson, Durbin, and Salinger. 173).

In *The Dark Side of the Internet*, Paul Bocij, a computer-crime expert, explains that,

> identity theft involves impersonating someone, often
> by using his or her personal information, such as a
> Social Security number, address, and credit-card
> details. Usually identity theft is carried out with the
> aim of obtaining money, goods, or services at the
> expense of the victim. (86)

Identity theft is centuries old. Before the electronic revolution, however, criminals relied on low-tech, relatively easily prevented methods to impersonate others and steal their names, money, and property. A favorite trick was to steal the victim's credit-card and bank statements directly from a home mail box, then to use that information to empty checking and savings accounts or to take out loans or credit cards in the victim's names. According to Robert Hammond, other scams involved filing change-of-address forms to divert mail to new locations or rifling through the victim's garbage for useful information. Using that data, the thief would then purchase—often for less than $100 each—forged driver's licenses, passports, Social Security cards, and other important documents needed to assume the victim's identity and rob him or her blind (22).

However, today's identity thieves use more devious, harder-to-defeat methods. According to an article in *Atlantic Monthly*, the FBI's Internet Complaint Center has reported that criminals using the Internet scammed $239 million from Americans in 2007:

> Fraud on auction sites like eBay caused the most

Margin annotations:

Citation for this paraphrased information includes name of authors followed by page number of article from which information was taken.

Signal phrase introduces a direct quotation as part of student's sentence.

Citation contains page number only because quotation has been introduced with author's name.

Block format is used for quotations longer than four lines.

Information is common knowledge, so no citation is necessary.

Information is introduced by a signal phrase that includes the author's name. Here, student wishes to distinguish Hammond's information from his own ideas, which began the paragraph.

Student does not make quotation part of his own sentence, so it is introduced with a colon, not a comma.

complaints. But with an average loss of $484 per incident, such schemes are small change compared with investment fraud ($3,548 per incident), check scams ($3,000 per incident), and Nigerian email "rope-a-dopes" ($1,923 per incident). ("CyberSuckers" 28)

Thieves are even taking advantage of social networks like Facebook to scam their victims. Indeed, according to *Consumer Reports*, Facebook and other social networks provide enormous exposure to identity theft ("Online Exposure" 29).

Illegally obtained personal information can be used to apply for a false driver's license or to rent an apartment in someone else's name and certainly without his or her permission. More often, however, thieves use this information to raid bank accounts, open new credit card accounts, or take out other types of loans. The problem is compounded because victims are often unaware that their money has been stolen or that a new account has been opened in their name until well into the process. Like Nina Russell, they find out only when their bank sends them a low-account-balance alert or when they receive a credit card statement listing a charge for something they never bought. In fact, some victims don't know that they have been scammed until they apply for a car loan or some other kind of credit, only to learn that their credit reports list hitherto unknown accounts, all of which contain large unpaid balances. But that's not the end of it. The victim now needs to file police reports, contact credit bureaus, cancel credit/debit card and bank accounts, and complete a number of other nerve-wracking tasks that wreak havoc on his or her emotional well-being. In fact, Anderson, Durbin, and Salinger report that for years following a theft, many victims are plagued by the suspicion that the con man is continuing to use their personal information for more scams (175).

All of this is more than disturbing to the average user of electronic media. A number of companies offer identity-theft insurance protection. Some will pay legal fees as well as the costs associated with repairing the victim's credit, but such policies can be expensive (Lankford).

Article is unsigned, so title (in quotation marks) is used in the citation.

Quotation is longer than four lines, so block format is used.

Article is unsigned, so title (in quotation marks) is used in the citation.

Writer uses both cause/effect and process analysis in this paragraph.

Signal phrase is used to introduce paraphrased information.

Lankford's article is not paginated, so no page number can be included.

On the other hand, such thievery can be thwarted even before it begins if only users of computers and of smart phones would exercise caution and common sense when accessing the Web, engaging in electronic shopping, making bank and brokerage transactions, responding to emails, and logging onto social networks. In short, the best way to protect against the effects of identity-theft is not to become a victim in the first place.

Thesis is stated. Note that writer has begun the paper by explaining a problem. The rest of the paper provides the solution.

The computer industry has flooded our vocabulary with new and often strange words such as "phishing" and "pharming," with the *f* in "fishing" and "farming" being replaced by *ph*. However odd these words may sound, the practices they name can have devastating results.

Information about "phishing" and "pharming" appears in various sources, so no citation is needed.

According to Paul Bocij, "'phishing' involves directing a potential victim to a false Web site using various techniques." "Phishers" send out thousands of emails that purport to come from legitimate sources such as banks or investment brokers. Such emails explain that a problem has occurred with the account and asks that, in order to help resolve the issue, the victim click on a link in the email. Of course, the link leads to a bogus site that asks him or her to supply account numbers, Social Security numbers or other personal information, which is then used by the "phisher" to steal the victim's identity (88).

Bocij's quotation contains a newly coined word, which is placed in single quotation marks.

"Spear phishing" is a variation on this theme. As its name implies, it uses what David H. Holtzman calls "a more targeted approach." "Spear phishers" make a point of researching particular individuals and, when sending out emails, they include personal information that those people will recognize. For example, the con artist might mention a friend's name and claim that he or she referred him to the victim. Scammers have also been known to include the victim's mother's last name and even his or her Social Security number (23).

Writer begins paragraph with a transitional sentence.

Process analysis is used here to explain how scam works.

In this paragraph, Da Rienzo both quotes and paraphrases Holtzman.

"Pharming" is a related scheme, whose objective is the same but whose methodology differs. According to Chris Risely, whose firm, Nominium, develops Internet security technology, "'phishing' is to 'pharming' what a guy with a rod and reel is to a Russian trawler" (qtd. in Delio). When an Internet user searches for a Web site, he or she usually clicks on a link or types the site's Uniform Resource Locater (URL) into a search

As noted in the citation, Risley was quoted in Delio, and not directly.

Article by Delio is not paginated, so no page number is included.

engine. This address usually consists of a company's, person's, or institution's name or title, followed by a domain name such as *org*, *net* or *com*. The URL is then converted to a numerical address so that the user's Web browser can locate the site. By changing a few digits—a practice called "domain name system (DNS) poisoning"—"Pharmers" can direct the victim to a fake site, which may look very much like a legitimate site the user has accessed before. The difference is that this time the user will be asked to divulge information that is sure to compromise his or her identity (Bocij 92; Delio).

This information is taken from both Bocij and Delio.

A type of fraud that US law-enforcement agencies find particularly hard to control comes through emails sent by people in other countries. According to Eugene Spafford, executive director of Purdue University's Center for Education for Research in Information Assurance and Security, "law enforcement is strongly bound to physical national boundaries." However, the Internet does not respect such boundaries, making "enforcement by local agencies very difficult" (qtd. in Gaidos 32).

Writer mentions Spafford's credentials to increase credibility.

As noted in the citation, Spafford was quoted in Gaidos, and not directly.

Among the most common types of email fraud is one known by several names including the "Nigerian Bank," "Nigerian Letter," and "Nigerian Prince" fraud. It is also known as the "419 Scam," the number 419 referring to a section of the Nigerian Criminal Code that prevents obtaining someone's money or property under false pretenses. It involves emails sent by someone posing as a Nigerian Prince. In another version, the emailer claims to work for an oil company that needs to get money out of Nigeria, and he asks to deposit that money in the victim's bank account. Of course, he promises to pay a handsome fee for this privilege. All he needs is an account number to which he promises to wire the money as well as the fee. Once the victim provides the necessary information, his or her money is as good as gone (Stickley 124).

Because this information is not introduced by a signal phrase, the citation must include the name of the author and the page number.

Another version of this scam, the "advance-fee fraud," involves an email that asks the victim to help access money in a foreign bank account held by the con man. The sender says that legal, political, or other problems prevent him from accessing money in a frozen bank account. He claims to need the cash desperately—to feed his family, to pay for a relative's operation,

or to fund another worthy cause. In exchange for a small investment—monies he will use to free up his account—he promises
the victim a handsome return. In some cases, the thief asks the
victim to wire the money; in others he also asks for personal
information, which can be used later to compromise the victim's identity (Christensen).

Another common Internet theft tool is the lottery scam.
The victim receives an email claiming he or she has won a
large amount of money or valuable prize like an automobile.
Of course the victim has no knowledge of ever buying a lottery
ticket for such a prize, but the email reassures the "winner" that
his or her email was selected randomly by a computer (Christensen). The scammer might also include links to what look like
the Web sites of legitimate lottery organizations that offer such
prizes. Victims are told that, before they collect their prizes,
they must respond by including Social Security numbers, bank
account numbers, and other vital information. They may even
be required to send money to defray the costs of processing
the award. Of course, there is no award, and the only thing
victims ever get is the anxiety of knowing their identities have
been hijacked.

There are a number of things one can do once the scam is
discovered. The first is to file a police report, which can help
protect the victim from the legal ramifications of identity theft.
The second is to contact the Motor Vehicle Agency to find out
whether a false driver's license has been taken out in the victim's name. Most importantly, victims should regularly check
their credit card statements, bank accounts, and credit reports
for any fraudulent activity (Kirchheimer 32).

The *Journal of Information Management* reports that, since
January 1, 2011, the Federal Trade Commission (FTC) has
enforced the Red Flags Rule, a law requiring that "all organizations subject to the Fair and Accurate Credit Transactions
Act of 2003 implement a written identity theft prevention program to detect, prevent, and mitigate identity theft" (Kunick
and Posnor 25). This is good news. However, the old adage "an
ounce of prevention is worth a pound of cure" applies, and there

---

Marginal notes:

Because the source is not paginated, no page number is included in the citation.

This paragraph combines information from Christensen with the author's own knowledge of the subject.

The writer draws on his personal knowledge here, so no citation is necessary.

Writer uses process analysis to explain how the scam works.

This summarized information is not introduced with the author's name, which must then appear in the citation.

Information is introduced with the journal's name. Still, citation must include the authors' names and the page number..